COMPILATION OF SELECTED
RAILROAD, PIPELINE, AND
HAZARDOUS MATERIALS
TRANSPORTATION LAWS
VOLUME 1 :
RAILROAD LAWS RELATING TO RAILROAD REGULATION

As amended through the 118th Congress.

Prepared By M. TWINCHEK

2025

Forward

T his Compilation of Selected United States Railroad, Pipeline, and Hazardous Materials Transportation Laws is a resource for those interested in U.S. laws governing railroad regulation; retirement; unemployment; and labor laws; and pipelines and hazardous materials. This compilation includes laws governing regional rail lines; AMTRAK; and passenger rail lines; rail labor issues; and pipeline safety; and hazardous materials.

The materials included comes from publicly available, open source information, prepared for the public by the Office of the Legislative Counsel of the U.S. House of Representatives and the Office of the Law Revision Counsel.

Items listed as a Statute Compilation do not appear in the U.S. Code or that have been classified to a title of the U.S. Code that has not been enacted into positive law. Each Statute Compilation incorporates the amendments made to the underlying statute since it was originally enacted and are current as of the date noted.

This compilation is not an official document and should not be cited as evidence of any law. The official version of Federal law is found in the United States Statutes at Large and in the U.S. Code, the legal effect of which is established in sections 112 and 204, respectively, of title 1, United States Code.

A special thanks is extended to the Office of Law Revision Counsel and the House Office of the Legislative Counsel for providing the U.S. Code and statute compilations; and to the Government Publications Office for hosting and making these available for use to the public. An additional thank you is offered to the staff of the House and Senate Committees who were gracious in responding to inquiries and providing background information on the legislation included. Questions and comments may be directed to:

M. Twinchek
Email: mtwinchek@outlook.com

Contents

Selected Provisions of

Title 49 U.S.C.
— Transportation

SUBTITLE I
DEPARTMENT OF TRANSPORTATION

TITLE 49—TRANSPORTATION

This title was enacted by Pub. L. 95–473, §1, Oct. 17, 1978, 92 Stat. 1337; Pub. L. 97–449, §1, Jan. 12, 1983, 96 Stat. 2413; Pub. L. 103–272, July 5, 1994, 108 Stat. 745

* * * * * * *

SUBTITLE I—DEPARTMENT OF TRANSPORTATION

* * * * * * *

5

CHAPTER 1—ORGANIZATION

§101. PURPOSE

(a) The national objectives of general welfare, economic growth and stability, and security of the United States require the development of transportation policies and programs that contribute to providing fast, safe, efficient, and convenient transportation at the lowest cost consistent with those and other national objectives, including the efficient use and conservation of the resources of the United States.

(b) A Department of Transportation is necessary in the public interest and to—

(1) ensure the coordinated and effective administration of the transportation programs of the United States Government;

(2) make easier the development and improvement of coordinated transportation service to be provided by private enterprise to the greatest extent feasible;

(3) encourage cooperation of Federal, State, and local governments, carriers, labor, and other interested persons to achieve transportation objectives;

(4) stimulate technological advances in transportation, through research and development or otherwise;

(5) provide general leadership in identifying and solving transportation problems; and

(6) develop and recommend to the President and Congress transportation policies and programs to achieve transportation objectives considering the needs of the public, users, carriers, industry, labor, and national defense.

(Pub. L. 97–449, §1(b), Jan. 12, 1983, 96 Stat. 2414; Pub. L. 102–240, title VI, §6018, Dec. 18, 1991, 105 Stat. 2183.)

§102. DEPARTMENT OF TRANSPORTATION

(a) The Department of Transportation (referred to in this section as the "Department") is an executive department of the United States Government at the seat of Government.

(b) The head of the Department is the Secretary of Transportation (referred to in this section as the "Secretary"). The Secretary is appointed by the President, by and with the advice and consent of the Senate.

(c) The Department has a Deputy Secretary of Transportation appointed by the President, by and with the advice and consent of the Senate. The Deputy Secretary—

(1) shall carry out duties and powers prescribed by the Secretary; and

(2) acts for the Secretary when the Secretary is absent or unable to serve or when the office of Secretary is vacant.

(d) The Department has an Under Secretary of Transportation for Policy appointed by the President, by and with the advice and consent of the Senate. The Under Secretary shall provide leadership in the development of policy for the Department, supervise the policy activities of Assistant Secretaries with primary responsibility for aviation, international, and other transportation policy development and carry out other powers and duties prescribed by the Secretary. The Under Secretary acts for the Secretary when the Secretary and the Deputy Secretary are absent or unable to serve, or when the offices of Secretary and Deputy Secretary are vacant.

(e) ASSISTANT SECRETARIES; GENERAL COUNSEL.—

(1) APPOINTMENT.—The Department has 8 Assistant Secretaries and a General Counsel, including—

(A) an Assistant Secretary for Aviation and International Affairs, an Assistant Secretary for Governmental Affairs, an Assistant Secretary for Research and Technology, an Assistant Secretary for Transportation Policy, and an Assistant Secretary for Aviation Consumer Protection, who shall each be appointed by the President, with the advice and consent of the Senate;

(B) an Assistant Secretary for Budget and Programs who shall be appointed by the President;

(C) an Assistant Secretary for Administration, who shall be appointed by the Secretary, with the approval of the President;

(D) an Assistant Secretary for Tribal Government Affairs, who shall be appointed by the President; and

(E) a General Counsel, who shall be appointed by the President, with the advice and consent of the Senate.

(2) DUTIES AND POWERS.—The officers set forth in paragraph (1) shall carry out duties and powers prescribed by the Secretary. An Assistant Secretary or the General Counsel, in the order prescribed by the Secretary, acts for the Secretary when the Secretary, Deputy Secretary, and Under Secretary of Transportation for Policy are absent or unable to serve, or when the offices of the Secretary, Deputy Secretary, and Under Secretary of Transportation for Policy are vacant.

(f) OFFICE OF TRIBAL GOVERNMENT AFFAIRS.—

(1) ESTABLISHMENT.—There is established in the Department an Office of Tribal Government Affairs, under the Assistant Secretary for Tribal Government Affairs—

(A) to oversee the tribal self-governance program under section 207 of title 23;

(B) to plan, coordinate, and implement policies and programs serving Indian Tribes and Tribal organizations;

(C) to coordinate Tribal transportation programs and activities in all offices and administrations of the Department; and

(D) to be a participant in any negotiated rulemakings relating to, or having an impact on, projects, programs, or funding associated with the Tribal transportation program under section 202 of title 23.

(2) RESERVATION OF TRUST OBLIGATIONS.—

(A) RESPONSIBILITY OF SECRETARY.—In carrying out this title, the Secretary shall be responsible to exercise the trust obligations of the United States to Indians and Indian tribes to ensure that the rights of a tribe or individual Indian are protected.

(B) PRESERVATION OF UNITED STATES RESPONSIBILITY.—Nothing in this title shall absolve the United States from any responsibility to Indians and Indian tribes, including responsibilities derived from the trust relationship and any treaty, executive order, or agreement between the United States and an Indian tribe.

(g) OFFICE OF CLIMATE CHANGE AND ENVIRONMENT.—

(1) ESTABLISHMENT.—There is established in the Department an Office of Climate Change and Environment to plan, coordinate, and implement—

(A) department-wide research, strategies, and actions under the Department's statutory authority to reduce transportation-related energy use and mitigate the effects of climate change; and

(B) department-wide research strategies and actions to address the impacts of climate change on transportation systems and infrastructure.

(2) CLEARINGHOUSE.—The Office shall establish a clearinghouse of solutions, including cost-effective congestion reduction approaches, to reduce air pollution and transportation-related energy use and mitigate the effects of climate change.

(h) INTERAGENCY INFRASTRUCTURE PERMITTING IMPROVEMENT CENTER.—

(1) DEFINITIONS.—In this subsection:

(A) CENTER.—The term "Center" means the Interagency Infrastructure Permitting Improvement Center established by paragraph (2).

(B) PROJECT.—The term "project" means a project authorized or funded under—

(i) this title; or

(ii) title 14, 23, 46, or 51.

(2) ESTABLISHMENT.—There is established within the Office of the Secretary a center, to be known as the "Interagency Infrastructure Permitting Improvement Center".

(3) PURPOSES.—The purposes of the Center shall be—

(A) to implement reforms to improve interagency coordination and expedite projects relating to the permitting and environmental review of major transportation infrastructure projects, including—

(i) developing and deploying information technology tools to track project schedules and metrics; and

(ii) improving the transparency and accountability of the permitting process;

(B)(i) to identify appropriate methods to assess environmental impacts; and

(ii) to develop innovative methods for reasonable mitigation;

(C) to reduce uncertainty and delays with respect to environmental reviews and permitting; and

(D) to reduce costs and risks to taxpayers in project delivery.

(4) EXECUTIVE DIRECTOR.—The Center shall be headed by an Executive Director, who shall—

(A) report to the Under Secretary of Transportation for Policy;

(B) be responsible for the management and oversight of the daily activities, decisions, operations, and personnel of the Center; and

(C) carry out such additional duties as the Secretary may prescribe.

(5) DUTIES.—The Center shall carry out the following duties:

(A) Coordinate and support implementation of priority reform actions for Federal agency permitting and reviews.

(B) Support modernization efforts at the operating administrations within the Department and interagency pilot programs relating to innovative approaches to the permitting and review of transportation infrastructure projects.

(C) Provide technical assistance and training to Department staff on policy changes, innovative approaches to project delivery, and other topics, as appropriate.

(D) Identify, develop, and track metrics for timeliness of permit reviews, permit decisions, and project outcomes.

(E) Administer and expand the use of online transparency tools providing for—

(i) tracking and reporting of metrics;

(ii) development and posting of schedules for permit reviews and permit decisions;

(iii) the sharing of best practices relating to efficient project permitting and reviews; and

(iv) the visual display of relevant geospatial data to support the permitting process.

(F) Submit to the Secretary reports describing progress made toward achieving—

(i) greater efficiency in permitting decisions and review of infrastructure projects; and

(ii) better outcomes for communities and the environment.

(6) INNOVATIVE BEST PRACTICES.—

(A) IN GENERAL.—The Center shall work with the operating administrations within the Department, eligible entities, and other public and private interests to develop and promote best practices for innovative project delivery.

(B) ACTIVITIES.—The Center shall support the Department and operating administrations in conducting environmental reviews and permitting, together with project sponsor technical assistance activities, by—

(i) carrying out activities that are appropriate and consistent with the goals and policies of the Department to improve the delivery timelines for projects;

(ii) serving as the Department liaison to—

(I) the Council on Environmental Quality; and

(II) the Federal Permitting Improvement Steering Council established by section 41002(a) of the Fixing America's Surface Transportation Act (42 U.S.C. 4370m–1(a));

(iii) supporting the National Surface Transportation and Innovative Finance Bureau (referred to in this paragraph as the "Bureau") in implementing activities to improve delivery timelines, as described in section 116(f), for projects carried out under the programs described in section 116(d)(1) for which the Bureau administers the application process;

(iv) leading activities to improve delivery timelines for projects carried out under programs not administered by the Bureau by—

(I) coordinating efforts to improve the efficiency and effectiveness of the environmental review and permitting process;

(II) providing technical assistance and training to field and headquarters staff of Federal agencies with respect to policy changes and innovative approaches to the delivery of projects; and

(III) identifying, developing, and tracking metrics for permit reviews and decisions by Federal agencies for projects under the National Environmental Policy Act of 1969 (42 U.S.C. 4321 et seq.).

(C) NEPA COMPLIANCE ASSISTANCE.—

(i) IN GENERAL.—Subject to clause (ii), at the request of an entity that is carrying out a project, the Center, in coordination with the appropriate operating administrations within the Department, shall provide technical assistance relating to compliance with the applicable requirements of the National Environmental Policy Act of 1969 (42 U.S.C. 4321 et seq.) and applicable Federal authorizations.

(ii) ASSISTANCE FROM THE BUREAU.—For projects carried out under the programs described in section 116(d)(1) for which the Bureau administers the application process, the Bureau, on request of the entity carrying out the project, shall provide the technical assistance described in clause (i).

(i) CHIEF TRAVEL AND TOURISM OFFICER.—

(1) ESTABLISHMENT.—There is established in the Office of the Secretary of Transportation a position, to be known as the "Chief Travel and Tourism Officer".

(2) DUTIES.—The Chief Travel and Tourism Officer shall collaborate with the Assistant Secretary for Aviation and International Affairs to carry out—

(A) the National Travel and Tourism Infrastructure Strategic Plan under section 1431(e) of Public Law 114–94 (49 U.S.C. 301 note); and

(B) other travel- and tourism-related matters involving the Department of Transportation.

(j) OFFICE OF AVIATION CONSUMER PROTECTION.—

(1) ESTABLISHMENT.—There is established in the Department an Office of Aviation

Consumer Protection (in this subsection referred to as the "Office") to administer and enforce the aviation consumer protection and civil rights authorities provided to the Department by statute, including the authorities under section 41712—
> (A) to assist, educate, and protect passengers; and
> (B) to monitor compliance with, conduct investigations relating to, and enforce, with support of attorneys in the Office of the General Counsel, including by taking appropriate action to address violations of aviation consumer protection and civil rights.

(2) LEADERSHIP.—The Office shall be headed by the Assistant Secretary for Aviation Consumer Protection (in this subsection referred to as the "Assistant Secretary").

(3) TRANSITION.—Not later than 180 days after funding is appropriated for an Office of Aviation Consumer Protection headed by an Assistant Secretary, the Office of Aviation Consumer Protection that is a unit within the Office of the General Counsel of the Department which is headed by the Assistant General Counsel for Aviation Consumer Protection shall cease to exist. The Secretary shall determine which employees are necessary to fulfill the responsibilities of the new Office of Aviation Consumer Protection and such employees shall be transferred from the Office of the General Counsel, as appropriate, to the newly established Office of Aviation Consumer Protection.

(4) COORDINATION.—The Assistant Secretary shall coordinate with the General Counsel appointed under subsection (e)(1)(E), in accordance with section 1.26 of title 49, Code of Federal Regulations (or a successor regulation), on all legal matters relating to—
> (A) aviation consumer protection; and
> (B) the duties and activities of the Office described in subparagraphs (A) through
> (C) [1] of paragraph (1).

(5) ANNUAL REPORT.—The Assistant Secretary shall submit to the Secretary, who shall submit to Congress and make publicly available on the website of the Department, an annual report that, with respect to matters under the jurisdiction of the Department, or otherwise within the statutory authority of the Department—
> (A) analyzes trends in aviation consumer protection, civil rights, and licensing;
> (B) identifies major challenges facing passengers; and
> (C) addresses any other relevant issues, as the Assistant Secretary determines to be appropriate.

(6) FUNDING.—There is authorized to be appropriated $12,000,000 for fiscal year 2024, $13,000,000 for fiscal year 2025, $14,000,000 for fiscal year 2026, $15,000,000 for fiscal year 2027, and $16,000,000 for fiscal year 2028 to carry out this subsection.

(Pub. L. 97–449, §1(b), Jan. 12, 1983, 96 Stat. 2414; Pub. L. 98–557, §26(a), Oct. 30, 1984, 98 Stat. 2873; Pub. L. 103–272, §4(j)(1), July 5, 1994, 108 Stat. 1365; Pub. L. 107–295, title II, §215(a), (c), Nov. 25, 2002, 116 Stat. 2101, 2102; Pub. L. 109–59, title I, §1119(l), Aug. 10, 2005, 119 Stat. 1189; Pub. L. 110–140, title XI, §1101(a), Dec. 19, 2007, 121 Stat. 1756; Pub. L. 112–166, §2(k)(1), Aug. 10, 2012, 126 Stat. 1286; Pub. L. 114–94, div. A, title VI, §6011(a), Dec. 4, 2015, 129 Stat. 1568; Pub. L. 117–58, div. A, title IV, §14009, div. B, title V, §§25009(a), 25018(b), Nov. 15, 2021, 135 Stat. 651, 852, 875; Pub. L. 118–63, title V, §501,

May 16, 2024, 138 Stat. 1186.)

    [1] *So in original. Paragraph (1) does not contain a subparagraph (C).*

§103. FEDERAL RAILROAD ADMINISTRATION

(a) IN GENERAL.—The Federal Railroad Administration is an administration in the Department of Transportation.

(b) SAFETY.—To carry out all railroad safety laws of the United States, the Administration is divided on a geographical basis into at least 8 safety offices. The Secretary of Transportation is responsible for all acts taken under those laws and for ensuring that the laws are uniformly administered and enforced among the safety offices.

(c) SAFETY AS HIGHEST PRIORITY.—In carrying out its duties, the Administration shall consider the assignment and maintenance of safety as the highest priority, recognizing the clear intent, encouragement, and dedication of Congress to the furtherance of the highest degree of safety in railroad transportation.

(d) ADMINISTRATOR.—The head of the Administration shall be the Administrator who shall be appointed by the President, by and with the advice and consent of the Senate, and shall be an individual with professional experience in railroad safety, hazardous materials safety, or other transportation safety. The Administrator shall report directly to the Secretary of Transportation.

(e) DEPUTY ADMINISTRATOR.—The Administration shall have a Deputy Administrator who shall be appointed by the Secretary. The Deputy Administrator shall carry out duties and powers prescribed by the Administrator.

(f) CHIEF SAFETY OFFICER.—The Administration shall have an Associate Administrator for Railroad Safety appointed in the career service by the Secretary. The Associate Administrator shall be the Chief Safety Officer of the Administration. The Associate Administrator shall carry out the duties and powers prescribed by the Administrator.

(g) DUTIES AND POWERS OF THE ADMINISTRATOR.—The Administrator shall carry out—

(1) duties and powers related to railroad safety vested in the Secretary by section 20134(c) and chapters 203 through 211 of this title, and by chapter 213 of this title for carrying out chapters 203 through 211;

(2) the duties and powers related to railroad policy and development under subsection (j); and

(3) other duties and powers prescribed by the Secretary.

(h) LIMITATION.—A duty or power specified in subsection (g)(1) may be transferred to another part of the Department of Transportation or another Federal Government entity only when specifically provided by law. A decision of the Administrator in carrying out the duties or powers of the Administration and involving notice and hearing required by law is administratively final.

(i) AUTHORITIES.—Subject to the provisions of subtitle I of title 40 and division C (except sections 3302, 3501(b), 3509, 3906, 4710, and 4711) of subtitle I of title 41, the Secretary of Transportation may make, enter into, and perform such contracts, grants, leases, cooperative agreements, and other similar transactions with Federal or other public agencies (including State and local governments) and private organizations and persons, and make such payments, by way of advance or reimbursement, as the Secretary may determine to be necessary or appropriate to carry out functions at the Administration. The authority of the Secretary granted by this subsection shall be carried out by the Administrator. Notwithstanding any other provision of this chapter, no authority to enter into contracts or to make payments under this subsection shall be effective, except as provided for in appropriations Acts.

(j) ADDITIONAL DUTIES OF THE ADMINISTRATOR.—The Administrator shall—

(1) provide assistance to States in developing State rail plans prepared under chapter 227 and review all State rail plans submitted under that section; [1]

(2) develop a long-range national rail plan that is consistent with approved State rail plans and the rail needs of the Nation, as determined by the Secretary in order to promote an integrated, cohesive, efficient, and optimized national rail system for the movement of goods and people;

(3) develop a preliminary national rail plan within a year after the date of enactment of the Passenger Rail Investment and Improvement Act of 2008;

(4) develop and enhance partnerships with the freight and passenger railroad industry, States, and the public concerning rail development;

(5) support rail intermodal development and high-speed rail development, including high speed rail planning;

(6) ensure that programs and initiatives developed under this section benefit the public and work toward achieving regional and national transportation goals; and

(7) facilitate and coordinate efforts to assist freight and passenger rail carriers, transit agencies and authorities, municipalities, and States in passenger-freight service integration on shared rights of way by providing neutral assistance at the joint request of affected rail service providers and infrastructure owners relating to operations and capacity analysis, capital requirements, operating costs, and other research and planning related to corridors shared by passenger or commuter rail service and freight rail operations.

(k) PERFORMANCE GOALS AND REPORTS.—

(1) PERFORMANCE GOALS.—In conjunction with the objectives established and activities undertaken under subsection (j) of this section, the Administrator shall develop a schedule for achieving specific, measurable performance goals.

(2) RESOURCE NEEDS.—The strategy and annual plans shall include estimates of the funds and staff resources needed to accomplish each goal and the additional duties required under subsection (j).

(3) SUBMISSION WITH PRESIDENT'S BUDGET.—Beginning with fiscal year 2010 and each fiscal year thereafter, the Secretary shall submit to the Committee on Transportation and Infrastructure of the House of Representatives and the Committee on Commerce, Science, and Transportation of the Senate, at the same time as the President's budget submission, the Administration's performance goals and schedule developed under paragraph (1), including an assessment of the progress of the Administration toward achieving its performance goals.

(Pub. L. 97–449, §1(b), Jan. 12, 1983, 96 Stat. 2414; Pub. L. 98–216, §2(2), Feb. 14, 1984, 98 Stat. 5; Pub. L. 103–272, §5(m)(1), July 5, 1994, 108 Stat. 1375; Pub. L. 103–440, title II, §216, Nov. 2, 1994, 108 Stat.

4624; Pub. L. 107–217, §3(n)(1), Aug. 21, 2002, 116 Stat. 1302; Pub. L. 110–432, div. A, title I, §101, div. B, title III, §307, Oct. 16, 2008, 122 Stat. 4851, 4953; Pub. L. 111–350, §5(o)(1), Jan. 4, 2011, 124 Stat. 3853.)

[1] *So in original. Probably should be "chapter;".*

* * * * * * *

§114. TRANSPORTATION SECURITY ADMINISTRATION

(a) IN GENERAL.—The Transportation Security Administration shall be an administration of the Department of Homeland Security.

(b) LEADERSHIP.—

(1) HEAD OF TRANSPORTATION SECURITY ADMINISTRATION.—

(A) APPOINTMENT.—The head of the Administration shall be the Administrator of the Transportation Security Administration (referred to in this section as the "Administrator"). The Administrator shall be appointed by the President, by and with the advice and consent of the Senate.

(B) QUALIFICATIONS.—The Administrator must—

(i) be a citizen of the United States; and

(ii) have experience in a field directly related to transportation or security.

(C) TERM.—Effective with respect to any individual appointment by the President, by and with the advice and consent of the Senate, after the date of enactment of the TSA Modernization Act, the term of office of an individual appointed as the Administrator shall be 5 years. The term of office of an individual serving as the Administrator on the date of enactment of the TSA Modernization Act shall be 5 years beginning on the date that the Administrator began serving.

(2) DEPUTY ADMINISTRATOR.—

(A) APPOINTMENT.—There is established in the Transportation Security Administration a Deputy Administrator, who shall assist the Administrator in the management of the Transportation Security Administration. The Deputy Administrator shall be appointed by the President.

(B) VACANCY.—The Deputy Administrator shall be Acting Administrator during the absence or incapacity of the Administrator or during a vacancy in the office of Administrator.

(C) QUALIFICATIONS.—The Deputy Administrator must—

(i) be a citizen of the United States; and

(ii) have experience in a field directly related to transportation or security.

(3) CHIEF COUNSEL.—

(A) APPOINTMENT.—There is established in the Transportation Security Administration a Chief Counsel, who shall advise the Administrator and other senior officials on all legal matters relating to the responsibilities, functions, and management of the Transportation Security Administration.

(B) QUALIFICATIONS.—The Chief Counsel must be a citizen of the United States.

(c) LIMITATION ON OWNERSHIP OF STOCKS AND BONDS.—The Administrator may not own stock in or bonds of a transportation or security enterprise or an enterprise that makes equipment that could be used for security purposes.

(d) FUNCTIONS.—The Administrator shall be responsible for security in all modes of transportation, including—

(1) carrying out chapter 449, relating to civil aviation security, and related research and development activities; and

(2) security responsibilities over other modes of transportation that are exercised by the Department of Transportation.

(e) SCREENING OPERATIONS.—The Administrator shall—

(1) be responsible for day-to-day Federal security screening operations for passenger air transportation and intrastate air transportation under sections 44901 and 44935;

(2) develop standards for the hiring and retention of security screening personnel;

(3) train and test security screening personnel; and

(4) be responsible for hiring and training personnel to provide security screening at all airports in the United States where screening is required under section 44901, in consultation with the Secretary of Transportation and the heads of other appropriate Federal agencies and departments.

(f) ADDITIONAL DUTIES AND POWERS.—In addition to carrying out the functions specified in subsections (d) and (e), the Administrator shall—

(1) receive, assess, and distribute intelligence information related to transportation security;

(2) assess threats to transportation;

(3) develop policies, strategies, and plans for dealing with threats to transportation security;

(4) make other plans related to transportation security, including coordinating countermeasures with appropriate departments, agencies, and instrumentalities of the United States Government;

(5) serve as the primary liaison for transportation security to the intelligence and law enforcement communities;

(6) on a day-to-day basis, manage and provide operational guidance to the field security resources of the Administration, including Federal Security Managers as provided by section 44933;

(7) enforce security-related regulations and requirements;

(8) identify and undertake research and development activities necessary to enhance transportation security;

(9) inspect, maintain, and test security facilities, equipment, and systems;

(10) ensure the adequacy of security measures for the transportation of cargo;

(11) oversee the implementation, and ensure the adequacy, of security measures at airports and other transportation facilities;

(12) require background checks for airport security screening personnel, individuals with access to secure areas of airports, and other transportation security personnel;

(13) work in conjunction with the Administrator of the Federal Aviation Administration with respect to any actions or activities that may affect aviation safety or air carrier operations;

(14) work with the International Civil Aviation Organization and appropriate aeronautic authorities of foreign governments under section 44907 to address security concerns on passenger flights by foreign air carriers in foreign air transportation;

(15) establish and maintain a National Deployment Office as required under section 44948 of this title; and

(16) carry out such other duties, and exercise such other powers, relating to transportation security as the Administrator considers appropriate, to the extent authorized by law.

(g) NATIONAL EMERGENCY RESPONSIBILITIES.—

(1) IN GENERAL.—Subject to the direction and control of the Secretary of Homeland Security, the Administrator, during a national emergency, shall have the following responsibilities:

(A) To coordinate domestic transportation, including aviation, rail, and other surface transportation, and maritime transportation (including port security).

(B) To coordinate and oversee the transportation-related responsibilities of other departments and agencies of the Federal Government other than the Department of Defense and the military departments.

(C) To coordinate and provide notice to other departments and agencies of the Federal Government, and appropriate agencies of State and local governments, including departments and agencies for transportation, law enforcement, and border control, about threats to transportation.

(D) To carry out such other duties, and exercise such other powers, relating to transportation during a national emergency as the Secretary of Homeland Security shall prescribe.

(2) AUTHORITY OF OTHER DEPARTMENTS AND AGENCIES.—The authority of the Administrator under this subsection shall not supersede the authority of any other department or agency of the Federal Government under law with respect to transportation or transportation-related matters, whether or not during a national emergency.

(3) CIRCUMSTANCES.—The Secretary of Homeland Security shall prescribe the circumstances constituting a national emergency for purposes of this subsection.

(h) MANAGEMENT OF SECURITY INFORMATION.—In consultation with the Transportation Security Oversight Board, the Administrator shall—

(1) enter into memoranda of understanding with Federal agencies or other entities to share or otherwise cross-check as necessary data on individuals identified on Federal agency databases who may pose a risk to transportation or national security;

(2) establish procedures for notifying the Administrator of the Federal Aviation Administration, appropriate State and local law enforcement officials, and airport or airline security officers of the identity of individuals known to pose, or suspected of

posing, a risk of air piracy or terrorism or a threat to airline or passenger safety;

(3) in consultation with other appropriate Federal agencies and air carriers, establish policies and procedures requiring air carriers—

(A) to use information from government agencies to identify individuals on passenger lists who may be a threat to civil aviation or national security; and

(B) if such an individual is identified, notify appropriate law enforcement agencies, prevent the individual from boarding an aircraft, or take other appropriate action with respect to that individual; and

(4) consider requiring passenger air carriers to share passenger lists with appropriate Federal agencies for the purpose of identifying individuals who may pose a threat to aviation safety or national security.

(i) VIEW OF NTSB.—In taking any action under this section that could affect safety, the Administrator shall give great weight to the timely views of the National Transportation Safety Board.

(j) ACQUISITIONS.—

(1) IN GENERAL.—The Administrator is authorized—

(A) to acquire (by purchase, lease, condemnation, or otherwise) such real property, or any interest therein, within and outside the continental United States, as the Administrator considers necessary;

(B) to acquire (by purchase, lease, condemnation, or otherwise) and to construct, repair, operate, and maintain such personal property (including office space and patents), or any interest therein, within and outside the continental United States, as the Administrator considers necessary;

(C) to lease to others such real and personal property and to provide by contract or otherwise for necessary facilities for the welfare of its employees and to acquire, maintain, and operate equipment for these facilities;

(D) to acquire services, including such personal services as the Secretary of Homeland Security determines necessary, and to acquire (by purchase, lease, condemnation, or otherwise) and to construct, repair, operate, and maintain research and testing sites and facilities; and

(E) in cooperation with the Administrator of the Federal Aviation Administration, to utilize the research and development facilities of the Federal Aviation Administration.

(2) TITLE.—Title to any property or interest therein acquired pursuant to this subsection shall be held by the Government of the United States.

(k) TRANSFERS OF FUNDS.—The Administrator is authorized to accept transfers of unobligated balances and unexpended balances of funds appropriated to other Federal agencies (as such term is defined in section 551(1) of title 5) to carry out functions assigned by law to the Administrator.

(l) REGULATIONS.—

(1) IN GENERAL.—The Administrator is authorized to issue, rescind, and revise such regulations as are necessary to carry out the functions of the Administration.

(2) EMERGENCY PROCEDURES.—

(A) IN GENERAL.—Notwithstanding any other provision of law or executive order (including an executive order requiring a cost-benefit analysis), if the Administrator determines that a regulation or security directive must be issued immediately in order to protect transportation security, the Administrator shall issue the regulation or security directive without providing notice or an opportunity for comment and without prior approval of the Secretary.

(B) REVIEW BY TRANSPORTATION SECURITY OVERSIGHT BOARD.—Any regulation or security directive issued under this paragraph shall be subject to review by the Transportation Security Oversight Board established under section 115. Any regulation or security directive issued under this paragraph shall remain effective for a period not to exceed 90 days unless ratified or disapproved by the Board or rescinded by the Administrator.

(3) FACTORS TO CONSIDER.—In determining whether to issue, rescind, or revise a regulation under this section, the Administrator shall consider, as a factor in the final determination, whether the costs of the regulation are excessive in relation to the enhancement of security the regulation will provide. The Administrator may waive requirements for an analysis that estimates the number of lives that will be saved by the regulation and the monetary value of such lives if the Administrator determines that it is not feasible to make such an estimate.

(4) AIRWORTHINESS OBJECTIONS BY FAA.—

(A) IN GENERAL.—The Administrator shall not take an aviation security action under this title if the Administrator of the Federal Aviation Administration notifies the Administrator that the action could adversely affect the airworthiness of an aircraft.

(B) REVIEW BY SECRETARY.—Notwithstanding subparagraph (A), the Administrator may take such an action, after receiving a notification concerning the action from the Administrator of the Federal Aviation Administration under subparagraph (A), if the Secretary of Transportation subsequently approves the action.

(m) PERSONNEL AND SERVICES; COOPERATION BY ADMINISTRATOR.—

(1) AUTHORITY OF ADMINISTRATOR.—In carrying out the functions of the Administration, the Administrator shall have the same authority as is provided to the Administrator of the Federal Aviation Administration under subsections (l) and (m) of section 106.

(2) AUTHORITY OF AGENCY HEADS.—The head of a Federal agency shall have the same authority to provide services, supplies, equipment, personnel, and facilities to the Administrator as the head has to provide services, supplies, equipment, personnel, and facilities to the Administrator of the Federal Aviation Administration under section 106(m).

(n) PERSONNEL MANAGEMENT SYSTEM.—

(1) IN GENERAL.—The personnel management system established by the Administrator of the Federal Aviation Administration under section 40122 shall apply to employees of the Transportation Security Administration, or, subject to the requirements

of such section, the Administrator may make such modifications to the personnel management system with respect to such employees as the Administrator considers appropriate, such as adopting aspects of other personnel systems of the Department of Homeland Security.

(2) MERITORIOUS EXECUTIVE OR DISTINGUISHED EXECUTIVE RANK AWARDS.—Notwithstanding section 40122(g)(2) of this title, the applicable sections of title 5 shall apply to the Transportation Security Administration personnel management system, except that—

(A) for purposes of applying such provisions to the personnel management system—

(i) the term "agency" means the Department of Homeland Security;

(ii) the term "senior executive" means a Transportation Security Administration executive serving on a Transportation Security Executive Service appointment;

(iii) the term "career appointee" means a Transportation Security Administration executive serving on a career Transportation Security Executive Service appointment; and

(iv) The [1] term "senior career employee" means a Transportation Security Administration employee covered by the Transportation Security Administration Core Compensation System at the L or M pay band;

(B) receipt by a career appointee or a senior career employee of the rank of Meritorious Executive or Meritorious Senior Professional entitles the individual to a lump-sum payment of an amount equal to 20 percent of annual basic pay, which shall be in addition to the basic pay paid under the applicable Transportation Security Administration pay system; and

(C) receipt by a career appointee or a senior career employee of the rank of Distinguished Executive or Distinguished Senior Professional entitles the individual to a lump-sum payment of an amount equal to 35 percent of annual basic pay, which shall be in addition to the basic pay paid under the applicable Transportation Security Administration pay system.

(3) DEFINITION OF APPLICABLE SECTIONS OF TITLE 5.—In this subsection, the term "applicable sections of title 5" means—

(A) subsections (b), (c) and (d) of section 4507 of title 5; and

(B) subsections (b) and (c) of section 4507a of title 5.

(o) AUTHORITY OF INSPECTOR GENERAL.—The Transportation Security Administration shall be subject to chapter 4 of title 5 and other laws relating to the authority of the Inspector General of the Department of Homeland Security.

(p) LAW ENFORCEMENT POWERS.—

(1) IN GENERAL.—The Administrator may designate an employee of the Transportation Security Administration or other Federal agency to serve as a law enforcement officer.

(2) POWERS.—While engaged in official duties of the Administration as required to fulfill the responsibilities under this section, a law enforcement officer designated under

paragraph (1) may—

(A) carry a firearm;

(B) make an arrest without a warrant for any offense against the United States committed in the presence of the officer, or for any felony cognizable under the laws of the United States if the officer has probable cause to believe that the person to be arrested has committed or is committing the felony; and

(C) seek and execute warrants for arrest or seizure of evidence issued under the authority of the United States upon probable cause that a violation has been committed.

(3) GUIDELINES ON EXERCISE OF AUTHORITY.—The authority provided by this subsection shall be exercised in accordance with guidelines prescribed by the Administrator, in consultation with the Attorney General of the United States, and shall include adherence to the Attorney General's policy on use of deadly force.

(4) REVOCATION OR SUSPENSION OF AUTHORITY.—The powers authorized by this subsection may be rescinded or suspended should the Attorney General determine that the Administrator has not complied with the guidelines prescribed in paragraph (3) and conveys the determination in writing to the Secretary of Homeland Security and the Administrator.

(q) AUTHORITY TO EXEMPT.—The Administrator may grant an exemption from a regulation prescribed in carrying out this section if the Administrator determines that the exemption is in the public interest.

(r) NONDISCLOSURE OF SECURITY ACTIVITIES.—

(1) IN GENERAL.—Notwithstanding section 552 of title 5, the Administrator shall prescribe regulations prohibiting the disclosure of information obtained or developed in carrying out security under authority of the Aviation and Transportation Security Act (Public Law 107–71) or under chapter 449 of this title if the Administrator decides that disclosing the information would—

(A) be an unwarranted invasion of personal privacy;

(B) reveal a trade secret or privileged or confidential commercial or financial information; or

(C) be detrimental to the security of transportation.

(2) AVAILABILITY OF INFORMATION TO CONGRESS.—Paragraph (1) does not authorize information to be withheld from a committee of Congress authorized to have the information.

(3) LIMITATION ON TRANSFERABILITY OF DUTIES.—Except as otherwise provided by law, the Administrator may not transfer a duty or power under this subsection to another department, agency, or instrumentality of the United States.

(4) LIMITATIONS.—Nothing in this subsection, or any other provision of law, shall be construed to authorize the designation of information as sensitive security information (as defined in section 1520.5 of title 49, Code of Federal Regulations)—

(A) to conceal a violation of law, inefficiency, or administrative error;

(B) to prevent embarrassment to a person, organization, or agency;

(C) to restrain competition; or

(D) to prevent or delay the release of information that does not require protection in the interest of transportation security, including basic scientific research information not clearly related to transportation security.

(s) TRANSPORTATION SECURITY STRATEGIC PLANNING.—

(1) IN GENERAL.—The Secretary of Homeland Security shall develop, prepare, implement, and update, as needed—

(A) a National Strategy for Transportation Security; and

(B) transportation modal security plans addressing security risks, including threats, vulnerabilities, and consequences, for aviation, railroad, ferry, highway, maritime, pipeline, public transportation, over-the-road bus, and other transportation infrastructure assets.

(2) ROLE OF SECRETARY OF TRANSPORTATION.—The Secretary of Homeland Security shall work jointly with the Secretary of Transportation in developing, revising, and updating the documents required by paragraph (1).

(3) CONTENTS OF NATIONAL STRATEGY FOR TRANSPORTATION SECURITY.—The National Strategy for Transportation Security shall include the following:

(A) An identification and evaluation of the transportation assets in the United States that, in the interests of national security and commerce, must be protected from attack or disruption by terrorist or other hostile forces, including modal security plans for aviation, bridge and tunnel, commuter rail and ferry, highway, maritime, pipeline, rail, mass transit, over-the-road bus, and other public transportation infrastructure assets that could be at risk of such an attack or disruption.

(B) The development of risk-based priorities, based on risk assessments conducted or received by the Secretary of Homeland Security (including assessments conducted under the Implementing Recommendations of the 9/11 Commission Act of 2007) across all transportation modes and realistic deadlines for addressing security needs associated with those assets referred to in subparagraph (A).

(C) The most appropriate, practical, and cost-effective means of defending those assets against threats to their security.

(D) A forward-looking strategic plan that sets forth the agreed upon roles and missions of Federal, State, regional, local, and tribal authorities and establishes mechanisms for encouraging cooperation and participation by private sector entities, including nonprofit employee labor organizations, in the implementation of such plan.

(E) A comprehensive delineation of prevention, response, and recovery responsibilities and issues regarding threatened and executed acts of terrorism within the United States and threatened and executed acts of terrorism outside the United States to the extent such acts affect United States transportation systems.

(F) A prioritization of research and development objectives that support transportation security needs, giving a higher priority to research and development directed toward protecting vital transportation assets. Transportation security research and development projects shall be based, to the extent practicable, on such prioritization. Nothing in the preceding sentence shall be construed to require the termination of any research or development project initiated by the Secretary of Homeland Security or the Secretary of Transportation before the date of enactment of the Implementing Recommendations of the 9/11 Commission Act of 2007.

(G) A 3- and 10-year budget for Federal transportation security programs that will achieve the priorities of the National Strategy for Transportation Security.

(H) Methods for linking the individual transportation modal security plans and the programs contained therein, and a plan for addressing the security needs of intermodal transportation.

(I) Transportation modal security plans described in paragraph (1)(B), including operational recovery plans to expedite, to the maximum extent practicable, the return to operation of an adversely affected transportation system following a major terrorist attack on that system or other incident. These plans shall be coordinated with the resumption of trade protocols required under section 202 of the SAFE Port Act (6 U.S.C. 942) and the National Maritime Transportation Security Plan required under section 70103(a) of title 46.

(4) SUBMISSION OF PLANS.—

(A) IN GENERAL.—The Secretary of Homeland Security shall submit the National Strategy for Transportation Security, including the transportation modal security plans and any revisions to the National Strategy for Transportation Security and the transportation modal security plans, to appropriate congressional committees not less frequently than April 1 of each even-numbered year.

(B) PERIODIC PROGRESS REPORT.—

(i) REQUIREMENT FOR REPORT.—Each year, in conjunction with the submission of the budget to Congress under section 1105(a) of title 31, United States Code, the Secretary of Homeland Security shall submit to the appropriate congressional committees an assessment of the progress made on implementing the National Strategy for Transportation Security, including the transportation modal security plans.

(ii) CONTENT.—Each progress report submitted under this subparagraph shall include, at a minimum, the following:

(I) Recommendations for improving and implementing the National Strategy for Transportation Security and the transportation modal and intermodal security plans that the Secretary of Homeland Security, in consultation with the Secretary of Transportation, considers appropriate.

(II) An accounting of all grants for transportation security, including grants and contracts for research and development, awarded by the Secretary of Homeland Security in the most recent fiscal year and a description of how such grants accomplished the goals of the National Strategy for Transportation Security.

(III) An accounting of all—

(aa) funds requested in the President's budget submitted pursuant to section 1105 of title 31 for the most recent fiscal year for transportation security, by mode;

(bb) personnel working on transportation security by mode, including the number of contractors; and (cc) information on the turnover in the previous year among senior staff of the Department of Homeland Security, including component agencies, working on transportation security issues. Such information shall include the number of employees who have permanently left the office, agency, or area in which they worked, and the amount of time that they worked for the Department of Homeland Security.

(iii) WRITTEN EXPLANATION OF TRANSPORTATION SECURITY ACTIVITIES NOT DELINEATED IN THE NATIONAL STRATEGY FOR TRANSPORTATION SECURITY.—At the end of each fiscal year, the Secretary of Homeland Security shall submit to the appropriate congressional committees a written explanation of any Federal transportation security activity that is inconsistent with the National Strategy for Transportation Security, including the amount of funds to be expended for the activity and the number of personnel involved.

(C) CLASSIFIED MATERIAL.—Any part of the National Strategy for Transportation Security or the transportation modal security plans that involve information that is properly classified under criteria established by Executive order shall be submitted to the appropriate congressional committees separately in a classified format.

(D) APPROPRIATE CONGRESSIONAL COMMITTEES DEFINED.—In this subsection, the term "appropriate congressional committees" means the Committee on Transportation and Infrastructure and the Committee on Homeland Security of the House of Representatives and the Committee on Commerce, Science, and Transportation, the Committee on Homeland Security and Governmental Affairs, and the Committee on Banking, Housing, and Urban Affairs of the Senate.

(5) PRIORITY STATUS.—

(A) IN GENERAL.—The National Strategy for Transportation Security shall be the governing document for Federal transportation security efforts.

(B) OTHER PLANS AND REPORTS.—The National Strategy for Transportation Security shall include, as an integral part or as an appendix—

(i) the current National Maritime Transportation Security Plan under section 70103 of title 46;

(ii) the report required by section 44938 of this title;

(iii) transportation modal security plans required under this section;

(iv) the transportation sector specific plan required under Homeland Security Presidential Directive–7; and

(v) any other transportation security plan or report that the Secretary of Homeland Security determines appropriate for inclusion.

(6) COORDINATION.—In carrying out the responsibilities under this section, the Secretary of Homeland Security, in coordination with the Secretary of Transportation, shall consult, as appropriate, with Federal, State, and local agencies, tribal governments, private sector entities (including nonprofit employee labor organizations), institutions of higher learning, and other entities.

(7) PLAN DISTRIBUTION.—The Secretary of Homeland Security shall make available and appropriately publicize an unclassified version of the National Strategy for Transportation Security, including its component transportation modal security plans, to Federal, State, regional, local and tribal authorities, transportation system owners or operators, private sector stakeholders, including nonprofit employee labor organizations representing transportation employees, institutions of higher learning, and other appropriate entities.

(t) TRANSPORTATION SECURITY INFORMATION SHARING PLAN.—

(1) DEFINITIONS.—In this subsection:

(A) APPROPRIATE CONGRESSIONAL COMMITTEES.—The term "appropriate congressional committees" has the meaning given that term in subsection (s)(4)(E).

(B) PLAN.—The term "Plan" means the Transportation Security Information Sharing Plan established under paragraph (2).

(C) PUBLIC AND PRIVATE STAKEHOLDERS.—The term "public and private stakeholders" means Federal, State, and local agencies, tribal governments, and appropriate private entities, including nonprofit employee labor organizations representing transportation employees.

(D) TRANSPORTATION SECURITY INFORMATION.—The term "transportation security information" means information relating to the risks to transportation modes, including aviation, public transportation, railroad, ferry, highway, maritime, pipeline, and over-the-road bus transportation, and may include specific and general intelligence products, as appropriate.

(2) ESTABLISHMENT OF PLAN.—The Secretary of Homeland Security, in consultation with the program manager of the information sharing environment established under section 1016 of the Intelligence Reform and Terrorism Prevention Act of 2004 (6 U.S.C. 485), the Secretary of Transportation, and public and private stakeholders, shall establish a Transportation Security Information Sharing Plan. In establishing the Plan, the Secretary of Homeland Security shall gather input on the development of the Plan from private and public stakeholders and the program manager of the information sharing environment established under section 1016 of the Intelligence Reform and Terrorism Prevention Act of 2004 (6 U.S.C. 485).

(3) PURPOSE OF PLAN.—The Plan shall promote sharing of transportation security information between the Department of Homeland Security and public and private stakeholders.

(4) CONTENT OF PLAN.—The Plan shall include—

(A) a description of how intelligence analysts within the Department of Homeland Security will coordinate their activities within the Department and with other Federal, State, and local agencies, and tribal governments, including coordination with existing modal information sharing centers and the center described in section 1410 of the Implementing Recommendations of the 9/11 Commission Act of 2007;

(B) the establishment of a point of contact, which may be a single point of contact within the Department of Homeland Security, for each mode of transportation for the sharing of transportation security information with public and private stakeholders, including an explanation and justification to the appropriate congressional committees if the point of contact established pursuant to this subparagraph differs from the agency within the Department of Homeland Security that has the primary authority, or has been delegated such authority by the Secretary of Homeland Security, to regulate the security of that transportation mode;

(C) a reasonable deadline by which the Plan will be implemented; and

(D) a description of resource needs for fulfilling the Plan.

(5) COORDINATION WITH INFORMATION SHARING.—The Plan shall be—

(A) implemented in coordination, as appropriate, with the program manager for the information sharing environment established under section 1016 of the Intelligence Reform and Terrorism Prevention Act of 2004 (6 U.S.C. 485); and

(B) consistent with the establishment of the information sharing environment and any policies, guidelines, procedures, instructions, or standards established by the President or the program manager for the implementation and management of the information sharing environment.

(6) ANNUAL REPORT ON PLAN.—The Secretary of Homeland Security shall annually submit to the appropriate congressional committees a report containing the Plan.

(7) SECURITY CLEARANCES.—The Secretary of Homeland Security shall, to the greatest extent practicable, take steps to expedite the security clearances needed for designated public and private stakeholders to receive and obtain access to classified information distributed under this section, as appropriate.

(8) CLASSIFICATION OF MATERIAL.—The Secretary of Homeland Security, to the greatest extent practicable, shall provide designated public and private stakeholders with transportation security information in an unclassified format.

(u) ENFORCEMENT OF REGULATIONS AND ORDERS OF THE SECRETARY OF HOMELAND SECURITY.—

(1) APPLICATION OF SUBSECTION.—

(A) IN GENERAL.—This subsection applies to the enforcement of regulations prescribed, and orders issued, by the Secretary of Homeland Security under a provision of chapter 701 of title 46 and under a provision of this title other than a provision of chapter 449 (in this subsection referred to as an "applicable provision of this title").

(B) VIOLATIONS OF CHAPTER 449.—The penalties for violations of regulations prescribed and orders issued by the Secretary of Homeland Security or the Administrator under chapter 449 of this title are provided under chapter 463 of this title.

(C) NONAPPLICATION TO CERTAIN VIOLATIONS.—

(i) Paragraphs (2) through (5) do not apply to violations of regulations prescribed, and orders issued, by the Secretary of Homeland Security under a provision of this title—

(I) involving the transportation of personnel or shipments of materials by contractors where the Department of Defense has assumed control and responsibility;

(II) by a member of the armed forces of the United States when performing official duties; or

(III) by a civilian employee of the Department of Defense when performing official duties.

(ii) Violations described in subclause (I), (II), or (III) of clause (i) shall be subject to penalties as determined by the Secretary of Defense or the Secretary of Defense's designee.

(2) CIVIL PENALTY.—

(A) IN GENERAL.—A person is liable to the United States Government for a civil penalty of not more than $10,000 for a violation of a regulation prescribed, or order issued, by the Secretary of Homeland Security under an applicable provision of this title.

(B) REPEAT VIOLATIONS.—A separate violation occurs under this paragraph for each day the violation continues.

(3) ADMINISTRATIVE IMPOSITION OF CIVIL PENALTIES.—

(A) IN GENERAL.—The Secretary of Homeland Security may impose a civil penalty for a violation of a regulation prescribed, or order issued, under an applicable provision of this title. The Secretary shall give written notice of the finding of a violation and the penalty.

(B) SCOPE OF CIVIL ACTION.—In a civil action to collect a civil penalty imposed by the Secretary of Homeland Security under this subsection, a court may not re-examine issues of liability or the amount of the penalty.

(C) JURISDICTION.—The district courts of the United States shall have exclusive jurisdiction of civil actions to collect a civil penalty imposed by the Secretary of Homeland Security under this subsection if—

(i) the amount in controversy is more than—

(I) $400,000, if the violation was committed by a person other than an individual or small business concern; or

(II) $50,000 if the violation was committed by an individual or small business concern;

(ii) the action is in rem or another action in rem based on the same violation has been brought; or

(iii) another action has been brought for an injunction based on the same violation.

(D) MAXIMUM PENALTY.—The maximum civil penalty the Secretary of Homeland Security administratively may impose under this paragraph is—

(i) $400,000, if the violation was committed by a person other than an individual or small business concern; or

(ii) $50,000, if the violation was committed by an individual or small business concern.

(E) NOTICE AND OPPORTUNITY TO REQUEST HEARING.—Before imposing a penalty under this section the Secretary of Homeland Security shall provide to the person against whom the penalty is to be imposed—
    (i) written notice of the proposed penalty; and
    (ii) the opportunity to request a hearing on the proposed penalty, if the Secretary of Homeland Security receives the request not later than 30 days after the date on which the person receives notice.

(4) COMPROMISE AND SETOFF.—
    (A) The Secretary of Homeland Security may compromise the amount of a civil penalty imposed under this subsection.
    (B) The Government may deduct the amount of a civil penalty imposed or compromised under this subsection from amounts it owes the person liable for the penalty.

(5) INVESTIGATIONS AND PROCEEDINGS.—Chapter 461 shall apply to investigations and proceedings brought under this subsection to the same extent that it applies to investigations and proceedings brought with respect to aviation security duties designated to be carried out by the Secretary of Homeland Security.

(6) DEFINITIONS.—In this subsection:
    (A) PERSON.—The term "person" does not include—
    (i) the United States Postal Service; or
    (ii) the Department of Defense.

    (B) SMALL BUSINESS CONCERN.—The term "small business concern" has the meaning given that term in section 3 of the Small Business Act (15 U.S.C. 632).

(7) ENFORCEMENT TRANSPARENCY.—
    (A) IN GENERAL.—The Secretary of Homeland Security shall—
    (i) provide an annual summary to the public of all enforcement actions taken by the Secretary under this subsection; and
    (ii) include in each such summary the docket number of each enforcement action, the type of alleged violation, the penalty or penalties proposed, and the final assessment amount of each penalty.

    (B) ELECTRONIC AVAILABILITY.—Each summary under this paragraph shall be made available to the public by electronic means.
    (C) RELATIONSHIP TO THE FREEDOM OF INFORMATION ACT AND THE PRIVACY ACT.—Nothing in this subsection shall be construed to require disclosure of information or records that are exempt from disclosure under sections 552 or 552a of title 5.

(v) AUTHORIZATION OF APPROPRIATIONS.—There are authorized to be appropriated to

the Transportation Security Administration for salaries, operations, and maintenance of the Administration—
(1) $7,849,247,000 for fiscal year 2019;
(2) $7,888,494,000 for fiscal year 2020; and
(3) $7,917,936,000 for fiscal year 2021.

(w) LEADERSHIP AND ORGANIZATION.—
(1) IN GENERAL.—For each of the areas described in paragraph (2), the Administrator of the Transportation Security Administration shall appoint at least 1 individual who shall—
(A) report directly to the Administrator or the Administrator's designated direct report; and
(B) be responsible and accountable for that area.

(2) AREAS DESCRIBED.—The areas described in this paragraph are as follows:
(A) Aviation security operations and training, including risk-based, adaptive security—
(i) focused on airport checkpoint and baggage screening operations;
(ii) workforce training and development programs; and
(iii) ensuring compliance with aviation security law, including regulations, and other specialized programs designed to secure air transportation.

(B) Surface transportation security operations and training, including risk-based, adaptive security—
(i) focused on accomplishing security systems assessments;
(ii) reviewing and prioritizing projects for appropriated surface transportation security grants;
(iii) operator compliance with surface transportation security law, including regulations, and voluntary industry standards; and
(iv) workforce training and development programs, and other specialized programs designed to secure surface transportation.

(C) Transportation industry engagement and planning, including the development, interpretation, promotion, and oversight of a unified effort regarding risk-based, risk-reducing security policies and plans (including strategic planning for future contingencies and security challenges) between government and transportation stakeholders, including airports, domestic and international airlines, general aviation, air cargo, mass transit and passenger rail, freight rail, pipeline, highway and motor carriers, and maritime.
(D) International strategy and operations, including agency efforts to work with international partners to secure the global transportation network.
(E) Trusted and registered traveler programs, including the management and marketing of the agency's trusted traveler initiatives, including the PreCheck Program, and coordination with trusted traveler programs of other Department of Homeland Security agencies and the private sector.

(F) Technology acquisition and deployment, including the oversight, development, testing, evaluation, acquisition, deployment, and maintenance of security technology and other acquisition programs.

(G) Inspection and compliance, including the integrity, efficiency and effectiveness of the agency's workforce, operations, and programs through objective audits, covert testing, inspections, criminal investigations, and regulatory compliance.

(H) Civil rights, liberties, and traveler engagement, including ensuring that agency employees and the traveling public are treated in a fair and lawful manner consistent with Federal laws and regulations protecting privacy and prohibiting discrimination and reprisal.

(I) Legislative and public affairs, including communication and engagement with internal and external audiences in a timely, accurate, and transparent manner, and development and implementation of strategies within the agency to achieve congressional approval or authorization of agency programs and policies.

(3) NOTIFICATION.—The Administrator shall submit to the appropriate committees of Congress—

(A) not later than 180 days after the date of enactment of the TSA Modernization Act, a list of the names of the individuals appointed under paragraph (1); and

(B) an update of the list not later than 5 days after any new individual is appointed under paragraph (1).

(x) TRANSPORTATION SECURITY PREPAREDNESS PLAN.—

(1) IN GENERAL.—Not later than two years after the date of the enactment of this subsection, the Secretary of Homeland Security, acting through the Administrator, in coordination with the Chief Medical Officer of the Department of Homeland Security, and in consultation with the partners identified under paragraphs (3)(A)(i) through (3)(A)(iv), shall develop a transportation security preparedness plan to address the event of a communicable disease outbreak. The Secretary, acting through the Administrator, shall ensure such plan aligns with relevant Federal plans and strategies for communicable disease outbreaks.

(2) CONSIDERATIONS.—In developing the plan required under paragraph (1), the Secretary, acting through the Administrator, shall consider each of the following:

(A) The findings of the survey required under section 6411 of the National Defense Authorization Act for Fiscal Year 2022.

(B) The findings of the analysis required under section 6414 of the National Defense Authorization Act for Fiscal Year 2022.

(C) The plan required under section 6415 of the National Defense Authorization Act for Fiscal Year 2022.

(D) All relevant reports and recommendations regarding the Administration's response to the COVID–19 pandemic, including any reports and recommendations issued by the Comptroller General and the Inspector General of the Department of Homeland Security.

(E) Lessons learned from Federal interagency efforts during the COVID–19 pandemic.

(3) CONTENTS OF PLAN.—The plan developed under paragraph (1) shall include each of the following:

(A) Plans for communicating and collaborating in the event of a communicable disease outbreak with the following partners:

(i) Appropriate Federal departments and agencies, including the Department of Health and Human Services, the Centers for Disease Control and Prevention, the Department of Transportation, the Department of Labor, and appropriate interagency task forces.

(ii) The workforce of the Administration, including through the labor organization certified as the exclusive representative of full- and part-time non-supervisory Administration personnel carrying out screening functions under section 44901 of this title.

(iii) International partners, including the International Civil Aviation Organization and foreign governments, airports, and air carriers.

(iv) Public and private stakeholders, as such term is defined under subsection (t)(1)(C).

(v) The traveling public.

(B) Plans for protecting the safety of the Transportation Security Administration workforce, including—

(i) reducing the risk of communicable disease transmission at screening checkpoints and within the Administration's workforce related to the Administration's transportation security operations and mission;

(ii) ensuring the safety and hygiene of screening checkpoints and other workstations;

(iii) supporting equitable and appropriate access to relevant vaccines, prescriptions, and other medical care; and

(iv) tracking rates of employee illness, recovery, and death.

(C) Criteria for determining the conditions that may warrant the integration of additional actions in the aviation screening system in response to the communicable disease outbreak and a range of potential roles and responsibilities that align with such conditions.

(D) Contingency plans for temporarily adjusting checkpoint operations to provide for passenger and employee safety while maintaining security during the communicable disease outbreak.

(E) Provisions setting forth criteria for establishing an interagency task force or other standing engagement platform with other appropriate Federal departments and agencies, including the Department of Health and Human Services and the Department of Transportation, to address such communicable disease outbreak.

(F) A description of scenarios in which the Administrator should consider exercising authorities provided under subsection (g) and for what purposes.

(G) Considerations for assessing the appropriateness of issuing security directives and emergency amendments to regulated parties in various modes of transportation, including surface transportation, and plans for ensuring compliance with such measures.

(H) A description of any potential obstacles, including funding constraints and limitations to authorities, that could restrict the ability of the Administration to respond appropriately to a communicable disease outbreak.

(4) DISSEMINATION.—Upon development of the plan required under paragraph (1), the Administrator shall disseminate the plan to the partners identified under paragraph (3)(A) and to the Committee on Homeland Security of the House of Representatives and the Committee on Homeland Security and Governmental Affairs and the Committee on Commerce, Science, and Transportation of the Senate.

(5) REVIEW OF PLAN.—Not later than two years after the date on which the plan is disseminated under paragraph (4), and biennially thereafter, the Secretary, acting through the Administrator and in coordination with the Chief Medical Officer of the Department of Homeland Security, shall review the plan and, after consultation with the partners identified under paragraphs (3)(A)(i) through (3)(A)(iv), update the plan as appropriate.

(Added Pub. L. 107–71, title I, §101(a), Nov. 19, 2001, 115 Stat. 597; amended Pub. L. 107–296, title XVI, §1601(b), title XVII, §1707, Nov. 25, 2002, 116 Stat. 2312, 2318; Pub. L. 108–7, div. I, title III, §351(d), Feb. 20, 2003, 117 Stat. 420; Pub. L. 108–458, title IV, §4001(a), Dec. 17, 2004, 118 Stat. 3710; Pub. L. 110–53, title XII, §§1202, 1203(a), title XIII, §1302(a), title XV, §1503(a), Aug. 3, 2007, 121 Stat. 381, 383, 390, 425; Pub. L. 110–161, div. E, title V, §568(a), Dec. 26, 2007, 121 Stat. 2092; Pub. L. 111–83, title V, §561(c)(1), Oct. 28, 2009, 123 Stat. 2182; Pub. L. 114–301, §2(d), Dec. 16, 2016, 130 Stat. 1514; Pub. L. 115–254, div. K, title I, §§1903, 1904(a), (b)(1), 1905, 1909, 1988(c), Oct. 5, 2018, 132 Stat. 3543, 3544, 3546, 3549, 3623; Pub. L. 117–81, div. F, title LXIV, §6412(a), Dec. 27, 2021, 135 Stat. 2409; Pub. L. 117–286, §4(b)(95), Dec. 27, 2022, 136 Stat. 4353.)

---

[1] *So in original. Probably should not be capitalized.*

§115. TRANSPORTATION SECURITY OVERSIGHT BOARD

(a) IN GENERAL.—There is established in the Department of Homeland Security a board to be known as the "Transportation Security Oversight Board".

(b) MEMBERSHIP.—

(1) NUMBER AND APPOINTMENT.—The Board shall be composed of 7 members as follows:

(A) The Secretary of Homeland Security, or the Secretary's designee.

(B) The Secretary of Transportation, or the Secretary's designee.

(C) The Attorney General, or the Attorney General's designee.

(D) The Secretary of Defense, or the Secretary's designee.

(E) The Secretary of the Treasury, or the Secretary's designee.

(F) The Director of National Intelligence, or the Director's designee.

(G) One member appointed by the President to represent the National Security Council.

(2) CHAIRPERSON.—The Chairperson of the Board shall be the Secretary of Homeland Security.

(c) DUTIES.—The Board shall—

(1) review and ratify or disapprove any regulation or security directive issued by the Administrator of the Transportation Security Administration under section 114(l)(2) within 30 days after the date of issuance of such regulation or directive;

(2) facilitate the coordination of intelligence, security, and law enforcement activities affecting transportation;

(3) facilitate the sharing of intelligence, security, and law enforcement information affecting transportation among Federal agencies and with carriers and other transportation providers as appropriate;

(4) explore the technical feasibility of developing a common database of individuals who may pose a threat to transportation or national security;

(5) review plans for transportation security;

(6) make recommendations to the Administrator regarding matters reviewed under paragraph (5).

(d) QUARTERLY MEETINGS.—The Board shall meet at least quarterly.

(e) CONSIDERATION OF SECURITY INFORMATION.—A majority of the Board may vote to close a meeting of the Board to the public, except that meetings shall be closed to the public whenever classified,[1] sensitive security information, or information protected in accordance with section 40119(b),[2] will be discussed.

(Added Pub. L. 107–71, title I, §102(a), Nov. 19, 2001, 115 Stat. 604; amended Pub. L. 107–296, title IV, §426(a), Nov. 25, 2002, 116 Stat. 2186; Pub. L. 111–259, title IV, §411, Oct. 7, 2010, 124 Stat. 2725; Pub. L. 115–254, div. K, title I, §1991(b), Oct. 5, 2018, 132 Stat. 3626.)

---

[1] *So in original. The word "information" probably should be inserted.*

[2] *See References in Text note below.*

§116. NATIONAL SURFACE TRANSPORTATION AND INNOVATIVE FINANCE BUREAU

(a) ESTABLISHMENT.— The Secretary of Transportation shall establish a National Surface Transportation and Innovative Finance Bureau in the Department.

(b) PURPOSES.—The purposes of the Bureau shall be—

(1) to provide assistance and communicate best practices and financing and funding opportunities to eligible entities for the programs referred to in subsection (d)(1);

(2) to administer the application processes for programs within the Department in accordance with subsection (d);

(3) to promote innovative financing best practices in accordance with subsection (e);

(4) to reduce uncertainty and delays with respect to environmental reviews and permitting in accordance with subsection (f); and

(5) to reduce costs and risks to taxpayers in project delivery and procurement in accordance with subsection (g).

(c) EXECUTIVE DIRECTOR.—

(1) APPOINTMENT.—The Bureau shall be headed by an Executive Director, who shall be appointed in the competitive service by the Secretary, with the approval of the President.

(2) DUTIES.—The Executive Director shall—

(A) report to the Under Secretary of Transportation for Policy;

(B) be responsible for the management and oversight of the daily activities, decisions, operations, and personnel of the Bureau;

(C) support the Council on Credit and Finance established under section 117 in accordance with this section; and

(D) carry out such additional duties as the Secretary may prescribe.

(d) ADMINISTRATION OF CERTAIN APPLICATION PROCESSES.—

(1) IN GENERAL.—The Bureau shall administer the application processes for the following programs:

(A) The infrastructure finance programs authorized under chapter 6 of title 23.

(B) The railroad rehabilitation and improvement financing program authorized under sections 22401 through 22403.

(C) Amount allocations authorized under section 142(m) of the Internal Revenue Code of 1986.

(D) The Rural and Tribal Assistance Pilot Program established under section 21205(b)(1) of the Surface Transportation Investment Act of 2021.

(2) CONGRESSIONAL NOTIFICATION.—The Executive Director shall ensure that the congressional notification requirements for each program referred to in paragraph (1) are followed in accordance with the statutory provisions applicable to the program.

(3) REPORTS.—The Executive Director shall ensure that the reporting requirements for each program referred to in paragraph (1) are followed in accordance with the statutory provisions applicable to the program.

(4) COORDINATION.—In administering the application processes for the programs referred to in paragraph (1), the Executive Director shall coordinate with appropriate officials in the Department and its modal administrations responsible for administering such programs.

(5) STREAMLINING APPROVAL PROCESSES.—Not later than 1 year after the date of enactment of this section, the Executive Director shall submit to the Committee on Transportation and Infrastructure of the House of Representatives and the Committee on Commerce, Science, and Transportation, the Committee on Banking, Housing, and Urban Affairs, and the Committee on Environment and Public Works of the Senate a report that—

(A) evaluates the application processes for the programs referred to in paragraph (1);

(B) identifies administrative and legislative actions that would improve the efficiency of the application processes without diminishing Federal oversight; and

(C) describes how the Executive Director will implement administrative actions identified under subparagraph (B) that do not require an Act of Congress.

(6) PROCEDURES AND TRANSPARENCY.—

(A) PROCEDURES.—With respect to the programs referred to in paragraph (1), the Executive Director shall—

(i) establish procedures for analyzing and evaluating applications and for utilizing the recommendations of the Council on Credit and Finance;

(ii) establish procedures for addressing late-arriving applications, as applicable, and communicating the Bureau's decisions for accepting or rejecting late applications to the applicant and the public; and

(iii) document major decisions in the application evaluation process through a decision memorandum or similar mechanism that provides a clear rationale for such decisions.

(B) REVIEW.—

(i) IN GENERAL.—The Comptroller General of the United States shall review the compliance of the Executive Director with the requirements of this paragraph.

(ii) RECOMMENDATIONS.—The Comptroller General may make recommendations to the Executive Director in order to improve compliance with the requirements of this paragraph.

(iii) REPORT.—Not later than 3 years after the date of enactment of this section, the Comptroller General shall submit to the Committee on Transportation and Infrastructure of the House of Representatives and the Committee on Environment and Public Works, the Committee on Banking, Housing, and Urban Affairs, and the Committee on Commerce, Science, and Transportation of the Senate a report on the results of the review conducted under clause (i), including findings and recommendations for improvement.

(e) INNOVATIVE FINANCING BEST PRACTICES.—

(1) IN GENERAL.—The Bureau shall work with the modal administrations within the Department, eligible entities, and other public and private interests to develop and promote best practices for innovative financing and public-private partnerships.

(2) ACTIVITIES.—The Bureau shall carry out paragraph (1)—

(A) by making Federal credit assistance programs more accessible to eligible recipients;

(B) by providing advice and expertise to eligible entities that seek to leverage public and private funding;

(C) by sharing innovative financing best practices and case studies from eligible entities with other eligible entities that are interested in utilizing innovative financing methods; and

(D) by developing and monitoring—

(i) best practices with respect to standardized State public-private partnership authorities and practices, including best practices related to—

(I) accurate and reliable assumptions for analyzing public-private partnership procurements;

(II) procedures for the handling of unsolicited bids;

(III) policies with respect to noncompete clauses; and

(IV) other significant terms of public-private partnership procurements, as determined appropriate by the Bureau;

(ii) standard contracts for the most common types of public-private partnerships for transportation facilities; and

(iii) analytical tools and other techniques to aid eligible entities in determining the appropriate project delivery model, including a value for money analysis.

(3) TRANSPARENCY.—The Bureau shall—

(A) ensure the transparency of a project receiving credit assistance under a program referred to in subsection (d)(1) and procured as a public-private partnership by—

(i) requiring the sponsor of the project to undergo a value for money analysis or a comparable analysis prior to deciding to advance the project as a public-private partnership;

(ii) requiring the analysis required under subparagraph (A), and other key terms of the relevant public-private partnership agreement, to be made publicly available by the project sponsor at an appropriate time;

(iii) not later than 3 years after the date of completion of the project, requiring the sponsor of the project to conduct a review regarding whether the private partner is meeting the terms of the relevant public-private partnership agreement; and

(iv) providing a publicly available summary of the total level of Federal assistance in such project; and

(B) develop guidance to implement this paragraph that takes into consideration variations in State and local laws and requirements related to public-private partnerships.

(4) SUPPORT TO PROJECT SPONSORS.—At the request of an eligible entity, the Bureau shall provide technical assistance to the eligible entity regarding proposed public-private partnership agreements for transportation facilities, including assistance in performing a value for money analysis or comparable analysis.

(f) ENVIRONMENTAL REVIEW AND PERMITTING.—

(1) IN GENERAL.—The Bureau shall take actions that are appropriate and consistent with the Department's goals and policies to improve the delivery timelines for projects carried out under the programs referred to in subsection (d)(1).

(2) ACTIVITIES.—The Bureau shall carry out paragraph (1)—

(A) by coordinating efforts to improve the efficiency and effectiveness of the environmental review and permitting process;

(B) by providing technical assistance and training to field and headquarters staff of Federal agencies on policy changes and innovative approaches to the delivery of projects; and

(C) by identifying, developing, and tracking metrics for permit reviews and decisions by Federal agencies for projects under the National Environmental Policy

Act of 1969.

(3) SUPPORT TO PROJECT SPONSORS.—At the request of an eligible entity that is carrying out a project under a program referred to in subsection (d)(1), the Bureau, in coordination with the appropriate modal administrations within the Department, shall provide technical assistance with regard to the compliance of the project with the requirements of the National Environmental Policy Act 1969 and relevant Federal environmental permits.

(g) PROJECT PROCUREMENT.—

(1) IN GENERAL.—The Bureau shall promote best practices in procurement for a project receiving assistance under a program referred to in subsection (d)(1) by developing, in coordination with modal administrations within the Department as appropriate, procurement benchmarks in order to ensure accountable expenditure of Federal assistance over the life cycle of the project.

(2) PROCUREMENT BENCHMARKS.—To the maximum extent practicable, the procurement benchmarks developed under paragraph (1) shall—

(A) establish maximum thresholds for acceptable project cost increases and delays in project delivery;

(B) establish uniform methods for States to measure cost and delivery changes over the life cycle of a project; and

(C) be tailored, as necessary, to various types of project procurements, including design-bid-build, design-build, and public-private partnerships.

(3) DATA COLLECTION.—The Bureau shall—

(A) collect information related to procurement benchmarks developed under paragraph (1), including project specific information detailed under paragraph (2); and

(B) provide on a publicly accessible Internet Web site of the Department a report on the information collected under subparagraph (A).

(h) ELIMINATION AND CONSOLIDATION OF DUPLICATIVE OFFICES.—

(1) ELIMINATION OF OFFICES.—The Secretary may eliminate any office within the Department if the Secretary determines that—

(A) the purposes of the office are duplicative of the purposes of the Bureau; and

(B) the elimination of the office does not adversely affect the obligations of the Secretary under any Federal law.

(2) CONSOLIDATION OF OFFICES AND OFFICE FUNCTIONS.—The Secretary may consolidate any office or office function within the Department into the Bureau that the Secretary determines has duties, responsibilities, resources, or expertise that support the purposes of the Bureau.

(3) STAFFING AND BUDGETARY RESOURCES.—

(A) IN GENERAL.—The Secretary shall ensure that the Bureau is adequately staffed and funded.

(B) STAFFING.—The Secretary may transfer to the Bureau a position within the

Department from any office that is eliminated or consolidated under this subsection if the Secretary determines that the position is necessary to carry out the purposes of the Bureau.

(C) SAVINGS PROVISION.—If the Secretary transfers a position to the Bureau under subparagraph (B), the Secretary, in coordination with the appropriate modal administration, shall ensure that the transfer of the position does not adversely affect the obligations of the modal administration under any Federal law.

(D) BUDGETARY RESOURCES.—

(i) TRANSFER OF FUNDS FROM ELIMINATED OR CONSOLIDATED OFFICES.—The Secretary may transfer to the Bureau funds allocated to any office or office function that is eliminated or consolidated under this subsection to carry out the purposes of the Bureau. Any such funds or limitation of obligations or portions thereof transferred to the Bureau may be transferred back to and merged with the original account.

(ii) TRANSFER OF FUNDS ALLOCATED TO ADMINISTRATIVE COSTS.—The Secretary may transfer to the Bureau funds allocated to the administrative costs of processing applications for the programs referred to in subsection (d)(1). Any such funds or limitation of obligations or portions thereof transferred to the Bureau may be transferred back to and merged with the original account.

(4) NOTIFICATION.—Not later than 90 days after the date of enactment of this section, and every 90 days thereafter, the Secretary shall notify the Committee on Transportation and Infrastructure of the House of Representatives and the Committee on Environment and Public Works, the Committee on Banking, Housing, and Urban Affairs, and the Committee on Commerce, Science, and Transportation of the Senate of—

(A) the offices eliminated under paragraph (1) and the rationale for elimination of the offices;

(B) the offices and office functions consolidated under paragraph (2) and the rationale for consolidation of the offices and office functions;

(C) the actions taken under paragraph (3) and the rationale for taking such actions; and

(D) any additional legislative actions that may be needed.

(i) SAVINGS PROVISIONS.—

(1) LAWS AND REGULATIONS.—Nothing in this section may be construed to change a law or regulation with respect to a program referred to in subsection (d)(1).

(2) RESPONSIBILITIES.—Nothing in this section may be construed to abrogate the responsibilities of an agency, operating administration, or office within the Department otherwise charged by a law or regulation with other aspects of program administration, oversight, or project approval or implementation for the programs and projects subject to this section.

(3) APPLICABILITY.—Nothing in this section may be construed to affect any pending application under 1 or more of the programs referred to in subsection (d)(1) that was received by the Secretary on or before the date of enactment of this section.

(j) DEFINITIONS.—In this section, the following definitions apply:

(1) BUREAU.—The term "Bureau" means the National Surface Transportation and Innovative Finance Bureau of the Department.

(2) DEPARTMENT.—The term "Department" means the Department of Transportation.

(3) ELIGIBLE ENTITY.—The term "eligible entity" means an eligible applicant receiving financial or credit assistance under 1 or more of the programs referred to in subsection (d)(1).

(4) EXECUTIVE DIRECTOR.—The term "Executive Director" means the Executive Director of the Bureau.

(5) MULTIMODAL PROJECT.—The term "multimodal project" means a project involving the participation of more than 1 modal administration or secretarial office within the Department.

(6) PROJECT.—The term "project" means a highway project, public transportation capital project, freight or passenger rail project, or multimodal project.

(Added Pub. L. 114–94, div. A, title IX, §9001(a), Dec. 4, 2015, 129 Stat. 1612; amended Pub. L. 115–56, div. D, §164(a), as added Pub. L. 115–123, div. B, §20101(2), Feb. 9, 2018, 132 Stat. 121; Pub. L. 117–58, div. B, title I, §§21101(d)(4), 21205(i), 21301(j)(4)(A), title V, §25009(b), Nov. 15, 2021, 135 Stat. 657, 682, 692, 854.)

§117. COUNCIL ON CREDIT AND FINANCE

(a) ESTABLISHMENT.—The Secretary of Transportation shall establish a Council on Credit and Finance in accordance with this section.

(b) MEMBERSHIP.—

(1) IN GENERAL.—The Council shall be composed of the following members:

(A) The Deputy Secretary of Transportation.

(B) The Under Secretary of Transportation for Policy.

(C) The Chief Financial Officer and Assistant Secretary for Budget and Programs.

(D) The General Counsel of the Department of Transportation.

(E) The Assistant Secretary for Transportation Policy.

(F) The Administrator of the Federal Highway Administration.

(G) The Administrator of the Federal Transit Administration.

(H) The Administrator of the Federal Railroad Administration.

(2) ADDITIONAL MEMBERS.—The Secretary may designate up to 3 additional officials of the Department to serve as at-large members of the Council.

(3) CHAIRPERSON AND VICE CHAIRPERSON.—

(A) CHAIRPERSON.—The Deputy Secretary of Transportation shall serve as the chairperson of the Council.

(B) VICE CHAIRPERSON.—The Chief Financial Officer and Assistant Secretary for Budget and Programs shall serve as the vice chairperson of the Council.

(4) EXECUTIVE DIRECTOR.—The Executive Director of the National Surface Transportation and Innovative Finance Bureau shall serve as a nonvoting member of the Council.

(c) DUTIES.—The Council shall—

(1) review applications for assistance submitted under the programs referred to in subparagraphs (A), (B), and (C) of section 116(d)(1);

(2) review applications for assistance submitted under the program referred to in section 116(d)(1)(D), as determined appropriate by the Secretary;

(3) make recommendations to the Secretary regarding the selection of projects to receive assistance under such programs;

(4) review, on a regular basis, projects that received assistance under such programs; and

(5) carry out such additional duties as the Secretary may prescribe.

(Added Pub. L. 114–94, div. A, title IX, §9002(a), Dec. 4, 2015, 129 Stat. 1618.)

* * * * * * *

SUBTITLE II
OTHER GOVERNMENT AGENCIES

SUBTITLE II—OTHER GOVERNMENT AGENCIES

CHAPTER 11—NATIONAL TRANSPORTATION SAFETY BOARD

SUBCHAPTER I—GENERAL

SUBCHAPTER II—ORGANIZATION AND ADMINISTRATIVE

SUBCHAPTER III—AUTHORITY

SUBCHAPTER IV—ENFORCEMENT AND PENALTIES

¹ Section catchline amended by Pub. L. 118–63 without corresponding amendment of chapter analysis.

SUBCHAPTER I—GENERAL

§1101. DEFINITIONS

(a) IN GENERAL.—In this chapter:

(1) ACCIDENT.—The term "accident" includes damage to or destruction of vehicles in surface or air transportation or pipelines, regardless of whether the initiating event is accidental or otherwise.

(2) STATE.—The term "State" means a State of the United States, the District of Columbia, Puerto Rico, the Virgin Islands, American Samoa, the Northern Mariana Islands, and Guam.

(b) APPLICABILITY OF OTHER DEFINITIONS.—Section 2101(23) of title 46 and section 40102(a) of this title shall apply to this chapter.

(Pub. L. 103–272, §1(d), July 5, 1994, 108 Stat. 746; Pub. L. 106–424, §2, Nov. 1, 2000, 114 Stat. 1883; Pub. L. 115–232, div. C, title XXXV, §3541(b)(17), Aug. 13, 2018, 132 Stat. 2324; Pub. L. 118–63, title XII, §1203, May 16, 2024, 138 Stat. 1422.)

SUBCHAPTER II—ORGANIZATION AND ADMINISTRATIVE

§1111. GENERAL ORGANIZATION

(a) ORGANIZATION.—The National Transportation Safety Board is an independent establishment of the United States Government.

(b) APPOINTMENT OF MEMBERS.—The Board is composed of 5 members appointed by the President, by and with the advice and consent of the Senate. Not more than 3 members may be appointed from the same political party. At least 3 members shall be appointed on the basis of technical qualification, professional standing, and demonstrated knowledge in accident reconstruction, safety engineering, human factors, transportation safety, or transportation regulation.

(c) TERMS OF OFFICE AND REMOVAL.—The term of office of each member is 5 years. An individual appointed to fill a vacancy occurring before the expiration of the term for which the predecessor of that individual was appointed, is appointed for the remainder of that term. When the term of office of a member ends, the member may continue to serve until a successor is appointed and qualified. The President may remove a member for inefficiency, neglect of duty, or malfeasance in office.

(d) CHAIRMAN AND VICE CHAIRMAN.—The President shall designate, by and with the advice and consent of the Senate, a Chairman of the Board. The President also shall designate a Vice Chairman of the Board. The terms of office of both the Chairman and Vice Chairman are 3 years. When the Chairman is absent or unable to serve or when the position of Chairman is vacant, the Vice Chairman acts as Chairman.

(e) DUTIES AND POWERS OF CHAIRMAN.—The Chairman is the chief executive and administrative officer of the Board. Subject to the general policies and decisions of the Board, the Chairman shall—

(1) appoint and supervise officers and employees, other than regular and full-time employees in the immediate offices of another member, necessary to carry out this chapter;

(2) fix the pay of officers and employees necessary to carry out this chapter;

(3) distribute business among the officers, employees, and administrative units of the Board; and

(4) supervise the expenditures of the Board.

(f) QUORUM.—Three members of the Board are a quorum in carrying out duties and powers of the Board.

(g) OFFICES, BUREAUS, AND DIVISIONS.—The Board shall establish offices necessary to carry out this chapter, including an office to investigate and report on the safe transportation of hazardous material. The Board shall establish distinct and appropriately staffed bureaus, divisions, or offices to investigate and report on accidents involving each of the following modes of transportation:

(1) aviation.

(2) highway and motor vehicle.

(3) rail and tracked vehicle.

(4) pipeline.

(5) marine.

(h) CHIEF FINANCIAL OFFICER.—The Chairman shall designate an officer or employee of the Board as the Chief Financial Officer. The Chief Financial Officer shall—

(1) report directly to the Chairman on financial management and budget execution;

(2) direct, manage, and provide policy guidance and oversight on financial management and property and inventory control; and

(3) review the fees, rents, and other charges imposed by the Board for services and things of value it provides, and suggest appropriate revisions to those charges to reflect costs incurred by the Board in providing those services and things of value.

(i) BOARD MEMBER STAFF.—Each member of the Board shall select and supervise regular and full-time employees in his or her immediate office as long as any such employee has been approved for employment by the designated agency ethics official under the same guidelines that apply to all employees of the Board. Except for the Chairman, the appointment authority provided by this subsection is limited to the number of full-time equivalent positions, in addition to 1 senior professional staff at a level not to exceed the GS 15 level and 1 administrative staff, allocated to each member through the Board's annual budget and allocation process.

(j) SEAL.—The Board shall have a seal that shall be judicially recognized.

(k) OPEN MEETINGS.—

(1) IN GENERAL.—The Board shall be deemed to be an agency for purposes of section

552b of title 5.

(2) NONPUBLIC COLLABORATIVE DISCUSSIONS.—

(A) IN GENERAL.—Notwithstanding section 552b of title 5, a majority of the members may hold a meeting that is not open to public observation to discuss official agency business if—

(i) no formal or informal vote or other official agency action is taken at the meeting;

(ii) each individual present at the meeting is a member or an employee of the Board;

(iii) at least 1 member of the Board from each political party is present at the meeting, if applicable; and

(iv) the General Counsel of the Board is present at the meeting.

(B) DISCLOSURE OF NONPUBLIC COLLABORATIVE DISCUSSIONS.—Except as provided under subparagraphs (C) and (D), not later than 2 business days after the conclusion of a meeting under subparagraph (A), the Board shall make available to the public, in a place easily accessible to the public—

(i) a list of the individuals present at the meeting; and

(ii) a summary of the matters, including key issues, discussed at the meeting, except for any matter the Board properly determines may be withheld from the public under section 552b(c) of title 5.

(C) SUMMARY.—If the Board properly determines a matter may be withheld from the public under section 552b(c) of title 5, the Board shall provide a summary with as much general information as possible on each matter withheld from the public.

(D) ACTIVE INVESTIGATIONS.—If a discussion under subparagraph (A) directly relates to an active investigation, the Board shall make the disclosure under subparagraph (B) on the date the Board adopts the final report.

(E) PRESERVATION OF OPEN MEETINGS REQUIREMENTS FOR AGENCY ACTION.—Nothing in this paragraph may be construed to limit the applicability of section 552b of title 5 with respect to a meeting of the members other than that described in this paragraph.

(F) STATUTORY CONSTRUCTION.—Nothing in this paragraph may be construed—

(i) to limit the applicability of section 552b of title 5 with respect to any information which is proposed to be withheld from the public under subparagraph (B)(ii); or

(ii) to authorize the Board to withhold from any individual any record that is accessible to that individual under section 552a of title 5.

(Pub. L. 103–272, §1(d), July 5, 1994, 108 Stat. 746; Pub. L. 106–424, §10, Nov. 1, 2000, 114 Stat. 1886; Pub. L. 109–443, §9(a), (d), Dec. 21, 2006, 120 Stat. 3301; Pub. L. 115–254, div. C, §1112(a), (b), Oct. 5, 2018, 132 Stat. 3436.)

§1112. SPECIAL BOARDS OF INQUIRY ON AIR TRANSPORTATION SAFETY

(a) ESTABLISHMENT.—If an accident involves a substantial question about public safety in air transportation, the National Transportation Safety Board may establish a special board of inquiry composed of—

(1) one member of the Board acting as chairman; and

(2) 2 members representing the public, appointed by the President on notification of the establishment of the special board of inquiry.

(b) QUALIFICATIONS AND CONFLICTS OF INTEREST.—The public members of a special board of inquiry must be qualified by training and experience to participate in the inquiry and may not have a pecuniary interest in an aviation enterprise involved in the accident to be investigated.

(c) AUTHORITY.—A special board of inquiry has the same authority that the Board has under this chapter.

(Pub. L. 103–272, §1(d), July 5, 1994, 108 Stat. 747.)

§1113. ADMINISTRATIVE

(a) GENERAL AUTHORITY.—(1) The National Transportation Safety Board, and when authorized by it, a member of the Board, an administrative law judge employed by or assigned to the Board, or an officer or employee designated by the Chairman of the Board, may conduct hearings to carry out this chapter, administer oaths, and require, by subpoena or otherwise, necessary witnesses and evidence.

(2) A witness or evidence in a hearing under paragraph (1) of this subsection may be summoned or required to be produced from any place in the United States to the designated place of the hearing. A witness summoned under this subsection is entitled to the same fee and mileage the witness would have been paid in a court of the United States.

(3) A subpoena shall be issued under the signature of the Chairman or the Chairman's delegate but may be served by any person designated by the Chairman.

(4) If a person disobeys a subpoena, order, or inspection notice of the Board, the Board may bring a civil action in a district court of the United States to enforce the subpoena, order, or notice. An action under this paragraph may be brought in the judicial district in which the person against whom the action is brought resides, is found, or does business. The court may punish a failure to obey an order of the court to comply with the subpoena, order, or notice as a contempt of court.

(b) ADDITIONAL POWERS.—(1) The Board may—

(A) procure the temporary or intermittent services of experts or consultants under section 3109 of title 5;

(B) make agreements and other transactions necessary to carry out this chapter without regard to section 6101(b) to (d) of title 41;

(C) use, when appropriate, available services, equipment, personnel, and facilities of a department, agency, or instrumentality of the United States Government on a reimbursable or other basis;

(D) confer with employees and use services, records, and facilities of State and local governmental authorities;

(E) appoint advisory committees composed of qualified private citizens and officials of the Government and State and local governments as appropriate;

(F) accept voluntary and uncompensated services notwithstanding another law;

(G) accept gifts of money and other property;

(H) make contracts with nonprofit entities to carry out studies related to duties and powers of the Board;

(I) negotiate and enter into agreements with individuals and private entities and departments, agencies, and instrumentalities of the Government, State and local governments, and governments of foreign countries for the provision of facilities, accident-related and technical services or training in accident investigation theory and techniques, and require that such entities provide appropriate consideration for the reasonable costs of any facilities, goods, services, or training provided by the Board;

(J) notwithstanding section 1343 of title 31, acquire 1 or more small unmanned aircraft (as defined in section 44801) for use in investigations under this chapter; and

(K) notwithstanding section 3301 of title 41, acquire training on emerging transportation technologies if such training—

(i) is required for an ongoing investigation; and

(ii) meets the criteria under section 3304(a)(7)(A) of title 41.

(2) The Board shall deposit in the Treasury amounts received under paragraph (1)(I) of this subsection to be credited as offsetting collections to the appropriation of the Board. The Board shall maintain an annual record of collections received under paragraph (1)(I) of this subsection.

(c) SUBMISSION OF CERTAIN COPIES TO CONGRESS.—When the Board submits to the President or the Director of the Office of Management and Budget a budget estimate, budget request, supplemental budget estimate, other budget information, a legislative recommendation, prepared testimony for congressional hearings, or comments on legislation, the Board must submit a copy to Congress at the same time. An officer, department, agency, or instrumentality of the Government may not require the Board to submit the estimate, request, information, recommendation, testimony, or comments to another officer, department, agency, or instrumentality of the Government for approval, comment, or review before being submitted to Congress. The Board shall develop and approve a process for the Board's review and comment or approval of documents submitted to the President, Director of the Office of Management and Budget, or Congress under this subsection.

(d) LIAISON COMMITTEES.—The Chairman may determine the number of committees that are appropriate to maintain effective liaison with other departments, agencies, and instrumentalities of the Government, State and local governmental authorities, and independent standard-setting authorities that carry out programs and activities related to transportation safety. The Board may designate representatives to serve on or assist those committees.

(e) INQUIRIES.—The Board, or an officer or employee of the Board designated by the Chairman, may conduct an inquiry to obtain information related to transportation safety after publishing notice of the inquiry in the Federal Register. The Board or designated officer or employee may require by order a department, agency, or instrumentality of the Government, a State or local governmental authority, or a person transporting individuals or property in commerce to submit to the Board a written report and answers to requests and questions related to a duty or power of the Board. The Board may prescribe the time within which the report and answers must be given to the Board or to the designated officer or employee. Copies of the report and answers shall be made available for public inspection.

(f) REGULATIONS.—The Board may prescribe regulations to carry out this chapter.

(g) OVERTIME PAY.—

(1) IN GENERAL.—Subject to the requirements of this section and notwithstanding paragraphs (1) and (2) of section 5542(a) of title 5, for an employee of the Board whose basic pay is at a rate which equals or exceeds the minimum rate of basic pay for GS–10 of the General Schedule, the Board may establish an overtime hourly rate of pay for the employee with respect to work performed at the scene of an accident (including travel to or from the scene) and other work that is critical to an accident investigation in an amount equal to one and one-half times the hourly rate of basic pay of the employee. All of such amount shall be considered to be premium pay.

(2) LIMITATION ON OVERTIME PAY TO AN EMPLOYEE.—An employee of the Board may not receive overtime pay under paragraph (1), for work performed in a calendar year, in an amount that exceeds 15 percent of the annual rate of basic pay of the employee for such calendar year.

(3) LIMITATION ON TOTAL AMOUNT OF OVERTIME PAY.—The Board may not make overtime payments under paragraph (1) for work performed in any fiscal year in a total amount that exceeds 1.5 percent of the amount appropriated to carry out this chapter for that fiscal year.

(4) BASIC PAY DEFINED.—In this subsection, the term "basic pay" includes any applicable locality-based comparability payment under section 5304 of title 5 (or similar provision of law) and any special rate of pay under section 5305 of title 5 (or similar provision of law).

(h) STRATEGIC WORKFORCE PLAN.—

(1) IN GENERAL.—The Board shall develop a strategic workforce plan that addresses the immediate and long-term workforce needs of the Board with respect to carrying out the authorities and duties of the Board under this chapter.

(2) ALIGNING THE WORKFORCE TO STRATEGIC GOALS.—In developing the strategic workforce plan under paragraph (1), the Board shall take into consideration—

(A) the current state and capabilities of the Board, including a high-level review of mission requirements, structure, workforce, and performance of the Board;

(B) the significant workforce trends, needs, issues, and challenges with respect to the Board and the transportation industry;

(C) with respect to employees involved in transportation safety work, the needs, issues, and challenges, including accident severity and risk, posed by each mode of transportation, and how the Board's staffing for each transportation mode reflects these aspects;

(D) the workforce policies, strategies, performance measures, and interventions to mitigate succession risks that guide the workforce investment decisions of the Board;

(E) a workforce planning strategy that identifies workforce needs, including the knowledge, skills, and abilities needed to recruit and retain skilled employees at the Board;

(F) a workforce management strategy that is aligned with the mission of the Board, including plans for continuity of leadership and knowledge sharing;

(G) an implementation system that addresses workforce competency gaps, particularly in mission-critical occupations; and

(H) a system for analyzing and evaluating the performance of the Board's workforce management policies, programs, and activities.

(3) PLANNING PERIOD.—The strategic workforce plan developed under paragraph (1) shall address a 5-year forecast period, but may include planning for longer periods based on information about emerging technologies or safety trends in transportation.

(4) PLAN UPDATES.—The Board shall update the strategic workforce plan developed under paragraph (1) not less than once every 5 years.

(5) RELATIONSHIP TO STRATEGIC PLAN.—The strategic workforce plan developed under paragraph (1) may be developed separately from, or incorporated into, the strategic plan required under section 306 of title 5.

(6) AVAILABILITY.—The strategic workforce plan under paragraph (1) and the strategic plan required under section 306 of title 5 shall be—

(A) submitted to the Committee on Transportation and Infrastructure of the House of Representatives and the Committee on Commerce, Science, and Transportation of the Senate; and

(B) made available to the public on a website of the Board.

(i) NON-ACCIDENT-RELATED TRAVEL BUDGET.—

(1) IN GENERAL.—The Board shall establish annual fiscal year budgets for non-accident-related travel expenditures for each Board member.

(2) NOTIFICATION.—The Board shall notify the Committee on Transportation and Infrastructure of the House of Representatives and the Committee on Commerce, Science, and Transportation of the Senate of any non-accident-related travel budget overrun for any Board member not later than 30 days of such overrun becoming known to the Board.

(Pub. L. 103–272, §1(d), July 5, 1994, 108 Stat. 747; Pub. L. 106–424, §§3(a), (b)(1), 4, Nov. 1, 2000, 114 Stat. 1883, 1884; Pub. L. 109–443, §9(e)–(g), Dec. 21, 2006, 120 Stat. 3301; Pub. L. 111–350, §5(o)(2), Jan. 4, 2011, 124 Stat. 3853; Pub. L. 115–254, div. C, §1112(c)–(e), Oct. 5, 2018, 132 Stat. 3437, 3438; Pub. L. 118–63, title XII, §§1204(a), 1205–1207(a), May 16, 2024, 138 Stat. 1422–1424.)

§1114. DISCLOSURE, AVAILABILITY, AND USE OF INFORMATION

(a) GENERAL.—(1) Except as provided in subsections (b), (c), (d), and (f) of this section, a copy of a record, information, or investigation submitted or received by the National Transportation Safety Board, or a member or employee of the Board, shall be made available to the public on identifiable request and at reasonable cost. This subsection does not require the release of information described by section 552(b) of title 5 or protected from disclosure by another law of the United States.

(2) The Board shall deposit in the Treasury amounts received under paragraph (1) to be credited to the appropriation of the Board as offsetting collections.

(b) CERTAIN CONFIDENTIAL INFORMATION.—(1) In general.—The Board may disclose confidential information described in section 1905 of title 18, including trade secrets, only—

(A) to another department, agency, or instrumentality of the United States Government when requested for official use;

(B) to a committee of Congress having jurisdiction over the subject matter to which the information is related, when requested by that committee;

(C) in a judicial proceeding under a court order that preserves the confidentiality of the information without impairing the proceeding; and

(D) to the public to protect health and safety after giving notice to any interested person to whom the information is related and an opportunity for that person to comment in writing, or orally in closed session, on the proposed disclosure, if the delay resulting from notice and opportunity for comment would not be detrimental to health and safety.

(2) Information disclosed under paragraph (1) of this subsection may be disclosed only in a way designed to preserve its confidentiality.

(3) PROTECTION OF VOLUNTARY SUBMISSION OF INFORMATION.—Notwithstanding any other provision of law, neither the Board, nor any agency receiving information from the Board, shall disclose voluntarily provided safety-related information if that information is not related to the exercise of the Board's accident or incident investigation authority under this chapter and if the Board finds that the disclosure of the information would inhibit the voluntary provision of that type of information.

(c) COCKPIT RECORDINGS AND TRANSCRIPTS.—

(1) CONFIDENTIALITY OF RECORDINGS.—Except as provided in paragraph (2), the Board may not disclose publicly any part of a cockpit voice or video recorder recording or transcript of oral communications by and between flight crew members and ground stations related to an accident or incident investigated by the Board.

(2) EXCEPTION.—Subject to subsections (b) and (g), the Board shall make public any part of a transcript, any written depiction of visual information obtained from a video recorder, or any still image obtained from a video recorder the Board decides is relevant to the accident or incident—

(A) if the Board holds a public hearing on the accident or incident, at the time of the hearing; or

(B) if the Board does not hold a public hearing, at the time a majority of the other factual reports on the accident or incident are placed in the public docket.

(3) REFERENCES TO INFORMATION IN MAKING SAFETY RECOMMENDATIONS.—This subsection does not prevent the Board from referring at any time to cockpit voice or video recorder information in making safety recommendations.

(d) SURFACE VEHICLE RECORDINGS AND TRANSCRIPTS.—

(1) CONFIDENTIALITY OF RECORDINGS.—Except as provided in paragraph (2), the Board may not disclose publicly any part of a surface vehicle voice or video recorder recording or transcript of oral communications by or among drivers, train employees, or other operating employees responsible for the movement and direction of the vehicle or vessel, or between such operating employees and company communication centers, related to an accident investigated by the Board.

(2) EXCEPTION.—Subject to subsections (b) and (g), the Board shall make public any part of a transcript, any written depiction of visual information obtained from a video

recorder, or any still image obtained from a video recorder the Board decides is relevant to the accident—

(A) if the Board holds a public hearing on the accident, at the time of the hearing; or

(B) if the Board does not hold a public hearing, at the time a majority of the other factual reports on the accident are placed in the public docket.

(3) REFERENCES TO INFORMATION IN MAKING SAFETY RECOMMENDATIONS.—This subsection does not prevent the Board from referring at any time to voice or video recorder information in making safety recommendations.

(e) DRUG TESTS.—(1) Notwithstanding section 503(e) of the Supplemental Appropriations Act, 1987 (Public Law 100–71, 101 Stat. 471), the Secretary of Transportation shall provide the following information to the Board when requested in writing by the Board:

(A) any report of a confirmed positive toxicological test, verified as positive by a medical review officer, conducted on an officer or employee of the Department of Transportation under post-accident, unsafe practice, or reasonable suspicion toxicological testing requirements of the Department, when the officer or employee is reasonably associated with the circumstances of an accident or incident under the investigative jurisdiction of the Board.

(B) any laboratory record documenting that the test is confirmed positive.

(2) Except as provided by paragraph (3) of this subsection, the Board shall maintain the confidentiality of, and exempt from disclosure under section 552(b)(3) of title 5—

(A) a laboratory record provided the Board under paragraph (1) of this subsection that reveals medical use of a drug allowed under applicable regulations; and

(B) medical information provided by the tested officer or employee related to the test or a review of the test.

(3) The Board may use a laboratory record made available under paragraph (1) of this subsection to develop an evidentiary record in an investigation of an accident or incident if—

(A) the fitness of the tested officer or employee is at issue in the investigation; and

(B) the use of that record is necessary to develop the evidentiary record.

(f) FOREIGN INVESTIGATIONS.—

(1) IN GENERAL.—Notwithstanding any other provision of law, neither the Board, nor any agency receiving information from the Board, shall disclose records or information relating to its participation in foreign aircraft accident investigations; except that—

(A) the Board shall release records pertaining to such an investigation when the country conducting the investigation issues its final report or 2 years following the date of the accident, whichever occurs first; and

(B) the Board may disclose records and information when authorized to do so by the country conducting the investigation.

(2) SAFETY RECOMMENDATIONS.—Nothing in this subsection shall restrict the Board at any time from referring to foreign accident investigation information in making safety recommendations.

(g) PRIVACY PROTECTIONS.—Before making public any still image obtained from a video recorder under subsection (c)(2) or subsection (d)(2), the Board shall take such action as appropriate to protect from public disclosure any information that readily identifies an individual, including a decedent.

(Pub. L. 103–272, §1(d), July 5, 1994, 108 Stat. 749; Pub. L. 104–291, title I, §§102, 103, Oct. 11, 1996, 110 Stat. 3452; Pub. L. 106–424, §§3(b)(2), 5(a), (b), Nov. 1, 2000, 114 Stat. 1884, 1885; Pub. L. 115–254, div. C, §1104(a), Oct. 5, 2018, 132 Stat. 3429; Pub. L. 118–63, title XII, §1208(a), May 16, 2024, 138 Stat. 1424.)

§1115. TRAINING

(a) DEFINITION.—In this section, "Institute" means the Transportation Safety Institute of the Department of Transportation and any successor organization of the Institute.

(b) USE OF INSTITUTE SERVICES.—The National Transportation Safety Board may use, on a reimbursable basis, the services of the Institute. The Secretary of Transportation shall make the Institute available to—

(1) the Board for safety training of employees of the Board in carrying out their duties and powers; and

(2) other safety personnel of the United States Government, State and local governments, governments of foreign countries, interstate authorities, and private organizations the Board designates in consultation with the Secretary.

(c) FEES.—(1) Training at the Institute for safety personnel (except employees of the Government) shall be provided at a reasonable fee established periodically by the Board in consultation with the Secretary. The fee shall be paid directly to the Secretary, and the Secretary shall deposit the fee in the Treasury. The amount of the fee—

(A) shall be credited to the appropriate appropriation (subject to the requirements of any annual appropriation); and

(B) is an offset against any annual reimbursement agreement between the Board and the Secretary to cover all reasonable costs of providing training under this subsection that the Secretary incurs in operating the Institute.

(2) The Board shall maintain an annual record of offsets under paragraph (1)(B) of this subsection.

(d) TRAINING OF BOARD EMPLOYEES AND OTHERS.—The Board may conduct training of its employees in those subjects necessary for the proper performance of accident investigation and in those subjects furthering the personnel and workforce development needs set forth in the strategic workforce plan of the Board as required under section 1113(h). The Board may also authorize attendance at courses given under this subsection by other government personnel, personnel of foreign governments, and personnel from industry or otherwise who have a requirement for accident investigation training. The Board may require non-

Board personnel to reimburse some or all of the training costs, and amounts so reimbursed shall be credited to the appropriation of the Board as offsetting collections.

(Pub. L. 103–272, §1(d), July 5, 1994, 108 Stat. 750; Pub. L. 104–291, title I, §104, Oct. 11, 1996, 110 Stat. 3453; Pub. L. 106–424, §3(b)(3), Nov. 1, 2000, 114 Stat. 1884; Pub. L. 118–63, title XII, §1204(b), May 16, 2024, 138 Stat. 1423.)

§1116. Reports, studies, and retrospective reviews

(a) Periodic Reports.—The National Transportation Safety Board shall report periodically to Congress, departments, agencies, and instrumentalities of the United States Government and State and local governmental authorities concerned with transportation safety, and other interested persons. The report shall—

(1) advocate meaningful responses to reduce the likelihood of transportation accidents similar to those investigated by the Board; and

(2) propose corrective action to make the transportation of individuals as safe and free from risk of injury as possible, including action to minimize personal injuries that occur in transportation accidents.

(b) Studies, Investigations, and Other Reports.—The Board also shall—

(1) carry out special studies and investigations about transportation safety, including avoiding personal injury;

(2) examine techniques and methods of accident investigation and periodically publish recommended procedures for accident investigations;

(3) prescribe requirements for persons reporting accidents and aviation incidents that—

(A) may be investigated by the Board under this chapter; or

(B) involve public aircraft (except aircraft of the armed forces and the intelligence agencies);

(4) evaluate, examine the effectiveness of, and publish the findings of the Board about the transportation safety consciousness of other departments, agencies, and instrumentalities of the Government and their effectiveness in preventing accidents; and

(5) evaluate the adequacy of safeguards and procedures for the transportation of hazardous material and the performance of other departments, agencies, and instrumentalities of the Government responsible for the safe transportation of that material.

(c) Annual Report.—The National Transportation Safety Board shall submit a report to Congress on July 1 of each year. The report shall include—

(1) a statistical and analytical summary of the transportation accident investigations conducted and reviewed by the Board during the prior calendar year;

(2) a survey and summary of the recommendations made by the Board to reduce the likelihood of recurrence of those accidents together with the observed response to each recommendation;

(3) a list of each recommendation made by the Board to the Secretary of Transportation or the Commandant of the Coast Guard that was closed in an

unacceptable status in the preceding 12 months, including—

(A) any explanation the Board received from the Secretary or Commandant; and

(B) any explanation from the Board as to why the recommendation was closed in an unacceptable status, including a discussion of why alternate means, if any, taken by the Secretary or Commandant to address the Board's recommendation were inadequate;

(4) a detailed appraisal of the accident investigation and accident prevention activities of other departments, agencies, and instrumentalities of the United States Government and State and local governmental authorities having responsibility for those activities under a law of the United States or a State;

(5) a description of the activities and operations of the National Transportation Safety Board Training Center during the prior calendar year;

(6) a list of accidents, during the prior calendar year, that the Board was required to investigate under section 1131 but did not investigate and an explanation of why they were not investigated; and

(7) a list of ongoing investigations that have exceeded the expected time allotted for completion by Board order and an explanation for the additional time required to complete each such investigation.

(d) Retrospective Reviews.—

(1) In general.—Subject to paragraph (2), not later than June 1, 2019, and at least every 5 years thereafter, the Chairman shall complete a retrospective review of recommendations issued by the Board that are classified as open by the Board.

(2) Contents.—A review under paragraph (1) shall include—

(A) a determination of whether the recommendation should be updated, closed, or reissued in light of—

(i) changed circumstances;

(ii) more recently issued recommendations;

(iii) the availability of new technologies; or

(iv) new information making the recommendation ineffective or insufficient for achieving its objective; and

(B) a justification for each determination under subparagraph (A).

(3) Report.—Not later than 180 days after the date a review under paragraph (1) is complete, the Chairman shall submit to the Committee on Commerce, Science, and Transportation of the Senate and the Committee on Transportation and Infrastructure of the House of Representatives a report that includes—

(A) the findings of the review under paragraph (1);

(B) each determination under paragraph (2)(A) and justification under paragraph (2)(B); and

(C) if applicable, a schedule for updating, closing, or reissuing a recommendation.

(Pub. L. 103–272, §1(d), July 5, 1994, 108 Stat. 751; Pub. L. 115–254, div. C, §§1107(a), 1111(a), Oct. 5, 2018, 132 Stat. 3432, 3436; Pub. L. 118–63, title XII, §1209, May 16, 2024, 138 Stat. 1425.)

§1117. Methodology

(a) In General.—Not later than 2 years after the date of enactment of the National Transportation Safety Board Reauthorization Act, the Chairman shall include with each investigative report in which a recommendation is issued by the Board a methodology section detailing the process and information underlying the selection of each recommendation.

(b) Elements.—Except as provided in subsection (c), the methodology section under subsection (a) shall include, for each recommendation—

(1) a brief summary of the Board's collection and analysis of the specific accident investigation information most relevant to the recommendation;

(2) a description of the Board's use of external information, including studies, reports, and experts, other than the findings of a specific accident investigation, if any were used to inform or support the recommendation, including a brief summary of the specific safety benefits and other effects identified by each study, report, or expert; and

(3) a brief summary of any examples of actions taken by regulated entities before the publication of the safety recommendation, to the extent such actions are known to the Board, that were consistent with the recommendation.

(c) Acceptable Limitation.—If the Board knows of more than 3 examples taken by regulated entities before the publication of the safety recommendation that were consistent with the recommendation, the brief summary under subsection (b)(3) may be limited to only 3 of those examples.

(d) Exception.—Subsection (a) shall not apply if the recommendation is only for a person to disseminate information on—

(1) an existing agency best practices document; or

(2) an existing regulatory requirement.

(e) Rule of Construction.—Nothing in this section may be construed to require any change to a recommendation made by the Board before the date of enactment of the National Transportation Safety Board Reauthorization Act, unless the recommendation is a repeat recommendation issued on or after the date of enactment of such Act.

(f) Savings Clause.—Nothing in this section may be construed—

(1) to delay publication of the findings, cause, or probable cause of a Board investigation;

(2) to delay the issuance of an urgent recommendation that the Board has determined must be issued to avoid immediate loss, death, or injury; or

(3) to limit the number of examples the Board may consider before issuing a recommendation.

(Pub. L. 103–272, §1(d), July 5, 1994, 108 Stat. 751; Pub. L. 104–66, title II, §2151, Dec. 21, 1995, 109 Stat. 731; Pub. L. 109–443, §2(a)(1), Dec. 21, 2006, 120 Stat. 3297; Pub. L. 115–254, div. C, §1107(b)(1), Oct. 5, 2018, 132 Stat. 3432.)

§1118. Authorization of appropriations

(a) In General.—

(1) Authorizations.—There is authorized to be appropriated for purposes of this

chapter—
> (A) $140,000,000 for fiscal year 2024;
> (B) $145,000,000 for fiscal year 2025;
> (C) $148,000,000 for fiscal year 2026;
> (D) $151,000,000 for fiscal year 2027; and
> (E) $154,000,000 for fiscal year 2028.

(2) AVAILABILITY.—Amounts authorized under paragraph (1) shall remain available until expended.

(b) EMERGENCY FUND.—The Board has an emergency fund of $2,000,000 available for necessary expenses of the Board, not otherwise provided for, for accident investigations. In addition, there are authorized to be appropriated such sums as may be necessary to increase the fund to, and maintain the fund at, a level not to exceed $4,000,000.

(c) FEES, REFUNDS, AND REIMBURSEMENTS.—

(1) IN GENERAL.—The Board may impose and collect such fees, refunds, and reimbursements as it determines to be appropriate for services provided by or through the Board.

(2) RECEIPTS CREDITED AS OFFSETTING COLLECTIONS.—Notwithstanding section 3302 of title 31, any fee, refund, or reimbursement collected under this subsection—

> (A) shall be credited as offsetting collections to the account that finances the activities and services for which the fee is imposed or with which the refund or reimbursement is associated;
> (B) shall be available for expenditure only to pay the costs of activities and services for which the fee is imposed or with which the refund or reimbursement is associated; and
> (C) shall remain available until expended.

(3) REFUNDS.—The Board may refund any fee paid by mistake or any amount paid in excess of that required.

(Pub. L. 103–272, §1(d), July 5, 1994, 108 Stat. 752; Pub. L. 103–411, §2, Oct. 25, 1994, 108 Stat. 4236; Pub. L. 104–291, title I, §105, Oct. 11, 1996, 110 Stat. 3453; Pub. L. 106–424, §13, Nov. 1, 2000, 114 Stat. 1888; Pub. L. 108–168, §2, Dec. 6, 2003, 117 Stat. 2032; Pub. L. 109–443, §8(a), (b)(1), (c), Dec. 21, 2006, 120 Stat. 3300; Pub. L. 115–254, div. C, §1103, Oct. 5, 2018, 132 Stat. 3429; Pub. L. 118–63, title XII, §1202, May 16, 2024, 138 Stat. 1422.)

§1119. ACCIDENT AND SAFETY DATA CLASSIFICATION AND PUBLICATION

(a) IN GENERAL.—Not later than 90 days after the date of the enactment of this section, the National Transportation Safety Board shall, in consultation and coordination with the Administrator of the Federal Aviation Administration, develop a system for classifying air carrier accident data maintained by the Board.

(b) REQUIREMENTS FOR CLASSIFICATION SYSTEM.—

(1) IN GENERAL.—The system developed under this section shall provide for the classification of accident and safety data in a manner that, in comparison to the system in effect on the date of the enactment of this section, provides for safety-related categories

that provide clearer descriptions of accidents associated with air transportation, including a more refined classification of accidents which involve fatalities, injuries, or substantial damage and which are only related to the operation of an aircraft.

(2) PUBLIC COMMENT.—In developing a system of classification under paragraph (1), the Board shall provide adequate opportunity for public review and comment.

(3) FINAL CLASSIFICATION.—After providing for public review and comment, and after consulting with the Administrator, the Board shall issue final classifications. The Board shall ensure that air travel accident covered under this section is classified in accordance with the final classifications issued under this section for data for calendar year 1997, and for each subsequent calendar year.

(4) PUBLICATION.—The Board shall publish on a periodic basis accident and safety data in accordance with the final classifications issued under paragraph (3).

(5) RECOMMENDATIONS OF THE ADMINISTRATOR.—The Administrator may, from time to time, request the Board to consider revisions (including additions to the classification system developed under this section). The Board shall respond to any request made by the Administrator under this section not later than 90 days after receiving that request.

(c) APPEALS.—

(1) NOTIFICATION OF RIGHTS.—In any case in which an employee of the Board determines that an occurrence associated with the operation of an aircraft constitutes an accident, the employee shall notify the owner or operator of that aircraft of the right to appeal that determination to the Board.

(2) PROCEDURE.—The Board shall establish and publish the procedures for appeals under this subsection.

(3) LIMITATION ON APPLICABILITY.—This subsection shall not apply in the case of an accident that results in a loss of life.

(Added Pub. L. 104–264, title IV, §407(a)(1), Oct. 9, 1996, 110 Stat. 3257; amended Pub. L. 108–168, §5, Dec. 6, 2003, 117 Stat. 2034.)

SUBCHAPTER III—AUTHORITY

§1131. GENERAL AUTHORITY

(a) GENERAL.—(1) The National Transportation Safety Board shall investigate or have investigated (in detail the Board prescribes) and establish the facts, circumstances, and cause or probable cause of—

(A) an aircraft accident the Board has authority to investigate under section 1132 of this title or an aircraft accident involving a public aircraft as defined by section 40102(a) of this title other than an aircraft operated by the Armed Forces or by an intelligence agency of the United States;

(B) a highway accident, including a railroad grade crossing accident, the Board selects, concurrent with any State investigation, in which case the Board and the relevant State agencies shall coordinate to ensure both the Board and State agencies have timely access to the information needed to conduct each such investigation, including any criminal and enforcement activities conducted by the relevant State agency;

(C) a railroad—
   (i) accident in which there is a fatality or substantial property damage, except—
      (I) a grade crossing accident or incident, unless selected by the Board; or
      (II) an accident or incident involving a trespasser, unless selected by the Board; or

   (ii) accident or incident that involves a passenger train, except in any case in which such accident or incident resulted in no fatalities or serious injuries to the passengers or crewmembers of such train, and—
      (I) was a grade crossing accident or incident, unless selected by the Board; or
      (II) such accident or incident involved a trespasser, unless selected by the Board;

(D) a pipeline accident in which there is a fatality, substantial property damage, or significant injury to the environment;

(E) a major marine casualty (except a casualty involving only public vessels) occurring on or under the navigable waters, internal waters, or the territorial sea of the United States as described in Presidential Proclamation No. 5928 of December 27, 1988, or involving a vessel of the United States (as defined in section 116 of title 46), under regulations prescribed jointly by the Board and the head of the department in which the Coast Guard is operating; and

(F) any other accident related to the transportation of individuals or property when the Board decides—
   (i) the accident is catastrophic;
   (ii) the accident involves problems of a recurring character; or
   (iii) the investigation of the accident would carry out this chapter.

(2)(A) Subject to the requirements of this paragraph, an investigation by the Board under paragraph (1)(A)–(D) or (F) of this subsection has priority over any investigation by another department, agency, or instrumentality of the United States Government. The Board shall provide for appropriate participation by other departments, agencies, or instrumentalities in the investigation. However, those departments, agencies, or instrumentalities may not participate in the decision of the Board about the probable cause of the accident.

(B) If the Attorney General, in consultation with the Chairman of the Board, determines and notifies the Board that circumstances reasonably indicate that the accident may have been caused by an intentional criminal act, the Board shall relinquish investigative priority to the Federal Bureau of Investigation. The relinquishment of investigative priority by the Board shall not otherwise affect the authority of the Board to continue its investigation under this section.

(C) If a Federal law enforcement agency suspects and notifies the Board that an accident being investigated by the Board under subparagraph (A), (B), (C), or (D) of paragraph (1) may have been caused by an intentional criminal act, the Board, in consultation with the law enforcement agency, shall take necessary actions to ensure that evidence of the criminal act is preserved.

(3) This section and sections 1113, 1116(b), 1133, and 1134(a) and (c)–(e) of this

title do not affect the authority of another department, agency, or instrumentality of the Government to investigate an accident under applicable law or to obtain information directly from the parties involved in, and witnesses to, the accident. The Board and other departments, agencies, and instrumentalities shall ensure that appropriate information developed about the accident is exchanged in a timely manner.

(b) ACCIDENTS INVOLVING PUBLIC VESSELS.—(1) The Board or the head of the department in which the Coast Guard is operating shall investigate and establish the facts, circumstances, and cause or probable cause of a marine accident involving a public vessel and any other vessel. The results of the investigation shall be made available to the public.

(2) Paragraph (1) of this subsection and subsection (a)(1)(E) of this section do not affect the responsibility, under another law of the United States, of the head of the department in which the Coast Guard is operating.

(c) ACCIDENTS NOT INVOLVING GOVERNMENT MISFEASANCE OR NONFEASANCE.—(1) When asked by the Board, the Secretary of Transportation or the Secretary of the department in which the Coast Guard is operating may—

(A) investigate an accident described under subsection (a) or (b) of this section in which misfeasance or nonfeasance by the Government has not been alleged; and

(B) report the facts and circumstances of the accident to the Board.

(2) The Board shall use the report in establishing cause or probable cause of an accident described under subsection (a) or (b) of this section.

(d) ACCIDENTS INVOLVING PUBLIC AIRCRAFT.—The Board, in furtherance of its investigative duties with respect to public aircraft accidents under subsection (a)(1)(A) of this section, shall have the same duties and powers as are specified for civil aircraft accidents under sections 1132(a), 1132(b), and 1134(a), (b), (d), and (f) of this title.

(e) ACCIDENT REPORTS.—The Board shall report on the facts and circumstances of each accident investigated by it under subsection (a) or (b) of this section. The Board shall make each report available to the public—

(1) in electronic form at no cost in a publicly accessible database on a website of the Board; and

(2) if the electronic form required in paragraph (1) is not printable, in printed form upon a reasonable request at a reasonable cost.

(f) TIMELINESS OF REPORTS.—If any accident report under subsection (e) is not completed within 2 years from the date of the accident, the Board shall submit to the Committee on Transportation and Infrastructure of the House of Representatives and the Committee on Commerce, Science, and Transportation of the Senate a report identifying such accident report and the reasons for which such report has not been completed. The Board shall report progress toward completion of the accident report to each such Committees every 90 days thereafter, until such time as the accident report is completed.

(Pub. L. 103–272, §1(d), July 5, 1994, 108 Stat. 752; Pub. L. 103–411, §3(c), Oct. 25, 1994, 108 Stat. 4237; Pub. L. 106–424, §§6(a), 7, Nov. 1, 2000, 114 Stat. 1885, 1886; Pub. L. 108–168, §7, Dec. 6, 2003, 117 Stat. 2034; Pub. L. 109–443, §9(b), (c), Dec. 21, 2006, 120 Stat. 3301; Pub. L. 115–254, div. C, §1113(b), Oct. 5, 2018, 132 Stat. 3438; Pub. L. 117–263, div. K, title CXVI, §11601(c)(3), Dec. 23, 2022, 136 Stat. 4146; Pub. L. 118–63, title XII, §§1210–1212, May 16, 2024, 138 Stat. 1425, 1426.)

§1132. CIVIL AIRCRAFT ACCIDENT INVESTIGATIONS

(a) GENERAL AUTHORITY.—(1) The National Transportation Safety Board shall investigate—

(A) each accident involving civil aircraft; and

(B) with the participation of appropriate military authorities, each accident involving both military and civil aircraft.

(2) A person employed under section 1113(b)(1) of this title that is conducting an investigation or hearing about an aircraft accident has the same authority to conduct the investigation or hearing as the Board.

(b) NOTIFICATION AND REPORTING.—The Board shall prescribe regulations governing the notification and reporting of accidents involving civil aircraft.

(c) PARTICIPATION OF SECRETARY.—The Board shall provide for the participation of the Secretary of Transportation in the investigation of an aircraft accident under this chapter when participation is necessary to carry out the duties and powers of the Secretary. However, the Secretary may not participate in establishing probable cause.

(d) ACCIDENTS INVOLVING ONLY MILITARY AIRCRAFT.—If an accident involves only military aircraft and a duty of the Secretary is or may be involved, the military authorities shall provide for the participation of the Secretary. In any other accident involving only military aircraft, the military authorities shall give the Board or Secretary information the military authorities decide would contribute to the promotion of air safety.

(Pub. L. 103–272, §1(d), July 5, 1994, 108 Stat. 753.)

§1133. REVIEW OF OTHER AGENCY ACTION

The National Transportation Safety Board shall review on appeal—

(1) the denial, amendment, modification, suspension, or revocation of a certificate issued by the Secretary of Transportation under section 44703, 44709, or 44710 of this title;

(2) the revocation of a certificate of registration under section 44106 of this title;

(3) a decision of the head of the department in which the Coast Guard is operating on an appeal from the decision of an administrative law judge denying, revoking, or suspending a license, certificate, document, or register in a proceeding under section 6101, 6301, or 7503, chapter 77, or section 9303 of title 46; and

(4) under section 46301(d)(5) of this title, an order imposing a penalty under section 46301.

(Pub. L. 103–272, §1(d), July 5, 1994, 108 Stat. 754.)

§1134. INSPECTIONS AND AUTOPSIES

(a) ENTRY AND INSPECTION.—An officer or employee of the National Transportation Safety Board—

(1) on display of appropriate credentials and written notice of inspection authority, may enter property where a transportation accident has occurred or wreckage from the accident is located and do anything necessary to conduct an investigation; and

(2) during reasonable hours, may inspect any record, including an electronic record,

process, control, or facility related to an accident investigation under this chapter.

(b) INSPECTION, TESTING, PRESERVATION, AND MOVING OF AIRCRAFT AND PARTS.—(1) In investigating an aircraft accident under this chapter, the Board may inspect and test, to the extent necessary, any civil aircraft, aircraft engine, propeller, appliance, or property on an aircraft involved in an accident in air commerce.

(2) Any civil aircraft, aircraft engine, propeller, appliance, or property on an aircraft involved in an accident in air commerce shall be preserved, and may be moved, only as provided by regulations of the Board.

(c) AVOIDING UNNECESSARY INTERFERENCE AND PRESERVING EVIDENCE.—In carrying out subsection (a)(1) of this section, an officer or employee may examine or test any vehicle, vessel, rolling stock, track, or pipeline component. The examination or test shall be conducted in a way that—

(1) does not interfere unnecessarily with transportation services provided by the owner or operator of the vehicle, vessel, rolling stock, track, or pipeline component; and

(2) to the maximum extent feasible, preserves evidence related to the accident, consistent with the needs of the investigation and with the cooperation of that owner or operator.

(d) EXCLUSIVE AUTHORITY OF BOARD.—Only the Board has the authority to decide on the way in which testing under this section will be conducted, including decisions on the person that will conduct the test, the type of test that will be conducted, and any individual who will witness the test. Those decisions are committed to the discretion of the Board. The Board shall make any of those decisions based on the needs of the investigation being conducted and, when applicable, subsections (a), (c), and (e) of this section.

(e) PROMPTNESS OF TESTS AND AVAILABILITY OF RESULTS.—An inspection, examination, or test under subsection (a) or (c) of this section shall be started and completed promptly, and the results shall be made available.

(f) AUTOPSIES.—(1) The Board may order an autopsy to be performed and have other tests made when necessary to investigate an accident under this chapter. However, local law protecting religious beliefs related to autopsies shall be observed to the extent consistent with the needs of the accident investigation.

(2) With or without reimbursement, the Board may obtain a copy of an autopsy report performed by a State or local official on an individual who died because of a transportation accident investigated by the Board under this chapter.

(g) RECORDERS AND DATA.—In investigating an accident under this chapter, the Board may require from a transportation operator or equipment manufacturer or the vendors, suppliers, subsidiaries, or parent companies of such manufacturer, or operator of a product or service which is subject to an investigation by the Board—

(1) any recorder or recorded information pertinent to the accident;

(2) without undue delay, information the Board determines necessary to enable the Board to read and interpret any recording device or recorded information pertinent to the accident; and

(3) design specifications or data related to the operation and performance of the equipment the Board determines necessary to enable the Board to perform independent

physics-based simulations and analyses of the accident situation.

(Pub. L. 103–272, §1(d), July 5, 1994, 108 Stat. 754; Pub. L. 115–254, div. C, §1105, Oct. 5, 2018, 132 Stat. 3431; Pub. L. 118–63, title XII, §1213, May 16, 2024, 138 Stat. 1426.)

§1135. SECRETARY OF TRANSPORTATION'S RESPONSES TO SAFETY RECOMMENDATIONS

(a) GENERAL.—When the National Transportation Safety Board submits a recommendation about transportation safety to the Secretary of Transportation, the Secretary shall give to the Board a formal written response to each recommendation not later than 90 days after receiving the recommendation. The response shall indicate whether the Secretary intends—

(1) to carry out procedures to adopt the complete recommendation;

(2) to carry out procedures to adopt a part of the recommendation; or

(3) to refuse to carry out procedures to adopt the recommendation.

(b) TIMETABLE FOR COMPLETING PROCEDURES AND REASONS FOR REFUSALS.—A response under subsection (a)(1) or (2) of this section shall include a copy of a proposed timetable for completing the procedures. A response under subsection (a)(2) of this section shall detail the reasons for the refusal to carry out procedures on the remainder of the recommendation. A response under subsection (a)(3) of this section shall detail the reasons for the refusal to carry out procedures.

(c) PUBLIC AVAILABILITY.—The Board shall make a copy of each recommendation and response available to the public—

(1) in electronic form at no cost in a publicly accessible database on a website of the Board; and

(2) if the electronic form required in paragraph (1) is not printable, in printed form upon a reasonable request at a reasonable cost.

(d) ANNUAL REPORT ON AIR CARRIER SAFETY RECOMMENDATIONS.—

(1) IN GENERAL.—The Secretary shall submit to Congress and the Board, on an annual basis, a report on the recommendations made by the Board to the Secretary regarding air carrier operations conducted under part 121 of title 14, Code of Federal Regulations.

(2) RECOMMENDATIONS TO BE COVERED.—The report shall cover—

(A) any recommendation for which the Secretary has developed, or intends to develop, procedures to adopt the recommendation or part of the recommendation, but has yet to complete the procedures; and

(B) any recommendation for which the Secretary, in the preceding year, has issued a response under subsection (a)(2) or (a)(3) refusing to carry out all or part of the procedures to adopt the recommendation.

(3) CONTENTS.—

(A) PLANS TO ADOPT RECOMMENDATIONS.—For each recommendation of the Board described in paragraph (2)(A), the report shall contain—

(i) a description of the recommendation;

(ii) a description of the procedures planned for adopting the recommendation or part of the recommendation;

(iii) the proposed date for completing the procedures; and

(iv) if the Secretary has not met a deadline contained in a proposed timeline developed in connection with the recommendation under subsection (b), an explanation for not meeting the deadline.

(B) REFUSALS TO ADOPT RECOMMENDATIONS.—For each recommendation of the Board described in paragraph (2)(B), the report shall contain—

(i) a description of the recommendation; and

(ii) a description of the reasons for the refusal to carry out all or part of the procedures to adopt the recommendation.

(Pub. L. 103–272, §1(d), July 5, 1994, 108 Stat. 755; Pub. L. 108–168, §6, Dec. 6, 2003, 117 Stat. 2034; Pub. L. 109–443, §2(b), Dec. 21, 2006, 120 Stat. 3298; Pub. L. 111–216, title II, §202, Aug. 1, 2010, 124 Stat. 2351; Pub. L. 111–249, §6(1), (2), Sept. 30, 2010, 124 Stat. 2628; Pub. L. 118–63, title XII, §§1214, 1220(a), May 16, 2024, 138 Stat. 1426, 1432.)

§1136. ASSISTANCE TO PASSENGERS INVOLVED IN AIRCRAFT ACCIDENTS AND FAMILIES OF SUCH PASSENGERS

(a) IN GENERAL.—As soon as practicable after being notified of an aircraft accident within United States airspace or airspace delegated to the United States involving an air carrier or foreign air carrier, resulting in any loss of life, and for which the National Transportation Safety Board will serve as the lead investigative agency, the Chairman of the Board shall—

(1) designate and publicize the name and phone number of a director of family support services who shall be an employee of the Board and shall be responsible for acting as a point of contact within the Federal Government for the families of passengers involved in the accident and a liaison between the air carrier or foreign air carrier and the families; and

(2) designate an independent nonprofit organization, with experience in disasters and posttrauma communication with families, which shall have primary responsibility for coordinating the emotional care, psychological care, and family support services of passengers involved in the accident and the families of such passengers.

(b) RESPONSIBILITIES OF THE BOARD.—The Board shall have primary Federal responsibility for facilitating the recovery and identification of fatally-injured passengers involved in an accident described in subsection (a).

(c) RESPONSIBILITIES OF DESIGNATED ORGANIZATION.—The organization designated for an accident under subsection (a)(2) shall have the following responsibilities with respect to passengers involved in the accident and the families of such passengers:

(1) To provide emotional care, psychological care, and family support services, in coordination with the disaster response team of the air carrier or foreign air carrier involved.

(2) To take such actions as may be necessary to provide an environment in which the families may grieve in private.

(3) To meet with passengers involved in the accident and the families of such

passengers who have traveled to the location of the accident, to contact the families unable to travel to such location, and to contact all passengers and affected families regularly thereafter until such time as the organization, in consultation with the director of family support services designated for the accident under subsection (a)(1), determines that further assistance is no longer needed.

(4) To communicate with the passengers and families as to the roles of the organization, government agencies, and the air carrier or foreign air carrier involved with respect to the accident and the post-accident activities.

(5) To arrange a suitable memorial service, in consultation with the families.

(d) PASSENGER LISTS.—

(1) REQUESTS FOR PASSENGER LISTS BY THE DIRECTOR OF FAMILY SERVICES.—

(A) REQUESTS BY DIRECTOR OF FAMILY SUPPORT SERVICES.—It shall be the responsibility of the director of family support services designated for an accident under subsection (a)(1) to request, as soon as practicable, from the air carrier or foreign air carrier involved in the accident a passenger list, which is based on the best available information at the time of the request.

(B) USE OF INFORMATION.—The director of family support services may not release to any person information on a list obtained under subparagraph (A), except that the director may, to the extent the director considers appropriate, provide information on the list about a passenger to—

(i) the family of the passenger; or

(ii) a local, Tribal, State, or Federal agency responsible for determining the whereabouts or welfare of a passenger.

(C) LIMITATION.—A local, Tribal, State, or Federal agency may not release to any person any information obtained under subparagraph (B)(ii), except if given express authority from the director of family support services.

(D) RULE OF CONSTRUCTION.—Nothing in subparagraph (C) shall be construed to preclude a local, Tribal, State, or Federal agency from releasing information that is lawfully obtained through other means independent of releases made by the director of family support services under subparagraph (B).

(2) REQUESTS FOR PASSENGER LISTS BY DESIGNATED ORGANIZATION.—

(A) REQUESTS BY DESIGNATED ORGANIZATION.—The organization designated for an accident under subsection (a)(2) may request from the air carrier or foreign air carrier involved in the accident a passenger list.

(B) USE OF INFORMATION.—The designated organization may not release to any person information on a passenger list but may provide information on the list about a passenger to the family of the passenger to the extent the organization considers appropriate.

(e) CONTINUING RESPONSIBILITIES OF THE BOARD.—In the course of its investigation of an accident described in subsection (a), the Board shall, to the maximum extent practicable, ensure that the families of passengers involved in the accident—

(1) are briefed, prior to any public briefing, about the accident, its causes, and any other findings from the investigation; and

(2) are individually informed of and allowed to attend any public hearings and meetings of the Board about the accident.

(f) USE OF AIR CARRIER RESOURCES.—To the extent practicable, the organization designated for an accident under subsection (a)(2) shall coordinate its activities with the air carrier or foreign air carrier involved in the accident so that the resources of the carrier can be used to the greatest extent possible to carry out the organization's responsibilities under this section.

(g) PROHIBITED ACTIONS.—

(1) ACTIONS TO IMPEDE THE BOARD.—No person (including a State or political subdivision) may impede the ability of the Board (including the director of family support services designated for an accident under subsection (a)(1)), or an organization designated for an accident under subsection (a)(2), to carry out its responsibilities under this section or the ability of passengers involved in the accident and the families of such passengers to have contact with one another.

(2) UNSOLICITED COMMUNICATIONS.—In the event of an accident involving an air carrier providing interstate or foreign air transportation and in the event of an accident involving a foreign air carrier that occurs within the United States, no unsolicited communication concerning a potential action for personal injury or wrongful death may be made by an attorney (including any associate, agent, employee, or other representative of an attorney) or any potential party to the litigation to an individual injured in the accident, or to a relative of an individual involved in the accident, before the 45th day following the date of the accident.

(3) PROHIBITION ON ACTIONS TO PREVENT CERTAIN CARE AND SUPPORT SERVICES.—No State or political subdivision thereof may prevent the employees, agents, or volunteers of an organization designated for an accident under subsection (a)(2) from providing emotional care, psychological care, and family support services under subsection (c)(1) in the 30-day period beginning on the date of the accident. The director of family support services designated for the accident under subsection (a)(1) may extend such period for not to exceed an additional 30 days if the director determines that the extension is necessary to meet the needs of the passengers and families and if State and local authorities are notified of the determination.

(h) DEFINITIONS.—In this section, the following definitions apply:

(1) AIRCRAFT ACCIDENT.—The term "aircraft accident" means any aviation disaster, regardless of its cause or suspected cause, for which the Board is the lead investigative agency.

(2) PASSENGER.—The term "passenger" includes—

(A) an employee of an air carrier or foreign air carrier aboard an aircraft;

(B) any other person aboard the aircraft without regard to whether the person paid for the transportation, occupied a seat, or held a reservation for the flight; and

(C) any other person injured or killed in the aircraft accident, as determined appropriate by the Board.

(3) PASSENGER LIST.—The term "passenger list" means a list based on the best available information at the time of a request, of the name of each passenger aboard the aircraft involved in the accident.

(i) STATUTORY CONSTRUCTION.—Nothing in this section may be construed as limiting the actions that an air carrier may take, or the obligations that an air carrier may have, in providing assistance to passengers involved in the aircraft accident and the families of such passengers.

(j) RELINQUISHMENT OF INVESTIGATIVE PRIORITY.—

(1) GENERAL RULE.—This section (other than subsection (g)) shall not apply to an aircraft accident if the Board has relinquished investigative priority under section 1131(a)(2)(B) and the Federal agency to which the Board relinquished investigative priority is willing and able to provide assistance to the victims and families of the passengers involved in the accident.

(2) BOARD ASSISTANCE.—If this section does not apply to an aircraft accident because the Board has relinquished investigative priority with respect to the accident, the Board shall assist, to the maximum extent possible, the agency to which the Board has relinquished investigative priority in assisting families with respect to the accident.

(Added Pub. L. 104–264, title VII, §702(a)(1), Oct. 9, 1996, 110 Stat. 3265; amended Pub. L. 106–181, title IV, §401(a)(1), (b)–(d), Apr. 5, 2000, 114 Stat. 129; Pub. L. 108–168, §3(a), Dec. 6, 2003, 117 Stat. 2033; Pub. L. 115–254, div. C, §1109(c), Oct. 5, 2018, 132 Stat. 3434; Pub. L. 118–63, title XII, §1215(a), May 16, 2024, 138 Stat. 1427.)

§1137. AUTHORITY OF THE INSPECTOR GENERAL

(a) IN GENERAL.—The Inspector General of the Department of Transportation, in accordance with the mission of the Inspector General to prevent and detect fraud and abuse, shall have authority to review only the financial management, property management, and business operations of the National Transportation Safety Board, including internal accounting and administrative control systems, to determine compliance with applicable Federal laws, rules, and regulations.

(b) DUTIES.—In carrying out this section, the Inspector General shall—

(1) keep the Chairman of the Board and Congress fully and currently informed about problems relating to administration of the internal accounting and administrative control systems of the Board;

(2) issue findings and recommendations for actions to address such problems; and

(3) report periodically to Congress on any progress made in implementing actions to address such problems.

(c) ACCESS TO INFORMATION.—In carrying out this section, the Inspector General may exercise authorities granted to the Inspector General under subsections (a) and (c) of section 406 of title 5.

(d) AUTHORIZATIONS OF APPROPRIATIONS.—

(1) FUNDING.—There are authorized to be appropriated to the Secretary of

Transportation for use by the Inspector General of the Department of Transportation such sums as may be necessary to cover expenses associated with activities pursuant to the authority exercised under this section.

(2) REIMBURSABLE AGREEMENT.—In the absence of an appropriation under this subsection for an expense referred to in paragraph (1), the Inspector General and the Board shall have a reimbursable agreement to cover such expense.

(Added Pub. L. 106–424, §12(a), Nov. 1, 2000, 114 Stat. 1887; amended Pub. L. 109–443, §4, Dec. 21, 2006, 120 Stat. 3299; Pub. L. 117–286, §4(b)(96), Dec. 27, 2022, 136 Stat. 4353.)

§1138. EVALUATION AND AUDIT OF NATIONAL TRANSPORTATION SAFETY BOARD

(a) IN GENERAL.—To promote economy, efficiency, and effectiveness in the administration of the programs, operations, and activities of the National Transportation Safety Board, the Comptroller General of the United States shall evaluate and audit the programs and expenditures of the Board. Such evaluation and audit shall be conducted as determined necessary by the Comptroller General or the appropriate congressional committees.

(b) RESPONSIBILITY OF COMPTROLLER GENERAL.—The Comptroller General shall evaluate and audit Board programs, operations, and activities, including—

(1) information management and security, including privacy protection of personally identifiable information;

(2) resource management;

(3) workforce development;

(4) procurement and contracting planning, practices and policies;

(5) the process and procedures to select an accident to investigate;

(6) the extent to which the Board follows leading practices in selected management areas; and

(7) the extent to which the Board addresses management challenges in completing accident investigations.

(c) APPROPRIATE CONGRESSIONAL COMMITTEES.—For purposes of this section the term "appropriate congressional committees" means the Committee on Commerce, Science, and Transportation of the Senate and the Committee on Transportation and Infrastructure of the House of Representatives.

(Added Pub. L. 109–443, §5(a), Dec. 21, 2006, 120 Stat. 3299; amended Pub. L. 113–188, title XV, §1502, Nov. 26, 2014, 128 Stat. 2025; Pub. L. 115–254, div. C, §1110, Oct. 5, 2018, 132 Stat. 3435; Pub. L. 118–63, title XII, §1221(a), May 16, 2024, 138 Stat. 1432.)

§1139. ASSISTANCE TO PASSENGERS INVOLVED IN RAIL PASSENGER ACCIDENTS AND FAMILIES OF SUCH PASSENGERS

(a) IN GENERAL.—As soon as practicable after being notified of a rail passenger accident within the United States involving a rail passenger carrier and resulting in any loss of life, and for which the National Transportation Safety Board will serve as the lead investigative agency, the Chairman of the Board shall—

(1) designate and publicize the name and telephone number of a director of family support services who shall be an employee of the Board and shall be responsible for acting as a point of contact within the Federal Government for the families of passengers involved in the accident and a liaison between the rail passenger carrier and the families; and

(2) designate an independent nonprofit organization, with experience in disasters and post-trauma communication with families, which shall have primary responsibility for coordinating the emotional care, psychological care, and family support services of passengers involved in the accident and the families of such passengers.

(b) RESPONSIBILITIES OF THE BOARD.—The Board shall have primary Federal responsibility for—

(1) facilitating the recovery and identification of fatally injured passengers involved in an accident described in subsection (a); and

(2) communicating with the families of passengers involved in the accident as to the roles, with respect to the accident and the post-accident activities, of—

(A) the organization designated for an accident under subsection (a)(2);

(B) Government agencies; and

(C) the rail passenger carrier involved.

(c) RESPONSIBILITIES OF DESIGNATED ORGANIZATION.—The organization designated for an accident under subsection (a)(2) shall have the following responsibilities with respect to passengers involved in the accident and the families of such passengers:

(1) To provide emotional care, psychological care, and family support services, in coordination with the disaster response team of the rail passenger carrier involved.

(2) To take such actions as may be necessary to provide an environment in which the families may grieve in private.

(3) To meet with passengers involved in the accident and the families of such passengers who have traveled to the location of the accident, to contact the families unable to travel to such location, and to contact all passengers and affected families periodically thereafter until such time as the organization, in consultation with the director of family support services designated for the accident under subsection (a)(1), determines that further assistance is no longer needed.

(4) To arrange a suitable memorial service, in consultation with the passengers and families.

(d) PASSENGER LISTS.—

(1) REQUESTS FOR PASSENGER LISTS BY THE DIRECTOR OF FAMILY SERVICES.—

(A) REQUESTS BY DIRECTOR OF FAMILY SUPPORT SERVICES.—It shall be the responsibility of the director of family support services designated for an accident under subsection (a)(1) to request, as soon as practicable, from the rail passenger carrier involved in the accident a passenger list, which is based on the best available information at the time of the request.

(B) USE OF INFORMATION.—The director of family support services may not release to any person information on a list obtained under subparagraph (A), except that the director may, to the extent the director considers appropriate, provide information on the list about a passenger to—

(i) the family of the passenger; or

(ii) a local, Tribal, State, or Federal agency responsible for determining the whereabouts or welfare of a passenger.

(C) LIMITATION.—A local, Tribal, State, or Federal agency may not release to any person any information obtained under subparagraph (B)(ii), except if given express authority from the director of family support services.

(D) RULE OF CONSTRUCTION.—Nothing in subparagraph (C) shall be construed to preclude a local, Tribal, State, or Federal agency from releasing information that is lawfully obtained through other means independent of releases made by the director of family support services under subparagraph (B).

(2) REQUESTS FOR PASSENGER LISTS BY DESIGNATED ORGANIZATION.—

(A) REQUESTS BY DESIGNATED ORGANIZATION.—The organization designated for an accident under subsection (a)(2) may request from the rail passenger carrier involved in the accident a passenger list.

(B) USE OF INFORMATION.—The designated organization may not release to any person information on a passenger list but may provide information on the list about a passenger to the family of the passenger to the extent the organization considers appropriate.

(e) CONTINUING RESPONSIBILITIES OF THE BOARD.—In the course of its investigation of an accident described in subsection (a), the Board shall, to the maximum extent practicable, ensure that the families of passengers involved in the accident—

(1) are briefed, prior to any public briefing, about the accident and any other findings from the investigation; and

(2) are individually informed of and allowed to attend any public hearings and meetings of the Board about the accident.

(f) USE OF RAIL PASSENGER CARRIER RESOURCES.—To the extent practicable, the organization designated for an accident under subsection (a)(2) shall coordinate its activities with the rail passenger carrier involved in the accident to facilitate the reasonable use of the resources of the carrier.

(g) PROHIBITED ACTIONS.—

(1) ACTIONS TO IMPEDE THE BOARD.—No person (including a State or political subdivision thereof) may impede the ability of the Board (including the director of family support services designated for an accident under subsection (a)(1)), or an organization designated for an accident under subsection (a)(2), to carry out its responsibilities under this section or the ability of passengers involved in the accident and the families of such passengers to have contact with one another.

(2) UNSOLICITED COMMUNICATIONS.—No unsolicited communication concerning a potential action or settlement offer for personal injury or wrongful death may be made

by an attorney (including any associate, agent, employee, or other representative of an attorney) or any potential party to the litigation, including the railroad carrier or rail passenger carrier, to an individual (other than an employee of the rail passenger carrier) injured in the accident, or to a relative of an individual involved in the accident, before the 45th day following the date of the accident.

(3) PROHIBITION ON ACTIONS TO PREVENT CERTAIN CARE AND SUPPORT SERVICES.—No State or political subdivision thereof may prevent the employees, agents, or volunteers of an organization designated for an accident under subsection (a)(2) from providing emotional care, psychological care, and family support services under subsection (c)(1) in the 30-day period beginning on the date of the accident. The director of family support services designated for the accident under subsection (a)(1) may extend such period for not to exceed an additional 30 days if the director determines that the extension is necessary to meet the needs of the passengers and families and if State and local authorities are notified of the determination.

(h) DEFINITIONS.—In this section:
(1) RAIL PASSENGER ACCIDENT.—The term "rail passenger accident" means any rail passenger disaster that—
(A) results in any loss of life;
(B) the Board will serve as the lead investigative agency for; and
(C) occurs in the provision of—
(i) interstate intercity rail passenger transportation (as such term is defined in section 24102); or
(ii) high-speed rail (as such term is defined in section 26105) transportation, regardless of its cause or suspected cause.

(2) RAIL PASSENGER CARRIER.—The term "rail passenger carrier" means a rail carrier providing—
(A) interstate intercity rail passenger transportation (as such term is defined in section 24102); or
(B) interstate or intrastate high-speed rail (as such term is defined in section 26105) transportation,

except that such term does not include a tourist, historic, scenic, or excursion rail carrier.
(3) PASSENGER.—The term "passenger" includes—
(A) an employee of a rail passenger carrier aboard a train;
(B) any other person aboard the train without regard to whether the person paid for the transportation, occupied a seat, or held a reservation for the rail transportation; and
(C) any other person injured or killed in a rail passenger accident, as determined appropriate by the Board.

(4) PASSENGER LIST.—The term "passenger list" means a list based on the best available information at the time of the request, of the name of each passenger aboard the rail passenger carrier's train involved in the accident. A rail passenger carrier shall use reasonable efforts, with respect to its unreserved trains, and passengers not holding

reservations on its other trains, to ascertain the names of passengers aboard a train involved in an accident.

(i) LIMITATION ON STATUTORY CONSTRUCTION.—Nothing in this section may be construed as limiting the actions that a rail passenger carrier may take, or the obligations that a rail passenger carrier may have, in providing assistance to the families of passengers involved in a rail passenger accident.

(j) RELINQUISHMENT OF INVESTIGATIVE PRIORITY.—

(1) GENERAL RULE.—This section (other than subsection (g)) shall not apply to a rail passenger accident if the Board has relinquished investigative priority under section 1131(a)(2)(B) and the Federal agency to which the Board relinquished investigative priority is willing and able to provide assistance to the victims and families of the passengers involved in the accident.

(2) BOARD ASSISTANCE.—If this section does not apply to a rail passenger accident because the Board has relinquished investigative priority with respect to the accident, the Board shall assist, to the maximum extent possible, the agency to which the Board has relinquished investigative priority in assisting families with respect to the accident.

(k) SAVINGS CLAUSE.—Nothing in this section shall be construed to abridge the authority of the Board or the Secretary of Transportation to investigate the causes or circumstances of any rail accident, including development of information regarding the nature of injuries sustained and the manner in which they were sustained for the purposes of determining compliance with existing laws and regulations or for identifying means of preventing similar injuries in the future, or both.

(Added Pub. L. 110–432, div. A, title V, §501(a), Oct. 16, 2008, 122 Stat. 4894; amended Pub. L. 114–94, div. A, title XI, §11316(a), Dec. 4, 2015, 129 Stat. 1676; Pub. L. 115–254, div. C, §1109(d), Oct. 5, 2018, 132 Stat. 3435; Pub. L. 118–63, title XII, §1215(c), May 16, 2024, 138 Stat. 1428.)

§1140. INFORMATION [1] INDIVIDUALS INVOLVED IN ACCIDENTS AND FAMILIES OF SUCH INDIVIDUALS

In the course of an investigation of an accident described in section 1131(a)(1), except an aircraft accident described in section 1136 or a rail passenger accident described in section 1139, the Board may, to the maximum extent practicable, ensure that individuals involved in accidents and the families of such individuals, and other individuals the Board deems appropriate—

(1) are informed as to the roles, with respect to the accident and the post-accident activities, of the Board;

(2) are briefed, before any public briefing, about the accident, its causes, and any other findings from the investigation; and

(3) are individually informed of and allowed to attend any public hearings and meetings of the Board about the accident.

(Added Pub. L. 115–254, div. C, §1109(e)(1), Oct. 5, 2018, 132 Stat. 3435; amended Pub. L. 118–63, title XII, §1215(e), May 16, 2024, 138 Stat. 1430.)

[1] So in original. Probably should be followed by "for".

SUBCHAPTER IV—ENFORCEMENT AND PENALTIES

§1151. AVIATION ENFORCEMENT

(a) CIVIL ACTIONS BY BOARD.—The National Transportation Safety Board may bring a civil action in a district court of the United States against a person to enforce section 1132, 1134(b) or (f)(1) (related to an aircraft accident), 1136(g)(2), or 1155(a) of this title or a regulation prescribed or order issued under any of those sections. An action under this subsection may be brought in the judicial district in which the person does business or the violation occurred.

(b) CIVIL ACTIONS BY ATTORNEY GENERAL.—On request of the Board, the Attorney General may bring a civil action in an appropriate court—

(1) to enforce section 1132, 1134(b) or (f)(1) (related to an aircraft accident), 1136(g)(2), or 1155(a) of this title or a regulation prescribed or order issued under any of those sections; and

(2) to prosecute a person violating those sections or a regulation prescribed or order issued under any of those sections.

(c) PARTICIPATION OF BOARD.—On request of the Attorney General, the Board may participate in a civil action to enforce section 1132, 1134(b) or (f)(1) (related to an aircraft accident), 1136(g)(2), or 1155(a) of this title.

(d) NOTIFICATION TO CONGRESS.—If the Board or Attorney General carry out such civil actions described in subsection (a) or (b) of this section against an airman employed at the time of the accident or incident by an air carrier operating under part 121 of title 14, Code of Federal Regulations, the Board shall immediately notify the Committee on Transportation and Infrastructure of the House of Representatives and the Committee on Commerce, Science, and Transportation of the Senate of such civil actions, including—

(1) the labor union representing the airman involved, if applicable;

(2) the air carrier at which the airman is employed;

(3) the docket information of the incident or accident in which the airman was involved;

(4) the date of such civil actions taken by the Board or Attorney General; and

(5) a description of why such civil actions were taken by the Board or Attorney General.

(e) SUBSEQUENT NOTIFICATION TO CONGRESS.—Not later than 15 days after the notification described in subsection (d), the Board shall submit a report to or brief the Committee on Transportation and Infrastructure of the House of Representatives and the Committee on Commerce, Science, and Transportation of the Senate describing the status of compliance with the civil actions taken.

(Pub. L. 103–272, §1(d), July 5, 1994, 108 Stat. 756; Pub. L. 106–181, title IV, §401(a)(2), Apr. 5, 2000, 114 Stat. 129; Pub. L. 118–63, title XII, §1208(b), May 16, 2024, 138 Stat. 1424.)

§1152. JOINDER AND INTERVENTION IN AVIATION PROCEEDINGS

A person interested in or affected by a matter under consideration in a proceeding or a civil action to enforce section 1132, 1134(b) or (f)(1) (related to an aircraft accident), or 1155(a) of this title, or a regulation prescribed or order issued under any of those sections, may be joined as a party or permitted to intervene in the proceeding or civil action.

(Pub. L. 103–272, §1(d), July 5, 1994, 108 Stat. 756.)

§1153. JUDICIAL REVIEW

(a) GENERAL.—The appropriate court of appeals of the United States or the United States Court of Appeals for the District of Columbia Circuit may review a final order of the National Transportation Safety Board under this chapter. A person disclosing a substantial interest in the order may apply for review by filing a petition not later than 60 days after the order of the Board is issued.

(b) PERSONS SEEKING JUDICIAL REVIEW OF AVIATION MATTERS.—(1) A person disclosing a substantial interest in an order related to an aviation matter issued by the Board under this chapter may apply for review of the order by filing a petition for review in the United States Court of Appeals for the District of Columbia Circuit or in the court of appeals of the United States for the circuit in which the person resides or has its principal place of business. The petition must be filed not later than 60 days after the order is issued. The court may allow the petition to be filed after the 60 days only if there was a reasonable ground for not filing within that 60-day period.

(2) When a petition is filed under paragraph (1) of this subsection, the clerk of the court immediately shall send a copy of the petition to the Board. The Board shall file with the court a record of the proceeding in which the order was issued.

(3) When the petition is sent to the Board, the court has exclusive jurisdiction to affirm, amend, modify, or set aside any part of the order and may order the Board to conduct further proceedings. After reasonable notice to the Board, the court may grant interim relief by staying the order or taking other appropriate action when cause for its action exists. Findings of fact by the Board, if supported by substantial evidence, are conclusive.

(4) In reviewing an order under this subsection, the court may consider an objection to an order of the Board only if the objection was made in the proceeding conducted by the Board or if there was a reasonable ground for not making the objection in the proceeding.

(5) A decision by a court under this subsection may be reviewed only by the Supreme Court under section 1254 of title 28.

(c) ADMINISTRATOR SEEKING JUDICIAL REVIEW OF AVIATION MATTERS.—When the Administrator of the Federal Aviation Administration decides that an order of the Board under section 44703(d), 44709, or 46301(d)(5) of this title will have a significant adverse impact on carrying out this chapter related to an aviation matter, the Administrator may obtain judicial review of the order under section 46110 of this title. The Administrator shall be made a party to the judicial review proceedings. Findings of fact of the Board are conclusive if supported by substantial evidence.

(d) COMMANDANT SEEKING JUDICIAL REVIEW OF MARITIME MATTERS.—If the Commandant of the Coast Guard decides that an order of the Board issued pursuant to a review of a Coast Guard action under section 1133 of this title will have an adverse impact on maritime safety or security, the Commandant may obtain judicial review of the order under subsection (a). The Commandant, in the official capacity of the Commandant, shall be a party to the judicial review proceedings.

(Pub. L. 103–272, §1(d), July 5, 1994, 108 Stat. 756; Pub. L. 108–293, title VI, §622, Aug. 9, 2004, 118 Stat. 1063; Pub. L. 112–95, title III, §301(b), Feb. 14, 2012, 126 Stat. 56.)

§1154. DISCOVERY AND USE OF COCKPIT AND SURFACE VEHICLE RECORDINGS AND TRANSCRIPTS

(a) IN GENERAL.—(1) Except as provided by this subsection, a party in a judicial proceeding may not use discovery to obtain—

(A) any still image that the National Transportation Safety Board has not made available to the public under section 1114(c) or 1114(d) of this title;

(B) any part of a cockpit or surface vehicle recorder transcript that the National Transportation Safety Board has not made available to the public under section 1114(c) or 1114(d) of this title; and

(C) a cockpit or surface vehicle recorder recording.

(2)(A) Except as provided in paragraph (4)(A) of this subsection, a court may allow discovery by a party of a cockpit or surface vehicle recorder transcript if, after an in camera review of the transcript, the court decides that—

(i) the part of the transcript made available to the public under section 1114(c) or 1114(d) of this title does not provide the party with sufficient information for the party to receive a fair trial; and

(ii) discovery of additional parts of the transcript is necessary to provide the party with sufficient information for the party to receive a fair trial.

(B) A court may allow discovery, or require production for an in camera review, of a cockpit or surface vehicle recorder transcript that the Board has not made available under section 1114(c) or 1114(d) of this title only if the cockpit or surface vehicle recorder recording is not available.

(3) Except as provided in paragraph (4)(A) of this subsection, a court may allow discovery by a party of a cockpit or surface vehicle recorder recording, including with regard to a video recording any still image that the National Transportation Safety Board has not made available to the public under section 1114(c) or 1114(d) of this title, if, after an in camera review of the recording, the court decides that—

(A) the parts of the transcript made available to the public under section 1114(c) or 1114(d) of this title and to the party through discovery under paragraph (2) of this subsection do not provide the party with sufficient information for the party to receive a fair trial; and

(B) discovery of the cockpit or surface vehicle recorder recording, including with regard to a video recording any still image that the National Transportation Safety Board has not made available to the public under section 1114(c) or 1114(d) of this title, is necessary to provide the party with sufficient information for the party to receive a fair trial.

(4)(A) When a court allows discovery in a judicial proceeding of a still image or a part of a cockpit or surface vehicle recorder transcript not made available to the public under section 1114(c) or 1114(d) of this title or a cockpit or surface vehicle recorder recording, the court shall issue a protective order—

(i) to limit the use of the still image, the part of the transcript, or the recording to the judicial proceeding; and

(ii) to prohibit dissemination of the still image, the part of the transcript, or the recording to any person that does not need access to the still image, the part of the transcript, or the recording for the proceeding.

(B) A court may allow a still image or a part of a cockpit or surface vehicle recorder transcript not made available to the public under section 1114(c) or 1114(d) of this title or a cockpit or surface vehicle recorder recording to be admitted into evidence in a judicial proceeding, only if the court places the still image, the part of the transcript, or the recording under seal to prevent the use of the still image, the part of the transcript, or the recording for purposes other than for the proceeding.

(5) This subsection does not prevent the Board from referring at any time to cockpit or surface vehicle recorder information in making safety recommendations.

(6) In this subsection:

(A) RECORDER.—The term "recorder" means a voice or video recorder.

(B) STILL IMAGE.—The term "still image" means any still image obtained from a video recorder.

(C) TRANSCRIPT.—The term "transcript" includes any written depiction of visual information obtained from a video recorder.

(b) REPORTS.—No part of a report of the Board, related to an accident or an investigation of an accident, may be admitted into evidence or used in a civil action for damages resulting from a matter mentioned in the report.

(Pub. L. 103–272, §1(d), July 5, 1994, 108 Stat. 757; Pub. L. 106–424, §5(c)(1), Nov. 1, 2000, 114 Stat. 1885; Pub. L. 115–254, div. C, §1104(b), Oct. 5, 2018, 132 Stat. 3430.)

§1155. PENALTIES

(a) CIVIL PENALTY.—(1) A person violating section 1132, section 1134(b), section 1134(f)(1), section 1136(g), or section 1139(g) of this title or a regulation prescribed or order issued under any of those sections is liable to the United States Government for a civil penalty of not more than $1,000. A separate violation occurs for each day a violation continues.

(2) This subsection does not apply to a member of the armed forces of the United States or an employee of the Department of Defense subject to the Uniform Code of Military Justice when the member or employee is performing official duties. The appropriate military authorities are responsible for taking necessary disciplinary action and submitting to the National Transportation Safety Board a timely report on action taken.

(3) The Board may compromise the amount of a civil penalty imposed under this subsection.

(4) The Government may deduct the amount of a civil penalty imposed or compromised

under this subsection from amounts it owes the person liable for the penalty.

(5) A civil penalty under this subsection may be collected by bringing a civil action against the person liable for the penalty. The action shall conform as nearly as practicable to a civil action in admiralty.

(b) CRIMINAL PENALTY.—A person that knowingly and without authority removes, conceals, or withholds a part of a civil aircraft involved in an accident, or property on the aircraft at the time of the accident, shall be fined under title 18, imprisoned for not more than 10 years, or both.

(Pub. L. 103–272, §1(d), July 5, 1994, 108 Stat. 758; Pub. L. 104–264, title VII, §702(b), Oct. 9, 1996, 110 Stat. 3267; Pub. L. 118–63, title XII, §1216(a), May 16, 2024, 138 Stat. 1431.)

CHAPTER 13—SURFACE TRANSPORTATION BOARD

I—ESTABLISHMENT [1]

II—ADMINISTRATIVE [1]

[1] *So in original. Does not conform to subchapter heading since word "SUBCHAPTER" does not appear.*

SUBCHAPTER I—ESTABLISHMENT

§1301. ESTABLISHMENT OF BOARD

(a) ESTABLISHMENT.—The Surface Transportation Board is an independent establishment of the United States Government.

(b) MEMBERSHIP.—(1) The Board shall consist of 5 members, to be appointed by the President, by and with the advice and consent of the Senate. Not more than 3 members may be appointed from the same political party.

(2) At all times—

(A) at least 3 members of the Board shall be individuals with professional standing and demonstrated knowledge in the fields of transportation, transportation regulation, or economic regulation; and

(B) at least 2 members shall be individuals with professional or business experience (including agriculture) in the private sector.

(3) The term of each member of the Board shall be 5 years and shall begin when the term of the predecessor of that member ends. An individual appointed to fill a vacancy occurring before the expiration of the term for which the predecessor of that individual was appointed, shall be appointed for the remainder of that term. When the term of office of a member ends, the member may continue to serve until a successor is appointed and qualified, but

for a period not to exceed one year. The President may remove a member for inefficiency, neglect of duty, or malfeasance in office.

(4) No individual may serve as a member of the Board for more than 2 terms. In the case of an individual appointed to fill a vacancy occurring before the expiration of the term for which the predecessor of that individual was appointed, such individual may not be appointed for more than one additional term.

(5) A member of the Board may not have a pecuniary interest in, hold an official relation to, or own stock in or bonds of, a carrier providing transportation by any mode and may not engage in another business, vocation, or employment.

(6) A vacancy in the membership of the Board does not impair the right of the remaining members to exercise all of the powers of the Board. The Board may designate a member to act as Chairman during any period in which there is no Chairman designated by the President.

(c) CHAIRMAN.—(1) There shall be at the head of the Board a Chairman, who shall be designated by the President from among the members of the Board. The Chairman shall receive compensation at the rate prescribed for level III of the Executive Schedule under section 5314 of title 5.

(2) Subject to the general policies, decisions, findings, and determinations of the Board, the Chairman shall be responsible for administering the Board. The Chairman may delegate the powers granted under this paragraph to an officer, employee, or office of the Board. The Chairman shall—

(A) appoint and supervise, other than regular and full-time employees in the immediate offices of another member, the officers and employees of the Board, including attorneys to provide legal aid and service to the Board and its members, and to represent the Board in any case in court;

(B) appoint the heads of offices with the approval of the Board;

(C) distribute Board business among officers and employees and offices of the Board;

(D) prepare requests for appropriations for the Board and submit those requests to the President and Congress with the prior approval of the Board; and

(E) supervise the expenditure of funds allocated by the Board for major programs and purposes.

(Added Pub. L. 104–88, title II, §201(a), Dec. 29, 1995, 109 Stat. 932, §701; amended Pub. L. 104–287, §5(5), Oct. 11, 1996, 110 Stat. 3389; renumbered §1301 and amended Pub. L. 114–110, §§3(a)(3), (b), 4, Dec. 18, 2015, 129 Stat. 2228, 2229.)

§1302. FUNCTIONS

Except as otherwise provided in the ICC Termination Act of 1995, or the amendments made thereby, the Board shall perform all functions that, immediately before January 1, 1996, were functions of the Interstate Commerce Commission or were performed by any officer or employee of the Interstate Commerce Commission in the capacity as such officer or employee.

(Added Pub. L. 104–88, title II, §201(a), Dec. 29, 1995, 109 Stat. 933, §702; amended Pub. L. 104–287, §5(6), Oct. 11, 1996, 110 Stat. 3389; renumbered §1302, Pub. L. 114–110, §3(a)(3), Dec. 18, 2015, 129 Stat. 2228.)

§1303. ADMINISTRATIVE PROVISIONS

(a) OPEN MEETINGS.—

(1) IN GENERAL.—The Board shall be deemed to be an agency for purposes of section 552b of title 5.

(2) NONPUBLIC COLLABORATIVE DISCUSSIONS.—

(A) IN GENERAL.—Notwithstanding section 552b of title 5, a majority of the members may hold a meeting that is not open to public observation to discuss official agency business if—

(i) no formal or informal vote or other official agency action is taken at the meeting;

(ii) each individual present at the meeting is a member or an employee of the Board; and

(iii) the General Counsel of the Board is present at the meeting.

(B) DISCLOSURE OF NONPUBLIC COLLABORATIVE DISCUSSIONS.—Except as provided under subparagraph (C), not later than 2 business days after the conclusion of a meeting under subparagraph (A), the Board shall make available to the public, in a place easily accessible to the public—

(i) a list of the individuals present at the meeting; and

(ii) a summary of the matters discussed at the meeting, except for any matters the Board properly determines may be withheld from the public under section 552b(c) of title 5.

(C) SUMMARY.—If the Board properly determines matters may be withheld from the public under section 555b(c) of title 5, the Board shall provide a summary with as much general information as possible on those matters withheld from the public.

(D) ONGOING PROCEEDINGS.—If a discussion under subparagraph (A) directly relates to an ongoing proceeding before the Board, the Board shall make the disclosure under subparagraph (B) on the date of the final Board decision.

(E) PRESERVATION OF OPEN MEETINGS REQUIREMENTS FOR AGENCY ACTION.—Nothing in this paragraph may be construed to limit the applicability of section 552b of title 5 with respect to a meeting of the members other than that described in this paragraph.

(F) STATUTORY CONSTRUCTION.—Nothing in this paragraph may be construed—

(i) to limit the applicability of section 552b of title 5 with respect to any information which is proposed to be withheld from the public under subparagraph (B)(ii); or

(ii) to authorize the Board to withhold from any individual any record that is accessible to that individual under section 552a of title 5, United States Code.

(b) REPRESENTATION BY ATTORNEYS.—Attorneys designated by the Chairman of the Board may appear for, and represent the Board in, any civil action brought in connection with any function carried out by the Board pursuant to this chapter or subtitle IV or as otherwise authorized by law.

(c) ADMISSION TO PRACTICE.—Subject to section 500 of title 5, the Board may regulate the admission of individuals to practice before it and may impose a reasonable admission fee.

(d) SUBMISSION OF CERTAIN DOCUMENTS TO CONGRESS.—

(1) IN GENERAL.—If the Board submits any budget estimate, budget request, supplemental budget estimate, or other budget information, legislative recommendation, prepared testimony for a congressional hearing, or comment on legislation to the President or to the Office of Management and Budget, the Board shall concurrently submit a copy of such document to—

(A) the Committee on Commerce, Science, and Transportation of the Senate; and

(B) the Committee on Transportation and Infrastructure of the House of Representatives.

(2) NO APPROVAL REQUIRED.—No officer or agency of the United States has any authority to require the Board to submit budget estimates or requests, legislative recommendations, prepared testimony for congressional hearings, or comments on legislation to any officer or agency of the United States for approval, comments, or review before submitting such recommendations, testimony, or comments to Congress.

(Added Pub. L. 104–88, title II, §201(a), Dec. 29, 1995, 109 Stat. 934, §703; renumbered §1303 and amended Pub. L. 114–110, §§3(a)(3), (c)(1), 5, Dec. 18, 2015, 129 Stat. 2228–2230.)

§1304. REPORTS

(a) ANNUAL REPORT.—The Board shall annually transmit to the Congress a report on its activities, including each instance in which the Board has initiated an investigation on its own initiative under this chapter or subtitle IV.

(b) RATE CASE REVIEW METRICS.—

(1) QUARTERLY REPORTS.—The Board shall post a quarterly report of rail rate review cases pending or completed by the Board during the previous quarter that includes—

(A) summary information of the case, including the docket number, case name, commodity or commodities involved, and rate review guideline or guidelines used;

(B) the date on which the rate review proceeding began;

(C) the date for the completion of discovery;

(D) the date for the completion of the evidentiary record;

(E) the date for the submission of closing briefs;

(F) the date on which the Board issued the final decision; and

(G) a brief summary of the final decision;

(2) WEBSITE POSTING.—Each quarterly report shall be posted on the Board's public website.

(c) COMPLAINTS.—

(1) IN GENERAL.—The Board shall establish and maintain a database of complaints received by the Board.

(2) QUARTERLY REPORTS.—The Board shall post a quarterly report of formal and

informal service complaints received by the Board during the previous quarter that includes—

(A) the date on which the complaint was received by the Board;

(B) a list of the type of each complaint;

(C) the geographic region of each complaint; and

(D) the resolution of each complaint, if appropriate.

(3) WRITTEN CONSENT.—The quarterly report may identify a complainant that submitted an informal complaint only upon the written consent of the complainant.

(4) WEBSITE POSTING.—Each quarterly report shall be posted on the Board's public website.

(Added Pub. L. 104–88, title II, §201(a), Dec. 29, 1995, 109 Stat. 934, §704; renumbered §1304 and amended Pub. L. 114–110, §§3(a)(3), 6, Dec. 18, 2015, 129 Stat. 2228, 2231.)

§1305. AUTHORIZATION OF APPROPRIATIONS

There are authorized to be appropriated for the activities of the Board—

(1) $33,000,000 for fiscal year 2016;

(2) $35,000,000 for fiscal year 2017;

(3) $35,500,000 for fiscal year 2018;

(4) $35,500,000 for fiscal year 2019; and

(5) $36,000,000 for fiscal year 2020.

(Added Pub. L. 104–88, title II, §201(a), Dec. 29, 1995, 109 Stat. 934, §705; renumbered §1305 and amended Pub. L. 114–110, §§3(a)(3), 7, Dec. 18, 2015, 129 Stat. 2228, 2232.)

§1306. REPORTING OFFICIAL ACTION

(a) REPORTS ON PROCEEDINGS.—The Board shall make a written report of each proceeding conducted on complaint or on its own initiative and furnish a copy to each party to that proceeding. The report shall include the findings, conclusions, and the order of the Board and, if damages are awarded, the findings of fact supporting the award. The Board may have its reports published for public use. A published report of the Board is competent evidence of its contents.

(b) SPECIAL RULES FOR MATTERS RELATED TO RAIL CARRIERS.—(1) When action of the Board in a matter related to a rail carrier is taken by the Board, an individual member of the Board, or another individual or group of individuals designated to take official action for the Board, the written statement of that action (including a report, order, decision and order, vote, notice, letter, policy statement, or regulation) shall indicate—

(A) the official designation of the individual or group taking the action;

(B) the name of each individual taking, or participating in taking, the action; and

(C) the vote or position of each participating individual.

(2) If an individual member of a group taking an official action referred to in paragraph (1) does not participate in it, the written statement of the action shall indicate that the member did not participate. An individual participating in taking an official action is

entitled to express the views of that individual as part of the written statement of the action. In addition to any publication of the written statement, it shall be made available to the public under section 552(a) of title 5.

(Added Pub. L. 104–88, title II, §201(a), Dec. 29, 1995, 109 Stat. 934, §706; renumbered §1306, Pub. L. 114–110, §3(a)(3), Dec. 18, 2015, 129 Stat. 2228.)

SUBCHAPTER II—ADMINISTRATIVE

§1321. POWERS

(a) IN GENERAL.—The Board shall carry out this chapter and subtitle IV. Enumeration of a power of the Board in this chapter or subtitle IV does not exclude another power the Board may have in carrying out this chapter or subtitle IV. The Board may prescribe regulations in carrying out this chapter and subtitle IV.

(b) INQUIRIES, REPORTS, AND ORDERS.—The Board may—

(1) inquire into and report on the management of the business of carriers providing transportation and services subject to subtitle IV;

(2) inquire into and report on the management of the business of a person controlling, controlled by, or under common control with those carriers to the extent that the business of that person is related to the management of the business of that carrier;

(3) obtain from those carriers and persons information the Board decides is necessary to carry out subtitle IV; and

(4) when necessary to prevent irreparable harm, issue an appropriate order without regard to subchapter II of chapter 5 of title 5.

(c) SUBPOENA WITNESSES.—(1) The Board may subpoena witnesses and records related to a proceeding of the Board from any place in the United States, to the designated place of the proceeding. If a witness disobeys a subpoena, the Board, or a party to a proceeding before the Board, may petition a court of the United States to enforce that subpoena.

(2) The district courts of the United States have jurisdiction to enforce a subpoena issued under this section. Trial is in the district in which the proceeding is conducted. The court may punish a refusal to obey a subpoena as a contempt of court.

(d) DEPOSITIONS.—(1) In a proceeding, the Board may take the testimony of a witness by deposition and may order the witness to produce records. A party to a proceeding pending before the Board may take the testimony of a witness by deposition and may require the witness to produce records at any time after a proceeding is at issue on petition and answer.

(2) If a witness fails to be deposed or to produce records under paragraph (1), the Board may subpoena the witness to take a deposition, produce the records, or both.

(3) A deposition may be taken before a judge of a court of the United States, a United States magistrate judge, a clerk of a district court, or a chancellor, justice, or judge of a supreme or superior court, mayor or chief magistrate of a city, judge of a county court, or court of common pleas of any State, or a notary public who is not counsel or attorney of a party or interested in the proceeding.

(4) Before taking a deposition, reasonable notice must be given in writing by the party or the attorney of that party proposing to take a deposition to the opposing party or the

attorney of record of that party, whoever is nearest. The notice shall state the name of the witness and the time and place of taking the deposition.

(5) The testimony of a person deposed under this subsection shall be taken under oath. The person taking the deposition shall prepare, or cause to be prepared, a transcript of the testimony taken. The transcript shall be subscribed by the deponent.

(6) The testimony of a witness who is in a foreign country may be taken by deposition before an officer or person designated by the Board or agreed on by the parties by written stipulation filed with the Board. A deposition shall be filed with the Board promptly.

(e) WITNESS FEES.—Each witness summoned before the Board or whose deposition is taken under this section and the individual taking the deposition are entitled to the same fees and mileage paid for those services in the courts of the United States.

(Added Pub. L. 104–88, title II, §201(a), Dec. 29, 1995, 109 Stat. 935, §721; renumbered §1321, Pub. L. 114–110, §3(a)(5), Dec. 18, 2015, 129 Stat. 2228.)

§1322. BOARD ACTION

(a) EFFECTIVE DATE OF ACTIONS.—Unless otherwise provided in subtitle IV, the Board may determine, within a reasonable time, when its actions, other than an action ordering the payment of money, take effect.

(b) TERMINATING AND CHANGING ACTIONS.—An action of the Board remains in effect under its own terms or until superseded. The Board may change, suspend, or set aside any such action on notice. Notice may be given in a manner determined by the Board. A court of competent jurisdiction may suspend or set aside any such action.

(c) RECONSIDERING ACTIONS.—The Board may, at any time on its own initiative because of material error, new evidence, or substantially changed circumstances—

(1) reopen a proceeding;

(2) grant rehearing, reargument, or reconsideration of an action of the Board; or

(3) change an action of the Board.

An interested party may petition to reopen and reconsider an action of the Board under this subsection under regulations of the Board.

(d) FINALITY OF ACTIONS.—Notwithstanding subtitle IV, an action of the Board under this section is final on the date on which it is served, and a civil action to enforce, enjoin, suspend, or set aside the action may be filed after that date.

(Added Pub. L. 104–88, title II, §201(a), Dec. 29, 1995, 109 Stat. 936, §722; renumbered §1322, Pub. L. 114–110, §3(a)(5), Dec. 18, 2015, 129 Stat. 2228.)

§1323. SERVICE OF NOTICE IN BOARD PROCEEDINGS

(a) DESIGNATION OF AGENT.—A carrier providing transportation subject to the jurisdiction of the Board under subtitle IV shall designate an agent on whom service of notices in a proceeding before, and of actions of, the Board may be made.

(b) FILING AND CHANGING DESIGNATIONS.—A designation under subsection (a) shall be in writing and filed with the Board. The designation may be changed at any time in the same manner as originally made.

(c) SERVICE OF NOTICE.—Except as otherwise provided, notices of the Board shall be served on its designated agent at the office or usual place of residence of that agent. A notice of action of the Board shall be served immediately on the agent or in another manner provided by law. If that carrier does not have a designated agent, service may be made by posting the notice in the office of the Board.

(d) SPECIAL RULE FOR RAIL CARRIERS.—In a proceeding involving the lawfulness of classifications, rates, or practices of a rail carrier that has not designated an agent under this section, service of notice of the Board on an attorney in fact for the carrier constitutes service of notice on the carrier.

(Added Pub. L. 104–88, title II, §201(a), Dec. 29, 1995, 109 Stat. 937, §723; renumbered §1323 and amended Pub. L. 114–110, §§3(a)(5), 8(a), Dec. 18, 2015, 129 Stat. 2228, 2232.)

§1324. SERVICE OF PROCESS IN COURT PROCEEDINGS

(a) DESIGNATION OF AGENT.—A carrier providing transportation subject to the jurisdiction of the Board under subtitle IV shall designate an agent on whom service of process in an action before a district court may be made. Except as otherwise provided, process in an action before a district court shall be served on the designated agent of that carrier at the office or usual place of residence of that agent. If the carrier does not have a designated agent, service may be made by posting the notice in the office of the Board.

(b) CHANGING DESIGNATION.—A designation under this section may be changed at any time in the same manner as originally made.

(Added Pub. L. 104–88, title II, §201(a), Dec. 29, 1995, 109 Stat. 937, §724; renumbered §1324 and amended Pub. L. 114–110, §§3(a)(5), 8(b), Dec. 18, 2015, 129 Stat. 2228, 2232.)

§1325. RAILROAD-SHIPPER TRANSPORTATION ADVISORY COUNCIL

(a) ESTABLISHMENT; MEMBERSHIP.—There is established the Railroad-Shipper Transportation Advisory Council (in this section referred to as the "Council") to be composed of 19 members, of which 15 members shall be appointed by the Chairman of the Board, after recommendation from rail carriers and shippers, within 60 days after December 29, 1995. The members of the Council shall be appointed as follows:

(1) The members of the Council shall be appointed from among citizens of the United States who are not regular full-time employees of the United States and shall be selected for appointment so as to provide as nearly as practicable a broad representation of the various segments of the railroad and rail shipper industries.

(2) Nine of the members shall be appointed from senior executive officers of organizations engaged in the railroad and rail shipping industries, which 9 members shall be the voting members of the Council. Council action and Council positions shall be determined by a majority vote of the members present. A majority of such voting members shall constitute a quorum. Of such 9 voting members—

(A) at least 4 shall be representative of small shippers (as determined by the Chairman); and

(B) at least 4 shall be representative of Class II or III railroads.

(3) The remaining 6 members of the Council shall serve in a nonvoting advisory capacity only, but shall be entitled to participate in Council deliberations. Of the remaining members—

(A) 3 shall be representative of Class I railroads; and

(B) 3 shall be representative of large shipper organizations (as determined by the Chairman).

(4) The Secretary of Transportation and the members of the Board shall serve as ex officio, nonvoting members of the Council. The Council shall not be subject to chapter 10 of title 5. A list of the members appointed to the Council shall be forwarded to the Chairmen and ranking members of the Committee on Commerce, Science, and Transportation of the Senate and the Committee on Transportation and Infrastructure of the House of Representatives.

(5) Each ex officio member of the Council may designate an alternate, who shall serve as a member of the Council whenever the ex officio member is unable to attend a meeting of the Council. Any such designated alternate shall be selected from individuals who exercise significant decision-making authority in the Federal agency involved.

(b) TERM OF OFFICE.—The members of the Council shall be appointed for a term of office of 3 years, except that of the members first appointed—

(1) 5 members shall be appointed for terms of 1 year; and

(2) 5 members shall be appointed for terms of 2 years,

as designated by the Chairman at the time of appointment. Any member appointed to fill a vacancy occurring before the expiration of the term for which the member's predecessor was appointed shall be appointed only for the remainder of such term. A member may serve after the expiration of his term until his successor has taken office. Vacancies on the Council shall be filled in the same manner in which the original appointments were made. No member of the Council shall be eligible to serve in excess of two consecutive terms.

(c) ELECTION AND DUTIES OF OFFICERS.—The Council Chairman and Vice Chairman and other appropriate officers of the Council shall be elected by and from the voting members of the Council. The Council Chairman shall serve as the Council's executive officer and shall direct the administration of the Council, assign officer and committee duties, and shall be responsible for issuing and communicating the reports, policy positions and statements of the Council. In the event that the Council Chairman is unable to serve, the Vice Chairman shall act as Council Chairman.

(d) EXPENSES.—(1) The members of the Council shall receive no compensation for their services as such, but upon request by the Council Chairman, based on a showing of significant economic burden, the Secretary of Transportation or the Chairman of the Board, to the extent provided in advance in appropriation Acts, may provide reasonable and necessary travel expenses for such individual Council members from Department or Board funding sources in order to foster balanced representation on the Council.

(2) Upon request by the Council Chairman, the Secretary or Chairman of the Board, to the extent provided in advance in appropriations Acts, may pay the reasonable and necessary expenses incurred by the Council in connection with the coordination of Council

activities, announcement and reporting of meetings, and preparation of such Council documents as are required or permitted by this section.

(3) The Council may solicit and use private funding for its activities, subject to this subsection.

(4) Prior to making any Federal funding requests, the Council Chairman shall undertake best efforts to fund such activities privately unless the Council Chairman determines that such private funding would create a conflict of interest, or the appearance thereof, or is otherwise impractical. The Council Chairman shall not request funding from any Federal agency without providing written justification as to why private funding would create any such conflict or appearance, or is otherwise impractical.

(5) To enable the Council to carry out its functions—

(A) the Council Chairman may request directly from any Federal agency such personnel, information, services, or facilities, on a compensated or uncompensated basis, as the Council Chairman determines necessary to carry out the functions of the Council;

(B) each Federal agency may, in its discretion, furnish the Council with such information, services, and facilities as the Council Chairman may request to the extent permitted by law and within the limits of available funds; and

(C) each Federal agency may, in its discretion, detail to temporary duty with the Council, such personnel as the Council Chairman may request for carrying out the functions of the Council, each such detail to be without loss of seniority, pay, or other employee status.

(e) MEETINGS.—The Council shall meet at least semi-annually and shall hold other meetings at the call of the Council Chairman. Appropriate Federal facilities, where available, may be used for such meetings. Whenever the Council, or a committee of the Council, considers matters that affect the jurisdictional interests of Federal agencies that are not represented on the Council, the Council Chairman may invite the heads of such agencies, or their designees, to participate in the deliberations of the Council.

(f) FUNCTIONS AND DUTIES; ANNUAL REPORT.—(1) The Council shall advise the Secretary, the Chairman, the Committee on Commerce, Science, and Transportation of the Senate, and the Committee on Transportation and Infrastructure of the House of Representatives with respect to rail transportation policy issues it considers significant, with particular attention to issues of importance to small shippers and small railroads, including car supply, rates, competition, and effective procedures for addressing legitimate shipper and other claims.

(2) To the extent the Council addresses specific grain car issues, it shall coordinate such activities with the National Grain Car Council. The Secretary and Chairman shall cooperate with the Council to provide research, technical and other reasonable support in developing any reports and policy statements required or authorized by this subsection.

(3) The Council shall endeavor to develop within the private sector mechanisms to prevent, or identify and effectively address, obstacles to the most effective and efficient transportation system practicable.

(4) The Council shall prepare an annual report concerning its activities and the results of Council efforts to resolve industry issues, and propose whatever regulatory or legislative relief it considers appropriate. The Council shall include in the annual report such

recommendations as it considers appropriate with respect to the performance of the Secretary and Chairman under this chapter, and with respect to the operation and effectiveness of meetings and industry developments relating to the Council's efforts, and such other information as it considers appropriate. Such annual reports shall be reviewed by the Secretary and Chairman, and shall include the Secretary's and Chairman's views or comments relating to—

(A) the accuracy of information therein;

(B) Council efforts and reasonableness of Council positions and actions; and

(C) any other aspects of the Council's work as they may consider appropriate.

The Council may prepare other reports or develop policy statements as the Council considers appropriate. An annual report shall be submitted for each fiscal year and shall be submitted to the Secretary and Chairman within 90 days after the end of the fiscal year. Other such reports and statements may be submitted as the Council considers appropriate.

(Added Pub. L. 104–88, title II, §201(a), Dec. 29, 1995, 109 Stat. 937, §726; amended Pub. L. 104–287, §5(7), Oct. 11, 1996, 110 Stat. 3389; renumbered §1325, Pub. L. 114–110, §3(a)(6), Dec. 18, 2015, 129 Stat. 2229; amended Pub. L. 117–286, §4(a)(303), Dec. 27, 2022, 136 Stat. 4339.)

§1326. AUTHORITY OF THE INSPECTOR GENERAL

(a) IN GENERAL.—The Inspector General of the Department of Transportation, in accordance with the mission of the Inspector General to prevent and detect fraud and abuse, shall have authority to review only the financial management, property management, and business operations of the Surface Transportation Board, including internal accounting and administrative control systems, to determine the Board's compliance with applicable Federal laws, rules, and regulations.

(b) DUTIES.—In carrying out this section, the Inspector General shall—

(1) keep the Chairman of the Board, the Committee on Commerce, Science, and Transportation of the Senate, and the Committee on Transportation and Infrastructure of the House of Representatives fully and currently informed about problems relating to administration of the internal accounting and administrative control systems of the Board;

(2) issue findings and recommendations for actions to address the problems referred to in paragraph (1); and

(3) submit periodic reports to the Committee on Commerce, Science, and Transportation of the Senate, and the Committee on Transportation and Infrastructure of the House of Representatives that describe any progress made in implementing actions to address the problems referred to in paragraph (1).

(c) ACCESS TO INFORMATION.—In carrying out this section, the Inspector General may exercise authorities granted to the Inspector General under subsections (a) and (c) of section 406 of title 5.

(d) AUTHORIZATION OF APPROPRIATIONS.—

(1) FUNDING.—There are authorized to be appropriated to the Secretary of Transportation for use by the Inspector General of the Department of Transportation such

sums as may be necessary to cover expenses associated with activities pursuant to the authority exercised under this section.

(2) REIMBURSABLE AGREEMENT.—In the absence of an appropriation under this subsection for an expense referred to in paragraph (1), the Inspector General and the Board shall have a reimbursement agreement to cover such expense.

(Added Pub. L. 114–110, §9, Dec. 18, 2015, 129 Stat. 2232; amended Pub. L. 117–286, §4(b)(97), Dec. 27, 2022, 136 Stat. 4353.)

SUBTITLE III
GENERAL AND INTERMODAL
PROGRAMS

SUBTITLE III—GENERAL AND INTERMODAL PROGRAMS

CHAPTER 55—INTERMODAL TRANSPORTATION

SUBCHAPTER I—GENERAL

SUBCHAPTER II—TERMINALS

SUBCHAPTER I—GENERAL

§5501. National Intermodal Transportation System policy

(a) GENERAL.—It is the policy of the United States Government to develop a National Intermodal Transportation System that is economically efficient and environmentally sound, provides the foundation for the United States to compete in the global economy, and will move individuals and property in an energy efficient way.

(b) SYSTEM CHARACTERISTICS.—(1) The National Intermodal Transportation System shall consist of all forms of transportation in a unified, interconnected manner, including the transportation systems of the future, to reduce energy consumption and air pollution while promoting economic development and supporting the United States' preeminent position in international commerce.

(2) The National Intermodal Transportation System shall include a National Highway System consisting of the Dwight D. Eisenhower System of Interstate and Defense Highways and those principal arterial roads that are essential for interstate and regional commerce and travel, national defense, intermodal transfer facilities, and international commerce and border crossings.

(3) The National Intermodal Transportation System shall include significant improvements in public transportation necessary to achieve national goals for improved

[§5502. Repealed. Pub. L. 117–58, div. B, title V, §25021(a), Nov. 15, 2021, 135 Stat. 878]

CHAPTER 55—INTERMODAL TRANSPORTATION

air quality, energy conservation, international competitiveness, and mobility for elderly individuals, individuals with disabilities, and economically disadvantaged individuals in urban and rural areas of the United States.

(4) The National Intermodal Transportation System shall provide improved access to ports and airports, the Nation's link to commerce.

(5) The National Intermodal Transportation System shall give special emphasis to the contributions of the transportation sectors to increased productivity growth. Social benefits must be considered with particular attention to the external benefits of reduced air pollution, reduced traffic congestion, and other aspects of the quality of life in the United States.

(6) The National Intermodal Transportation System must be operated and maintained with insistent attention to the concepts of innovation, competition, energy efficiency, productivity, growth, and accountability. Practices that resulted in the lengthy and overly costly construction of the Dwight D. Eisenhower System of Interstate and Defense Highways must be confronted and stopped.

(7) The National Intermodal Transportation System shall be adapted to "intelligent vehicles", "magnetic levitation systems", and other new technologies, wherever feasible and economical, with benefit cost estimates given special emphasis on safety considerations and techniques for cost allocation.

(8) When appropriate, the National Intermodal Transportation System will be financed, as regards Government apportionments and reimbursements, by the Highway Trust Fund. Financial assistance will be provided to State and local governments and their instrumentalities to help carry out national goals related to mobility for elderly individuals, individuals with disabilities, and economically disadvantaged individuals.

(9) The National Intermodal Transportation System must be the centerpiece of a national investment commitment to create the new wealth of the United States for the 21st century.

(c) DISTRIBUTION AND POSTING.—The Secretary of Transportation shall distribute copies of the policy in subsections (a) and (b) of this section to each employee of the Department of Transportation and ensure that the policy is posted in all offices of the Department.

(Pub. L. 103–272, §1(d), July 5, 1994, 108 Stat. 848.)

[§5502. REPEALED. PUB. L. 117–58, DIV. B, TITLE V, §25021(A), NOV. 15, 2021, 135 STAT. 878]

Section, Pub. L. 103–272, §1(d), July 5, 1994, 108 Stat. 849; Pub. L. 109–59, title IV, §4145(a), Aug. 10, 2005, 119 Stat. 1749, related to Intermodal Transportation Advisory Board.

[§5503. REPEALED. PUB. L. 114–94, DIV. A, TITLE VI, §6015(A), DEC. 4, 2015, 129 STAT. 1571]

Section, Pub. L. 103–272, §1(d), July 5, 1994, 108 Stat. 850; Pub. L. 105–178, title V, §5109(b), June 9, 1998, 112 Stat. 440; Pub. L. 108–426, §4(c), Nov. 30, 2004, 118 Stat. 2425; Pub. L. 109–59, title IV, §4149, Aug. 10, 2005, 119 Stat. 1750; Pub. L. 110–244, title III, §301(k), June 6, 2008, 122 Stat. 1616; Pub. L. 113–76, div. L, title I, Jan. 17, 2014, 128 Stat. 574, related to the Office of Intermodalism.

§5504. MODEL INTERMODAL TRANSPORTATION PLANS

(a) GRANTS.—The Secretary of Transportation shall make grants to States to develop model State intermodal transportation plans that are consistent with the policy set forth in section 302(e) of this title. The model plans shall include systems for collecting data related to intermodal transportation.

(b) DISTRIBUTION.—The Secretary shall award grants to States under this section that represent a variety of geographic regions and transportation needs, patterns, and modes.

(c) PLAN SUBMISSION.—As a condition to a State receiving a grant under this section, the Secretary shall require that the State provide assurances that the State will submit to the Secretary a State intermodal transportation plan not later than 18 months after the date of receipt of the grant.

(d) GRANT AMOUNTS.—The Secretary shall reserve, from amounts deducted under section 104(a) of title 23, $3,000,000 to make grants under this section. The total amount that a State may receive in grants under this section may not be more than $500,000.

(Pub. L. 103–272, §1(d), July 5, 1994, 108 Stat. 850.)

§5505. UNIVERSITY TRANSPORTATION CENTERS PROGRAM

(a) UNIVERSITY TRANSPORTATION CENTERS PROGRAM.—

(1) ESTABLISHMENT AND OPERATION.—The Secretary of Transportation, acting through the Assistant Secretary for Research and Technology (referred to in this section as the "Secretary"), shall make grants under this section to eligible nonprofit institutions of higher education to establish and operate university transportation centers.

(2) ROLE OF CENTERS.—The role of each university transportation center referred to in paragraph (1) shall be—

(A) to advance transportation expertise and technology in the varied disciplines that comprise the field of transportation through education, research, and technology transfer activities;

(B) to provide for a critical multimodal transportation knowledge base outside of the Department of Transportation; and

(C) to address critical workforce needs and educate the next generation of transportation leaders with respect to the matters described in subparagraphs (A) through (G) of section 6503(c)(1).

(b) COMPETITIVE SELECTION PROCESS.—

(1) APPLICATIONS.—To receive a grant under this section, a consortium of nonprofit institutions of higher education shall submit to the Secretary an application that is in such form and contains such information as the Secretary may require.

(2) RESTRICTION.—

(A) LIMITATION.—A lead institution of a consortium of nonprofit institutions of higher education, as applicable, may only receive 1 grant per fiscal year as a lead institution under this section, except as provided in subparagraph (B).

(B) EXCEPTION FOR CONSORTIUM MEMBERS THAT ARE NOT LEAD INSTITUTIONS.—Subparagraph (A) shall not apply to a nonprofit institution of higher education that is a member of a consortium of nonprofit institutions of higher education but not the lead institution of such consortium.

(3) COORDINATION.—The Secretary shall solicit grant applications for national transportation centers, regional transportation centers, and Tier 1 university transportation centers with identical advertisement schedules and deadlines.

(4) GENERAL SELECTION CRITERIA.—

(A) IN GENERAL.—Except as otherwise provided by this section, the Secretary shall award grants under this section in nonexclusive candidate topic areas established by the Secretary that address the research priorities described in subparagraphs (A) through (G) of section 6503(c)(1).

(B) CRITERIA.—The Secretary, in consultation with the heads of the modal administrations of the Department of Transportation, as appropriate, shall select each recipient of a grant under this section through a competitive process based on the assessment of the Secretary relating to—

(i) the demonstrated ability of the recipient to address each specific topic area described in the research and strategic plans of the recipient;

(ii) the demonstrated research, technology transfer, and education resources available to the recipient to carry out this section;

(iii) the ability of the recipient to provide leadership in solving immediate and long-range national and regional transportation problems;

(iv) the ability of the recipient to carry out research, education, and technology transfer activities that are multimodal and multidisciplinary in scope;

(v) the demonstrated commitment of the recipient to carry out transportation workforce development programs through—

(I) degree-granting programs or programs that provide other industry-recognized credentials; and

(II) outreach activities to attract new entrants into the transportation field, including women and underrepresented populations;

(vi) the demonstrated ability of the recipient to disseminate results and spur the implementation of transportation research and education programs through national or statewide continuing education programs;

(vii) the demonstrated commitment of the recipient to the use of peer review principles and other research best practices in the selection, management, and dissemination of research projects;

(viii) the strategic plan submitted by the recipient describing the proposed research to be carried out by the recipient and the performance metrics to be used in assessing the performance of the recipient in meeting the stated research, technology transfer, education, and outreach goals; and

(ix) the ability of the recipient to implement the proposed program in a cost-efficient manner, such as through cost sharing and overall reduced overhead, facilities, and administrative costs.

(5) TRANSPARENCY.—

(A) IN GENERAL.—The Secretary shall provide to each applicant, upon request, any materials, including copies of reviews (with any information that would identify a reviewer redacted), used in the evaluation process of the proposal of the applicant.

(B) REPORTS.—The Secretary shall make available to the public on a website of the Department of Transportation a report describing the overall review process under paragraph (4) that includes—

(i) specific criteria of evaluation used in the review;

(ii) descriptions of the review process; and

(iii) explanations of the selected awards.

(6) OUTSIDE STAKEHOLDERS.—The Secretary shall, to the maximum extent practicable, consult external stakeholders, including the Transportation Research Board of the National Research Council of the National Academies, to evaluate and competitively review all proposals.

(c) GRANTS.—

(1) IN GENERAL.—Not later than 1 year after the date of enactment of this section, the Secretary shall select grant recipients under subsection (b) and make grant amounts available to the selected recipients.

(2) NATIONAL TRANSPORTATION CENTERS.—

(A) IN GENERAL.—Subject to subparagraph (B), the Secretary shall provide grants to 5 consortia that the Secretary determines best meet the criteria described in subsection (b)(4).

(B) RESTRICTIONS.—

(i) IN GENERAL.—For each fiscal year, a grant made available under this paragraph shall be not greater than $4,000,000 and not less than $2,000,000 per recipient.

(ii) FOCUSED RESEARCH.—A consortium receiving a grant under this paragraph shall focus research on 1 of the transportation issue areas specified in section 6503(c).

(C) MATCHING REQUIREMENT.—

(i) IN GENERAL.—As a condition of receiving a grant under this paragraph, a grant recipient shall match 100 percent of the amounts made available under the grant.

(ii) SOURCES.—The matching amounts referred to in clause (i) may include amounts made available to the recipient under—

(I) section 504(b) of title 23; or

(II) section 505 of title 23.

(3) REGIONAL UNIVERSITY TRANSPORTATION CENTERS.—

(A) LOCATION OF REGIONAL CENTERS.—One regional university transportation center shall be located in each of the 10 Federal regions that comprise the Standard Federal Regions established by the Office of Management and Budget in the document entitled "Standard Federal Regions" and dated April 1974 (circular A–105).

(B) SELECTION CRITERIA.—In conducting a competition under subsection (b), the

Secretary shall provide grants to 10 consortia on the basis of—

(i) the criteria described in subsection (b)(4);

(ii) the location of the lead center within the Federal region to be served; and

(iii) whether the consortium of institutions demonstrates that the consortium has a well-established, nationally recognized program in transportation research and education, as evidenced by—

(I) recent expenditures by the institution in highway or public transportation research;

(II) a historical track record of awarding graduate degrees in professional fields closely related to highways and public transportation; and

(III) an experienced faculty who specialize in professional fields closely related to highways and public transportation.

(C) RESTRICTIONS.—For each fiscal year, a grant made available under this paragraph shall be not greater than $3,000,000 and not less than $1,500,000 per recipient.

(D) MATCHING REQUIREMENTS.—

(i) IN GENERAL.—As a condition of receiving a grant under this paragraph, a grant recipient shall match 100 percent of the amounts made available under the grant.

(ii) SOURCES.—The matching amounts referred to in clause (i) may include amounts made available to the recipient under—

(I) section 504(b) of title 23; or

(II) section 505 of title 23.

(E) FOCUSED RESEARCH.—

(i) IN GENERAL.—A regional university transportation center receiving a grant under this paragraph shall carry out research focusing on 1 or more of the matters described in subparagraphs (A) through (G) of section 6503(c)(1).

(ii) FOCUSED OBJECTIVES.—The Secretary shall make a grant to 1 of the 10 regional university transportation centers established under this paragraph for the purpose of furthering the objectives described in subsection (a)(2) in the field of comprehensive transportation safety, congestion, connected vehicles, connected infrastructure, and autonomous vehicles, including the cybersecurity implications of technologies relating to connected vehicles, connected infrastructure, and autonomous vehicles.

(4) TIER 1 UNIVERSITY TRANSPORTATION CENTERS.—

(A) IN GENERAL.—The Secretary shall provide grants of not greater than $2,000,000 and not less than $1,000,000 to not more than 20 recipients to carry out this paragraph.

(B) MATCHING REQUIREMENT.—

(i) IN GENERAL.—As a condition of receiving a grant under this paragraph, a grant recipient shall match 50 percent of the amounts made available under the grant.

(ii) SOURCES.—The matching amounts referred to in clause (i) may include amounts made available to the recipient under—

(I) section 504(b) of title 23; or

(II) section 505 of title 23.

(C) FOCUSED RESEARCH.—In awarding grants under this section, consideration shall be given to minority institutions, as defined by section 365 of the Higher Education Act of 1965 (20 U.S.C. 1067k), or consortia that include such institutions that have demonstrated an ability in transportation-related research.

(d) PROGRAM COORDINATION.—
(1) IN GENERAL.—The Secretary shall—
(A) coordinate the research, education, and technology transfer activities carried out by grant recipients under this section; and
(B) disseminate the results of that research through the establishment and operation of a publicly accessible online information clearinghouse.

(2) REVIEW AND EVALUATION.—Not less frequently than biennially, and consistent with the plan developed under section 6503, the Secretary shall—
(A) review and evaluate the programs carried out under this section by grant recipients; and
(B) make available to the public on a website of the Department of Transportation a report describing that review and evaluation.

(3) PROGRAM EVALUATION AND OVERSIGHT.—For each of fiscal years 2022 through 2026, the Secretary shall expend not more than 1 and a half percent of the amounts made available to the Secretary to carry out this section for any coordination, evaluation, and oversight activities of the Secretary under this section.

(e) LIMITATION ON AVAILABILITY OF AMOUNTS.—Amounts made available to the Secretary to carry out this section shall remain available for obligation by the Secretary for a period of 3 years after the last day of the fiscal year for which the amounts are authorized.

(f) INFORMATION COLLECTION.—Any survey, questionnaire, or interview that the Secretary determines to be necessary to carry out reporting requirements relating to any program assessment or evaluation activity under this section, including customer satisfaction assessments, shall not be subject to chapter 35 of title 44.

(Added and amended Pub. L. 105–178, title V, §5110(a), (d), June 9, 1998, 112 Stat. 441; Pub. L. 105–206, title IX, §9011(d), July 22, 1998, 112 Stat. 863; Pub. L. 109–59, title V, §5401(a), Aug. 10, 2005, 119 Stat. 1814; Pub. L. 112–141, div. E, title II, §52009(a), July 6, 2012, 126 Stat. 882; Pub. L. 114–94, div. A, title VI, §6016, Dec. 4, 2015, 129 Stat. 1571; Pub. L. 117–58, div. B, title V, §25017, Nov. 15, 2021, 135 Stat. 873.)

§5506. ADVANCED TRANSPORTATION RESEARCH INITIATIVE

(a) DEFINITION OF ELIGIBLE ENTITY.—In this section, the term "eligible entity" means—
(1) a State agency;
(2) a local government agency;
(3) an institution of higher education (as defined in section 102 of the Higher

Education Act of 1965 (20 U.S.C. 1002)), including a university transportation center established under section 5505;

(4) a nonprofit organization, including a nonprofit research organization; and

(5) a private sector organization working in collaboration with an entity described in any of paragraphs (1) through (4).

(b) PILOT PROGRAM.—The Secretary of Transportation (referred to in this section as the "Secretary") shall establish an advanced transportation research pilot program under which the Secretary—

(1) shall establish a process for eligible entities to submit to the Secretary unsolicited research proposals; and

(2) may enter into arrangements with 1 or more eligible entities to fund research proposed under paragraph (1), in accordance with this section.

(c) ELIGIBLE RESEARCH.—The Secretary may enter into an arrangement with an eligible entity under this section to fund research that—

(1) addresses—

(A) a research need identified by—

(i) the Secretary; or

(ii) the Administrator of a modal administration of the Department of Transportation; or

(B) an issue that the Secretary determines to be important; and

(2) is not duplicative of—

(A) any other Federal research project; or

(B) any project for which funding is provided by another Federal agency.

(d) PROJECT REVIEW.—The Secretary shall—

(1) review each research proposal submitted under the pilot program established under subsection (b); and

(2)(A) if funding is denied for the research proposal—

(i) provide to the eligible entity that submitted the proposal a written notice of the denial that, as applicable—

(I) explains why the research proposal was not selected, including whether the research proposal fails to cover an area of need; and

(II) recommends that the research proposal be submitted to another research program; and

(ii) if the Secretary recommends that the research proposal be submitted to another research program under clause (i)(II), provide guidance and direction to—

(I) the eligible entity; and

(II) the proposed research program office; or

(B) if the research proposal is selected for funding—

(i) provide to the eligible entity that submitted the proposal a written notice of the selection; and

(ii) seek to enter into an arrangement with the eligible entity to provide funding for the proposed research.

(e) COORDINATION.—

(1) IN GENERAL.—The Secretary shall ensure that the activities carried out under subsection (c) are coordinated with, and do not duplicate the efforts of, programs of the Department of Transportation and other Federal agencies.

(2) INTRAAGENCY COORDINATION.—The Secretary shall coordinate the research carried out under this section with—

(A) the research, education, and technology transfer activities carried out by grant recipients under section 5505; and

(B) the research, development, demonstration, and commercial application activities of other relevant programs of the Department of Transportation, including all modal administrations of the Department.

(3) INTERAGENCY COLLABORATION.—The Secretary shall coordinate, as appropriate, regarding fundamental research with the potential for application in the transportation sector with—

(A) the Director of the Office of Science and Technology Policy;

(B) the Director of the National Science Foundation;

(C) the Secretary of Energy;

(D) the Director of the National Institute of Standards and Technology;

(E) the Secretary of Homeland Security;

(F) the Administrator of the National Oceanic and Atmospheric Administration;

(G) the Secretary of Defense; and

(H) the heads of other appropriate Federal agencies, as determined by the Secretary.

(f) REVIEW, EVALUATION, AND REPORT.—Not less frequently than biennially, in accordance with the plan developed under section 6503, the Secretary shall—

(1) review and evaluate the pilot program established under subsection (b), including the research carried out under that pilot program; and

(2) make public on a website of the Department of Transportation a report describing the review and evaluation under paragraph (1).

(g) FEDERAL SHARE.—

(1) IN GENERAL.—The Federal share of the cost of an activity carried out under this section shall not exceed 80 percent.

(2) NON-FEDERAL SHARE.—All costs directly incurred by the non-Federal partners (including personnel, travel, facility, and hardware development costs) shall be credited toward the non-Federal share of the cost of an activity carried out under this section.

(h) LIMITATION ON CERTAIN EXPENSES.—Of any amounts made available to carry out this section for a fiscal year, the Secretary may use not more than 1.5 percent for coordination, evaluation, and oversight activities under this section.

(i) AUTHORIZATION OF APPROPRIATIONS.—There is authorized to be appropriated to the Secretary to carry out this section $50,000,000 for each of fiscal years 2022 through 2026.

(Added Pub. L. 117–58, div. B, title V, §25013(a), Nov. 15, 2021, 135 Stat. 867.)

§5507. TRANSPORTATION WORKFORCE OUTREACH PROGRAM

(a) IN GENERAL.—The Secretary of Transportation (referred to in this section as the "Secretary") shall establish and administer a transportation workforce outreach program, under which the Secretary shall carry out a series of public service announcement campaigns during each of fiscal years 2022 through 2026.

(b) PURPOSES.—The purpose of the campaigns carried out under the program under this section shall be—

(1) to increase awareness of career opportunities in the transportation sector, including aviation pilots, safety inspectors, mechanics and technicians, air traffic controllers, flight attendants, truck and bus drivers, engineers, transit workers, railroad workers, and other transportation professionals; and

(2) to target awareness of professional opportunities in the transportation sector to diverse segments of the population, including with respect to race, sex, ethnicity, ability (including physical and mental ability), veteran status, and socioeconomic status.

(c) ADVERTISING.—The Secretary may use, or authorize the use of, amounts made available to carry out the program under this section for the development, production, and use of broadcast, digital, and print media advertising and outreach in carrying out a campaign under this section.

(d) FUNDING.—The Secretary may use to carry out this section any amounts otherwise made available to the Secretary, not to exceed $5,000,000, for each of fiscal years 2022 through 2026.

(Added Pub. L. 117–58, div. B, title V, §25020(c)(1), Nov. 15, 2021, 135 Stat. 877.)

SUBCHAPTER II—TERMINALS

§5561. DEFINITION

In this chapter, "civic and cultural activities" includes libraries, musical and dramatic presentations, art exhibits, adult education programs, public meeting places, and other facilities for carrying on an activity any part of which is supported under a law of the United States.

(Pub. L. 103–272, §1(d), July 5, 1994, 108 Stat. 851.)

§5562. ASSISTANCE PROJECTS

(a) REQUIREMENTS TO PROVIDE ASSISTANCE.—The Secretary of Transportation shall provide financial, technical, and advisory assistance under this chapter to—

(1) promote, on a feasibility demonstration basis, the conversion of at least 3 rail passenger terminals into intermodal transportation terminals;

(2) preserve rail passenger terminals that reasonably are likely to be converted or maintained pending preparation of plans for their reuse;

(3) acquire and use space in suitable buildings of historic or architectural significance but only if use of the space is feasible and prudent when compared to available alternatives; and

(4) encourage State and local governments, local and regional transportation authorities, common carriers, philanthropic organizations, and other responsible persons to develop plans to convert rail passenger terminals into intermodal transportation terminals and civic and cultural activity centers.

(b) EFFECT ON ELIGIBILITY.—This chapter does not affect the eligibility of any rail passenger terminal for preservation or reuse assistance under another program or law.

(c) ACQUIRING SPACE.—The Secretary may acquire space under subsection (a)(3) of this section only after consulting with the Advisory Council on Historic Preservation and the Chairman of the National Endowment for the Arts.

(Pub. L. 103–272, §1(d), July 5, 1994, 108 Stat. 851.)

§5563. CONVERSION OF CERTAIN RAIL PASSENGER TERMINALS

(a) AUTHORITY TO PROVIDE ASSISTANCE.—The Secretary of Transportation may provide financial assistance to convert a rail passenger terminal to an intermodal transportation terminal under section 5562(a)(1) of this title only if—

(1) the terminal can be converted to accommodate other modes of transportation the Secretary of Transportation decides are appropriate, including—

(A) motorbus transportation;

(B) mass transit (rail or rubber tire); and

(C) airline ticket offices and passenger terminals providing direct transportation to area airports;

(2) the terminal is listed on the National Register of Historic Places maintained by the Secretary of the Interior;

(3) the architectural integrity of the terminal will be preserved;

(4) to the extent practicable, the use of the terminal facilities for transportation may be combined with use of those facilities for other civic and cultural activities, especially when another activity is recommended by—

(A) the Advisory Council on Historic Preservation;

(B) the Chairman of the National Endowment for the Arts; or

(C) consultants retained under subsection (b) of this section; and

(5) the terminal and the conversion project meet other criteria prescribed by the Secretary of Transportation after consultation with the Council and Chairman.

(b) ARCHITECTURAL INTEGRITY.—The Secretary of Transportation must employ consultants on whether the architectural integrity of the rail passenger terminal will be preserved under subsection (a)(3) of this section. The Secretary may decide that the architectural integrity will be preserved only if the consultants concur. The Council and Chairman shall recommend consultants to be employed by the Secretary. The consultants also may make recommendations referred to in subsection (a)(4) of this section.

(c) GOVERNMENT'S SHARE OF COSTS.—The Secretary of Transportation may not make a grant under this section for more than 80 percent of the total cost of converting a rail passenger terminal into an intermodal transportation terminal.

(Pub. L. 103–272, §1(d), July 5, 1994, 108 Stat. 851.)

§5564. INTERIM PRESERVATION OF CERTAIN RAIL PASSENGER TERMINALS

(a) GENERAL GRANT AUTHORITY.—Subject to subsection (b) of this section, the Secretary of Transportation may make a grant of financial assistance to a responsible person (including a governmental authority) to preserve a rail passenger terminal under section 5562(a)(2) of this title. To receive assistance under this section, the person must be qualified, prepared, committed, and authorized by law to maintain (and prevent the demolition, dismantling, or further deterioration of) the terminal until plans for its reuse are prepared.

(b) GRANT REQUIREMENTS.—The Secretary of Transportation may make a grant of financial assistance under this section only if—

(1) the Secretary decides the rail passenger terminal has a reasonable likelihood of being converted to, or conditioned for reuse as, an intermodal transportation terminal, a civic or cultural activities center, or both; and

(2) planning activity directed toward conversion or reuse has begun and is proceeding in a competent way.

(c) MAXIMIZING PRESERVATION OF TERMINALS.—(1) Amounts appropriated to carry out this section and section 5562(a)(2) of this title shall be expended in the way most likely to maximize the preservation of rail passenger terminals that are—

(A) reasonably capable of conversion to intermodal transportation terminals;

(B) listed in the National Register of Historic Places maintained by the Secretary of the Interior; or

(C) recommended (on the basis of architectural integrity and quality) by the Advisory Council on Historic Preservation or the Chairman of the National Endowment for the Arts.

(2) The Secretary of Transportation may not make a grant under this section for more than 80 percent of the total cost of maintaining the terminal for an interim period of not more than 5 years.

(Pub. L. 103–272, §1(d), July 5, 1994, 108 Stat. 852.)

§5565. ENCOURAGING THE DEVELOPMENT OF PLANS FOR CONVERTING CERTAIN RAIL PASSENGER TERMINALS

(a) GENERAL GRANT AUTHORITY.—The Secretary of Transportation may make a grant of financial assistance to a qualified person (including a governmental authority) to encourage the development of plans for converting a rail passenger terminal under section 5562(a)(4) of this title. To receive assistance under this section, the person must—

(1) be prepared to develop practicable plans that meet zoning, land use, and other requirements of the applicable State and local jurisdictions in which the terminal is

located;

(2) incorporate into the designs and plans proposed for converting the terminal, features that reasonably appear likely to attract private investors willing to carry out the planned conversion and its subsequent maintenance and operation; and

(3) complete the designs and plans for the conversion within the period of time prescribed by the Secretary.

(b) PREFERENCE.—In making a grant under this section, the Secretary of Transportation shall give preferential consideration to an applicant whose completed designs and plans will be carried out within 3 years after their completion.

(c) MAXIMIZING CONVERSION AND CONTINUED PUBLIC USE.—(1) Amounts appropriated to carry out this section and section 5562(a)(4) of this title shall be expended in the way most likely to maximize the conversion and continued public use of rail passenger terminals that are—

(A) listed in the National Register of Historic Places maintained by the Secretary of the Interior; or

(B) recommended (on the basis of architectural integrity and quality) by the Advisory Council on Historic Preservation or the Chairman of the National Endowment for the Arts.

(2) The Secretary of Transportation may not make a grant under this section for more than 80 percent of the total cost of the project for which the financial assistance is provided.

(Pub. L. 103–272, §1(d), July 5, 1994, 108 Stat. 853; Pub. L. 103–429, §6(15), Oct. 31, 1994, 108 Stat. 4379.)

§5566. RECORDS AND AUDITS

(a) RECORD REQUIREMENTS.—Each recipient of financial assistance under this chapter shall keep records required by the Secretary of Transportation. The records shall disclose—

(1) the amount, and disposition by the recipient, of the proceeds of the assistance;

(2) the total cost of the project for which the assistance was given or used;

(3) the amount of that part of the cost of the project supplied by other sources; and

(4) any other records that will make an effective audit easier.

(b) AUDITS AND INSPECTIONS.—For 3 years after a project is completed, the Secretary and the Comptroller General may audit and inspect records of a recipient that the Secretary or Comptroller General decides may be related or pertinent to the financial assistance.

(Pub. L. 103–272, §1(d), July 5, 1994, 108 Stat. 853.)

§5567. PREFERENCE FOR PRESERVING BUILDINGS OF HISTORIC OR ARCHITECTURAL SIGNIFICANCE

Amtrak shall give preference to the use of rail passenger terminal facilities that will preserve buildings of historic or architectural significance.

(Pub. L. 103–272, §1(d), July 5, 1994, 108 Stat. 854.)

§5568. Authorization of appropriations

(a) General.—The following amounts may be appropriated to the Secretary of Transportation:

(1) not more than $15,000,000 to carry out section 5562(a)(1) and (3) of this title.

(2) not more than $2,500,000 to carry out section 5562(a)(2) of this title.

(3) not more than $2,500,000 to carry out section 5562(a)(4) of this title.

(b) Availability of Amounts.—Amounts appropriated to carry out this chapter remain available until expended.

(Pub. L. 103–272, §1(d), July 5, 1994, 108 Stat. 854.)

* * * * * * *

CHAPTER 59—INTERMODAL SAFE CONTAINER TRANSPORTATION

Sec.

§5901. DEFINITIONS

In this chapter—

(1) except as otherwise provided in this chapter, the definitions in sections 10102 and 13102 of this title apply.

(2) "beneficial owner" means a person not having title to property but having ownership rights in the property, including a trustee of property in transit from an overseas place of origin that is domiciled or doing business in the United States, except that a carrier, agent of a carrier, broker, customs broker, freight forwarder, warehouser, or terminal operator is not a beneficial owner only because of providing or arranging for any part of the intermodal transportation of property.

(3) "carrier" means—

(A) a motor carrier, water carrier, and rail carrier providing transportation of property in commerce; and

(B) an ocean common carrier (as defined in section 40102 of title 46) providing transportation of property in commerce.

(4) "container" has the meaning given the term "freight container" by the International Standards Organization in Series 1, Freight Containers, 3d Edition (reference number ISO668–1979(E)), including successive revisions, and similar containers that are used in providing transportation in interstate commerce.

(5) "first carrier" means the first carrier transporting a loaded container or trailer in intermodal transportation.

(6) "gross cargo weight" means the weight of the cargo, packaging materials (including ice), pallets, and dunnage.

(7) "intermodal transportation" means the successive transportation of a loaded container or trailer from its place of origin to its place of destination by more than one mode of transportation in interstate or foreign commerce, whether under a single bill of lading or under separate bills of lading.

(8) "trailer" means a nonpower, property-carrying, trailing unit that is designed for use in combination with a truck tractor.

(Pub. L. 103–272, §1(d), July 5, 1994, 108 Stat. 859; Pub. L. 104–291, title II, §203, Oct. 11, 1996, 110 Stat.

3453; Pub. L. 109–304, §17(h)(2), Oct. 6, 2006, 120 Stat. 1709.)

§5902. NOTIFICATIONS AND CERTIFICATIONS

(a) PRIOR NOTIFICATION.—If the first carrier to which any loaded container or trailer having a projected gross cargo weight of more than 29,000 pounds is tendered for intermodal transportation is a motor carrier, the person tendering the container or trailer shall give the motor carrier a notification of the gross cargo weight and a reasonable description of the contents of the container or trailer before the tendering of the container or trailer. The notification may be transmitted electronically or by telephone. This subsection applies to any person within the United States who tenders a container or trailer subject to this chapter for intermodal transportation if the first carrier is a motor carrier.

(b) CERTIFICATION.—

(1) IN GENERAL.—A person who tenders a loaded container or trailer with an actual gross cargo weight of more than 29,000 pounds to a first carrier for intermodal transportation shall provide a certification of the contents of the container or trailer in writing, or electronically, before or when the container or trailer is so tendered.

(2) CONTENTS OF CERTIFICATION.—The certification required by paragraph (1) shall include—

(A) the actual gross cargo weight;

(B) a reasonable description of the contents of the container or trailer;

(C) the identity of the certifying party;

(D) the container or trailer number; and

(E) the date of certification or transfer of data to another document, as provided for in paragraph (3).

(3) TRANSFER OF CERTIFICATION DATA.—A carrier who receives a certification may transfer the information contained in the certification to another document or to electronic format for forwarding to a subsequent carrier. The person transferring the information shall state on the forwarded document the date on which the data was transferred and the identity of the party who performed the transfer.

(4) SHIPPING DOCUMENTS.—For purposes of this chapter, a shipping document, prepared by the person who tenders a container or trailer to a first carrier, that contains the information required by paragraph (2) meets the requirements of paragraph (1).

(5) USE OF "FREIGHT ALL KINDS" TERM.—The term "Freight All Kinds" or "FAK" may not be used for the purpose of certification under section 5902(b) after December 31, 2000, as a commodity description for a trailer or container if the weight of any commodity in the trailer or container equals or exceeds 20 percent of the total weight of the contents of the trailer or container. This subsection does not prohibit the use of the term after that date for rating purposes.

(6) SEPARATE DOCUMENT MARKING.—If a separate document is used to meet the requirements of paragraph (1), it shall be conspicuously marked "INTERMODAL CERTIFICATION".

(7) APPLICABILITY.—This subsection applies to any person, domestic or foreign, who first tenders a container or trailer subject to this chapter for intermodal transportation within the United States.

(c) FORWARDING CERTIFICATIONS TO SUBSEQUENT CARRIERS.—A carrier, agent of a carrier, broker, customs broker, freight forwarder, warehouser, or terminal operator shall forward the certification provided under subsection (b) of this section to a subsequent carrier transporting the container or trailer in intermodal transportation before or when the loaded intermodal container or trailer is tendered to the subsequent carrier. If no certification is received by the subsequent carrier before or when the container or trailer is tendered to it, the subsequent carrier may presume that no certification is required. The act of forwarding the certification may not be construed as a verification or affirmation of the accuracy or completeness of the information in the certification. If a person inaccurately transfers the information on the certification, or fails to forward the certification to a subsequent carrier, then that person is liable to any person who incurs any bond, fine, penalty, cost (including storage), or interest for any such fine, penalty, cost (including storage), or interest incurred as a result of the inaccurate transfer of information or failure to forward the certification. A subsequent carrier who incurs a bond, fine, penalty, or cost (including storage), or interest as a result of the inaccurate transfer of the information, or the failure to forward the certification, shall have a lien against the contents of the container or trailer under section 5905 in the amount of the bond, fine, penalty, or cost (including storage), or interest and all court costs and legal fees incurred by the carrier as a result of such inaccurate transfer or failure.

(d) LIABILITY TO OWNER OR BENEFICIAL OWNER.—If—

(1) a person inaccurately transfers information on a certification required by subsection (b)(1), or fails to forward a certification to the subsequent carrier;

(2) as a result of the inaccurate transfer of such information or a failure to forward a certification, the subsequent carrier incurs a bond, fine, penalty, or cost (including storage), or interest; and

(3) that subsequent carrier exercises its rights to a lien under section 5905,

then that person is liable to the owner or beneficial owner, or to any other person paying the amount of the lien to the subsequent carrier, for the amount of the lien and all costs related to the imposition of the lien, including court costs and legal fees incurred in connection with it.

(e) NONAPPLICATION.—(1) The notification and certification requirements of subsections (a) and (b) of this section do not apply to any intermodal container or trailer containing consolidated shipments loaded by a motor carrier if that motor carrier—

(A) performs the highway portion of the intermodal movement; or

(B) assumes the responsibility for any weight-related fine or penalty incurred by any other motor carrier that performs a part of the highway transportation.

(2) Subsections (a) and (b) of this section and section 5903(c) of this title do not apply to a carrier when the carrier is transferring a loaded container or trailer to another carrier during intermodal transportation, unless the carrier is also the person tendering the loaded container or trailer to the first carrier.

(3) A carrier, agent of a carrier, broker, customs broker, freight forwarder, warehouser, or terminal operator is deemed not to be a person tendering a loaded container or trailer

to a first carrier under this section, unless the carrier, agent, broker, customs broker, freight forwarder, warehouser, or terminal operator assumes legal responsibility for loading property into the container or trailer.

(Pub. L. 103–272, §1(d), July 5, 1994, 108 Stat. 860; Pub. L. 104–291, title II, §204, Oct. 11, 1996, 110 Stat. 3453.)

§5903. PROHIBITIONS

(a) PROVIDING ERRONEOUS INFORMATION.—A person, To [1] whom section 5902(b) applies, tendering a loaded container or trailer may not provide erroneous information in a certification required by section 5902(b) of this title.

(b) TRANSPORTING PRIOR TO RECEIVING CERTIFICATION.—

(1) PRESUMPTION.—If no certification is received by a motor carrier before or when a loaded intermodal container or trailer is tendered to it, the motor carrier may presume that the gross cargo weight of the container or trailer is less than 29,001 pounds.

(2) COPY OF CERTIFICATION NOT REQUIRED TO ACCOMPANY CONTAINER OR TRAILER.—Notwithstanding any other provision of this chapter to the contrary, a copy of the certification required by section 5902(b) is not required to accompany the intermodal container or trailer.

(c) UNLAWFUL COERCION.—(1) A person may not coerce or attempt to coerce a person participating in intermodal transportation to transport a loaded container or trailer having an actual gross cargo weight of more than 29,000 pounds before the certification required by section 5902(b) of this title is provided.

(2) A person, knowing that the weight of a loaded container or trailer or the weight of a tractor-trailer combination carrying the container or trailer is more than the weight allowed by applicable State law, may not coerce or attempt to coerce a carrier to transport the container or trailer or to operate the tractor-trailer combination in violation of that State law.

(d) NOTICE TO LEASED OPERATORS.—

(1) IN GENERAL.—If a motor carrier knows that the gross cargo weight of an intermodal container or trailer subject to the certification requirements of section 5902(b) would result in a violation of applicable State gross vehicle weight laws, then—

(A) the motor carrier shall give notice to the operator of a vehicle which is leased by the vehicle operator to a motor carrier that transports an intermodal container or trailer of the gross cargo weight of the container or trailer as certified to the motor carrier under section 5902(b);

(B) the notice shall be provided to the operator prior to the operator being tendered the container or trailer;

(C) the notice required by this subsection shall be in writing, but may be transmitted electronically; and

(D) the motor carrier shall bear the burden of proof to establish that it tendered the required notice to the operator.

(2) REIMBURSEMENT.—If the operator of a leased vehicle transporting a container or trailer subject to this chapter is fined because of a violation of a State's gross vehicle

weight laws or regulations and the lessee motor carrier cannot establish that it tendered to the operator the notice required by paragraph (1) of this subsection, then the operator shall be entitled to reimbursement from the motor carrier in the amount of any fine and court costs resulting from the failure of the motor carrier to tender the notice to the operator.

(Pub. L. 103–272, §1(d), July 5, 1994, 108 Stat. 860; Pub. L. 104–291, title II, §205, Oct. 11, 1996, 110 Stat. 3456.)

[1] *So in original. Probably should not be capitalized.*

§5904. State enforcement

(a) General.—A State may enact a law to permit the State or a political subdivision of the State—

(1) to impose a fine or penalty, for a violation of a State highway weight law or regulation by a tractor-trailer combination carrying a loaded container or trailer for which a certification is required by section 5902(b) of this title, against the person tendering the loaded container or trailer to the first carrier if the violation results from the person's having provided erroneous information in the certification in violation of section 5903(a) of this title; and

(2) to impound the container or trailer until the fine or penalty has been paid by the owner or beneficial owner of the contents of the container or trailer or the person tendering the loaded container or trailer to the first carrier.

(b) Limitation.—This chapter does not require a person tendering a loaded container or trailer to a first carrier to ensure that the first carrier or any other carrier involved in the intermodal transportation will comply with any State highway weight law or regulation, other than as required by this chapter.

(Pub. L. 103–272, §1(d), July 5, 1994, 108 Stat. 861.)

§5905. Liens

(a) General.—If a person involved in the intermodal transportation of a loaded container or trailer for which a certification is required by section 5902(b) of this title is required, because of a violation of a State's gross vehicle weight laws or regulations, to post a bond or pay a fine, penalty, cost (including storage), or interest resulting from—

(1) erroneous information provided by the certifying party in the certification to the first carrier in violation of section 5903(a) of this title;

(2) the failure of the party required to provide the certification to the first carrier to provide it;

(3) the failure of a person required under section 5902(c) to forward the certification to forward it; or

(4) an error occurring in the transfer of information on the certification to another document under section 5902(b)(3) or (c),

then the person posting the bond, or paying the fine, penalty, costs (including storage), or interest has a lien against the contents equal to the amount of the bond, fine, penalty, cost

SUBTITLE IV
INTERSTATE TRANSPORTATION

(including storage), or interest incurred, until the person receives a payment of that amount from the owner or beneficial owner of the contents, or from the person responsible for making or forwarding the certification, or transferring the information from the certification to another document.

(b) LIMITATIONS.—(1) A lien under this section does not authorize a person to dispose of the contents of a loaded container or trailer until the person who tendered the container or trailer to the first carrier, or the owner or beneficial owner of the contents, is given a reasonable opportunity to establish responsibility for the bond, fine, penalty, cost (including storage), or interest. The lien shall remain in effect until the lien holder has received payment for all costs and expenses described in subsection (a) of this section.

(2) In this section, an owner or beneficial owner of the contents of a container or trailer or a person tendering a container or trailer to the first carrier is deemed not to be a person involved in the intermodal transportation of the container or trailer.

(Pub. L. 103–272, §1(d), July 5, 1994, 108 Stat. 861; Pub. L. 104–291, title II, §206, Oct. 11, 1996, 110 Stat. 3457.)

§5906. PERISHABLE AGRICULTURAL COMMODITIES

Section 5905 of this title does not apply to a container or trailer the contents of which are perishable agricultural commodities (as defined in the Perishable Agricultural Commodities Act, 1930 (7 U.S.C. 499a et seq.)).

(Pub. L. 103–272, §1(d), July 5, 1994, 108 Stat. 861; Pub. L. 104–291, title II, §207, Oct. 11, 1996, 110 Stat. 3457.)

§5907. EFFECTIVE DATE

This chapter shall take effect 180 days after the date of enactment of the Intermodal Safe Container Transportation Amendments Act of 1996.

(Pub. L. 103–272, §1(d), July 5, 1994, 108 Stat. 862; Pub. L. 104–291, title II, §208(a), Oct. 11, 1996, 110 Stat. 3457.)

§5908. RELATIONSHIP TO OTHER LAWS

Nothing in this chapter affects—

(1) chapter 51 (relating to transportation of hazardous material) or the regulations promulgated under that chapter; or

(2) any State highway weight or size law or regulation applicable to tractor-trailer combinations.

(Added Pub. L. 104–291, title II, §209(a), Oct. 11, 1996, 110 Stat. 3458.)

* * * * * * *

SUBTITLE IV—INTERSTATE TRANSPORTATION

PART A—RAIL

* * * * * * *

PART A—RAIL

CHAPTER 101—GENERAL PROVISIONS

Sec.
10101.   Rail transportation policy.
10102.   Definitions.

§10101. RAIL TRANSPORTATION POLICY

In regulating the railroad industry, it is the policy of the United States Government—

(1) to allow, to the maximum extent possible, competition and the demand for services to establish reasonable rates for transportation by rail;

(2) to minimize the need for Federal regulatory control over the rail transportation system and to require fair and expeditious regulatory decisions when regulation is required;

(3) to promote a safe and efficient rail transportation system by allowing rail carriers to earn adequate revenues, as determined by the Board;

(4) to ensure the development and continuation of a sound rail transportation system with effective competition among rail carriers and with other modes, to meet the needs of the public and the national defense;

(5) to foster sound economic conditions in transportation and to ensure effective competition and coordination between rail carriers and other modes;

(6) to maintain reasonable rates where there is an absence of effective competition and where rail rates provide revenues which exceed the amount necessary to maintain the rail system and to attract capital;

(7) to reduce regulatory barriers to entry into and exit from the industry;

(8) to operate transportation facilities and equipment without detriment to the public health and safety;

(9) to encourage honest and efficient management of railroads;

(10) to require rail carriers, to the maximum extent practicable, to rely on individual rate increases, and to limit the use of increases of general applicability;

(11) to encourage fair wages and safe and suitable working conditions in the railroad industry;

(12) to prohibit predatory pricing and practices, to avoid undue concentrations of market power, and to prohibit unlawful discrimination;

(13) to ensure the availability of accurate cost information in regulatory proceedings, while minimizing the burden on rail carriers of developing and maintaining the capability of providing such information;

(14) to encourage and promote energy conservation; and

(15) to provide for the expeditious handling and resolution of all proceedings required or permitted to be brought under this part.

(Added Pub. L. 104–88, title I, §102(a), Dec. 29, 1995, 109 Stat. 805.)

§10102. Definitions

In this part—

(1) "Board" means the Surface Transportation Board;

(2) "car service" includes (A) the use, control, supply, movement, distribution, exchange, interchange, and return of locomotives, cars, other vehicles, and special types of equipment used in the transportation of property by a rail carrier, and (B) the supply of trains by a rail carrier;

(3) "control", when referring to a relationship between persons, includes actual control, legal control, and the power to exercise control, through or by (A) common directors, officers, stockholders, a voting trust, or a holding or investment company, or (B) any other means;

(4) "person", in addition to its meaning under section 1 of title 1, includes a trustee, receiver, assignee, or personal representative of a person;

(5) "rail carrier" means a person providing common carrier railroad transportation for compensation, but does not include street, suburban, or interurban electric railways not operated as part of the general system of rail transportation;

(6) "railroad" includes—

(A) a bridge, car float, lighter, ferry, and intermodal equipment used by or in connection with a railroad;

(B) the road used by a rail carrier and owned by it or operated under an agreement; and

(C) a switch, spur, track, terminal, terminal facility, and a freight depot, yard, and ground, used or necessary for transportation;

(7) "rate" means a rate or charge for transportation;

(8) "State" means a State of the United States and the District of Columbia;

(9) "transportation" includes—

(A) a locomotive, car, vehicle, vessel, warehouse, wharf, pier, dock, yard, property, facility, instrumentality, or equipment of any kind related to the movement of passengers or property, or both, by rail, regardless of ownership or an agreement concerning use; and

(B) services related to that movement, including receipt, delivery, elevation, transfer in transit, refrigeration, icing, ventilation, storage, handling, and interchange of passengers and property; and

(10) "United States" means the States of the United States and the District of Columbia.

(Added Pub. L. 104–88, title I, §102(a), Dec. 29, 1995, 109 Stat. 806.)

CHAPTER 105—JURISDICTION

§10501. GENERAL JURISDICTION

(a)(1) Subject to this chapter, the Board has jurisdiction over transportation by rail carrier that is—

(A) only by railroad; or

(B) by railroad and water, when the transportation is under common control, management, or arrangement for a continuous carriage or shipment.

(2) Jurisdiction under paragraph (1) applies only to transportation in the United States between a place in—

(A) a State and a place in the same or another State as part of the interstate rail network;

(B) a State and a place in a territory or possession of the United States;

(C) a territory or possession of the United States and a place in another such territory or possession;

(D) a territory or possession of the United States and another place in the same territory or possession;

(E) the United States and another place in the United States through a foreign country; or

(F) the United States and a place in a foreign country.

(b) The jurisdiction of the Board over—

(1) transportation by rail carriers, and the remedies provided in this part with respect to rates, classifications, rules (including car service, interchange, and other operating rules), practices, routes, services, and facilities of such carriers; and

(2) the construction, acquisition, operation, abandonment, or discontinuance of spur, industrial, team, switching, or side tracks, or facilities, even if the tracks are located, or intended to be located, entirely in one State,

is exclusive. Except as otherwise provided in this part, the remedies provided under this part with respect to regulation of rail transportation are exclusive and preempt the remedies provided under Federal or State law.

(c)(1) In this subsection—

(A) the term "local governmental authority"—

(i) has the same meaning given that term by section 5302 of this title; and

(ii) includes a person or entity that contracts with the local governmental authority to provide transportation services; and

(B) the term "public transportation" means transportation services described in section

5302 of this title that are provided by rail.

(2) Except as provided in paragraph (3), the Board does not have jurisdiction under this part over—

(A) public transportation provided by a local government authority; or

(B) a solid waste rail transfer facility as defined in section 10908 of this title, except as provided under sections 10908 and 10909 of this title.

(3)(A) Notwithstanding paragraph (2) of this subsection, a local governmental authority, described in paragraph (2), is subject to applicable laws of the United States related to—

(i) safety;

(ii) the representation of employees for collective bargaining; and

(iii) employment, retirement, annuity, and unemployment systems or other provisions related to dealings between employees and employers.

(B) The Board has jurisdiction under sections 11102 and 11103 of this title over transportation provided by a local governmental authority only if the Board finds that such governmental authority meets all of the standards and requirements for being a rail carrier providing transportation subject to the jurisdiction of the Interstate Commerce Commission that were in effect immediately before January 1, 1996. The enactment of the ICC Termination Act of 1995 shall neither expand nor contract coverage of employees and employers by the Railway Labor Act, the Railroad Retirement Act of 1974, the Railroad Retirement Tax Act, and the Railroad Unemployment Insurance Act.

(Added Pub. L. 104–88, title I, §102(a), Dec. 29, 1995, 109 Stat. 807; amended Pub. L. 104–287, §5(21), Oct. 11, 1996, 110 Stat. 3390; Pub. L. 110–432, div. A, title VI, §602, Oct. 16, 2008, 122 Stat. 4900; Pub. L. 114–94, div. A, title III, §3030(g), Dec. 4, 2015, 129 Stat. 1497.)

§10502. Authority to exempt rail carrier transportation

(a) In a matter related to a rail carrier providing transportation subject to the jurisdiction of the Board under this part, the Board, to the maximum extent consistent with this part, shall exempt a person, class of persons, or a transaction or service whenever the Board finds that the application in whole or in part of a provision of this part—

(1) is not necessary to carry out the transportation policy of section 10101 of this title; and

(2) either—

(A) the transaction or service is of limited scope; or

(B) the application in whole or in part of the provision is not needed to protect shippers from the abuse of market power.

(b) The Board may, where appropriate, begin a proceeding under this section on its own initiative or on application by the Secretary of Transportation or an interested party. The Board shall, within 90 days after receipt of any such application, determine whether to begin an appropriate proceeding. If the Board decides not to begin a class exemption proceeding, the reasons for the decision shall be published in the Federal Register. Any proceeding begun as a result of an application under this subsection shall be completed within 9 months after it is begun.

(c) The Board may specify the period of time during which an exemption granted under this section is effective.

(d) The Board may revoke an exemption, to the extent it specifies, when it finds that application in whole or in part of a provision of this part to the person, class, or transportation is necessary to carry out the transportation policy of section 10101 of this title. The Board shall, within 90 days after receipt of a request for revocation under this subsection, determine whether to begin an appropriate proceeding. If the Board decides not to begin a proceeding to revoke a class exemption, the reasons for the decision shall be published in the Federal Register. Any proceeding begun as a result of a request under this subsection shall be completed within 9 months after it is begun.

(e) No exemption order issued pursuant to this section shall operate to relieve any rail carrier from an obligation to provide contractual terms for liability and claims which are consistent with the provisions of section 11706 of this title. Nothing in this subsection or section 11706 of this title shall prevent rail carriers from offering alternative terms nor give the Board the authority to require any specific level of rates or services based upon the provisions of section 11706 of this title.

(f) The Board may exercise its authority under this section to exempt transportation that is provided by a rail carrier as part of a continuous intermodal movement.

(g) The Board may not exercise its authority under this section to relieve a rail carrier of its obligation to protect the interests of employees as required by this part.

(Added Pub. L. 104–88, title I, §102(a), Dec. 29, 1995, 109 Stat. 808.)

CHAPTER 107—RATES

SUBCHAPTER I—GENERAL AUTHORITY

SUBCHAPTER II—SPECIAL CIRCUMSTANCES

SUBCHAPTER III—LIMITATIONS

SUBCHAPTER I—GENERAL AUTHORITY

§10701. STANDARDS FOR RATES, CLASSIFICATIONS, THROUGH ROUTES, RULES, AND PRACTICES

(a) A through route established by a rail carrier must be reasonable. Divisions of joint rates by rail carriers must be made without unreasonable discrimination against a participating carrier and must be reasonable.

(b) A rail carrier providing transportation subject to the jurisdiction of the Board under this part may not discriminate in its rates against a connecting line of another rail carrier providing transportation subject to the jurisdiction of the Board under this part or unreasonably discriminate against that line in the distribution of traffic that is not routed specifically by the shipper.

(c) Except as provided in subsection (d) of this section and unless a rate is prohibited by a provision of this part, a rail carrier providing transportation subject to the jurisdiction of the Board under this part may establish any rate for transportation or other service provided by the rail carrier.

(d)(1) If the Board determines, under section 10707 of this title, that a rail carrier has market dominance over the transportation to which a particular rate applies, the rate established by such carrier for such transportation must be reasonable.

(2) In determining whether a rate established by a rail carrier is reasonable for purposes of this section, the Board shall give due consideration to—

(A) the amount of traffic which is transported at revenues which do not contribute to going concern value and the efforts made to minimize such traffic;

(B) the amount of traffic which contributes only marginally to fixed costs and the extent to which, if any, rates on such traffic can be changed to maximize the revenues from such traffic; and

(C) the carrier's mix of rail traffic to determine whether one commodity is paying an unreasonable share of the carrier's overall revenues,

recognizing the policy of this part that rail carriers shall earn adequate revenues, as established by the Board under section 10704(a)(2) of this title.

(3) The Board shall maintain 1 or more simplified and expedited methods for determining the reasonableness of challenged rates in those cases in which a full stand-alone cost presentation is too costly, given the value of the case.

(Added Pub. L. 104–88, title I, §102(a), Dec. 29, 1995, 109 Stat. 809; amended Pub. L. 104–287, §5(22), Oct. 11, 1996, 110 Stat. 3390; Pub. L. 114–110, §11(a), Dec. 18, 2015, 129 Stat. 2233.)

§10702. AUTHORITY FOR RAIL CARRIERS TO ESTABLISH RATES, CLASSIFICATIONS, RULES, AND PRACTICES

A rail carrier providing transportation or service subject to the jurisdiction of the Board under this part shall establish reasonable—

(1) rates, to the extent required by section 10707, divisions of joint rates, and classifications for transportation and service it may provide under this part; and

(2) rules and practices on matters related to that transportation or service.

(Added Pub. L. 104–88, title I, §102(a), Dec. 29, 1995, 109 Stat. 810.)

§10703. AUTHORITY FOR RAIL CARRIERS TO ESTABLISH THROUGH ROUTES

Rail carriers providing transportation subject to the jurisdiction of the Board under this part shall establish through routes (including physical connections) with each other and with water carriers providing transportation subject to chapter 137, shall establish rates and classifications applicable to those routes, and shall establish rules for their operation and provide—

(1) reasonable facilities for operating the through route; and

(2) reasonable compensation to persons entitled to compensation for services related to the through route.

(Added Pub. L. 104–88, title I, §102(a), Dec. 29, 1995, 109 Stat. 810.)

§10704. AUTHORITY AND CRITERIA: RATES, CLASSIFICATIONS, RULES, AND PRACTICES PRESCRIBED BY BOARD

(a)(1) When the Board, after a full hearing, decides that a rate charged or collected by a rail carrier for transportation subject to the jurisdiction of the Board under this part, or that a classification, rule, or practice of that carrier, does or will violate this part, the Board may prescribe the maximum rate, classification, rule, or practice to be followed. The Board may order the carrier to stop the violation. When a rate, classification, rule, or practice is prescribed under this subsection, the affected carrier may not publish, charge, or collect a different rate and shall adopt the classification and observe the rule or practice prescribed by the Board.

(2) The Board shall maintain and revise as necessary standards and procedures for establishing revenue levels for rail carriers providing transportation subject to its jurisdiction under this part that are adequate, under honest, economical, and efficient management, for the infrastructure and investment needed to meet the present and future demand for rail services and to cover total operating expenses, including depreciation and obsolescence, plus a reasonable and economic profit or return (or both) on capital employed in the business. The Board shall make an adequate and continuing effort to assist those carriers in attaining revenue levels prescribed under this paragraph. Revenue levels established under this paragraph should—

(A) provide a flow of net income plus depreciation adequate to support prudent capital outlays, assure the repayment of a reasonable level of debt, permit the raising of needed equity capital, and cover the effects of inflation; and

(B) attract and retain capital in amounts adequate to provide a sound transportation system in the United States.

(3) On the basis of the standards and procedures described in paragraph (2), the Board shall annually determine which rail carriers are earning adequate revenues.

(b) The Board may begin a proceeding under this section only on complaint. A complaint under subsection (a) of this section must be made under section 11701 of this title, but the proceeding may also be in extension of a complaint pending before the Board.

(c) In a proceeding to challenge the reasonableness of a rate, the Board shall make its determination as to the reasonableness of the challenged rate—

(1) within 9 months after the close of the administrative record if the determination is based upon a stand-alone cost presentation; or

(2) within 6 months after the close of the administrative record if the determination is based upon the methodology adopted by the Board pursuant to section 10701(d)(3).

(d)(1) The Board shall maintain procedures to ensure the expeditious handling of challenges to the reasonableness of railroad rates. The procedures shall include appropriate measures for avoiding delay in the discovery and evidentiary phases of such proceedings and exemption or revocation proceedings, including appropriate sanctions for such delay, and for ensuring prompt disposition of motions and interlocutory administrative appeals.

(2)(A) Except as provided under subparagraph (B), in a stand-alone cost rate challenge, the Board shall comply with the following timeline:

(i) Discovery shall be completed not later than 150 days after the date on which the challenge is initiated.

(ii) The development of the evidentiary record shall be completed not later than 155 days after the date on which discovery is completed under clause (i).

(iii) The closing brief shall be submitted not later than 60 days after the date on which the development of the evidentiary record is completed under clause (ii).

(iv) A final Board decision shall be issued not later than 180 days after the date on which the evidentiary record is completed under clause (ii).

(B) The Board may extend a timeline under subparagraph (A) after a request from any party or in the interest of due process.

(Added Pub. L. 104–88, title I, §102(a), Dec. 29, 1995, 109 Stat. 810; amended Pub. L. 104–287, §5(23), Oct. 11, 1996, 110 Stat. 3390; Pub. L. 114–110, §§11(b), 16, Dec. 18, 2015, 129 Stat. 2233, 2238.)

§10705. AUTHORITY: THROUGH ROUTES, JOINT CLASSIFICATIONS, RATES, AND DIVISIONS PRESCRIBED BY BOARD

(a)(1) The Board may, and shall when it considers it desirable in the public interest, prescribe through routes, joint classifications, joint rates, the division of joint rates, and the conditions under which those routes must be operated, for a rail carrier providing transportation subject to the jurisdiction of the Board under this part.

(2) The Board may require a rail carrier to include in a through route substantially less than the entire length of its railroad and any intermediate railroad operated with it under common management or control if that intermediate railroad lies between the terminals of the through route only when—

(A) required under section 10741, 10742, or 11102 of this title;

(B) inclusion of those lines would make the through route unreasonably long when compared with a practicable alternative through route that could be established; or

(C) the Board decides that the proposed through route is needed to provide adequate, and more efficient or economic, transportation.

The Board shall give reasonable preference, subject to this subsection, to the rail carrier originating the traffic when prescribing through routes.

(b) The Board shall prescribe the division of joint rates to be received by a rail carrier providing transportation subject to its jurisdiction under this part when it decides that a division of joint rates established by the participating carriers under section 10703 of this title, or under a decision of the Board under subsection (a) of this section, does or will violate section 10701 of this title.

(c) If a division of a joint rate prescribed under a decision of the Board is later found to violate section 10701 of this title, the Board may decide what division would have been reasonable and order adjustment to be made retroactive to the date the complaint was filed, the date the order for an investigation was made, or a later date that the Board decides is justified. The Board may make a decision under this subsection effective as part of its original decision.

(Added Pub. L. 104–88, title I, §102(a), Dec. 29, 1995, 109 Stat. 811.)

§10706. Rate agreements: exemption from antitrust laws

(a)(1) In this subsection—

(A) the term "affiliate" means a person controlling, controlled by, or under common control or ownership with another person and "ownership" refers to equity holdings in a business entity of at least 5 percent;

(B) the term "single-line rate" refers to a rate or allowance proposed by a single rail carrier that is applicable only over its line and for which the transportation (exclusive of terminal services by switching, drayage or other terminal carriers or agencies) can be provided by that carrier; and

(C) the term "practicably participates in the movement" shall have such meaning as the Board shall by regulation prescribe.

(2)(A) A rail carrier providing transportation subject to the jurisdiction of the Board under this part that is a party to an agreement of at least 2 rail carriers that relates to rates (including charges between rail carriers and compensation paid or received for the use of facilities and equipment), classifications, divisions, or rules related to them, or procedures for joint consideration, initiation, publication, or establishment of them, shall apply to the Board for approval of that agreement under this subsection. The Board shall approve the agreement only when it finds that the making and carrying out of the agreement will further the transportation policy of section 10101 of this title and may require compliance with conditions necessary to make the agreement further that policy as a condition of its approval. If the Board approves the agreement, it may be made and carried out under its terms and under the conditions required by the Board, and the Sherman Act (15 U.S.C. 1, et seq.), the Clayton Act (15 U.S.C. 12, et seq.), the Federal Trade Commission Act (15 U.S.C. 41, et seq.), sections 73 and 74 of the Wilson Tariff Act (15 U.S.C. 8 and 9), and the Act of June 19, 1936 (15 U.S.C. 13, 13a, 13b, 21a) do not apply to parties and other persons with respect to making or carrying out the agreement. However, the Board may not approve or continue approval of an agreement when the conditions required by it are not met or if it does not receive a verified statement under subparagraph (B) of this paragraph.

(B) The Board may approve an agreement under subparagraph (A) of this paragraph only when the rail carriers applying for approval file a verified statement with the Board. Each statement must specify for each rail carrier that is a party to the agreement—

(i) the name of the carrier;

(ii) the mailing address and telephone number of its headquarter's office; and

(iii) the names of each of its affiliates and the names, addresses, and affiliates of each of its officers and directors and of each person, together with an affiliate, owning or controlling any debt, equity, or security interest in it having a value of at least $1,000,000.

(3)(A) An organization established or continued under an agreement approved under this subsection shall make a final disposition of a rule or rate docketed with it by the 120th day after the proposal is docketed. Such an organization may not—

(i) permit a rail carrier to discuss, to participate in agreements related to, or to vote on single-line rates proposed by another rail carrier, except that for purposes of general rate increases and broad changes in rates, classifications, rules, and practices only, if the Board finds at any time that the implementation of this clause is not feasible, it may delay or suspend such implementation in whole or in part;

(ii) permit a rail carrier to discuss, to participate in agreements related to, or to vote on rates related to a particular interline movement unless that rail carrier practicably participates in the movement; or

(iii) if there are interline movements over two or more routes between the same end points, permit a carrier to discuss, to participate in agreements related to, or to vote on rates except with a carrier which forms part of a particular single route. If the Board finds at any time that the implementation of this clause is not feasible, it may delay or suspend such implementation in whole or in part.

(B)(i) In any proceeding in which a party alleges that a rail carrier voted or agreed on a rate or allowance in violation of this subsection, that party has the burden of showing that the vote or agreement occurred. A showing of parallel behavior does not satisfy that burden by itself.

(ii) In any proceeding in which it is alleged that a carrier was a party to an agreement, conspiracy, or combination in violation of a Federal law cited in subsection (a)(2)(A) of this section or of any similar State law, proof of an agreement, conspiracy, or combination may not be inferred from evidence that two or more rail carriers acted together with respect to an interline rate or related matter and that a party to such action took similar action with respect to a rate or related matter on another route or traffic. In any proceeding in which such a violation is alleged, evidence of a discussion or agreement between or among such rail carrier and one or more other rail carriers, or of any rate or other action resulting from such discussion or agreement, shall not be admissible if the discussion or agreement—

(I) was in accordance with an agreement approved under paragraph (2) of this subsection; or

(II) concerned an interline movement of the rail carrier, and the discussion or agreement would not, considered by itself, violate the laws referred to in the first sentence of this clause.

In any proceeding before a jury, the court shall determine whether the requirements of subclause (I) or (II) are satisfied before allowing the introduction of any such evidence.

(C) An organization described in subparagraph (A) of this paragraph shall provide that transcripts or sound recordings be made of all meetings, that records of votes be made, and that such transcripts or recordings and voting records be submitted to the Board and made available to other Federal agencies in connection with their statutory responsibilities over rate bureaus, except that such material shall be kept confidential and shall not be subject to disclosure under section 552 of title 5, United States Code.

(4) Notwithstanding any other provision of this subsection, one or more rail carriers may

enter into an agreement, without obtaining prior Board approval, that provides solely for compilation, publication, and other distribution of rates in effect or to become effective. The Sherman Act (15 U.S.C. 1 et seq.), the Clayton Act (15 U.S.C. 12 et seq.), the Federal Trade Commission Act (15 U.S.C. 41 et seq.), sections 73 and 74 of the Wilson Tariff Act (15 U.S.C. 8 and 9), and the Act of June 19, 1936 (15 U.S.C. 13, 13a, 13b, 21a) shall not apply to parties and other persons with respect to making or carrying out such agreement. However, the Board may, upon application or on its own initiative, investigate whether the parties to such an agreement have exceeded its scope, and upon a finding that they have, the Board may issue such orders as are necessary, including an order dissolving the agreement, to ensure that actions taken pursuant to the agreement are limited as provided in this paragraph.

(5)(A) Whenever two or more shippers enter into an agreement to discuss among themselves that relates to the amount of compensation such shippers propose to be paid by rail carriers providing transportation subject to the jurisdiction of the Board under this part, for use by such rail carriers of rolling stock owned or leased by such shippers, the shippers shall apply to the Board for approval of that agreement under this paragraph. The Board shall approve the agreement only when it finds that the making and carrying out of the agreement will further the transportation policy set forth in section 10101 of this title and may require compliance with conditions necessary to make the agreement further that policy as a condition of approval. If the Board approves the agreement, it may be made and carried out under its terms and under the terms required by the Board, and the antitrust laws set forth in paragraph (2) of this subsection do not apply to parties and other persons with respect to making or carrying out the agreement. The Board shall approve or disapprove an agreement under this paragraph within one year after the date application for approval of such agreement is made.

(B) If the Board approves an agreement described in subparagraph (A) of this paragraph and the shippers entering into such agreement and the rail carriers proposing to use rolling stock owned or leased by such shippers, under payment by such carriers or under a published allowance, are unable to agree upon the amount of compensation to be paid for the use of such rolling stock, any party directly involved in the negotiations may require that the matter be settled by submitting the issues in dispute to the Board. The Board shall render a binding decision, based upon a standard of reasonableness and after taking into consideration any past precedents on the subject matter of the negotiations, no later than 90 days after the date of the submission of the dispute to the Board.

(C) Nothing in this paragraph shall be construed to change the law in effect prior to October 1, 1980, with respect to the obligation of rail carriers to utilize rolling stock owned or leased by shippers.

(b) The Board may require an organization established or continued under an agreement approved under this section to maintain records and submit reports. The Board may inspect a record maintained under this section.

(c) The Board may review an agreement approved under subsection (a) of this section and shall change the conditions of approval or terminate it when necessary to comply with the public interest and subsection (a). The Board shall postpone the effective date of a change of an agreement under this subsection for whatever period it determines to be reasonably necessary to avoid unreasonable hardship.

(d) The Board may begin a proceeding under this section on its own initiative or on application. Action of the Board under this section—

(1) approving an agreement;

(2) denying, ending, or changing approval;

(3) prescribing the conditions on which approval is granted; or

(4) changing those conditions,

has effect only as related to application of the antitrust laws referred to in subsection (a) of this section.

(e)(1) The Federal Trade Commission, in consultation with the Antitrust Division of the Department of Justice, shall prepare periodically an assessment of, and shall report to the Board on—

(A) possible anticompetitive features of—

(i) agreements approved or submitted for approval under subsection (a) of this section; and

(ii) an organization operating under those agreements; and

(B) possible ways to alleviate or end an anticompetitive feature, effect, or aspect in a manner that will further the goals of this part and of the transportation policy of section 10101 of this title.

(2) Reports received by the Board under this subsection shall be published and made available to the public under section 552(a) of title 5.

(Added Pub. L. 104–88, title I, §102(a), Dec. 29, 1995, 109 Stat. 812; amended Pub. L. 104–287, §5(24), Oct. 11, 1996, 110 Stat. 3390.)

§10707. DETERMINATION OF MARKET DOMINANCE IN RAIL RATE PROCEEDINGS

(a) In this section, "market dominance" means an absence of effective competition from other rail carriers or modes of transportation for the transportation to which a rate applies.

(b) When a rate for transportation by a rail carrier providing transportation subject to the jurisdiction of the Board under this part is challenged as being unreasonably high, the Board shall determine whether the rail carrier proposing the rate has market dominance over the transportation to which the rate applies. The Board may make that determination on its own initiative or on complaint. A finding by the Board that the rail carrier does not have market dominance is determinative in a proceeding under this part related to that rate or transportation unless changed or set aside by the Board or set aside by a court of competent jurisdiction.

(c) When the Board finds in any proceeding that a rail carrier proposing or defending a rate for transportation has market dominance over the transportation to which the rate applies, it may then determine that rate to be unreasonable if it exceeds a reasonable maximum for that transportation. However, a finding of market dominance does not establish a presumption that the proposed rate exceeds a reasonable maximum.

(d)(1)(A) In making a determination under this section, the Board shall find that the rail carrier establishing the challenged rate does not have market dominance over the transportation to which the rate applies if such rail carrier proves that the rate charged results in a revenue-variable cost percentage for such transportation that is less than 180 percent.

(B) For purposes of this section, variable costs for a rail carrier shall be determined only by using such carrier's unadjusted costs, calculated using the Uniform Rail Costing System cost finding methodology (or an alternative methodology adopted by the Board in lieu thereof) and indexed quarterly to account for current wage and price levels in the region in which the carrier operates, with adjustments specified by the Board. A rail carrier may meet its burden of proof under this subsection by establishing its variable costs in accordance with this paragraph, but a shipper may rebut that showing by evidence of such type, and in accordance with such burden of proof, as the Board shall prescribe.

(2) A finding by the Board that a rate charged by a rail carrier results in a revenue-variable cost percentage for the transportation to which the rate applies that is equal to or greater than 180 percent does not establish a presumption that—

(A) such rail carrier has or does not have market dominance over such transportation; or

(B) the proposed rate exceeds or does not exceed a reasonable maximum.

(Added Pub. L. 104–88, title I, §102(a), Dec. 29, 1995, 109 Stat. 815.)

§10708. Rail cost adjustment factor

(a) The Board shall, as often as practicable, but in no event less often than quarterly, publish a rail cost adjustment factor which shall be a fraction, the numerator of which is the latest published Index of Railroad Costs (which index shall be compiled or verified by the Board, with appropriate adjustments to reflect the change in composition of railroad costs, including the quality and mix of material and labor) and the denominator of which is the same index for the fourth quarter of every fifth year, beginning with the fourth quarter of 1992.

(b) The rail cost adjustment factor published by the Board under subsection (a) of this section shall take into account changes in railroad productivity. The Board shall also publish a similar index that does not take into account changes in railroad productivity.

(Added Pub. L. 104–88, title I, §102(a), Dec. 29, 1995, 109 Stat. 816.)

§10709. Contracts

(a) One or more rail carriers providing transportation subject to the jurisdiction of the Board under this part may enter into a contract with one or more purchasers of rail services to provide specified services under specified rates and conditions.

(b) A party to a contract entered into under this section shall have no duty in connection with services provided under such contract other than those duties specified by the terms of the contract.

(c)(1) A contract that is authorized by this section, and transportation under such contract, shall not be subject to this part, and may not be subsequently challenged before the Board or in any court on the grounds that such contract violates a provision of this part.

(2) The exclusive remedy for any alleged breach of a contract entered into under this section shall be an action in an appropriate State court or United States district court, unless the parties otherwise agree. This section does not confer original jurisdiction on the district courts of the United States based on section 1331 or 1337 of title 28, United States Code.

(d)(1) A summary of each contract for the transportation of agricultural products (including grain, as defined in section 3 of the United States Grain Standards Act (7 U.S.C. 75) and products thereof) entered into under this section shall be filed with the Board, containing such nonconfidential information as the Board prescribes. The Board shall publish special rules for such contracts in order to ensure that the essential terms of the contract are available to the general public.

(2) Documents, papers, and records (and any copies thereof) relating to a contract described in subsection (a) shall not be subject to the mandatory disclosure requirements of section 552 of title 5.

(e) Any lawful contract between a rail carrier and one or more purchasers of rail service that was in effect on October 1, 1980, shall be considered a contract authorized by this section.

(f) A rail carrier that enters into a contract as authorized by this section remains subject to the common carrier obligation set forth in section 11101, with respect to rail transportation not provided under such a contract.

(g)(1) No later than 30 days after the date of filing of a summary of a contract under this section, the Board may, on complaint, begin a proceeding to review such contract on the grounds described in this subsection.

(2)(A) A complaint may be filed under this subsection—

(i) by a shipper on the grounds that such shipper individually will be harmed because the proposed contract unduly impairs the ability of the contracting rail carrier or carriers to meet their common carrier obligations to the complainant under section 11101 of this title; or

(ii) by a port only on the grounds that such port individually will be harmed because the proposed contract will result in unreasonable discrimination against such port.

(B) In addition to the grounds for a complaint described in subparagraph (A) of this paragraph, a complaint may be filed by a shipper of agricultural commodities on the grounds that such shipper individually will be harmed because—

(i) the rail carrier has unreasonably discriminated by refusing to enter into a contract with such shipper for rates and services for the transportation of the same type of commodity under similar conditions to the contract at issue, and that shipper was ready, willing, and able to enter into such a contract at a time essentially contemporaneous with the period during which the contract at issue was offered; or

(ii) the proposed contract constitutes a destructive competitive practice under this part.

In making a determination under clause (ii) of this subparagraph, the Board shall consider the difference between contract rates and published single car rates.

(C) For purposes of this paragraph, the term "unreasonable discrimination" has the same meaning as such term has under section 10741 of this title.

(3)(A) Within 30 days after the date a proceeding is commenced under paragraph

(1) of this subsection, or within such shorter time period after such date as the Board may establish, the Board shall determine whether the contract that is the subject of such proceeding is in violation of this section.

(B) If the Board determines, on the basis of a complaint filed under paragraph (2)(B)(i) of this subsection, that the grounds for a complaint described in such paragraph have been established with respect to a rail carrier, the Board shall, subject to the provisions of this section, order such rail carrier to provide rates and service substantially similar to the contract at issue with such differentials in terms and conditions as are justified by the evidence.

(Added Pub. L. 104–88, title I, §102(a), Dec. 29, 1995, 109 Stat. 817; amended Pub. L. 104–287, §5(24), Oct. 11, 1996, 110 Stat. 3390; Pub. L. 114–110, §11(d), Dec. 18, 2015, 129 Stat. 2234.)

SUBCHAPTER II—SPECIAL CIRCUMSTANCES

§10721. GOVERNMENT TRAFFIC

A rail carrier providing transportation or service for the United States Government may transport property or individuals for the United States Government without charge or at a rate reduced from the applicable commercial rate. Section 6101(b) to (d) of title 41 does not apply when transportation for the United States Government can be obtained from a rail carrier lawfully operating in the area where the transportation would be provided.

(Added Pub. L. 104–88, title I, §102(a), Dec. 29, 1995, 109 Stat. 819; amended Pub. L. 111–350, §5(o)(4), Jan. 4, 2011, 124 Stat. 3853.)

§10722. CAR UTILIZATION

In order to encourage more efficient use of freight cars, notwithstanding any other provision of this part, rail carriers shall be permitted to establish premium charges for special services or special levels of services not otherwise applicable to the movement. The Board shall facilitate development of such charges so as to increase the utilization of equipment.

(Added Pub. L. 104–88, title I, §102(a), Dec. 29, 1995, 109 Stat. 819.)

SUBCHAPTER III—LIMITATIONS

§10741. PROHIBITIONS AGAINST DISCRIMINATION BY RAIL CARRIERS

(a)(1) A rail carrier providing transportation or service subject to the jurisdiction of the Board under this part may not subject a person, place, port, or type of traffic to unreasonable discrimination.

(2) For purposes of this section, a rail carrier engages in unreasonable discrimination when it charges or receives from a person a different compensation for a service rendered, or to be rendered, in transportation the rail carrier may perform under this part than it charges or receives from another person for performing a like and contemporaneous service in the transportation of a like kind of traffic under substantially similar circumstances.

(b) This section shall not apply to—

(1) contracts described in section 10709 of this title;

(2) rail rates applicable to different routes; or

(3) discrimination against the traffic of another carrier providing transportation by any mode.

(c) Differences between rates, classifications, rules, and practices of rail carriers do not constitute a violation of this section if such differences result from different services provided by rail carriers.

(Added Pub. L. 104–88, title I, §102(a), Dec. 29, 1995, 109 Stat. 819.)

§10742. FACILITIES FOR INTERCHANGE OF TRAFFIC

A rail carrier providing transportation subject to the jurisdiction of the Board under this part shall provide reasonable, proper, and equal facilities that are within its power to provide for the interchange of traffic between, and for the receiving, forwarding, and delivering of passengers and property to and from, its respective line and a connecting line of another rail carrier or of a water carrier providing transportation subject to chapter 137.

(Added Pub. L. 104–88, title I, §102(a), Dec. 29, 1995, 109 Stat. 819.)

§10743. LIABILITY FOR PAYMENT OF RATES

(a)(1) Liability for payment of rates for transportation for a shipment of property by a shipper or consignor to a consignee other than the shipper or consignor, is determined under this subsection when the transportation is provided by a rail carrier under this part. When the shipper or consignor instructs the rail carrier transporting the property to deliver it to a consignee that is an agent only, not having beneficial title to the property, the consignee is liable for rates billed at the time of delivery for which the consignee is otherwise liable, but not for additional rates that may be found to be due after delivery if the consignee gives written notice to the delivering carrier before delivery of the property—

(A) of the agency and absence of beneficial title; and

(B) of the name and address of the beneficial owner of the property if it is reconsigned or diverted to a place other than the place specified in the original bill of lading.

(2) When the consignee is liable only for rates billed at the time of delivery under paragraph (1) of this subsection, the shipper or consignor, or, if the property is reconsigned or diverted, the beneficial owner, is liable for those additional rates regardless of the bill of lading or contract under which the property was transported. The beneficial owner is liable for all rates when the property is reconsigned or diverted by an agent but is refused or abandoned at its ultimate destination if the agent gave the rail carrier in the reconsignment or diversion order a notice of agency and the name and address of the beneficial owner. A consignee giving the rail carrier, and a reconsignor or diverter giving a rail carrier, erroneous information about the identity of the beneficial owner of the property is liable for the additional rates.

(b) Liability for payment of rates for transportation for a shipment of property by a shipper or consignor, named in the bill of lading as consignee, is determined under this subsection when the transportation is provided by a rail carrier under this part. When the shipper or consignor gives written notice, before delivery of the property, to the line-haul rail carrier that is to make ultimate delivery—

(1) to deliver the property to another party identified by the shipper or consignor as the beneficial owner of the property; and

(2) that delivery is to be made to that party on payment of all applicable transportation rates;

that party is liable for the rates billed at the time of delivery and for additional rates that may be found to be due after delivery if that party does not pay the rates required to be paid under paragraph (2) of this subsection on delivery. However, if the party gives written notice to the delivering rail carrier before delivery that the party is not the beneficial owner of the property and gives the rail carrier the name and address of the beneficial owner, then the party is not liable for those additional rates. A shipper, consignor, or party to whom delivery is made that gives the delivering rail carrier erroneous information about the identity of the beneficial owner, is liable for the additional rates regardless of the bill of lading or contract under which the property was transported. This subsection does not apply to a prepaid shipment of property.

(c)(1) A rail carrier may bring an action to enforce liability under subsection (a) of this section. That rail carrier must bring the action during the period provided in section 11705(a) of this title or by the end of the 6th month after final judgment against it in an action against the consignee, or the beneficial owner named by the consignee or agent, under that section.

(2) A rail carrier may bring an action to enforce liability under subsection (b) of this section. That carrier must bring the action during the period provided in section 11705(a) of this title or by the end of the 6th month after final judgment against it in an action against the shipper, consignor, or other party under that section.

(Added Pub. L. 104–88, title I, §102(a), Dec. 29, 1995, 109 Stat. 819.)

§10744. CONTINUOUS CARRIAGE OF FREIGHT

A rail carrier providing transportation or service subject to the jurisdiction of the Board under this part may not enter a combination or arrangement to prevent the carriage of freight from being continuous from the place of shipment to the place of destination whether by change of time schedule, carriage in different cars, or by other means. The carriage of freight by those rail carriers is considered to be a continuous carriage from the place of shipment to the place of destination when a break of bulk, stoppage, or interruption is not made in good faith for a necessary purpose, and with the intent of avoiding or unnecessarily interrupting the continuous carriage or of evading this part.

(Added Pub. L. 104–88, title I, §102(a), Dec. 29, 1995, 109 Stat. 821.)

§10745. Transportation services or facilities furnished by shipper

A rail carrier providing transportation or service subject to the jurisdiction of the Board under this part may establish a charge or allowance for transportation or service for property when the owner of the property, directly or indirectly, furnishes a service related to or an instrumentality used in the transportation or service. The Board may prescribe the maximum reasonable charge or allowance a rail carrier subject to its jurisdiction may pay for a service or instrumentality furnished under this section. The Board may begin a proceeding under this section on its own initiative or on application.

(Added Pub. L. 104–88, title I, §102(a), Dec. 29, 1995, 109 Stat. 821.)

§10746. Demurrage charges

A rail carrier providing transportation subject to the jurisdiction of the Board under this part shall compute demurrage charges, and establish rules related to those charges, in a way that fulfills the national needs related to—

(1) freight car use and distribution; and

(2) maintenance of an adequate supply of freight cars to be available for transportation of property.

(Added Pub. L. 104–88, title I, §102(a), Dec. 29, 1995, 109 Stat. 821.)

§10747. Designation of certain routes by shippers

(a)(1) When a person delivers property to a rail carrier for transportation subject to the jurisdiction of the Board under this part, the person may direct the rail carrier to transport the property over an established through route. When competing rail lines constitute a part of the route, the person shipping the property may designate the lines over which the property will be transported. The designation must be in writing. A rail carrier may be directed to transport property over a particular through route when—

(A) there are at least 2 through routes over which the property could be transported;

(B) a through rate has been established for transportation over each of those through routes; and

(C) the rail carrier is a party to those routes and rates.

(2) A rail carrier directed to route property transported under paragraph (1) of this subsection must issue a through bill of lading containing the routing instructions and transport the property according to the instructions. When the property is delivered to a connecting rail carrier, that rail carrier must also receive and transport it according to the routing instructions and deliver it to the next succeeding rail carrier or consignee according to the instructions.

(b) The Board may prescribe exceptions to the authority of a person to direct the movement of traffic under subsection (a) of this section.

(Added Pub. L. 104–88, title I, §102(a), Dec. 29, 1995, 109 Stat. 821.)

CHAPTER 109—LICENSING

§10901. AUTHORIZING CONSTRUCTION AND OPERATION OF RAILROAD LINES

(a) A person may—

(1) construct an extension to any of its railroad lines;

(2) construct an additional railroad line;

(3) provide transportation over, or by means of, an extended or additional railroad line; or

(4) in the case of a person other than a rail carrier, acquire a railroad line or acquire or operate an extended or additional railroad line,

only if the Board issues a certificate authorizing such activity under subsection (c).

(b) A proceeding to grant authority under subsection (a) of this section begins when an application is filed. On receiving the application, the Board shall give reasonable public notice, including notice to the Governor of any affected State, of the beginning of such proceeding.

(c) The Board shall issue a certificate authorizing activities for which such authority is requested in an application filed under subsection (b) unless the Board finds that such activities are inconsistent with the public convenience and necessity. Such certificate may approve the application as filed, or with modifications, and may require compliance with conditions (other than labor protection conditions) the Board finds necessary in the public interest.

(d)(1) When a certificate has been issued by the Board under this section authorizing the construction or extension of a railroad line, no other rail carrier may block any construction or extension authorized by such certificate by refusing to permit the carrier to cross its property if—

(A) the construction does not unreasonably interfere with the operation of the crossed line;

(B) the operation does not materially interfere with the operation of the crossed line; and

(C) the owner of the crossing line compensates the owner of the crossed line.

(2) If the parties are unable to agree on the terms of operation or the amount of payment for purposes of paragraph (1) of this subsection, either party may submit the matters in dispute to the Board for determination. The Board shall make a determination under this paragraph within 120 days after the dispute is submitted for determination.

(Added Pub. L. 104–88, title I, §102(a), Dec. 29, 1995, 109 Stat. 822.)

§10902. SHORT LINE PURCHASES BY CLASS II AND CLASS III RAIL CARRIERS

(a) A Class II or Class III rail carrier providing transportation subject to the jurisdiction of the Board under this part may acquire or operate an extended or additional rail line under this section only if the Board issues a certificate authorizing such activity under subsection (c).

(b) A proceeding to grant authority under subsection (a) of this section begins when an application is filed. On receiving the application, the Board shall give reasonable public notice of the beginning of such proceeding.

(c) The Board shall issue a certificate authorizing activities for which such authority is requested in an application filed under subsection (b) unless the Board finds that such activities are inconsistent with the public convenience and necessity. Such certificate may approve the application as filed, or with modifications, and may require compliance with conditions (other than labor protection conditions) the Board finds necessary in the public interest.

(d) The Board shall require any Class II rail carrier which receives a certificate under subsection (c) of this section to provide a fair and equitable arrangement for the protection of the interests of employees who may be affected thereby. The arrangement shall consist exclusively of one year of severance pay, which shall not exceed the amount of earnings from railroad employment of the employee during the 12-month period immediately preceding the date on which the application for such certificate is filed with the Board. The amount of such severance pay shall be reduced by the amount of earnings from railroad employment of the employee with the acquiring carrier during the 12-month period immediately following the effective date of the transaction to which the certificate applies. The parties may agree to terms other than as provided in this subsection. The Board shall not require such an arrangement from a Class III rail carrier which receives a certificate under subsection (c) of this section.

(Added Pub. L. 104–88, title I, §102(a), Dec. 29, 1995, 109 Stat. 823.)

§10903. FILING AND PROCEDURE FOR APPLICATION TO ABANDON OR DISCONTINUE

(a)(1) A rail carrier providing transportation subject to the jurisdiction of the Board under this part who intends to—

(A) abandon any part of its railroad lines; or

(B) discontinue the operation of all rail transportation over any part of its railroad lines, must file an application relating thereto with the Board. An abandonment or discontinuance may be carried out only as authorized under this chapter.

(2) When a rail carrier providing transportation subject to the jurisdiction of the Board under this part files an application, the application shall include—

(A) an accurate and understandable summary of the rail carrier's reasons for the proposed abandonment or discontinuance;

(B) a statement indicating that each interested person is entitled to make recommendations to the Board on the future of the rail line; and

(C)(i) a statement that the line is available for subsidy or sale in accordance with section 10904 of this title, (ii) a statement that the rail carrier will promptly provide to each interested party an estimate of the annual subsidy and minimum purchase price, calculated in accordance with section 10904 of this title, and (iii) the name and business address of the person who is authorized to discuss the subsidy or sale terms for the rail carrier.

(3) The rail carrier shall—

(A) send by certified mail notice of the application to the chief executive officer of each State that would be directly affected by the proposed abandonment or discontinuance;

(B) post a copy of the notice in each terminal and station on each portion of a railroad line proposed to be abandoned or over which all transportation is to be discontinued;

(C) publish a copy of the notice for 3 consecutive weeks in a newspaper of general circulation in each county in which each such portion is located;

(D) mail a copy of the notice, to the extent practicable, to all shippers that have made significant use (as designated by the Board) of the railroad line during the 12 months preceding the filing of the application; and

(E) attach to the application filed with the Board an affidavit certifying the manner in which subparagraphs (A) through (D) of this paragraph have been satisfied, and certifying that subparagraphs (A) through (D) have been satisfied within the most recent 30 days prior to the date the application is filed.

(b)(1) Except as provided in subsection (d), abandonment and discontinuance may occur as provided in section 10904.

(2) The Board shall require as a condition of any abandonment or discontinuance under this section provisions to protect the interests of employees. The provisions shall be at least as beneficial to those interests as the provisions established under sections 11326(a) and 24706(c) [1] of this title before May 31, 1998.

(c)(1) In this subsection, the term "potentially subject to abandonment" has the meaning given the term in regulations of the Board. The regulations may include standards that vary by region of the United States and by railroad or group of railroads.

(2) Each rail carrier shall maintain a complete diagram of the transportation system operated, directly or indirectly, by the rail carrier. The rail carrier shall submit to the Board and publish amendments to its diagram that are necessary to maintain the accuracy of the diagram. The diagram shall—

(A) include a detailed description of each of its railroad lines potentially subject to abandonment; and

(B) identify each railroad line for which the rail carrier plans to file an application to abandon or discontinue under subsection (a) of this section.

(d) A rail carrier providing transportation subject to the jurisdiction of the Board under this part may—

(1) abandon any part of its railroad lines; or

(2) discontinue the operation of all rail transportation over any part of its railroad lines;

only if the Board finds that the present or future public convenience and necessity require or permit the abandonment or discontinuance. In making the finding, the Board shall consider whether the abandonment or discontinuance will have a serious, adverse impact on rural and community development.

(e) Subject to this section and sections 10904 and 10905 of this title, if the Board—

(1) finds public convenience and necessity, it shall—

(A) approve the application as filed; or

(B) approve the application with modifications and require compliance with conditions that the Board finds are required by public convenience and necessity; or

(2) fails to find public convenience and necessity, it shall deny the application.

(Added Pub. L. 104–88, title I, §102(a), Dec. 29, 1995, 109 Stat. 823; amended Pub. L. 112–141, div. C, title II, §32932(b), July 6, 2012, 126 Stat. 829.)

[1] See References in Text note below.

§10904. Offers of financial assistance to avoid abandonment and discontinuance

(a) In this section—

(1) the term "avoidable cost" means all expenses that would be incurred by a rail carrier in providing transportation that would not be incurred if the railroad line over which the transportation was provided were abandoned or if the transportation were discontinued. Expenses include cash inflows foregone and cash outflows incurred by the rail carrier as a result of not abandoning or discontinuing the transportation. Cash inflows foregone and cash outflows incurred include—

(A) working capital and required capital expenditure;

(B) expenditures to eliminate deferred maintenance;

(C) the current cost of freight cars, locomotives, and other equipment; and

(D) the foregone tax benefits from not retiring properties from rail service and other effects of applicable Federal and State income taxes; and

(2) the term "reasonable return" means—

(A) if a rail carrier is not in reorganization, the cost of capital to the rail carrier, as determined by the Board; and

(B) if a rail carrier is in reorganization, the mean cost of capital of rail carriers not in reorganization, as determined by the Board.

(b) Any rail carrier which has filed an application for abandonment or discontinuance shall provide promptly to a party considering an offer of financial assistance and shall provide concurrently to the Board—

(1) an estimate of the annual subsidy and minimum purchase price required to keep the line or a portion of the line in operation;

(2) its most recent reports on the physical condition of that part of the railroad line involved in the proposed abandonment or discontinuance;

(3) traffic, revenue, and other data necessary to determine the amount of annual financial assistance which would be required to continue rail transportation over that part of the railroad line; and

(4) any other information that the Board considers necessary to allow a potential offeror to calculate an adequate subsidy or purchase offer.

(c) Within 4 months after an application is filed under section 10903, any person may offer to subsidize or purchase the railroad line that is the subject of such application. Such offer shall be filed concurrently with the Board. If the offer to subsidize or purchase is less than the carrier's estimate stated pursuant to subsection (b)(1), the offer shall explain the basis of the disparity, and the manner in which the offer is calculated.

(d)(1) Unless the Board, within 15 days after the expiration of the 4-month period described in subsection (c), finds that one or more financially responsible persons (including a governmental authority) have offered financial assistance regarding that part of the railroad line to be abandoned or over which all rail transportation is to be discontinued, abandonment or discontinuance may be carried out in accordance with section 10903.

(2) If the Board finds that such an offer or offers of financial assistance has been made within such period, abandonment or discontinuance shall be postponed until—

(A) the carrier and a financially responsible person have reached agreement on a transaction for subsidy or sale of the line; or

(B) the conditions and amount of compensation are established under subsection (f).

(e) Except as provided in subsection (f)(3), if the rail carrier and a financially responsible person (including a governmental authority) fail to agree on the amount or terms of the subsidy or purchase, either party may, within 30 days after the offer is made, request that the Board establish the conditions and amount of compensation.

(f)(1) Whenever the Board is requested to establish the conditions and amount of compensation under this section—

(A) the Board shall render its decision within 30 days;

(B) for proposed sales, the Board shall determine the price and other terms of sale, except that in no case shall the Board set a price which is below the fair market value of the line (including, unless otherwise mutually agreed, all facilities on the line or portion necessary to provide effective transportation services); and

(C) for proposed subsidies, the Board shall establish the compensation as the difference between the revenues attributable to that part of the railroad line and the avoidable cost of providing rail freight transportation on the line, plus a reasonable return on the value of the line.

(2) The decision of the Board shall be binding on both parties, except that the person who has offered to subsidize or purchase the line may withdraw his offer within 10 days of the Board's decision. In such a case, the abandonment or discontinuance may be carried out immediately, unless other offers are being considered pursuant to paragraph (3) of this subsection.

(3) If a rail carrier receives more than one offer to subsidize or purchase, it shall select the offeror with whom it wishes to transact business, and complete the subsidy or sale agreement, or request that the Board establish the conditions and amount of compensation before the 40th day after the expiration of the 4-month period described in subsection (c). If no agreement on subsidy or sale is reached within such 40-day period and the Board has not been requested to establish the conditions and amount of compensation, any other offeror whose offer was made within the 4-month period described in subsection (c) may request that the Board establish the conditions and amount of compensation. If the Board has established the conditions and amount of compensation, and the original offer has been withdrawn, any other offeror whose offer was made within the 4-month period described in subsection (c) may accept the Board's decision within 20 days after such decision, and the Board shall require the carrier to enter into a subsidy or sale agreement with such offeror, if such subsidy or sale agreement incorporates the Board's decision.

(4)(A) No purchaser of a line or portion of line sold under this section may transfer or discontinue service on such line prior to the end of the second year after consummation of the sale, nor may such purchaser transfer such line, except to the rail carrier from whom it was purchased, prior to the end of the fifth year after consummation of the sale.

(B) No subsidy arrangement approved under this section shall remain in effect for more than one year, unless otherwise mutually agreed by the parties.

(g) Upon abandonment of a railroad line under this chapter, the obligation of the rail carrier abandoning the line to provide transportation on that line, as required by section 11101(a), is extinguished.

(Added Pub. L. 104–88, title I, §102(a), Dec. 29, 1995, 109 Stat. 825.)

§10905. OFFERING ABANDONED RAIL PROPERTIES FOR SALE FOR PUBLIC PURPOSES

When the Board approves an application to abandon or discontinue under section 10903, the Board shall find whether the rail properties that are involved in the proposed abandonment or discontinuance are appropriate for use for public purposes, including highways, other forms of mass transportation, conservation, energy production or transmission, or recreation. If the Board finds that the rail properties proposed to be abandoned are appropriate for public purposes and not required for continued rail operations, the properties may be sold, leased, exchanged, or otherwise disposed of only under conditions provided in the order of the Board. The conditions may include a prohibition on any such disposal for a period of not more than 180 days after the effective date of the order, unless the properties have first been offered, on reasonable terms, for sale for public purposes.

(Added Pub. L. 104–88, title I, §102(a), Dec. 29, 1995, 109 Stat. 827.)

§10906. Exception

Notwithstanding section 10901 and subchapter II of chapter 113 of this title, and without the approval of the Board, a rail carrier providing transportation subject to the jurisdiction of the Board under this part may enter into arrangements for the joint ownership or joint use of spur, industrial, team, switching, or side tracks. The Board does not have authority under this chapter over construction, acquisition, operation, abandonment, or discontinuance of spur, industrial, team, switching, or side tracks.

(Added Pub. L. 104–88, title I, §102(a), Dec. 29, 1995, 109 Stat. 827.)

§10907. Railroad development

(a) In this section, the term "financially responsible person" means a person who—

(1) is capable of paying the constitutional minimum value of the railroad line proposed to be acquired; and

(2) is able to assure that adequate transportation will be provided over such line for a period of not less than 3 years.

Such term includes a governmental authority but does not include a Class I or Class II rail carrier.

(b)(1) When the Board finds that—

(A)(i) the public convenience and necessity require or permit the sale of a particular railroad line under this section; or

(ii) a railroad line is on a system diagram map as required under section 10903 of this title, but the rail carrier owning such line has not filed an application to abandon such line under section 10903 of this title before an application to purchase such line, or any required preliminary filing with respect to such application, is filed under this section; and

(B) an application to purchase such line has been filed by a financially responsible person,

the Board shall require the rail carrier owning the railroad line to sell such line to such financially responsible person at a price not less than the constitutional minimum value.

(2) For purposes of this subsection, the constitutional minimum value of a particular railroad line shall be presumed to be not less than the net liquidation value of such line or the going concern value of such line, whichever is greater.

(c)(1) For purposes of this section, the Board may determine that the public convenience and necessity require or permit the sale of a railroad line if the Board determines, after a hearing on the record, that—

(A) the rail carrier operating such line refuses within a reasonable time to make the necessary efforts to provide adequate service to shippers who transport traffic over such line;

(B) the transportation over such line is inadequate for the majority of shippers who transport traffic over such line;

(C) the sale of such line will not have a significantly adverse financial effect on the rail carrier operating such line;

(D) the sale of such line will not have an adverse effect on the overall operational performance of the rail carrier operating such line; and

(E) the sale of such line will be likely to result in improved railroad transportation for shippers that transport traffic over such line.

(2) In a proceeding under this subsection, the burden of proving that the public convenience and necessity require or permit the sale of a particular railroad line is on the person filing the application to acquire such line. If the Board finds under this subsection that the public convenience and necessity require or permit the sale of a particular railroad line, the Board shall concurrently notify the parties of such finding and publish such finding in the Federal Register.

(d) In the case of any railroad line subject to sale under subsection (a) of this section, the Board shall, upon the request of the acquiring carrier, require the selling carrier to provide to the acquiring carrier trackage rights to allow a reasonable interchange with the selling carrier or to move power equipment or empty rolling stock between noncontiguous feeder lines operated by the acquiring carrier. The Board shall require the acquiring carrier to provide the selling carrier reasonable compensation for any such trackage rights.

(e) The Board shall require, to the maximum extent practicable, the use of the employees who would normally have performed work in connection with a railroad line subject to a sale under this section.

(f) In the case of a railroad line which carried less than 3,000,000 gross ton miles of traffic per mile in the preceding calendar year, whenever a purchasing carrier under this section petitions the Board for joint rates applicable to traffic moving over through routes in which the purchasing carrier may practicably participate, the Board shall, within 30 days after the date such petition is filed and pursuant to section 10705(a) of this title, require the establishment of reasonable joint rates and divisions over such route.

(g)(1) Any person operating a railroad line acquired under this section may elect to be exempt from any of the provisions of this part, except that such a person may not be exempt from the provisions of chapter 107 of this title with respect to transportation under a joint rate.

(2) The provisions of paragraph (1) of this subsection shall apply to any line of railroad which was abandoned during the 18-month period immediately prior to October 1, 1980, and was subsequently purchased by a financially responsible person.

(h) If a purchasing carrier under this section proposes to sell or abandon all or any portion of a purchased railroad line, such purchasing carrier shall offer the right of first refusal with respect to such line or portion thereof to the carrier which sold such line under this section. Such offer shall be made at a price equal to the sum of the price paid by such purchasing carrier to such selling carrier for such line or portion thereof and the fair market value (less deterioration) of any improvements made, as adjusted to reflect inflation.

(i) Any person operating a railroad line acquired under this section may determine preconditions, such as payment of a subsidy, which must be met by shippers in order to obtain service over such lines, but such operator must notify the shippers on the line of its intention to impose such preconditions.

(Added Pub. L. 104–88, title I, §102(a), Dec. 29, 1995, 109 Stat. 828.)

§10908. REGULATION OF SOLID WASTE RAIL TRANSFER FACILITIES

(a) IN GENERAL.—Each solid waste rail transfer facility shall be subject to and shall comply with all applicable Federal and State requirements, both substantive and procedural, including judicial and administrative orders and fines, respecting the prevention and abatement of pollution, the protection and restoration of the environment, and the protection of public health and safety, including laws governing solid waste, to the same extent as required for any similar solid waste management facility, as defined in section 1004(29) of the Solid Waste Disposal Act (42 U.S.C. 6903(29)) [1] that is not owned or operated by or on behalf of a rail carrier, except as provided for in section 10909 of this chapter.

(b) EXISTING FACILITIES.—

(1) STATE LAWS AND STANDARDS.—Not later than 90 days after the date of enactment of the Clean Railroads Act of 2008, a solid waste rail transfer facility operating as of such date of enactment shall comply with all Federal and State requirements pursuant to subsection (a) other than those provisions requiring permits.

(2) PERMIT REQUIREMENTS.—

(A) STATE NON-SITING PERMITS.—Any solid waste rail transfer facility operating as of the date of enactment of the Clean Railroads Act of 2008 that does not possess a permit required pursuant to subsection (a), other than a siting permit for the facility, as of the date of enactment of the Clean Railroads Act of 2008 shall not be required to possess any such permits in order to operate the facility—

(i) if, within 180 days after such date of enactment, the solid waste rail transfer facility has submitted, in good faith, a complete application for all permits, except siting permits, required pursuant to subsection (a) to the appropriate permitting agency authorized to grant such permits; and

(ii) until the permitting agency has either approved or denied the solid waste rail transfer facility's application for each permit.

(B) SITING PERMITS AND REQUIREMENTS.—A solid waste rail transfer facility operating as of the date of enactment of the Clean Railroads Act of 2008 that does not possess a State siting permit required pursuant to subsection (a) as of such date of enactment shall not be required to possess any siting permit to continue to operate or comply with any State land use requirements. The Governor of a State in which the facility is located, or his or her designee, may petition the Board to require the facility to apply for a land-use exemption pursuant to section 10909 of this chapter. The Board shall accept the petition, and the facility shall be required to have a Board-issued land-use exemption in order to continue to operate, pursuant to section 10909 of this chapter.

(c) COMMON CARRIER OBLIGATION.—No prospective or current rail carrier customer may demand solid waste rail transfer service from a rail carrier at a solid waste rail transfer facility that does not already possess the necessary Federal land-use exemption and State permits at the location where service is requested.

(d) NON-WASTE COMMODITIES.—Nothing in this section or section 10909 of this chapter shall affect a rail carrier's ability to conduct transportation-related activities with respect to commodities other than solid waste.

(e) DEFINITIONS.—

(1) IN GENERAL.—In this section:

(A) COMMERCIAL AND RETAIL WASTE.—The term "commercial and retail waste" means material discarded by stores, offices, restaurants, warehouses, nonmanufacturing activities at industrial facilities, and other similar establishments or facilities.

(B) CONSTRUCTION AND DEMOLITION DEBRIS.—The term "construction and demolition debris" means waste building materials, packaging, and rubble resulting from construction, remodeling, repair, and demolition operations on pavements, houses, commercial buildings, and other structures.

(C) HOUSEHOLD WASTE.—The term "household waste" means material discarded by residential dwellings, hotels, motels, and other similar permanent or temporary housing establishments or facilities.

(D) INDUSTRIAL WASTE.—The term "industrial waste" means the solid waste generated by manufacturing and industrial and research and development processes and operations, including contaminated soil, nonhazardous oil spill cleanup waste and dry nonhazardous pesticides and chemical waste, but does not include hazardous waste regulated under subtitle C of the Solid Waste Disposal Act (42 U.S.C. 6921 et seq.), mining or oil and gas waste.

(E) INSTITUTIONAL WASTE.—The term "institutional waste" means material discarded by schools, nonmedical waste discarded by hospitals, material discarded by nonmanufacturing activities at prisons and government facilities, and material discarded by other similar establishments or facilities.

(F) MUNICIPAL SOLID WASTE.—The term "municipal solid waste" means—

(i) household waste;

(ii) commercial and retail waste; and

(iii) institutional waste.

(G) SOLID WASTE.—With the exception of waste generated by a rail carrier during track, track structure, or right-of-way construction, maintenance, or repair (including railroad ties and line-side poles) or waste generated as a result of a railroad accident, incident, or derailment, the term "solid waste" means—

(i) construction and demolition debris;

(ii) municipal solid waste;

(iii) household waste;

(iv) commercial and retail waste;

(v) institutional waste;

(vi) sludge;

(vii) industrial waste; and

(viii) other solid waste, as determined appropriate by the Board.

(H) Solid waste rail transfer facility.—The term "solid waste rail transfer facility"—

(i) means the portion of a facility owned or operated by or on behalf of a rail carrier (as defined in section 10102 of this title) where solid waste, as a commodity to be transported for a charge, is collected, stored, separated, processed, treated, managed, disposed of, or transferred, when the activity takes place outside of original shipping containers; but

(ii) does not include—

(I) the portion of a facility to the extent that activities taking place at such portion are comprised solely of the railroad transportation of solid waste after the solid waste is loaded for shipment on or in a rail car, including railroad transportation for the purpose of interchanging railroad cars containing solid waste shipments; or

(II) a facility where solid waste is solely transferred or transloaded from a tank truck directly to a rail tank car.

(I) Sludge.—The term "sludge" means any solid, semi-solid or liquid waste generated from a municipal, commercial, or industrial wastewater treatment plant, water supply treatment plant, or air pollution control facility exclusive of the treated effluent from a wastewater treatment plant.

(2) Exceptions.—Notwithstanding paragraph (1), the terms "household waste", "commercial and retail waste", and "institutional waste" do not include—

(A) yard waste and refuse-derived fuel;

(B) used oil;

(C) wood pallets;

(D) clean wood;

(E) medical or infectious waste; or

(F) motor vehicles (including motor vehicle parts or vehicle fluff).

(3) State requirements.—In this section the term "State requirements" does not include the laws, regulations, ordinances, orders, or other requirements of a political subdivision of a State, including a locality or municipality, unless a State expressly delegates such authority to such political subdivision.

(Added Pub. L. 110–432, div. A, title VI, §603(a), Oct. 16, 2008, 122 Stat. 4900.)

---

[1] *So in original. Probably should be followed by a comma.*

§10909. Solid waste rail transfer facility land-use exemption

(a) Authority.—The Board may issue a land-use exemption for a solid waste rail transfer facility that is or is proposed to be operated by or on behalf of a rail carrier if—

(1) the Board finds that a State, local, or municipal law, regulation, order, or other requirement affecting the siting of such facility unreasonably burdens the interstate

transportation of solid waste by railroad, discriminates against the railroad transportation of solid waste and a solid waste rail transfer facility, or a rail carrier that owns or operates such a facility petitions the Board for such an exemption; or

(2) the Governor of a State in which a facility that is operating as of the date of enactment of the Clean Railroads Act of 2008 is located, or his or her designee, petitions the Board to initiate a permit proceeding for that particular facility.

(b) LAND-USE EXEMPTION PROCEDURES.—Not later than 90 days after the date of enactment of the Clean Railroads Act of 2008, the Board shall publish procedures governing the submission and review of applications for solid waste rail transfer facility land-use exemptions. At a minimum, the procedures shall address—

(1) the information that each application should contain to explain how the solid waste rail transfer facility will not pose an unreasonable risk to public health, safety, or the environment;

(2) the opportunity for public notice and comment including notification of the municipality, the State, and any relevant Federal or State regional planning entity in the jurisdiction of which the solid waste rail transfer facility is proposed to be located;

(3) the timeline for Board review, including a requirement that the Board approve or deny an exemption within 90 days after the full record for the application is developed;

(4) the expedited review timelines for petitions for modifications, amendments, or revocations of granted exemptions;

(5) the process for a State to petition the Board to require a solid waste transfer facility or a rail carrier that owns or operates such a facility to apply for a siting permit; and

(6) the process for a solid waste transfer facility or a rail carrier that owns or operates such a facility to petition the Board for a land-use exemption.

(c) STANDARD FOR REVIEW.—

(1) The Board may only issue a land-use exemption if it determines that the facility at the existing or proposed location does not pose an unreasonable risk to public health, safety, or the environment. In deciding whether a solid waste rail transfer facility that is or proposed to be constructed or operated by or on behalf of a rail carrier poses an unreasonable risk to public health, safety, or the environment, the Board shall weigh the particular facility's potential benefits to and the adverse impacts on public health, public safety, the environment, interstate commerce, and transportation of solid waste by rail.

(2) The Board may not grant a land-use exemption for a solid waste rail transfer facility proposed to be located on land within any unit of or land affiliated with the National Park System, the National Wildlife Refuge System, the National Wilderness Preservation System, the National Trails System, the National Wild and Scenic Rivers System, a National Reserve, a National Monument, or lands referenced in Public Law 108–421 for which a State has implemented a conservation management plan, if operation of the facility would be inconsistent with restrictions placed on such land.

(d) CONSIDERATIONS.—When evaluating an application under this section, the Board shall consider and give due weight to the following, as applicable:

(1) the land-use, zoning, and siting regulations or solid waste planning requirements of

the State or State subdivision in which the facility is or will be located that are applicable to solid waste transfer facilities, including those that are not owned or operated by or on behalf of a rail carrier;

(2) the land-use, zoning, and siting regulations or solid waste planning requirements applicable to the property where the solid waste rail transfer facility is proposed to be located;

(3) regional transportation planning requirements developed pursuant to Federal and State law;

(4) regional solid waste disposal plans developed pursuant to State or Federal law;

(5) any Federal and State environmental protection laws or regulations applicable to the site;

(6) any unreasonable burdens imposed on the interstate transportation of solid waste by railroad, or the potential for discrimination against the railroad transportation of solid waste, a solid waste rail transfer facility, or a rail carrier that owns or operates such a facility; and

(7) any other relevant factors, as determined by the Board.

(e) EXISTING FACILITIES.—Upon the granting of a petition from the State in which a solid waste rail transfer facility is operating as of the date of enactment of the Clean Railroads Act of 2008 by the Board, the facility shall submit a complete application for a siting permit to the Board pursuant to the procedures issued pursuant to subsection (b). No State may enforce a law, regulation, order, or other requirement affecting the siting of a facility that is operating as of the date of enactment of the Clean Railroads Act of 2008 until the Board has approved or denied a permit pursuant to subsection (c).

(f) EFFECT OF LAND-USE EXEMPTION.—If the Board grants a land-use exemption to a solid waste rail transfer facility, all State laws, regulations, orders, or other requirements affecting the siting of a facility are preempted with regard to that facility. An exemption may require compliance with such State laws, regulations, orders, or other requirements.

(g) INJUNCTIVE RELIEF.—Nothing in this section precludes a person from seeking an injunction to enjoin a solid waste rail transfer facility from being constructed or operated by or on behalf of a rail carrier if that facility has materially violated, or will materially violate, its land-use exemption or if it failed to receive a valid land-use exemption under this section.

(h) FEES.—The Board may charge permit applicants reasonable fees to implement this section, including the costs of third-party consultants.

(i) DEFINITIONS.—In this section the terms "solid waste", "solid waste rail transfer facility", and "State requirements" have the meaning given such terms in section 10908(e).

(Added Pub. L. 110–432, div. A, title VI, §604(a), Oct. 16, 2008, 122 Stat. 4903; amended Pub. L. 114–94, div. A, title XI, §11316(b), Dec. 4, 2015, 129 Stat. 1676.)

§10910. EFFECT ON OTHER STATUTES AND AUTHORITIES

Nothing in section 10908 or 10909 is intended to affect the traditional police powers of the State to require a rail carrier to comply with State and local environmental, public health, and public safety standards that are not unreasonably burdensome to interstate commerce and do not discriminate against rail carriers.

(Added Pub. L. 110–432, div. A, title VI, §605(a), Oct. 16, 2008, 122 Stat. 4905.)

SUBCHAPTER I—GENERAL REQUIREMENTS

§11101. COMMON CARRIER TRANSPORTATION, SERVICE, AND RATES

(a) A rail carrier providing transportation or service subject to the jurisdiction of the Board under this part shall provide the transportation or service on reasonable request. A rail carrier shall not be found to have violated this section because it fulfills its reasonable commitments under contracts authorized under section 10709 of this title before responding to reasonable requests for service. Commitments which deprive a carrier of its ability to respond to reasonable requests for common carrier service are not reasonable.

(b) A rail carrier shall also provide to any person, on request, the carrier's rates and other service terms. The response by a rail carrier to a request for the carrier's rates and other service terms shall be—

(1) in writing and forwarded to the requesting person promptly after receipt of the

153

request; or

(2) promptly made available in electronic form.

(c) A rail carrier may not increase any common carrier rates or change any common carrier service terms unless 20 days have expired after written or electronic notice is provided to any person who, within the previous 12 months—

(1) has requested such rates or terms under subsection (b); or

(2) has made arrangements with the carrier for a shipment that would be subject to such increased rates or changed terms.

(d) With respect to transportation of agricultural products, in addition to the requirements of subsections (a), (b), and (c), a rail carrier shall publish, make available, and retain for public inspection its common carrier rates, schedules of rates, and other service terms, and any proposed and actual changes to such rates and service terms. For purposes of this subsection, agricultural products shall include grain as defined in section 3 of the United States Grain Standards Act (7 U.S.C. 75) and all products thereof, and fertilizer.

(e) A rail carrier shall provide transportation or service in accordance with the rates and service terms, and any changes thereto, as published or otherwise made available under subsection (b), (c), or (d).

(f) The Board shall, by regulation, establish rules to implement this section. The regulations shall provide for immediate disclosure and dissemination of rates and service terms, including classifications, rules, and practices, and their effective dates. Final regulations shall be adopted by the Board not later than 180 days after January 1, 1996.

(Added Pub. L. 104–88, title I, §102(a), Dec. 29, 1995, 109 Stat. 830; amended Pub. L. 104–287, §5(25), Oct. 11, 1996, 110 Stat. 3390.)

§11102. USE OF TERMINAL FACILITIES

(a) The Board may require terminal facilities, including main-line tracks for a reasonable distance outside of a terminal, owned by a rail carrier providing transportation subject to the jurisdiction of the Board under this part, to be used by another rail carrier if the Board finds that use to be practicable and in the public interest without substantially impairing the ability of the rail carrier owning the facilities or entitled to use the facilities to handle its own business. The rail carriers are responsible for establishing the conditions and compensation for use of the facilities. However, if the rail carriers cannot agree, the Board may establish conditions and compensation for use of the facilities under the principle controlling compensation in condemnation proceedings. The compensation shall be paid or adequately secured before a rail carrier may begin to use the facilities of another rail carrier under this section.

(b) A rail carrier whose terminal facilities are required to be used by another rail carrier under this section is entitled to recover damages from the other rail carrier for injuries sustained as the result of compliance with the requirement or for compensation for the use, or both as appropriate, in a civil action, if it is not satisfied with the conditions for use of the facilities or if the amount of the compensation is not paid promptly.

(c)(1) The Board may require rail carriers to enter into reciprocal switching agreements, where it finds such agreements to be practicable and in the public interest, or where such agreements are necessary to provide competitive rail service. The rail carriers entering into such an agreement shall establish the conditions and compensation applicable to such agreement, but, if the rail carriers cannot agree upon such conditions and compensation within a reasonable period of time, the Board may establish such conditions and compensation.

(2) The Board may require reciprocal switching agreements entered into by rail carriers pursuant to this subsection to contain provisions for the protection of the interests of employees affected thereby.

(d) The Board shall complete any proceeding under subsection (a) or (b) within 180 days after the filing of the request for relief.

(Added Pub. L. 104–88, title I, §102(a), Dec. 29, 1995, 109 Stat. 831.)

§11103. Switch connections and tracks

(a) On application of the owner of a lateral branch line of railroad, or of a shipper tendering interstate traffic for transportation, a rail carrier providing transportation subject to the jurisdiction of the Board under this part shall construct, maintain, and operate, on reasonable conditions, a switch connection to connect that branch line or private side track with its railroad and shall furnish cars to move that traffic to the best of its ability without discrimination in favor of or against the shipper when the connection—

(1) is reasonably practicable;

(2) can be made safely; and

(3) will furnish sufficient business to justify its construction and maintenance.

(b) If a rail carrier fails to install and operate a switch connection after application is made under subsection (a) of this section, the owner of the lateral branch line of railroad or the shipper may file a complaint with the Board under section 11701 of this title. The Board shall investigate the complaint and decide the safety, practicability, justification, and compensation to be paid for the connection. The Board may direct the rail carrier to comply with subsection (a) of this section only after a full hearing.

(Added Pub. L. 104–88, title I, §102(a), Dec. 29, 1995, 109 Stat. 831.)

SUBCHAPTER II—CAR SERVICE

§11121. Criteria

(a)(1) A rail carrier providing transportation subject to the jurisdiction of the Board under this part shall furnish safe and adequate car service and establish, observe, and enforce reasonable rules and practices on car service. The Board may require a rail carrier to provide facilities and equipment that are reasonably necessary to furnish safe and adequate car service if the Board decides that the rail carrier has materially failed to furnish that service. The Board may begin a proceeding under this paragraph when an interested person files an application with it. The Board may act only after a hearing on the record and an affirmative finding, based on the evidence presented, that—

(A) providing the facilities or equipment will not materially and adversely affect the ability of the rail carrier to provide safe and adequate transportation;

(B) the amount spent for the facilities or equipment, including a return equal to the rail carrier's current cost of capital, will be recovered; and

(C) providing the facilities or equipment will not impair the ability of the rail carrier to attract adequate capital.

(2) The Board may require a rail carrier to file its car service rules with the Board.

(b) The Board may designate and appoint agents and agencies to make and carry out its directions related to car service and matters under sections 11123 and 11124(a)(1) of this title.

(c) The Board shall consult, as it considers necessary, with the National Grain Car Council on matters within the charter of that body.

(Added Pub. L. 104–88, title I, §102(a), Dec. 29, 1995, 109 Stat. 832.)

§11122. COMPENSATION AND PRACTICE

(a) The regulations of the Board on car service shall encourage the purchase, acquisition, and efficient use of freight cars. The regulations may include—

(1) the compensation to be paid for the use of a locomotive, freight car, or other vehicle;

(2) the other terms of any arrangement for the use by a rail carrier of a locomotive, freight car, or other vehicle not owned by the rail carrier using the locomotive, freight car, or other vehicle, whether or not owned by another carrier, shipper, or third person; and

(3) sanctions for nonobservance.

(b) The rate of compensation to be paid for each type of freight car shall be determined by the expense of owning and maintaining that type of freight car, including a fair return on its cost giving consideration to current costs of capital, repairs, materials, parts, and labor. In determining the rate of compensation, the Board shall consider the transportation use of each type of freight car, the national level of ownership of each type of freight car, and other factors that affect the adequacy of the national freight car supply.

(Added Pub. L. 104–88, title I, §102(a), Dec. 29, 1995, 109 Stat. 832.)

§11123. SITUATIONS REQUIRING IMMEDIATE ACTION TO SERVE THE PUBLIC

(a) When the Board determines that shortage of equipment, congestion of traffic, unauthorized cessation of operations, failure of existing commuter rail passenger transportation operations caused by a cessation of service by the National Railroad Passenger Corporation, or other failure of traffic movement exists which creates an emergency situation of such magnitude as to have substantial adverse effects on shippers, or on rail service in a region of the United States, or that a rail carrier providing transportation subject to the jurisdiction of the Board under this part cannot transport the traffic offered to it in a manner that properly serves the public, the Board may, to promote commerce and service to the public, for a period not to exceed 30 days—

(1) direct the handling, routing, and movement of the traffic of a rail carrier and its distribution over its own or other railroad lines;

(2) require joint or common use of railroad facilities;

(3) prescribe temporary through routes;

(4) give directions for—

(A) preference or priority in transportation;

(B) embargoes; or

(C) movement of traffic under permits; or

(5) in the case of a failure of existing freight or commuter rail passenger transportation operations caused by a cessation of service by the National Railroad Passenger Corporation, direct the continuation of the operations and dispatching, maintenance, and other necessary infrastructure functions related to the operations.

(b)(1) Except with respect to proceedings under paragraph (2) of this subsection, the Board may act under this section on its own initiative or on application without regard to subchapter II of chapter 5 of title 5.

(2) Rail carriers may establish between themselves the terms of compensation for operations, and use of facilities and equipment, required under this section. When rail carriers do not agree on the terms of compensation under this section, the Board may establish the terms for them. The Board may act under subsection (a) before conducting a proceeding under this paragraph.

(3)(A) Except as provided in subparagraph (B), when a rail carrier is directed under this section to operate the lines of another rail carrier due to that carrier's cessation of operations, compensation for the directed operations shall derive only from revenues generated by the directed operations.

(B) In the case of a failure of existing freight or commuter rail passenger transportation operations caused by a cessation of service by the National Railroad Passenger Corporation, the Board shall provide funding to fully reimburse the directed service provider for its costs associated with the activities directed under subsection (a), including the payment of increased insurance premiums. The Board shall order complete indemnification against any and all claims associated with the provision of service to which the directed rail carrier may be exposed.

(c)(1) The Board may extend any action taken under subsection (a) of this section beyond 30 days if the Board finds that a transportation emergency described in subsection (a) continues to exist. Action by the Board under subsection (a) of this section may not remain in effect for more than 240 days beyond the initial 30-day period.

(2) The Board may not take action under this section that would—

(A) cause a rail carrier to operate in violation of this part; or

(B) impair substantially the ability of a rail carrier to serve its own customers adequately, or to fulfill its common carrier obligations.

(3) A rail carrier directed by the Board to take action under this section is not responsible,

as a result of that action, for debts of any other rail carrier.

(4) In the case of a failure of existing freight or commuter rail passenger transportation operations caused by cessation of service by the National Railroad Passenger Corporation, the Board may not direct a rail carrier to undertake activities under subsection (a) to continue such operations unless—

(A) the Board first affirmatively finds that the rail carrier is operationally capable of conducting the directed service in a safe and efficient manner; and

(B) the funding for such directed service required by subparagraph (B) of subsection (b)(3) is provided in advance in appropriations Acts.

(d) In carrying out this section, the Board shall require, to the maximum extent practicable, the use of employees who would normally have performed work in connection with the traffic subject to the action of the Board.

(e) For purposes of this section, the National Railroad Passenger Corporation and any entity providing commuter rail passenger transportation shall be considered rail carriers subject to the Board's jurisdiction.

(f) For purposes of this section, the term "commuter rail passenger transportation" has the meaning given that term in section 24102(4).[1]

(Added Pub. L. 104–88, title I, §102(a), Dec. 29, 1995, 109 Stat. 833; amended Pub. L. 108–199, div. F, title I, §150(1), Jan. 23, 2004, 118 Stat. 302.)

---

[1] *See References in Text note below.*

§11124. WAR EMERGENCIES; EMBARGOES IMPOSED BY CARRIERS

(a)(1) When the President, during time of war or threatened war, notifies the Board that it is essential to the defense and security of the United States to give preference or priority to the movement of certain traffic, the Board shall direct that preference or priority be given to that traffic.

(2) When the President, during time of war or threatened war, demands that preference and precedence be given to the transportation of troops and material of war over all other traffic, all rail carriers providing transportation subject to the jurisdiction of the Board under this part shall adopt every means within their control to facilitate and expedite the military traffic.

(b) An embargo imposed by any such rail carrier does not apply to shipments consigned to agents of the United States Government for its use. The rail carrier shall deliver those shipments as promptly as possible.

(Added Pub. L. 104–88, title I, §102(a), Dec. 29, 1995, 109 Stat. 834.)

SUBCHAPTER III—REPORTS AND RECORDS

§11141. DEFINITIONS

In this subchapter—

(1) the terms "rail carrier" and "lessor" include a receiver or trustee of a rail carrier and

lessor, respectively;

(2) the term "lessor" means a person owning a railroad that is leased to and operated by a carrier providing transportation subject to the jurisdiction of the Board under this part; and

(3) the term "association" means an organization maintained by or in the interest of a group of rail carriers providing transportation or service subject to the jurisdiction of the Board under this part that performs a service, or engages in activities, related to transportation under this part.

(Added Pub. L. 104–88, title I, §102(a), Dec. 29, 1995, 109 Stat. 834.)

§11142. UNIFORM ACCOUNTING SYSTEM

The Board may prescribe a uniform accounting system for classes of rail carriers providing transportation subject to the jurisdiction of the Board under this part. To the maximum extent practicable, the Board shall conform such system to generally accepted accounting principles, and shall administer this subchapter in accordance with such principles.

(Added Pub. L. 104–88, title I, §102(a), Dec. 29, 1995, 109 Stat. 834.)

§11143. DEPRECIATION CHARGES

The Board shall, for a class of rail carriers providing transportation subject to its jurisdiction under this part, prescribe, and change when necessary, those classes of property for which depreciation charges may be included under operating expenses and a rate of depreciation that may be charged to a class of property. The Board may classify those rail carriers for purposes of this section. A rail carrier for whom depreciation charges and rates of depreciation are in effect under this section for any class of property may not—

(1) charge to operating expenses a depreciation charge on a class of property other than that prescribed by the Board;

(2) charge another rate of depreciation; or

(3) include other depreciation charges in operating expenses.

(Added Pub. L. 104–88, title I, §102(a), Dec. 29, 1995, 109 Stat. 834.)

§11144. RECORDS: FORM; INSPECTION; PRESERVATION

(a) The Board may prescribe the form of records required to be prepared or compiled under this subchapter—

(1) by rail carriers and lessors, including records related to movement of traffic and receipts and expenditures of money; and

(2) by persons furnishing cars to or for a rail carrier providing transportation subject to the jurisdiction of the Board under this part to the extent related to those cars or that service.

(b) The Board, or an employee designated by the Board, may on demand and display of proper credentials—

(1) inspect and examine the lands, buildings, and equipment of a rail carrier or lessor; and

(2) inspect and copy any record of—

(A) a rail carrier, lessor, or association;

(B) a person controlling, controlled by, or under common control with a rail carrier if the Board considers inspection relevant to that person's relation to, or transaction with, that rail carrier; and

(C) a person furnishing cars to or for a rail carrier if the Board prescribed the form of that record.

(c) The Board may prescribe the time period during which operating, accounting, and financial records must be preserved by rail carriers, lessors, and persons furnishing cars.

(Added Pub. L. 104–88, title I, §102(a), Dec. 29, 1995, 109 Stat. 835.)

§11145. REPORTS BY RAIL CARRIERS, LESSORS, AND ASSOCIATIONS

(a) The Board may require—

(1) rail carriers, lessors, and associations, or classes of them as the Board may prescribe, to file annual, periodic, and special reports with the Board containing answers to questions asked by it; and

(2) a person furnishing cars to a rail carrier to file reports with the Board containing answers to questions about those cars.

(b)(1) An annual report shall contain an account, in as much detail as the Board may require, of the affairs of the rail carrier, lessor, or association for the 12-month period ending on December 31 of each year.

(2) An annual report shall be filed with the Board by the end of the third month after the end of the year for which the report is made unless the Board extends the filing date or changes the period covered by the report. The annual report and, if the Board requires, any other report made under this section, shall be made under oath.

(Added Pub. L. 104–88, title I, §102(a), Dec. 29, 1995, 109 Stat. 835.)

SUBCHAPTER IV—RAILROAD COST ACCOUNTING

§11161. IMPLEMENTATION OF COST ACCOUNTING PRINCIPLES

The Board shall periodically review its cost accounting rules and shall make such changes in those rules as are required to achieve the regulatory purposes of this part. The Board shall insure that the rules promulgated under this section are the most efficient and least burdensome means by which the required information may be developed for regulatory purposes. To the maximum extent practicable, the Board shall conform such rules to generally accepted accounting principles.

(Added Pub. L. 104–88, title I, §102(a), Dec. 29, 1995, 109 Stat. 835.)

§11162. Rail carrier cost accounting system

(a) Each rail carrier shall have and maintain a cost accounting system that is in compliance with the rules promulgated by the Board under section 11161 of this title. A rail carrier may, after notifying the Board, make modifications in such system unless, within 60 days after the date of notification, the Board finds such modifications to be inconsistent with the rules promulgated by the Board under section 11161 of this title.

(b) For purposes of determining whether the cost accounting system of a rail carrier is in compliance with the rules promulgated by the Board, the Board shall have the right to examine and make copies of any documents, papers, or records of such rail carrier relating to compliance with such rules. Such documents, papers, and records (and any copies thereof) shall not be subject to the mandatory disclosure requirements of section 552 of title 5.

(Added Pub. L. 104–88, title I, §102(a), Dec. 29, 1995, 109 Stat. 836.)

§11163. Cost availability

As required by the rules of the Board governing discovery in Board proceedings, rail carriers shall make relevant cost data available to shippers, States, ports, communities, and other interested parties that are a party to a Board proceeding in which such data are required.

(Added Pub. L. 104–88, title I, §102(a), Dec. 29, 1995, 109 Stat. 836.)

§11164. Accounting and cost reporting

To obtain expense and revenue information for regulatory purposes, the Board may promulgate reasonable rules for rail carriers providing transportation subject to the jurisdiction of the Board under this part, prescribing expense and revenue accounting and reporting requirements consistent with generally accepted accounting principles uniformly applied to such carriers. Such requirements shall be cost effective and compatible with and not duplicative of the managerial and responsibility accounting requirements of those carriers.

(Added Pub. L. 104–88, title I, §102(a), Dec. 29, 1995, 109 Stat. 836.)

CHAPTER 113—FINANCE

SUBCHAPTER I—EQUIPMENT TRUSTS AND SECURITY INTERESTS

SUBCHAPTER II—COMBINATIONS

SUBCHAPTER I—EQUIPMENT TRUSTS AND SECURITY INTERESTS

§11301. EQUIPMENT TRUSTS: RECORDATION; EVIDENCE OF INDEBTEDNESS

(a) A mortgage (other than a mortgage under chapter 313 of title 46), lease, equipment trust agreement, conditional sales agreement, or other instrument evidencing the mortgage, lease, conditional sale, or bailment of or security interest in vessels, railroad cars, locomotives, or other rolling stock, or accessories used on such railroad cars, locomotives, or other rolling stock (including superstructures and racks), intended for a use related to interstate commerce shall be filed with the Board in order to perfect the security interest that is the subject of such instrument. An assignment of a right or interest under one of those instruments and an amendment to that instrument or assignment including a release, discharge, or satisfaction of any part of it shall also be filed with the Board. The instrument, assignment, or amendment must be in writing, executed by the parties to it, and acknowledged or verified under Board regulations. When filed under this section, that document is notice to, and enforceable against, all persons. A document filed under this section does not have to be filed, deposited, registered, or recorded under another law of the United States, a State (or its political subdivisions), or territory or possession of the United States, related to filing, deposit, registration, or recordation of those documents. This section does not change chapter 313 of title 46.

(b) The Board shall maintain a system for recording each document filed under subsection (a) of this section and mark each of them with a consecutive number and the date and hour of their recordation. The Board shall maintain and keep open for public inspection an index of documents filed under that subsection. That index shall include the name and address of the principal debtors, trustees, guarantors, and other parties to those documents and may include other facts that will assist in determining the rights of the parties to those transactions.

(c) The Board may to the greatest extent practicable perform its functions under this section through contracts with private sector entities.

(d) A mortgage, lease, equipment trust agreement, conditional sales agreement, or other instrument evidencing the mortgage, lease, conditional sale, or bailment of or security interest in vessels, railroad cars, locomotives, or other rolling stock, or accessories used on such railroad cars, locomotives, or other rolling stock (including superstructures and racks), or any assignment thereof, which—

(1) is duly constituted under the laws of a country other than the United States; and

(2) relates to property that bears the reporting marks and identification numbers of any person domiciled in or corporation organized under the laws of such country,

shall be recognized with the same effect as having been filed under this section.

(e) Interests with respect to which documents are filed or recognized under this section are deemed perfected in all jurisdictions, and shall be governed by applicable State or foreign law in all matters not specifically governed by this section.

(f) The Board shall collect, maintain, and keep open for public inspection a railway equipment register consistent with the manner and format maintained by the Interstate Commerce Commission as of January 1, 1996.

(Added Pub. L. 104–88, title I, §102(a), Dec. 29, 1995, 109 Stat. 837; amended Pub. L. 104–287, §5(25), Oct. 11, 1996, 110 Stat. 3390.)

SUBCHAPTER II—COMBINATIONS

§11321. Scope of authority

(a) The authority of the Board under this subchapter is exclusive. A rail carrier or corporation participating in or resulting from a transaction approved by or exempted by the Board under this subchapter may carry out the transaction, own and operate property, and exercise control or franchises acquired through the transaction without the approval of a State authority. A rail carrier, corporation, or person participating in that approved or exempted transaction is exempt from the antitrust laws and from all other law, including State and municipal law, as necessary to let that rail carrier, corporation, or person carry out the transaction, hold, maintain, and operate property, and exercise control or franchises acquired through the transaction. However, if a purchase and sale, a lease, or a corporate consolidation or merger is involved in the transaction, the carrier or corporation may carry out the transaction only with the assent of a majority, or the number required under applicable State law, of the votes of the holders of the capital stock of that corporation entitled to vote. The vote must occur at a regular meeting, or special meeting called for that purpose, of those stockholders and the notice of the meeting must indicate its purpose.

(b) A power granted under this subchapter to a carrier or corporation is in addition to and changes its powers under its corporate charter and under State law. Action under this subchapter does not establish or provide for establishing a corporation under the laws of the

United States.

(Added Pub. L. 104–88, title I, §102(a), Dec. 29, 1995, 109 Stat. 838.)

§11322. LIMITATION ON POOLING AND DIVISION OF TRANSPORTATION OR EARNINGS

(a) A rail carrier providing transportation subject to the jurisdiction of the Board under this part may not agree or combine with another of those rail carriers to pool or divide traffic or services or any part of their earnings without the approval of the Board under this section or section 11123 of this title. The Board may approve and authorize the agreement or combination if the rail carriers involved assent to the pooling or division and the Board finds that a pooling or division of traffic, services, or earnings—

(1) will be in the interest of better service to the public or of economy of operation; and

(2) will not unreasonably restrain competition.

(b) The Board may impose conditions governing the pooling or division and may approve and authorize payment of a reasonable consideration between the rail carriers.

(c) The Board may begin a proceeding under this section on its own initiative or on application.

(Added Pub. L. 104–88, title I, §102(a), Dec. 29, 1995, 109 Stat. 838.)

§11323. CONSOLIDATION, MERGER, AND ACQUISITION OF CONTROL

(a) The following transactions involving rail carriers providing transportation subject to the jurisdiction of the Board under this part may be carried out only with the approval and authorization of the Board:

(1) Consolidation or merger of the properties or franchises of at least 2 rail carriers into one corporation for the ownership, management, and operation of the previously separately owned properties.

(2) A purchase, lease, or contract to operate property of another rail carrier by any number of rail carriers.

(3) Acquisition of control of a rail carrier by any number of rail carriers.

(4) Acquisition of control of at least 2 rail carriers by a person that is not a rail carrier.

(5) Acquisition of control of a rail carrier by a person that is not a rail carrier but that controls any number of rail carriers.

(6) Acquisition by a rail carrier of trackage rights over, or joint ownership in or joint use of, a railroad line (and terminals incidental to it) owned or operated by another rail carrier.

(b) A person may carry out a transaction referred to in subsection (a) of this section or participate in achieving the control or management, including the power to exercise control or management, in a common interest of more than one of those rail carriers, regardless of how that result is reached, only with the approval and authorization of the Board under this subchapter. In addition to other transactions, each of the following transactions are considered achievements of control or management:

(1) A transaction by a rail carrier that has the effect of putting that rail carrier and person affiliated with it, taken together, in control of another rail carrier.

(2) A transaction by a person affiliated with a rail carrier that has the effect of putting that rail carrier and persons affiliated with it, taken together, in control of another rail carrier.

(3) A transaction by at least 2 persons acting together (one of whom is a rail carrier or is affiliated with a rail carrier) that has the effect of putting those persons and rail carriers and persons affiliated with any of them, or with any of those affiliated rail carriers, taken together, in control of another rail carrier.

(c) A person is affiliated with a rail carrier under this subchapter if, because of the relationship between that person and a rail carrier, it is reasonable to believe that the affairs of another rail carrier, control of which may be acquired by that person, will be managed in the interest of the other rail carrier.

(Added Pub. L. 104–88, title I, §102(a), Dec. 29, 1995, 109 Stat. 838.)

§11324. Consolidation, merger, and acquisition of control: conditions of approval

(a) The Board may begin a proceeding to approve and authorize a transaction referred to in section 11323 of this title on application of the person seeking that authority. When an application is filed with the Board, the Board shall notify the chief executive officer of each State in which property of the rail carriers involved in the proposed transaction is located and shall notify those rail carriers. The Board shall hold a public hearing unless the Board determines that a public hearing is not necessary in the public interest.

(b) In a proceeding under this section which involves the merger or control of at least two Class I railroads, as defined by the Board, the Board shall consider at least—

(1) the effect of the proposed transaction on the adequacy of transportation to the public;

(2) the effect on the public interest of including, or failing to include, other rail carriers in the area involved in the proposed transaction;

(3) the total fixed charges that result from the proposed transaction;

(4) the interest of rail carrier employees affected by the proposed transaction; and

(5) whether the proposed transaction would have an adverse effect on competition among rail carriers in the affected region or in the national rail system.

(c) The Board shall approve and authorize a transaction under this section when it finds the transaction is consistent with the public interest. The Board may impose conditions governing the transaction, including the divestiture of parallel tracks or requiring the granting of trackage rights and access to other facilities. Any trackage rights and related conditions imposed to alleviate anticompetitive effects of the transaction shall provide for operating terms and compensation levels to ensure that such effects are alleviated. When the transaction contemplates a guaranty or assumption of payment of dividends or of fixed charges or will result in an increase of total fixed charges, the Board may approve and authorize the transaction only if it finds that the guaranty, assumption, or increase is consistent with the public interest. The Board may require inclusion of other rail carriers located in the area involved in the transaction if they apply for inclusion and the Board finds their inclusion to be consistent with the public interest.

(d) In a proceeding under this section which does not involve the merger or control of at least two Class I railroads, as defined by the Board, the Board shall approve such an application unless it finds that—

(1) as a result of the transaction, there is likely to be substantial lessening of competition, creation of a monopoly, or restraint of trade in freight surface transportation in any region of the United States; and

(2) the anticompetitive effects of the transaction outweigh the public interest in meeting significant transportation needs.

In making such findings, the Board shall, with respect to any application that is part of a plan or proposal developed under section 333(a)–(d) of this title, accord substantial weight to any recommendations of the Attorney General.

(e) No transaction described in section 11326(b) may have the effect of avoiding a collective bargaining agreement or shifting work from a rail carrier with a collective bargaining agreement to a rail carrier without a collective bargaining agreement.

(f)(1) To the extent provided in this subsection, a proceeding under this subchapter relating to a transaction involving at least one Class I rail carrier shall not be considered an adjudication required by statute to be determined on the record after opportunity for an agency hearing, for the purposes of subchapter II of chapter 5 of title 5, United States Code.

(2) Ex parte communications, as defined in section 551(14) of title 5, United States Code, shall be permitted in proceedings described in paragraph (1) of this subsection, subject to the requirements of paragraph (3) of this subsection.

(3)(A) Any member or employee of the Board who makes or receives a written ex parte communication concerning the merits of a proceeding described in paragraph (1) shall promptly place the communication in the public docket of the proceeding.

(B) Any member or employee of the Board who makes or receives an oral ex parte communication concerning the merits of a proceeding described in paragraph (1) shall promptly place a written summary of the oral communication in the public docket of the proceeding.

(4) Nothing in this subsection shall be construed to require the Board or any of its members or employees to engage in any ex parte communication with any person. Nothing in this subsection or any other law shall be construed to limit the authority of the members or employees of the Board, in their discretion, to note in the docket or otherwise publicly the occurrence and substance of an ex parte communication.

(Added Pub. L. 104–88, title I, §102(a), Dec. 29, 1995, 109 Stat. 839.)

§11325. Consolidation, merger, and acquisition of control: procedure

(a) The Board shall publish notice of the application under section 11324 in the Federal

Register by the end of the 30th day after the application is filed with the Board. However, if the application is incomplete, the Board shall reject it by the end of that period. The order of rejection is a final action of the Board. The published notice shall indicate whether the application involves—

(1) the merger or control of at least two Class I railroads, as defined by the Board, to be decided within the time limits specified in subsection (b) of this section;

(2) transactions of regional or national transportation significance, to be decided within the time limits specified in subsection (c) of this section; or

(3) any other transaction covered by this section, to be decided within the time limits specified in subsection (d) of this section.

(b) If the application involves the merger or control of two or more Class I railroads, as defined by the Board, the following conditions apply:

(1) Written comments about an application may be filed with the Board within 45 days after notice of the application is published under subsection (a) of this section. Copies of such comments shall be served on the Attorney General and the Secretary of Transportation, who may decide to intervene as a party to the proceeding. That decision must be made by the 15th day after the date of receipt of the written comments, and if the decision is to intervene, preliminary comments about the application must be sent to the Board by the end of the 15th day after the date of receipt of the written comments.

(2) The Board shall require that applications inconsistent with an application, notice of which was published under subsection (a) of this section, and applications for inclusion in the transaction, be filed with it by the 90th day after publication of notice under that subsection.

(3) The Board must conclude evidentiary proceedings by the end of 1 year after the date of publication of notice under subsection (a) of this section. The Board must issue a final decision by the 90th day after the date on which it concludes the evidentiary proceedings.

(c) If the application involves a transaction other than the merger or control of at least two Class I railroads, as defined by the Board, which the Board has determined to be of regional or national transportation significance, the following conditions apply:

(1) Written comments about an application, including comments of the Attorney General and the Secretary of Transportation, may be filed with the Board within 30 days after notice of the application is published under subsection (a) of this section.

(2) The Board shall require that applications inconsistent with an application, notice of which was published under subsection (a) of this section, and applications for inclusion in the transaction, be filed with it by the 60th day after publication of notice under that subsection.

(3) The Board must conclude any evidentiary proceedings by the 180th day after the date of publication of notice under subsection (a) of this section. The Board must issue a final decision by the 90th day after the date on which it concludes the evidentiary proceedings.

(d) For all applications under this section other than those specified in subsections (b) and (c) of this section, the following conditions apply:

(1) Written comments about an application, including comments of the Attorney General and the Secretary of Transportation, may be filed with the Board within 30 days after notice of the application is published under subsection (a) of this section.

(2) The Board must conclude any evidentiary proceedings by the 105th day after the date of publication of notice under subsection (a) of this section. The Board must issue a final decision by the 45th day after the date on which it concludes the evidentiary proceedings.

(Added Pub. L. 104–88, title I, §102(a), Dec. 29, 1995, 109 Stat. 841.)

§11326. EMPLOYEE PROTECTIVE ARRANGEMENTS IN TRANSACTIONS INVOLVING RAIL CARRIERS

(a) Except as otherwise provided in this section, when approval is sought for a transaction under sections 11324 and 11325 of this title, the Board shall require the rail carrier to provide a fair arrangement at least as protective of the interests of employees who are affected by the transaction as the terms imposed under section 5(2)(f) of the Interstate Commerce Act before February 5, 1976, and the terms established under section 24706(c) [1] of this title. Notwithstanding this part, the arrangement may be made by the rail carrier and the authorized representative of its employees. The arrangement and the order approving the transaction must require that the employees of the affected rail carrier will not be in a worse position related to their employment as a result of the transaction during the 4 years following the effective date of the final action of the Board (or if an employee was employed for a lesser period of time by the rail carrier before the action became effective, for that lesser period).

(b) When approval is sought under sections 11324 and 11325 for a transaction involving one Class II and one or more Class III rail carriers, there shall be an arrangement as required under subsection (a) of this section, except that such arrangement shall be limited to one year of severance pay, which shall not exceed the amount of earnings from the railroad employment of that employee during the 12-month period immediately preceding the date on which the application for approval of such transaction is filed with the Board. The amount of such severance pay shall be reduced by the amount of earnings from railroad employment of that employee with the acquiring carrier during the 12-month period immediately following the effective date of the transaction. The parties may agree to terms other than as provided in this subsection.

(c) When approval is sought under sections 11324 and 11325 for a transaction involving only Class III rail carriers, this section shall not apply.

(Added Pub. L. 104–88, title I, §102(a), Dec. 29, 1995, 109 Stat. 842.)

[1] See References in Text note below.

§11327. SUPPLEMENTAL ORDERS

When cause exists, the Board may make appropriate orders supplemental to an order made in a proceeding under sections 11322 through 11326 of this title.

(Added Pub. L. 104–88, title I, §102(a), Dec. 29, 1995, 109 Stat. 843.)

§11328. RESTRICTIONS ON OFFICERS AND DIRECTORS

(a) A person may hold the position of officer or director of more than one rail carrier only when authorized by the Board. The Board may authorize a person to hold the position of officer or director of more than one of those carriers when public or private interests will not be adversely affected.

(b) This section shall not apply to an individual holding the position of officer or director only of Class III rail carriers.

(Added Pub. L. 104–88, title I, §102(a), Dec. 29, 1995, 109 Stat. 843.)

CHAPTER 115—FEDERAL-STATE RELATIONS

§11501. TAX DISCRIMINATION AGAINST RAIL TRANSPORTATION PROPERTY

(a) In this section—

(1) the term "assessment" means valuation for a property tax levied by a taxing district;

(2) the term "assessment jurisdiction" means a geographical area in a State used in determining the assessed value of property for ad valorem taxation;

(3) the term "rail transportation property" means property, as defined by the Board, owned or used by a rail carrier providing transportation subject to the jurisdiction of the Board under this part; and

(4) the term "commercial and industrial property" means property, other than transportation property and land used primarily for agricultural purposes or timber growing, devoted to a commercial or industrial use and subject to a property tax levy.

(b) The following acts unreasonably burden and discriminate against interstate commerce, and a State, subdivision of a State, or authority acting for a State or subdivision of a State may not do any of them:

(1) Assess rail transportation property at a value that has a higher ratio to the true market value of the rail transportation property than the ratio that the assessed value of other commercial and industrial property in the same assessment jurisdiction has to the true market value of the other commercial and industrial property.

(2) Levy or collect a tax on an assessment that may not be made under paragraph (1) of this subsection.

(3) Levy or collect an ad valorem property tax on rail transportation property at a tax rate that exceeds the tax rate applicable to commercial and industrial property in the same assessment jurisdiction.

(4) Impose another tax that discriminates against a rail carrier providing transportation subject to the jurisdiction of the Board under this part.

(c) Notwithstanding section 1341 of title 28 and without regard to the amount in controversy or citizenship of the parties, a district court of the United States has jurisdiction, concurrent with other jurisdiction of courts of the United States and the States, to prevent a violation of subsection (b) of this section. Relief may be granted under this subsection only if the ratio of assessed value to true market value of rail transportation property exceeds by at least 5 percent the ratio of assessed value to true market value of other commercial and industrial property in the same assessment jurisdiction. The burden of proof in determining assessed value and true market value is governed by State law. If the ratio of the assessed value of other commercial and industrial property in the assessment jurisdiction to the true market value of all other commercial and industrial property cannot be determined to the satisfaction of the district court through the random-sampling method known as a sales assessment ratio study (to be carried out under statistical principles applicable to such a study), the court shall find, as a violation of this section—

(1) an assessment of the rail transportation property at a value that has a higher ratio to the true market value of the rail transportation property than the assessed value of all other property subject to a property tax levy in the assessment jurisdiction has to the true market value of all other commercial and industrial property; and

(2) the collection of an ad valorem property tax on the rail transportation property at a tax rate that exceeds the tax ratio rate applicable to taxable property in the taxing district.

(Added Pub. L. 104–88, title I, §102(a), Dec. 29, 1995, 109 Stat. 843.)

§11502. WITHHOLDING STATE AND LOCAL INCOME TAX BY RAIL CARRIERS

(a) No part of the compensation paid by a rail carrier providing transportation subject to the jurisdiction of the Board under this part to an employee who performs regularly assigned duties as such an employee on a railroad in more than one State shall be subject to the income tax laws of any State or subdivision of that State, other than the State or subdivision thereof of the employee's residence.

(b) A rail carrier withholding pay from an employee under subsection (a) of this section shall file income tax information returns and other reports only with the State and subdivision of residence of the employee.

(Added Pub. L. 104–88, title I, §102(a), Dec. 29, 1995, 109 Stat. 844.)

CHAPTER 117—ENFORCEMENT: INVESTIGATIONS, RIGHTS, AND REMEDIES

---

[1] So in original. Does not conform to section catchline.

§11701. GENERAL AUTHORITY

(a) Except as otherwise provided in this part, the Board may begin an investigation under this part on the Board's own initiative or upon receiving a complaint pursuant to subsection (b). If the Board finds that a rail carrier is violating this part, the Board shall take appropriate action to compel compliance with this part. If the Board finds a violation of this part in a proceeding brought on its own initiative, any remedy from such proceeding may only be applied prospectively.

(b) A person, including a governmental authority, may file with the Board a complaint about a violation of this part by a rail carrier providing transportation or service subject to the jurisdiction of the Board under this part. The complaint must state the facts that are the subject of the violation. The Board may dismiss a complaint it determines does not state reasonable grounds for investigation and action. However, the Board may not dismiss a complaint made against a rail carrier providing transportation subject to the jurisdiction of the Board under this part because of the absence of direct damage to the complainant.

(c) A formal investigative proceeding begun by the Board under subsection (a) of this section is dismissed automatically unless it is concluded by the Board with administrative finality by the end of the third year after the date on which it was begun.

(d) In any investigation commenced on the Board's own initiative, the Board shall—

(1) not later than 30 days after initiating the investigation, provide written notice to the parties under investigation, which shall state the basis for such investigation;

(2) only investigate issues that are of national or regional significance;

(3) permit the parties under investigation to file a written statement describing any or all facts and circumstances concerning a matter which may be the subject of such investigation;

(4) make available to the parties under investigation and Board members—

(A) any recommendations made as a result of the investigation; and

(B) a summary of the findings that support such recommendations;

(5) to the extent practicable, separate the investigative and decisionmaking functions of staff;

(6) dismiss any investigation that is not concluded by the Board with administrative finality within 1 year after the date on which it was commenced; and

(7) not later than 90 days after receiving the recommendations and summary of findings under paragraph (4)—

(A) dismiss the investigation if no further action is warranted; or

(B) initiate a proceeding to determine if a provision under this part has been violated.

(e)(1) Any parties to an investigation against whom a violation is found as a result of an investigation begun on the Board's own initiative may, not later than 60 days after the date of the order of the Board finding such a violation, institute an action in the United States court of appeals for the appropriate judicial circuit for de novo review of such order in accordance with chapter 7 of title 5.

(2) The court—

(A) shall have jurisdiction to enter a judgment affirming, modifying, or setting aside, in whole or in part, the order of the Board; and

(B) may remand the proceeding to the Board for such further action as the court may direct.

(Added Pub. L. 104–88, title I, §102(a), Dec. 29, 1995, 109 Stat. 845; amended Pub. L. 114–110, §12(a), (b), Dec. 18, 2015, 129 Stat. 2234.)

§11702. ENFORCEMENT BY THE BOARD

The Board may bring a civil action—

(1) to enjoin a rail carrier from violating sections 10901 through 10906 of this title, or a regulation prescribed or order or certificate issued under any of those sections;

(2) to enforce subchapter II of chapter 113 of this title and to compel compliance with an order of the Board under that subchapter; and

(3) to enforce an order of the Board, except a civil action to enforce an order for the payment of money, when it is violated by a rail carrier providing transportation subject to the jurisdiction of the Board under this part.

(Added Pub. L. 104–88, title I, §102(a), Dec. 29, 1995, 109 Stat. 845.)

§11703. ENFORCEMENT BY THE ATTORNEY GENERAL

(a) The Attorney General may, and on request of the Board shall, bring court proceedings to enforce this part, or a regulation or order of the Board or certificate issued under this part, and to prosecute a person violating this part or a regulation or order of the Board or certificate issued under this part.

(b) The United States Government may bring a civil action on behalf of a person to compel a rail carrier providing transportation subject to the jurisdiction of the Board under this part to provide that transportation to that person in compliance with this part at the same rate charged, or on conditions as favorable as those given by the rail carrier, for like traffic under similar conditions to another person.

(Added Pub. L. 104–88, title I, §102(a), Dec. 29, 1995, 109 Stat. 845.)

§11704. RIGHTS AND REMEDIES OF PERSONS INJURED BY RAIL CARRIERS

(a) A person injured because a rail carrier providing transportation or service subject to the jurisdiction of the Board under this part does not obey an order of the Board, except an order for the payment of money, may bring a civil action in a United States District Court to enforce that order under this subsection.

(b) A rail carrier providing transportation subject to the jurisdiction of the Board under this part is liable for damages sustained by a person as a result of an act or omission of that carrier in violation of this part. A rail carrier providing transportation subject to the jurisdiction of the Board under this part is liable to a person for amounts charged that exceed the applicable rate for the transportation.

(c)(1) A person may file a complaint with the Board under section 11701(b) of this title or bring a civil action under subsection (b) of this section to enforce liability against a rail carrier providing transportation subject to the jurisdiction of the Board under this part.

(2) When the Board makes an award under subsection (b) of this section, the Board shall order the rail carrier to pay the amount awarded by a specific date. The Board may order a rail carrier providing transportation subject to the jurisdiction of the Board under this part to pay damages only when the proceeding is on complaint. The person for whose benefit an order of the Board requiring the payment of money is made may bring a civil action to enforce that order under this paragraph if the rail carrier does not pay the amount awarded by the date payment was ordered to be made.

(d)(1) When a person begins a civil action under subsection (b) of this section to enforce an order of the Board requiring the payment of damages by a rail carrier providing transportation subject to the jurisdiction of the Board under this part, the text of the order of the Board must be included in the complaint. In addition to the district courts of the United States, a State court of general jurisdiction having jurisdiction of the parties has jurisdiction to enforce an order under this paragraph. The findings and order of the Board are competent evidence of the facts stated in them. Trial in a civil action brought in a district court of the United States under this paragraph is in the judicial district—

(A) in which the plaintiff resides;

(B) in which the principal operating office of the rail carrier is located; or

(C) through which the railroad line of that carrier runs.

In a civil action under this paragraph, the plaintiff is liable for only those costs that accrue on an appeal taken by the plaintiff.

(2) All parties in whose favor the award was made may be joined as plaintiffs in a civil action brought in a district court of the United States under this subsection and all the rail carriers that are parties to the order awarding damages may be joined as defendants. Trial in the action is in the judicial district in which any one of the plaintiffs could bring the action against any one of the defendants. Process may be served on a defendant at its principal operating office when that defendant is not in the district in which the action is brought. A judgment ordering recovery may be made in favor of any of those plaintiffs against the

defendant found to be liable to that plaintiff.

(3) The district court shall award a reasonable attorney's fee as a part of the damages for which a rail carrier is found liable under this subsection. The district court shall tax and collect that fee as a part of the costs of the action.

(Added Pub. L. 104–88, title I, §102(a), Dec. 29, 1995, 109 Stat. 846.)

§11705. LIMITATION ON ACTIONS BY AND AGAINST RAIL CARRIERS

(a) A rail carrier providing transportation or service subject to the jurisdiction of the Board under this part must begin a civil action to recover charges for transportation or service provided by the carrier within 3 years after the claim accrues.

(b) A person must begin a civil action to recover overcharges under section 11704(b) of this title within 3 years after the claim accrues, whether or not a complaint is filed under section 11704(c)(1).

(c) A person must file a complaint with the Board to recover damages under section 11704(b) of this title within 2 years after the claim accrues.

(d) The limitation period under subsection (b) of this section is extended for 6 months from the time written notice is given to the claimant by the rail carrier of disallowance of any part of the claim specified in the notice if a written claim is given to the rail carrier within that limitation period. The limitation periods under subsections (b) and (c) of this section are extended for 90 days from the time the rail carrier begins a civil action under subsection (a) of this section to recover charges related to the same transportation or service, or collects (without beginning a civil action under that subsection) the charge for that transportation or service if that action is begun or collection is made within the appropriate period.

(e) A person must begin a civil action to enforce an order of the Board against a rail carrier for the payment of money within one year after the date the order required the money to be paid.

(f) This section applies to transportation for the United States Government. The time limitations under this section are extended, as related to transportation for or on behalf of the United States Government, for 3 years from the date of—

(1) payment of the rate for the transportation or service involved;

(2) subsequent refund for overpayment of that rate; or

(3) deduction made under section 3726 of title 31, whichever is later.

(g) A claim related to a shipment of property accrues under this section on delivery or tender of delivery by the rail carrier.

(Added Pub. L. 104–88, title I, §102(a), Dec. 29, 1995, 109 Stat. 847.)

§11706. LIABILITY OF RAIL CARRIERS UNDER RECEIPTS AND BILLS OF LADING

(a) A rail carrier providing transportation or service subject to the jurisdiction of the Board under this part shall issue a receipt or bill of lading for property it receives for transportation under this part. That rail carrier and any other carrier that delivers the property and is providing transportation or service subject to the jurisdiction of the Board under this part are liable to the person entitled to recover under the receipt or bill of lading. The liability imposed under this subsection is for the actual loss or injury to the property caused by—

(1) the receiving rail carrier;

(2) the delivering rail carrier; or

(3) another rail carrier over whose line or route the property is transported in the United States or from a place in the United States to a place in an adjacent foreign country when transported under a through bill of lading.

Failure to issue a receipt or bill of lading does not affect the liability of a rail carrier. A delivering rail carrier is deemed to be the rail carrier performing the line-haul transportation nearest the destination but does not include a rail carrier providing only a switching service at the destination.

(b) The rail carrier issuing the receipt or bill of lading under subsection (a) of this section or delivering the property for which the receipt or bill of lading was issued is entitled to recover from the rail carrier over whose line or route the loss or injury occurred the amount required to be paid to the owners of the property, as evidenced by a receipt, judgment, or transcript, and the amount of its expenses reasonably incurred in defending a civil action brought by that person.

(c)(1) A rail carrier may not limit or be exempt from liability imposed under subsection (a) of this section except as provided in this subsection. A limitation of liability or of the amount of recovery or representation or agreement in a receipt, bill of lading, contract, or rule in violation of this section is void.

(2) A rail carrier of passengers may limit its liability under its passenger rate for loss or injury of baggage carried on trains carrying passengers.

(3) A rail carrier providing transportation or service subject to the jurisdiction of the Board under this part may establish rates for transportation of property under which—

(A) the liability of the rail carrier for such property is limited to a value established by written declaration of the shipper or by a written agreement between the shipper and the carrier; or

(B) specified amounts are deducted, pursuant to a written agreement between the shipper and the carrier, from any claim against the carrier with respect to the transportation of such property.

(d)(1) A civil action under this section may be brought in a district court of the United States or in a State court.

(2)(A) A civil action under this section may only be brought—

(i) against the originating rail carrier, in the judicial district in which the point of origin is located;

(ii) against the delivering rail carrier, in the judicial district in which the principal place of business of the person bringing the action is located if the delivering carrier operates a railroad or a route through such judicial district, or in the judicial district in which the point of destination is located; and

(iii) against the carrier alleged to have caused the loss or damage, in the judicial district in which such loss or damage is alleged to have occurred.

(B) In this section, "judicial district" means (i) in the case of a United States district court, a judicial district of the United States, and (ii) in the case of a State court, the applicable geographic area over which such court exercises jurisdiction.

(e) A rail carrier may not provide by rule, contract, or otherwise, a period of less than 9 months for filing a claim against it under this section and a period of less than 2 years for bringing a civil action against it under this section. The period for bringing a civil action is computed from the date the carrier gives a person written notice that the carrier has disallowed any part of the claim specified in the notice. For the purposes of this subsection—

(1) an offer of compromise shall not constitute a disallowance of any part of the claim unless the carrier, in writing, informs the claimant that such part of the claim is disallowed and provides reasons for such disallowance; and

(2) communications received from a carrier's insurer shall not constitute a disallowance of any part of the claim unless the insurer, in writing, informs the claimant that such part of the claim is disallowed, provides reasons for such disallowance, and informs the claimant that the insurer is acting on behalf of the carrier.

(Added Pub. L. 104–88, title I, §102(a), Dec. 29, 1995, 109 Stat. 847.)

§11707. LIABILITY WHEN PROPERTY IS DELIVERED IN VIOLATION OF ROUTING INSTRUCTIONS

(a)(1) When a rail carrier providing transportation subject to the jurisdiction of the Board under this part diverts or delivers property to another rail carrier in violation of routing instructions in the bill of lading, both of those rail carriers are jointly and severally liable to the rail carrier that was deprived of its right to participate in hauling that property for the total amount of the rate it would have received if it participated in hauling the property.

(2) A rail carrier is not liable under paragraph (1) of this subsection when it diverts or delivers property in compliance with an order or regulation of the Board.

(3) A rail carrier to whom property is transported is not liable under this subsection if it shows that it had no notice of the routing instructions before transporting the property. The burden of proving lack of notice is on that rail carrier.

(b) The court shall award a reasonable attorney's fee to the plaintiff in a judgment against the defendant rail carrier under subsection (a) of this section. The court shall tax and collect that fee as a part of the costs of the action.

(Added Pub. L. 104–88, title I, §102(a), Dec. 29, 1995, 109 Stat. 849.)

§11708. VOLUNTARY ARBITRATION OF CERTAIN RAIL RATES AND PRACTICES DISPUTES

(a) IN GENERAL.—Not later than 1 year after the date of the enactment of the Surface Transportation Board Reauthorization Act of 2015, the Board shall promulgate regulations to establish a voluntary and binding arbitration process to resolve rail rate and practice complaints subject to the jurisdiction of the Board.

(b) COVERED DISPUTES.—The voluntary and binding arbitration process established pursuant to subsection (a)—

(1) shall apply to disputes involving—

(A) rates, demurrage, accessorial charges, misrouting, or mishandling of rail cars; or

(B) a carrier's published rules and practices as applied to particular rail transportation;

(2) shall not apply to disputes—

(A) to obtain the grant, denial, stay, or revocation of any license, authorization, or exemption;

(B) to prescribe for the future any conduct, rules, or results of general, industry-wide applicability;

(C) to enforce a labor protective condition; or

(D) that are solely between 2 or more rail carriers; and

(3) shall not prevent parties from independently seeking or utilizing private arbitration services to resolve any disputes the parties may have.

(c) ARBITRATION PROCEDURES.—

(1) IN GENERAL.—The Board—

(A) may make the voluntary and binding arbitration process established pursuant to subsection (a) available only to the relevant parties;

(B) may make the voluntary and binding arbitration process available only—

(i) after receiving the written consent to arbitrate from all relevant parties; and

(ii)(I) after the filing of a written complaint; or

(II) through other procedures adopted by the Board in a rulemaking proceeding;

(C) with respect to rate disputes, may make the voluntary and binding arbitration process available only to the relevant parties if the rail carrier has market dominance (as determined under section 10707); and

(D) may initiate the voluntary and binding arbitration process not later than 40 days after the date on which a written complaint is filed or through other procedures adopted by the Board in a rulemaking proceeding.

(2) LIMITATION.—Initiation of the voluntary and binding arbitration process shall preclude the Board from separately reviewing a complaint or dispute related to the same rail rate or practice in a covered dispute involving the same parties.

(3) RATES.—In resolving a covered dispute involving the reasonableness of a rail carrier's rates, the arbitrator or panel of arbitrators, as applicable, shall consider the Board's methodologies for setting maximum lawful rates, giving due consideration to the need for differential pricing to permit a rail carrier to collect adequate revenues (as determined under section 10704(a)(2)).

(d) ARBITRATION DECISIONS.—Any decision reached in an arbitration process under this section—

(1) shall be consistent with sound principles of rail regulation economics;

(2) shall be in writing;

(3) shall contain findings of fact and conclusions;

(4) shall be binding upon the parties; and

(5) shall not have any precedential effect in any other or subsequent arbitration dispute.

(e) TIMELINES.—

(1) SELECTION.—An arbitrator or panel of arbitrators shall be selected not later than 14 days after the date of the Board's decision to initiate arbitration.

(2) EVIDENTIARY PROCESS.—The evidentiary process of the voluntary and binding arbitration process shall be completed not later than 90 days after the date on which the arbitration process is initiated unless—

(A) a party requests an extension; and

(B) the arbitrator or panel of arbitrators, as applicable, grants such extension request.

(3) DECISION.—The arbitrator or panel of arbitrators, as applicable, shall issue a decision not later than 30 days after the date on which the evidentiary record is closed.

(4) EXTENSIONS.—The Board may extend any of the timelines under this subsection upon the agreement of all parties in the dispute.

(f) ARBITRATORS.—

(1) IN GENERAL.—Unless otherwise agreed by all of the parties, an arbitration under this section shall be conducted by an arbitrator or panel of arbitrators, which shall be selected from a roster, maintained by the Board, of persons with rail transportation, economic regulation, professional or business experience, including agriculture, in the private sector.

(2) INDEPENDENCE.—In an arbitration under this section, the arbitrators shall perform their duties with diligence, good faith, and in a manner consistent with the requirements of impartiality and independence.

(3) SELECTION.—

(A) IN GENERAL.—If the parties cannot mutually agree on an arbitrator, or the lead arbitrator of a panel of arbitrators, the parties shall select the arbitrator or lead arbitrator from the roster by alternately striking names from the roster until only 1 name remains meeting the criteria set forth in paragraph (1).

(B) PANEL OF ARBITRATORS.—If the parties agree to select a panel of arbitrators, instead of a single arbitrator, the panel shall be selected under this subsection as follows:

(i) The parties to a dispute may mutually select 1 arbitrator from the roster to serve as the lead arbitrator of the panel of arbitrators.

(ii) If the parties cannot mutually agree on a lead arbitrator, the parties shall select a lead arbitrator using the process described in subparagraph (A).

(iii) In addition to the lead arbitrator selected under this subparagraph, each party to a dispute shall select 1 additional arbitrator from the roster, regardless of whether the other party struck out the arbitrator's name under subparagraph (A).

(4) Cost.—The parties shall share the costs incurred by the Board and arbitrators equally, with each party responsible for paying its own legal and other associated arbitration costs.

(g) Relief.—

(1) In general.—Subject to the limitations set forth in paragraphs (2) and (3), an arbitral decision under this section may award the payment of damages or rate prescriptive relief.

(2) Practice disputes.—The damage award for practice disputes may not exceed $2,000,000.

(3) Rate disputes.—

(A) Monetary limit.—The damage award for rate disputes, including any rate prescription, may not exceed $25,000,000.

(B) Time limit.—Any rate prescription shall be limited to not longer than 5 years from the date of the arbitral decision.

(h) Board Review.—If a party appeals a decision under this section to the Board, the Board may review the decision under this section to determine if—

(1) the decision is consistent with sound principles of rail regulation economics;

(2) a clear abuse of arbitral authority or discretion occurred;

(3) the decision directly contravenes statutory authority; or

(4) the award limitation under subsection (g) was violated.

(Added Pub. L. 114–110, §13(a), Dec. 18, 2015, 129 Stat. 2235.)

CHAPTER 119—CIVIL AND CRIMINAL PENALTIES

§11901. GENERAL CIVIL PENALTIES

(a) Except as otherwise provided in this section, a rail carrier providing transportation subject to the jurisdiction of the Board under this part, an officer or agent of that rail carrier, or a receiver, trustee, lessee, or agent of one of them, knowingly violating this part or an order of the Board under this part is liable to the United States Government for a civil penalty of not more than $5,000 for each violation. Liability under this subsection is incurred for each distinct violation. A separate violation occurs for each day the violation continues.

(b) A rail carrier providing transportation subject to the jurisdiction of the Board under this part, or a receiver or trustee of that rail carrier, violating a regulation or order of the Board under section 11124(a)(2) or (b) of this title is liable to the United States Government for a civil penalty of $500 for each violation and for $25 for each day the violation continues.

(c) A person knowingly authorizing, consenting to, or permitting a violation of sections 10901 through 10906 of this title or of a requirement or a regulation under any of those sections, is liable to the United States Government for a civil penalty of not more than $5,000.

(d) A rail carrier, receiver, or operating trustee violating an order or direction of the Board under section 11123 or 11124(a)(1) of this title is liable to the United States Government for a civil penalty of at least $100 but not more than $500 for each violation and for $50 for each day the violation continues.

(e)(1) A person required under subchapter III of chapter 111 of this title to make, prepare, preserve, or submit to the Board a record concerning transportation subject to the jurisdiction of the Board under this part that does not make, prepare, preserve, or submit that record as required under that subchapter, is liable to the United States Government for a civil penalty of $500 for each violation.

(2) A rail carrier providing transportation subject to the jurisdiction of the Board under this part, and a lessor, receiver, or trustee of that rail carrier, violating section 11144(b)(1) of this title, is liable to the United States Government for a civil penalty of $100 for each violation.

(3) A rail carrier providing transportation subject to the jurisdiction of the Board under this part, a lessor, receiver, or trustee of that rail carrier, a person furnishing cars, and an

officer, agent, or employee of one of them, required to make a report to the Board or answer a question that does not make the report or does not specifically, completely, and truthfully answer the question, is liable to the United States Government for a civil penalty of $100 for each violation.

(4) A separate violation occurs for each day a violation under this subsection continues.

(f) Trial in a civil action under subsections (a) through (e) of this section is in the judicial district in which the rail carrier has its principal operating office or in a district through which the railroad of the rail carrier runs.

(Added Pub. L. 104–88, title I, §102(a), Dec. 29, 1995, 109 Stat. 849.)

§11902. Interference with railroad car supply

(a) A person that offers or gives anything of value to another person acting for or employed by a rail carrier providing transportation subject to the jurisdiction of the Board under this part intending to influence an action of that other person related to supply, distribution, or movement of cars, vehicles, or vessels used in the transportation of property, or because of the action of that other person, shall be fined not more than $1,000, imprisoned for not more than 2 years, or both.

(b) A person acting for or employed by a rail carrier providing transportation subject to the jurisdiction of the Board under this part that solicits, accepts, or receives anything of value—

(1) intending to be influenced by it in an action of that person related to supply, distribution, or movement of cars, vehicles, or vessels used in the transportation of property; or

(2) because of the action of that person,

shall be fined not more than $1,000, imprisoned for not more than 2 years, or both.

(Added Pub. L. 104–88, title I, §102(a), Dec. 29, 1995, 109 Stat. 850.)

§11903. Record keeping and reporting violations

A person required to make a report to the Board, or make, prepare, or preserve a record, under subchapter III of chapter 111 of this title about transportation subject to the jurisdiction of the Board under this part that knowingly and willfully—

(1) makes a false entry in the report or record;

(2) destroys, mutilates, changes, or by another means falsifies the record;

(3) does not enter business related facts and transactions in the record;

(4) makes, prepares, or preserves the record in violation of a regulation or order of the Board; or

(5) files a false report or record with the Board,

shall be fined not more than $5,000, imprisoned for not more than 2 years, or both.

(Added Pub. L. 104–88, title I, §102(a), Dec. 29, 1995, 109 Stat. 851.)

§11904. UNLAWFUL DISCLOSURE OF INFORMATION

(a) A—

(1) rail carrier providing transportation subject to the jurisdiction of the Board under this part, or an officer, agent, or employee of that rail carrier, or another person authorized to receive information from that rail carrier, that knowingly discloses to another person, except the shipper or consignee; or

(2) person who solicits or knowingly receives,

information described in subsection (b) without the consent of the shipper or consignee shall be fined not more than $1,000.

(b) The information referred to in subsection (a) is information about the nature, kind, quantity, destination, consignee, or routing of property tendered or delivered to that rail carrier for transportation provided under this part, or information about the contents of a contract authorized under section 10709 of this title, that may be used to the detriment of the shipper or consignee or may disclose improperly, to a competitor, the business transactions of the shipper or consignee.

(c) This part does not prevent a rail carrier providing transportation subject to the jurisdiction of the Board under this part from giving information—

(1) in response to legal process issued under authority of a court of the United States or a State;

(2) to an officer, employee, or agent of the United States Government, a State, or a territory or possession of the United States; or

(3) to another rail carrier or its agent to adjust mutual traffic accounts in the ordinary course of business.

(d) An employee of the Board delegated to make an inspection or examination under section 11144 of this title who knowingly discloses information acquired during that inspection or examination, except as directed by the Board, a court, or a judge of that court, shall be fined not more than $500, imprisoned for not more than 6 months, or both.

(e) A person that knowingly discloses confidential data made available to such person under section 11163 of this title by a rail carrier providing transportation subject to the jurisdiction of the Board under this part shall be fined not more than $50,000.

(Added Pub. L. 104–88, title I, §102(a), Dec. 29, 1995, 109 Stat. 851; amended Pub. L. 105–102, §2(6), Nov. 20, 1997, 111 Stat. 2204.)

§11905. DISOBEDIENCE TO SUBPOENAS

A person not obeying a subpoena or requirement of the Board to appear and testify or produce records shall be fined at least $100 but not more than $5,000, imprisoned for not more than one year, or both.

(Added Pub. L. 104–88, title I, §102(a), Dec. 29, 1995, 109 Stat. 852.)

§11906. GENERAL CRIMINAL PENALTY WHEN SPECIFIC PENALTY NOT PROVIDED

When another criminal penalty is not provided under this chapter, a rail carrier providing transportation subject to the jurisdiction of the Board under this part, and when that rail carrier is a corporation, a director or officer of the corporation, or a receiver, trustee, lessee, or person acting for or employed by the corporation that, alone or with another person, willfully violates this part or an order prescribed under this part, shall be fined not more than $5,000. The person may be imprisoned for not more than 2 years in addition to being fined under this section. A separate violation occurs each day a violation of this part continues.

(Added Pub. L. 104–88, title I, §102(a), Dec. 29, 1995, 109 Stat. 852; amended Pub. L. 105–102, §2(7), Nov. 20, 1997, 111 Stat. 2204.)

§11907. PUNISHMENT OF CORPORATION FOR VIOLATIONS COMMITTED BY CERTAIN INDIVIDUALS

An act or omission that would be a violation of this part if committed by a director, officer, receiver, trustee, lessee, agent, or employee of a rail carrier providing transportation or service subject to the jurisdiction of the Board under this part that is a corporation is also a violation of this part by that corporation. The penalties of this chapter apply to that violation. When acting in the scope of their employment, the actions and omissions of individuals acting for or employed by that rail carrier are considered to be the actions and omissions of that rail carrier as well as that individual.

(Added Pub. L. 104–88, title I, §102(a), Dec. 29, 1995, 109 Stat. 852.)

§11908. RELATION TO OTHER FEDERAL CRIMINAL PENALTIES

Notwithstanding section 3571 of title 18, United States Code, the criminal penalties provided for in this chapter are the exclusive criminal penalties for violations of this part.

(Added Pub. L. 104–88, title I, §102(a), Dec. 29, 1995, 109 Stat. 852.)

* * * * * * *

SUBTITLE V
RAIL PROGRAMS

SUBTITLE V—RAIL PROGRAMS

PART A—SAFETY

PART B—ASSISTANCE

PART C—PASSENGER TRANSPORTATION

PART D—HIGH-SPEED RAIL

PART E—MISCELLANEOUS

[1] So in original. Probably should be "Railroad Rehabilitation and Improvement Financing".

[2] So in original. Probably should be "State Rail Plans".

[3] So in original. Probably should be "Project Delivery".

[4] So in original. Probably should be "Passenger Rail Planning".

PART A—SAFETY

CHAPTER 201—GENERAL

SUBCHAPTER I—GENERAL

SUBCHAPTER II—PARTICULAR ASPECTS OF SAFETY

[1] *Section catchline amended by Pub. L. 110–53 without corresponding amendment of chapter analysis.*

[2] *So in original. Does not conform to section catchline.*

SUBCHAPTER I—GENERAL

§20101. Purpose

The purpose of this chapter is to promote safety in every area of railroad operations and reduce railroad-related accidents and incidents.

(Pub. L. 103–272, §1(e), July 5, 1994, 108 Stat. 863.)

§20102. DEFINITIONS

In this part—

(1) "Class I railroad", "Class II railroad", and "Class III railroad" mean railroad carriers that have annual carrier operating revenues that meet the threshold amount for Class I carriers, Class II carriers, and Class III carriers, respectively, as determined by the Surface Transportation Board under section 1201.1–1 of title 49, Code of Federal Regulations.

(2) "railroad"—

(A) means any form of nonhighway ground transportation that runs on rails or electromagnetic guideways, including—

(i) commuter or other short-haul railroad passenger service in a metropolitan or suburban area and commuter railroad service that was operated by the Consolidated Rail Corporation on January 1, 1979; and

(ii) high speed ground transportation systems that connect metropolitan areas, without regard to whether those systems use new technologies not associated with traditional railroads; but

(B) does not include rapid transit operations in an urban area that are not connected to the general railroad system of transportation.

(3) "railroad carrier" means a person providing railroad transportation, except that, upon petition by a group of commonly controlled railroad carriers that the Secretary determines is operating within the United States as a single, integrated rail system, the Secretary may by order treat the group of railroad carriers as a single railroad carrier for purposes of one or more provisions of part A, subtitle V of this title and implementing regulations and order, subject to any appropriate conditions that the Secretary may impose.

(4) "safety-related railroad employee" means—

(A) a railroad employee who is subject to chapter 211;

(B) another operating railroad employee who is not subject to chapter 211;

(C) an employee who maintains the right of way of a railroad;

(D) an employee of a railroad carrier who is a hazmat employee as defined in section 5102(3) of this title;

(E) an employee who inspects, repairs, or maintains locomotives, passenger cars, or freight cars; and

(F) any other employee of a railroad carrier who directly affects railroad safety, as determined by the Secretary.

(Pub. L. 103–272, §1(e), July 5, 1994, 108 Stat. 863; Pub. L. 110–432, div. A, §2(b), title IV, §407, Oct. 16, 2008, 122 Stat. 4850, 4886.)

§20103. GENERAL AUTHORITY

(a) REGULATIONS AND ORDERS.—The Secretary of Transportation, as necessary, shall prescribe regulations and issue orders for every area of railroad safety supplementing laws and regulations in effect on October 16, 1970. When prescribing a security regulation or issuing a security order that affects the safety of railroad operations, the Secretary of

Homeland Security shall consult with the Secretary.

(b) REGULATIONS OF PRACTICE FOR PROCEEDINGS.—The Secretary shall prescribe regulations of practice applicable to each proceeding under this chapter. The regulations shall reflect the varying nature of the proceedings and include time limits for disposition of the proceedings. The time limit for disposition of a proceeding may not be more than 12 months after the date it begins.

(c) CONSIDERATION OF INFORMATION AND STANDARDS.—In prescribing regulations and issuing orders under this section, the Secretary shall consider existing relevant safety information and standards.

(d) NONEMERGENCY WAIVERS.—

(1) IN GENERAL.—The Secretary of Transportation may waive, or suspend the requirement to comply with, any part of a regulation prescribed or an order issued under this chapter if such waiver or suspension is in the public interest and consistent with railroad safety.

(2) NOTICE REQUIRED.—The Secretary shall—

(A) provide timely public notice of any request for a waiver under this subsection or for a suspension under subpart E of part 211 of title 49, Code of Federal Regulations, or successor regulations;

(B) make available the application for such waiver or suspension and any nonconfidential underlying data to interested parties;

(C) provide the public with notice and a reasonable opportunity to comment on a proposed waiver or suspension under this subsection before making a final decision; and

(D) publish on a publicly accessible website the reasons for granting each such waiver or suspension.

(3) INFORMATION PROTECTION.—Nothing in this subsection may be construed to require the release of information protected by law from public disclosure.

(4) RULEMAKING.—

(A) IN GENERAL.—Not later than 1 year after the first day on which a waiver under this subsection or a suspension under subpart E of part 211 of title 49, Code of Federal Regulations, or successor regulations, has been in continuous effect for a 6-year period, the Secretary shall complete a review and analysis of such waiver or suspension to determine whether issuing a rule that is consistent with the waiver is—

(i) in the public interest; and

(ii) consistent with railroad safety.

(B) FACTORS.—In conducting the review and analysis under subparagraph (A), the Secretary shall consider—

(i) the relevant safety record under the waiver or suspension;

(ii) the likelihood that other entities would have similar safety outcomes;

(iii) the materials submitted in the applications, including any comments regarding such materials; and

(iv) related rulemaking activity.

(C) NOTICE AND COMMENT.—

(i) IN GENERAL.—The Secretary shall publish the review and analysis required under this paragraph in the Federal Register, which shall include a summary of the data collected and all relevant underlying data, if the Secretary decides not to initiate a regulatory update under subparagraph (D).

(ii) NOTICE OF PROPOSED RULEMAKING.—The review and analysis under this paragraph shall be included as part of the notice of proposed rulemaking if the Secretary initiates a regulatory update under subparagraph (D).

(D) REGULATORY UPDATE.—The Secretary may initiate a rulemaking to incorporate relevant aspects of a waiver under this subsection or a suspension under subpart E of part 211 of title 49, Code of Federal Regulations, or successor regulations, into the relevant regulation, to the extent the Secretary considers appropriate.

(5) RULE OF CONSTRUCTION.—Nothing in this subsection may be construed to delay any waiver granted pursuant to this subsection that is in the public interest and consistent with railroad safety.

(e) HEARINGS.—The Secretary shall conduct a hearing as provided by section 553 of title 5 when prescribing a regulation or issuing an order under this part, including a regulation or order establishing, amending, or providing a waiver, described in subsection (d), of compliance with a railroad safety regulation prescribed or order issued under this part. An opportunity for an oral presentation shall be provided.

(f) TOURIST RAILROAD CARRIERS.—In prescribing regulations that pertain to railroad safety that affect tourist, historic, scenic, or excursion railroad carriers, the Secretary of Transportation shall take into consideration any financial, operational, or other factors that may be unique to such railroad carriers. The Secretary shall submit a report to Congress not later than September 30, 1995, on actions taken under this subsection.

(g) EMERGENCY WAIVERS.—

(1) IN GENERAL.—The Secretary may waive compliance with any part of a regulation prescribed or order issued under this part without prior notice and comment if the Secretary determines that—

(A) it is in the public interest to grant the waiver;

(B) the waiver is not inconsistent with railroad safety; and

(C) the waiver is necessary to address an actual or impending emergency situation or emergency event.

(2) PERIOD OF WAIVER.—A waiver under this subsection may be issued for a period of not more than 60 days and may be renewed upon application to the Secretary only after notice and an opportunity for a hearing on the waiver. The Secretary shall immediately revoke the waiver if continuation of the waiver would not be consistent with the goals and objectives of this part.

(3) STATEMENT OF REASONS.—The Secretary shall state in the decision issued under this subsection the reasons for granting the waiver.

(4) CONSULTATION.—In granting a waiver under this subsection, the Secretary shall

consult and coordinate with other Federal agencies, as appropriate, for matters that may impact such agencies.

(5) EMERGENCY SITUATION; EMERGENCY EVENT.—In this subsection, the terms "emergency situation" and "emergency event" mean a natural or manmade disaster, such as a hurricane, flood, earthquake, mudslide, forest fire, snowstorm, terrorist act, biological outbreak, release of a dangerous radiological, chemical, explosive, or biological material, or a war-related activity, that poses a risk of death, serious illness, severe injury, or substantial property damage. The disaster may be local, regional, or national in scope.

(Pub. L. 103–272, §1(e), July 5, 1994, 108 Stat. 863; Pub. L. 103–440, title II, §217, Nov. 2, 1994, 108 Stat. 4624; Pub. L. 107–296, title XVII, §1710(b), Nov. 25, 2002, 116 Stat. 2319; Pub. L. 110–432, div. A, title III, §308, Oct. 16, 2008, 122 Stat. 4881; Pub. L. 117–58, div. B, title II, §22411, Nov. 15, 2021, 135 Stat. 742.)

§20104. EMERGENCY AUTHORITY

(a) ORDERING RESTRICTIONS AND PROHIBITIONS.—(1) If, through testing, inspection, investigation, or research carried out under this chapter, the Secretary of Transportation decides that an unsafe condition or practice, or a combination of unsafe conditions and practices, causes an emergency situation involving a hazard of death, personal injury, or significant harm to the environment, the Secretary immediately may order restrictions and prohibitions, without regard to section 20103(e) of this title, that may be necessary to abate the situation.

(2) The order shall describe the condition or practice, or a combination of conditions and practices, that causes the emergency situation and prescribe standards and procedures for obtaining relief from the order. This paragraph does not affect the Secretary's discretion under this section to maintain the order in effect for as long as the emergency situation exists.

(b) REVIEW OF ORDERS.—After issuing an order under this section, the Secretary shall provide an opportunity for review of the order under section 554 of title 5. If a petition for review is filed and the review is not completed by the end of the 30-day period beginning on the date the order was issued, the order stops being effective at the end of that period unless the Secretary decides in writing that the emergency situation still exists.

(c) CIVIL ACTIONS TO COMPEL ISSUANCE OF ORDERS.—An employee of a railroad carrier engaged in interstate or foreign commerce who may be exposed to imminent physical injury during that employment because of the Secretary's failure, without any reasonable basis, to issue an order under subsection (a) of this section, or the employee's authorized representative, may bring a civil action against the Secretary in a district court of the United States to compel the Secretary to issue an order. The action must be brought in the judicial district in which the emergency situation is alleged to exist, in which that employing carrier has its principal executive office, or for the District of Columbia. The Secretary's failure to issue an order under subsection (a) of this section may be reviewed only under section 706 of title 5.

(Pub. L. 103–272, §1(e), July 5, 1994, 108 Stat. 864; Pub. L. 110–432, div. A, title III, §304, Oct. 16, 2008, 122 Stat. 4879.)

§20105. STATE PARTICIPATION

(a) INVESTIGATIVE AND SURVEILLANCE ACTIVITIES.—The Secretary concerned may prescribe investigative and surveillance activities necessary to enforce the safety regulations prescribed and orders issued by the Secretary [1] that apply to railroad equipment, facilities, rolling stock, and operations in a State. The State may participate in those activities when the safety practices for railroad equipment, facilities, rolling stock, and operations in the State are regulated by a State authority and the authority submits to the Secretary concerned an annual certification as provided in subsection (b) of this section.

(b) ANNUAL CERTIFICATION.—(1) A State authority's annual certification must include—
(A) a certification that the authority—
(i) has regulatory jurisdiction over the safety practices for railroad equipment, facilities, rolling stock, and operations in the State;
(ii) was given a copy of each safety regulation prescribed and order issued by the Secretary concerned, that applies to the equipment, facilities, rolling stock, or operations, as of the date of certification; and
(iii) is conducting the investigative and surveillance activities prescribed by the Secretary concerned under subsection (a) of this section; and

(B) a report, in the form the Secretary concerned prescribes by regulation, that includes—
(i) the name and address of each railroad carrier subject to the safety jurisdiction of the authority;
(ii) each accident or incident reported during the prior 12 months by a railroad carrier involving a fatality, personal injury requiring hospitalization, or property damage of more than $750 (or a higher amount prescribed by the Secretary concerned), and a summary of the authority's investigation of the cause and circumstances surrounding the accident or incident;
(iii) the record maintenance, reporting, and inspection practices conducted by the authority to aid the Secretary concerned in enforcing railroad safety regulations prescribed and orders issued by the Secretary concerned, including the number of inspections made of railroad equipment, facilities, rolling stock, and operations by the authority during the prior 12 months; and
(iv) other information the Secretary concerned requires.

(2) An annual certification applies to a safety regulation prescribed or order issued after the date of the certification only if the State authority submits an appropriate certification to provide the necessary investigative and surveillance activities.

(3) If, after receipt of an annual certification, the Secretary concerned decides the State authority is not complying satisfactorily with the investigative and surveillance activities prescribed under subsection (a) of this section, the Secretary concerned may reject any part of the certification or take other appropriate action to achieve adequate enforcement. The Secretary concerned must give the authority notice and an opportunity for a hearing before taking action under this paragraph. When the Secretary concerned gives notice, the burden of proof is on the authority to show that it is complying satisfactorily with the investigative and surveillance activities prescribed by the Secretary concerned.

(c) AGREEMENT WHEN CERTIFICATION NOT RECEIVED.—(1) If the Secretary concerned does not receive an annual certification under subsection (a) of this section related to any railroad equipment, facility, rolling stock, or operation, the Secretary concerned may make an agreement with a State authority for the authority to provide any part of the investigative and surveillance activities prescribed by the Secretary concerned as necessary to enforce the safety regulations and orders applicable to the equipment, facility, rolling stock, or operation.

(2) The Secretary concerned may terminate any part of an agreement made under this subsection on finding that the authority has not provided every part of the investigative and surveillance activities to which the agreement relates. The Secretary concerned must give the authority notice and an opportunity for a hearing before making such a finding. The finding and termination shall be published in the Federal Register and may not become effective for at least 15 days after the date of publication.

(d) AGREEMENT FOR INVESTIGATIVE AND SURVEILLANCE ACTIVITIES.—In addition to providing for State participation under this section, the Secretary concerned may make an agreement with a State to provide investigative and surveillance activities related to the duties under chapters 203–213 of this title (in the case of the Secretary of Transportation) and duties under section 114 of this title (in the case of the Secretary of Homeland Security).

(e) PAYMENT.—On application by a State authority that has submitted a certification under subsections (a) and (b) of this section or made an agreement under subsection (c) or (d) of this section, the Secretary concerned shall pay not more than 50 percent of the cost of the personnel, equipment, and activities of the authority needed, during the next fiscal year, to carry out a safety program under the certification or agreement. However, the Secretary concerned may pay an authority only when the authority assures the Secretary concerned that it will provide the remaining cost of the safety program and that the total State money expended for the safety program, excluding grants of the United States Government, will be at least as much as the average amount expended for the fiscal years that ended June 30, 1969, and June 30, 1970.

(f) MONITORING.—The Secretary concerned may monitor State investigative and surveillance practices and carry out other inspections and investigations necessary to help enforce this chapter (in the case of the Secretary of Transportation) and duties under section 114 of this title (in the case of the Secretary of Homeland Security).

(g) DEFINITIONS.—In this section—

(1) the term "safety" includes security; and

(2) the term "Secretary concerned" means—

(A) the Secretary of Transportation, with respect to railroad safety matters concerning such Secretary under laws administered by that Secretary; and

(B) the Secretary of Homeland Security, with respect to railroad safety matters concerning such Secretary under laws administered by that Secretary.

(Pub. L. 103–272, §1(e), July 5, 1994, 108 Stat. 864; Pub. L. 107–296, title XVII, §1710(a), Nov. 25, 2002, 116 Stat. 2319.)

---

[1] So in original. Probably should be "Secretary concerned".

§20106. PREEMPTION

(a) NATIONAL UNIFORMITY OF REGULATION.—(1) Laws, regulations, and orders related to railroad safety and laws, regulations, and orders related to railroad security shall be nationally uniform to the extent practicable.

(2) A State may adopt or continue in force a law, regulation, or order related to railroad safety or security until the Secretary of Transportation (with respect to railroad safety matters), or the Secretary of Homeland Security (with respect to railroad security matters), prescribes a regulation or issues an order covering the subject matter of the State requirement. A State may adopt or continue in force an additional or more stringent law, regulation, or order related to railroad safety or security when the law, regulation, or order—

(A) is necessary to eliminate or reduce an essentially local safety or security hazard;

(B) is not incompatible with a law, regulation, or order of the United States Government; and

(C) does not unreasonably burden interstate commerce.

(b) CLARIFICATION REGARDING STATE LAW CAUSES OF ACTION.—(1) Nothing in this section shall be construed to preempt an action under State law seeking damages for personal injury, death, or property damage alleging that a party—

(A) has failed to comply with the Federal standard of care established by a regulation or order issued by the Secretary of Transportation (with respect to railroad safety matters), or the Secretary of Homeland Security (with respect to railroad security matters), covering the subject matter as provided in subsection (a) of this section;

(B) has failed to comply with its own plan, rule, or standard that it created pursuant to a regulation or order issued by either of the Secretaries; or

(C) has failed to comply with a State law, regulation, or order that is not incompatible with subsection (a)(2).

(2) This subsection shall apply to all pending State law causes of action arising from events or activities occurring on or after January 18, 2002.

(c) JURISDICTION.—Nothing in this section creates a Federal cause of action on behalf of an injured party or confers Federal question jurisdiction for such State law causes of action.

(Pub. L. 103–272, §1(e), July 5, 1994, 108 Stat. 866; Pub. L. 107–296, title XVII, §1710(c), Nov. 25, 2002, 116 Stat. 2319; Pub. L. 110–53, title XV, §1528, Aug. 3, 2007, 121 Stat. 453.)

§20107. INSPECTION AND INVESTIGATION

(a) GENERAL.—To carry out this part, the Secretary of Transportation may take actions the Secretary considers necessary, including—

(1) conduct investigations, make reports, issue subpenas, require the production of documents, take depositions, and prescribe recordkeeping and reporting requirements; and

(2) delegate to a public entity or qualified person the inspection, examination, and testing of railroad equipment, facilities, rolling stock, operations, and persons.

(b) ENTRY AND INSPECTION.—In carrying out this part, an officer, employee, or agent of the Secretary, at reasonable times and in a reasonable way, may enter and inspect railroad equipment, facilities, rolling stock, operations, and relevant records. When requested, the officer, employee, or agent shall display proper credentials. During an inspection, the officer, employee, or agent is an employee of the United States Government under chapter 171 of title 28.

(c) RAILROAD RADIO COMMUNICATIONS.—

(1) IN GENERAL.—To carry out the Secretary's responsibilities under this part and under chapter 51, the Secretary may authorize officers, employees, or agents of the Secretary to conduct, with or without making their presence known, the following activities in circumstances the Secretary finds to be reasonable:

(A) Intercepting a radio communication, with or without the consent of the sender or other receivers of the communication, but only where such communication is broadcast or transmitted over a radio frequency which is—

(i) authorized for use by one or more railroad carriers by the Federal Communications Commission; and

(ii) primarily used by such railroad carriers for communications in connection with railroad operations.

(B) Communicating the existence, contents, substance, purport, effect, or meaning of the communication, subject to the restrictions in paragraph (3).

(C) Receiving or assisting in receiving the communication (or any information therein contained).

(D) Disclosing the contents, substance, purport, effect, or meaning of the communication (or any part thereof of such communication) or using the communication (or any information contained therein), subject to the restrictions in paragraph (3), after having received the communication or acquired knowledge of the contents, substance, purport, effect, or meaning of the communication (or any part thereof).

(E) Recording the communication by any means, including writing and tape recording.

(2) ACCIDENT AND INCIDENT PREVENTION AND INVESTIGATION.—The Secretary, and officers, employees, and agents of the Department of Transportation authorized by the Secretary, may engage in the activities authorized by paragraph (1) for the purpose of accident and incident prevention and investigation.

(3) USE OF INFORMATION.—(A) Information obtained through activities authorized by paragraphs (1) and (2) shall not be admitted into evidence in any administrative or judicial proceeding except—

(i) in a prosecution of a felony under Federal or State criminal law; or

(ii) to impeach evidence offered by a party other than the Federal Government regarding the existence, electronic characteristics, content, substance, purport, effect, meaning, or timing of, or identity of parties to, a communication intercepted pursuant to paragraphs (1) and (2) in proceedings pursuant to section 5122, 5123, 20702(b), 20111, 20112, 20113, or 20114 of this title.

(B) If information obtained through activities set forth in paragraphs (1) and (2) is admitted into evidence for impeachment purposes in accordance with subparagraph (A), the court, administrative law judge, or other officer before whom the proceeding is conducted may make such protective orders regarding the confidentiality or use of the information as may be appropriate in the circumstances to protect privacy and administer justice.

(C) No evidence shall be excluded in an administrative or judicial proceeding solely because the government would not have learned of the existence of or obtained such evidence but for the interception of information that is not admissible in such proceeding under subparagraph (A).

(D) Information obtained through activities set forth in paragraphs (1) and (2) shall not be subject to publication or disclosure, or search or review in connection therewith, under section 552 of title 5.

(E) Nothing in this subsection shall be construed to impair or otherwise affect the authority of the United States to intercept a communication, and collect, retain, analyze, use, and disseminate the information obtained thereby, under a provision of law other than this subsection.

(4) APPLICATION WITH OTHER LAW.—Section 705 of the Communications Act of 1934 (47 U.S.C. 605) and chapter 119 of title 18 shall not apply to conduct authorized by and pursuant to this subsection.

(Pub. L. 103–272, §1(e), July 5, 1994, 108 Stat. 866; Pub. L. 110–432, div. A, title III, §306, Oct. 16, 2008, 122 Stat. 4880.)

§20108. RESEARCH, DEVELOPMENT, TESTING, AND TRAINING

(a) GENERAL.—The Secretary of Transportation shall carry out, as necessary, research, development, testing, evaluation, and training for every area of railroad safety.

(b) CONTRACTS.—To carry out this part, the Secretary may make contracts for, and carry out, research, development, testing, evaluation, and training (particularly for those areas of railroad safety found to need prompt attention).

(c) AMOUNTS FROM NON-GOVERNMENT SOURCES FOR TRAINING SAFETY EMPLOYEES.—The Secretary may request, receive, and expend amounts received from non-United States Government sources for expenses incurred in training safety employees of private industry, State and local authorities, or other public authorities, except State rail safety inspectors participating in training under section 20105 of this title.

(d) FACILITIES.—The Secretary may erect, alter, and repair buildings and make other public improvements to carry out necessary railroad research, safety, and training activities at the Transportation Technology Center in Pueblo, Colorado.

(e) OFFSETTING COLLECTIONS.—The Secretary may collect fees or rents from facility users to offset appropriated amounts for the cost of providing facilities or research, development, testing, training, or other services, including long-term sustainment of the on-site physical plant.

(f) REVOLVING FUND.—Amounts appropriated to carry out subsection (d) and all fees and rents collected pursuant to subsection (e) shall be credited to a revolving fund and remain available until expended. The Secretary may use such fees and rents for operation, maintenance, repair, or improvement of the Transportation Technology Center.

(g) LEASES AND CONTRACTS.—Notwithstanding section 1302 of title 40, the Secretary may lease to others or enter into contracts for terms of up to 20 years, for such consideration and subject to such terms and conditions as the Secretary determines to be in the best interests of the Government of the United States, for the operation, maintenance, repair, and improvement of the Transportation Technology Center.

(h) PROPERTY AND CASUALTY LOSS INSURANCE.—The Secretary may allow its lessees and contractors to purchase property and casualty loss insurance for its assets and activities at the Transportation Technology Center to mitigate the lessee's or contractor's risk associated with operating a facility.

(i) ENERGY PROJECTS.—Notwithstanding section 1341 of title 31, the Secretary may enter into contracts or agreements, or commit to obligations in connection with third-party contracts or agreements, including contingent liability for the purchase of electric power in connection with such contracts or agreements, for terms not to exceed 20 years, to enable the use of the land at the Transportation Technology Center for projects to produce energy from renewable sources.

(j) RAIL RESEARCH AND DEVELOPMENT CENTER OF EXCELLENCE.—

(1) CENTER OF EXCELLENCE.—The Secretary shall award grants to establish and maintain a center of excellence to advance research and development that improves the safety, efficiency, and reliability of passenger and freight rail transportation.

(2) ELIGIBILITY.—An institution of higher education (as defined in section 101 of the Higher Education Act of 1965 (20 U.S.C. 1001)) or a consortium of nonprofit institutions of higher education shall be eligible to receive a grant from the center established pursuant to paragraph (1).

(3) SELECTION CRITERIA.—In awarding a grant under this subsection, the Secretary shall—

(A) give preference to applicants with strong past performance related to rail research, education, and workforce development activities;

(B) consider the extent to which the applicant would involve public and private sector passenger and freight railroad operators; and

(C) consider the regional and national impacts of the applicant's proposal.

(4) USE OF FUNDS.—Grant funds awarded pursuant to this subsection shall be used for basic and applied research, evaluation, education, workforce development, and training efforts related to safety, project delivery, efficiency, reliability, resiliency, and sustainability of urban commuter, intercity high-speed, and freight rail transportation, to include advances in rolling stock, advanced positive train control, human factors, rail infrastructure, shared corridors, grade crossing safety, inspection technology, remote sensing, rail systems maintenance, network resiliency, operational reliability, energy efficiency, and other advanced technologies.

(5) FEDERAL SHARE.—The Federal share of a grant awarded under this subsection shall be 50 percent of the cost of establishing and operating the center of excellence and related research activities carried out by the grant recipient.

(Pub. L. 103–272, §1(e), July 5, 1994, 108 Stat. 867; Pub. L. 117–58, div. B, title II, §§22412, 22413, Nov. 15, 2021, 135 Stat. 743, 744.)

§20109. EMPLOYEE PROTECTIONS

(a) IN GENERAL.—A railroad carrier engaged in interstate or foreign commerce, a contractor or a subcontractor of such a railroad carrier, or an officer or employee of such a railroad carrier, may not discharge, demote, suspend, reprimand, or in any other way discriminate against an employee if such discrimination is due, in whole or in part, to the employee's lawful, good faith act done, or perceived by the employer to have been done or about to be done—

(1) to provide information, directly cause information to be provided, or otherwise directly assist in any investigation regarding any conduct which the employee reasonably believes constitutes a violation of any Federal law, rule, or regulation relating to railroad safety or security, or gross fraud, waste, or abuse of Federal grants or other public funds intended to be used for railroad safety or security, if the information or assistance is provided to or an investigation stemming from the provided information is conducted by—

(A) a Federal, State, or local regulatory or law enforcement agency (including an office of the Inspector General under chapter 4 of title 5; [1]

(B) any Member of Congress, any committee of Congress, or the Government Accountability Office; or

(C) a person with supervisory authority over the employee or such other person who has the authority to investigate, discover, or terminate the misconduct;

(2) to refuse to violate or assist in the violation of any Federal law, rule, or regulation relating to railroad safety or security;

(3) to file a complaint, or directly cause to be brought a proceeding related to the enforcement of this part or, as applicable to railroad safety or security, chapter 51 or 57 of this title, or to testify in that proceeding;

(4) to notify, or attempt to notify, the railroad carrier or the Secretary of Transportation of a work-related personal injury or work-related illness of an employee;

(5) to cooperate with a safety or security investigation by the Secretary of Transportation, the Secretary of Homeland Security, or the National Transportation Safety Board;

(6) to furnish information to the Secretary of Transportation, the Secretary of Homeland Security, the National Transportation Safety Board, or any Federal, State, or local regulatory or law enforcement agency as to the facts relating to any accident or incident resulting in injury or death to an individual or damage to property occurring in connection with railroad transportation; or

(7) to accurately report hours on duty pursuant to chapter 211.

(b) HAZARDOUS SAFETY OR SECURITY CONDITIONS.—(1) A railroad carrier engaged in interstate or foreign commerce, or an officer or employee of such a railroad carrier, shall not discharge, demote, suspend, reprimand, or in any other way discriminate against an employee for—

(A) reporting, in good faith, a hazardous safety or security condition;

(B) refusing to work when confronted by a hazardous safety or security condition related to the performance of the employee's duties, if the conditions described in paragraph (2) exist; or

(C) refusing to authorize the use of any safety-related equipment, track, or structures, if the employee is responsible for the inspection or repair of the equipment, track, or structures, when the employee believes that the equipment, track, or structures are in a hazardous safety or security condition, if the conditions described in paragraph (2) exist.

(2) A refusal is protected under paragraph (1)(B) and (C) if—

(A) the refusal is made in good faith and no reasonable alternative to the refusal is available to the employee;

(B) a reasonable individual in the circumstances then confronting the employee would conclude that—

(i) the hazardous condition presents an imminent danger of death or serious injury; and

(ii) the urgency of the situation does not allow sufficient time to eliminate the danger without such refusal; and

(C) the employee, where possible, has notified the railroad carrier of the existence of the hazardous condition and the intention not to perform further work, or not to authorize the use of the hazardous equipment, track, or structures, unless the condition is corrected immediately or the equipment, track, or structures are repaired properly or replaced.

(3) In this subsection, only paragraph (1)(A) shall apply to security personnel employed by a railroad carrier to protect individuals and property transported by railroad.

(c) PROMPT MEDICAL ATTENTION.—

(1) PROHIBITION.—A railroad carrier or person covered under this section may not deny, delay, or interfere with the medical or first aid treatment of an employee who is injured during the course of employment. If transportation to a hospital is requested by an employee who is injured during the course of employment, the railroad shall promptly arrange to have the injured employee transported to the nearest hospital where the employee can receive safe and appropriate medical care.

(2) DISCIPLINE.—A railroad carrier or person covered under this section may not discipline, or threaten discipline to, an employee for requesting medical or first aid treatment, or for following orders or a treatment plan of a treating physician, except that a railroad carrier's refusal to permit an employee to return to work following medical treatment shall not be considered a violation of this section if the refusal is pursuant to Federal Railroad Administration medical standards for fitness of duty or, if there are no pertinent Federal Railroad Administration standards, a carrier's medical standards for fitness for duty. For purposes of this paragraph, the term "discipline" means to bring charges against a person in a disciplinary proceeding, suspend, terminate, place on probation, or make note of reprimand on an employee's record.

(d) ENFORCEMENT ACTION.—

(1) IN GENERAL.—An employee who alleges discharge, discipline, or other discrimination in violation of subsection (a), (b), or (c) of this section, may seek relief in accordance with the provisions of this section, with any petition or other request for

relief under this section to be initiated by filing a complaint with the Secretary of Labor.

(2) PROCEDURE.—

(A) IN GENERAL.—Any action under paragraph (1) shall be governed under the rules and procedures set forth in section 42121(b), including:

(i) BURDENS OF PROOF.—Any action brought under (d)(1) [2] shall be governed by the legal burdens of proof set forth in section 42121(b).

(ii) STATUTE OF LIMITATIONS.—An action under paragraph (1) shall be commenced not later than 180 days after the date on which the alleged violation of subsection (a), (b), or (c) of this section occurs.

(iii) CIVIL ACTIONS TO ENFORCE.—If a person fails to comply with an order issued by the Secretary of Labor pursuant to the procedures in section 42121(b), the Secretary of Labor may bring a civil action to enforce the order in the district court of the United States for the judicial district in which the violation occurred, as set forth in 42121. [3]

(B) EXCEPTION.—Notification made under section 42121(b)(1) shall be made to the person named in the complaint and the person's employer.

(3) DE NOVO REVIEW.—With respect to a complaint under paragraph (1), if the Secretary of Labor has not issued a final decision within 210 days after the filing of the complaint and if the delay is not due to the bad faith of the employee, the employee may bring an original action at law or equity for de novo review in the appropriate district court of the United States, which shall have jurisdiction over such an action without regard to the amount in controversy, and which action shall, at the request of either party to such action, be tried by the court with a jury.

(4) APPEALS.—Any person adversely affected or aggrieved by an order issued pursuant to the procedures in section 42121(b), [4] may obtain review of the order in the United States court of appeals for the circuit in which the violation, with respect to which the order was issued, allegedly occurred or the circuit in which the complainant resided on the date of such violation. The petition for review must be filed not later than 60 days after the date of the issuance of the final order of the Secretary of Labor. The review shall conform to chapter 7 of title 5. The commencement of proceedings under this paragraph shall not, unless ordered by the court, operate as a stay of the order.

(e) REMEDIES.—

(1) IN GENERAL.—An employee prevailing in any action under subsection (d) shall be entitled to all relief necessary to make the employee whole.

(2) DAMAGES.—Relief in an action under subsection (d) (including an action described in subsection (d)(3)) shall include—

(A) reinstatement with the same seniority status that the employee would have had, but for the discrimination;

(B) any backpay, with interest; and

(C) compensatory damages, including compensation for any special damages sustained as a result of the discrimination, including litigation costs, expert witness fees, and reasonable attorney fees.

(3) POSSIBLE RELIEF.—Relief in any action under subsection (d) may include punitive damages in an amount not to exceed $250,000.

(f) ELECTION OF REMEDIES.—An employee may not seek protection under both this section and another provision of law for the same allegedly unlawful act of the railroad carrier.

(g) NO PREEMPTION.—Nothing in this section preempts or diminishes any other safeguards against discrimination, demotion, discharge, suspension, threats, harassment, reprimand, retaliation, or any other manner of discrimination provided by Federal or State law.

(h) RIGHTS RETAINED BY EMPLOYEE.—Nothing in this section shall be deemed to diminish the rights, privileges, or remedies of any employee under any Federal or State law or under any collective bargaining agreement. The rights and remedies in this section may not be waived by any agreement, policy, form, or condition of employment.

(i) DISCLOSURE OF IDENTITY.—

(1) Except as provided in paragraph (2) of this subsection, or with the written consent of the employee, the Secretary of Transportation or the Secretary of Homeland Security may not disclose the name of an employee of a railroad carrier who has provided information about an alleged violation of this part or, as applicable to railroad safety or security, chapter 51 or 57 of this title, or a regulation prescribed or order issued under any of those provisions.

(2) The Secretary of Transportation or the Secretary of Homeland Security shall disclose to the Attorney General the name of an employee described in paragraph (1) if the matter is referred to the Attorney General for enforcement. The Secretary making such disclosures shall provide reasonable advance notice to the affected employee if disclosure of that person's identity or identifying information is to occur.

(j) PROCESS FOR REPORTING SECURITY PROBLEMS TO THE DEPARTMENT OF HOMELAND SECURITY.—

(1) ESTABLISHMENT OF PROCESS.—The Secretary of Homeland Security shall establish through regulations, after an opportunity for notice and comment, a process by which any person may report to the Secretary of Homeland Security regarding railroad security problems, deficiencies, or vulnerabilities.

(2) ACKNOWLEDGMENT OF RECEIPT.—If a report submitted under paragraph (1) identifies the person making the report, the Secretary of Homeland Security shall respond promptly to such person and acknowledge receipt of the report.

(3) STEPS TO ADDRESS PROBLEM.—The Secretary of Homeland Security shall review and consider the information provided in any report submitted under paragraph (1) and shall take appropriate steps to address any problems or deficiencies identified.

(Pub. L. 103–272, §1(e), July 5, 1994, 108 Stat. 867; Pub. L. 110–53, title XV, §1521, Aug. 3, 2007, 121 Stat. 444; Pub. L. 110–432, div. A, title IV, §419, Oct. 16, 2008, 122 Stat. 4892; Pub. L. 117–286, §4(b)(98), Dec. 27, 2022, 136 Stat. 4353.)

---

¹ So in original. A closing parenthesis probably should precede the semicolon.

[2] *So in original. Probably should be preceded by "subsection".*

[3] *So in original. Probably should be preceded by "section".*

[4] *So in original. The comma probably should not appear.*

§20110. EFFECT ON EMPLOYEE QUALIFICATIONS AND COLLECTIVE BARGAINING

This chapter does not—

(1) authorize the Secretary of Transportation to prescribe regulations and issue orders related to qualifications of employees, except qualifications specifically related to safety; or

(2) prohibit the bargaining representatives of railroad carriers and their employees from making collective bargaining agreements under the Railway Labor Act (45 U.S.C. 151 et seq.), including agreements related to qualifications of employees, that are not inconsistent with regulations prescribed and orders issued under this chapter.

(Pub. L. 103–272, §1(e), July 5, 1994, 108 Stat. 868.)

§20111. ENFORCEMENT BY THE SECRETARY OF TRANSPORTATION

(a) EXCLUSIVE AUTHORITY.—The Secretary of Transportation has exclusive authority—

(1) to impose and compromise a civil penalty for a violation of a railroad safety regulation prescribed or order issued by the Secretary;

(2) except as provided in section 20113 of this title, to request an injunction for a violation of a railroad safety regulation prescribed or order issued by the Secretary; and

(3) to recommend appropriate action be taken under section 20112(a) of this title.

(b) COMPLIANCE ORDERS.—The Secretary may issue an order directing compliance with this part or with a railroad safety regulation prescribed or order issued under this part.

(c) ORDERS PROHIBITING INDIVIDUALS FROM PERFORMING SAFETY-SENSITIVE FUNCTIONS.—

(1) If an individual's violation of this part, chapter 51 of this title, or a regulation prescribed, or an order issued, by the Secretary under this part or chapter 51 of this title is shown to make that individual unfit for the performance of safety-sensitive functions, the Secretary, after providing notice and an opportunity for a hearing, may issue an order prohibiting the individual from performing safety-sensitive functions in the railroad industry for a specified period of time or until specified conditions are met.

(2) This subsection does not affect the Secretary's authority under section 20104 of this title to act on an emergency basis.

(d) REGULATIONS REQUIRING REPORTING OF REMEDIAL ACTIONS.—(1) The Secretary shall prescribe regulations to require that a railroad carrier notified by the Secretary that imposition of a civil penalty will be recommended for a failure to comply with this part, chapter 51 or 57 of this title, or a regulation prescribed or order issued under any of those provisions, shall report to the Secretary, not later than the 30th day after the end of the month in which the notification is received—

(A) actions taken to remedy the failure; or

(B) if appropriate remedial actions cannot be taken by that 30th day, an explanation of the reasons for the delay.

(2) The Secretary—

(A) not later than June 3, 1993, shall issue a notice of a regulatory proceeding for proposed regulations to carry out this subsection; and

(B) not later than September 3, 1994, shall prescribe final regulations to carry out this subsection.

(Pub. L. 103–272, §1(e), July 5, 1994, 108 Stat. 868; Pub. L. 103–440, title II, §205, Nov. 2, 1994, 108 Stat. 4620; Pub. L. 110–432, div. A, title III, §305, Oct. 16, 2008, 122 Stat. 4879.)

§20112. Enforcement by the Attorney General

(a) Civil Actions.—At the request of the Secretary of Transportation, the Attorney General may bring a civil action in a district court of the United States—

(1) to enjoin a violation of, or to enforce, this part, except for section 20109 of this title, or a railroad safety regulation prescribed or order issued by the Secretary;

(2) to collect a civil penalty imposed or an amount agreed on in compromise under section 21301, 21302, or 21303 of this title; or

(3) to enforce a subpoena, request for admissions, request for production of documents or other tangible things, or request for testimony by deposition issued by the Secretary under this part.

(b) Venue.—(1) Except as provided in paragraph (2) of this subsection, a civil action under this section may be brought in the judicial district in which the violation occurred or the defendant has its principal executive office. If an action to collect a penalty is against an individual, the action also may be brought in the judicial district in which the individual resides.

(2) A civil action to enforce a subpena issued by the Secretary or a compliance order issued under section 20111(b) of this title may be brought in the judicial district in which the defendant resides, does business, or is found.

(Pub. L. 103–272, §1(e), July 5, 1994, 108 Stat. 869; Pub. L. 110–432, div. A, title III, §309, Oct. 16, 2008, 122 Stat. 4882.)

§20113. Enforcement by the States

(a) Injunctive Relief.—If the Secretary of Transportation does not begin a civil action under section 20112 of this title to enjoin the violation of a railroad safety regulation prescribed or order issued by the Secretary not later than 15 days after the date the Secretary receives notice of the violation and a request from a State authority participating in investigative and surveillance activities under section 20105 of this title that the action be brought, the authority may bring a civil action in a district court of the United States to enjoin the violation. This subsection does not apply if the Secretary makes an affirmative written finding that the violation did not occur or that the action is not necessary because of other enforcement action taken by the Secretary related to the violation.

(b) Imposition and Collection of Civil Penalties.—If the Secretary does not impose the applicable civil penalty for a violation of a railroad safety regulation prescribed or order issued by the Secretary not later than 60 days after the date of receiving notice from a State authority participating in investigative and surveillance activities under section 20105 of this title, the authority may bring a civil action in a district court of the United States to impose and collect the penalty. This paragraph does not apply if the Secretary makes an affirmative written finding that the violation did not occur.

(c) VENUE.—A civil action under this section may be brought in the judicial district in which the violation occurred or the defendant has its principal executive office. However, a State authority may not bring an action under this section outside the State.

(Pub. L. 103–272, §1(e), July 5, 1994, 108 Stat. 869.)

§20114. JUDICIAL PROCEDURES

(a) CRIMINAL CONTEMPT.—In a trial for criminal contempt for violating an injunction or restraining order issued under this chapter, the violation of which is also a violation of this chapter, the defendant may demand a jury trial. The defendant shall be tried as provided in rule 42(b) of the Federal Rules of Criminal Procedure (18 App. U.S.C.).

(b) SUBPENAS FOR WITNESSES.—A subpena for a witness required to attend a district court of the United States in an action brought under this chapter may be served in any judicial district.

(c) REVIEW OF AGENCY ACTION.—Except as provided in section 20104(c) of this title, a proceeding to review a final action of the Secretary of Transportation under this part or, as applicable to railroad safety, chapter 51 or 57 of this title shall be brought in the appropriate court of appeals as provided in chapter 158 of title 28.

(Pub. L. 103–272, §1(e), July 5, 1994, 108 Stat. 870.)

§20115. USER FEES

(a) SCHEDULE OF FEES.—The Secretary of Transportation shall prescribe by regulation a schedule of fees for railroad carriers subject to this chapter. The fees—

(1) shall cover the costs of carrying out this chapter (except section 20108(a));

(2) shall be imposed fairly on the railroad carriers, in reasonable relationship to an appropriate combination of criteria such as revenue ton-miles, track miles, passenger miles, or other relevant factors; and

(3) may not be based on that part of industry revenues attributable to a railroad carrier or class of railroad carriers.

(b) COLLECTION PROCEDURES.—The Secretary shall prescribe procedures to collect the fees. The Secretary may use the services of a department, agency, or instrumentality of the United States Government or of a State or local authority to collect the fees, and may reimburse the department, agency, or instrumentality a reasonable amount for its services.

(c) COLLECTION, DEPOSIT, AND USE.—(1) The Secretary shall impose and collect fees under this section for each fiscal year before the end of the fiscal year.

(2) Fees collected under this section shall be deposited in the general fund of the Treasury as offsetting receipts. The fees may be used, to the extent provided in advance in an appropriation law, only to carry out this chapter.

(3) Fees prescribed under this section shall be imposed in an amount sufficient to pay for the costs of activities under this chapter. However, the total fees received for a fiscal year may not be more than 105 percent of the total amount of the appropriations for the fiscal year for activities to be financed by the fees.

(d) ANNUAL REPORT.—(1) Not later than 90 days after the end of each fiscal year in which fees are collected under this section, the Secretary shall report to Congress on—

(A) the amount of fees collected during that fiscal year;

(B) the impact of the fees on the financial health of the railroad industry and its competitive position relative to each competing mode of transportation; and

(C) the total cost of Government safety activities for each other competing mode of transportation, including any part of that total cost defrayed by Government user fees.

(2) Not later than 90 days after submitting a report for a fiscal year, the Secretary shall submit to Congress recommendations for corrective legislation if the report includes a finding that—

(A) there has been an impact from the fees on the financial health of the railroad industry or its competitive position relative to each competing mode of transportation; or

(B) there is a significant difference in the burden of Government user fees on the railroad industry and other competing modes of transportation.

(e) EXPIRATION.—This section expires on September 30, 1995.

(Pub. L. 103–272, §1(e), July 5, 1994, 108 Stat. 870.)

§20116. RULEMAKING PROCESS

No rule or order issued by the Secretary under this part shall be effective if it incorporates by reference a code, rule, standard, requirement, or practice issued by an association or other entity that is not an agency of the Federal Government, unless—

(1) the date on which the code, rule, standard, requirement, or practice was adopted is specifically cited in the rule or order; or

(2) the code, rule, standard, requirement, or practice has been subject to notice and comment under a rule or order issued under this part.

(Added Pub. L. 110–432, div. A, title I, §107(a), Oct. 16, 2008, 122 Stat. 4859; amended Pub. L. 114–94, div. A, title XI, §11316(c), Dec. 4, 2015, 129 Stat. 1676.)

§20117. AUTHORIZATION OF APPROPRIATIONS

(a) IN GENERAL.—(1) There are authorized to be appropriated to the Secretary of Transportation to carry out this part and to carry out responsibilities under chapter 51 as delegated or authorized by the Secretary—

(A) $225,000,000 for fiscal year 2009;

(B) $245,000,000 for fiscal year 2010;

(C) $266,000,000 for fiscal year 2011;

(D) $289,000,000 for fiscal year 2012; and

(E) $293,000,000 for fiscal year 2013.

(2) With amounts appropriated pursuant to paragraph (1), the Secretary shall purchase Gage Restraint Measurement System vehicles and track geometry vehicles or other comparable technology as needed to assess track safety consistent with the results of the track inspection study required by section 403 of the Rail Safety Improvement Act of 2008.

(3) There are authorized to be appropriated to the Secretary $18,000,000 for the period encompassing fiscal years 2009 through 2013 to design, develop, and construct the Facility for Underground Rail Station and Tunnel at the Transportation Technology Center in Pueblo, Colorado. The facility shall be used to test and evaluate the vulnerabilities of above-ground and underground rail tunnels to prevent accidents and incidents in such tunnels, to mitigate and remediate the consequences of any such accidents or incidents, and to provide a realistic scenario for training emergency responders.

(4) Such sums as may be necessary from the amount appropriated pursuant to paragraph (1) for each of the fiscal years 2009 through 2013 shall be made available to the Secretary for personnel in regional offices and in Washington, D.C., whose duties primarily involve rail security.

(b) GRADE CROSSING SAFETY.—Not more than $1,000,000 may be appropriated to the Secretary for improvements in grade crossing safety, except demonstration projects under section 20134(c) of this title. Amounts appropriated under this subsection remain available until expended.

(c) RESEARCH AND DEVELOPMENT, AUTOMATED TRACK INSPECTION, AND STATE PARTICIPATION GRANTS.—Amounts appropriated under this section for research and development, automated track inspection, and grants under section 20105(e) of this title remain available until expended.

(d) MINIMUM AVAILABLE FOR CERTAIN PURPOSES.—At least 50 percent of the amounts appropriated to the Secretary for a fiscal year to carry out railroad research and development programs under this chapter or another law shall be available for safety research, improved track inspection and information acquisition technology, improved railroad freight transportation, and improved railroad passenger systems.

(e) OPERATION LIFESAVER.—In addition to amounts otherwise authorized by law, there are authorized to be appropriated for railroad research and development $300,000 for fiscal year 1995, $500,000 for fiscal year 1996, and $750,000 for fiscal year 1997, to support Operation Lifesaver, Inc.

(Pub. L. 103–272, §1(e), July 5, 1994, 108 Stat. 872; Pub. L. 103–440, title II, §§202, 218, Nov. 2, 1994, 108 Stat. 4619, 4625; Pub. L. 110–432, div. A, §3, Oct. 16, 2008, 122 Stat. 4850.)

§20118. PROHIBITION ON PUBLIC DISCLOSURE OF RAILROAD SAFETY ANALYSIS RECORDS

(a) IN GENERAL.—Except as necessary for the Secretary of Transportation or another Federal agency to enforce or carry out any provision of Federal law, any part of any record (including, but not limited to, a railroad carrier's analysis of its safety risks and its statement of the mitigation measures it has identified with which to address those risks) that the Secretary has obtained pursuant to a provision of, or regulation or order under, this chapter related to the establishment, implementation, or modification of a railroad safety risk reduction program or pilot program is exempt from the requirements of section 552 of title 5 if the record is—

(1) supplied to the Secretary pursuant to that safety risk reduction program or pilot program; or

(2) made available for inspection and copying by an officer, employee, or agent of the Secretary pursuant to that safety risk reduction program or pilot program.

(b) Exception.—Notwithstanding subsection (a), the Secretary may disclose any part of any record comprised of facts otherwise available to the public if, in the Secretary's sole discretion, the Secretary determines that disclosure would be consistent with the confidentiality needed for that safety risk reduction program or pilot program.

(c) Discretionary Prohibition of Disclosure.—The Secretary may prohibit the public disclosure of risk analyses or risk mitigation analyses that the Secretary has obtained under other provisions of, or regulations or orders under, this chapter if the Secretary determines that the prohibition of public disclosure is necessary to promote railroad safety.

(Added Pub. L. 110–432, div. A, title I, §109(a), Oct. 16, 2008, 122 Stat. 4866.)

§20119. Study on use of certain reports and surveys

(a) Study.—The Federal Railroad Administration shall complete a study to evaluate whether it is in the public interest, including public safety and the legal rights of persons injured in railroad accidents, to withhold from discovery or admission into evidence in a Federal or State court proceeding for damages involving personal injury or wrongful death against a carrier any report, survey, schedule, list, or data compiled or collected for the purpose of evaluating, planning, or implementing a railroad safety risk reduction program required under this chapter, including a railroad carrier's analysis of its safety risks and its statement of the mitigation measures with which it will address those risks. In conducting this study, the Secretary shall solicit input from the railroads, railroad non-profit employee labor organizations, railroad accident victims and their families, and the general public.

(b) Authority.—Following completion of the study required under subsection (a), the Secretary, if in the public interest, including public safety and the legal rights of persons injured in railroad accidents, may prescribe a rule subject to notice and comment to address the results of the study. Any such rule prescribed pursuant to this subsection shall not become effective until 1 year after its adoption.

(Added Pub. L. 110–432, div. A, title I, §109(a), Oct. 16, 2008, 122 Stat. 4867.)

§20120. Enforcement report

(a) [1] In General.—Beginning not later than December 31, 2009, the Secretary of Transportation shall make available to the public and publish on its public Web site an annual report that—

(1) provides a summary of railroad safety and hazardous materials compliance inspections and audits that Federal or State inspectors conducted in the prior fiscal year organized by type of alleged violation, including track, motive power and equipment, signal, grade crossing, operating practices, accident and incident reporting, and hazardous materials;

(2) provides a summary of all enforcement actions taken by the Secretary or the Federal Railroad Administration during the prior fiscal year, including—

(A) the number of civil penalties assessed;

(B) the initial amount of civil penalties assessed;

(C) the number of civil penalty cases settled;

(D) the final amount of civil penalties assessed;

(E) the difference between the initial and final amounts of civil penalties assessed;

(F) the number of administrative hearings requested and completed related to hazardous materials transportation law violations or enforcement actions against individuals;

(G) the number of cases referred to the Attorney General for civil or criminal prosecution; and

(H) the number and subject matter of all compliance orders, emergency orders, or precursor agreements;

(3) analyzes the effect of the number of inspections conducted and enforcement actions taken on the number and rate of reported accidents and incidents and railroad safety;

(4) provide [2] the information required by paragraphs (2) and (3)—

(A) for each Class I railroad individually; and

(B) in the aggregate for—

(i) Class II railroads;

(ii) Class III railroads;

(iii) hazardous materials shippers; and

(iv) individuals;

(5) identifies the number of locomotive engineer certification denial or revocation cases appealed to and the average length of time it took to be decided by—

(A) the Locomotive Engineer Review Board;

(B) an administrative hearing officer or administrative law judge; or

(C) the Administrator of the Federal Railroad Administration;

(6) provides an explanation regarding any changes in the Secretary's or the Federal Railroad Administration's enforcement programs or policies that may substantially affect the information reported; and

(7) includes any additional information that the Secretary determines is useful to improve the transparency of its enforcement program.

(Added Pub. L. 110–432, div. A, title III, §303(a), Oct. 16, 2008, 122 Stat. 4878; amended Pub. L. 114–94, div. A, title XI, §11316(d), Dec. 4, 2015, 129 Stat. 1676.)

---

[1] *So in original. No subsec. (b) has been enacted.*

[2] *So in original. Probably should be "provides".*

§20121. Repair and replacement of damaged track inspection equipment

The Secretary of Transportation may receive and expend cash, or receive and utilize spare parts and similar items, from non-United States Government sources to repair damages to or replace United States Government-owned automated track inspection cars and equipment as a result of third-party liability for such damages, and any amounts collected under this section shall be credited directly to the Railroad Safety and Operations account of the Federal Railroad Administration and shall remain available until expended for the repair, operation, and maintenance of automated track inspection cars and equipment in connection with the automated track inspection program.

(Added Pub. L. 114–94, div. A, title XI, §11413(a), Dec. 4, 2015, 129 Stat. 1688.)

SUBCHAPTER II—PARTICULAR ASPECTS OF SAFETY

§20131. Restricted access to rolling equipment

The Secretary of Transportation shall prescribe regulations and issue orders that may be necessary to require that when railroad carrier employees (except train or yard crews) assigned to inspect, test, repair, or service rolling equipment have to work on, under, or between that equipment, every manually operated switch, including each crossover switch, providing access to the track on which the equipment is located is lined against movement to that track and secured by an effective locking device that can be removed only by the class or craft of employees performing the inspection, testing, repair, or service.

(Pub. L. 103–272, §1(e), July 5, 1994, 108 Stat. 872.)

§20132. Visible markers for rear cars

(a) General.—The Secretary of Transportation shall prescribe regulations and issue orders that may be necessary to require that—

(1) the rear car of each passenger and commuter train has at least one highly visible marker that is lighted during darkness and when weather conditions restrict clear visibility; and

(2) the rear car of each freight train has highly visible markers during darkness and when weather conditions restrict clear visibility.

(b) Preemption.—Notwithstanding section 20106 of this title, subsection (a) of this section does not prohibit a State from continuing in force a law, regulation, or order in effect on July 8, 1976, related to lighted markers on the rear car of a freight train except to the extent it would cause the car to be in violation of this section.

(Pub. L. 103–272, §1(e), July 5, 1994, 108 Stat. 873.)

§20133. Passenger cars

(a) Minimum Standards.—The Secretary of Transportation shall prescribe regulations establishing minimum standards for the safety of cars used by railroad carriers to transport passengers. Before prescribing such regulations, the Secretary shall consider—

(1) the crashworthiness of the cars;

(2) interior features (including luggage restraints, seat belts, and exposed surfaces) that may affect passenger safety;

(3) maintenance and inspection of the cars;

(4) emergency response procedures and equipment; and

(5) any operating rules and conditions that directly affect safety not otherwise governed by regulations.

The Secretary may make applicable some or all of the standards established under this subsection to cars existing at the time the regulations are prescribed, as well as to new cars, and the Secretary shall explain in the rulemaking document the basis for making such standards applicable to existing cars.

(b) INITIAL AND FINAL REGULATIONS.—(1) The Secretary shall prescribe initial regulations under subsection (a) within 3 years after November 2, 1994. The initial regulations may exempt equipment used by tourist, historic, scenic, and excursion railroad carriers to transport passengers.

(2) The Secretary shall prescribe final regulations under subsection (a) within 5 years after November 2, 1994.

(c) PERSONNEL.—The Secretary may establish within the Department of Transportation 2 additional full-time equivalent positions beyond the number permitted under existing law to assist with the drafting, prescribing, and implementation of regulations under this section.

(d) CONSULTATION.—In prescribing regulations, issuing orders, and making amendments under this section, the Secretary may consult with Amtrak, public authorities operating railroad passenger service, other railroad carriers transporting passengers, organizations of passengers, and organizations of employees. A consultation is not subject to chapter 10 of title 5, but minutes of the consultation shall be placed in the public docket of the regulatory proceeding.

(Pub. L. 103–272, §1(e), July 5, 1994, 108 Stat. 873; Pub. L. 103–440, title II, §215(a), Nov. 2, 1994, 108 Stat. 4623; Pub. L. 104–287, §5(47), Oct. 11, 1996, 110 Stat. 3393; Pub. L. 117–286, §4(a)(306), Dec. 27, 2022, 136 Stat. 4339.)

§20134. GRADE CROSSINGS AND RAILROAD RIGHTS OF WAY

(a) GENERAL.—To the extent practicable, the Secretary of Transportation shall maintain a coordinated effort to develop and carry out solutions to the railroad grade crossing problem and measures to protect pedestrians in densely populated areas along railroad rights of way. To carry out this subsection, the Secretary may use the authority of the Secretary under this chapter and over highway, traffic, and motor vehicle safety and over highway construction. The Secretary may purchase items of nominal value and distribute them to the public without charge as part of an educational or awareness program to accomplish the purposes of this section and of any other sections of this title related to improving the safety of highway-rail crossings and to preventing trespass on railroad rights of way, and the Secretary shall prescribe guidelines for the administration of this authority.

(b) SIGNAL SYSTEMS AND OTHER DEVICES.—Not later than June 22, 1989, the Secretary shall prescribe regulations and issue orders to ensure the safe maintenance, inspection, and testing of signal systems and devices at railroad highway grade crossings.

(c) DEMONSTRATION PROJECTS.—(1) The Secretary shall establish demonstration projects to evaluate whether accidents and incidents involving trains would be reduced by—

(A) reflective markers installed on the road surface or on a signal post at railroad grade crossings;

(B) stop signs or yield signs installed at grade crossings; and

(C) speed bumps or rumble strips installed on the road surfaces at the approaches to grade crossings.

(2) Not later than June 22, 1990, the Secretary shall submit a report on the results of the demonstration projects to the Committee on Transportation and Infrastructure of the House of Representatives and the Committee on Commerce, Science, and Transportation of the Senate.

(Pub. L. 103–272, §1(e), July 5, 1994, 108 Stat. 873; Pub. L. 104–287, §5(48), Oct. 11, 1996, 110 Stat. 3393; Pub. L. 110–432, div. A, title II, §208(c), Oct. 16, 2008, 122 Stat. 4876.)

§20135. LICENSING OR CERTIFICATION OF LOCOMOTIVE OPERATORS

(a) GENERAL.—The Secretary of Transportation shall prescribe regulations and issue orders to establish a program requiring the licensing or certification, after one year after the program is established, of any operator of a locomotive.

(b) PROGRAM REQUIREMENTS.—The program established under subsection (a) of this section—

(1) shall be carried out through review and approval of each railroad carrier's operator qualification standards;

(2) shall provide minimum training requirements;

(3) shall require comprehensive knowledge of applicable railroad carrier operating practices and rules;

(4) except as provided in subsection (c)(1) of this section, shall require consideration, to the extent the information is available, of the motor vehicle driving record of each individual seeking licensing or certification, including—

(A) any denial, cancellation, revocation, or suspension of a motor vehicle operator's license by a State for cause within the prior 5 years; and

(B) any conviction within the prior 5 years of an offense described in section 30304(a)(3)(A) or (B) of this title;

(5) may require, based on the individual's driving record, disqualification or the granting of a license or certification conditioned on requirements the Secretary prescribes; and

(6) shall require an individual seeking a license or certification—

(A) to request the chief driver licensing official of each State in which the individual has held a motor vehicle operator's license within the prior 5 years to provide information about the individual's driving record to the individual's employer, prospective employer, or the Secretary, as the Secretary requires; and

(B) to make the request provided for in section 30305(b)(4) of this title for information to be sent to the individual's employer, prospective employer, or the Secretary, as the Secretary requires.

(c) WAIVERS.—(1) The Secretary shall prescribe standards and establish procedures for waiving subsection (b)(4) of this section for an individual or class of individuals who the Secretary decides are not currently unfit to operate a locomotive. However, the Secretary may waive subsection (b)(4) for an individual or class of individuals with a conviction, cancellation, revocation, or suspension described in paragraph (2)(A) or (B) of this subsection only if the individual or class, after the conviction, cancellation, revocation, or suspension, successfully completes a rehabilitation program established by a railroad carrier or approved by the Secretary.

(2) If an individual, after the conviction, cancellation, revocation, or suspension, successfully completes a rehabilitation program established by a railroad carrier or approved by the Secretary, the individual may not be denied a license or certification under subsection (b)(4) of this section because of—

(A) a conviction for operating a motor vehicle when under the influence of, or impaired by, alcohol or a controlled substance; or

(B) the cancellation, revocation, or suspension of the individual's motor vehicle operator's license for operating a motor vehicle when under the influence of, or impaired by, alcohol or a controlled substance.

(d) OPPORTUNITY FOR HEARING.—An individual denied a license or certification or whose license or certification is conditioned on requirements prescribed under subsection (b)(4) of this section shall be entitled to a hearing under section 20103(e) of this title to decide whether the license has been properly denied or conditioned.

(e) OPPORTUNITY TO EXAMINE AND COMMENT ON INFORMATION.—The Secretary, employer, or prospective employer, as appropriate, shall make information obtained under subsection (b)(6) of this section available to the individual. The individual shall be given an opportunity to comment in writing about the information. Any comment shall be included in any record or file maintained by the Secretary, employer, or prospective employer that contains information to which the comment is related.

(Pub. L. 103–272, §1(e), July 5, 1994, 108 Stat. 874.)

§20136. AUTOMATIC TRAIN CONTROL AND RELATED SYSTEMS

The Secretary of Transportation shall prescribe regulations and issue orders to require that—

(1) an individual performing a test of an automatic train stop, train control, or cab signal apparatus required by the Secretary to be performed before entering territory where the apparatus will be used shall certify in writing that the test was performed properly; and

(2) the certification required under clause (1) of this section shall be maintained in the same way and place as the daily inspection report for the locomotive.

(Pub. L. 103–272, §1(e), July 5, 1994, 108 Stat. 875; Pub. L. 103–429, §6(19), Oct. 31, 1994, 108 Stat. 4379.)

§20137. EVENT RECORDERS

(a) DEFINITION.—In this section, "event recorder" means a device that—

(1) records train speed, hot box detection, throttle position, brake application, brake operations, and any other function the Secretary of Transportation considers necessary to record to assist in monitoring the safety of train operation, such as time and signal indication; and

(2) is designed to resist tampering.

(b) REGULATIONS AND ORDERS.—Not later than December 22, 1989, the Secretary shall prescribe regulations and issue orders that may be necessary to enhance safety by requiring that a train be equipped with an event recorder not later than one year after the regulations are prescribed and the orders are issued. However, if the Secretary finds it is impracticable to equip trains within that one-year period, the Secretary may extend the period to a date that is not later than 18 months after the regulations are prescribed and the orders are issued.

(Pub. L. 103–272, §1(e), July 5, 1994, 108 Stat. 875.)

§20138. TAMPERING WITH SAFETY AND OPERATIONAL MONITORING DEVICES

(a) GENERAL.—The Secretary of Transportation shall prescribe regulations and issue orders to prohibit the willful tampering with, or disabling of, any specified railroad safety or operational monitoring device.

(b) PENALTIES.—(1) A railroad carrier operating a train on which a safety or operational monitoring device is tampered with or disabled in violation of a regulation prescribed or order issued under subsection (a) of this section is liable to the United States Government for a civil penalty under section 21301 of this title.

(2) An individual tampering with or disabling a safety or operational monitoring device in violation of a regulation prescribed or order issued under subsection (a) of this section, or knowingly operating or allowing to be operated a train on which such a device has been tampered with or disabled, is liable for penalties established by the Secretary. The penalties may include—

(A) a civil penalty under section 21301 of this title;

(B) suspension from work; and

(C) suspension or loss of a license or certification issued under section 20135 of this title.

(Pub. L. 103–272, §1(e), July 5, 1994, 108 Stat. 876.)

§20139. MAINTENANCE-OF-WAY OPERATIONS ON RAILROAD BRIDGES

Not later than June 22, 1989, the Secretary of Transportation shall prescribe regulations and issue orders for the safety of maintenance-of-way employees on railroad bridges. The Secretary at least shall provide in those regulations standards for bridge safety equipment, including nets, walkways, handrails, and safety lines, and requirements for the use of vessels when work is performed on bridges located over bodies of water.

(Pub. L. 103–272, §1(e), July 5, 1994, 108 Stat. 876.)

§20140. ALCOHOL AND CONTROLLED SUBSTANCES TESTING

(a) DEFINITION.—In this section, "controlled substance" means any substance under section 102 of the Comprehensive Drug Abuse Prevention and Control Act of 1970 (21

U.S.C. 802) specified by the Secretary of Transportation.

(b) GENERAL.—(1) In the interest of safety, the Secretary of Transportation shall prescribe regulations and issue orders, not later than October 28, 1992, related to alcohol and controlled substances use in railroad operations. The regulations shall establish a program requiring—

(A) a railroad carrier to conduct preemployment, reasonable suspicion, random, and post-accident testing of all railroad employees responsible for safety-sensitive functions (as decided by the Secretary) for the use of a controlled substance in violation of law or a United States Government regulation, and to conduct reasonable suspicion, random, and post-accident testing of such employees for the use of alcohol in violation of law or a United States Government regulation; the regulations shall permit such railroad carriers to conduct preemployment testing of such employees for the use of alcohol; and

(B) when the Secretary considers it appropriate, disqualification for an established period of time or dismissal of any employee found—

(i) to have used or been impaired by alcohol when on duty; or

(ii) to have used a controlled substance, whether or not on duty, except as allowed for medical purposes by law or a regulation or order under this chapter.

(2) When the Secretary of Transportation considers it appropriate in the interest of safety, the Secretary may prescribe regulations and issue orders requiring railroad carriers to conduct periodic recurring testing of railroad employees responsible for safety-sensitive functions (as decided by the Secretary) for the use of alcohol or a controlled substance in violation of law or a Government regulation.

(c) TESTING AND LABORATORY REQUIREMENTS.—In carrying out this section, the Secretary of Transportation shall develop requirements that shall—

(1) promote, to the maximum extent practicable, individual privacy in the collection of specimens;

(2) for laboratories and testing procedures for controlled substances, incorporate the Department of Health and Human Services scientific and technical guidelines dated April 11, 1988, and any amendments to those guidelines, including mandatory guidelines establishing—

(A) comprehensive standards for every aspect of laboratory controlled substances testing and laboratory procedures to be applied in carrying out this section, including standards requiring the use of the best available technology to ensure the complete reliability and accuracy of controlled substances tests and strict procedures governing the chain of custody of specimens collected for controlled substances testing;

(B) the minimum list of controlled substances for which individuals may be tested; and

(C) appropriate standards and procedures for periodic review of laboratories and criteria for certification and revocation of certification of laboratories to perform controlled substances testing in carrying out this section;

(3) require that a laboratory involved in controlled substances testing under this section have the capability and facility, at the laboratory, of performing screening and confirmation tests;

(4) provide that all tests indicating the use of alcohol or a controlled substance in violation of law or a Government regulation be confirmed by a scientifically recognized method of testing capable of providing quantitative information about alcohol or a controlled substance;

(5) provide that each specimen be subdivided, secured, and labeled in the presence of the tested individual and that a part of the specimen be retained in a secure manner to prevent the possibility of tampering, so that if the individual's confirmation test results are positive the individual has an opportunity to have the retained part tested by a 2d confirmation test done independently at another certified laboratory if the individual requests the 2d confirmation test not later than 3 days after being advised of the results of the first confirmation test;

(6) ensure appropriate safeguards for testing to detect and quantify alcohol in breath and body fluid samples, including urine and blood, through the development of regulations that may be necessary and in consultation with the Secretary of Health and Human Services;

(7) provide for the confidentiality of test results and medical information (other than information about alcohol or a controlled substance) of employees, except that this clause does not prevent the use of test results for the orderly imposition of appropriate sanctions under this section; and

(8) ensure that employees are selected for tests by nondiscriminatory and impartial methods, so that no employee is harassed by being treated differently from other employees in similar circumstances.

(d) REHABILITATION.—The Secretary of Transportation shall prescribe regulations or issue orders establishing requirements for rehabilitation programs that at least provide for the identification and opportunity for treatment of railroad employees responsible for safety-sensitive functions (as decided by the Secretary) in need of assistance in resolving problems with the use of alcohol or a controlled substance in violation of law or a Government regulation. The Secretary shall decide on the circumstances under which employees shall be required to participate in a program. Each railroad carrier is encouraged to make such a program available to all of its employees in addition to employees responsible for safety-sensitive functions. This subsection does not prevent a railroad carrier from establishing a program under this subsection in cooperation with another railroad carrier.

(e) INTERNATIONAL OBLIGATIONS AND FOREIGN LAWS AND REGULATIONS.—In carrying out this section, the Secretary of Transportation—

(1) shall establish only requirements that are consistent with international obligations of the United States; and

(2) shall consider applicable laws and regulations of foreign countries.

(f) OTHER REGULATIONS ALLOWED.—This section does not prevent the Secretary of Transportation from continuing in effect, amending, or further supplementing a regulation prescribed or order issued before October 28, 1991, governing the use of alcohol or a controlled substance in railroad operations.

(Pub. L. 103–272, §1(e), July 5, 1994, 108 Stat. 876; Pub. L. 104–59, title III, §342(b), Nov. 28, 1995, 109

Stat. 609.)

§20141. Power brake safety

(a) Review and Revision of Existing Regulations.—The Secretary of Transportation shall review existing regulations on railroad power brakes and, not later than December 31, 1993, revise the regulations based on safety information presented during the review. Where applicable, the Secretary shall prescribe regulations that establish standards on dynamic braking equipment.

(b) 2-Way End-of-Train Devices.—(1) The Secretary shall require 2-way end-of-train devices (or devices able to perform the same function) on road trains, except locals, road switchers, or work trains, to enable the initiation of emergency braking from the rear of a train. The Secretary shall prescribe regulations as soon as possible, but not later than December 31, 1993, requiring the 2-way end-of-train devices. The regulations at least shall—

(A) establish standards for the devices based on performance;

(B) prohibit a railroad carrier, on or after the date that is one year after the regulations are prescribed, from acquiring any end-of-train device for use on trains that is not a 2-way device meeting the standards established under clause (A) of this paragraph;

(C) require that the trains be equipped with 2-way end-of-train devices meeting those standards not later than 4 years after the regulations are prescribed; and

(D) provide that any 2-way end-of-train device acquired for use on trains before the regulations are prescribed shall be deemed to meet the standards.

(2) The Secretary may consider petitions to amend the regulations prescribed under paragraph (1) of this subsection to allow the use of alternative technologies that meet the same basic performance requirements established by the regulations.

(3) In developing the regulations required by paragraph (1) of this subsection, the Secretary shall consider information presented under subsection (a) of this section.

(c) Exclusions.—The Secretary may exclude from regulations prescribed under subsections (a) and (b) of this section any category of trains or rail operations if the Secretary decides that the exclusion is in the public interest and is consistent with railroad safety. The Secretary shall make public the reasons for the exclusion. The Secretary at least shall exclude from the regulations prescribed under subsection (b)—

(1) trains that have manned cabooses;

(2) passenger trains with emergency brakes;

(3) trains that operate only on track that is not part of the general railroad system;

(4) trains that do not exceed 30 miles an hour and do not operate on heavy grades, except for any categories of trains specifically designated by the Secretary; and

(5) trains that operate in a push mode.

(Pub. L. 103–272, §1(e), July 5, 1994, 108 Stat. 878.)

§20142. Track safety

(a) Review of Existing Regulations.—Not later than March 3, 1993, the Secretary of Transportation shall begin a review of Department of Transportation regulations related to track safety standards. The review at least shall include an evaluation of—

(1) procedures associated with maintaining and installing continuous welded rail and its attendant structure, including cold weather installation procedures;

(2) the need for revisions to regulations on track excepted from track safety standards; and

(3) employee safety.

(b) REVISION OF REGULATIONS.—Not later than September 1, 1995, the Secretary shall prescribe regulations and issue orders to revise track safety standards, considering safety information presented during the review under subsection (a) of this section and the report of the Comptroller General submitted under subsection (c) of this section.

(c) COMPTROLLER GENERAL'S STUDY AND REPORT.—The Comptroller General shall study the effectiveness of the Secretary's enforcement of track safety standards, with particular attention to recent relevant railroad accident experience and information. Not later than September 3, 1993, the Comptroller General shall submit a report to Congress and the Secretary on the results of the study, with recommendations for improving enforcement of those standards.

(d) IDENTIFICATION OF INTERNAL RAIL DEFECTS.—In carrying out subsections (a) and (b), the Secretary shall consider whether or not to prescribe regulations and issue orders concerning—

(1) inspection procedures to identify internal rail defects, before they reach imminent failure size, in rail that has significant shelling; and

(2) any specific actions that should be taken when a rail surface condition, such as shelling, prevents the identification of internal defects.

(e) TRACK STANDARDS.—

(1) IN GENERAL.—Within 90 days after the date of enactment of this subsection, the Federal Railroad Administration shall—

(A) require each track owner using continuous welded rail track to include procedures (in its procedures filed with the Administration pursuant to section 213.119 of title 49, Code of Federal Regulations) to improve the identification of cracks in rail joint bars;

(B) instruct Administration track inspectors to obtain copies of the most recent continuous welded rail programs of each railroad within the inspectors' areas of responsibility and require that inspectors use those programs when conducting track inspections; and

(C) establish a program to review continuous welded rail joint bar inspection data from railroads and Administration track inspectors periodically.

(2) INSPECTION.—Whenever the Administration determines that it is necessary or appropriate, the Administration may require railroads to increase the frequency of inspection, or improve the methods of inspection, of joint bars in continuous welded rail.

(Pub. L. 103–272, §1(e), July 5, 1994, 108 Stat. 879; Pub. L. 103–440, title II, §208, Nov. 2, 1994, 108 Stat. 4621; Pub. L. 109–59, title IX, §9005(a), Aug. 10, 2005, 119 Stat. 1924.)

§20143. LOCOMOTIVE VISIBILITY

(a) DEFINITION.—In this section, "locomotive visibility" means the enhancement of day and night visibility of the front end unit of a train, considering in particular the visibility and perspective of a driver of a motor vehicle at a grade crossing.

(b) INTERIM REGULATIONS.—Not later than December 31, 1992, the Secretary of Transportation shall prescribe temporary regulations identifying ditch, crossing, strobe, and oscillating lights as temporary locomotive visibility measures and authorizing and encouraging the installation and use of those lights. Subchapter II of chapter 5 of title 5 does not apply to a temporary regulation or to an amendment to a temporary regulation.

(c) REVIEW OF REGULATIONS.—The Secretary shall review the Secretary's regulations on locomotive visibility. Not later than December 31, 1993, the Secretary shall complete the current research of the Department of Transportation on locomotive visibility. In conducting the review, the Secretary shall collect relevant information from operational experience by rail carriers using enhanced visibility measures.

(d) REGULATORY PROCEEDING.—Not later than June 30, 1994, the Secretary shall begin a regulatory proceeding to prescribe final regulations requiring substantially enhanced locomotive visibility measures. In the proceeding, the Secretary shall consider at least—

(1) revisions to the existing locomotive headlight standards, including standards for placement and intensity;

(2) requiring the use of reflective material to enhance locomotive visibility;

(3) requiring the use of additional alerting lights, including ditch, crossing, strobe, and oscillating lights;

(4) requiring the use of auxiliary lights to enhance locomotive visibility when viewed from the side;

(5) the effect of an enhanced visibility measure on the vision, health, and safety of train crew members; and

(6) separate standards for self-propelled, push-pull, and multi-unit passenger operations without a dedicated head end locomotive.

(e) FINAL REGULATIONS.—(1) Not later than June 30, 1995, the Secretary shall prescribe final regulations requiring enhanced locomotive visibility measures. The Secretary shall require that not later than December 31, 1997, a locomotive not excluded from the regulations be equipped with temporary visibility measures under subsection (b) of this section or the visibility measures the final regulations require.

(2) In prescribing regulations under paragraph (1) of this subsection, the Secretary may exclude a category of trains or rail operations from a specific visibility requirement if the Secretary decides the exclusion is in the public interest and is consistent with rail safety, including grade-crossing safety.

(3) A locomotive equipped with temporary visibility measures prescribed under subsection (b) of this section when final regulations are prescribed under paragraph (1) of this subsection is deemed to be complying with the final regulations for 4 years after the final regulations are prescribed.

(Pub. L. 103–272, §1(e), July 5, 1994, 108 Stat. 880.)

§20144. BLUE SIGNAL PROTECTION FOR ON-TRACK VEHICLES

The Secretary of Transportation shall prescribe regulations applying blue signal protection to on-track vehicles where rest is provided.

(Pub. L. 103–272, §1(e), July 5, 1994, 108 Stat. 881.)

§20145. REPORT ON BRIDGE DISPLACEMENT DETECTION SYSTEMS

Not later than 18 months after November 2, 1994, the Secretary of Transportation shall transmit to the Committee on Commerce, Science, and Transportation of the Senate and the Committee on Transportation and Infrastructure of the House of Representatives a report concerning any action that has been taken by the Secretary on railroad bridge displacement detection systems.

(Added Pub. L. 103–440, title II, §207(a), Nov. 2, 1994, 108 Stat. 4621; amended Pub. L. 104–287, §5(48), (49), Oct. 11, 1996, 110 Stat. 3393.)

§20146. INSTITUTE FOR RAILROAD SAFETY

The Secretary of Transportation, in conjunction with a university or college having expertise in transportation safety, shall establish, within one year after November 2, 1994, an Institute for Railroad Safety. The Institute shall research, develop, fund, and test measures for reducing the number of fatalities and injuries relevant to railroad operations. There are authorized to be appropriated to the Secretary $1,000,000 for each of the fiscal years 1996 through 2000 to fund activities carried out under this section by the Institute, which shall report at least once each year on its use of such funds in carrying out such activities and the results thereof to the Secretary of Transportation and the Congress.

(Added Pub. L. 103–440, title II, §210(a), Nov. 2, 1994, 108 Stat. 4621; amended Pub. L. 104–287, §5(49), Oct. 11, 1996, 110 Stat. 3393.)

§20147. WARNING OF CIVIL LIABILITY

The Secretary of Transportation shall encourage railroad carriers to warn the public about potential liability for violation of regulations related to vandalism of railroad signs, devices, and equipment and to trespassing on railroad property.

(Added Pub. L. 103–440, title II, §211(a), Nov. 2, 1994, 108 Stat. 4622.)

§20148. RAILROAD CAR VISIBILITY

(a) REVIEW OF RULES.—The Secretary of Transportation shall conduct a review of the Department of Transportation's rules with respect to railroad car visibility. As part of this review, the Secretary shall collect relevant data from operational experience by railroads having enhanced visibility measures in service.

(b) REGULATIONS.—If the review conducted under subsection (a) establishes that enhanced railroad car visibility would likely improve safety in a cost-effective manner, the Secretary shall initiate a rulemaking proceeding to prescribe regulations requiring enhanced visibility standards for newly manufactured and remanufactured railroad cars. In such proceeding the Secretary shall consider, at a minimum—

(1) visibility of railroad cars from the perspective of nonrailroad traffic;

(2) whether certain railroad car paint colors should be prohibited or required;

(3) the use of reflective materials;

(4) the visibility of lettering on railroad cars;

(5) the effect of any enhanced visibility measures on the health and safety of train crew members; and

(6) the cost/benefit ratio of any new regulations.

(c) EXCLUSIONS.—In prescribing regulations under subsection (b), the Secretary may exclude from any specific visibility requirement any category of trains or railroad operations if the Secretary determines that such an exclusion is in the public interest and is consistent with railroad safety.

(Added Pub. L. 103–440, title II, §212(a), Nov. 2, 1994, 108 Stat. 4622.)

§20149. COORDINATION WITH THE DEPARTMENT OF LABOR

The Secretary of Transportation shall consult with the Secretary of Labor on a regular basis to ensure that all applicable laws affecting safe working conditions for railroad employees are appropriately enforced to ensure a safe and productive working environment for the railroad industry.

(Added Pub. L. 103–440, title II, §213(a), Nov. 2, 1994, 108 Stat. 4623.)

§20150. POSITIVE TRAIN CONTROL SYSTEM PROGRESS REPORT

The Secretary of Transportation shall submit a report to the Congress on the development, deployment, and demonstration of positive train control systems by December 31, 1995.

(Added Pub. L. 103–440, title II, §214(a), Nov. 2, 1994, 108 Stat. 4623.)

§20151. RAILROAD TRESPASSING, VANDALISM, AND HIGHWAY-RAIL GRADE CROSSING WARNING SIGN VIOLATION PREVENTION STRATEGY

(a) EVALUATION OF EXISTING LAWS.—In consultation with affected parties, the Secretary of Transportation shall evaluate and review current local, State, and Federal laws regarding trespassing on railroad property, vandalism affecting railroad safety, and violations of highway-rail grade crossing signs, signals, markings, or other warning devices and develop model prevention strategies and enforcement laws to be used for the consideration of State and local legislatures and governmental entities. The first such evaluation and review shall be completed within 1 year after the date of enactment of the Rail Safety Improvement Act of 2008. The Secretary shall revise the model prevention strategies and enforcement codes periodically.

(b) OUTREACH PROGRAM FOR TRESPASSING AND VANDALISM PREVENTION.—The Secretary shall develop and maintain a comprehensive outreach program to improve communications among Federal railroad safety inspectors, State inspectors certified by the Federal Railroad Administration, railroad police, and State and local law enforcement officers, for the purpose of addressing trespassing and vandalism problems on railroad property, and strengthening relevant enforcement strategies. This program shall be designed to increase public and police awareness of the illegality of, dangers inherent in, and the extent of, trespassing on railroad rights-of-way, to develop strategies to improve the prevention of trespassing and vandalism, and to improve the enforcement of laws relating to railroad trespass, vandalism, and safety.

(c) MODEL LEGISLATION.—(1) Within 18 months after November 2, 1994, the Secretary, after consultation with State and local governments and railroad carriers, shall develop and make available to State and local governments model State legislation providing for—

(A) civil or criminal penalties, or both, for vandalism of railroad equipment or property which could affect the safety of the public or of railroad employees; and

(B) civil or criminal penalties, or both, for trespassing on a railroad owned or leased right-of-way.

(2) Not later than 18 months after the date of enactment of the Rail Safety Improvement Act of 2008, the Secretary, after consultation with State and local governments and railroad carriers, shall develop and make available to State and local governments model State legislation providing for civil or criminal penalties, or both, for violations of highway-rail grade crossing signs, signals, markings, or other warning devices.

(d) DEFINITION.—In this section, the term "violation of highway-rail grade crossing signs, signals, markings, or other warning devices" includes any action by a motorist, unless directed by an authorized safety officer—

(1) to drive around a grade crossing gate in a position intended to block passage over railroad tracks;

(2) to drive through a flashing grade crossing signal;

(3) to drive through a grade crossing with passive warning signs without ensuring that the grade crossing could be safely crossed before any train arrived; and

(4) in the vicinity of a grade crossing, who creates a hazard of an accident involving injury or property damage at the grade crossing.

(Added Pub. L. 103–440, title II, §219(a), Nov. 2, 1994, 108 Stat. 4625; amended Pub. L. 104–287, §5(49), Oct. 11, 1996, 110 Stat. 3393; Pub. L. 110–432, div. A, title II, §208(a), Oct. 16, 2008, 122 Stat. 4875.)

§20152. NOTIFICATION OF GRADE CROSSING PROBLEMS

(a) IN GENERAL.—Not later than 18 months after the date of enactment of the Rail Safety Improvement Act of 2008, the Secretary of Transportation shall require each railroad carrier to—

(1) establish and maintain a toll-free telephone service for rights-of-way over which it dispatches trains, to directly receive calls reporting—

(A) malfunctions of signals, crossing gates, and other devices to promote safety at the grade crossing of railroad tracks on those rights-of-way and public or private roads;

(B) disabled vehicles blocking railroad tracks at such grade crossings;

(C) obstructions to the view of a pedestrian or a vehicle operator for a reasonable distance in either direction of a train's approach; or

(D) other safety information involving such grade crossings;

(2) upon receiving a report pursuant to paragraph (1)(A) or (B), immediately contact trains operating near the grade crossing to warn them of the malfunction or disabled vehicle;

(3) upon receiving a report pursuant to paragraph (1)(A) or (B), and after contacting trains pursuant to paragraph (2), contact, as necessary, appropriate public safety officials having jurisdiction over the grade crossing to provide them with the information necessary for them to direct traffic, assist in the removal of the disabled vehicle, or carry out other activities as appropriate;

(4) upon receiving a report pursuant to paragraph (1)(C) or (D), timely investigate the report, remove the obstruction if possible, or correct the unsafe circumstance; and

(5) ensure the placement at each grade crossing on rights-of-way that it owns of appropriately located signs, on which shall appear, at a minimum—

(A) a toll-free telephone number to be used for placing calls described in paragraph (1) to the railroad carrier dispatching trains on that right-of-way;

(B) an explanation of the purpose of that toll-free telephone number; and

(C) the grade crossing number assigned for that crossing by the National Highway-Rail Crossing Inventory established by the Department of Transportation.

(b) WAIVER.—The Secretary may waive the requirement that the telephone service be toll-free for Class II and Class III rail carriers if the Secretary determines that toll-free service would be cost prohibitive or unnecessary.

(Added Pub. L. 103–440, title III, §301(a), Nov. 2, 1994, 108 Stat. 4626; amended Pub. L. 104–287, §5(50), Oct. 11, 1996, 110 Stat. 3393; Pub. L. 110–432, div. A, title II, §205(a), Oct. 16, 2008, 122 Stat. 4872.)

§20153. AUDIBLE WARNINGS AT HIGHWAY-RAIL GRADE CROSSINGS

(a) DEFINITIONS.—As used in this section—

(1) the term "highway-rail grade crossing" includes any street or highway crossing over a line of railroad at grade;

(2) the term "locomotive horn" refers to a train-borne audible warning device meeting standards specified by the Secretary of Transportation; and

(3) the term "supplementary safety measure" refers to a safety system or procedure, provided by the appropriate traffic control authority or law enforcement authority responsible for safety at the highway-rail grade crossing, that is determined by the Secretary to be an effective substitute for the locomotive horn in the prevention of highway-rail casualties. A traffic control arrangement that prevents careless movement over the crossing (e.g., as where adequate median barriers prevent movement around crossing gates extending over the full width of the lanes in the particular direction of travel), and that conforms to standards prescribed by the Secretary under this subsection, shall be deemed to constitute a supplementary safety measure. The following do not, individually or in combination, constitute supplementary safety measures within the meaning of this subsection: standard traffic control devices or arrangements such as reflectorized crossbucks, stop signs, flashing lights, flashing lights with gates that do not completely block travel over the line of railroad, or traffic signals.

(b) REQUIREMENT.—The Secretary of Transportation shall prescribe regulations requiring that a locomotive horn shall be sounded while each train is approaching and entering upon each public highway-rail grade crossing.

(c) EXCEPTION.—(1) In issuing such regulations, the Secretary may except from the requirement to sound the locomotive horn any categories of rail operations or categories of highway-rail grade crossings (by train speed or other factors specified by regulation)—

(A) that the Secretary determines not to present a significant risk with respect to loss of life or serious personal injury;

(B) for which use of the locomotive horn as a warning measure is impractical; or

(C) for which, in the judgment of the Secretary, supplementary safety measures fully compensate for the absence of the warning provided by the locomotive horn.

(2) In order to provide for safety and the quiet of communities affected by train operations, the Secretary may specify in such regulations that any supplementary safety measures must be applied to all highway-rail grade crossings within a specified distance along the railroad in order to be excepted from the requirement of this section.

(d) APPLICATION FOR WAIVER OR EXEMPTION.—Notwithstanding any other provision of this subchapter, the Secretary may not entertain an application for waiver or exemption of the regulations issued under this section unless such application shall have been submitted jointly by the railroad carrier owning, or controlling operations over, the crossing and by the appropriate traffic control authority or law enforcement authority. The Secretary shall not grant any such application unless, in the judgment of the Secretary, the application demonstrates that the safety of highway users will not be diminished.

(e) DEVELOPMENT OF SUPPLEMENTARY SAFETY MEASURES.—(1) In order to promote the quiet of communities affected by rail operations and the development of innovative safety measures at highway-rail grade crossings, the Secretary may, in connection with demonstration of proposed new supplementary safety measures, order railroad carriers operating over one or more crossings to cease temporarily the sounding of locomotive horns at such crossings. Any such measures shall have been subject to testing and evaluation and deemed necessary by the Secretary prior to actual use in lieu of the locomotive horn.

(2) The Secretary may include in regulations issued under this subsection special procedures for approval of new supplementary safety measures meeting the requirements of subsection (c)(1) of this section following successful demonstration of those measures.

(f) SPECIFIC RULES.—The Secretary may, by regulation, provide that the following crossings over railroad lines shall be subject, in whole or in part, to the regulations required under this section:

(1) Private highway-rail grade crossings.

(2) Pedestrian crossings.

(3) Crossings utilized primarily by nonmotorized vehicles and other special vehicles.

Regulations issued under this subsection shall not apply to any location where persons are not authorized to cross the railroad.

(g) ISSUANCE.—The Secretary shall issue regulations required by this section pertaining to categories of highway-rail grade crossings that in the judgment of the Secretary pose

[§20154. Repealed. Pub. L. 114–94, div. A, title XI, §11301(c)(1), Dec. 4, 2015, 129 Stat. 1648]

CHAPTER 201—GENERAL

the greatest safety hazard to rail and highway users not later than 24 months following November 2, 1994. The Secretary shall issue regulations pertaining to any other categories of crossings not later than 48 months following November 2, 1994.

(h) IMPACT OF REGULATIONS.—The Secretary shall include in regulations prescribed under this section a concise statement of the impact of such regulations with respect to the operation of section 20106 of this title (national uniformity of regulation).

(i) REGULATIONS.—In issuing regulations under this section, the Secretary—

(1) shall take into account the interest of communities that—

(A) have in effect restrictions on the sounding of a locomotive horn at highway-rail grade crossings; or

(B) have not been subject to the routine (as defined by the Secretary) sounding of a locomotive horn at highway-rail grade crossings;

(2) shall work in partnership with affected communities to provide technical assistance and shall provide a reasonable amount of time for local communities to install supplementary safety measures, taking into account local safety initiatives (such as public awareness initiatives and highway-rail grade crossing traffic law enforcement programs) subject to such terms and conditions as the Secretary deems necessary, to protect public safety; and

(3) may waive (in whole or in part) any requirement of this section (other than a requirement of this subsection or subsection (j)) that the Secretary determines is not likely to contribute significantly to public safety.

(j) EFFECTIVE DATE OF REGULATIONS.—Any regulations under this section shall not take effect before the 365th day following the date of publication of the final rule.

(Added Pub. L. 103–440, title III, §302(a), Nov. 2, 1994, 108 Stat. 4626; amended Pub. L. 104–264, title XII, §1218(a), Oct. 9, 1996, 110 Stat. 3285; Pub. L. 104–287, §5(51), Oct. 11, 1996, 110 Stat. 3393.)

[§20154. REPEALED. PUB. L. 114–94, DIV. A, TITLE XI, §11301(C)(1), DEC. 4, 2015, 129 STAT. 1648]

Section, Pub. L. 109–59, title IX, §9002(a)(1), Aug. 10, 2005, 119 Stat. 1919, related to capital grants for rail line relocation projects.

§20155. TANK CARS

(a) STANDARDS.—The Federal Railroad Administration shall—

(1) validate a predictive model to quantify the relevant dynamic forces acting on railroad tank cars under accident conditions within 1 year after the date of enactment of this section; and

(2) initiate a rulemaking to develop and implement appropriate design standards for pressurized tank cars within 18 months after the date of enactment of this section.

(b) OLDER TANK CAR IMPACT RESISTANCE ANALYSIS AND REPORT.—Within 1 year after the date of enactment of this section the Federal Railroad Administration shall conduct a comprehensive analysis to determine the impact resistance of the steels in the shells of pressure tank cars constructed before 1989. Within 6 months after completing that analysis the Administration shall transmit a report, including recommendations for reducing any risk of catastrophic fracture and separation of such cars, to the Committee on Commerce, Science, and Transportation of the Senate and the Committee on Transportation and Infrastructure of the House of Representatives.

(Added Pub. L. 109–59, title IX, §9005(b)(1), Aug. 10, 2005, 119 Stat. 1924.)

§20156. RAILROAD SAFETY RISK REDUCTION PROGRAM

(a) IN GENERAL.—

(1) PROGRAM REQUIREMENT.—Not later than 4 years after the date of enactment of the Rail Safety Improvement Act of 2008, the Secretary of Transportation, by regulation, shall require each railroad carrier that is a Class I railroad, a railroad carrier that has inadequate safety performance (as determined by the Secretary), or a railroad carrier that provides intercity rail passenger or commuter rail passenger transportation—

(A) to develop a railroad safety risk reduction program under subsection (d) that systematically evaluates railroad safety risks on its system and manages those risks in order to reduce the numbers and rates of railroad accidents, incidents, injuries, and fatalities;

(B) to submit its program, including any required plans, to the Secretary for review and approval; and

(C) to implement the program and plans approved by the Secretary.

(2) RELIANCE ON PILOT PROGRAM.—The Secretary may conduct behavior-based safety and other research, including pilot programs, before promulgating regulations under this subsection and thereafter. The Secretary shall use any information and experience gathered through such research and pilot programs under this subsection in developing regulations under this section.

(3) REVIEW AND APPROVAL.—The Secretary shall review and approve or disapprove railroad safety risk reduction program plans within a reasonable period of time. If the proposed plan is not approved, the Secretary shall notify the affected railroad carrier as to the specific areas in which the proposed plan is deficient, and the railroad carrier shall correct all deficiencies within a reasonable period of time following receipt of written notice from the Secretary. The Secretary shall annually conduct a review to ensure that the railroad carriers are complying with their plans.

(4) VOLUNTARY COMPLIANCE.—A railroad carrier that is not required to submit a railroad safety risk reduction program under this section may voluntarily submit a program that meets the requirements of this section to the Secretary. The Secretary shall approve or disapprove any program submitted under this paragraph.

(b) CERTIFICATION.—The chief official responsible for safety of each railroad carrier required to submit a railroad safety risk reduction program under subsection (a) shall certify that the contents of the program are accurate and that the railroad carrier will implement the contents of the program as approved by the Secretary.

(c) Risk Analysis.—In developing its railroad safety risk reduction program, each railroad carrier required to submit such a program pursuant to subsection (a) shall identify and analyze the aspects of its railroad, including operating rules and practices, infrastructure, equipment, employee levels and schedules, safety culture, management structure, employee training, and other matters, including those not covered by railroad safety regulations or other Federal regulations, that impact railroad safety.

(d) Program Elements.—

(1) In general.—Each railroad carrier required to submit a railroad safety risk reduction program under subsection (a) shall develop a comprehensive safety risk reduction program to improve safety by reducing the number and rates of accidents, incidents, injuries, and fatalities that is based on the risk analysis required by subsection (c) through—

(A) the mitigation of aspects that increase risks to railroad safety; and

(B) the enhancement of aspects that decrease risks to railroad safety.

(2) Required components.—Each railroad carrier's safety risk reduction program shall include a risk mitigation plan in accordance with this section, a technology implementation plan that meets the requirements of subsection (e), and a fatigue management plan that meets the requirements of subsection (f).

(e) Technology Implementation Plan.—

(1) In general.—As part of its railroad safety risk reduction program, a railroad carrier required to submit a railroad safety risk reduction program under subsection (a) shall develop, and periodically update as necessary, a 10-year technology implementation plan that describes the railroad carrier's plan for development, adoption, implementation, maintenance, and use of current, new, or novel technologies on its system over a 10-year period to reduce safety risks identified under the railroad safety risk reduction program. Any updates to the plan are subject to review and approval by the Secretary.

(2) Technology analysis.—A railroad carrier's technology implementation plan shall include an analysis of the safety impact, feasibility, and cost and benefits of implementing technologies, including processor-based technologies, positive train control systems (as defined in section 20157(i)), electronically controlled pneumatic brakes, rail integrity inspection systems, rail integrity warning systems, switch position monitors and indicators, trespasser prevention technology, highway-rail grade crossing technology, and other new or novel railroad safety technology, as appropriate, that may mitigate risks to railroad safety identified in the risk analysis required by subsection (c).

(3) Implementation schedule.—A railroad carrier's technology implementation plan shall contain a prioritized implementation schedule for the development, adoption, implementation, and use of current, new, or novel technologies on its system to reduce safety risks identified under the railroad safety risk reduction program.

(4) Positive train control.—Except as required by section 20157 (relating to the requirements for implementation of positive train control systems), the Secretary shall ensure that—

(A) each railroad carrier's technology implementation plan required under paragraph (1) that includes a schedule for implementation of a positive train control system complies with that schedule; and

(B) each railroad carrier required to submit such a plan implements a positive train control system pursuant to such plan by December 31, 2018.

(f) FATIGUE MANAGEMENT PLAN.—

(1) IN GENERAL.—As part of its railroad safety risk reduction program, a railroad carrier required to submit a railroad safety risk reduction program under subsection (a) shall develop and update at least once every 2 years a fatigue management plan that is designed to reduce the fatigue experienced by safety-related railroad employees and to reduce the likelihood of accidents, incidents, injuries, and fatalities caused by fatigue. Any such update shall be subject to review and approval by the Secretary.

(2) TARGETED FATIGUE COUNTERMEASURES.—A railroad carrier's fatigue management plan shall take into account the varying circumstances of operations by the railroad on different parts of its system, and shall prescribe appropriate fatigue countermeasures to address those varying circumstances.

(3) ADDITIONAL ELEMENTS.—A railroad shall consider the need to include in its fatigue management plan elements addressing each of the following items, as applicable:

(A) Employee education and training on the physiological and human factors that affect fatigue, as well as strategies to reduce or mitigate the effects of fatigue, based on the most current scientific and medical research and literature.

(B) Opportunities for identification, diagnosis, and treatment of any medical condition that may affect alertness or fatigue, including sleep disorders.

(C) Effects on employee fatigue of an employee's short-term or sustained response to emergency situations, such as derailments and natural disasters, or engagement in other intensive working conditions.

(D) Scheduling practices for employees, including innovative scheduling practices, on-duty call practices, work and rest cycles, increased consecutive days off for employees, changes in shift patterns, appropriate scheduling practices for varying types of work, and other aspects of employee scheduling that would reduce employee fatigue and cumulative sleep loss.

(E) Methods to minimize accidents and incidents that occur as a result of working at times when scientific and medical research have shown increased fatigue disrupts employees' circadian rhythm.

(F) Alertness strategies, such as policies on napping, to address acute drowsiness and fatigue while an employee is on duty.

(G) Opportunities to obtain restful sleep at lodging facilities, including employee sleeping quarters provided by the railroad carrier.

(H) The increase of the number of consecutive hours of off-duty rest, during which an employee receives no communication from the employing railroad carrier or its managers, supervisors, officers, or agents.

(I) Avoidance of abrupt changes in rest cycles for employees.

(J) Additional elements that the Secretary considers appropriate.

(g) CONSENSUS.—

(1) IN GENERAL.—Each railroad carrier required to submit a railroad safety risk reduction program under subsection (a) shall consult with, employ good faith, and use its best efforts to reach agreement with, all of its directly affected employees, including any nonprofit employee labor organization representing a class or craft of directly affected employees of the railroad carrier, on the contents of the safety risk reduction program.

(2) STATEMENT.—If the railroad carrier and its directly affected employees, including any nonprofit employee labor organization representing a class or craft of directly affected employees of the railroad carrier, cannot reach consensus on the proposed contents of the plan, then directly affected employees and such organization may file a statement with the Secretary explaining their views on the plan on which consensus was not reached. The Secretary shall consider such views during review and approval of the program.

(h) ENFORCEMENT.—The Secretary shall have the authority to assess civil penalties pursuant to chapter 213 for a violation of this section, including the failure to submit, certify, or comply with a safety risk reduction program, risk mitigation plan, technology implementation plan, or fatigue management plan.

(Added Pub. L. 110–432, div. A, title I, §103(a), Oct. 16, 2008, 122 Stat. 4853; amended Pub. L. 114–94, div. A, title XI, §11316(e), Dec. 4, 2015, 129 Stat. 1676.)

§20157. IMPLEMENTATION OF POSITIVE TRAIN CONTROL SYSTEMS

(a) IN GENERAL.—

(1) PLAN REQUIRED.—Not later than 90 days after the date of enactment of the Positive Train Control Enforcement and Implementation Act of 2015, each Class I railroad carrier and each entity providing regularly scheduled intercity or commuter rail passenger transportation shall submit to the Secretary of Transportation a revised plan for implementing a positive train control system by December 31, 2018, governing operations on—

(A) its main line over which intercity rail passenger transportation or commuter rail passenger transportation, as defined in section 24102, is regularly provided;

(B) its main line over which poison- or toxic-by-inhalation hazardous materials, as defined in sections 171.8, 173.115, and 173.132 of title 49, Code of Federal Regulations, are transported; and

(C) such other tracks as the Secretary may prescribe by regulation or order.

(2) IMPLEMENTATION.—

(A) CONTENTS OF REVISED PLAN.—A revised plan required under paragraph (1) shall—

(i) describe—

(I) how the positive train control system will provide for interoperability of the system with the movements of trains of other railroad carriers over its lines; and

(II) how, to the extent practical, the positive train control system will be implemented in a manner that addresses areas of greater risk before areas of lesser risk;

(ii) comply with the positive train control system implementation plan content requirements under section 236.1011 of title 49, Code of Federal Regulations; and

(iii) provide—

(I) the calendar year or years in which spectrum will be acquired and will be available for use in each area as needed for positive train control system implementation, if such spectrum is not already acquired and available for use;

(II) the total amount of positive train control system hardware that will be installed for implementation, with totals separated by each major hardware category;

(III) the total amount of positive train control system hardware that will be installed by the end of each calendar year until the positive train control system is implemented, with totals separated by each hardware category;

(IV) the total number of employees required to receive training under the applicable positive train control system regulations;

(V) the total number of employees that will receive the training, as required under the applicable positive train control system regulations, by the end of each calendar year until the positive train control system is implemented;

(VI) a summary of any remaining technical, programmatic, operational, or other challenges to the implementation of a positive train control system, including challenges with—

(aa) availability of public funding;

(bb) interoperability;

(cc) spectrum;

(dd) software;

(ee) permitting; and

(ff) testing, demonstration, and certification; and

(VII) a schedule and sequence for implementing a positive train control system by the deadline established under paragraph (1).

(B) ALTERNATIVE SCHEDULE AND SEQUENCE.—Notwithstanding the implementation deadline under paragraph (1) and in lieu of a schedule and sequence under paragraph (2)(A)(iii)(VII), a railroad carrier or other entity subject to paragraph (1) may include in its revised plan an alternative schedule and sequence for implementing a positive train control system, subject to review under paragraph (3). Such schedule and sequence shall provide for implementation of a positive train control system as soon as practicable, but not later than the date that is 24 months after the implementation deadline under paragraph (1).

(C) AMENDMENTS.—A railroad carrier or other entity subject to paragraph (1) may file a request to amend a revised plan, including any alternative schedule and sequence, as applicable, in accordance with section 236.1021 of title 49, Code of Federal Regulations.

(D) COMPLIANCE.—A railroad carrier or other entity subject to paragraph (1) shall implement a positive train control system in accordance with its revised plan, including any amendments or any alternative schedule and sequence approved by the Secretary under paragraph (3).

(3) SECRETARIAL REVIEW.—

(A) NOTIFICATION.—A railroad carrier or other entity that submits a revised plan under paragraph (1) and proposes an alternative schedule and sequence under paragraph (2)(B) shall submit to the Secretary a written notification when such railroad carrier or other entity is prepared for review under subparagraph (B).

(B) CRITERIA.—Not later than 90 days after a railroad carrier or other entity submits a notification under subparagraph (A), the Secretary shall review the alternative schedule and sequence submitted pursuant to paragraph (2)(B) and determine whether the railroad carrier or other entity has demonstrated, to the satisfaction of the Secretary, that such carrier or entity has—

(i) installed all positive train control system hardware consistent with the plan contents provided pursuant to paragraph (2)(A)(iii)(II) on or before the implementation deadline under paragraph (1);

(ii) acquired all spectrum necessary for implementation of a positive train control system, consistent with the plan contents provided pursuant to paragraph (2)(A)(iii)(I) on or before the implementation deadline under paragraph (1);

(iii) completed employee training required under the applicable positive train control system regulations;

(iv) included in its revised plan an alternative schedule and sequence for implementing a positive train control system as soon as practicable, pursuant to paragraph (2)(B);

(v) certified to the Secretary in writing that it will be in full compliance with the requirements of this section on or before the date provided in an alternative schedule and sequence, subject to approval by the Secretary;

(vi) in the case of a Class I railroad carrier and Amtrak, implemented a positive train control system or initiated revenue service demonstration on the majority of territories, such as subdivisions or districts, or route miles that are owned or controlled by such carrier and required to have operations governed by a positive train control system; and

(vii) in the case of any other railroad carrier or other entity not subject to clause (vi)—

(I) initiated revenue service demonstration on at least 1 territory that is required to have operations governed by a positive train control system; or

(II) met any other criteria established by the Secretary.

(C) DECISION.—

(i) IN GENERAL.—Not later than 90 days after the receipt of the notification from a railroad carrier or other entity under subparagraph (A), the Secretary shall—

(I) approve an alternative schedule and sequence submitted pursuant to paragraph (2)(B) if the railroad carrier or other entity meets the criteria in subparagraph (B); and

(II) notify in writing the railroad carrier or other entity of the decision.

(ii) DEFICIENCIES.—Not later than 45 days after the receipt of the notification under subparagraph (A), the Secretary shall provide to the railroad carrier or other entity a written notification of any deficiencies that would prevent approval under clause (i) and provide the railroad carrier or other entity an opportunity to correct deficiencies before the date specified in such clause.

(D) REVISED DEADLINES.—

(i) PENDING REVIEWS.—For a railroad carrier or other entity that submits a notification under subparagraph (A), the deadline for implementation of a positive train control system required under paragraph (1) shall be extended until the date on which the Secretary approves or disapproves the alternative schedule and sequence, if such date is later than the implementation date under paragraph (1).

(ii) ALTERNATIVE SCHEDULE AND SEQUENCE DEADLINE.—If the Secretary approves a railroad carrier or other entity's alternative schedule and sequence under subparagraph (C)(i), the railroad carrier or other entity's deadline for implementation of a positive train control system required under paragraph (1) shall be the date specified in that railroad carrier or other entity's alternative schedule and sequence. The Secretary may not approve a date for implementation that is later than 24 months from the deadline in paragraph (1).

(b) TECHNICAL ASSISTANCE.—The Secretary may provide technical assistance and guidance to railroad carriers in developing the plans required under subsection (a).

(c) PROGRESS REPORTS AND REVIEW.—

(1) PROGRESS REPORTS.—Each railroad carrier or other entity subject to subsection (a) shall, not later than March 31, 2016, and annually thereafter until such carrier or entity has completed implementation of a positive train control system, submit to the Secretary a report on the progress toward implementing such systems, including—

(A) the information on spectrum acquisition provided pursuant to subsection (a)(2)(A)(iii)(I);

(B) the totals provided pursuant to subclauses (III) and (V) of subsection (a)(2)(A)(iii), by territory, if applicable;

(C) the extent to which the railroad carrier or other entity is complying with the implementation schedule under subsection (a)(2)(A)(iii)(VII) or subsection (a)(2)(B);

(D) any update to the information provided under subsection (a)(2)(A)(iii)(VI);

(E) for each entity providing regularly scheduled intercity or commuter rail passenger transportation, a description of the resources identified and allocated to implement a positive train control system;

(F) for each railroad carrier or other entity subject to subsection (a), the total number of route miles on which a positive train control system has been initiated for revenue service demonstration or implemented, as compared to the total number of route miles required to have a positive train control system under subsection (a); and

(G) any other information requested by the Secretary.

(2) PLAN REVIEW.—The Secretary shall at least annually conduct reviews to ensure

that railroad carriers or other entities are complying with the revised plan submitted under subsection (a), including any amendments or any alternative schedule and sequence approved by the Secretary. Such railroad carriers or other entities shall provide such information as the Secretary determines necessary to adequately conduct such reviews.

(3) PUBLIC AVAILABILITY.—Not later than 60 days after receipt, the Secretary shall make available to the public on the Internet Web site of the Department of Transportation any report submitted pursuant to paragraph (1) or subsection (d), but may exclude, as the Secretary determines appropriate—

(A) proprietary information; and

(B) security-sensitive information, including information described in section 1520.5(a) of title 49, Code of Federal Regulations.

(d) REPORT TO CONGRESS.—Not later than July 1, 2018, the Secretary shall transmit to the Committee on Transportation and Infrastructure of the House of Representatives and the Committee on Commerce, Science, and Transportation of the Senate a report on the progress of each railroad carrier or other entity subject to subsection (a) in implementing a positive train control system.

(e) ENFORCEMENT.—The Secretary is authorized to assess civil penalties pursuant to chapter 213 for—

(1) a violation of this section;

(2) the failure to submit or comply with the revised plan required under subsection (a), including the failure to comply with the totals provided pursuant to subclauses (III) and (V) of subsection (a)(2)(A)(iii) and the spectrum acquisition dates provided pursuant to subsection (a)(2)(A)(iii)(I);

(3) failure to comply with any amendments to such revised plan pursuant to subsection (a)(2)(C); and

(4) the failure to comply with an alternative schedule and sequence submitted under subsection (a)(2)(B) and approved by the Secretary under subsection (a)(3)(C).

(f) OTHER RAILROAD CARRIERS.—Nothing in this section restricts the discretion of the Secretary to require railroad carriers other than those specified in subsection (a) to implement a positive train control system pursuant to this section or section 20156, or to specify the period by which implementation shall occur that does not exceed the time limits established in this section or section 20156. In exercising such discretion, the Secretary shall, at a minimum, consider the risk to railroad employees and the public associated with the operations of the railroad carrier.

(g) REGULATIONS.—

(1) IN GENERAL.—The Secretary shall prescribe regulations or issue orders necessary to implement this section, including regulations specifying in appropriate technical detail the essential functionalities of positive train control systems, and the means by which those systems will be qualified.

(2) CONFORMING REGULATORY AMENDMENTS.—Immediately after the date of the enactment of the Positive Train Control Enforcement and Implementation Act of 2015, the Secretary—

(A) shall remove or revise the date-specific deadlines in the regulations or orders implementing this section to the extent necessary to conform with the amendments made by such Act; and

(B) may not enforce any such date-specific deadlines or requirements that are inconsistent with the amendments made by such Act.

(3) REVIEW.—Nothing in the Positive Train Control Enforcement and Implementation Act of 2015, or the amendments made by such Act, shall be construed to require the Secretary to issue regulations to implement such Act or amendments other than the regulatory amendments required to conform with this section.

(4) CLARIFICATION.—

(A) PROHIBITIONS.—The Secretary is prohibited from—

(i) approving or disapproving a revised plan submitted under subsection (a)(1);

(ii) considering a revised plan under subsection (a)(1) as a request for amendment under section 236.1021 of title 49, Code of Federal Regulations; or

(iii) requiring the submission, as part of the revised plan under subsection (a)(1), of—

(I) only a schedule and sequence under subsection (a)(2)(A)(iii)(VII); or

(II) both a schedule and sequence under subsection (a)(2)(A)(iii)(VII) and an alternative schedule and sequence under subsection (a)(2)(B).

(B) CIVIL PENALTY AUTHORITY.—Except as provided in paragraph (2) and this paragraph, nothing in this subsection shall be construed to limit the Secretary's authority to assess civil penalties pursuant to subsection (e), consistent with the requirements of this section.

(C) RETAINED REVIEW AUTHORITY.—The Secretary retains the authority to review revised plans submitted under subsection (a)(1) and is authorized to require modifications of those plans to the extent necessary to ensure that such plans include the descriptions under subsection (a)(2)(A)(i), the contents under subsection (a)(2)(A)(ii), and the year or years, totals, and summary under subsection (a)(2)(A)(iii)(I) through (VI).

(h) CERTIFICATION.—

(1) IN GENERAL.—The Secretary shall not permit the installation of any positive train control system or component in revenue service unless the Secretary has certified that any such system or component has been approved through the approval process set forth in part 236 of title 49, Code of Federal Regulations, and complies with the requirements of that part.

(2) PROVISIONAL OPERATION.—Notwithstanding the requirements of paragraph (1), the Secretary may authorize a railroad carrier or other entity to commence operation in revenue service of a positive train control system or component to the extent necessary to enable the safe implementation and operation of a positive train control system in phases.

(i) DEFINITIONS.—In this section:

(1) EQUIVALENT OR GREATER LEVEL OF SAFETY.—The term "equivalent or greater level of safety" means the compliance of a railroad carrier with—

(A) appropriate operating rules in place immediately prior to the use or implementation of such carrier's positive train control system, except that such rules may be changed by such carrier to improve safe operations; and

(B) all applicable safety regulations, except as specified in subsection (j).

(2) HARDWARE.—The term "hardware" means a locomotive apparatus, a wayside interface unit (including any associated legacy signal system replacements), switch position monitors needed for a positive train control system, physical back office system equipment, a base station radio, a wayside radio, a locomotive radio, or a communication tower or pole.

(3) INTEROPERABILITY.—The term "interoperability" means the ability to control locomotives of the host railroad and tenant railroad to communicate with and respond to the positive train control system, including uninterrupted movements over property boundaries.

(4) MAIN LINE.—The term "main line" means a segment or route of railroad tracks over which 5,000,000 or more gross tons of railroad traffic is transported annually, except that—

(A) the Secretary may, through regulations under subsection (g), designate additional tracks as main line as appropriate for this section; and

(B) for intercity rail passenger transportation or commuter rail passenger transportation routes or segments over which limited or no freight railroad operations occur, the Secretary shall define the term "main line" by regulation.

(5) POSITIVE TRAIN CONTROL SYSTEM.—The term "positive train control system" means a system designed to prevent train-to-train collisions, over-speed derailments, incursions into established work zone limits, and the movement of a train through a switch left in the wrong position.

(j) EARLY ADOPTION.—

(1) OPERATIONS.—From the date of enactment of the Positive Train Control Enforcement and Implementation Act of 2015 through the 1-year period beginning on the date on which the last Class I railroad carrier's positive train control system subject to subsection (a) is certified by the Secretary under subsection (h)(1) of this section and is implemented on all of that railroad carrier's lines required to have operations governed by a positive train control system, any railroad carrier, including any railroad carrier that has its positive train control system certified by the Secretary, shall not be subject to the operational restrictions set forth in sections 236.567 and 236.1029 of title 49, Code of Federal Regulations, that would apply where a controlling locomotive that is operating in, or is to be operated in, a positive train control-equipped track segment experiences a positive train control system failure, a positive train control operated consist is not provided by another railroad carrier when provided in interchange, or a positive train control system otherwise fails to initialize, cuts out, or malfunctions, provided that such carrier operates at an equivalent or greater level of safety than the level achieved immediately prior to the use or implementation of its positive train control system.

(2) SAFETY ASSURANCE.—During the period described in paragraph (1), if a positive

train control system that has been certified and implemented fails to initialize, cuts out, or malfunctions, the affected railroad carrier or other entity shall make reasonable efforts to determine the cause of the failure and adjust, repair, or replace any faulty component causing the system failure in a timely manner.

(3) PLANS.—The positive train control safety plan for each railroad carrier or other entity shall describe the safety measures, such as operating rules and actions to comply with applicable safety regulations, that will be put in place during any system failure.

(4) NOTIFICATION.—During the period described in paragraph (1), if a positive train control system that has been certified and implemented fails to initialize, cuts out, or malfunctions, the affected railroad carrier or other entity shall submit a notification to the appropriate regional office of the Federal Railroad Administration within 7 days of the system failure, or under alternative location and deadline requirements set by the Secretary, and include in the notification a description of the safety measures the affected railroad carrier or other entity has in place.

(k) SMALL RAILROADS.—Not later than 120 days after the date of the enactment of this Act,[1] the Secretary shall amend section 236.1006(b)(4)(iii)(B) of title 49, Code of Federal Regulations (relating to equipping locomotives for applicable Class II and Class III railroads operating in positive train control territory) to extend each deadline under such section by 3 years.

(l) REVENUE SERVICE DEMONSTRATION.—When a railroad carrier or other entity subject to (a)(1)[2] notifies the Secretary it is prepared to initiate revenue service demonstration, it shall also notify any applicable tenant railroad carrier or other entity subject to subsection (a)(1).

(m) REPORTS ON POSITIVE TRAIN CONTROL SYSTEM PERFORMANCE.—

(1) IN GENERAL.—Each host railroad subject to this section or subpart I of part 236 of title 49, Code of Federal Regulations, shall electronically submit to the Secretary of Transportation a Report of PTC System Performance on Form FRA F 6180.152, which shall be submitted on or before the applicable due date set forth in paragraph (3) and contain the information described in paragraph (2), which shall be separated by the host railroad, each applicable tenant railroad, and each positive train control-governed track segment, consistent with the railroad's positive train control Implementation Plan described in subsection (a)(1).

(2) REQUIRED INFORMATION.—Each report submitted pursuant to paragraph (1) shall include, for the applicable reporting period—

(A) the number of positive train control system initialization failures, disaggregated by the number of initialization failures for which the source or cause was the onboard subsystem, the wayside subsystem, the communications subsystem, the back office subsystem, or a non-positive train control component;

(B) the number of positive train control system cut outs, disaggregated by each component listed in subparagraph (A) that was the source or cause of such cut outs;

(C) the number of positive train control system malfunctions, disaggregated by each component listed in subparagraph (A) that was the source or cause of such malfunctions;

(D) the number of enforcements by the positive train control system;

(E) the number of enforcements by the positive train control system in which it is reasonable to assume an accident or incident was prevented;

(F) the number of scheduled attempts at initialization of the positive train control system;

(G) the number of train miles governed by the positive train control system; and

(H) a summary of any actions the host railroad and its tenant railroads are taking to reduce the frequency and rate of initialization failures, cut outs, and malfunctions, such as any actions to correct or eliminate systemic issues and specific problems.

(3) DUE DATES.—

(A) IN GENERAL.—Except as provided in subparagraph (B), each host railroad shall electronically submit the report required under paragraph (1) not later than—

(i) April 30, for the period from January 1 through March 31;

(ii) July 31, for the period from April 1 through June 30;

(iii) October 31, for the period from July 1 through September 30; and

(iv) January 31, for the period from October 1 through December 31 of the prior calendar year.

(B) FREQUENCY REDUCTION.—Beginning on the date that is 3 years after the date of enactment of the Passenger Rail Expansion and Rail Safety Act of 2021, the Secretary shall reduce the frequency with which host railroads are required to submit the report described in paragraph (1) to not less frequently than twice per year, unless the Secretary—

(i) determines that quarterly reporting is in the public interest; and

(ii) publishes a justification for such determination in the Federal Register.

(4) TENANT RAILROADS.—Each tenant railroad that operates on a host railroad's positive train control-governed main line and is not currently subject to an exception under section 236.1006(b) of title 49, Code of Federal Regulations, shall submit the information described in paragraph (2) to each applicable host railroad on a continuous basis.

(5) ENFORCEMENTS.—Any railroad operating a positive train control system classified under Federal Railroad Administration Type Approval number FRA–TA–2010–001 or FRA–TA–2013–003 shall begin submitting the metric required under paragraph (2)(D) not later than January 31, 2023.

(Added Pub. L. 110–432, div. A, title I, §104(a), Oct. 16, 2008, 122 Stat. 4856; amended Pub. L. 114–73, title I, §1302(b), (c), Oct. 29, 2015, 129 Stat. 576, 582; Pub. L. 114–94, div. A, title XI, §11315(d), Dec. 4, 2015, 129 Stat. 1675; Pub. L. 117–58, div. B, title II, §22414, Nov. 15, 2021, 135 Stat. 744.)

[1] See References in Text note below.

[2] So in original. Probably should be preceded by "subsection".

§20158. RAILROAD SAFETY TECHNOLOGY GRANTS

(a) GRANT PROGRAM.—The Secretary of Transportation shall establish a grant program for the deployment of train control technologies, train control component technologies, processor-based technologies, electronically controlled pneumatic brakes, rail integrity inspection systems, rail integrity warning systems, switch position indicators and monitors, remote control power switch technologies, track integrity circuit technologies, and other new or novel railroad safety technology.

(b) GRANT CRITERIA.—

(1) ELIGIBILITY.—Grants shall be made under this section to eligible passenger and freight railroad carriers, railroad suppliers, and State and local governments for projects described in subsection (a) that have a public benefit of improved safety and network efficiency.

(2) CONSIDERATIONS.—Priority shall be given to projects that—

(A) focus on making technologies interoperable between railroad systems, such as train control technologies;

(B) accelerate train control technology deployment on high-risk corridors, such as those that have high volumes of hazardous materials shipments or over which commuter or passenger trains operate; or

(C) benefit both passenger and freight safety and efficiency.

(3) IMPLEMENTATION PLANS.—Grants may not be awarded under this section to entities that fail to develop and submit to the Secretary the plans required by sections 20156(e)(2) and 20157.

(4) MATCHING REQUIREMENTS.—Federal funds for any eligible project under this section shall not exceed 80 percent of the total cost of such project.

(c) AUTHORIZATION OF APPROPRIATIONS.—There are authorized to be appropriated to the Secretary of Transportation $50,000,000 for each of fiscal years 2009 through 2013 to carry out this section. Amounts appropriated pursuant to this section shall remain available until expended.

(Added Pub. L. 110–432, div. A, title I, §105(a), Oct. 16, 2008, 122 Stat. 4858.)

§20159. ROADWAY USER SIGHT DISTANCE AT HIGHWAY-RAIL GRADE CROSSINGS

Not later than 18 months after the date of enactment of the Rail Safety Improvement Act of 2008, the Secretary of Transportation, after consultation with the Federal Railroad Administration, the Federal Highway Administration, and States, shall develop and make available to States model legislation providing for improving safety by addressing sight obstructions, including vegetation growth, topographic features, structures, and standing railroad equipment, at highway-rail grade crossings that are equipped solely with passive warnings, as recommended by the Inspector General of the Department of Transportation in Report No. MH–2007–044.

(Added Pub. L. 110–432, div. A, title II, §203(a), Oct. 16, 2008, 122 Stat. 4869; amended Pub. L. 114–94, div. A, title XI, §11316(f), Dec. 4, 2015, 129 Stat. 1676.)

§20160. NATIONAL CROSSING INVENTORY

(a) INITIAL REPORTING OF INFORMATION ABOUT PREVIOUSLY UNREPORTED CROSSINGS.—Not later than 1 year after the date of enactment of the Rail Safety Improvement Act of 2008 or 6 months after a new crossing becomes operational, whichever occurs later, each railroad carrier shall—

(1) report to the Secretary of Transportation current information, including information about warning devices and signage, as specified by the Secretary, concerning each previously unreported crossing through which it operates with respect to the trackage over which it operates; or

(2) ensure that the information has been reported to the Secretary by another railroad carrier that operates through the crossing.

(b) UPDATING OF CROSSING INFORMATION.—

(1) On a periodic basis beginning not later than 2 years after the date of enactment of the Rail Safety Improvement Act of 2008 and on or before September 30 of every year thereafter, or as otherwise specified by the Secretary, each railroad carrier shall—

(A) report to the Secretary current information, including information about warning devices and signage, as specified by the Secretary, concerning each crossing through which it operates with respect to the trackage over which it operates; or

(B) ensure that the information has been reported to the Secretary by another railroad carrier that operates through the crossing.

(2) A railroad carrier that sells a crossing or any part of a crossing on or after the date of enactment of the Rail Safety Improvement Act of 2008 shall, not later than the date that is 18 months after the date of enactment of that Act or 3 months after the sale, whichever occurs later, or as otherwise specified by the Secretary, report to the Secretary current information, as specified by the Secretary, concerning the change in ownership of the crossing or part of the crossing.

(c) RULEMAKING AUTHORITY.—The Secretary shall prescribe the regulations necessary to implement this section. The Secretary may enforce each provision of the Department of Transportation's statement of the national highway-rail crossing inventory policy, procedures, and instruction for States and railroads that is in effect on the date of enactment of the Rail Safety Improvement Act of 2008, until such provision is superseded by a regulation issued under this section.

(d) DEFINITIONS.—In this section:

(1) CROSSING.—The term "crossing" means a location within a State, other than a location where one or more railroad tracks cross one or more railroad tracks either at grade or grade-separated, where—

(A) a public highway, road, or street, or a private roadway, including associated sidewalks and pathways, crosses one or more railroad tracks either at grade or grade-separated; or

(B) a pathway explicitly authorized by a public authority or a railroad carrier that is dedicated for the use of nonvehicular traffic, including pedestrians, bicyclists, and others, that is not associated with a public highway, road, or street, or a private

243

roadway, crosses one or more railroad tracks either at grade or grade-separated.

(2) STATE.—The term "State" means a State of the United States, the District of Columbia, or the Commonwealth of Puerto Rico.

(Added Pub. L. 110–432, div. A, title II, §204(a), Oct. 16, 2008, 122 Stat. 4869; amended Pub. L. 114–94, div. A, title XI, §11316(g), Dec. 4, 2015, 129 Stat. 1676.)

§20161. FOSTERING INTRODUCTION OF NEW TECHNOLOGY TO IMPROVE SAFETY AT HIGHWAY-RAIL GRADE CROSSINGS

(a) FINDINGS.—

(1) Collisions between highway users and trains at highway-rail grade crossings continue to cause an unacceptable loss of life, serious personal injury, and property damage.

(2) While elimination of at-grade crossings through consolidation of crossings and grade separations offers the greatest long-term promise for optimizing the safety and efficiency of the two modes of transportation, over 140,000 public grade crossings remain on the general rail system—approximately one for each route mile on the general rail system.

(3) Conventional highway traffic control devices such as flashing lights and gates are often effective in warning motorists of a train's approach to an equipped crossing.

(4) Since enactment of the Highway Safety Act of 1973, over $4,200,000,000 of Federal funding has been invested in safety improvements at highway-rail grade crossings, yet a majority of public highway-rail grade crossings are not yet equipped with active warning systems.

(5) The emergence of new technologies presents opportunities for more effective and affordable warnings and safer passage of highway users and trains at remaining highway-rail grade crossings.

(6) Implementation of new crossing safety technology will require extensive cooperation between highway authorities and railroad carriers.

(7) Federal Railroad Administration regulations establishing performance standards for processor-based signal and train control systems provide a suitable framework for qualification of new or novel technology at highway-rail grade crossings, and the Federal Highway Administration's Manual on Uniform Traffic Control Devices provides an appropriate means of determining highway user interface with such new technology.

(b) POLICY.—It is the policy of the United States to encourage the development of new technology that can prevent loss of life and injuries at highway-rail grade crossings. The Secretary of Transportation is designated to carry out this policy in consultation with States and necessary public and private entities.

(c) SUBMISSION OF NEW TECHNOLOGY PROPOSALS.—Railroad carriers and railroad suppliers may submit for review and approval to the Secretary such new technology designed to improve safety at highway-rail grade crossings. The Secretary shall approve by order the new technology designed to improve safety at highway-rail grade crossings in accordance with Federal Railroad Administration standards for the development and use of processor-based signal and train control systems and shall consider the effects on safety of highway-user interface with the new technology.

(d) EFFECT OF SECRETARIAL APPROVAL.—If the Secretary approves by order new technology to provide warning to highway users at a highway-rail grade crossing and such technology is installed at a highway-rail grade crossing in accordance with the conditions of the approval, this determination preempts any State statute or regulation concerning the adequacy of the technology in providing warning at the crossing.

(Added Pub. L. 110–432, div. A, title II, §210(a), Oct. 16, 2008, 122 Stat. 4876.)

§20162. MINIMUM TRAINING STANDARDS AND PLANS

(a) IN GENERAL.—The Secretary of Transportation shall, not later than 1 year after the date of enactment of the Rail Safety Improvement Act of 2008, establish—

(1) minimum training standards for each class and craft of safety-related railroad employee (as defined in section 20102) and equivalent railroad carrier contractor and subcontractor employees, which shall require railroad carriers, contractors, and subcontractors to qualify or otherwise document the proficiency of such employees in each such class and craft regarding their knowledge of, and ability to comply with, Federal railroad safety laws and regulations and railroad carrier rules and procedures promulgated to implement those Federal railroad safety laws and regulations;

(2) a requirement that railroad carriers, contractors, and subcontractors develop and submit training and qualification plans to the Secretary for approval, including training programs and information deemed necessary by the Secretary to ensure that all safety-related railroad employees receive appropriate training in a timely manner; and

(3) a minimum training curriculum, and ongoing training criteria, testing, and skills evaluation measures to ensure that safety-related railroad employees, and contractor and subcontractor employees, charged with the inspection of track or railroad equipment are qualified to assess railroad carrier compliance with Federal standards to identify defective conditions and initiate immediate remedial action to correct critical safety defects that are known to contribute to derailments, accidents, incidents, or injuries, and, in implementing the requirements of this paragraph, take into consideration existing training programs of railroad carriers.

(b) APPROVAL.—The Secretary shall review and approve the plans required under subsection (a)(2) utilizing an approval process required for programs to certify the qualification of locomotive engineers pursuant to part 240 of title 49, Code of Federal Regulations.

(c) EXEMPTION.—The Secretary may exempt railroad carriers and railroad carrier contractors and subcontractors from submitting training plans for which the Secretary has issued training regulations before the date of enactment of the Rail Safety Improvement Act of 2008.

(Added Pub. L. 110–432, div. A, title IV, §401(a), Oct. 16, 2008, 122 Stat. 4883; amended Pub. L. 114–94, div. A, title XI, §11316(h), Dec. 4, 2015, 129 Stat. 1677.)

§20163. CERTIFICATION OF TRAIN CONDUCTORS

(a) REGULATIONS.—Not later than 18 months after the date of enactment of the Rail Safety Improvement Act of 2008, the Secretary of Transportation shall prescribe regulations to establish a program requiring the certification of train conductors. In prescribing such regulations, the Secretary shall require that train conductors be trained, in accordance with the training standards developed pursuant to section 20162.

(b) PROGRAM REQUIREMENTS.—In developing the regulations required by subsection (a), the Secretary may consider the requirements of section 20135(b) through (e).

(Added Pub. L. 110–432, div. A, title IV, §402(a), Oct. 16, 2008, 122 Stat. 4884.)

§20164. DEVELOPMENT AND USE OF RAIL SAFETY TECHNOLOGY

(a) IN GENERAL.—Not later than 1 year after the date of enactment of the Rail Safety Improvement Act of 2008, the Secretary of Transportation shall prescribe standards, guidance, regulations, or orders governing the development, use, and implementation of rail safety technology in dark territory, in arrangements not defined in section 20501 or otherwise not covered by Federal standards, guidance, regulations, or orders that ensure the safe operation of such technology, such as—

(1) switch position monitoring devices or indicators;

(2) radio, remote control, or other power-assisted switches;

(3) hot box, high water, or earthquake detectors;

(4) remote control locomotive zone limiting devices;

(5) slide fences;

(6) grade crossing video monitors;

(7) track integrity warning systems; or

(8) other similar rail safety technologies, as determined by the Secretary.

(b) DARK TERRITORY DEFINED.—In this section, the term "dark territory" means any territory in a railroad system that does not have a signal or train control system installed or operational.

(Added Pub. L. 110–432, div. A, title IV, §406(a), Oct. 16, 2008, 122 Stat. 4886; amended Pub. L. 114–94, div. A, title XI, §11316(i), Dec. 4, 2015, 129 Stat. 1677.)

§20165. LIMITATIONS ON NON-FEDERAL ALCOHOL AND DRUG TESTING

(a) TESTING REQUIREMENTS.—Any non-Federal alcohol and drug testing program of a railroad carrier must provide that all post-employment tests of the specimens of employees who are subject to both the program and chapter 211 of this title be conducted using a scientifically recognized method of testing capable of determining the presence of the specific analyte at a level above the cut-off level established by the carrier.

(b) REDRESS PROCESS.—Each railroad carrier that has a non-Federal alcohol and drug testing program must provide a redress process to its employees who are subject to both the alcohol and drug testing program and chapter 211 of this title for such an employee to petition for and receive a carrier hearing to review his or her specimen test results that were determined to be in violation of the program. A dispute or grievance raised by a railroad carrier or its employee, except a probationary employee, in connection with the carrier's alcohol and drug testing program and the application of this section is subject to resolution under section 3 of the Railway Labor Act (45 U.S.C. 153).

(Added Pub. L. 110–432, div. A, title IV, §409(a), Oct. 16, 2008, 122 Stat. 4887.)

§20166. Emergency escape breathing apparatus

Not later than 18 months after the date of enactment of the Rail Safety Improvement Act of 2008, the Secretary of Transportation shall prescribe regulations that require railroad carriers—

(1) to provide emergency escape breathing apparatus suitable to provide head and neck coverage with respiratory protection for all crewmembers in locomotive cabs on freight trains carrying hazardous materials that would pose an inhalation hazard in the event of release;

(2) to provide convenient storage in each freight train locomotive to enable crewmembers to access such apparatus quickly;

(3) to maintain such equipment in proper working condition; and

(4) to provide their crewmembers with appropriate training for using the breathing apparatus.

(Added Pub. L. 110–432, div. A, title IV, §413(a), Oct. 16, 2008, 122 Stat. 4889.)

§20167. Reports on highway-rail grade crossing safety

(a) Report.—Not later than 4 years after the date by which States are required to submit State highway-rail grade crossing action plans under section 11401(b) of the Fixing America's Surface Transportation Act (49 U.S.C. 22907 note), the Administrator of the Federal Railroad Administration, in consultation with the Administrator of the Federal Highway Administration, shall submit a report to the Committee on Commerce, Science, and Transportation of the Senate and the Committee on Transportation and Infrastructure of the House of Representatives that summarizes the State highway-rail grade crossing action plans, including—

(1) an analysis and evaluation of each State railway-highway crossings program under section 130 of title 23, including—

(A) compliance with section 11401 of the Fixing America's Surface Transportation Act and section 130(g) of title 23; and

(B) the specific strategies identified by each State to improve safety at highway-rail grade crossings, including crossings with multiple accidents or incidents;

(2) the progress of each State in implementing its State highway-rail grade crossings action plan;

(3) the number of highway-rail grade crossing projects undertaken pursuant to section 130 of title 23, including the distribution of such projects by cost range, road system, nature of treatment, and subsequent accident experience at improved locations;

(4) which States are not in compliance with their schedule of projects under section

130(d) of title 23; and

(5) any recommendations for future implementation of the railway-highway crossings program under section 130 of title 23.

(b) UPDATES.—Not later than 5 years after the submission of the report required under subsection (a), the Administrator of the Federal Railroad Administration, in consultation with the Administrator of the Federal Highway Administration, shall—

(1) update the report based on the State annual reports submitted pursuant to section 130(g) of title 23 and any other information obtained by or available to the Administrator of the Federal Railroad Administration; and

(2) submit the updated report to the Committee on Commerce, Science, and Transportation of the Senate and the Committee on Transportation and Infrastructure of the House of Representatives.

(c) DEFINITIONS.—In this section:

(1) HIGHWAY-RAIL GRADE CROSSING.—The term "highway-rail grade crossing" means a location within a State, other than a location at which 1 or more railroad tracks cross 1 or more railroad tracks at grade, at which—

(A) a public highway, road, or street, or a private roadway, including associated sidewalks and pathways, crosses 1 or more railroad tracks, either at grade or grade-separated; or

(B) a pathway explicitly authorized by a public authority or a railroad carrier that—

(i) is dedicated for the use of nonvehicular traffic, including pedestrians, bicyclists, and others;

(ii) is not associated with a public highway, road, or street, or a private roadway; and

(iii) crosses 1 or more railroad tracks, either at grade or grade-separated.

(2) STATE.—The term "State" means a State of the United States or the District of Columbia.

(Added Pub. L. 117–58, div. B, title II, §22403(b)(1), Nov. 15, 2021, 135 Stat. 735.)

§20168. INSTALLATION OF AUDIO AND IMAGE RECORDING DEVICES

(a) IN GENERAL.—Not later than 2 years after the date of enactment of the Passenger Rail Reform and Investment Act of 2015, the Secretary of Transportation shall promulgate regulations to require each railroad carrier that provides regularly scheduled intercity rail passenger or commuter rail passenger transportation to the public to install inward- and outward-facing image recording devices in all controlling locomotive cabs and cab car operating compartments in such passenger trains.

(b) DEVICE STANDARDS.—Each inward- and outward-facing image recording device shall—

(1) have a minimum 12-hour continuous recording capability;

(2) have crash and fire protections for any in-cab image recordings that are stored only within a controlling locomotive cab or cab car operating compartment; and

(3) have recordings accessible for review during an accident or incident investigation.

(c) Review.—The Secretary shall establish a process to review and approve or disapprove an inward- or outward-facing image recording device for compliance with the standards described in subsection (b).

(d) Uses.—A railroad carrier subject to the requirements of subsection (a) that has installed an inward- or outward-facing image recording device approved under subsection (c) may use recordings from that inward- or outward-facing image recording device for the following purposes:

(1) Verifying that train crew actions are in accordance with applicable safety laws and the railroad carrier's operating rules and procedures, including a system-wide program for such verification.

(2) Assisting in an investigation into the causation of a reportable accident or incident.

(3) Documenting a criminal act or monitoring unauthorized occupancy of the controlling locomotive cab or car operating compartment.

(4) Other purposes that the Secretary considers appropriate.

(e) Discretion.—

(1) In general.—The Secretary may—

(A) require in-cab audio recording devices for the purposes described in subsection (d); and

(B) define in appropriate technical detail the essential features of the devices required under subparagraph (A).

(2) Exemptions.—The Secretary may exempt any railroad carrier subject to the requirements of subsection (a) or any part of the carrier's operations from the requirements under subsection (a) if the Secretary determines that the carrier has implemented an alternative technology or practice that provides an equivalent or greater safety benefit or that is better suited to the risks of the operation.

(f) Tampering.—

(1) In general.—Except as provided in paragraph (2), a railroad carrier subject to the requirements of subsection (a) may take appropriate enforcement or administrative action against any employee that tampers with or disables an audio or inward- or outward-facing image recording device installed by the railroad carrier.

(2) Temporarily obscuring field of view of an image recording device while expressing breast milk.—

(A) In general.—For purposes of expressing breast milk, an employee may temporarily obscure the field of view of an image recording device required under this section if the passenger train on which such device is installed is not in motion.

(B) Resuming operation.—The crew of a passenger train on which an image recording device has been obscured pursuant to subparagraph (A) shall ensure that such image recording device is no longer obscured immediately after the employee has finished expressing breast milk and before resuming operation of the passenger train.

(g) PRESERVATION OF DATA.—Each railroad carrier subject to the requirements of subsection (a) shall preserve recording device data for 1 year after the date of a reportable accident or incident.

(h) INFORMATION PROTECTIONS.—The Secretary may not disclose publicly any part of an in-cab audio or image recording or transcript of oral communications by or among train employees or other operating employees responsible for the movement and direction of the train, or between such operating employees and company communication centers, related to an accident or incident investigated by the Secretary. The Secretary may make public any part of a transcript or any written depiction of visual information that the Secretary determines is relevant to the accident at the time a majority of the other factual reports on the accident or incident are released to the public.

(i) PROHIBITED USE.—An in-cab audio or image recording obtained by a railroad carrier under this section may not be used to retaliate against an employee.

(j) SAVINGS CLAUSE.—Nothing in this section may be construed as requiring a railroad carrier to cease or restrict operations upon a technical failure of an inward- or outward-facing image recording device or in-cab audio device. Such railroad carrier shall repair or replace the failed inward- or outward-facing image recording device as soon as practicable.

(Added Pub. L. 114–94, div. A, title XI, §11411(a), Dec. 4, 2015, 129 Stat. 1686; amended Pub. L. 117–328, div. KK, §102(c), Dec. 29, 2022, 136 Stat. 6096.)

§20169. SPEED LIMIT ACTION PLANS

(a) IN GENERAL.—Not later than March 3, 2016, each railroad carrier providing intercity rail passenger transportation or commuter rail passenger transportation, in consultation with any applicable host railroad carrier, shall survey its entire system and identify each main track location where there is a reduction of more than 20 miles per hour from the approach speed to a curve, bridge, or tunnel and the maximum authorized operating speed for passenger trains at that curve, bridge, or tunnel.

(b) ACTION PLANS.—Not later than 120 days after the date that the survey under subsection (a) is complete, a railroad carrier described in subsection (a) shall submit to the Secretary of Transportation an action plan that—

(1) identifies each main track location where there is a reduction of more than 20 miles per hour from the approach speed to a curve, bridge, or tunnel and the maximum authorized operating speed for passenger trains at that curve, bridge, or tunnel;

(2) describes appropriate actions to enable warning and enforcement of the maximum authorized speed for passenger trains at each location identified under paragraph (1), including—

(A) modification to automatic train control systems, if applicable, or other signal systems;

(B) increased crew size;

(C) installation of signage alerting train crews of the maximum authorized speed for passenger trains in each location identified under paragraph (1);

(D) installation of alerters;

(E) increased crew communication; and

(F) other practices;

(3) contains milestones and target dates for implementing each appropriate action described under paragraph (2); and

(4) ensures compliance with the maximum authorized speed at each location identified under paragraph (1).

(c) APPROVAL.—Not later than 90 days after the date on which an action plan is submitted under subsection (b) or (d)(2), the Secretary shall approve, approve with conditions, or disapprove the action plan.

(d) PERIODIC REVIEWS AND UPDATES.—Each railroad carrier that submits an action plan to the Secretary pursuant to subsection (b) shall—

(1) not later than 1 year after the date of enactment of the Passenger Rail Expansion and Rail Safety Act of 2021, and annually thereafter, review such plan to ensure the effectiveness of actions taken to enable warning and enforcement of the maximum authorized speed for passenger trains at each location identified pursuant to subsection (b)(1); and

(2) not later than 90 days before implementing any significant operational or territorial operating change, including initiating a new service or route, submit to the Secretary a revised action plan, after consultation with any applicable host railroad, that addresses such operational or territorial operating change.

(e) NEW SERVICE.—If a railroad carrier providing intercity rail passenger transportation or commuter rail passenger transportation did not exist on the date of enactment of the FAST Act (Public Law 114–94; 129 Stat. 1312), such railroad carrier, in consultation with any applicable host railroad carrier, shall—

(1) survey its routes pursuant to subsection (a) not later than 90 days after the date of enactment of the Passenger Rail Expansion and Rail Safety Act of 2021; and

(2) develop an action plan pursuant to subsection (b) not later than 120 days after the date on which such survey is complete.

(f) ALTERNATIVE SAFETY MEASURES.   The Secretary may exempt from the requirements under this section each segment of track for which operations are governed by a positive train control system certified under section 20157, or any other safety technology or practice that would achieve an equivalent or greater level of safety in reducing derailment risk.

(g) PROHIBITION.—No new intercity or commuter rail passenger service may begin operation unless the railroad carrier providing such service is in compliance with the requirements under this section.

(h) SAVINGS CLAUSE.—Nothing in this section may be construed to prohibit the Secretary from applying the requirements under this section to other segments of track at high risk of overspeed derailment.

(Added Pub. L. 117–58, div. B, title II, §22415(a), Nov. 15, 2021, 135 Stat. 746.)

§20170. PRE-REVENUE SERVICE SAFETY VALIDATION PLAN

(a) PLAN SUBMISSION.—Any railroad providing new, regularly scheduled, intercity or commuter rail passenger transportation, an extension of existing service, or a renewal of service that has been discontinued for more than 180 days shall develop and submit for review a comprehensive pre-revenue service safety validation plan to the Secretary of Transportation not later than 60 days before initiating such revenue service. Such plan shall include pertinent safety milestones and a minimum period of simulated revenue service to ensure operational readiness and that all safety sensitive personnel are properly trained and qualified.

(b) COMPLIANCE.—After submitting a plan pursuant to subsection (a), the railroad shall adopt and comply with such plan and may not amend the plan without first notifying the Secretary of the proposed amendment. Revenue service may not begin until the railroad has completed the requirements of its plan, including the minimum simulated service period required by the plan.

(c) RULEMAKING.—The Secretary shall promulgate regulations to carry out this section, including—

(1) requiring that any identified safety deficiencies be addressed and corrected before the initiation of revenue service; and

(2) establishing appropriate deadlines to enable the Secretary to review and approve the pre-revenue service safety validation plan to ensure that service is not unduly delayed.

(Added Pub. L. 117–58, div. B, title II, §22416(a), Nov. 15, 2021, 135 Stat. 747.)

§20171. REQUIREMENTS FOR RAILROAD FREIGHT CARS PLACED INTO SERVICE IN THE UNITED STATES

(a) DEFINITIONS.—In this section:

(1) COMPONENT.—The term "component" means a part or subassembly of a railroad freight car.

(2) CONTROL.—The term "control" means the power, whether direct or indirect and whether or not exercised, through the ownership of a majority or a dominant minority of the total outstanding voting interest in an entity, representation on the board of directors of an entity, proxy voting on the board of directors of an entity, a special share in the entity, a contractual arrangement with the entity, a formal or informal arrangement to act in concert with an entity, or any other means, to determine, direct, make decisions, or cause decisions to be made for the entity.

(3) COST OF SENSITIVE TECHNOLOGY.—The term "cost of sensitive technology" means the aggregate cost of the sensitive technology located on a railroad freight car.

(4) COUNTRY OF CONCERN.—The term "country of concern" means a country that—

(A) is identified by the Department of Commerce as a nonmarket economy country (as defined in section 771(18) of the Tariff Act of 1930 (19 U.S.C. 1677(18))) as of the date of enactment of the Passenger Rail Expansion and Rail Safety Act of 2021;

(B) was identified by the United States Trade Representative in the most recent report required by section 182 of the Trade Act of 1974 (19 U.S.C. 2242) as a foreign country included on the priority watch list (as defined in subsection (g)(3) of such section); and

(C) is subject to monitoring by the Trade Representative under section 306 of the Trade Act of 1974 (19 U.S.C. 2416).

(5) NET COST.—The term "net cost" has the meaning given such term in chapter 4 of the USMCA or any subsequent free trade agreement between the United States, Mexico, and Canada.

(6) QUALIFIED FACILITY.—The term "qualified facility" means a facility that is not owned or under the control of a state-owned enterprise.

(7) QUALIFIED MANUFACTURER.—The term "qualified manufacturer" means a railroad freight car manufacturer that is not owned or under the control of a state-owned enterprise.

(8) RAILROAD FREIGHT CAR.—The term "railroad freight car" means a car designed to carry freight or railroad personnel by rail, including—

(A) a box car;

(B) a refrigerator car;

(C) a ventilator car;

(D) an intermodal well car;

(E) a gondola car;

(F) a hopper car;

(G) an auto rack car;

(H) a flat car;

(I) a special car;

(J) a caboose car;

(K) a tank car; and

(L) a yard car.

(9) SENSITIVE TECHNOLOGY.—The term "sensitive technology" means any device embedded with electronics, software, sensors, or other connectivity, that enables the device to connect to, collect data from, or exchange data with another device, including—

(A) onboard telematics;

(B) remote monitoring software;

(C) firmware;

(D) analytics;

(E) global positioning system satellite and cellular location tracking systems;

(F) event status sensors;

(G) predictive component condition and performance monitoring sensors; and

(H) similar sensitive technologies embedded into freight railcar components and sub-assemblies.

(10) STATE-OWNED ENTERPRISE.—The term "state-owned enterprise" means—

(A) an entity that is owned by, or under the control of, a national, provincial, or local government of a country of concern, or an agency of such government; or

(B) an individual acting under the direction or influence of a government or agency described in subparagraph (A).

(11) SUBSTANTIALLY TRANSFORMED.—The term "substantially transformed" means a component of a railroad freight car that undergoes an applicable change in tariff classification as a result of the manufacturing process, as described in chapter 4 and related annexes of the USMCA or any subsequent free trade agreement between the United States, Mexico, and Canada.

(12) USMCA.—The term "USMCA" has the meaning given the term in section 3 of the United States-Mexico-Canada Agreement Implementation Act (19 U.S.C. 4502).

(b) REQUIREMENTS FOR RAILROAD FREIGHT CARS.—

(1) LIMITATION ON RAILROAD FREIGHT CARS.—A railroad freight car wholly manufactured on or after the date that is 1 year after the date of issuance of the regulations required under subsection (c)(1) may only operate on the United States general railroad system of transportation if—

(A) the railroad freight car is manufactured, assembled, and substantially transformed, as applicable, by a qualified manufacturer in a qualified facility;

(B) none of the sensitive technology located on the railroad freight car, including components necessary to the functionality of the sensitive technology, originates from a country of concern or is sourced from a state-owned enterprise; and

(C) none of the content of the railroad freight car, excluding sensitive technology, originates from a country of concern or is sourced from a state-owned enterprise that has been determined by a recognized court or administrative agency of competent jurisdiction and legal authority to have violated or infringed valid United States intellectual property rights of another including such a finding by a Federal district court under title 35 or the U.S. International Trade Commission under section 337 of the Tariff Act of 1930 (19 U.S.C. 1337).

(2) LIMITATION ON RAILROAD FREIGHT CAR CONTENT.—

(A) PERCENTAGE LIMITATION.—

(i) INITIAL LIMITATION.—Not later than 1 year after the date of issuance of the regulations required under subsection (c)(1), a railroad freight car described in paragraph (1) may operate on the United States general railroad system of transportation only if not more than 20 percent of the content of the railroad freight car, calculated by the net cost of all components of the car and excluding the cost of sensitive technology, originates from a country of concern or is sourced from a state-owned enterprise.

(ii) SUBSEQUENT LIMITATION.—Effective beginning on the date that is 3 years after the date of issuance of the regulations required under subsection (c)(1), a railroad freight car described in paragraph (1) may operate on the United States general railroad system of transportation only if not more than 15 percent of the content of the railroad freight car, calculated by the net cost of all components of the car and excluding the cost of sensitive technology, originates from a country of concern or is sourced from a state-owned enterprise.

(B) CONFLICT.—The percentages specified in clauses (i) and (ii) of subparagraph (A), as applicable, shall apply notwithstanding any apparent conflict with provisions of chapter 4 of the USMCA.

(c) REGULATIONS AND PENALTIES.—

(1) REGULATIONS REQUIRED.—Not later than 2 years after the date of enactment of the Passenger Rail Expansion and Rail Safety Act of 2021, the Secretary of Transportation shall issue such regulations as are necessary to carry out this section, including for the monitoring and sensitive technology requirements of this section.

(2) CERTIFICATION REQUIRED.—To be eligible to provide a railroad freight car for operation on the United States general railroad system of transportation, the manufacturer of such car shall annually certify to the Secretary of Transportation that any railroad freight cars to be so provided meet the requirements under this section.

(3) COMPLIANCE.—

(A) VALID CERTIFICATION REQUIRED.—At the time a railroad freight car begins operation on the United States general railroad system of transportation, the manufacturer of such railroad freight car shall have valid certification described in paragraph (2) for the year in which such car begins operation.

(B) REGISTRATION OF NONCOMPLIANT CARS PROHIBITED.—A railroad freight car manufacturer may not register, or cause to be registered, a railroad freight car that does not comply with the requirements under this section in the Association of American Railroad's [1] Umler system.

(4) CIVIL PENALTIES.—

(A) IN GENERAL.—Pursuant to section 21301, the Secretary of Transportation may assess a civil penalty of not less than $100,000, but not more than $250,000, for each violation of this section for each railroad freight car.

(B) PROHIBITION ON OPERATION FOR VIOLATIONS.—The Secretary of Transportation may prohibit a railroad freight car manufacturer with respect to which the Secretary has assessed more than 3 violations under subparagraph (A) from providing additional railroad freight cars for operation on the United States general railroad system of transportation until the Secretary determines—

(i) such manufacturer is in compliance with this section; and

(ii) all civil penalties assessed to such manufacturer pursuant to subparagraph (A) have been paid in full.

(Added Pub. L. 117–58, div. B, title II, §22425(a), Nov. 15, 2021, 135 Stat. 753.)

---

[1] *So in original. Probably should be "Association of American Railroads' ".*

CHAPTER 203—SAFETY APPLIANCES

§20301. DEFINITION AND NONAPPLICATION

(a) DEFINITION.—In this chapter, "vehicle" means a car, locomotive, tender, or similar vehicle.

(b) NONAPPLICATION.—This chapter does not apply to the following:

(1) a train of 4-wheel coal cars.

(2) a train of 8-wheel standard logging cars if the height of each car from the top of the rail to the center of the coupling is not more than 25 inches.

(3) a locomotive used in hauling a train referred to in clause (2) of this subsection when the locomotive and cars of the train are used only to transport logs.

(4) a car, locomotive, or train used on a street railway.

(Pub. L. 103–272, §1(e), July 5, 1994, 108 Stat. 881; Pub. L. 104–287, §5(52), Oct. 11, 1996, 110 Stat. 3393.)

§20302. GENERAL REQUIREMENTS

(a) GENERAL.—Except as provided in subsection (c) of this section and section 20303 of this title, a railroad carrier may use or allow to be used on any of its railroad lines—

(1) a vehicle only if it is equipped with—

(A) couplers coupling automatically by impact, and capable of being uncoupled, without the necessity of individuals going between the ends of the vehicles;

(B) secure sill steps and efficient hand brakes; and

(C) secure ladders and running boards when required by the Secretary of Transportation, and, if ladders are required, secure handholds or grab irons on its roof at the top of each ladder;

(2) except as otherwise ordered by the Secretary, a vehicle only if it is equipped with secure grab irons or handholds on its ends and sides for greater security to individuals in coupling and uncoupling vehicles;

(3) a vehicle only if it complies with the standard height of drawbars required by regulations prescribed by the Secretary;

(4) a locomotive only if it is equipped with a power-driving wheel brake and appliances for operating the train-brake system; and

(5) a train only if—

(A) enough of the vehicles in the train are equipped with power or train brakes so that the engineer on the locomotive hauling the train can control the train's speed without the necessity of brake operators using the common hand brakes for that purpose; and

(B) at least 50 percent of the vehicles in the train are equipped with power or train brakes and the engineer is using the power or train brakes on those vehicles and on all other vehicles equipped with them that are associated with those vehicles in the train.

(b) REFUSAL TO RECEIVE VEHICLES NOT PROPERLY EQUIPPED.—A railroad carrier complying with subsection (a)(5)(A) of this section may refuse to receive from a railroad line of a connecting railroad carrier or a shipper a vehicle that is not equipped with power or train brakes that will work and readily interchange with the power or train brakes in use on the vehicles of the complying railroad carrier.

(c) COMBINED VEHICLES LOADING AND HAULING LONG COMMODITIES.—Notwithstanding subsection (a)(1)(B) of this section, when vehicles are combined to load and haul long commodities, only one of the vehicles must have hand brakes during the loading and hauling.

(d) AUTHORITY TO CHANGE REQUIREMENTS.—The Secretary may—

(1) change the number, dimensions, locations, and manner of application prescribed by the Secretary for safety appliances required by subsection (a)(1)(B) and (C) and (2) of this section only for good cause and after providing an opportunity for a full hearing;

(2) amend regulations for installing, inspecting, maintaining, and repairing power and train brakes only for the purpose of achieving safety; and

(3) increase, after an opportunity for a full hearing, the minimum percentage of vehicles in a train that are required by subsection (a)(5)(B) of this section to be equipped and used with power or train brakes.

(e) SERVICES OF ASSOCIATION OF AMERICAN RAILROADS.—In carrying out subsection (d)(2) and (3) of this section, the Secretary may use the services of the Association of American Railroads.

(Pub. L. 103–272, §1(e), July 5, 1994, 108 Stat. 881.)

§20303. MOVING DEFECTIVE AND INSECURE VEHICLES NEEDING REPAIRS

(a) GENERAL.—A vehicle that is equipped in compliance with this chapter whose equipment becomes defective or insecure nevertheless may be moved when necessary to make repairs, without a penalty being imposed under section 21302 of this title, from the place at which the defect or insecurity was first discovered to the nearest available place at which the repairs can be made—

(1) on the railroad line on which the defect or insecurity was discovered; or

(2) at the option of a connecting railroad carrier, on the railroad line of the connecting carrier, if not farther than the place of repair described in clause (1) of this subsection.

(b) USE OF CHAINS INSTEAD OF DRAWBARS.—A vehicle in a revenue train or in association with commercially-used vehicles may be moved under this section with chains instead of drawbars only when the vehicle contains livestock or perishable freight.

(c) LIABILITY.—The movement of a vehicle under this section is at the risk only of the railroad carrier doing the moving. This section does not relieve a carrier from liability in a proceeding to recover damages for death or injury of a railroad employee arising from the movement of a vehicle with equipment that is defective, insecure, or not maintained in compliance with this chapter.

(Pub. L. 103–272, §1(e), July 5, 1994, 108 Stat. 882.)

§20304. Assumption of risk by employees

An employee of a railroad carrier injured by a vehicle or train used in violation of section 20302(a)(1)(A), (2), (4), or (5)(A) of this title does not assume the risk of injury resulting from the violation, even if the employee continues to be employed by the carrier after learning of the violation.

(Pub. L. 103–272, §1(e), July 5, 1994, 108 Stat. 883.)

§20305. Inspection of mail cars

The Secretary of Transportation shall inspect the construction, adaptability, design, and condition of mail cars used on railroads in the United States. The Secretary shall make a report on the inspection and submit a copy of the report to the United States Postal Service.

(Pub. L. 103–272, §1(e), July 5, 1994, 108 Stat. 883.)

§20306. Exemption for technological improvements

(a) General.—Subject to subsection (b) of this section, the Secretary of Transportation may exempt from the requirements of this chapter railroad equipment or equipment that will be operated on rails, when those requirements preclude the development or implementation of more efficient railroad transportation equipment or other transportation innovations under existing law.

(b) Conditions for Exemption.—The Secretary may grant an exemption under subsection (a) of this section only on the basis of—

(1) findings based on evidence developed at a hearing; or

(2) an agreement between national railroad labor representatives and the developer of the new equipment or technology.

(Pub. L. 103–272, §1(e), July 5, 1994, 108 Stat. 883.)

CHAPTER 205—SIGNAL SYSTEMS

§20501. DEFINITION

In this chapter, "signal system" means a block signal system, an interlocking, automatic train stop, train control, or cab-signal device, or a similar appliance, method, device, or system intended to promote safety in railroad operations.

(Pub. L. 103–272, §1(e), July 5, 1994, 108 Stat. 883.)

§20502. REQUIREMENTS FOR INSTALLATION AND USE

(a) INSTALLATION.—(1) When the Secretary of Transportation decides after an investigation that it is necessary in the public interest, the Secretary may order a railroad carrier to install, on any part of its railroad line, a signal system that complies with requirements of the Secretary. The order must allow the carrier a reasonable time to complete the installation. A carrier may discontinue or materially alter a signal system required under this paragraph only with the approval of the Secretary.

(2) A railroad carrier ordered under paragraph (1) of this subsection to install a signal system on one part of its railroad line may not be held negligent for not installing the system on any part of its line that was not included in the order. If an accident or incident occurs on a part of the line on which the signal system was not required to be installed and was not installed, the use of the system on another part of the line may not be considered in a civil action brought because of the accident or incident.

(b) USE.—A railroad carrier may allow a signal system to be used on its railroad line only when the system, including its controlling and operating appurtenances—

(1) may be operated safely without unnecessary risk of personal injury; and

(2) has been inspected and can meet any test prescribed under this chapter.

(Pub. L. 103–272, §1(e), July 5, 1994, 108 Stat. 883.)

§20503. AMENDING REGULATIONS AND CHANGING REQUIREMENTS

The Secretary of Transportation may amend a regulation or change a requirement applicable to a railroad carrier for installing, maintaining, inspecting, or repairing a signal system under this chapter—

(1) when the carrier files with the Secretary a request for the amendment or change and the Secretary approves the request; or

(2) on the Secretary's own initiative for good cause shown.

(Pub. L. 103–272, §1(e), July 5, 1994, 108 Stat. 884.)

§20504. Inspection, testing, and investigation

(a) Systems in Use.—(1) The Secretary of Transportation may—
    (A) inspect and test a signal system used by a railroad carrier; and
    (B) decide whether the system is in safe operating condition.

(2) In carrying out this subsection, the Secretary may employ only an individual who—
    (A) has no interest in a patented article required to be used on or with a signal system; and
    (B) has no financial interest in a railroad carrier or in a concern dealing in railroad supplies.

(b) Systems Submitted for Investigation and Testing.—The Secretary may investigate, test, and report on the use of and need for a signal system, without cost to the United States Government, when the system is submitted in completed shape for investigation and testing.

(Pub. L. 103–272, §1(e), July 5, 1994, 108 Stat. 884.)

§20505. Reports of malfunctions and accidents

In the way and to the extent required by the Secretary of Transportation, a railroad carrier shall report to the Secretary a failure of a signal system to function as intended. If the failure results in an accident or incident causing injury to an individual or property that is required to be reported under regulations prescribed by the Secretary, the carrier owning or maintaining the signal system shall report to the Secretary immediately in writing the fact of the accident or incident.

(Pub. L. 103–272, §1(e), July 5, 1994, 108 Stat. 884.)

CHAPTER 207—LOCOMOTIVES

§20701. REQUIREMENTS FOR USE

A railroad carrier may use or allow to be used a locomotive or tender on its railroad line only when the locomotive or tender and its parts and appurtenances—

(1) are in proper condition and safe to operate without unnecessary danger of personal injury;

(2) have been inspected as required under this chapter and regulations prescribed by the Secretary of Transportation under this chapter; and

(3) can withstand every test prescribed by the Secretary under this chapter.

(Pub. L. 103–272, §1(e), July 5, 1994, 108 Stat. 885.)

§20702. INSPECTIONS, REPAIRS, AND INSPECTION AND REPAIR REPORTS

(a) GENERAL.—The Secretary of Transportation shall—

(1) become familiar, so far as practicable, with the condition of every locomotive and tender and its parts and appurtenances;

(2) inspect every locomotive and tender and its parts and appurtenances as necessary to carry out this chapter, but not necessarily at stated times or at regular intervals; and

(3) ensure that every railroad carrier makes inspections of locomotives and tenders and their parts and appurtenances as required by regulations prescribed by the Secretary and repairs every defect that is disclosed by an inspection before a defective locomotive, tender, part, or appurtenance is used again.

(b) NONCOMPLYING LOCOMOTIVES, TENDERS, AND PARTS.—(1) When the Secretary finds that a locomotive, tender, or locomotive or tender part or appurtenance owned or operated by a railroad carrier does not comply with this chapter or a regulation prescribed under this chapter, the Secretary shall give the carrier written notice describing any defect resulting in noncompliance. Not later than 5 days after receiving the notice of noncompliance, the carrier may submit a written request for a reinspection. On receiving the request, the Secretary shall provide for the reinspection by an officer or employee of the Department of Transportation who did not make the original inspection. The reinspection shall be made not later than 15 days after the date the Secretary gives the notice of noncompliance.

(2) Immediately after the reinspection is completed, the Secretary shall give written notice to the railroad carrier stating whether the locomotive, tender, part, or appurtenance is in compliance. If the original finding of noncompliance is sustained, the carrier has 30 days after receipt of the notice to file an appeal with the Secretary. If the carrier files an appeal, the Secretary, after providing an opportunity for a proceeding, may revise or set aside the finding of noncompliance.

(3) A locomotive, tender, part, or appurtenance found not in compliance under this

subsection may be used only after it is—

    (A) repaired to comply with this chapter and regulations prescribed under this chapter; or

    (B) found on reinspection or appeal to be in compliance.

    (c) REPORTS.—A railroad carrier shall make and keep, in the way the Secretary prescribes by regulation, a report of every—

    (1) inspection made under regulations prescribed by the Secretary; and

    (2) repair made of a defect disclosed by such an inspection.

    (d) CHANGES IN INSPECTION PROCEDURES.—A railroad carrier may change a rule or instruction of the carrier governing the inspection by the carrier of the locomotives and tenders and locomotive and tender parts and appurtenances of the carrier when the Secretary approves a request filed by the carrier to make the change.

(Pub. L. 103–272, §1(e), July 5, 1994, 108 Stat. 885.)

§20703. ACCIDENT REPORTS AND INVESTIGATIONS

    (a) ACCIDENT REPORTS AND SCENE PRESERVATION.—When the failure of a locomotive, tender, or locomotive or tender part or appurtenance results in an accident or incident causing serious personal injury or death, the railroad carrier owning or operating the locomotive or tender—

    (1) immediately shall file with the Secretary of Transportation a written statement of the fact of the accident or incident; and

    (2) when the locomotive is disabled to the extent it cannot be operated under its own power, shall preserve intact all parts affected by the accident or incident, if possible without interfering with traffic, until an investigation of the accident or incident is completed.

    (b) INVESTIGATIONS.—The Secretary shall—

    (1) investigate each accident and incident reported under subsection (a) of this section;

    (2) inspect each part affected by the accident or incident; and

    (3) make a complete and detailed report on the cause of the accident or incident.

    (c) PUBLICATION AND USE OF INVESTIGATION REPORTS.—When the Secretary considers publication to be in the public interest, the Secretary may publish a report of an investigation made under this section, stating the cause of the accident or incident and making appropriate recommendations. No part of a report may be admitted into evidence or used in a civil action for damages resulting from a matter mentioned in the report.

(Pub. L. 103–272, §1(e), July 5, 1994, 108 Stat. 886.)

CHAPTER 209—ACCIDENTS AND INCIDENTS

Sec.
20901. Reports.
20902. Investigations.
20903. Reports not evidence in civil actions for damages.

§20901. REPORTS

(a) GENERAL REQUIREMENTS.—Not later than 30 days after the end of each month, a railroad carrier shall file a report with the Secretary of Transportation on all accidents and incidents resulting in injury or death to an individual or damage to equipment or a roadbed arising from the carrier's operations during the month. The report shall be under oath and shall state the nature, cause, and circumstances of each reported accident or incident. If a railroad carrier assigns human error as a cause, the report shall include, at the option of each employee whose error is alleged, a statement by the employee explaining any factors the employee alleges contributed to the accident or incident.

(b) MONETARY THRESHOLD FOR REPORTING.—(1) In establishing or changing a monetary threshold for the reporting of a railroad accident or incident, the Secretary shall base damage cost calculations only on publicly available information obtained from—

(A) the Bureau of Labor Statistics; or

(B) another department, agency, or instrumentality of the United States Government if the information has been collected through objective, statistically sound survey methods or has been previously subject to a public notice and comment process in a proceeding of a Government department, agency, or instrumentality.

(2) If information is not available as provided in paragraph (1)(A) or (B) of this subsection, the Secretary may use any other source to obtain the information. However, use of the information shall be subject to public notice and an opportunity for written comment.

(Pub. L. 103–272, §1(e), July 5, 1994, 108 Stat. 886.)

§20902. INVESTIGATIONS

(a) GENERAL AUTHORITY.—The Secretary of Transportation, or an impartial investigator authorized by the Secretary, may investigate—

(1) an accident or incident resulting in serious injury to an individual or to railroad property, occurring on the railroad line of a railroad carrier; and

(2) an accident or incident reported under section 20505 of this title.

(b) OTHER DUTIES AND POWERS.—In carrying out an investigation, the Secretary or authorized investigator may subpoena witnesses, require the production of records, exhibits, and other evidence, administer oaths, and take testimony. If the accident or incident is investigated by a commission of the State in which it occurred, the Secretary, if convenient, shall carry out the investigation at the same time as, and in coordination with, the commission's investigation. The railroad carrier on whose railroad line the accident or incident occurred shall provide reasonable facilities to the Secretary for the investigation.

(c) Reports.—When in the public interest, the Secretary shall make a report of the investigation, stating the cause of the accident or incident and making recommendations the Secretary considers appropriate. The Secretary shall publish the report in a way the Secretary considers appropriate.

(d) Gathering Information and Technical Expertise.—

(1) In general.—The Secretary shall create a standard process for investigators to use during accident and incident investigations conducted under this section for determining when it is appropriate and the appropriate method for—

(A) gathering information about an accident or incident under investigation from railroad carriers, contractors or employees of railroad carriers or representatives of employees of railroad carriers, and others, as determined relevant by the Secretary; and

(B) consulting with railroad carriers, contractors or employees of railroad carriers or representatives of employees of railroad carriers, and others, as determined relevant by the Secretary, for technical expertise on the facts of the accident or incident under investigation.

(2) Confidentiality.—In developing the process required under paragraph (1), the Secretary shall factor in ways to maintain the confidentiality of any entity identified under paragraph (1) if—

(A) such entity requests confidentiality;

(B) such entity was not involved in the accident or incident; and

(C) maintaining such entity's confidentiality does not adversely affect an investigation of the Federal Railroad Administration.

(3) Applicability.—This subsection shall not apply to any investigation carried out by the National Transportation Safety Board.

(Pub. L. 103–272, §1(e), July 5, 1994, 108 Stat. 887; Pub. L. 117–58, div. B, title II, §22417, Nov. 15, 2021, 135 Stat. 748.)

§20903. Reports not evidence in civil actions for damages

No part of an accident or incident report filed by a railroad carrier under section 20901 of this title or made by the Secretary of Transportation under section 20902 of this title may be used in a civil action for damages resulting from a matter mentioned in the report.

(Pub. L. 103–272, §1(e), July 5, 1994, 108 Stat. 887.)

CHAPTER 211—HOURS OF SERVICE

§21101. DEFINITIONS

In this chapter—

(1) "designated terminal" means the home or away-from-home terminal for the assignment of a particular crew.

(2) "dispatching service employee" means an operator, train dispatcher, or other train employee who by the use of an electrical or mechanical device dispatches, reports, transmits, receives, or delivers orders related to or affecting train movements.

(3) "employee" means a dispatching service employee, a signal employee, or a train employee.

(4) "signal employee" means an individual who is engaged in installing, repairing, or maintaining signal systems.

(5) "train employee" means an individual engaged in or connected with the movement of a train, including a hostler.

(Pub. L. 103–272, §1(e), July 5, 1994, 108 Stat. 888; Pub. L. 110–432, div. A, title I, §108(a), Oct. 16, 2008, 122 Stat. 4860.)

§21102. NONAPPLICATION, EXEMPTION, AND ALTERNATE HOURS OF SERVICE REGIME

(a) GENERAL.—This chapter does not apply to a situation involving any of the following:

(1) a casualty.

(2) an unavoidable accident.

(3) an act of God.

(4) a delay resulting from a cause unknown and unforeseeable to a railroad carrier or its officer or agent in charge of the employee when the employee left a terminal.

(b) EXEMPTION.—The Secretary of Transportation may exempt a railroad carrier having not more than 15 employees covered by this chapter from the limitations imposed by this chapter. The Secretary may allow the exemption after a full hearing, for good cause shown, and on deciding that the exemption is in the public interest and will not affect safety adversely. The exemption shall be for a specific period of time and is subject to review at least annually. The exemption may not authorize a carrier to require or allow its employees to be on duty more than a total of 16 hours in a 24-hour period.

(c) APPLICATION OF HOURS OF SERVICE REGIME TO COMMUTER AND INTERCITY PASSENGER RAILROAD TRAIN EMPLOYEES.—

(1) When providing commuter rail passenger transportation or intercity rail passenger transportation, the limitations on duty hours for train employees of railroad carriers, including public authorities operating passenger service, shall be solely governed by old section 21103 until the earlier of—

(A) the effective date of regulations prescribed by the Secretary under section 21109(b) of this chapter; or

(B) the date that is 3 years following the date of enactment of the Rail Safety Improvement Act of 2008.

(2) After the date on which old section 21103 ceases to apply, pursuant to paragraph (1), to the limitations on duty hours for train employees of railroad carriers with respect to the provision of commuter rail passenger transportation or intercity rail passenger transportation, the limitations on duty hours for train employees of such railroad carriers shall be governed by new section 21103, except as provided in paragraph (3).

(3) After the effective date of the regulations prescribed by the Secretary under section 21109(b) of this title, such carriers shall—

(A) comply with the limitations on duty hours for train employees with respect to the provision of commuter rail passenger transportation or intercity rail passenger transportation as prescribed by such regulations; and

(B) be exempt from complying with the provisions of old section 21103 and new section 21103 for such employees.

(4) In this subsection:

(A) The terms "commuter rail passenger transportation" and "intercity rail passenger transportation" have the meaning given those terms in section 24102 of this title.

(C) [1] The term "new section 21103" means section 21103 of this chapter as amended by the Rail Safety Improvement Act of 2008.

(D) The term "old section 21103" means section 21103 of this chapter as it was in effect on the day before the enactment of that Act.

(Pub. L. 103–272, §1(e), July 5, 1994, 108 Stat. 888; Pub. L. 110–432, div. A, title I, §108(d)(1), Oct. 16, 2008, 122 Stat. 4863.)

[1] So in original. No subpar. (B) has been enacted.

§21103. LIMITATIONS ON DUTY HOURS OF TRAIN EMPLOYEES

(a) IN GENERAL.—Except as provided in subsection (d) of this section, a railroad carrier and its officers and agents may not require or allow a train employee to—

(1) remain on duty, go on duty, wait for deadhead transportation, be in deadhead transportation from a duty assignment to the place of final release, or be in any other mandatory service for the carrier in any calendar month where the employee has spent a total of 276 hours—

(A) on duty;

(B) waiting for deadhead transportation, or in deadhead transportation from a duty assignment to the place of final release; or

(C) in any other mandatory service for the carrier;

(2) remain or go on duty for a period in excess of 12 consecutive hours;

(3) remain or go on duty unless that employee has had at least 10 consecutive hours off duty during the prior 24 hours; or

(4) remain or go on duty after that employee has initiated an on-duty period each day for—

(A) 6 consecutive days, unless that employee has had at least 48 consecutive hours off duty at the employee's home terminal during which time the employee is unavailable for any service for any railroad carrier except that—

(i) an employee may work a seventh consecutive day if that employee completed his or her final period of on-duty time on his or her sixth consecutive day at a terminal other than his or her home terminal; and

(ii) any employee who works a seventh consecutive day pursuant to subparagraph (i) shall have at least 72 consecutive hours off duty at the employee's home terminal during which time the employee is unavailable for any service for any railroad carrier; or

(B) except as provided in subparagraph (A), 7 consecutive days, unless that employee has had at least 72 consecutive hours off duty at the employee's home terminal during which time the employee is unavailable for any service for any railroad carrier, if—

(i) for a period of 18 months following the date of enactment of the Rail Safety Improvement Act of 2008, an existing collective bargaining agreement expressly provides for such a schedule or, following the expiration of 18 months after the date of enactment of the Rail Safety Improvement Act of 2008, collective bargaining agreements entered into during such period expressly provide for such a schedule;

(ii) such a schedule is provided for by a pilot program authorized by a collective bargaining agreement; or

(iii) such a schedule is provided for by a pilot program under section 21108 of this chapter related to employees' work and rest cycles.

The Secretary may waive paragraph (4), consistent with the procedural requirements of section 20103, if a collective bargaining agreement provides a different arrangement and such an arrangement is in the public interest and consistent with railroad safety.

(b) DETERMINING TIME ON DUTY.—In determining under subsection (a) of this section the time a train employee is on or off duty, the following rules apply:

(1) Time on duty begins when the employee reports for duty and ends when the employee is finally released from duty.

(2) Time the employee is engaged in or connected with the movement of a train is time on duty.

(3) Time spent performing any other service for the railroad carrier during a 24-hour

period in which the employee is engaged in or connected with the movement of a train is time on duty.

(4) Time spent in deadhead transportation to a duty assignment is time on duty, but time spent in deadhead transportation from a duty assignment to the place of final release is neither time on duty nor time off duty.

(5) An interim period available for rest at a place other than a designated terminal is time on duty.

(6) An interim period available for less than 4 hours rest at a designated terminal is time on duty.

(7) An interim period available for at least 4 hours rest at a place with suitable facilities for food and lodging is not time on duty when the employee is prevented from getting to the employee's designated terminal by any of the following:

(A) a casualty.

(B) a track obstruction.

(C) an act of God.

(D) a derailment or major equipment failure resulting from a cause that was unknown and unforeseeable to the railroad carrier or its officer or agent in charge of that employee when that employee left the designated terminal.

(c) LIMBO TIME LIMITATION AND ADDITIONAL REST REQUIREMENT.—

(1) A railroad carrier may not require or allow an employee—

(A) to exceed a total of 40 hours per calendar month spent—

(i) waiting for deadhead transportation; or

(ii) in deadhead transportation from a duty assignment to the place of final release,

following a period of 12 consecutive hours on duty that is neither time on duty nor time off duty, not including interim rest periods, during the period from the date of enactment of the Rail Safety Improvement Act of 2008 to one year after such date of enactment; and

(B) to exceed a total of 30 hours per calendar month spent—

(i) waiting for deadhead transportation; or

(ii) in deadhead transportation from a duty assignment to the place of final release,

following a period of 12 consecutive hours on duty that is neither time on duty nor time off duty, not including interim rest periods, during the period beginning one year after the date of enactment of the Rail Safety Improvement Act of 2008 except that the Secretary may further limit the monthly limitation pursuant to regulations prescribed under section 21109.

(2) The limitations in paragraph (1) shall apply unless the train carrying the employee is directly delayed by—

(A) a casualty;

(B) an accident;

(C) an act of God;

(D) a derailment;

(E) a major equipment failure that prevents the train from advancing; or

(F) a delay resulting from a cause unknown and unforeseeable to a railroad carrier or its officer or agent in charge of the employee when the employee left a terminal.

(3) Each railroad carrier shall report to the Secretary, in accordance with procedures established by the Secretary, each instance where an employee subject to this section spends time waiting for deadhead transportation or in deadhead transportation from a duty assignment to the place of final release in excess of the requirements of paragraph (1).

(4) If—

(A) the time spent waiting for deadhead transportation or in deadhead transportation from a duty assignment to the place of final release that is not time on duty, plus

(B) the time on duty,

exceeds 12 consecutive hours, the railroad carrier and its officers and agents shall provide the employee with additional time off duty equal to the number of hours by which such sum exceeds 12 hours.

(d) EMERGENCIES.—A train employee on the crew of a wreck or relief train may be allowed to remain or go on duty for not more than 4 additional hours in any period of 24 consecutive hours when an emergency exists and the work of the crew is related to the emergency. In this subsection, an emergency ends when the track is cleared and the railroad line is open for traffic.

(e) COMMUNICATION DURING TIME OFF DUTY.—During a train employee's minimum off-duty period of 10 consecutive hours, as provided under subsection (a) or during an interim period of at least 4 consecutive hours available for rest under subsection (b)(7) or during additional off-duty hours under subsection (c)(4), a railroad carrier, and its officers and agents, shall not communicate with the train employee by telephone, by pager, or in any other manner that could reasonably be expected to disrupt the employee's rest. Nothing in this subsection shall prohibit communication necessary to notify an employee of an emergency situation, as defined by the Secretary. The Secretary may waive the requirements of this paragraph for commuter or intercity passenger railroads if the Secretary determines that such a waiver will not reduce safety and is necessary to maintain such railroads' efficient operations and on-time performance of its trains.

(Pub. L. 103–272, §1(e), July 5, 1994, 108 Stat. 888; Pub. L. 110–432, div. A, title I, §108(b), Oct. 16, 2008, 122 Stat. 4860.)

§21104. LIMITATIONS ON DUTY HOURS OF SIGNAL EMPLOYEES

(a) IN GENERAL.—Except as provided in subsection (c) of this section, a railroad carrier and its officers and agents may not require or allow its signal employees to remain or go on duty and a contractor or subcontractor to a railroad carrier and its officers and agents may not require or allow its signal employees to remain or go on duty—

(1) for a period in excess of 12 consecutive hours; or

(2) unless that employee has had at least 10 consecutive hours off duty during the prior

24 hours.

(b) Determining Time on Duty.—In determining under subsection (a) of this section the time a signal employee is on duty or off duty, the following rules apply:

(1) Time on duty begins when the employee reports for duty and ends when the employee is finally released from duty.

(2) Time spent performing any other service for the railroad carrier during a 24-hour period in which the employee is engaged in installing, repairing, or maintaining signal systems is time on duty.

(3) Time spent returning from a trouble call, whether the employee goes directly to the employee's residence or by way of the employee's headquarters, is neither time on duty nor time off duty.

(4) If, at the end of scheduled duty hours, an employee has not completed the trip from the final outlying worksite of the duty period to the employee's headquarters or directly to the employee's residence, the time after the scheduled duty hours necessarily spent in completing the trip to the residence or headquarters is neither time on duty nor time off duty.

(5) If an employee is released from duty at an outlying worksite before the end of the employee's scheduled duty hours to comply with this section, the time necessary for the trip from the worksite to the employee's headquarters or directly to the employee's residence is neither time on duty nor time off duty.

(6) Time spent in transportation on an ontrack vehicle, including time referred to in paragraphs (3)–(5) of this subsection, is time on duty.

(7) A regularly scheduled meal period or another release period of at least 30 minutes but not more than one hour is time off duty and does not break the continuity of service of the employee under this section, but a release period of more than one hour is time off duty and does break the continuity of service.

(c) Emergencies.—A signal employee may be allowed to remain or go on duty for not more than 4 additional hours in any period of 24 consecutive hours when an emergency exists and the work of that employee is related to the emergency. In this subsection, an emergency ends when the signal system is restored to service. A signal employee may not be allowed to remain or go on duty under the emergency authority provided under this subsection to conduct routine repairs, routine maintenance, or routine inspection of signal systems.

(d) Communication During Time Off Duty.—During a signal employee's minimum off-duty period of 10 consecutive hours, as provided under subsection (a), a railroad carrier or a contractor or subcontractor to a railroad carrier, and its officers and agents, shall not communicate with the signal employee by telephone, by pager, or in any other manner that could reasonably be expected to disrupt the employee's rest. Nothing in this subsection shall prohibit communication necessary to notify an employee of an emergency situation, as defined by the Secretary.

(e) Exclusivity.—The hours of service, duty hours, and rest periods of signal employees shall be governed exclusively by this chapter. Signal employees operating motor vehicles shall not be subject to any hours of service rules, duty hours or rest period rules promulgated by any Federal authority, including the Federal Motor Carrier Safety Administration, other than the Federal Railroad Administration.

(Pub. L. 103–272, §1(e), July 5, 1994, 108 Stat. 889; Pub. L. 110–432, div. A, title I, §108(c), Oct. 16, 2008, 122 Stat. 4862.)

§21105. LIMITATIONS ON DUTY HOURS OF DISPATCHING SERVICE EMPLOYEES

(a) APPLICATION.—This section applies, rather than section 21103 or 21104 of this title, to a train employee or signal employee during any period of time the employee is performing duties of a dispatching service employee.

(b) GENERAL.—Except as provided in subsection (d) of this section, a dispatching service employee may not be required or allowed to remain or go on duty for more than—

(1) a total of 9 hours during a 24-hour period in a tower, office, station, or place at which at least 2 shifts are employed; or

(2) a total of 12 hours during a 24-hour period in a tower, office, station, or place at which only one shift is employed.

(c) DETERMINING TIME ON DUTY.—Under subsection (b) of this section, time spent performing any other service for the railroad carrier during a 24-hour period in which the employee is on duty in a tower, office, station, or other place is time on duty in that tower, office, station, or place.

(d) EMERGENCIES.—When an emergency exists, a dispatching service employee may be allowed to remain or go on duty for not more than 4 additional hours during a period of 24 consecutive hours for not more than 3 days during a period of 7 consecutive days.

(Pub. L. 103–272, §1(e), July 5, 1994, 108 Stat. 890.)

§21106. LIMITATIONS ON EMPLOYEE SLEEPING QUARTERS

(a) IN GENERAL.—A railroad carrier and its officers and agents—

(1) may provide sleeping quarters (including crew quarters, camp or bunk cars, and trailers) for employees, and any individuals employed to maintain the right of way of a railroad carrier, only if the sleeping quarters are clean, safe, and sanitary, give those employees and individuals an opportunity for rest free from the interruptions caused by noise under the control of the carrier, and provide indoor toilet facilities, potable water, and other features to protect the health of employees; and

(2) may not begin, after July 7, 1976, construction or reconstruction of sleeping quarters referred to in clause (1) of this section in an area or in the immediate vicinity of an area, as determined under regulations prescribed by the Secretary of Transportation, in which railroad switching or humping operations are performed.

(b) CAMP CARS.—Not later than December 31, 2009, any railroad carrier that uses camp cars shall fully retrofit or replace such cars in compliance with subsection (a).

(c) REGULATIONS.—Not later than April 1, 2010, the Secretary of Transportation, in coordination with the Secretary of Labor, shall prescribe regulations to implement subsection (a)(1) to protect the safety and health of any employees and individuals employed to maintain the right of way of a railroad carrier that uses camp cars, which shall require that all camp cars comply with those regulations by December 31, 2010.

In prescribing the regulations, the Secretary shall assess the action taken by any railroad carrier to fully retrofit or replace its camp cars pursuant to this section.

(d) COMPLIANCE AND ENFORCEMENT.—The Secretary shall determine whether a railroad carrier has fully retrofitted or replaced a camp car pursuant to subsection (b) and shall prohibit the use of any non-compliant camp car. The Secretary may assess civil penalties pursuant to chapter 213 for violations of this section.

(Pub. L. 103–272, §1(e), July 5, 1994, 108 Stat. 891; Pub. L. 110–432, div. A, title IV, §420, Oct. 16, 2008, 122 Stat. 4893.)

§21107. MAXIMUM DUTY HOURS AND SUBJECTS OF COLLECTIVE BARGAINING

The number of hours established by this chapter that an employee may be required or allowed to be on duty is the maximum number of hours consistent with safety. Shorter hours of service and time on duty of an employee are proper subjects for collective bargaining between a railroad carrier and its employees.

(Pub. L. 103–272, §1(e), July 5, 1994, 108 Stat. 891.)

§21108. PILOT PROJECTS

(a) IN GENERAL.—As of the date of enactment of the Rail Safety Improvement Act of 2008, a railroad carrier or railroad carriers and all nonprofit employee labor organizations representing any class or craft of directly affected covered service employees of the railroad carrier or railroad carriers, may jointly petition the Secretary of Transportation for approval of—

(1) a waiver of compliance with this chapter as in effect on the date of enactment of the Rail Safety Improvement Act of 2008; or

(2) a waiver of compliance with this chapter as it will be effective 9 months after the enactment of the Rail Safety Improvement Act of 2008,

to enable the establishment of one or more pilot projects to demonstrate the possible benefits of implementing alternatives to the strict application of the requirements of this chapter, including requirements concerning maximum on-duty and minimum off-duty periods.

(b) GRANTING OF WAIVERS.—The Secretary may, after notice and opportunity for comment, approve such waivers described in subsection (a) for a period not to exceed two years, if the Secretary determines that such a waiver of compliance is in the public interest and is consistent with railroad safety.

(c) EXTENSIONS.—Any such waiver, based on a new petition, may be extended for additional periods of up to two years, after notice and opportunity for comment. An explanation of any waiver granted under this section shall be published in the Federal Register.

(d) REPORT.—The Secretary of Transportation shall submit to the Committee on Commerce, Science, and Transportation of the Senate and the Committee on Transportation and Infrastructure of the House of Representatives, no later than December 31, 2012, or, if no projects are completed prior to December 31, 2012, no later than 6 months after the completion of a pilot project, a report that—

(1) explains and analyzes the effectiveness of any pilot project established pursuant to

a waiver granted under subsection (a);

(2) describes the status of all other waivers granted under subsection (a) and their related pilot projects, if any; and

(3) recommends any appropriate legislative changes to this chapter.

(e) DEFINITION.—For purposes of this section, the term "directly affected covered service employees" means covered service employees to whose hours of service the terms of the waiver petitioned for specifically apply.

(Added Pub. L. 103–440, title II, §203(a), Nov. 2, 1994, 108 Stat. 4619; amended Pub. L. 110–432, div. A, title I, §110, Oct. 16, 2008, 122 Stat. 4867.)

§21109. REGULATORY AUTHORITY

(a) IN GENERAL.—In order to improve safety and reduce employee fatigue, the Secretary may prescribe regulations—

(1) to reduce the maximum hours an employee may be required or allowed to go or remain on duty to a level less than the level established under this chapter;

(2) to increase the minimum hours an employee may be required or allowed to rest to a level greater than the level established under this chapter;

(3) to limit or eliminate the amount of time an employee spends waiting for deadhead transportation or in deadhead transportation from a duty assignment to the place of final release that is considered neither on duty nor off duty under this chapter;

(4) for signal employees—

(A) to limit or eliminate the amount of time that is considered to be neither on duty nor off duty under this chapter that an employee spends returning from an outlying worksite after scheduled duty hours or returning from a trouble call to the employee's headquarters or directly to the employee's residence; and

(B) to increase the amount of time that constitutes a release period, that does not break the continuity of service and is considered time off duty; and

(5) to require other changes to railroad operating and scheduling practices, including unscheduled duty calls, that could affect employee fatigue and railroad safety.

(b) REGULATIONS GOVERNING THE HOURS OF SERVICE OF TRAIN EMPLOYEES OF COMMUTER AND INTERCITY PASSENGER RAILROAD CARRIERS.—Within 3 years after the date of enactment of the Rail Safety Improvement Act of 2008, the Secretary shall prescribe regulations and issue orders to establish hours of service requirements for train employees engaged in commuter rail passenger transportation and intercity rail passenger transportation (as defined in section 24102 of this title) that may differ from the requirements of this chapter. Such regulations and orders may address railroad operating and scheduling practices, including unscheduled duty calls, communications during time off duty, and time spent waiting for deadhead transportation or in deadhead transportation from a duty assignment to the place of final release, that could affect employee fatigue and railroad safety.

(c) CONSIDERATIONS.—In issuing regulations under subsection (a) the Secretary shall consider scientific and medical research related to fatigue and fatigue abatement, railroad scheduling and operating practices that improve safety or reduce employee fatigue, a railroad's use of new or novel technology intended to reduce or eliminate human error, the variations in freight and passenger railroad scheduling practices and operating conditions, the variations in duties and operating conditions for employees subject to this chapter, a railroad's required or voluntary use of fatigue management plans covering employees subject to this chapter, and any other relevant factors.

(d) TIME LIMITS.—

(1) If the Secretary determines that regulations are necessary under subsection (a), the Secretary shall first request that the Railroad Safety Advisory Committee develop proposed regulations and, if the Committee accepts the task, provide the Committee with a reasonable time period in which to complete the task.

(2) If the Secretary requests that the Railroad Safety Advisory Committee accept the task of developing regulations under subsection (b) and the Committee accepts the task, the Committee shall reach consensus on the rulemaking within 18 months after accepting the task. If the Committee does not reach consensus within 18 months after the Secretary makes the request, the Secretary shall prescribe appropriate regulations within 18 months.

(3) If the Secretary does not request that the Railroad Safety Advisory Committee accept the task of developing regulations under subsection (b), the Secretary shall prescribe regulations within 3 years after the date of enactment of the Rail Safety Improvement Act of 2008.

(e) PILOT PROJECTS.—

(1) IN GENERAL.—Not later than 2 years after the date of enactment of the Rail Safety Improvement Act of 2008, the Secretary shall conduct at least 2 pilot projects of sufficient size and scope to analyze specific practices which may be used to reduce fatigue for train and engine and other railroad employees as follows:

(A) A pilot project at a railroad or railroad facility to evaluate the efficacy of communicating to employees notice of their assigned shift time 10 hours prior to the beginning of their assigned shift as a method for reducing employee fatigue.

(B) A pilot project at a railroad or railroad facility to evaluate the efficacy of requiring railroads who use employee scheduling practices that subject employees to periods of unscheduled duty calls to assign employees to defined or specific unscheduled call shifts that are followed by shifts not subject to call, as a method for reducing employee fatigue.

(2) WAIVER.—The Secretary may temporarily waive the requirements of this section, if necessary, to complete a pilot project under this subsection.

(f) DUTY CALL DEFINED.—In this section the term "duty call" means a telephone call that a railroad places to an employee to notify the employee of his or her assigned shift time.

(Added Pub. L. 110–432, div. A, title I, §108(e)(1), Oct. 16, 2008, 122 Stat. 4864.)

CHAPTER 213—PENALTIES

SUBCHAPTER I—CIVIL PENALTIES

SUBCHAPTER II—CRIMINAL PENALTIES

SUBCHAPTER I—CIVIL PENALTIES

§21301. CHAPTER 201 GENERAL VIOLATIONS

(a) PENALTY.—(1) A person may not fail to comply with section 20160 or with a regulation prescribed or order issued by the Secretary of Transportation under chapter 201 of this title. Subject to section 21304 of this title, a person violating section 20160 of this title or a regulation prescribed or order issued by the Secretary under chapter 201 is liable to the United States Government for a civil penalty. The Secretary shall impose the penalty applicable under paragraph (2) of this subsection. A separate violation occurs for each day the violation continues.

(2) The Secretary shall include in, or make applicable to, each regulation prescribed and order issued under chapter 201 of this title a civil penalty for a violation. The Secretary shall impose a civil penalty for a violation of section 20160 of this title. The amount of the penalty shall be at least $500 but not more than $25,000. However, when a grossly negligent violation or a pattern of repeated violations has caused an imminent hazard of death or injury to individuals, or has caused death or injury, the amount may be not more than $100,000.

(3) The Secretary may find that a person has violated this chapter or a regulation prescribed or order, special permit, or approval issued under this chapter only after notice and an opportunity for a hearing. The Secretary shall impose a penalty under this section by giving the person written notice of the amount of the penalty. The Secretary may compromise the amount of a civil penalty by settlement agreement without issuance of an order. In determining the amount of a compromise, the Secretary shall consider—

(A) the nature, circumstances, extent, and gravity of the violation;

(B) with respect to the violator, the degree of culpability, any history of violations, the ability to pay, and any effect on the ability to continue to do business; and

(C) other matters that justice requires.

(4) The Attorney General may bring a civil action in an appropriate district court of the United States to collect a civil penalty imposed or compromise under this section and any

accrued interest on the civil penalty. In the civil action, the amount and appropriateness of the civil penalty shall not be subject to review.

(b) SETOFF.—The Government may deduct the amount of a civil penalty imposed or compromised under this section from amounts it owes the person liable for the penalty.

(c) DEPOSIT IN TREASURY.—A civil penalty collected under this section or section 20113(b) of this title shall be deposited in the Treasury as miscellaneous receipts.

(Pub. L. 103–272, §1(e), July 5, 1994, 108 Stat. 891; Pub. L. 104–287, §5(53), Oct. 11, 1996, 110 Stat. 3393; Pub. L. 110–432, div. A, title II, §204(d), title III, §302(a), Oct. 16, 2008, 122 Stat. 4871, 4878; Pub. L. 117–58, div. B, title II, §22418, Nov. 15, 2021, 135 Stat. 749.)

§21302. CHAPTER 201 ACCIDENT AND INCIDENT VIOLATIONS AND CHAPTER 203–209 VIOLATIONS

(a) PENALTY.—(1) Subject to section 21304 of this title, a person violating a regulation prescribed or order issued under chapter 201 of this title related to accident and incident reporting or investigation, or violating chapters 203–209 of this title or a regulation or requirement prescribed or order issued under chapters 203–209, is liable to the United States Government for a civil penalty. An act by an individual that causes a railroad carrier to be in violation is a violation. A separate violation occurs for each day the violation continues.

(2) The Secretary of Transportation imposes a civil penalty under this subsection. The amount of the penalty shall be at least $500 but not more than $25,000. However, when a grossly negligent violation or a pattern of repeated violations has caused an imminent hazard of death or injury to individuals, or has caused death or injury, the amount may be not more than $100,000.

(3) The Secretary may compromise the amount of the civil penalty under section 3711 of title 31. In determining the amount of a compromise, the Secretary shall consider—

(A) the nature, circumstances, extent, and gravity of the violation;

(B) with respect to the violator, the degree of culpability, any history of violations, the ability to pay, and any effect on the ability to continue to do business; and

(C) other matters that justice requires.

(4) If the Secretary does not compromise the amount of the civil penalty, the Secretary shall refer the matter to the Attorney General for collection.

(b) CIVIL ACTIONS TO COLLECT.—The Attorney General shall bring a civil action in a district court of the United States to collect a civil penalty that is referred to the Attorney General for collection under subsection (a) of this section. The action may be brought in the judicial district in which the violation occurred or the defendant has its principal executive office. If the action is against an individual, the action also may be brought in the judicial district in which the individual resides.

(Pub. L. 103–272, §1(e), July 5, 1994, 108 Stat. 892; Pub. L. 110–432, div. A, title III, §302(b), Oct. 16, 2008, 122 Stat. 4878.)

§21303. CHAPTER 211 VIOLATIONS

(a) PENALTY.—(1) Subject to section 21304 of this title, a person violating chapter 211 of this title, including section 21103 (as such section was in effect on the day before the date of enactment of the Rail Safety Improvement Act of 2008), or violating any provision of a waiver applicable to that person that has been granted under section 21108 of this title, is liable to the United States Government for a civil penalty. An act by an individual that causes a railroad carrier to be in violation is a violation. For a violation of section 21106 of this title, a separate violation occurs for each day a facility is not in compliance.

(2) The Secretary of Transportation imposes a civil penalty under this subsection. The amount of the penalty shall be at least $500 but not more than $25,000. However, when a grossly negligent violation or a pattern of repeated violations has caused an imminent hazard of death or injury to individuals, or has caused death or injury, the amount may be not more than $100,000.

(3) The Secretary may compromise the amount of the civil penalty under section 3711 of title 31. In determining the amount of a compromise, the Secretary shall consider—

(A) the nature, circumstances, extent, and gravity of the violation;

(B) with respect to the violator, the degree of culpability, any history of violations, the ability to pay, and any effect on the ability to continue to do business; and

(C) other matters that justice requires.

(4) If the Secretary does not compromise the amount of the civil penalty, the Secretary shall refer the matter to the Attorney General for collection.

(b) CIVIL ACTIONS TO COLLECT.—(1) The Attorney General shall bring a civil action in a district court of the United States to collect a civil penalty that is referred to the Attorney General for collection under subsection (a) of this section after satisfactory information is presented to the Attorney General. The action may be brought in the judicial district in which the violation occurred or the defendant has its principal executive office. If the action is against an individual, the action also may be brought in the judicial district in which the individual resides.

(2) A civil action under this subsection must be brought not later than 2 years after the date of the violation unless administrative notification under section 3711 of title 31 is given within that 2-year period to the person committing the violation. However, even if notification is given, the action must be brought within the period specified in section 2462 of title 28.

(c) IMPUTATION OF KNOWLEDGE.—In any proceeding under this section, a railroad carrier is deemed to know the acts of its officers and agents.

(Pub. L. 103–272, §1(e), July 5, 1994, 108 Stat. 892; Pub. L. 103–440, title II, §204, Nov. 2, 1994, 108 Stat. 4620; Pub. L. 104–287, §5(54), Oct. 11, 1996, 110 Stat. 3393; Pub. L. 110–432, div. A, title I, §108(e)(2)(B), title III, §302(c), Oct. 16, 2008, 122 Stat. 4866, 4878.)

§21304. WILLFULNESS REQUIREMENT FOR PENALTIES AGAINST INDIVIDUALS

A civil penalty under this subchapter may be imposed against an individual only for a willful violation. An individual is deemed not to have committed a willful violation if the individual was following the direct order of a railroad carrier official or supervisor under protest communicated to the official or supervisor. The individual is entitled to document the protest.

(Pub. L. 103–272, §1(e), July 5, 1994, 108 Stat. 893.)

SUBCHAPTER II—CRIMINAL PENALTIES

§21311. RECORDS AND REPORTS

(a) RECORDS AND REPORTS UNDER CHAPTER 201.—A person shall be fined under title 18, imprisoned for not more than 2 years, or both, if the person knowingly and willfully—

(1) makes a false entry in a record or report required to be made or preserved under chapter 201 of this title;

(2) destroys, mutilates, changes, or by another means falsifies such a record or report;

(3) does not enter required specified facts and transactions in such a record or report;

(4) makes or preserves such a record or report in violation of a regulation prescribed or order issued under chapter 201 of this title; or

(5) files a false record or report with the Secretary of Transportation.

(b) ACCIDENT AND INCIDENT REPORTS.—A railroad carrier not filing a report in violation of section 20901 of this title shall be fined not more than $2,500. A separate violation occurs for each day the violation continues.

(Pub. L. 103–272, §1(e), July 5, 1994, 108 Stat. 893; Pub. L. 110–432, div. A, title III, §310, Oct. 16, 2008, 122 Stat. 4882.)

PART B—ASSISTANCE

CHAPTER 221—LOCAL RAIL FREIGHT ASSISTANCE

§22101. FINANCIAL ASSISTANCE FOR STATE PROJECTS

(a) GENERAL.—The Secretary of Transportation shall provide financial assistance to a State, as provided under this chapter, for a rail freight assistance project of the State when a rail carrier subject to part A of subtitle IV of this title maintains a rail line in the State. The assistance is for the cost of—

(1) acquiring, in any way the State considers appropriate, an interest in a rail line or rail property to maintain existing, or to provide future, rail freight transportation, but only if the Surface Transportation Board has authorized, or exempted from the requirements of that authorization, the abandonment of, or the discontinuance of rail transportation on, the rail line related to the project;

(2) improving and rehabilitating rail property on a rail line to the extent necessary to allow adequate and efficient rail freight transportation on the line, but only if the rail carrier certifies that the rail line related to the project carried not more than 5,000,000 gross ton-miles of freight a mile in the prior year; and

(3) building rail or rail-related facilities (including new connections between at least 2 existing rail lines, intermodal freight terminals, sidings, bridges, and relocation of existing lines) to improve the quality and efficiency of the rail freight transportation, but only if the rail carrier certifies that the rail line related to the project carried not more than 5,000,000 gross ton-miles of freight a mile in the prior year.

(b) CALCULATING COST-BENEFIT RATIO.—The Secretary shall establish a methodology for calculating the ratio of benefits to costs of projects proposed under this chapter. In establishing the methodology, the Secretary shall consider the need for equitable treatment of different regions of the United States and different commodities transported by rail. The establishment of the methodology is committed to the discretion of the Secretary.

(c) CONDITIONS.—(1) Assistance for a project shall be provided under this chapter only if—

(A) a rail carrier certifies that the rail line related to the project carried more than 20 carloads a mile during the most recent year during which transportation was provided by the carrier on the line; and

(B) the ratio of benefits to costs for the project, as calculated using the methodology established under subsection (b) of this section, is more than 1.0.

(2) If the rail carrier that provided the transportation on the rail line is no longer in existence, the applicant for the project shall provide the information required by the certification under paragraph (1)(A) of this subsection in the way the Secretary prescribes.

(3) The Secretary may waive the requirement of paragraph (1)(A) or (2) of this subsection if the Secretary—

(A) decides that the rail line has contractual guarantees of at least 40 carloads a mile for each of the first 2 years of operation of the proposed project; and

(B) finds that there is a reasonable expectation that the contractual guarantees will be fulfilled.

(d) LIMITATIONS ON AMOUNTS.—A State may not receive more than 15 percent of the amounts provided in a fiscal year under this chapter. Not more than 20 percent of the amounts available under this chapter may be provided in a fiscal year for any one project.

(Pub. L. 103–272, §1(e), July 5, 1994, 108 Stat. 894; Pub. L. 104–88, title III, §308(f)(1), (2), Dec. 29, 1995, 109 Stat. 947.)

§22102. ELIGIBILITY

A State is eligible to receive financial assistance under this chapter only when the State complies with regulations the Secretary of Transportation prescribes under this chapter and the Secretary decides that—

(1) the State has an adequate plan for rail transportation in the State and a suitable process for updating, revising, and modifying the plan;

(2) the State plan is administered or coordinated by a designated State authority and provides for a fair distribution of resources;

(3) the State authority—

(A) is authorized to develop, promote, supervise, and support safe, adequate, and efficient rail transportation;

(B) employs or will employ sufficient qualified and trained personnel;

(C) maintains or will maintain adequate programs of investigation, research, promotion, and development with opportunity for public participation; and

(D) is designated and directed to take all practicable steps (by itself or with other State authorities) to improve rail transportation safety and reduce energy use and pollution related to transportation; and

(4) the State has ensured that it maintains or will maintain adequate procedures for financial control, accounting, and performance evaluation for the proper use of assistance provided by the United States Government.

(Pub. L. 103–272, §1(e), July 5, 1994, 108 Stat. 895.)

§22103. APPLICATIONS

(a) FILING.—A State must file an application with the Secretary of Transportation for financial assistance for a project described under section 22101(a) of this title not later than January 1 of the fiscal year for which amounts have been appropriated. However, for a fiscal year for which the authorization of appropriations for assistance under this chapter has not been enacted by the first day of the fiscal year, the State must file the application not later than 90 days after the date of enactment of a law authorizing the appropriations for that fiscal year. The Secretary shall prescribe the form of the application.

(b) CONSIDERATIONS.—In considering an application under this subsection, the Secretary shall consider the following:

(1) the percentage of rail lines that rail carriers have identified to the Surface Transportation Board for abandonment or potential abandonment in the State.

(2) the likelihood of future abandonments in the State.

(3) the ratio of benefits to costs for a proposed project calculated using the methodology established under section 22101(b) of this title.

(4) the likelihood that the rail line will continue operating with assistance.

(5) the impact of rail bankruptcies, rail restructuring, and rail mergers on the State.

(Pub. L. 103–272, §1(e), July 5, 1994, 108 Stat. 896; Pub. L. 104–88, title III, §308(f)(3), Dec. 29, 1995, 109 Stat. 947.)

§22104. STATE RAIL PLAN FINANCING

(a) ENTITLEMENT AND USES.—On the first day of each fiscal year, each State is entitled to $36,000 of the amounts made available under section 22108 [1] of this title during that fiscal year to be used—

(1) to establish, update, revise, and modify the State plan required by section 22102 of this title; or

(2) to carry out projects described in section 22101(a)(1), (2), or (3) of this title, as designated by the State, if those projects meet the requirements of section 22101(c)(1)(B) of this title.

(b) APPLICATIONS.—Each State must apply for amounts under this section not later than the first day of the fiscal year for which the amounts are available. However, for any fiscal year for which the authorization of appropriations for financial assistance under this chapter has not been enacted by the first day of the fiscal year, the State must apply for amounts under this section not later than 60 days after the date of enactment of a law authorizing the appropriations for that fiscal year. Not later than 60 days after receiving an application, the Secretary of Transportation shall consider the application and notify the State of the approval or disapproval of the application.

(c) AVAILABILITY OF AMOUNTS.—Amounts provided under this section remain available to a State for obligation for the first 3 months after the end of the fiscal year for which the amounts were made available. Amounts not applied for under this section or that remain unobligated after the first 3 months after the end of the fiscal year for which the amounts were made available are available to the Secretary for projects meeting the requirements of this chapter.

(Pub. L. 103–272, §1(e), July 5, 1994, 108 Stat. 896.)

[1] See References in Text note below.

§22105. SHARING PROJECT COSTS

(a) GENERAL.—(1) The United States Government's share of the costs of financial assistance for a project under this chapter is 50 percent, except that for assistance provided under section 22101(a)(2) of this title, the Government's share is 70 percent. The State may pay its share of the costs in cash or through the following benefits, to the extent that the benefits otherwise would not be provided:

(A) forgiveness of taxes imposed on a rail carrier or its property.

(B) real and tangible personal property (provided by the State or a person for the State) necessary for the safe and efficient operation of rail freight transportation.

(C) track rights secured by the State for a rail carrier.

(D) the cash equivalent of State salaries for State employees working on the State project, except overhead and general administrative costs.

(2) A State may pay more than its required percentage share of the costs of a project under this chapter. When a State, or a person acting for a State, pays more than the State share of the costs of its projects during a fiscal year, the excess amount shall be applied to the State share for the costs of the State projects for later fiscal years.

(b) AGREEMENTS TO COMBINE AMOUNTS.—States may agree to combine any part of the amounts made available under this chapter to carry out a project that is eligible for assistance under this chapter when—

(1) the project will benefit each State making the agreement; and

(2) the agreement is not a violation of State law.

(Pub. L. 103–272, §1(e), July 5, 1994, 108 Stat. 897.)

§22106. LIMITATIONS ON FINANCIAL ASSISTANCE

(a) GRANTS AND LOANS.—A State shall use financial assistance for projects under this chapter to make a grant or lend money to the owner of rail property, or a rail carrier providing rail transportation, related to a project being assisted.

(b) STATE USE OF REPAID FUNDS AND CONTINGENT INTEREST RECOVERIES.—The State shall place the United States Government's share of money that is repaid and any contingent interest that is recovered in an interest-bearing account. The repaid money, contingent interest, and any interest thereon shall be considered to be State funds. The State shall use such funds to make other grants and loans, consistent with the purposes for which financial assistance may be used under subsection (a), as the State considers to be appropriate.

(c) ENCOURAGING PARTICIPATION.—To the maximum extent possible, the State shall encourage the participation of shippers, rail carriers, and local communities in paying the State share of assistance costs.

(Pub. L. 103–272, §1(e), July 5, 1994, 108 Stat. 897; Pub. L. 104–287, §5(55), Oct. 11, 1996, 110 Stat. 3393; Pub. L. 110–432, div. A, title VII, §701(a), Oct. 16, 2008, 122 Stat. 4905; Pub. L. 114–94, div. A, title XI, §11316(k), Dec. 4, 2015, 129 Stat. 1678.)

§22107. RECORDS, AUDITS, AND INFORMATION

(a) RECORDS.—Each recipient of financial assistance through an arrangement under this chapter shall keep records required by the Secretary of Transportation. The records shall be

[§22108. Repealed. Pub. L. 114–94, div. A, title XI, §11301(c)(4), Dec. 4, 2015, 129 Stat. 1648]

CHAPTER 221—LOCAL RAIL FREIGHT ASSISTANCE

kept for 3 years after a project is completed and shall disclose—

(1) the amount of, and disposition by the recipient, of the assistance;

(2) the total costs of the project for which the assistance was given or used;

(3) the amount of that part of the costs of the project paid by other sources; and

(4) any other records that will make an effective audit easier.

(b) Audits.—The Secretary shall make regular financial and performance audits, as provided under chapter 75 of title 31, of activities and transactions assisted under this chapter.

(c) Information.—The Surface Transportation Board shall provide the Secretary with information the Secretary requests to assist in carrying out this chapter. The Board shall provide the information not later than 30 days after receiving a request from the Secretary.

(d) List of Rail Lines.—Not later than August 1 of each year, each rail carrier subject to part A of subtitle IV of this title shall submit to the Secretary a list of the rail lines of the carrier that carried not more than 5,000,000 gross ton-miles of freight a mile in the prior year.

(Pub. L. 103–272, §1(e), July 5, 1994, 108 Stat. 898; Pub. L. 104–88, title III, §308(f)(4), (5), Dec. 29, 1995, 109 Stat. 947; Pub. L. 104–316, title I, §127(c), Oct. 19, 1996, 110 Stat. 3840.)

[§22108. Repealed. Pub. L. 114–94, div. A, title XI, §11301(c)(4), Dec. 4, 2015, 129 Stat. 1648]

Section, Pub. L. 103–272, §1(e), July 5, 1994, 108 Stat. 898; Pub. L. 103–429, §6(20), Oct. 31, 1994, 108 Stat. 4379; Pub. L. 104–287, §5(48), Oct. 11, 1996, 110 Stat. 3393, related to authorization of appropriations.

CHAPTER 223—CAPITAL GRANTS FOR CLASS II AND CLASS III RAILROADS

§22301. CAPITAL GRANTS FOR CLASS II AND CLASS III RAILROADS

(a) ESTABLISHMENT OF PROGRAM.—

(1) ESTABLISHMENT.—The Secretary of Transportation shall establish a program for making capital grants to class II and class III railroads. Such grants shall be for projects in the public interest that—

(A)(i) rehabilitate, preserve, or improve railroad track (including roadbed, bridges, and related track structures) used primarily for freight transportation;

(ii) facilitate the continued or greater use of railroad transportation for freight shipments; and

(iii) reduce the use of less fuel efficient modes of transportation in the transportation of such shipments; or

(B) demonstrate innovative technologies and advanced research and development that increase fuel economy, reduce greenhouse gas emissions, and lower the costs of operation.

(2) PROVISION OF GRANTS.—Grants may be provided under this chapter—

(A) directly to the class II or class III railroad; or

(B) with the concurrence of the class II or class III railroad, to a State or local government.

(3) STATE COOPERATION.—Class II and class III railroad applicants for a grant under this chapter are encouraged to utilize the expertise and assistance of State transportation agencies in applying for and administering such grants. State transportation agencies are encouraged to provide such expertise and assistance to such railroads.

(4) REGULATIONS.—Not later than October 1, 2008, the Secretary shall issue final regulations to implement the program under this section.

(b) MAXIMUM FEDERAL SHARE.—The maximum Federal share for carrying out a project under this section shall be 80 percent of the project cost. The non-Federal share may be provided by any non-Federal source in cash, equipment, or supplies. Other in-kind contributions may be approved by the Secretary on a case-by-case basis consistent with this chapter.

(c) USE OF FUNDS.—Grants provided under this section shall be used to implement track capital projects as soon as possible. In no event shall grant funds be contractually obligated for a project later than the end of the third Federal fiscal year following the year in which the grant was awarded. Any funds not so obligated by the end of such fiscal year shall be returned to the Secretary for reallocation.

(d) EMPLOYEE PROTECTION.—The Secretary shall require as a condition of any grant made under this section that the recipient railroad provide a fair arrangement at least as protective of the interests of employees who are affected by the project to be funded with the grant as the terms imposed under section 11326(a), as in effect on the date of the enactment of this chapter.

(e) LABOR STANDARDS.—

(1) PREVAILING WAGES.—The Secretary shall ensure that laborers and mechanics employed by contractors and subcontractors in construction work financed by a grant made under this section will be paid wages not less than those prevailing on similar construction in the locality, as determined by the Secretary of Labor under subchapter IV of chapter 31 of title 40 (commonly known as the "Davis-Bacon Act"). The Secretary shall make a grant under this section only after being assured that required labor standards will be maintained on the construction work.

(2) WAGE RATES.—Wage rates in a collective bargaining agreement negotiated under the Railway Labor Act (45 U.S.C. 151 et seq.) are deemed for purposes of this subsection to comply with the [1] subchapter IV of chapter 31 of title 40.

(f) STUDY.—The Secretary shall conduct a study of the projects carried out with grant assistance under this section to determine the extent to which the program helps promote a reduction in fuel use associated with the transportation of freight and demonstrates innovative technologies that increase fuel economy, reduce greenhouse gas emissions, and lower the costs of operation. Not later than March 31, 2009, the Secretary shall submit a report to the Committee on Transportation and Infrastructure of the House of Representatives and the Committee on Commerce, Science, and Transportation of the Senate on the study, including any recommendations the Secretary considers appropriate regarding the program.

(g) AUTHORIZATION OF APPROPRIATIONS.—There is authorized to be appropriated to the Secretary $50,000,000 for each of fiscal years 2008 through 2011 for carrying out this section.

(Added Pub. L. 110–140, title XI, §1112(a), Dec. 19, 2007, 121 Stat. 1758; amended Pub. L. 110–432, div. A, title VII, §701(b), Oct. 16, 2008, 122 Stat. 4906.)

---

[1] So in original. The word "the" probably should not appear.

CHAPTER 224—RAILROAD REHABILITATION AND IMPROVEMENT FINANCING

§22401. DEFINITIONS

In this chapter:

(1) COST.—

(A) The term "cost" means the estimated long-term cost to the Government of a direct loan or loan guarantee or modification thereof, calculated on a net present value basis, excluding administrative costs and any incidental effects on governmental receipts or outlays.

(B) The cost of a direct loan shall be the net present value, at the time when the direct loan is disbursed, of the following estimated cash flows:

(i) Loan disbursements.

(ii) Repayments of principal.

(iii) Payments of interest and other payments by or to the Government over the life of the loan after adjusting for estimated defaults, prepayments, fees, penalties, and other recoveries.

Calculation of the cost of a direct loan shall include the effects of changes in loan terms resulting from the exercise by the borrower of an option included in the loan contract.

(C) The cost of a loan guarantee shall be the net present value, at the time when the guaranteed loan is disbursed, of the following estimated cash flows:

(i) Payments by the Government to cover defaults and delinquencies, interest subsidies, or other payments.

(ii) Payments to the Government, including origination and other fees, penalties, and recoveries.

Calculation of the cost of a loan guarantee shall include the effects of changes in loan terms resulting from the exercise by the guaranteed lender of an option included in the loan guarantee contract, or by the borrower of an option included in the guaranteed loan contract.

(D) The cost of a modification is the difference between the current estimate of the net present value of the remaining cash flows under the terms of a direct loan or loan guarantee contract, and the current estimate of the net present value of the remaining cash flows under the terms of the contract, as modified.

(E) In estimating net present values, the discount rate shall be the average interest rate on marketable Treasury securities of similar maturity to the cash flows of the direct loan or loan guarantee for which the estimate is being made.

(F) When funds are obligated for a direct loan or loan guarantee, the estimated cost shall be based on the current assumptions, adjusted to incorporate the terms of the loan contract, for the fiscal year in which the funds are obligated.

(2) CURRENT.—The term "current" has the same meaning as in section 250(c)(9) of the Balanced Budget and Emergency Deficit Control Act of 1985.

(3) DIRECT LOAN.—The term "direct loan" means a disbursement of funds by the Government to a non-Federal borrower under a contract that requires the repayment of such funds. The term includes the purchase of, or participation in, a loan made by another lender and financing arrangements that defer payment for more than 90 days, including the sale of a Government asset on credit terms. The term does not include the acquisition of a federally guaranteed loan in satisfaction of default claims.

(4) DIRECT LOAN OBLIGATION.—The term "direct loan obligation" means a binding agreement by the Secretary to make a direct loan when specified conditions are fulfilled by the borrower.

(5) INTERMODAL.—The term "intermodal" means of or relating to the connection between rail service and other modes of transportation, including all parts of facilities at which such connection is made.

(6) INVESTMENT-GRADE RATING.—The term "investment-grade rating" means a rating of BBB minus, Baa 3, bbb minus, BBB(low), or higher assigned by a rating agency.

(7) LOAN GUARANTEE.—The term "loan guarantee" means any guarantee, insurance, or other pledge with respect to the payment of all or a part of the principal or interest on any debt obligation of a non-Federal borrower to a non-Federal lender, but does not include the insurance of deposits, shares, or other withdrawable accounts in financial institutions.

(8) LOAN GUARANTEE COMMITMENT.—The term "loan guarantee commitment" means a binding agreement by the Secretary to make a loan guarantee when specified conditions are fulfilled by the borrower, the lender, or any other party to the guarantee agreement.

(9) MASTER CREDIT AGREEMENT.—The term "master credit agreement" means an agreement to make 1 or more direct loans or loan guarantees at future dates for a program of related projects on terms acceptable to the Secretary.

(10) MODIFICATION.—The term "modification" means any Government action that alters the estimated cost of an outstanding direct loan (or direct loan obligation) or an outstanding loan guarantee (or loan guarantee commitment) from the current estimate of cash flows. This includes the sale of loan assets, with or without recourse, and the purchase of guaranteed loans. This also includes any action resulting from new legislation, or from the exercise of administrative discretion under existing law, that directly or indirectly alters the estimated cost of outstanding direct loans (or direct loan obligations) or loan guarantees (or loan guarantee commitments) such as a change in collection procedures.

(11) PROJECT OBLIGATION.—The term "project obligation" means a note, bond, debenture, or other debt obligation issued by a borrower in connection with the financing of a project, other than a direct loan or loan guarantee under this chapter.

(12) RAILROAD.—The term "railroad" includes—

(A) any railroad or railroad carrier (as such terms are defined in section 20102); and

(B) any rail carrier (as defined in section 24102).

(13) RATING AGENCY.—The term "rating agency" means a credit rating agency registered with the Securities and Exchange Commission as a nationally recognized statistical rating organization (as defined in section 3(a) of the Securities Exchange Act of 1934 (15 U.S.C. 78c(a))).

(14) SECRETARY.—The term "Secretary" means the Secretary of Transportation.

(15) SUBSTANTIAL COMPLETION.—The term "substantial completion" means—

(A) the opening of a project to passenger or freight traffic; or

(B) a comparable event, as determined by the Secretary and specified in the terms of the direct loan or loan guarantee provided by the Secretary.

(Added and amended Pub. L. 117–58, div. B, title I, §21301(a)(2), (3), (c), Nov. 15, 2021, 135 Stat. 683.)

§22402. DIRECT LOANS AND LOAN GUARANTEES

(a) GENERAL AUTHORITY.—The Secretary shall provide direct loans and loan guarantees to—

(1) State and local governments;

(2) entities implementing interstate compacts consented to by Congress under section 410(a) of the Amtrak Reform and Accountability Act of 1997 (49 U.S.C. 24101 note);

(3) government sponsored authorities and corporations;

(4) railroads;

(5) entities participating in joint ventures that include at least 1 of the entities described in paragraph (1), (2), (3), (4), or (6);

(6) limited option freight shippers that own or operate a plant or other facility, solely for the purpose of constructing a rail connection between a plant or facility and a railroad; and

(7) private entities with controlling ownership in 1 or more freight railroads other than Class I carriers.

(b) ELIGIBLE PURPOSES.—

(1) IN GENERAL.—Direct loans and loan guarantees authorized under this section shall be used—

(A) to acquire, improve, or rehabilitate intermodal or rail equipment or facilities, including track, components of track, cuts and fills, stations, tunnels, bridges, yards, buildings, and shops, and to finance costs related to those activities, including preconstruction costs;

(B) to develop or establish new intermodal or railroad facilities;

(C) to develop landside port infrastructure for seaports serviced by rail;

(D) to refinance outstanding debt incurred for the purposes described in subparagraph (A) , (B), or (C);

(E) to reimburse planning, permitting, and design expenses relating to activities described in subparagraph (A), (B), or (C); or

(F) to finance economic development, including commercial and residential development, and related infrastructure and activities, that—

(i) incorporates private investment of greater than 20 percent of total project costs;

(ii) is physically connected to, or is within ½ mile of, a fixed guideway transit station, an intercity bus station, a passenger rail station, or a multimodal station, provided that the location includes service by a railroad;

(iii) demonstrates the ability of the applicant to commence the contracting process for construction not later than 90 days after the date on which the direct loan or loan guarantee is obligated for the project under this chapter; and

(iv) demonstrates the ability to generate new revenue for the relevant passenger rail station or service by increasing ridership, increasing tenant lease payments, or carrying out other activities that generate revenue exceeding costs.

(2) OPERATING EXPENSES NOT ELIGIBLE.—Direct loans and loan guarantees under this section shall not be used for railroad operating expenses.

(c) PRIORITY PROJECTS.—In granting applications for direct loans or guaranteed loans under this section, the Secretary shall give priority to projects that—

(1) enhance public safety, including projects for the installation of a positive train control system (as defined in section 20157(i));

(2) promote economic development;

(3) enhance the environment;

(4) enable United States companies to be more competitive in international markets;

(5) are endorsed by the plans prepared under section 135 of title 23 or chapter 227 of this title by the State or States in which they are located;

(6) improve railroad stations and passenger facilities and increase transit-oriented development;

(7) preserve or enhance rail or intermodal service to small communities or rural areas;

(8) enhance service and capacity in the national rail system; or

(9) would materially alleviate rail capacity problems which degrade the provision of service to shippers and would fulfill a need in the national transportation system.

(d) EXTENT OF AUTHORITY.—The aggregate unpaid principal amounts of obligations under direct loans and loan guarantees made under this section shall not exceed $35,000,000,000 at any one time. Of this amount, not less than $7,000,000,000 shall be available solely for projects primarily benefiting freight railroads other than Class I carriers. The Secretary shall not establish any limit on the proportion of the unused amount authorized under this subsection that may be used for 1 loan or loan guarantee.

(e) RATES OF INTEREST.—

(1) DIRECT LOANS.—The interest rate on a direct loan under this section shall be not less than the yield on United States Treasury securities of a similar maturity to the maturity of the secured loan on the date of execution of the loan agreement.

(2) LOAN GUARANTEES.—The Secretary shall not make a loan guarantee under this section if the interest rate for the loan exceeds that which the Secretary determines to be reasonable, taking into consideration the prevailing interest rates and customary fees incurred under similar obligations in the private capital market.

(f) INFRASTRUCTURE PARTNERS.—

(1) AUTHORITY OF SECRETARY.—In lieu of or in combination with appropriations of budget authority to cover the costs of direct loans and loan guarantees as required under section 504(b)(1) of the Federal Credit Reform Act of 1990, including the cost of a modification thereof, the Secretary may accept on behalf of an applicant for assistance under this section a commitment from a non-Federal source, including a State or local government or agency or public benefit corporation or public authority thereof, to fund in whole or in part credit risk premiums and modification costs with respect to the loan that is the subject of the application or modification. In no event shall the aggregate of appropriations of budget authority and credit risk premiums described in this paragraph with respect to a direct loan or loan guarantee be less than the cost of that direct loan or loan guarantee.

(2) CREDIT RISK PREMIUM AMOUNT.—The Secretary shall determine the amount required for credit risk premiums under this subsection on the basis of—

(A) the circumstances of the applicant, including the amount of collateral offered, if any;

(B) the proposed schedule of loan disbursements;

(C) historical data on the repayment history of similar borrowers;

(D) consultation with the Congressional Budget Office; and

(E) any other factors the Secretary considers relevant.

(3) CREDITWORTHINESS.—Upon receipt of a proposal from an applicant under this section, the Secretary shall accept as a basis for determining the amount of the credit risk premium under paragraph (2) any of the following in addition to the value of any collateral described in paragraph (6):

(A) The net present value of a future stream of State or local subsidy income or other dedicated revenues to secure the direct loan or loan guarantee.

(B) Adequate coverage requirements to ensure repayment, on a non-recourse basis, from cash flows generated by the project or any other dedicated revenue source, including—

(i) tolls;

(ii) user fees, including operating or tenant charges, facility rents, or other fees paid by transportation service providers or operators for access to, or the use of, infrastructure, including rail lines, bridges, tunnels, yards, or stations; or

(iii) payments owing to the obligor under a public-private partnership.

(C) An investment-grade rating on the direct loan or loan guarantee, as applicable, except that if the total amount of the direct loan or loan guarantee is greater than $150,000,000, the applicant shall have an investment-grade rating from at least 2 rating agencies on the direct loan or loan guarantee.

(D) Revenue from projected freight or passenger demand for the project based on regionally developed economic forecasts, including projections of any modal diversion resulting from the project.

(4) PAYMENT OF PREMIUMS.—Credit risk premiums under this subsection shall be paid to the Secretary before the disbursement of loan amounts (and in the case of a modification, before the modification is executed), to the extent appropriations are not available to the Secretary to meet the costs of direct loans and loan guarantees, including costs of modifications thereof.

(5) COHORTS OF LOANS.—Subject to the availability of funds appropriated by Congress under section 22406(a)(2), for any direct loan issued before the date of enactment of the Fixing America's Surface Transportation Act (Public Law 114–94) pursuant to sections 501 through 504 of the Railroad Revitalization and Regulatory Reform Act of 1976 (Public Law 94–210), the Secretary shall repay the credit risk premiums of such loan, with interest accrued thereon, not later than—

(A) 60 days after the date of enactment of the Surface Transportation Investment Act of 2021 if the borrower has satisfied all obligations attached to such loan; or

(B) if the borrower has not yet satisfied all obligations attached to such loan, 60 days after the date on which all obligations attached to such loan have been satisfied.

(6) COLLATERAL.—

(A) TYPES OF COLLATERAL.—An applicant or infrastructure partner may propose tangible and intangible assets as collateral, exclusive of goodwill. The Secretary, after evaluating each such asset—

(i) shall accept a net liquidation value of collateral; and

(ii) shall consider and may accept—

(I) the market value of collateral; or

(II) in the case of a blanket pledge or assignment of an entire operating asset or basket of assets as collateral, the market value of assets, or, the market value of the going concern, considering—

(aa) inclusion in the pledge of all the assets necessary for independent operational utility of the collateral, including tangible assets such as real property, track and structure, motive power, equipment and rolling stock, stations, systems and maintenance facilities and intangible assets such as long-term shipping agreements, easements, leases and access rights such as for trackage and haulage;

(bb) interchange commitments; and

(cc) the value of the asset as determined through the cost or market approaches, or the market value of the going concern, with the latter considering discounted cash flows for a period not to exceed the term of the direct loan or loan guarantee.

(B) APPRAISAL STANDARDS.—In evaluating appraisals of collateral under subparagraph (A), the Secretary shall consider—

(i) adherence to the substance and principles of the Uniform Standards of Professional Appraisal Practice, as developed by the Appraisal Standards Board of the Appraisal Foundation; and

(ii) the qualifications of the appraisers to value the type of collateral offered.

(7) REPAYMENT OF CREDIT RISK PREMIUMS.—The Secretary shall return credit risk

premiums paid, and interest accrued on such premiums, to the original source when all obligations of a loan or loan guarantee have been satisfied. This paragraph applies to any project that has been granted assistance under this section after the date of enactment of the Surface Transportation Investment Act of 2021.

(g) PREREQUISITES FOR ASSISTANCE.—The Secretary shall not make a direct loan or loan guarantee under this section unless the Secretary has made a finding in writing that—
(1) repayment of the obligation is required to be made within a term that is not longer than the shorter of—
(A) 75 years after the date of substantial completion of the project;
(B) the estimated useful life of the rail equipment or facilities to be acquired, rehabilitated, improved, developed, or established, subject to an adequate determination of long-term risk; or
(C) for projects determined to have an estimated useful life that is longer than 35 years, the period that is equal to the sum of—
(i) 35 years; and
(ii) the product of—
(I) the difference between the estimated useful life and 35 years; multiplied by
(II) 75 percent.

(2) the direct loan or loan guarantee is justified by the present and probable future demand for rail services or intermodal facilities;
(3) the applicant has given reasonable assurances that the facilities or equipment to be acquired, rehabilitated, improved, developed, or established with the proceeds of the obligation will be economically and efficiently utilized;
(4) the obligation can reasonably be repaid, using an appropriate combination of credit risk premiums and collateral offered by the applicant to protect the Federal Government; and
(5) the purposes of the direct loan or loan guarantee are consistent with subsection (b).

(h) CONDITIONS OF ASSISTANCE.—
(1) The Secretary shall, before granting assistance under this section, require the applicant to agree to such terms and conditions as are sufficient, in the judgment of the Secretary, to ensure that, as long as any principal or interest is due and payable on such obligation, the applicant, and any railroad or railroad partner for whose benefit the assistance is intended—
(A) will not use any funds or assets from railroad or intermodal operations for purposes not related to such operations, if such use would impair the ability of the applicant, railroad, or railroad partner to provide rail or intermodal services in an efficient and economic manner, or would adversely affect the ability of the applicant, railroad, or railroad partner to perform any obligation entered into by the applicant under this section;
(B) will, consistent with its capital resources, maintain its capital program, equipment, facilities, and operations on a continuing basis; and
(C) will not make any discretionary dividend payments that unreasonably conflict

with the purposes stated in subsection (b).

(2) The Secretary shall not require an applicant for a direct loan or loan guarantee under this section to provide collateral. Any collateral provided or thereafter enhanced shall be valued as a going concern after giving effect to the present value of improvements contemplated by the completion and operation of the project, if applicable. The Secretary shall not require that an applicant for a direct loan or loan guarantee under this section have previously sought the financial assistance requested from another source.

(3) The Secretary shall require recipients of direct loans or loan guarantees under this section to comply with—

(A) the standards of section 24312, as in effect on September 1, 2002, with respect to the project in the same manner that Amtrak is required to comply with such standards for construction work financed under an agreement made under section 24308(a); and

(B) the protective arrangements established under section 22404, with respect to employees affected by actions taken in connection with the project to be financed by the loan or loan guarantee.

(4) The Secretary shall require each recipient of a direct loan or loan guarantee under this section for a project described in subsection (b)(1)(F) to provide a non-Federal match of not less than 25 percent of the total amount expended by the recipient for such project.

(i) APPLICATION PROCESSING PROCEDURES.—

(1) APPLICATION STATUS NOTICES.—Not later than 30 days after the date that the Secretary receives an application under this section, or additional information and material under paragraph (2)(B), the Secretary shall provide the applicant written notice as to whether the application is complete or incomplete.

(2) INCOMPLETE APPLICATIONS.—If the Secretary determines that an application is incomplete, the Secretary shall—

(A) provide the applicant with a description of all of the specific information or material that is needed to complete the application, including any information required by an independent financial analyst; and

(B) allow the applicant to resubmit the application with the information and material described under subparagraph (A) to complete the application.

(3) APPLICATION APPROVALS AND DISAPPROVALS.—

(A) IN GENERAL.—Not later than 60 days after the date the Secretary notifies an applicant that an application is complete under paragraph (1), the Secretary shall provide the applicant written notice as to whether the Secretary has approved or disapproved the application.

(B) ACTIONS BY THE OFFICE OF MANAGEMENT AND BUDGET.—In order to enable compliance with the time limit under subparagraph (A), the Office of Management and Budget shall take any action required with respect to the application within that 60-day period.

(4) STREAMLINED APPLICATION REVIEW PROCESS.—

(A) IN GENERAL.—Not later than 180 days after the date of enactment of the Surface Transportation Investment Act of 2021, the Secretary shall implement procedures and measures to economize and make available an streamlined application process or processes at the request of applicants seeking loans or loan guarantees.

(B) CRITERIA.—Applicants seeking loans and loan guarantees under this section shall—

(i) seek a total loan or loan guarantee value not exceeding $150,000,000;

(ii) meet eligible project purposes described in subparagraphs (A) and (B) of subsection (b)(1); and

(iii) meet other criteria considered appropriate by the Secretary, in consultation with the Council on Credit and Finance of the Department of Transportation.

(C) EXPEDITED CREDIT REVIEW.—The total period between the submission of an application and the approval or disapproval of an application for a direct loan or loan guarantee under this paragraph may not exceed 90 days. If an application review conducted under this paragraph exceeds 90 days, the Secretary shall—

(i) provide written notice to the applicant, including a justification for the delay and updated estimate of the time needed for approval or disapproval; and

(ii) publish the notice on the dashboard described in paragraph (5).

(5) DASHBOARD.—The Secretary shall post on the Department of Transportation's Internet Web site a monthly report that includes, for each application—

(A) the applicant type;

(B) the location of the project;

(C) a brief description of the project, including its purpose;

(D) the requested direct loan or loan guarantee amount;

(E) the date on which the Secretary provided application status notice under paragraph (1);

(F) the date that the Secretary provided notice of approval or disapproval under paragraph (3); and

(G) whether the project utilized the streamlined application process under paragraph (4).

(6) CREDITWORTHINESS REVIEW STATUS.—

(A) IN GENERAL.—The Secretary shall maintain status information related to each application for a loan or loan guarantee, which shall be provided to the applicant upon request, including—

(i) the total value of the proposed loan or loan guarantee;

(ii) the name of the applicant or applicants submitting the application;

(iii) the proposed capital structure of the project to which the loan or loan guarantee would be applied, including the proposed Federal and non-Federal shares of the total project cost;

(iv) the type of activity to receive credit assistance, including whether the project is new construction, the rehabilitation of existing rail equipment or facilities, or the refinancing an existing loan or loan guarantee;

(v) if a deferred payment is proposed, the length of such deferment;

(vi) the credit rating or ratings provided for the applicant;

(vii) if other credit instruments are involved, the proposed subordination relationship and a description of such other credit instruments;

(viii) a schedule for the readiness of proposed investments for financing;

(ix) a description of any Federal permits required, including under the National Environmental Policy Act of 1969 (42 U.S.C. 4321 et seq.) and any waivers under section 5323(j) (commonly known as the "Buy America Act");

(x) other characteristics of the proposed activity to be financed, borrower, key agreements, or the nature of the credit that the Secretary considers to be fundamental to the creditworthiness review;

(xi) the status of the application in the pre-application review and selection process;

(xii) the cumulative amounts paid by the Secretary to outside advisors related to the application, including financial and legal advisors;

(xiii) a description of the key rating factors used by the Secretary to determine credit risk, including—

(I) the factors used to determine risk for the proposed application;

(II) an adjectival risk rating for each identified factor, ranked as either low, moderate, or high;

(xiv) a nonbinding estimate of the credit risk premium, which may be in the form of—

(I) a range, based on the assessment of risk factors described in clause (xiii); or

(II) a justification for why the estimate of the credit risk premium cannot be determined based on available information; and

(xv) a description of the key information the Secretary needs from the applicant to complete the credit review process and make a final determination of the credit risk premium.

(B) REPORT UPON REQUEST.—The Secretary shall provide the information described in subparagraph (A) not later than 30 days after a request from the applicant.

(C) EXCEPTION.—Applications processed using the streamlined application review process under paragraph (4) are not subject to the requirements under this paragraph.

(j) REPAYMENT SCHEDULES.—

(1) IN GENERAL.—The Secretary shall establish a repayment schedule requiring payments to commence not later than 5 years after the date of substantial completion.

(2) ACCRUAL.—Interest shall accrue as of the date of disbursement, and shall be amortized over the remaining term of the loan beginning at the time the payments begin.

(3) DEFERRED PAYMENTS.—

(A) IN GENERAL.—If at any time after the date of substantial completion the obligor is unable to pay the scheduled loan repayments of principal and interest on a direct loan provided under this section, the Secretary, subject to subparagraph (B), may allow, for a maximum aggregate time of 1 year over the duration of the direct loan, the obligor to add unpaid principal and interest to the outstanding balance of the direct loan.

(B) INTEREST.—A payment deferred under subparagraph (A) shall—

(i) continue to accrue interest under paragraph (2) until the loan is fully repaid; and

(ii) be scheduled to be amortized over the remaining term of the loan.

(4) PREPAYMENTS.—

(A) USE OF EXCESS REVENUES.—With respect to a direct loan provided by the Secretary under this section, any excess revenues that remain after satisfying scheduled debt service requirements on the project obligations and direct loan and all deposit requirements under the terms of any trust agreement, bond resolution, or similar agreement securing project obligations may be applied annually to prepay the direct loan without penalty.

(B) USE OF PROCEEDS OF REFINANCING.—The direct loan may be prepaid at any time without penalty from the proceeds of refinancing from non-Federal funding sources.

(k) SALE OF DIRECT LOANS.—

(1) IN GENERAL.—Subject to paragraph (2) and as soon as practicable after substantial completion of a project, the Secretary, after notifying the obligor, may sell to another entity or reoffer into the capital markets a direct loan for the project if the Secretary determines that the sale or reoffering has a high probability of being made on favorable terms.

(2) CONSENT OF OBLIGOR.—In making a sale or reoffering under paragraph (1), the Secretary may not change the original terms and conditions of the secured loan without the prior written consent of the obligor.

(l) NONSUBORDINATION.—

(1) IN GENERAL.—Except as provided in paragraph (2), a direct loan provided by the Secretary under this section shall not be subordinated to the claims of any holder of project obligations in the event of bankruptcy, insolvency, or liquidation of the obligor.

(2) PREEXISTING INDENTURES.—

(A) IN GENERAL.—The Secretary may waive the requirement under paragraph (1) for a public agency borrower that is financing ongoing capital programs and has outstanding senior bonds under a preexisting indenture if—

(i) the direct loan is rated in the A category or higher;

(ii) the direct loan is secured and payable from pledged revenues not affected by project performance, such as a tax-based revenue pledge or a system-backed pledge of project revenues; and

(iii) the program share, under this chapter, of eligible project costs is 50 percent or less.

(B) LIMITATION.—The Secretary may impose limitations for the waiver of the nonsubordination requirement under this paragraph if the Secretary determines that such limitations would be in the financial interest of the Federal Government.

(m) MASTER CREDIT AGREEMENTS.—

(1) IN GENERAL.—Subject to subsection (d) and paragraph (2) of this subsection, the Secretary may enter into a master credit agreement that is contingent on all of the conditions for the provision of a direct loan or loan guarantee, as applicable, under this chapter and other applicable requirements being satisfied prior to the issuance of the direct loan or loan guarantee.

(2) CONDITIONS.—Each master credit agreement shall—

(A) establish the maximum amount and general terms and conditions of each applicable direct loan or loan guarantee;

(B) identify 1 or more dedicated non-Federal revenue sources that will secure the repayment of each applicable direct loan or loan guarantee;

(C) provide for the obligation of funds for the direct loans or loan guarantees contingent on and after all requirements have been met for the projects subject to the master credit agreement; and

(D) provide 1 or more dates, as determined by the Secretary, before which the master credit agreement results in each of the direct loans or loan guarantees or in the release of the master credit agreement.

(n) NON-FEDERAL SHARE.—The proceeds of a loan provided under this section may be used as the non-Federal share of project costs for any grant program administered by the Secretary if such loan is repayable from non-Federal funds.

(Added and amended Pub. L. 117–58, div. B, title I, §21301(a)(2), (4), (d), Nov. 15, 2021, 135 Stat. 683, 684.)

§22403. ADMINISTRATION OF DIRECT LOANS AND LOAN GUARANTEES

(a) APPLICATIONS.—

(1) IN GENERAL.—The Secretary shall prescribe the form and contents required of applications for assistance under section 22402, to enable the Secretary to determine the eligibility of the applicant's proposal, and shall establish terms and conditions for direct loans and loan guarantees made under that section, including a program guide, a standard term sheet, and specific timetables.

(2) DOCUMENTATION.—An applicant meeting the size standard for small business concerns established under section 3(a)(2) of the Small Business Act (15 U.S.C. 632(a)(2)) may provide unaudited financial statements as documentation of historical financial information if such statements are accompanied by the applicant's Federal tax returns and Internal Revenue Service tax verifications for the corresponding years.

(b) FULL FAITH AND CREDIT.—All guarantees entered into by the Secretary under section 22402 shall constitute general obligations of the United States of America backed by the full faith and credit of the United States of America.

(c) ASSIGNMENT OF LOAN GUARANTEES.—The holder of a loan guarantee made under section 22402 may assign the loan guarantee in whole or in part, subject to such requirements as the Secretary may prescribe.

(d) MODIFICATIONS.—The Secretary may approve the modification of any term or condition of a direct loan, loan guarantee, direct loan obligation, or loan guarantee commitment, including the rate of interest, time of payment of interest or principal, or security requirements, if the Secretary finds in writing that—

(1) the modification is equitable and is in the overall best interests of the United States;

(2) consent has been obtained from the applicant and, in the case of a loan guarantee or loan guarantee commitment, the holder of the obligation; and

(3) the modification cost has been covered under section 22402(f).

(e) COMPLIANCE.—The Secretary shall assure compliance, by an applicant, any other party to the loan, and any railroad or railroad partner for whose benefit assistance is intended, with the provisions of this chapter, regulations issued hereunder, and the terms and conditions of the direct loan or loan guarantee, including through regular periodic inspections.

(f) COMMERCIAL VALIDITY.—For purposes of claims by any party other than the Secretary, a loan guarantee or loan guarantee commitment shall be conclusive evidence that the underlying obligation is in compliance with the provisions of this chapter, and that such obligation has been approved and is legal as to principal, interest, and other terms. Such a guarantee or commitment shall be valid and incontestable in the hands of a holder thereof, including the original lender or any other holder, as of the date when the Secretary granted the application therefor, except as to fraud or material misrepresentation by such holder.

(g) DEFAULT.—The Secretary shall prescribe regulations setting forth procedures in the event of default on a loan made or guaranteed under section 22402. The Secretary shall ensure that each loan guarantee made under that section contains terms and conditions that provide that—

(1) if a payment of principal or interest under the loan is in default for more than 30 days, the Secretary shall pay to the holder of the obligation, or the holder's agent, the amount of unpaid guaranteed interest;

(2) if the default has continued for more than 90 days, the Secretary shall pay to the holder of the obligation, or the holder's agent, 90 percent of the unpaid guaranteed principal;

(3) after final resolution of the default, through liquidation or otherwise, the Secretary shall pay to the holder of the obligation, or the holder's agent, any remaining amounts guaranteed but which were not recovered through the default's resolution;

(4) the Secretary shall not be required to make any payment under paragraphs (1) through (3) if the Secretary finds, before the expiration of the periods described in such paragraphs, that the default has been remedied; and

(5) the holder of the obligation shall not receive payment or be entitled to retain payment in a total amount which, together with all other recoveries (including any recovery based upon a security interest in equipment or facilities) exceeds the actual loss of such holder.

(h) RIGHTS OF THE SECRETARY.—

(1) SUBROGATION.—If the Secretary makes payment to a holder, or a holder's agent, under subsection (g) in connection with a loan guarantee made under section 22402, the Secretary shall be subrogated to all of the rights of the holder with respect to the obligor under the loan.

(2) DISPOSITION OF PROPERTY.—The Secretary may complete, recondition, reconstruct, renovate, repair, maintain, operate, charter, rent, sell, or otherwise dispose of any property or other interests obtained pursuant to this section. The Secretary shall not be subject to any Federal or State regulatory requirements when carrying out this paragraph.

(i) ACTION AGAINST OBLIGOR.—The Secretary may bring a civil action in an appropriate Federal court in the name of the United States in the event of a default on a direct loan made under section 22402, or in the name of the United States or of the holder of the obligation in the event of a default on a loan guaranteed under section 22402. The holder of a guarantee shall make available to the Secretary all records and evidence necessary to prosecute the civil action. The Secretary may accept property in full or partial satisfaction of any sums owed as a result of a default. If the Secretary receives, through the sale or other disposition of such property, an amount greater than the aggregate of—

(1) the amount paid to the holder of a guarantee under subsection (g) of this section; and

(2) any other cost to the United States of remedying the default,

the Secretary shall pay such excess to the obligor.

(j) BREACH OF CONDITIONS.—The Attorney General shall commence a civil action in an appropriate Federal court to enjoin any activity which the Secretary finds is in violation of this chapter, regulations issued hereunder, or any conditions which were duly agreed to, and to secure any other appropriate relief.

(k) ATTACHMENT.—No attachment or execution may be issued against the Secretary, or any property in the control of the Secretary, prior to the entry of final judgment to such effect in any State, Federal, or other court.

(l) CHARGES AND LOAN SERVICING.—

(1) PURPOSES.—The Secretary may collect from each applicant, obligor, or loan party a reasonable charge for—

(A) the cost of evaluating the application, amendments, modifications, and waivers, including for evaluating project viability, applicant creditworthiness, and the appraisal of the value of the equipment or facilities for which the direct loan or loan guarantee is sought, and for making necessary determinations and findings;

(B) the cost of award management and project management oversight;

(C) the cost of services from expert firms, including counsel, and independent financial advisors to assist in the underwriting, auditing, servicing, and exercise of rights with respect to direct loans and loan guarantees; and

(D) the cost of all other expenses incurred as a result of a breach of any term or condition or any event of default on a direct loan or loan guarantee.

(2) STANDARDS.—The Secretary may charge different amounts under this subsection based on the different costs incurred under paragraph (1).

(3) SERVICER.—

(A) IN GENERAL.—The Secretary may appoint a financial entity to assist the Secretary in servicing a direct loan or loan guarantee under this chapter.

(B) DUTIES.—A servicer appointed under subparagraph (A) shall act as the agent of the Secretary in servicing a direct loan or loan guarantee under this chapter.

(C) FEES.—A servicer appointed under subparagraph (A) shall receive a servicing fee from the obligor or other loan party, subject to approval by the Secretary.

(4) NATIONAL SURFACE TRANSPORTATION AND INNOVATIVE FINANCE BUREAU ACCOUNT.—Amounts collected under this subsection shall—

(A) be credited directly to the National Surface Transportation and Innovative Finance Bureau account; and

(B) remain available until expended to pay for the costs described in this subsection.

(m) FEES AND CHARGES.—Except as provided in this chapter, the Secretary may not assess any fees, including user fees, or charges in connection with a direct loan or loan guarantee provided under section 22402.

(Added and amended Pub. L. 117–58, div. B, title I, §21301(a)(2), (5), (e), Nov. 15, 2021, 135 Stat. 683, 689.)

§22404. EMPLOYEE PROTECTION

(a) GENERAL.—Fair and equitable arrangements shall be provided, in accordance with this section, to protect the interests of any employees who may be affected by actions taken pursuant to authorizations or approval obtained under this chapter. Such arrangements shall be determined by the execution of an agreement between the representatives of the railroads and the representatives of their employees, not later than 120 days after February 5, 1976. In the absence of such an executed agreement, the Secretary of Labor shall prescribe the applicable protective arrangements, not later than 150 days after February 5, 1976.

(b) TERMS.—The arrangements required by subsection (a) of this section shall apply to each employee who has an employment relationship with a railroad on the date on which such railroad first applies for applicable financial assistance under this chapter. Such arrangements shall include such provisions as may be necessary for the negotiation and execution of agreements as to the manner in which the protective arrangements shall be applied, including notice requirements. Such agreements shall be executed prior to implementation of work funded from financial assistance under this chapter. If such an agreement is not reached within 30 days after the date on which an application for such assistance is approved, either party to the dispute may submit the issue for final and binding arbitration. The decision on any such arbitration shall be rendered within 30 days after such submission. Such arbitration decision shall in no way modify the protection afforded in the protective arrangements established pursuant to this section, shall be final and binding on the parties thereto, and shall become a part of the agreement. Such arrangements shall also include such provisions as may be necessary—

(1) for the preservation of compensation (including subsequent general wage increases, vacation allowances, and monthly compensation guarantees), rights,

privileges, and benefits (including fringe benefits such as pensions, hospitalization, and vacations, under the same conditions and so long as such benefits continue to be accorded to other employees of the employing railroad in active service or on furlough, as the case may be) to such employees under existing collective-bargaining agreements or otherwise;

(2) to provide for final and binding arbitration of any dispute which cannot be settled by the parties, with respect to the interpretation, application, or enforcement of the provisions of the protective arrangements;

(3) to provide that an employee who is unable to secure employment by the exercise of his or her seniority rights, as a result of actions taken with financial assistance obtained under this chapter, shall be offered reassignment and, where necessary, retraining to fill a position comparable to the position held at the time of such adverse effect and for which he is, or by training and retraining can become, physically and mentally qualified, so long as such offer is not in contravention of collective bargaining agreements relating thereto; and

(4) to provide that the protection afforded pursuant to this section shall not be applicable to employees benefited solely as a result of the work which is financed by funds provided pursuant to this chapter.

(c) SUBCONTRACTING.—The arrangements which are required to be negotiated by the parties or prescribed by the Secretary of Labor, pursuant to subsections (a) and (b) of this section, shall include provisions regulating subcontracting by the railroads of work which is financed by funds provided pursuant to this chapter.

(Added and amended Pub. L. 117–58, div. B, title I, §21301(a)(2), (6), (f), Nov. 15, 2021, 135 Stat. 683, 690.)

§22405. SUBSTANTIVE CRITERIA AND STANDARDS

The Secretary shall—

(1) publish in the Federal Register and post on a website of the Department of Transportation the substantive criteria and standards used by the Secretary to determine whether to approve or disapprove applications submitted under section 22402; and

(2) ensure that adequate procedures and guidelines are in place to permit the filing of complete applications not later than 30 days after the publication referred to in paragraph (1).

(Added Pub. L. 117–58, div. B, title I, §21301(g), Nov. 15, 2021, 135 Stat. 690.)

§22406. AUTHORIZATION OF APPROPRIATIONS.[1]

(a) AUTHORIZATION.—

(1) IN GENERAL.—There is authorized to be appropriated for credit assistance under this chapter, which shall be provided at the discretion of the Secretary, $50,000,000 for each of fiscal years 2022 through 2026.

(2) REFUND OF PREMIUM.—There is authorized to be appropriated to the Secretary $70,000,000 to repay the credit risk premium in accordance with section 22402(f)(5).

(3) AVAILABILITY.—Amounts appropriated pursuant to this subsection shall remain available until expended.

(b) USE OF FUNDS.—

(1) IN GENERAL.—Credit assistance provided under subsection (a) may not exceed $20,000,000 for any loan or loan guarantee.

(2) ADMINISTRATIVE COSTS.—Not less than 3 percent of the amounts appropriated pursuant to subsection (a) in each fiscal year shall be made available to the Secretary for use in place of charges collected under section 22403(l)(1) for passenger railroads and freight railroads other than Class I carriers.

(3) SHORT LINE SET-ASIDE.—Not less than 50 percent of the amounts appropriated pursuant to subsection (a)(1) for each fiscal year shall be set aside for freight railroads other than Class I carriers.

(Added Pub. L. 117–58, div. B, title I, §21301(h), Nov. 15, 2021, 135 Stat. 690.)

---

[1] So in original. The period probably should not appear.

[CHAPTER 225—REPEALED]

[§§22501 TO 22505. REPEALED. PUB. L. 114–94, DIV. A, TITLE XI, §11301(C)(3), DEC. 4, 2015, 129 STAT. 1648]

Section 22501, Pub. L. 110–432, div. A, title II, §207(a), Oct. 16, 2008, 122 Stat. 4873, related to financial assistance to States for certain projects.

Section 22502, Pub. L. 110–432, div. A, title II, §207(a), Oct. 16, 2008, 122 Stat. 4874, related to distribution of grants.

Section 22503, Pub. L. 110–432, div. A, title II, §207(a), Oct. 16, 2008, 122 Stat. 4874, related to standards for awarding grants.

Section 22504, Pub. L. 110–432, div. A, title II, §207(a), Oct. 16, 2008, 122 Stat. 4874, related to use of grant funds.

Section 22505, Pub. L. 110–432, div. A, title II, §207(a), Oct. 16, 2008, 122 Stat. 4874, related to authorization of appropriations.

CHAPTER 227—STATE RAIL PLANS

§22701. DEFINITIONS

In this subchapter: [1]

  (1) PRIVATE BENEFIT.—

    (A) IN GENERAL.—The term "private benefit"—

    (i) means a benefit accrued to a person or private entity, other than Amtrak, that directly improves the economic and competitive condition of that person or entity through improved assets, cost reductions, service improvements, or any other means as defined by the Secretary; and

    (ii) shall be determined on a project-by-project basis, based upon an agreement between the parties.

    (B) CONSULTATION.—The Secretary may seek the advice of the States and rail carriers in further defining this term.

  (2) PUBLIC BENEFIT.—

    (A) IN GENERAL.—The term "public benefit"—

    (i) means a benefit accrued to the public, including Amtrak, in the form of enhanced mobility of people or goods, environmental protection or enhancement, congestion mitigation, enhanced trade and economic development, improved air quality or land use, more efficient energy use, enhanced public safety or security, reduction of public expenditures due to improved transportation efficiency or infrastructure preservation, and any other positive community effects as defined by the Secretary; and

    (ii) shall be determined on a project-by-project basis, based upon an agreement between the parties.

    (B) CONSULTATION.—The Secretary may seek the advice of the States and rail carriers in further defining this term.

  (3) STATE.—The term "State" means any of the 50 States and the District of Columbia.

  (4) STATE RAIL TRANSPORTATION AUTHORITY.—The term "State rail transportation authority" means the State agency or official responsible under the direction of the Governor of the State or a State law for preparation, maintenance, coordination, and administration of the State rail plan.

(Added Pub. L. 110–432, div. B, title III, §303(a), Oct. 16, 2008, 122 Stat. 4947.)

> [1] *So in original. Probably should be "chapter:".*

§22702. AUTHORITY

(a) IN GENERAL.—Each State may prepare and maintain a State rail plan in accordance with the provisions of this chapter.

(b) REQUIREMENTS.—The Secretary shall establish the minimum requirements for the preparation and periodic revision of a State rail plan, including that a State shall—

(1) establish or designate a State rail transportation authority to prepare, maintain, coordinate, and administer the plan;

(2) establish or designate a State rail plan approval authority to approve the plan;

(3) submit the State's approved plan to the Secretary of Transportation for review; and

(4) revise and resubmit a State-approved plan no less frequently than once every 4 years for acceptance by the Secretary.

(Added Pub. L. 110–432, div. B, title III, §303(a), Oct. 16, 2008, 122 Stat. 4948; amended Pub. L. 114–94, div. A, title XI, §11315(a)(1), Dec. 4, 2015, 129 Stat. 1674.)

§22703. PURPOSES

(a) PURPOSES.—The purposes of a State rail plan are as follows:

(1) To set forth State policy involving freight and passenger rail transportation, including commuter rail operations, in the State.

(2) To establish the period covered by the State rail plan.

(3) To present priorities and strategies to enhance rail service in the State that benefits the public.

(4) To serve as the basis for Federal and State rail investments within the State.

(b) COORDINATION.—A State rail plan shall be coordinated with other State transportation planning goals and programs, including the plan required under section 135 of title 23, and set forth rail transportation's role within the State transportation system.

(Added Pub. L. 110–432, div. B, title III, §303(a), Oct. 16, 2008, 122 Stat. 4948.)

§22704. TRANSPARENCY; COORDINATION; REVIEW

(a) PREPARATION.—A State shall provide adequate and reasonable notice and opportunity for comment and other input to the public, rail carriers, commuter and transit authorities operating in, or affected by rail operations within the State, units of local government, and other interested parties in the preparation and review of its State rail plan.

(b) INTERGOVERNMENTAL COORDINATION.—A State shall review the freight and passenger rail service activities and initiatives by regional planning agencies, regional transportation authorities, and municipalities within the State, or in the region in which the State is located, while preparing the plan, and shall include any recommendations made by such agencies, authorities, and municipalities as deemed appropriate by the State.

(Added Pub. L. 110–432, div. B, title III, §303(a), Oct. 16, 2008, 122 Stat. 4949.)

§22705. CONTENT

(a) IN GENERAL.—Each State rail plan shall, at a minimum, contain the following:

(1) An inventory of the existing overall rail transportation system and rail services and facilities within the State and an analysis of the role of rail transportation within the State's surface transportation system.

(2) A review of all rail lines within the State, including proposed high-speed rail corridors and significant rail line segments not currently in service.

(3) A statement of the State's passenger rail service objectives, including minimum service levels, for rail transportation routes in the State.

(4) A general analysis of rail's transportation, economic, and environmental impacts in the State, including congestion mitigation, trade and economic development, air quality, land-use, energy-use, and community impacts.

(5) A long-range rail investment program for current and future freight and passenger infrastructure in the State that meets the requirements of subsection (b).

(6) A statement of public financing issues for rail projects and service in the State, including a list of current and prospective public capital and operating funding resources, public subsidies, State taxation, and other financial policies relating to rail infrastructure development.

(7) An identification of rail infrastructure issues within the State that reflects consultation with all relevant stakeholders.

(8) A review of major passenger and freight intermodal rail connections and facilities within the State, including seaports, and prioritized options to maximize service integration and efficiency between rail and other modes of transportation within the State.

(9) A review of publicly funded projects within the State to improve rail transportation safety and security, including all major projects funded under section 130 of title 23.

(10) A performance evaluation of passenger rail services operating in the State, including possible improvements in those services, and a description of strategies to achieve those improvements.

(11) A compilation of studies and reports on high-speed rail corridor development within the State not included in a previous plan under this subchapter,[1] and a plan for funding any recommended development of such corridors in the State.

(b) LONG-RANGE SERVICE AND INVESTMENT PROGRAM.—

(1) PROGRAM CONTENT.—A long-range rail investment program included in a State rail plan under subsection (a)(5) shall, at a minimum, include the following matters:

(A) A list of any rail capital projects expected to be undertaken or supported in whole or in part by the State.

(B) A detailed funding plan for those projects.

(2) PROJECT LIST CONTENT.—The list of rail capital projects shall contain—

(A) a description of the anticipated public and private benefits of each such project; and

(B) a statement of the correlation between—

(i) public funding contributions for the projects; and

    (ii) the public benefits.

    (3) CONSIDERATIONS FOR PROJECT LIST.—In preparing the list of freight and intercity passenger rail capital projects, a State rail transportation authority should take into consideration the following matters:

    (A) Contributions made by non-Federal and non-State sources through user fees, matching funds, or other private capital involvement.

    (B) Rail capacity and congestion effects.

    (C) Effects on highway, aviation, and maritime capacity, congestion, or safety.

    (D) Regional balance.

    (E) Environmental impact.

    (F) Economic and employment impacts.

    (G) Projected ridership and other service measures for passenger rail projects.

(Added Pub. L. 110–432, div. B, title III, §303(a), Oct. 16, 2008, 122 Stat. 4949; amended Pub. L. 114–94, div. A, title XI, §11315(a)(2), Dec. 4, 2015, 129 Stat. 1674.)

---

    [1] So in original. Probably should be "chapter,".

§22706. REVIEW

    The Secretary shall prescribe procedures for States to submit State rail plans for review under this title, including standardized format and data requirements. State rail plans completed before the date of enactment of the Passenger Rail Investment and Improvement Act of 2008 that substantially meet the requirements of this chapter, as determined by the Secretary, shall be deemed by the Secretary to have met the requirements of this chapter.

(Added Pub. L. 110–432, div. B, title III, §303(a), Oct. 16, 2008, 122 Stat. 4950.)

CHAPTER 229—RAIL IMPROVEMENT GRANTS

[1] *So in original. Does not conform to section catchline.*

§22901. DEFINITIONS

In this chapter:

(1) APPLICANT.—The term "applicant" means a State (including the District of Columbia), a group of States, an Interstate Compact, or a public agency established by one or more States and having responsibility for providing intercity passenger rail service.

(2) CAPITAL PROJECT.—The term "capital project" means a project or program in a State rail plan developed under chapter 227 of this title for—

(A) acquiring, constructing, improving, or inspecting equipment, track and track structures, or a facility for use in or for the primary benefit of intercity passenger rail service, expenses incidental to the acquisition or construction (including designing, engineering, location surveying, mapping, environmental studies, and acquiring rights-of-way), payments for the capital portions of rail trackage rights agreements, highway-rail grade crossing improvements related to intercity passenger rail service, mitigating environmental impacts, communication and signalization improvements, relocation assistance, acquiring replacement housing sites, and acquiring, constructing, relocating, and rehabilitating replacement housing;

(B) rehabilitating, remanufacturing or overhauling rail rolling stock and facilities used primarily in intercity passenger rail service;

(C) costs associated with developing State rail plans; and

(D) the first-dollar liability costs for insurance related to the provision of intercity passenger rail service under section 22904.

(3) INTERCITY PASSENGER RAIL SERVICE.—The term "intercity passenger rail service" means intercity rail passenger transportation, as defined in section 24102 of this title.

(Added Pub. L. 110–432, div. B, title III, §301(a), Oct. 16, 2008, 122 Stat. 4935, §24401; renumbered §22901 and amended Pub. L. 115–420, §7(a)(1), (b)(2)(A), Jan. 3, 2019, 132 Stat. 5445, 5446.)

§22902. Capital Investment Grants to Support Intercity Passenger Rail Service

(a) General Authority.—

(1) The Secretary of Transportation may make grants under this section to an applicant to assist in financing the capital costs of facilities, infrastructure, and equipment necessary to provide or improve intercity passenger rail transportation.

(2) Consistent with the requirements of this chapter, the Secretary shall require that a grant under this section be subject to the terms, conditions, requirements, and provisions the Secretary decides are necessary or appropriate for the purposes of this section, including requirements for the disposition of net increases in value of real property resulting from the project assisted under this section and shall prescribe procedures and schedules for the awarding of grants under this title, including application and qualification procedures and a record of decision on applicant eligibility. The Secretary shall issue a final rule establishing such procedures not later than 2 years after the date of enactment of the Passenger Rail Investment and Improvement Act of 2008. For the period prior to the earlier of the issuance of such a rule or 2 years after the date of enactment of such Act, the Secretary shall issue interim guidance to applicants covering such procedures, and administer the grant program authorized under this section pursuant to such guidance.

(b) Project as Part of State Rail Plan.—

(1) The Secretary may not approve a grant for a project under this section unless the Secretary finds that the project is part of a State rail plan developed under chapter 227 of this title, or under the plan required by section 211 of the Passenger Rail Investment and Improvement Act of 2008, and that the applicant or recipient has or will have the legal, financial, and technical capacity to carry out the project, satisfactory continuing control over the use of the equipment or facilities, and the capability and willingness to maintain the equipment or facilities.

(2) An applicant shall provide sufficient information upon which the Secretary can make the findings required by this subsection.

(3) If an applicant has not selected the proposed operator of its service competitively, the applicant shall provide written justification to the Secretary showing why the proposed operator is the best, taking into account price and other factors, and that use of the proposed operator will not unnecessarily increase the cost of the project.

(c) Project Selection Criteria.—The Secretary, in selecting the recipients of financial assistance to be provided under subsection (a), shall—

(1) require—

(A) that the project be part of a State rail plan developed under chapter 227 of this title, or under the plan required by section 211 of the Passenger Rail Investment and Improvement Act of 2008;

(B) that the applicant or recipient has or will have the legal, financial, and technical capacity to carry out the project, satisfactory continuing control over the use of the equipment or facilities, and the capability and willingness to maintain the equipment or facilities;

(C) that the applicant provides sufficient information upon which the Secretary can make the findings required by this subsection;

(D) that if an applicant has selected the proposed operator of its service competitively, that the applicant provide written justification to the Secretary showing why the proposed operator is the best, taking into account costs and other factors;

(E) that each proposed project meet all safety and security requirements that are applicable to the project under law; and

(F) that each project be compatible with, and operated in conformance with—

(i) plans developed pursuant to the requirements of section 135 of title 23, United States Code; and

(ii) the national rail plan (if it is available);

(2) select projects—

(A) that are anticipated to result in significant improvements to intercity rail passenger service, including, but not limited to, consideration of—

(i) the project's levels of estimated ridership, increased on-time performance, reduced trip time, additional service frequency to meet anticipated or existing demand, or other significant service enhancements as measured against minimum standards developed under section 207 of the Passenger Rail Investment and Improvement Act of 2008;

(ii) the project's anticipated favorable impact on air or highway traffic congestion, capacity, or safety; and

(iii) identification of the project by the Surface Transportation Board as necessary to improve the on-time performance and reliability of intercity passenger rail under section 24308(f);

(B) for which there is a high degree of confidence that the proposed project is feasible and will result in the anticipated benefits, as indicated by—

(i) the project's precommencement compliance with environmental protection requirements;

(ii) the readiness of the project to be commenced;

(iii) the timing and amount of the project's future noncommitted investments;

(iv) the commitment of any affected host rail carrier to ensure the realization of the anticipated benefits; and

(v) other relevant factors as determined by the Secretary; and

(C) for which the level of the anticipated benefits compares favorably to the amount of Federal funding requested under this chapter; and

(3) give greater consideration to projects—

(A) that are anticipated to result in benefits to other modes of transportation and to the public at large, including, but not limited to, consideration of the project's—

(i) encouragement of intermodal connectivity through provision of direct connections between train stations, airports, bus terminals, subway stations, ferry ports, and other modes of transportation;

    (ii) anticipated improvement of freight or commuter rail operations;

    (iii) encouragement of the use of positive train control technologies;

    (iv) environmental benefits, including projects that involve the purchase of environmentally sensitive, fuel-efficient, and cost-effective passenger rail equipment;

    (v) anticipated positive economic and employment impacts;

    (vi) encouragement of State and private contributions toward station development, energy and environmental efficiency, and economic benefits; and

    (vii) falling under the description in section 5302(a)(1)(G) [1] of this title as defined to support intercity passenger rail service; and

  (B) that incorporate equitable financial participation in the project's financing, including, but not limited to, consideration of—

    (i) donated property interests or services;

    (ii) financial contributions by freight and commuter rail carriers commensurate with the benefit expected to their operations; and

    (iii) financial commitments from host railroads, non-Federal governmental entities, nongovernmental entities, and others.

  (d) STATE RAIL PLANS.—State rail plans completed before the date of enactment of the Passenger Rail Investment and Improvement Act of 2008 that substantially meet the requirements of chapter 227 of this title, as determined by the Secretary pursuant to section 22506 [1] of this title, shall be deemed by the Secretary to have met the requirements of subsection (c)(1)(A) of this section.

  (e) AMTRAK ELIGIBILITY.—To receive a grant under this section, Amtrak may enter into a cooperative agreement with 1 or more States to carry out 1 or more projects on a State rail plan's ranked list of rail capital projects developed under section 22504(a)(5) [1] of this title. For such a grant, Amtrak may not use Federal funds authorized under section 101(a) or (c) of the Passenger Rail Investment and Improvement Act of 2008 to fulfill the non-Federal share requirements under subsection (g) of this section.

  (f) LETTERS OF INTENT AND EARLY SYSTEMS WORK AGREEMENTS.—

  (1) The Secretary may issue a letter of intent to an applicant announcing an intention to obligate, for a major capital project under this section, an amount from future available budget authority specified in law that is not more than the amount stipulated as the financial participation of the Secretary in the project.

  (2) At least 30 days before issuing a letter under paragraph (1) of this subsection, the Secretary shall notify in writing the Committee on Transportation and Infrastructure of the House of Representatives, the Committee on Commerce, Science, and Transportation of the Senate, and the House and Senate Committees on Appropriations of the proposed letter or agreement. The Secretary shall include with the notification a copy of the proposed letter or agreement, the criteria used in subsection (c) for selecting the project for a grant award, and a description of how the project meets such criteria.

(3) An obligation or administrative commitment may be made only when amounts are appropriated. The letter of intent shall state that the contingent commitment is not an obligation of the Federal Government, and is subject to the availability of appropriations under Federal law and to Federal laws in force or enacted after the date of the contingent commitment.

(g) FEDERAL SHARE OF NET PROJECT COST.—

(1)(A) Based on engineering studies, studies of economic feasibility, and information on the expected use of equipment or facilities, the Secretary shall estimate the net project cost.

(B) A grant for the project shall not exceed 80 percent of the project net capital cost.

(C) The Secretary shall give priority in allocating future obligations and contingent commitments to incur obligations to grant requests seeking a lower Federal share of the project net capital cost.

(2) Up to an additional 20 percent of the required non-Federal funds may be funded from amounts appropriated to or made available to a department or agency of the Federal Government that are eligible to be expended for transportation.

(3) The following amounts, not to exceed $15,000,000 per fiscal year, shall be available to each applicant as a credit toward an applicant's matching requirement for a grant awarded under this section—

(A) in each of fiscal years 2009, 2010, and 2011—

(i) 50 percent of the average of amounts expended in fiscal years 2002 through 2008 by an applicant for capital projects related to intercity passenger rail service; and

(ii) 50 percent of the average of amounts expended in fiscal years 2002 through 2008 by an applicant for operating costs of such service; and

(B) in each of fiscal years 2010, 2011 and 2012, 50 percent of the amount by which the amounts expended for capital projects and operating costs related to intercity passenger rail service by an applicant in the prior fiscal year exceed the average capital and operating expenditures made for such service in fiscal years 2006, 2007, and 2008.

The Secretary may require such information as necessary to verify such expenditures. Credits made available to an applicant in a fiscal year under this paragraph may only be applied towards grants awarded in that fiscal year.

(4) The Federal share of expenditures for capital improvements under this chapter may not exceed 100 percent.

(h) 2-YEAR AVAILABILITY.—Funds appropriated under this section shall remain available until expended. If any amount provided as a grant under this section is not obligated or expended for the purposes described in subsection (a) within 2 years after the date on which the State received the grant, such sums shall be returned to the Secretary for other intercity passenger rail development projects under this section at the discretion of the Secretary.

(i) COOPERATIVE AGREEMENTS.—

(1) IN GENERAL.—A metropolitan planning organization, State transportation

department, or other project sponsor may enter into an agreement with any public, private, or nonprofit entity to cooperatively implement any project funded with a grant under this chapter.

(2) FORMS OF PARTICIPATION.—Participation by an entity under paragraph (1) may consist of—

(A) ownership or operation of any land, facility, locomotive, rail car, vehicle, or other physical asset associated with the project;

(B) cost-sharing of any project expense;

(C) carrying out administration, construction management, project management, project operation, or any other management or operational duty associated with the project; and

(D) any other form of participation approved by the Secretary.

(3) SUBALLOCATION.—A State may allocate funds under this section to any entity described in paragraph (1).

(j) LARGE CAPITAL PROJECT REQUIREMENTS.—

(1) IN GENERAL.—For a grant awarded under this chapter for an amount in excess of $1,000,000,000, the following conditions shall apply:

(A) The Secretary may not obligate any funding unless the applicant demonstrates, to the satisfaction of the Secretary, that the applicant has committed, and will be able to fulfill, the non-Federal share required for the grant within the applicant's proposed project completion timetable.

(B) The Secretary may not obligate any funding for work activities that occur after the completion of final design unless—

(i) the applicant submits a financial plan to the Secretary that generally identifies the sources of the non-Federal funding required for any subsequent segments or phases of the corridor service development program covering the project for which the grant is awarded;

(ii) the grant will result in a useable segment, a transportation facility, or equipment, that has operational independence; and

(iii) the intercity passenger rail benefits anticipated to result from the grant, such as increased speed, improved on-time performance, reduced trip time, increased frequencies, new service, safety improvements, improved accessibility, or other significant enhancements, are detailed by the grantee and approved by the Secretary.

(C)(i) The Secretary shall ensure that the project is maintained to the level of utility that is necessary to support the benefits approved under subparagraph (B)(iii) for a period of 20 years from the date on which the useable segment, transportation facility, or equipment described in subparagraph (B)(ii) is placed in service.

(ii) If the project property is not maintained as required under clause (i) for a 12-month period, the grant recipient shall refund a pro-rata share of the Federal contribution, based upon the percentage remaining of the 20-year period that commenced when the project property was placed in service.

(2) EARLY WORK.—The Secretary may allow a grantee subject to this subsection to engage in at-risk work activities subsequent to the conclusion of final design if the Secretary determines that such work activities are reasonable and necessary.

(k) SMALL CAPITAL PROJECTS.—The Secretary shall make not less than 5 percent annually available from the amounts authorized under section 101(c) of the Passenger Rail Investment and Improvement Act of 2008 beginning in fiscal year 2009 for grants for capital projects eligible under this section not exceeding $2,000,000, including costs eligible under section 209(d) [1] of that Act. For grants awarded under this subsection, the Secretary may waive requirements of this section, including State rail plan requirements, as appropriate.

(l) NONMOTORIZED TRANSPORTATION ACCESS AND STORAGE.—Grants under this chapter may be used to provide access to rolling stock for nonmotorized transportation, including bicycles, and recreational equipment, and to provide storage capacity in trains for such transportation, equipment, and other luggage, to ensure passenger safety.

(Added Pub. L. 110–432, div. B, title III, §301(a), Oct. 16, 2008, 122 Stat. 4936, §24402; amended Pub. L. 114–94, div. A, title XI, §§11303(b)(1)(C), 11309, Dec. 4, 2015, 129 Stat. 1654, 1669; renumbered §22902 and amended Pub. L. 115–420, §7(a)(1), (b)(1)(A), Jan. 3, 2019, 132 Stat. 5445, 5446.)

[1] *See References in Text note below.*

§22903. PROJECT MANAGEMENT OVERSIGHT

(a) PROJECT MANAGEMENT PLAN REQUIREMENTS.—To receive Federal financial assistance for a major capital project under this chapter, an applicant must prepare and carry out a project management plan approved by the Secretary of Transportation. The plan shall provide for—

(1) adequate recipient staff organization with well-defined reporting relationships, statements of functional responsibilities, job descriptions, and job qualifications;

(2) a budget covering the project management organization, appropriate consultants, property acquisition, utility relocation, systems demonstration staff, audits, and miscellaneous payments the recipient may be prepared to justify;

(3) a construction schedule for the project;

(4) a document control procedure and recordkeeping system;

(5) a change order procedure that includes a documented, systematic approach to handling the construction change orders;

(6) organizational structures, management skills, and staffing levels required throughout the construction phase;

(7) quality control and quality assurance functions, procedures, and responsibilities for construction, system installation, and integration of system components;

(8) material testing policies and procedures;

(9) internal plan implementation and reporting requirements;

(10) criteria and procedures to be used for testing the operational system or its major components;

(11) periodic updates of the plan, especially related to project budget and project

schedule, financing, and ridership estimates; and

(12) the recipient's commitment to submit periodically a project budget and project schedule to the Secretary.

[(b) Repealed. Pub. L. 114–94, div. A, title XI, §11316(p), Dec. 4, 2015, 129 Stat. 1679]

(c) ACCESS TO SITES AND RECORDS.—Each recipient of assistance under this chapter shall provide the Secretary and a contractor the Secretary chooses under subsection (b) of this section with access to the construction sites and records of the recipient when reasonably necessary.

(Added Pub. L. 110–432, div. B, title III, §301(a), Oct. 16, 2008, 122 Stat. 4941, §24403; amended Pub. L. 114–94, div. A, title XI, §11316(p), Dec. 4, 2015, 129 Stat. 1679; renumbered §22903, Pub. L. 115–420, §7(a)(1), Jan. 3, 2019, 132 Stat. 5445.)

§22904. USE OF CAPITAL GRANTS TO FINANCE FIRST-DOLLAR LIABILITY OF GRANT PROJECT

Notwithstanding the requirements of section 22902 of this chapter, the Secretary of Transportation may approve the use of a capital assistance grant under this chapter to fund self-insured retention of risk for the first tier of liability insurance coverage for rail passenger service associated with the grant, but the coverage may not exceed $20,000,000 per occurrence or $20,000,000 in aggregate per year.

(Added Pub. L. 110–432, div. B, title III, §301(a), Oct. 16, 2008, 122 Stat. 4942, §24404; renumbered §22904 and amended Pub. L. 115–420, §7(a)(1), (b)(2)(B), Jan. 3, 2019, 132 Stat. 5445, 5446.)

§22905. GRANT CONDITIONS

(a) BUY AMERICA.—(1) The Secretary of Transportation may obligate an amount that may be appropriated to carry out this chapter for a project only if the steel, iron, and manufactured goods used in the project are produced in the United States.

(2) The Secretary of Transportation may waive paragraph (1) of this subsection if the Secretary finds that—

(A) applying paragraph (1) would be inconsistent with the public interest;

(B) the steel, iron, and goods produced in the United States are not produced in a sufficient and reasonably available amount or are not of a satisfactory quality;

(C) rolling stock or power train equipment cannot be bought and delivered in the United States within a reasonable time; or

(D) including domestic material will increase the cost of the overall project by more than 25 percent.

(3) For purposes of this subsection, in calculating the components' costs, labor costs involved in final assembly shall not be included in the calculation.

(4) If the Secretary determines that it is necessary to waive the application of paragraph (1) based on a finding under paragraph (2), the Secretary shall, before the date on which such finding takes effect—

(A) publish in the Federal Register a detailed written justification as to why the waiver is needed; and

(B) provide notice of such finding and an opportunity for public comment on such finding for a reasonable period of time not to exceed 15 days.

(5) Not later than December 31, 2012, the Secretary shall submit to the Committee on Transportation and Infrastructure of the House of Representatives and the Committee on Commerce, Science, and Transportation of the Senate a report on any waivers granted under paragraph (2).

(6) The Secretary of Transportation may not make a waiver under paragraph (2) of this subsection for goods produced in a foreign country if the Secretary, in consultation with the United States Trade Representative, decides that the government of that foreign country—

(A) has an agreement with the United States Government under which the Secretary has waived the requirement of this subsection; and

(B) has violated the agreement by discriminating against goods to which this subsection applies that are produced in the United States and to which the agreement applies.

(7) A person is ineligible to receive a contract or subcontract made with amounts authorized under this chapter if a court or department, agency, or instrumentality of the Government decides the person intentionally—

(A) affixed a "Made in America" label, or a label with an inscription having the same meaning, to goods sold in or shipped to the United States that are used in a project to which this subsection applies but not produced in the United States; or

(B) represented that goods described in subparagraph (A) of this paragraph were produced in the United States.

(8) The Secretary may not impose any limitation on assistance provided under this chapter that restricts a State from imposing more stringent requirements than this subsection on the use of articles, materials, and supplies mined, produced, or manufactured in foreign countries in projects carried out with that assistance or restricts a recipient of that assistance from complying with those State-imposed requirements.

(9) The Secretary may allow a manufacturer or supplier of steel, iron, or manufactured goods to correct after bid opening any certification of noncompliance or failure to properly complete the certification (but not including failure to sign the certification) under this subsection if such manufacturer or supplier attests under penalty of perjury that such manufacturer or supplier submitted an incorrect certification as a result of an inadvertent or clerical error. The burden of establishing inadvertent or clerical error is on the manufacturer or supplier.

(10) A party adversely affected by an agency action under this subsection shall have the right to seek review under section 702 of title 5.

(11) The requirements of this subsection shall only apply to projects for which the costs exceed $100,000.

(b) OPERATORS DEEMED RAIL CARRIERS AND EMPLOYERS FOR CERTAIN PURPOSES.—A person that conducts rail operations over rail infrastructure constructed or improved with funding provided in whole or in part in a grant made under this chapter shall be considered a rail carrier as defined in section 10102(5) of this title for purposes of this title and any other statute that adopts that definition or in which that definition applies, including—

(1) the Railroad Retirement Act of 1974 (45 U.S.C. 231 et seq.);

(2) the Railway Labor Act (45 U.S.C. 151 et seq.); and

(3) the Railroad Unemployment Insurance Act (45 U.S.C. 351 et seq.).

(c) GRANT CONDITIONS.—The Secretary shall require as a condition of making any grant under this chapter for a project that uses rights-of-way owned by a railroad that—

(1) a written agreement exist between the applicant and the railroad regarding such use and ownership, including—

(A) any compensation for such use;

(B) assurances regarding the adequacy of infrastructure capacity to accommodate both existing and future freight and passenger operations;

(C) an assurance by the railroad that collective bargaining agreements with the railroad's employees (including terms regulating the contracting of work) will remain in full force and effect according to their terms for work performed by the railroad on the railroad transportation corridor; and

(D) an assurance that an applicant complies with liability requirements consistent with section 28103 of this title; and

(2) the applicant agrees to comply with—

(A) the standards of section 24312 of this title, as such section was in effect on September 1, 2003, with respect to the project in the same manner that Amtrak is required to comply with those standards for construction work financed under an agreement made under section 24308(a) of this title; and

(B) the protective arrangements that are equivalent to the protective arrangements established under section 22404 with respect to employees affected by actions taken in connection with the project to be financed in whole or in part by grants under this chapter.

(d) REPLACEMENT OF EXISTING INTERCITY PASSENGER RAIL SERVICE.—

(1) COLLECTIVE BARGAINING AGREEMENT FOR INTERCITY PASSENGER RAIL PROJECTS.—Any entity providing intercity passenger railroad transportation that begins operations after the date of enactment of this Act [1] on a project funded in whole or in part by grants made under this chapter and replaces intercity rail passenger service that was provided by Amtrak, unless such service was provided solely by Amtrak to another entity or unless Amtrak ceased providing intercity passenger railroad transportation over the affected route more than 3 years before the commencement of new service, as of such date shall enter into an agreement with the authorized bargaining agent or agents for adversely affected employees of the predecessor provider that—

(A) gives each such qualified employee of the predecessor provider priority in hiring according to the employee's seniority on the predecessor provider for each position with the replacing entity that is in the employee's craft or class and is available within 3 years after the termination of the service being replaced;

(B) establishes a procedure for notifying such an employee of such positions;

(C) establishes a procedure for such an employee to apply for such positions; and

(D) establishes rates of pay, rules, and working conditions.

(2) IMMEDIATE REPLACEMENT SERVICE.—

(A) NEGOTIATIONS.—If the replacement of preexisting intercity rail passenger service occurs concurrent with or within a reasonable time before the commencement of the replacing entity's rail passenger service, the replacing entity shall give written notice of its plan to replace existing rail passenger service to the authorized collective bargaining agent or agents for the potentially adversely affected employees of the predecessor provider at least 90 days before the date on which it plans to commence service. Within 5 days after the date of receipt of such written notice, negotiations between the replacing entity and the collective bargaining agent or agents for the employees of the predecessor provider shall commence for the purpose of reaching agreement with respect to all matters set forth in subparagraphs (A) through (D) of paragraph (1). The negotiations shall continue for 30 days or until an agreement is reached, whichever is sooner. If at the end of 30 days the parties have not entered into an agreement with respect to all such matters, the unresolved issues shall be submitted for arbitration in accordance with the procedure set forth in subparagraph (B).

(B) ARBITRATION.—If an agreement has not been entered into with respect to all matters set forth in subparagraphs (A) through (D) of paragraph (1) as described in subparagraph (A) of this paragraph, the parties shall select an arbitrator. If the parties are unable to agree upon the selection of such arbitrator within 5 days, either or both parties shall notify the National Mediation Board, which shall provide a list of seven arbitrators with experience in arbitrating rail labor protection disputes. Within 5 days after such notification, the parties shall alternately strike names from the list until only 1 name remains, and that person shall serve as the neutral arbitrator. Within 45 days after selection of the arbitrator, the arbitrator shall conduct a hearing on the dispute and shall render a decision with respect to the unresolved issues among the matters set forth in subparagraphs (A) through (D) of paragraph (1). The arbitrator shall be guided by prevailing national standard rates of pay, benefits, and working conditions for comparable work. This decision shall be final, binding, and conclusive upon the parties. The salary and expenses of the arbitrator shall be borne equally by the parties; all other expenses shall be paid by the party incurring them.

(3) SERVICE COMMENCEMENT.—A replacing entity under this subsection shall commence service only after an agreement is entered into with respect to the matters set forth in subparagraphs (A) through (D) of paragraph (1) or the decision of the arbitrator has been rendered.

(4) SUBSEQUENT REPLACEMENT OF SERVICE.—If the replacement of existing rail passenger service takes place within 3 years after the replacing entity commences intercity passenger rail service, the replacing entity and the collective bargaining agent or agents for the adversely affected employees of the predecessor provider shall enter into an agreement with respect to the matters set forth in subparagraphs (A) through (D) of paragraph (1). If the parties have not entered into an agreement with respect to all such matters within 60 days after the date on which the replacing entity replaces

the predecessor provider, the parties shall select an arbitrator using the procedures set forth in paragraph (2)(B), who shall, within 20 days after the commencement of the arbitration, conduct a hearing and decide all unresolved issues. This decision shall be final, binding, and conclusive upon the parties.

(e) INAPPLICABILITY TO CERTAIN RAIL OPERATIONS.—Nothing in this section applies to—

(1) commuter rail passenger transportation (as defined in section 24102) operations of a State or local governmental authority (as those terms are defined in section 5302) eligible to receive financial assistance under section 5307 of this title, or to its contractor performing services in connection with commuter rail passenger operations (as so defined);

(2) the Alaska Railroad or its contractors; or

(3) Amtrak's access rights to railroad rights of way and facilities under current law.

(f) LIMITATION.—No grants shall be provided under this chapter for commuter rail passenger transportation (as defined in section 24102(3)).

(Added Pub. L. 110–432, div. B, title III, §301(a), Oct. 16, 2008, 122 Stat. 4942, §24405; amended Pub. L. 114–94, div. A, title XI, §11303(b)(1)(D), Dec. 4, 2015, 129 Stat. 1654; renumbered §22905 and amended Pub. L. 115–420, §7(a)(1), (b)(1)(B), (2)(C), Jan. 3, 2019, 132 Stat. 5445, 5446; Pub. L. 117–58, div. B, title I, §21301(j)(4)(D), Nov. 15, 2021, 135 Stat. 693.)

[1] *See References in Text note below.*

§22906. AUTHORIZATION OF APPROPRIATIONS

There are authorized to be appropriated to the Secretary of Transportation for capital grants under this chapter the following amounts:

(1) For fiscal year 2009, $100,000,000.

(2) For fiscal year 2010, $300,000,000.

(3) For fiscal year 2011, $400,000,000.

(4) For fiscal year 2012, $500,000,000.

(5) For fiscal year 2013, $600,000,000.

(Added Pub. L. 110–432, div. B, title III, §301(a), Oct. 16, 2008, 122 Stat. 4946, §24406; renumbered §22906, Pub. L. 115–420, §7(a)(1), Jan. 3, 2019, 132 Stat. 5445.)

§22907. CONSOLIDATED RAIL INFRASTRUCTURE AND SAFETY IMPROVEMENTS

(a) GENERAL AUTHORITY.—The Secretary may make grants under this section to an eligible recipient to assist in financing the cost of improving passenger and freight rail transportation systems in terms of safety, efficiency, or reliability.

(b) ELIGIBLE RECIPIENTS.—The following entities are eligible to receive a grant under this section:

(1) A State (including the District of Columbia).

(2) A group of States.

(3) An Interstate Compact.

(4) A public agency or publicly chartered authority established by 1 or more States.

(5) A political subdivision of a State.

(6) Amtrak or another rail carrier that provides intercity rail passenger transportation (as rail carrier and intercity rail passenger transportation are defined in section 24102).

(7) A Class II railroad or Class III railroad (as those terms are defined in section 20102).

(8) An association representing 1 or more railroads described in paragraph (7).

(9) A federally recognized Indian Tribe.

(10) Any rail carrier or rail equipment manufacturer in partnership with at least 1 of the entities described in paragraphs (1) through (5).

(11) The Transportation Research Board and any entity with which it contracts in the development of rail-related research, including cooperative research programs.

(12) A University transportation center engaged in rail-related research.

(13) A non-profit labor organization representing a class or craft of employees of rail carriers or rail carrier contractors.

(c) ELIGIBLE PROJECTS.—The following projects are eligible to receive grants under this section:

(1) Deployment of railroad safety technology, including positive train control and rail integrity inspection systems.

(2) A capital project as defined in section 22901(2), except that a project shall not be required to be in a State rail plan developed under chapter 227.

(3) A capital project identified by the Secretary as being necessary to address congestion or safety challenges affecting rail service.

(4) A capital project identified by the Secretary as being necessary to reduce congestion and facilitate ridership growth in intercity passenger rail transportation along heavily traveled rail corridors.

(5) A highway-rail grade crossing improvement project, including installation, repair, or improvement of grade separations, railroad crossing signals, gates, and related technologies, highway traffic signalization, highway lighting and crossing approach signage, roadway improvements such as medians or other barriers, railroad crossing panels and surfaces, and safety engineering improvements to reduce risk in quiet zones or potential quiet zones.

(6) A rail line relocation or improvement project.

(7) A capital project to improve short-line or regional railroad infrastructure.

(8) The preparation of regional rail and corridor service development plans and corresponding environmental analyses.

(9) Any project that the Secretary considers necessary to enhance multimodal connections or facilitate service integration between rail service and other modes, including between intercity rail passenger transportation and intercity bus service or commercial air service.

(10) The development and implementation of a safety program or institute designed to improve rail safety.

(11) The development and implementation of measures to prevent trespassing and reduce associated injuries and fatalities.

(12) Any research that the Secretary considers necessary to advance any particular aspect of rail-related capital, operations, or safety improvements.

(13) Workforce development and training activities, coordinated to the extent practicable with the existing local training programs supported by the Department of Transportation, the Department of Labor, and the Department of Education.

(14) Research, development, and testing to advance and facilitate innovative rail projects, including projects using electromagnetic guideways in an enclosure in a very low-pressure environment.

(15) The preparation of emergency plans for communities through which hazardous materials are transported by rail.

(16) Rehabilitating, remanufacturing, procuring, or overhauling locomotives, provided that such activities result in a significant reduction of emissions.

(d) APPLICATION PROCESS.—The Secretary shall prescribe the form and manner of filing an application under this section.

(e) PROJECT SELECTION CRITERIA.—

(1) IN GENERAL.—In selecting a recipient of a grant for an eligible project, the Secretary shall—

(A) give preference to a proposed project for which the proposed Federal share of total project costs does not exceed 50 percent; and

(B) after factoring in preference to projects under subparagraph (A), select projects that will maximize the net benefits of the funds appropriated for use under this section, considering the cost-benefit analysis of the proposed project, including anticipated private and public benefits relative to the costs of the proposed project and factoring in the other considerations described in paragraph (2).

(2) OTHER CONSIDERATIONS.—The Secretary shall also consider the following:

(A) The degree to which the proposed project's business plan considers potential private sector participation in the financing, construction, or operation of the project.

(B) The recipient's past performance in developing and delivering similar projects, and previous financial contributions.

(C) Whether the recipient has or will have the legal, financial, and technical capacity to carry out the proposed project, satisfactory continuing control over the use of the equipment or facilities, and the capability and willingness to maintain the equipment or facilities.

(D) If applicable, the consistency of the proposed project with planning guidance and documents set forth by the Secretary or required by law or State rail plans developed under chapter 227.

(E) If applicable, any technical evaluation ratings the proposed project received under previous competitive grant programs administered by the Secretary.

(F) Such other factors as the Secretary considers relevant to the successful delivery of the project.

(3) BENEFITS.—The benefits described in paragraph (1)(B) may include the effects on system and service performance, including measures such as improved safety,

competitiveness, reliability, trip or transit time, resilience, efficiencies from improved integration with other modes, the ability to meet existing or anticipated demand, and any other benefits.

(f) PERFORMANCE MEASURES.—The Secretary shall establish performance measures for each grant recipient to assess progress in achieving strategic goals and objectives. The Secretary may require a grant recipient to periodically report information related to such performance measures.

(g) RURAL AREAS.—

(1) IN GENERAL.—Of the amounts appropriated under this section, at least 25 percent shall be available for projects in rural areas. The Secretary shall consider a project to be in a rural area if all or the majority of the project (determined by the geographic location or locations where the majority of the project funds will be spent) is located in a rural area.

(2) DEFINITION OF RURAL AREA.—In this subsection, the term "rural area" means any area not in an urbanized area, as defined by the Bureau of the Census.

(h) FEDERAL SHARE OF TOTAL PROJECT COSTS.—

(1) TOTAL PROJECT COSTS.—The Secretary shall estimate the total costs of a project under this section based on the best available information, including any available engineering studies, studies of economic feasibility, environmental analyses, and information on the expected use of equipment or facilities.

(2) FEDERAL SHARE.—The Federal share of total project costs under this section shall not exceed 80 percent.

(3) TREATMENT OF PASSENGER RAIL REVENUE.—If Amtrak or another rail carrier is an applicant under this section, Amtrak or the other rail carrier, as applicable, may use ticket and other revenues generated from its operations and other sources to satisfy the non-Federal share requirements.

(4) GRADE CROSSING AND TRESPASSING PROJECTS.—Applicants may use costs incurred previously for preliminary engineering associated with highway-rail grade crossing improvement projects under subsection (c)(5) and trespassing prevention projects under subsection (c)(11) to satisfy the non-Federal share requirements.

(i) APPLICABILITY.—Except as specifically provided in this section, the use of any amounts appropriated for grants under this section shall be subject to the requirements of this chapter.

(j) AVAILABILITY.—Amounts appropriated for carrying out this section shall remain available until expended.

(k) LIMITATION.—The requirements under sections 22902, 22903, and 22904, and the definition contained in section 22901(1) shall not apply to this section.

(l) SPECIAL TRANSPORTATION CIRCUMSTANCES.—

(1) IN GENERAL.—In carrying out this chapter, the Secretary shall allocate an appropriate portion of the amounts available to programs in this chapter to provide grants to States—

(A) in which there is no intercity passenger rail service, for the purpose of funding freight rail capital projects that are on a State rail plan developed under chapter 227, including highway construction over rail facilities as an alternative to construction or improvement of a highway-rail grade crossing, that provide public benefits (as defined in chapter 227), as determined by the Secretary; or

(B) in which the rail transportation system is not physically connected to rail systems in the continental United States or may not otherwise qualify for a grant under this section due to the unique characteristics of the geography of that State or other relevant considerations, for the purpose of funding transportation-related capital projects.

(2) DEFINITION.—For the purposes of this subsection, the term "appropriate portion" means a share, for each State subject to paragraph (1), not less than the share of the total railroad route miles in such State of the total railroad route miles in the United States, excluding from all totals the route miles exclusively used for tourist, scenic, and excursion railroad operations.

(Added Pub. L. 114–94, div. A, title XI, §11301(a), Dec. 4, 2015, 129 Stat. 1644, §24407; renumbered §22907 and amended Pub. L. 115–420, §7(a)(1), (b)(2)(D), Jan. 3, 2019, 132 Stat. 5445, 5446; Pub. L. 117–58, div. B, title II, §22303(a), (c)(1), Nov. 15, 2021, 135 Stat. 718.)

§22908. RESTORATION AND ENHANCEMENT GRANTS

(a) DEFINITIONS.—In this section:

(1) APPLICANT.—Notwithstanding section 22901(1), the term "applicant" means—

(A) a State, including the District of Columbia;

(B) a group of States;

(C) an entity implementing an interstate compact;

(D) a public agency or publicly chartered authority established by 1 or more States;

(E) a political subdivision of a State;

(F) a federally recognized Indian Tribe;

(G) Amtrak or another rail carrier that provides intercity rail passenger transportation;

(H) any rail carrier in partnership with at least 1 of the entities described in subparagraphs (A) through (F); and

(I) any combination of the entities described in subparagraphs (A) through (F).

(2) OPERATING ASSISTANCE.—The term "operating assistance", with respect to any route subject to section 209 of the Passenger Rail Investment and Improvement Act of 2008 (Public Law 110–432), means any cost allocated, or that may be allocated, to a route pursuant to the cost methodology established under such section or under section 24712.

(b) GRANTS AUTHORIZED.—The Secretary of Transportation shall develop and implement a program for issuing operating assistance grants to applicants, on a competitive basis, for the purpose of initiating, restoring, or enhancing intercity rail passenger transportation.

(c) APPLICATION.—An applicant for a grant under this section shall submit to the Secretary—

(1) a capital and mobilization plan that—

(A) describes any capital investments, service planning actions (such as environmental reviews), and mobilization actions (such as qualification of train crews) required for initiation of intercity rail passenger transportation; and

(B) includes the timeline for undertaking and completing each of the investments and actions referred to in subparagraph (A);

(2) an operating plan that describes the planned operation of the service, including—

(A) the identity and qualifications of the train operator;

(B) the identity and qualifications of any other service providers;

(C) service frequency;

(D) the planned routes and schedules;

(E) the station facilities that will be utilized;

(F) projected ridership, revenues, and costs;

(G) descriptions of how the projections under subparagraph (F) were developed;

(H) the equipment that will be utilized, how such equipment will be acquired or refurbished, and where such equipment will be maintained; and

(I) a plan for ensuring safe operations and compliance with applicable safety regulations;

(3) a funding plan that—

(A) describes the funding of initial capital costs and operating costs for the first 6 years of operation;

(B) includes a commitment by the applicant to provide the funds described in subparagraph (A) to the extent not covered by Federal grants and revenues; and

(C) describes the funding of operating costs and capital costs, to the extent necessary, after the first 6 years of operation; and

(4) a description of the status of negotiations and agreements with—

(A) each of the railroads or regional transportation authorities whose tracks or facilities would be utilized by the service;

(B) the anticipated railroad carrier, if such entity is not part of the applicant group; and

(C) any other service providers or entities expected to provide services or facilities that will be used by the service, including any required access to Amtrak systems, stations, and facilities if Amtrak is not part of the applicant group.

(d) PRIORITIES.—In awarding grants under this section, the Secretary shall give priority to applications—

(1) for which planning, design, any environmental reviews, negotiation of agreements, acquisition of equipment, construction, and other actions necessary for initiation of service have been completed or nearly completed;

(2) that would restore service over routes formerly operated by Amtrak, including

routes described in section 11304 of the Passenger Rail Reform and Investment Act of 2015;

(3) that would provide daily or daytime service over routes where such service did not previously exist;

(4) that include funding (including funding from railroads), or other significant participation by State, local, and regional governmental and private entities;

(5) that include a funding plan that demonstrates the intercity rail passenger service will be financially sustainable beyond the 3-year grant period;

(6) that would provide service to regions and communities that are underserved or not served by other intercity public transportation;

(7) that would foster economic development, particularly in rural communities and for disadvantaged populations;

(8) that would provide other non-transportation benefits;

(9) that would enhance connectivity and geographic coverage of the existing national network of intercity rail passenger service; and

(10) for routes selected under the Corridor Identification and Development Program and operated by Amtrak.

(e) LIMITATIONS.—

(1) DURATION.—Federal operating grants authorized under this section for any individual intercity rail passenger transportation route may not provide funding for more than 6 years (including for any such routes selected for funding before the date of enactment of the Passenger Rail Expansion and Rail Safety Act of 2021) and may not be renewed.

(2) LIMITATION.—Not more than 6 of the operating assistance grants awarded pursuant to subsection (b) may be simultaneously active.

(3) MAXIMUM FUNDING.—Grants described in paragraph (1) may not exceed—

(A) 90 percent of the projected net operating costs for the first year of service;

(B) 80 percent of the projected net operating costs for the second year of service;

(C) 70 percent of the projected net operating costs for the third year of service;

(D) 60 percent of the projected net operating costs for the fourth year of service;

(E) 50 percent of the projected net operating costs for the fifth year of service; and

(F) 30 percent of the projected net operating costs for the sixth year of service.

(f) USE WITH CAPITAL GRANTS AND OTHER FEDERAL FUNDING.—A recipient of an operating assistance grant under subsection (b) may use that grant in combination with other Federal grants awarded that would benefit the applicable service.

(g) AVAILABILITY.—Amounts appropriated for carrying out this section shall remain available until expended.

(h) COORDINATION WITH AMTRAK.—If the Secretary awards a grant under this section to a rail carrier other than Amtrak, Amtrak may be required consistent with section 24711(c)(1) of this title to provide access to its reservation system, stations, and facilities that are directly related to operations to such carrier, to the extent necessary to carry out the purposes of this section. The Secretary may award an appropriate portion of the grant to Amtrak as compensation for this access.

(i) CONDITIONS.—

(1) GRANT AGREEMENT.—The Secretary shall require a grant recipient under this section to enter into a grant agreement that requires such recipient to provide similar information regarding the route performance, financial, and ridership projections, and capital and business plans that Amtrak is required to provide, and such other data and information as the Secretary considers necessary.

(2) INSTALLMENTS; TERMINATION.—The Secretary may—

(A) award grants under this section in installments, as the Secretary considers appropriate; and

(B) terminate any grant agreement upon—

(i) the cessation of service; or

(ii) the violation of any other term of the grant agreement.

(3) GRANT CONDITIONS.—The Secretary shall require each recipient of a grant under this section to comply with the grant requirements of section 22905.

(j) REPORT.—Not later than 4 years after the date of enactment of the Passenger Rail Reform and Investment Act of 2015, the Secretary, after consultation with grant recipients under this section, shall submit to Congress a report that describes—

(1) the implementation of this section;

(2) the status of the investments and operations funded by such grants;

(3) the performance of the routes funded by such grants;

(4) the plans of grant recipients for continued operation and funding of such routes; and

(5) any legislative recommendations.

(Added Pub. L. 114–94, div. A, title XI, §11303(a), Dec. 4, 2015, 129 Stat. 1651, §24408; renumbered §22908 and amended Pub. L. 115–420, §7(a)(1), (b)(2)(E), Jan. 3, 2019, 132 Stat. 5445, 5446; Pub. L. 117–58, div. B, title II, §22304, Nov. 15, 2021, 135 Stat. 719.)

§22909. RAILROAD CROSSING ELIMINATION PROGRAM

(a) IN GENERAL.—The Secretary of Transportation, in cooperation with the Administrator of the Federal Railroad Administration, shall establish a competitive grant program (referred to in this section as the "Program") under which the Secretary shall award grants to eligible recipients described in subsection (c) for highway-rail or pathway-rail grade crossing improvement projects that focus on improving the safety and mobility of people and goods.

(b) GOALS.—The goals of the Program are—

(1) to eliminate highway-rail grade crossings that are frequently blocked by trains;

(2) to improve the health and safety of communities;

(3) to reduce the impacts that freight movement and railroad operations may have on underserved communities; and

(4) to improve the mobility of people and goods.

(c) ELIGIBLE RECIPIENTS.—The following entities are eligible to receive a grant under this section:

(1) A State, including the District of Columbia, Puerto Rico, and other United States territories and possessions.

(2) A political subdivision of a State.

(3) A federally recognized Indian Tribe.

(4) A unit of local government or a group of local governments.

(5) A public port authority.

(6) A metropolitan planning organization.

(7) A group of entities described in any of paragraphs (1) through (6).

(d) ELIGIBLE PROJECTS.—The Secretary may award a grant under the Program for a highway-rail or pathway-rail grade crossing improvement project (including acquiring real property interests) involving—

(1) grade separation or closure, including through the use of a bridge, embankment, tunnel, or combination thereof;

(2) track relocation;

(3) the improvement or installation of protective devices, signals, signs, or other measures to improve safety, provided that such activities are related to a separation or relocation project described in paragraph (1) or (2);

(4) other means to improve the safety and mobility of people and goods at highway-rail grade crossings (including technological solutions);

(5) a group of related projects described in paragraphs (1) through (4) that would collectively improve the mobility of people and goods; or

(6) the planning, environmental review, and design of an eligible project described in paragraphs (1) through (5).

(e) APPLICATION PROCESS.—

(1) IN GENERAL.—An eligible entity seeking a grant under the Program shall submit an application to the Secretary at such time, in such manner, and containing such information as the Secretary may require.

(2) RAILROAD APPROVALS.—

(A) IN GENERAL.—Except as provided in subparagraph (B), the Secretary shall require applicants to obtain the necessary approvals from any impacted rail carriers or real property owners before proceeding with the construction of a project funded by a grant under the Program.

(B) EXCEPTION.—The requirement under subparagraph (A) shall not apply to planning projects described in subsection (d)(6) if the applicant agrees to work collaboratively with rail carriers and right-of-way owners.

(f) PROJECT SELECTION CRITERIA.—

(1) IN GENERAL.—In awarding grants under the Program, the Secretary shall evaluate the extent to which proposed projects would—

(A) improve safety at highway-rail or pathway-rail grade crossings;

(B) grade separate, eliminate, or close highway-rail or pathway-rail grade crossings;

(C) improve the mobility of people and goods;

(D) reduce emissions, protect the environment, and provide community benefits, including noise reduction;

(E) improve access to emergency services;

(F) provide economic benefits; and

(G) improve access to communities separated by rail crossings.

(2) ADDITIONAL CONSIDERATIONS.—In awarding grants under the Program, the Secretary shall consider—

(A) the degree to which the proposed project will use—

(i) innovative technologies;

(ii) innovative design and construction techniques; or

(iii) construction materials that reduce greenhouse gas emissions;

(B) the applicant's planned use of contracting incentives to employ local labor, to the extent permissible under Federal law;

(C) whether the proposed project will improve the mobility of—

(i) multiple modes of transportation, including ingress and egress from freight facilities; or

(ii) users of nonvehicular modes of transportation, such as pedestrians, bicyclists, and public transportation;

(D) whether the proposed project is identified in—

(i) the freight investment plan component of a State freight plan, as required under section 70202(b)(9);

(ii) a State rail plan prepared in accordance with chapter 227; or

(iii) a State highway-rail grade crossing action plan, as required under section 11401(b) of the Passenger Rail Reform and Investment Act of 2015 (title XI of Public Law 114–94); and

(E) the level of financial support provided by impacted rail carriers.

(3) AWARD DISTRIBUTION.—In selecting grants for Program funds in any fiscal year, the Secretary shall comply with the following limitations:

(A) GRANT FUNDS.—Not less than 20 percent of the grant funds available for the Program in any fiscal year shall be reserved for projects located in rural areas or on Tribal lands. The requirement under section 22907(1), which applies to this section, shall not apply to grant funds reserved specifically under this subparagraph. Not less than 5 percent of the grant funds reserved under this subparagraph shall be reserved for projects in counties with 20 or fewer residents per square mile, according to the most recent decennial census, provided that sufficient eligible applications have been submitted.

(B) PLANNING GRANTS.—Not less than 25 percent of the grant funds set aside for planning projects in any fiscal year pursuant to section 22104(b) of the Passenger Rail Expansion and Rail Safety Act of 2021 shall be awarded for projects located in rural areas or on tribal lands.

(C) STATE LIMITATION.—Not more than 20 percent of the grant funds available for the Program in any fiscal year may be selected for projects in any single State.

(D) MINIMUM SIZE.—No grant awarded under this section shall be for less than $1,000,000, except for a planning grant described in subsection (d)(6).

(g) COST SHARE.—Except as provided in paragraph (2),[1] the Federal share of the cost of a project carried out using a grant under the Program may not exceed 80 percent of the total cost of the project. Applicants may count costs incurred for preliminary engineering associated with highway-rail and pathway-rail grade crossing improvement projects as part of the total project costs.

(h) CONGRESSIONAL NOTIFICATION.—Not later than 3 days before awarding a grant for a project under the Program, the Secretary shall submit written notification of the proposed grant to the Committee on Commerce, Science, and Transportation of the Senate and the Committee on Transportation and Infrastructure of the House of Representatives, which shall include—

(1) a summary of the project; and

(2) the amount of the proposed grant award.

(i) ANNUAL REPORT.—Not later than 60 days after each round of award notifications, the Secretary shall post, on the public website of the Department of Transportation—

(1) a list of all eligible applicants that submitted an application for funding under the Program during the current fiscal year;

(2) a list of the grant recipients and projects that received grant funding under the Program during such fiscal year; and

(3) a list of the proposed projects and applicants that were determined to be ineligible.

(j) COMMUTER RAIL ELIGIBILITY AND GRANT CONDITIONS.—

(1) IN GENERAL.—Section 22905(f) shall not apply to grants awarded under this section for commuter rail passenger transportation projects.

(2) ADMINISTRATION OF FUNDS.—The Secretary of Transportation shall transfer amounts awarded under this section for commuter rail passenger transportation projects to the Federal Transit Administration, which shall administer such funds in accordance with chapter 53.

(3) PROTECTIVE ARRANGEMENTS.—

(A) IN GENERAL.—Notwithstanding paragraph (2) and section 22905(e)(1), as a condition of receiving a grant under this section, any employee covered by the Railway Labor Act (45 U.S.C. 151 et seq.) and the Railroad Retirement Act of 1974 (45 U.S.C. 231 et seq.) who is adversely affected by actions taken in connection with the project financed in whole or in part by such grant shall be covered by employee protective arrangements required to be established under section 22905(c)(2)(B).

(B) IMPLEMENTATION.—A grant recipient under this section, and the successors, assigns, and contractors of such grant recipient—

(i) shall be bound by the employee protective arrangements required under subparagraph (A); and

(ii) shall be responsible for the implementation of such arrangements and for the obligations under such arrangements, but may arrange for another entity to take initial responsibility for compliance with the conditions of such arrangement.

(k) DEFINED TERM.—In this section, the term "rural area" means any area that is not within an area designated as an urbanized area by the Bureau of the Census.

(Added Pub. L. 117–58, div. B, title II, §22305(a), Nov. 15, 2021, 135 Stat. 720.)

---

[1] So in original. No par. (2) has been enacted.

§22910. INTERSTATE RAIL COMPACTS GRANT PROGRAM

(a) GRANTS AUTHORIZED.—The Secretary of Transportation shall establish a competitive grant program to provide financial assistance to entities implementing interstate rail compacts pursuant to section 410 of the Amtrak Reform and Accountability Act of 1997 (49 U.S.C. 24101 note) for—

(1) costs of administration;

(2) systems planning, including studying the impacts on freight rail operations and ridership;

(3) promotion of intercity passenger rail operation;

(4) preparation of applications for competitive Federal grant programs; and

(5) operations coordination.

(b) MAXIMUM AMOUNT.—The Secretary may not award a grant under this section in an amount exceeding $1,000,000 per year.

(c) SELECTION CRITERIA.—In selecting a recipient of a grant for an eligible project under this section, the Secretary shall consider—

(1) the amount of funding received (including funding from a rail carrier (as defined in section 24102)) or other participation by State, local, and regional governments and the private sector;

(2) the applicant's work to foster economic development through rail service, particularly in rural communities;

(3) whether the applicant seeks to restore service over routes formerly operated by Amtrak, including routes described in section 11304(a) of the Passenger Rail Reform and Investment Act of 2015 (title XI of division A of Public Law 114–94);

(4) the applicant's dedication to providing intercity passenger rail service to regions and communities that are underserved or not served by other intercity public transportation;

(5) whether the applicant is enhancing connectivity and geographic coverage of the existing national network of intercity passenger rail service;

(6) whether the applicant has prepared regional rail or corridor service development plans and corresponding environmental analysis; and

(7) whether the applicant has engaged with appropriate government entities and transportation providers to identify projects necessary to enhance multimodal connections or facilitate service integration between rail service and other modes, including between intercity passenger rail service and intercity bus service or

commercial air service.

(d) NUMERICAL LIMITATION.—The Secretary may not award grants under this section for more than 10 interstate rail compacts in any fiscal year.

(e) OPERATOR LIMITATION.—The Secretary may only award grants under this section to applicants with eligible expenses related to intercity passenger rail service to be operated by Amtrak.

(f) NON-FEDERAL MATCH.—The Secretary shall require each recipient of a grant under this section to provide a non-Federal match of not less than 50 percent of the eligible expenses of carrying out the interstate rail compact under this section.

(g) REPORT.—Not later than 3 years after the date of enactment of the Passenger Rail Expansion and Rail Safety Act of 2021, the Secretary, after consultation with grant recipients under this section, shall submit a report to the Committee on Commerce, Science, and Transportation of the Senate and the Committee on Transportation and Infrastructure of the House of Representatives that describes—

(1) the implementation of this section;

(2) the status of the planning efforts and coordination funded by grants awarded under this section;

(3) the plans of grant recipients for continued implementation of the interstate rail compacts;

(4) the status of, and data regarding, any new, restored, or enhanced rail services initiated under the interstate rail compacts; and

(5) any legislative recommendations.

(Added Pub. L. 117–58, div. B, title II, §22306(a), Nov. 15, 2021, 135 Stat. 723.)

PART C—PASSENGER TRANSPORTATION

CHAPTER 241—GENERAL

§24101. FINDINGS, MISSION, AND GOALS

(a) FINDINGS.—(1) Public convenience and necessity require that Amtrak, to the extent its budget allows, provide modern, cost-efficient, and energy-efficient intercity rail passenger transportation throughout the United States.

(2) Rail passenger transportation can help alleviate overcrowding of airways and airports and on highways.

(3) A traveler in the United States should have the greatest possible choice of transportation most convenient to the needs of the traveler.

(4) A greater degree of cooperation is necessary among Amtrak, other rail carriers, State, regional, and local governments, the private sector, labor organizations, and suppliers of services and equipment in order to meet the intercity passenger rail needs of the United States.

(5) Modern and efficient intercity passenger and commuter rail passenger transportation is important to the viability and well-being of major urban and rural areas and to the energy conservation and self-sufficiency goals of the United States.

(6) As a rail passenger transportation entity, Amtrak should be available to operate commuter rail passenger transportation through its subsidiary, Amtrak Commuter, under contract with commuter authorities that do not provide the transportation themselves as part of the governmental function of the State.

(7) The Northeast Corridor is a valuable resource of the United States used by intercity and commuter rail passenger transportation and freight transportation.

(8) Greater coordination between intercity and commuter rail passenger transportation is required.

(9) Long-distance routes are valuable resources of the United States that are used by rural and urban communities.

(b) MISSION.—The mission of Amtrak is to provide efficient and effective intercity passenger rail mobility consisting of high quality service that is trip-time competitive with other intercity travel options and that is consistent with the goals set forth in subsection (c).

(c) GOALS.—Amtrak shall—

(1) use its best business judgment in acting to maximize the benefits of Federal investments, including—

(A) offering competitive fares;

(B) increasing revenue from the transportation of mail and express;

(C) offering food service that meets the needs of its customers;

(D) improving its contracts with rail carriers over whose tracks Amtrak operates;

(E) controlling or reducing management and operating costs; and

(F) providing economic benefits to the communities it serves;

(2) minimize Government subsidies by encouraging State, regional, and local governments and the private sector, separately or in combination, to share the cost of providing rail passenger transportation, including the cost of operating facilities;

(3) carry out strategies to achieve immediately maximum productivity and efficiency consistent with safe and efficient transportation;

(4) operate Amtrak trains, to the maximum extent feasible, to all station stops within 15 minutes of the time established in public timetables;

(5) develop transportation on rail corridors subsidized by States and private parties;

(6) implement schedules based on a systemwide average speed of at least 60 miles an hour that can be achieved with a degree of reliability and passenger comfort;

(7) encourage rail carriers to assist in improving intercity rail passenger transportation;

(8) improve generally the performance of Amtrak through comprehensive and systematic operational programs and employee incentives;

(9) provide additional or complementary intercity transportation service to ensure mobility in times of national disaster or other instances where other travel options are not adequately available;

(10) carry out policies that ensure equitable access to the Northeast Corridor by intercity and commuter rail passenger transportation;

(11) coordinate the uses of the Northeast Corridor, particularly intercity and commuter rail passenger transportation;

(12) maximize the use of its resources, including the most cost-effective use of employees, facilities, and real property; and

(13) support and maintain established long-distance routes to provide value to the Nation by serving customers throughout the United States and connecting urban and rural communities.

(d) INCREASING REVENUES.—Amtrak is encouraged to make agreements with private sector entities and to undertake initiatives that are consistent with good business judgment and designed to generate additional revenues to advance the goals described in subsection (c).

(Pub. L. 103–272, §1(e), July 5, 1994, 108 Stat. 899; Pub. L. 105–134, title I, §105(b), title II, §201, Dec. 2, 1997, 111 Stat. 2573, 2578; Pub. L. 110–432, div. B, title II, §§201(e)(1), 218(a)(1), Oct. 16, 2008, 122 Stat. 4910, 4930; Pub. L. 114–94, div. A, title XI, §11316(l), Dec. 4, 2015, 129 Stat. 1678; Pub. L. 117–58, div. B, title II, §22201, Nov. 15, 2021, 135 Stat. 696.)

§24102. DEFINITIONS

In this part—

(1) "auto-ferry transportation" means intercity rail passenger transportation—

(A) of automobiles or recreational vehicles and their occupants; and

(B) when space is available, of used unoccupied vehicles.

(2) "commuter authority" means a State, local, or regional entity established to provide, or make a contract providing for, commuter rail passenger transportation.

(3) "commuter rail passenger transportation" means short-haul rail passenger transportation in metropolitan and suburban areas usually having reduced fare, multiple-ride, and commuter tickets and morning and evening peak period operations.

(4) "intercity rail passenger transportation" means rail passenger transportation, except commuter rail passenger transportation.

(5) "long-distance route" means a route described in subparagraph (C) of paragraph (7).

(6) "National Network" includes long-distance routes and State-supported routes.

(7) "national rail passenger transportation system" means—

(A) the segment of the continuous Northeast Corridor railroad line between Boston, Massachusetts, and Washington, District of Columbia;

(B) rail corridors that have been designated by the Secretary of Transportation as high-speed rail corridors (other than corridors described in subparagraph (A)), but only after regularly scheduled intercity service over a corridor has been established;

(C) long-distance routes of more than 750 miles between endpoints operated by Amtrak as of the date of enactment of the Passenger Rail Investment and Improvement Act of 2008; and

(D) short-distance corridors, or routes of not more than 750 miles between endpoints, operated by—

(i) Amtrak; or

(ii) another rail carrier that receives funds under chapter 229.

(8) "Northeast Corridor" means Connecticut, Delaware, the District of Columbia, Maryland, Massachusetts, New Jersey, New York, Pennsylvania, and Rhode Island.

(9) "rail carrier" means a person, including a unit of State or local government, providing rail transportation for compensation.

(10) "rate" means a rate, fare, or charge for rail transportation.

(11) "regional transportation authority" means an entity established to provide passenger transportation in a region.

(12) "state-of-good-repair" means a condition in which physical assets, both individually and as a system, are—

(A) performing at a level at least equal to that called for in their as-built or as-modified design specification during any period when the life cycle cost of maintaining the assets is lower than the cost of replacing them; and

(B) sustained through regular maintenance and replacement programs.

(13) "State-supported route" means a route described in subparagraph (B) or (D) of paragraph (7), or in section 24702, that is operated by Amtrak, excluding those trains operated by Amtrak on the routes described in paragraph (7)(A).

(Pub. L. 103–272, §1(e), July 5, 1994, 108 Stat. 900; Pub. L. 105–134, title IV, §407, Dec. 2, 1997, 111 Stat. 2586; Pub. L. 110–432, div. B, title II, §201(a), Oct. 16, 2008, 122 Stat. 4909; Pub. L. 114–94, div. A, title XI, §11006(a), Dec. 4, 2015, 129 Stat. 1624; Pub. L. 115–420, §7(b)(3)(A)(i)(I), Jan. 3, 2019, 132 Stat.

5446.)

§24103. Enforcement

(a) General.—(1) Except as provided in paragraph (2) of this subsection, only the Attorney General may bring a civil action for equitable relief in a district court of the United States when Amtrak or a rail carrier—

(A) engages in or adheres to an action, practice, or policy inconsistent with this part or chapter 229;

(B) obstructs or interferes with an activity authorized under this part or chapter 229;

(C) refuses, fails, or neglects to discharge its duties and responsibilities under this part or chapter 229; or

(D) threatens—

(i) to engage in or adhere to an action, practice, or policy inconsistent with this part or chapter 229;

(ii) to obstruct or interfere with an activity authorized by this part or chapter 229; or

(iii) to refuse, fail, or neglect to discharge its duties and responsibilities under this part or chapter 229.

(2) An employee affected by any conduct or threat referred to in paragraph (1) of this subsection, or an authorized employee representative, may bring the civil action if the conduct or threat involves a labor agreement.

(b) Review of Discontinuance or Reduction.—A discontinuance of a route, a train, or transportation, or a reduction in the frequency of transportation, by Amtrak is reviewable only in a civil action for equitable relief brought by the Attorney General.

(c) Venue.—Except as otherwise prohibited by law, a civil action under this section may be brought in the judicial district in which Amtrak or the rail carrier resides or is found.

(Pub. L. 103–272, §1(e), July 5, 1994, 108 Stat. 901; Pub. L. 115–420, §7(b)(3)(A)(i)(II), Jan. 3, 2019, 132 Stat. 5447.)

[§24104. Repealed. Pub. L. 114–94, div. A, title XI, §11202(c)(2), Dec. 4, 2015, 129 Stat. 1630]

Section, Pub. L. 103–272, §1(e), July 5, 1994, 108 Stat. 902; Pub. L. 105–134, title III, §301(a), Dec. 2, 1997, 111 Stat. 2585, authorized certain appropriations for the benefit of Amtrak.

[§24105. Repealed. Pub. L. 114–94, div. A, title XI, §11301(c)(2), Dec. 4, 2015, 129 Stat. 1648]

Section, Pub. L. 110–432, div. B, title III, §302(a), Oct. 16, 2008, 122 Stat. 4947, related to congestion grants.

CHAPTER 242—PROJECT DELIVERY

§24201. EFFICIENT ENVIRONMENTAL REVIEWS

(a) EFFICIENT ENVIRONMENTAL REVIEWS.—

(1) IN GENERAL.—The Secretary of Transportation shall apply the project development procedures, to the greatest extent feasible, described in section 139 of title 23 to any railroad project that requires the approval of the Secretary under the National Environmental Policy Act of 1969 (42 U.S.C. 4321 et seq.).

(2) REGULATIONS AND PROCEDURES.—In carrying out paragraph (1), the Secretary shall incorporate into agency regulations and procedures pertaining to railroad projects described in paragraph (1) aspects of such project development procedures, or portions thereof, determined appropriate by the Secretary in a manner consistent with this section, that increase the efficiency of the review of railroad projects.

(3) DISCRETION.—The Secretary may choose not to incorporate into agency regulations and procedures pertaining to railroad projects described in paragraph (1) such project development procedures that could only feasibly apply to highway projects, public transportation capital projects, and multimodal projects.

(4) APPLICABILITY.—Subsection (l) of section 139 of title 23 shall apply to railroad projects described in paragraph (1), except that the limitation on claims of 150 days shall be 2 years.

(b) ADDITIONAL CATEGORICAL EXCLUSIONS.—Not later than 6 months after the date of enactment of the Passenger Rail Reform and Investment Act of 2015, the Secretary shall—

(1) survey the use by the Federal Railroad Administration of categorical exclusions in transportation projects since 2005; and

(2) publish in the Federal Register for notice and public comment a review of the survey that includes a description of—

(A) the types of actions categorically excluded; and

(B) any actions the Secretary is considering for new categorical exclusions, including those that would conform to those of other modal administrations.

(c) NEW CATEGORICAL EXCLUSIONS.—Not later than 1 year after the date of enactment of the Passenger Rail Reform and Investment Act of 2015, the Secretary shall publish a notice of proposed rulemaking to propose new and existing categorical exclusions for railroad projects that require the approval of the Secretary under the National Environmental Policy Act of 1969 (42 U.S.C. 4321 et seq.), including those identified under subsection (b), and develop a process for considering new categorical exclusions to the extent that the categorical exclusions meet the criteria for a categorical exclusion under section 1508.4 of title 40, Code of Federal Regulations.

(d) TRANSPARENCY.—The Secretary shall maintain and make publicly available, including on the Internet, a database that identifies project-specific information on the use of a categorical exclusion on any railroad project carried out under this title.

(e) PROTECTIONS FOR EXISTING AGREEMENTS AND NEPA.—Nothing in subtitle E of the Passenger Rail Reform and Investment Act of 2015, or any amendment made by such subtitle, shall affect any existing environmental review process, program, agreement, or funding arrangement approved by the Secretary under title 49, as that title was in effect on the day preceding the date of enactment of such subtitle.

(Added Pub. L. 114–94, div. A, title XI, §11503(a), Dec. 4, 2015, 129 Stat. 1691.)

§24202. RAILROAD RIGHTS-OF-WAY

(a) IN GENERAL.—Not later than 1 year after the date of enactment of the Passenger Rail Reform and Investment Act of 2015, the Secretary shall submit a proposed exemption of railroad rights-of-way from the review under section 306108 of title 54 to the Advisory Council on Historic Preservation for consideration, consistent with the exemption for interstate highways approved on March 10, 2005 (70 Fed. Reg. 11,928).

(b) FINAL EXEMPTION.—Not later than 180 days after the date on which the Secretary submits the proposed exemption under subsection (a) to the Council, the Council shall issue a final exemption of railroad rights-of-way from review under chapter 3061 of title 54 consistent with the exemption for interstate highways approved on March 10, 2005 (70 Fed. Reg. 11,928).

(Added Pub. L. 114–94, div. A, title XI, §11504(a), Dec. 4, 2015, 129 Stat. 1692.)

CHAPTER 243—AMTRAK

[1] So in original. Does not conform to section catchline.

§24301. STATUS AND APPLICABLE LAWS

(a) STATUS.—Amtrak—

(1) is a railroad carrier under section 20102(2) [1] and chapters 261 and 281 of this title;

(2) shall be operated and managed as a for-profit corporation; and

(3) is not a department, agency, or instrumentality of the United States Government, and shall not be subject to title 31.

(b) PRINCIPAL OFFICE AND PLACE OF BUSINESS.—The principal office and place of business of Amtrak are in the District of Columbia. Amtrak is qualified to do business in each State in which Amtrak carries out an activity authorized under this part. Amtrak shall accept service of process by certified mail addressed to the secretary of Amtrak at its principal office and place of business. Amtrak is a citizen only of the District of Columbia when deciding original jurisdiction of the district courts of the United States in a civil action.

(c) APPLICATION OF SUBTITLE IV.—Subtitle IV of this title shall not apply to Amtrak, except for sections 11123, 11301, 11322(a), 11502, and 11706. Notwithstanding the preceding sentence, Amtrak shall continue to be considered an employer under the Railroad Retirement Act of 1974, the Railroad Unemployment Insurance Act, and the Railroad Retirement Tax Act.

(d) APPLICATION OF SAFETY AND EMPLOYEE RELATIONS LAWS AND REGULATIONS.—Laws and regulations governing safety, employee representation for collective bargaining purposes, the handling of disputes between carriers and employees, employee retirement, annuity, and unemployment systems, and other dealings with employees that apply to a rail carrier subject to part A of subtitle IV of this title apply to Amtrak.

(e) APPLICATION OF CERTAIN ADDITIONAL LAWS.—Section 552 of title 5, this part, and, to the extent consistent with this part, the District of Columbia Business Corporation Act (D.C. Code §29–301 et seq.) apply to Amtrak. Section 552 of title 5, United States Code, applies to Amtrak for any fiscal year in which Amtrak receives a Federal subsidy.

(f) TAX EXEMPTION FOR CERTAIN COMMUTER AUTHORITIES.—A commuter authority that was eligible to make a contract with Amtrak Commuter to provide commuter rail passenger transportation but which decided to provide its own rail passenger transportation beginning January 1, 1983, is exempt, effective October 1, 1981, from paying a tax or fee to the same extent Amtrak is exempt.

(g) NONAPPLICATION OF RATE, ROUTE, AND SERVICE LAWS.—A State or other law related to rates, routes, or service does not apply to Amtrak in connection with rail passenger transportation.

(h) NONAPPLICATION OF PAY PERIOD LAWS.—A State or local law related to pay periods or days for payment of employees does not apply to Amtrak. Except when otherwise provided under a collective bargaining agreement, an employee of Amtrak shall be paid at least as frequently as the employee was paid on October 1, 1979.

(i) PREEMPTION RELATED TO EMPLOYEE WORK REQUIREMENTS.—A State may not adopt or continue in force a law, rule, regulation, order, or standard requiring Amtrak to employ a specified number of individuals to perform a particular task, function, or operation.

(j) NONAPPLICATION OF LAWS ON JOINT USE OR OPERATION OF FACILITIES AND EQUIPMENT.—Prohibitions of law applicable to an agreement for the joint use or operation of facilities and equipment necessary to provide quick and efficient rail passenger transportation do not apply to a person making an agreement with Amtrak to the extent necessary to allow the person to make and carry out obligations under the agreement.

(k) EXEMPTION FROM ADDITIONAL TAXES.—(1) In this subsection—

(A) "additional tax" means a tax or fee—

(i) on the acquisition, improvement, ownership, or operation of personal property by Amtrak; and

(ii) on real property, except a tax or fee on the acquisition of real property or on the value of real property not attributable to improvements made, or the operation of those improvements, by Amtrak.

(B) "Amtrak" includes a rail carrier subsidiary of Amtrak and a lessor or lessee of Amtrak or one of its rail carrier subsidiaries.

(2) Amtrak is not required to pay an additional tax because of an expenditure to acquire or improve real property, equipment, a facility, or right-of-way material or structures used in providing rail passenger transportation, even if that use is indirect.

(l) EXEMPTION FROM TAXES LEVIED AFTER SEPTEMBER 30, 1981.—(1) IN GENERAL.—Amtrak, a rail carrier subsidiary of Amtrak, and any passenger or other customer of Amtrak or such subsidiary, are exempt from a tax, fee, head charge, or other charge, imposed or levied by a State, political subdivision, or local taxing authority on Amtrak, a rail carrier subsidiary of Amtrak, or on persons traveling in intercity rail passenger transportation or on mail or express transportation provided by Amtrak or such a subsidiary, or on the carriage of such persons, mail, or express, or on the sale of any such transportation, or on the gross receipts derived therefrom after September 30, 1981. In the case of a tax or fee that Amtrak was required to pay as of September 10, 1982, Amtrak is not exempt from such tax or fee if it was assessed before April 1, 1997.

(2) The district courts of the United States have original jurisdiction over a civil action Amtrak brings to enforce this subsection and may grant equitable or declaratory relief requested by Amtrak.

(m) WASTE DISPOSAL.—(1) An intercity rail passenger car manufactured after October 14, 1990, shall be built to provide for the discharge of human waste only at a servicing facility. Amtrak shall retrofit each of its intercity rail passenger cars that was manufactured after May 1, 1971, and before October 15, 1990, with a human waste disposal system that provides for the discharge of human waste only at a servicing facility. Subject to appropriations—

(A) the retrofit program shall be completed not later than October 15, 2001; and

(B) a car that does not provide for the discharge of human waste only at a servicing facility shall be removed from service after that date.

(2) Section 361 of the Public Health Service Act (42 U.S.C. 264) and other laws of the United States, States, and local governments do not apply to waste disposal from rail carrier vehicles operated in intercity rail passenger transportation. The district courts of the United States have original jurisdiction over a civil action Amtrak brings to enforce this paragraph and may grant equitable or declaratory relief requested by Amtrak.

(n) RAIL TRANSPORTATION TREATED EQUALLY.—When authorizing transportation in the continental United States for an officer, employee, or member of the uniformed services of a department, agency, or instrumentality of the Government, the head of that department, agency, or instrumentality shall consider rail transportation (including transportation by extra-fare trains) the same as transportation by another authorized mode. The Administrator of General Services shall include Amtrak in the contract air program of the Administrator in markets in which transportation provided by Amtrak is competitive with other carriers on fares and total trip times.

(o) APPLICABILITY OF DISTRICT OF COLUMBIA LAW.—Any lease or contract entered into between Amtrak and the State of Maryland, or any department or agency of the State of Maryland, after the date of the enactment of this subsection shall be governed by the laws of the District of Columbia.

(Pub. L. 103–272, §1(e), July 5, 1994, 108 Stat. 904; Pub. L. 104–88, title III, §308(g), Dec. 29, 1995, 109

Stat. 947; Pub. L. 105–134, title I, §§106(b), 110(a), title II, §208, title IV, §§401, 402, 415(d)(1), Dec. 2, 1997, 111 Stat. 2573, 2574, 2584, 2585, 2590; Pub. L. 108–199, div. F, title I, §150(2), Jan. 23, 2004, 118 Stat. 303; Pub. L. 110–53, title XV, §1527, Aug. 3, 2007, 121 Stat. 452.)

[1] *See References in Text note below.*

§24302. BOARD OF DIRECTORS

(a) COMPOSITION AND TERMS.—

(1) The Amtrak Board of Directors (referred to in this section as the "Board") is composed of the following 10 directors, each of whom must be a citizen of the United States:

(A) The Secretary of Transportation.

(B) The Chief Executive Officer of Amtrak, who shall serve as a nonvoting member of the Board.

(C) 8 individuals appointed by the President of the United States, by and with the advice and consent of the Senate, with general business and financial experience, experience or qualifications in transportation, freight and passenger rail transportation, travel, hospitality, cruise line, or passenger air transportation businesses, or representatives of employees or users of passenger rail transportation or a State government, at least 1 of whom shall be an individual with a disability (as defined in section 3 of the Americans with Disabilities Act of 1990 (42 U.S.C. 12102)) who has a demonstrated history of, or experience with, accessibility, mobility, and inclusive transportation in passenger rail or commuter rail.

(2) In selecting individuals described in paragraph (1) for nominations for appointments to the Board, the President shall consult with the Speaker of the House of Representatives, the minority leader of the House of Representatives, the majority leader of the Senate, and the minority leader of the Senate.

(3) An individual appointed under paragraph (1)(C) of this subsection shall be appointed for a term of 5 years. Such term may be extended until the individual's successor is appointed and qualified. Not more than 5 individuals appointed under paragraph (1)(C) may be members of the same political party.

(4) Of the individuals appointed pursuant to paragraph (1)(C)—

(A) 2 individuals shall reside in or near a location served by a regularly scheduled Amtrak service along the Northeast Corridor;

(B) 4 individuals shall reside in or near regions of the United States that are geographically distributed outside of the Northeast Corridor, of whom—

(i) 2 individuals shall reside in States served by a long-distance route operated by Amtrak;

(ii) 2 individuals shall reside in States served by a State-supported route operated by Amtrak; and

(iii) an individual who resides in a State that is served by a State-supported route and a long-distance route may be appointed to serve either position referred to in clauses (i) and (ii);

(C) 2 individuals shall reside either—

(i) in or near a location served by a regularly scheduled Amtrak service on the Northeast Corridor; or

(ii) in a State served by long-distance or a State-supported route; and

(D) each individual appointed to the Board pursuant to this paragraph may only fill 1 of the allocations set forth in subparagraphs (A) through (C).

(5) The Board shall elect a chairperson and vice chairperson, other than the Chief Executive Officer of Amtrak, from among its membership. The vice chairperson shall act as chairperson in the absence of the chairperson.

(6) The Board shall meet at least annually with—

(A) representatives of Amtrak employees;

(B) representatives of persons with disabilities; and

(C) the general public, in an open meeting with a virtual attendance option, to discuss financial performance and service results.

(7) The Secretary may be represented at Board meetings by the Secretary's designee.

(b) PAY AND EXPENSES.—Each director not employed by the United States Government or Amtrak is entitled to reasonable pay when performing Board duties. Each director not employed by the United States Government is entitled to reimbursement from Amtrak for necessary travel, reasonable secretarial and professional staff support, and subsistence expenses incurred in attending Board meetings.

(c) TRAVEL.—(1) Each director not employed by the United States Government shall be subject to the same travel and reimbursable business travel expense policies and guidelines that apply to Amtrak's executive management when performing Board duties.

(2) Not later than 60 days after the end of each fiscal year, the Board shall submit a report describing all travel and reimbursable business travel expenses paid to each director when performing Board duties to the Committee on Transportation and Infrastructure of the House of Representatives and the Committee on Commerce, Science, and Transportation of the Senate.

(3) The report submitted under paragraph (2) shall include a detailed justification for any travel or reimbursable business travel expense that deviates from Amtrak's travel and reimbursable business travel expense policies and guidelines.

(d) VACANCIES.—A vacancy on the Board is filled in the same way as the original selection, except that an individual appointed by the President of the United States under subsection (a)(1)(C) of this section to fill a vacancy occurring before the end of the term for which the predecessor of that individual was appointed is appointed for the remainder of that term. A vacancy required to be filled by appointment under subsection (a)(1)(C) must be filled not later than 120 days after the vacancy occurs.

(e) QUORUM.—A majority of the members serving who are eligible to vote shall constitute a quorum for doing business.

(f) BYLAWS.—The Board may adopt and amend bylaws governing the operation of Amtrak. The bylaws shall be consistent with this part and the articles of incorporation.

(Pub. L. 103–272, §1(e), July 5, 1994, 108 Stat. 906; Pub. L. 105–134, title IV, §411(a), Dec. 2, 1997, 111

Stat. 2588; Pub. L. 110–432, div. B, title II, §202(a), Oct. 16, 2008, 122 Stat. 4911; Pub. L. 114–94, div. A, title XI, §11205, Dec. 4, 2015, 129 Stat. 1637; Pub. L. 117–58, div. B, title II, §22202(a), Nov. 15, 2021, 135 Stat. 697.)

§24303. OFFICERS

(a) APPOINTMENT AND TERMS.—Amtrak has a President and other officers that are named and appointed by the board of directors of Amtrak. An officer of Amtrak must be a citizen of the United States. Officers of Amtrak serve at the pleasure of the board.

(b) PAY.—The board may fix the pay of the officers of Amtrak. An officer may not be paid more than the general level of pay for officers of rail carriers with comparable responsibility. The preceding sentence shall not apply for any fiscal year for which no Federal assistance is provided to Amtrak.

(c) CONFLICTS OF INTEREST.—When employed by Amtrak, an officer may not have a financial or employment relationship with another rail carrier, except that holding securities issued by a rail carrier is not deemed to be a violation of this subsection if the officer holding the securities makes a complete public disclosure of the holdings and does not participate in any decision directly affecting the rail carrier.

(Pub. L. 103–272, §1(e), July 5, 1994, 108 Stat. 907; Pub. L. 105–134, title II, §207, Dec. 2, 1997, 111 Stat. 2584.)

§24304. EMPLOYEE STOCK OWNERSHIP PLANS

In issuing stock pursuant to applicable corporate law, Amtrak is encouraged to include employee stock ownership plans.

(Pub. L. 103–272, §1(e), July 5, 1994, 108 Stat. 908; Pub. L. 105–134, title IV, §415(a)(1), Dec. 2, 1997, 111 Stat. 2590.)

§24305. GENERAL AUTHORITY

(a) ACQUISITION AND OPERATION OF EQUIPMENT AND FACILITIES.—(1) Amtrak may acquire, operate, maintain, and make contracts for the operation and maintenance of equipment and facilities necessary for intercity and commuter rail passenger transportation, the transportation of mail and express, and auto-ferry transportation.

(2) Amtrak shall operate and control directly, to the extent practicable, all aspects of the rail passenger transportation it provides.

(3)(A) Except as provided in subsection (d)(2), Amtrak may enter into a contract with a motor carrier of passengers for the intercity transportation of passengers by motor carrier over regular routes only—

(i) if the motor carrier is not a public recipient of governmental assistance, as such term is defined in section 13902(b)(8)(A) of this title, other than a recipient of funds under section 5311 of this title;

(ii) for passengers who have had prior movement by rail or will have subsequent movement by rail; and

(iii) if the buses, when used in the provision of such transportation, are used exclusively for the transportation of passengers described in clause (ii).

(B) Subparagraph (A) shall not apply to transportation funded predominantly by a State or local government, or to ticket selling agreements.

(b) MAINTENANCE AND REHABILITATION.—Amtrak may maintain and rehabilitate rail passenger equipment and shall maintain a regional maintenance plan that includes—

(1) a review panel at the principal office of Amtrak consisting of members the President of Amtrak designates;

(2) a systemwide inventory of spare equipment parts in each operational region;

(3) enough maintenance employees for cars and locomotives in each region;

(4) a systematic preventive maintenance program;

(5) periodic evaluations of maintenance costs, time lags, and parts shortages and corrective actions; and

(6) other elements or activities Amtrak considers appropriate.

(c) MISCELLANEOUS AUTHORITY.—Amtrak may—

(1) make and carry out appropriate agreements;

(2) transport mail and express and shall use all feasible methods to obtain the bulk mail business of the United States Postal Service;

(3) improve its reservation system and advertising;

(4) provide food and beverage services on its trains;

(5) conduct research, development, and demonstration programs related to the mission of Amtrak; and

(6) buy or lease rail rolling stock and develop and demonstrate improved rolling stock.

(d) THROUGH ROUTES AND JOINT FARES.—(1) Establishing through routes and joint fares between Amtrak and other intercity rail passenger carriers and motor carriers of passengers is consistent with the public interest and the transportation policy of the United States. Congress encourages establishing those routes and fares.

(2) Amtrak may establish through routes and joint fares with any domestic or international motor carrier, air carrier, or water carrier.

(3) Congress encourages Amtrak and motor common carriers of passengers to use the authority conferred in sections 11322 and 14302 of this title for the purpose of providing improved service to the public and economy of operation.

(e) RAIL POLICE.—Amtrak may directly employ or contract with rail police to provide security for rail passengers and property of Amtrak. Rail police directly employed by or contracted by Amtrak who have complied with a State law establishing requirements applicable to rail police or individuals employed in a similar position may be directly employed or contracted without regard to the law of another State containing those requirements.

(f) DOMESTIC BUYING PREFERENCES.—(1) In this subsection, "United States" means the States, territories, and possessions of the United States and the District of Columbia.

(2) Amtrak shall buy only—

(A) unmanufactured articles, material, and supplies mined or produced in the United States; or

(B) manufactured articles, material, and supplies manufactured in the United States substantially from articles, material, and supplies mined, produced, or manufactured in the United States.

(3) Paragraph (2) of this subsection applies only when the cost of those articles, material, or supplies bought is at least $1,000,000.

(4) On application of Amtrak, the Secretary of Transportation may exempt Amtrak from this subsection if the Secretary decides that—

(A) for particular articles, material, or supplies—

(i) the requirements of paragraph (2) of this subsection are inconsistent with the public interest;

(ii) the cost of imposing those requirements is unreasonable; or

(iii) the articles, material, or supplies, or the articles, material, or supplies from which they are manufactured, are not mined, produced, or manufactured in the United States in sufficient and reasonably available commercial quantities and are not of a satisfactory quality; or

(B) rolling stock or power train equipment cannot be bought and delivered in the United States within a reasonable time.

(Pub. L. 103–272, §1(e), July 5, 1994, 108 Stat. 909; Pub. L. 105–134, title I, §107, Dec. 2, 1997, 111 Stat. 2573; Pub. L. 114–94, div. A, title XI, §11412(c)(1), Dec. 4, 2015, 129 Stat. 1688; Pub. L. 117–58, div. B, title II, §22208(a), Nov. 15, 2021, 135 Stat. 706.)

§24306. MAIL, EXPRESS, AND AUTO-FERRY TRANSPORTATION

(a) ACTIONS TO INCREASE REVENUES.—Amtrak shall take necessary action to increase its revenues from the transportation of mail and express. To increase its revenues, Amtrak may provide auto-ferry transportation as part of the basic passenger transportation authorized by this part.

(b) AUTHORITY OF OTHERS TO PROVIDE AUTO-FERRY TRANSPORTATION.—State and local laws and regulations that impair the provision of auto-ferry transportation do not apply to Amtrak or a rail carrier providing auto-ferry transportation. A rail carrier may not refuse to participate with Amtrak in providing auto-ferry transportation because a State or local law or regulation makes the transportation unlawful.

(Pub. L. 103–272, §1(e), July 5, 1994, 108 Stat. 910; Pub. L. 105–134, title I, §102, Dec. 2, 1997, 111 Stat. 2572.)

§24307. SPECIAL TRANSPORTATION

(a) REDUCED FARE PROGRAM.—Amtrak shall maintain a reduced fare program for the following:

(1) individuals at least 65 years of age.

(2) individuals (except alcoholics and drug abusers) who—

(A) have a physical or mental impairment that substantially limits a major life activity of the individual;

(B) have a record of an impairment; or

(C) are regarded as having an impairment.

(b) EMPLOYEE TRANSPORTATION.—(1) In this subsection, "rail carrier employee" means—

(A) an active full-time employee of a rail carrier or terminal company and includes an employee on furlough or leave of absence;

(B) a retired employee of a rail carrier or terminal company; and

(C) a dependent of an employee referred to in clause (A) or (B) of this paragraph.

(2) Amtrak shall ensure that a rail carrier employee eligible for free or reduced-rate rail transportation on April 30, 1971, under an agreement in effect on that date is eligible, to the greatest extent practicable, for free or reduced-rate intercity rail passenger transportation provided by Amtrak under this part, if space is available, on terms similar to those available on that date under the agreement. However, Amtrak may apply to all rail carrier employees eligible to receive free or reduced-rate transportation under any agreement a single systemwide schedule of terms that Amtrak decides applied to a majority of employees on that date under all those agreements. Unless Amtrak and a rail carrier make a different agreement, the carrier shall reimburse Amtrak at the rate of 25 percent of the systemwide average monthly yield of each revenue passenger-mile. The reimbursement is in place of costs Amtrak incurs related to free or reduced-rate transportation, including liability related to travel of a rail carrier employee eligible for free or reduced-rate transportation.

(3) This subsection does not prohibit the Surface Transportation Board from ordering retroactive relief in a proceeding begun or reopened after October 1, 1981.

(Pub. L. 103–272, §1(e), July 5, 1994, 108 Stat. 911; Pub. L. 105–134, title IV, §406(b), Dec. 2, 1997, 111 Stat. 2586; Pub. L. 112–141, div. C, title II, §32932(c)(1), July 6, 2012, 126 Stat. 829.)

§24308. Use of facilities and providing services to Amtrak

(a) General Authority.—(1) Amtrak may make an agreement with a rail carrier or regional transportation authority to use facilities of, and have services provided by, the carrier or authority under terms on which the parties agree. The terms shall include a penalty for untimely performance.

(2)(A) If the parties cannot agree and if the Surface Transportation Board finds it necessary to carry out this part, the Board shall—

(i) order that the facilities be made available and the services provided to Amtrak; and

(ii) prescribe reasonable terms and compensation for using the facilities and providing the services.

(B) When prescribing reasonable compensation under subparagraph (A) of this paragraph, the Board shall consider quality of service as a major factor when determining whether, and the extent to which, the amount of compensation shall be greater than the incremental costs of using the facilities and providing the services.

(C) The Board shall decide the dispute not later than 90 days after Amtrak submits the dispute to the Board.

(3) Amtrak's right to use the facilities or have the services provided is conditioned on payment of the compensation. If the compensation is not paid promptly, the rail carrier or authority entitled to it may bring an action against Amtrak to recover the amount owed.

(4) Amtrak shall seek immediate and appropriate legal remedies to enforce its contract rights when track maintenance on a route over which Amtrak operates falls below the contractual standard.

(b) OPERATING DURING EMERGENCIES.—To facilitate operation by Amtrak during an emergency, the Board, on application by Amtrak, shall require a rail carrier to provide facilities immediately during the emergency. The Board then shall promptly prescribe reasonable terms, including indemnification of the carrier by Amtrak against personal injury risk to which the carrier may be exposed. The rail carrier shall provide the facilities for the duration of the emergency.

(c) PREFERENCE OVER FREIGHT TRANSPORTATION.—Except in an emergency, intercity and commuter rail passenger transportation provided by or for Amtrak has preference over freight transportation in using a rail line, junction, or crossing unless the Board orders otherwise under this subsection. A rail carrier affected by this subsection may apply to the Board for relief. If the Board, after an opportunity for a hearing under section 553 of title 5, decides that preference for intercity and commuter rail passenger transportation materially will lessen the quality of freight transportation provided to shippers, the Board shall establish the rights of the carrier and Amtrak on reasonable terms.

(d) ACCELERATED SPEEDS.—If a rail carrier refuses to allow accelerated speeds on trains operated by or for Amtrak, Amtrak may apply to the Board for an order requiring the carrier to allow the accelerated speeds. The Board shall decide whether accelerated speeds are unsafe or impracticable and which improvements would be required to make accelerated speeds safe and practicable. After an opportunity for a hearing, the Board shall establish the maximum allowable speeds of Amtrak trains on terms the Board decides are reasonable.

(e) ADDITIONAL TRAINS.—(1) When a rail carrier does not agree to provide, or allow Amtrak to provide, for the operation of additional trains over a rail line of the carrier, Amtrak may apply to the Board for an order requiring the carrier to provide or allow for the operation of the requested trains. After a hearing on the record, the Board may order the carrier, within 60 days, to provide or allow for the operation of the requested trains on a schedule based on legally permissible operating times. However, if the Board decides not to hold a hearing, the Board, not later than 30 days after receiving the application, shall publish in the Federal Register the reasons for the decision not to hold the hearing.

(2) The Board shall consider—

(A) when conducting a hearing, whether an order would impair unreasonably freight transportation of the rail carrier, with the carrier having the burden of demonstrating that the additional trains will impair the freight transportation; and

(B) when establishing scheduled running times, the statutory goal of Amtrak to implement schedules that attain a system-wide average speed of at least 60 miles an hour that can be adhered to with a high degree of reliability and passenger comfort.

(3) Unless the parties have an agreement that establishes the compensation Amtrak will pay the carrier for additional trains provided under an order under this subsection, the Board shall decide the dispute under subsection (a) of this section.

(f) PASSENGER TRAIN PERFORMANCE AND OTHER STANDARDS.—

(1) INVESTIGATION OF SUBSTANDARD PERFORMANCE.—If the on-time performance of any intercity passenger train averages less than 80 percent for any 2 consecutive calendar quarters, or the service quality of intercity passenger train operations for which minimum standards are established under section 207 of the Passenger Rail Investment and Improvement Act of 2008 fails to meet those standards for 2 consecutive calendar

quarters, the Surface Transportation Board (referred to in this section as the "Board") may initiate an investigation, or upon the filing of a complaint by Amtrak, an intercity passenger rail operator, a host freight railroad over which Amtrak operates, or an entity for which Amtrak operates intercity passenger rail service, the Board shall initiate such an investigation, to determine whether and to what extent delays or failure to achieve minimum standards are due to causes that could reasonably be addressed by a rail carrier over whose tracks the intercity passenger train operates or reasonably addressed by Amtrak or other intercity passenger rail operators. As part of its investigation, the Board has authority to review the accuracy of the train performance data and the extent to which scheduling and congestion contribute to delays. In making its determination or carrying out such an investigation, the Board shall obtain information from all parties involved and identify reasonable measures and make recommendations to improve the service, quality, and on-time performance of the train.

(2) PROBLEMS CAUSED BY HOST RAIL CARRIER.—If the Board determines that delays or failures to achieve minimum standards investigated under paragraph (1) are attributable to a rail carrier's failure to provide preference to Amtrak over freight transportation as required under subsection (c), the Board may award damages against the host rail carrier, including prescribing such other relief to Amtrak as it determines to be reasonable and appropriate pursuant to paragraph (3) of this subsection.

(3) DAMAGES AND RELIEF.—In awarding damages and prescribing other relief under this subsection the Board shall consider such factors as—

(A) the extent to which Amtrak suffers financial loss as a result of host rail carrier delays or failure to achieve minimum standards; and

(B) what reasonable measures would adequately deter future actions which may reasonably be expected to be likely to result in delays to Amtrak on the route involved.

(4) USE OF DAMAGES.—The Board shall, as it deems appropriate, order the host rail carrier to remit the damages awarded under this subsection to Amtrak or to an entity for which Amtrak operates intercity passenger rail service. Such damages shall be used for capital or operating expenditures on the routes over which delays or failures to achieve minimum standards were the result of a rail carrier's failure to provide preference to Amtrak over freight transportation as determined in accordance with paragraph (2).

(Pub. L. 103–272, §1(e), July 5, 1994, 108 Stat. 911; 110–432, div. B, title II, §213(a), (d), Oct. 16, 2008, 122 Stat. 4925, 4926.)

§24309. RETAINING AND MAINTAINING FACILITIES

(a) DEFINITIONS.—In this section—

(1) "facility" means a rail line, right of way, fixed equipment, facility, or real property related to a rail line, right of way, fixed equipment, or facility, including a signal system, passenger station and repair tracks, a station building, a platform, and a related facility, including a water, fuel, steam, electric, and air line.

(2) downgrading a facility means reducing a track classification as specified in the Federal Railroad Administration track safety standards or altering a facility so that the time required for rail passenger transportation to be provided over the route on which a facility is located may be increased.

(b) APPROVAL REQUIRED FOR DOWNGRADING OR DISPOSAL.—A facility of a rail carrier or regional transportation authority that Amtrak used to provide rail passenger transportation on February 1, 1979, or on January 1, 1997, may be downgraded or disposed of only after approval by the Secretary of Transportation under this section.

(c) NOTIFICATION AND ANALYSIS.—(1) A rail carrier intending to downgrade or dispose of a facility Amtrak currently is not using to provide transportation shall notify Amtrak of its intention. If, not later than 60 days after Amtrak receives the notice, Amtrak and the carrier do not agree to retain or maintain the facility or to convey an interest in the facility to Amtrak, the carrier may apply to the Secretary for approval to downgrade or dispose of the facility.

(2) After a rail carrier notifies Amtrak of its intention to downgrade or dispose of a facility, Amtrak shall survey population centers with rail passenger transportation facilities to assist in preparing a valid and timely analysis of the need for the facility and shall update the survey as appropriate. Amtrak also shall maintain a system for collecting information gathered in the survey. The system shall collect the information based on geographic regions and on whether the facility would be part of a short haul or long haul route. The survey should facilitate an analysis of—

(A) ridership potential by ascertaining existing and changing travel patterns that would provide maximum efficient rail passenger transportation;

(B) the quality of transportation of competitors or likely competitors;

(C) the likelihood of Amtrak offering transportation at a competitive fare;

(D) opportunities to target advertising and fares to potential classes of riders;

(E) economic characteristics of rail passenger transportation related to the facility and the extent to which the characteristics are consistent with sound economic principles of short haul or long haul rail transportation; and

(F) the feasibility of applying effective internal cost controls to the facility and route served by the facility to improve the ratio of passenger revenue to transportation expenses (excluding maintenance of tracks, structures, and equipment and depreciation).

(d) APPROVAL OF APPLICATION AND PAYMENT OF AVOIDABLE COSTS.—(1) If Amtrak does not object to an application not later than 30 days after it is submitted, the Secretary shall approve the application promptly.

(2) If Amtrak objects to an application, the Secretary shall decide by not later than 180 days after the objection those costs the rail carrier may avoid if it does not have to retain or maintain a facility in the condition Amtrak requests. If Amtrak does not agree by not later than 60 days after the decision to pay the carrier these avoidable costs, the Secretary shall approve the application. When deciding whether to pay a carrier the avoidable costs of retaining or maintaining a facility, Amtrak shall consider—

(A) the potential importance of restoring rail passenger transportation on the route on which the facility is located;

(B) the market potential of the route;

(C) the availability, adequacy, and energy efficiency of an alternate rail line or alternate mode of transportation to provide passenger transportation to or near the places that would be served by the route;

(D) the extent to which major population centers would be served by the route;

(E) the extent to which providing transportation over the route would encourage the expansion of an intercity rail passenger system in the United States; and

(F) the possibility of increased ridership on a rail line that connects with the route.

(e) COMPLIANCE WITH OTHER OBLIGATIONS.—Downgrading or disposing of a facility under this section does not relieve a rail carrier from complying with its other common carrier or legal obligations related to the facility.

(Pub. L. 103–272, §1(e), July 5, 1994, 108 Stat. 913; Pub. L. 105–134, title I, §162, Dec. 2, 1997, 111 Stat. 2578.)

§24310. MANAGEMENT ACCOUNTABILITY

(a) IN GENERAL.—Within 3 years after the date of enactment of the Passenger Rail Investment and Improvement Act of 2008, and 2 years thereafter, the Inspector General of the Department of Transportation shall complete an overall assessment of the progress made by Amtrak management and the Department of Transportation in implementing the provisions of that Act.

(b) ASSESSMENT.—The management assessment undertaken by the Inspector General may include a review of—

(1) effectiveness in improving annual financial planning;

(2) effectiveness in implementing improved financial accounting;

(3) efforts to implement minimum train performance standards;

(4) progress maximizing revenues, minimizing Federal subsidies, and improving financial results; and

(5) any other aspect of Amtrak operations the Inspector General finds appropriate to review.

(Added Pub. L. 110–432, div. B, title II, §221(a), Oct. 16, 2008, 122 Stat. 4931.)

§24311. ACQUIRING INTERESTS IN PROPERTY BY EMINENT DOMAIN

(a) GENERAL AUTHORITY.—(1) To the extent financial resources are available, Amtrak may acquire by eminent domain under subsection (b) of this section interests in property—

(A) necessary for intercity rail passenger transportation, except property of a rail carrier, a State, a political subdivision of a State, or a governmental authority; or

(B) requested by the Secretary of Transportation in carrying out the Secretary's duty to design and build an intermodal transportation terminal at Union Station in the District of Columbia if the Secretary assures Amtrak that the Secretary will reimburse Amtrak.

(2) Amtrak may exercise the power of eminent domain only if it cannot—

(A) acquire the interest in the property by contract; or

(B) agree with the owner on the purchase price for the interest.

(b) CIVIL ACTIONS.—(1) A civil action to acquire an interest in property by eminent domain under subsection (a) of this section must be brought in the district court of the United States for the judicial district in which the property is located or, if a single piece of property is located in more than one judicial district, in any judicial district in which any piece of the property is located. An interest is condemned and taken by Amtrak for its use when a declaration of taking is filed under this subsection and an amount of money estimated in the declaration to be just compensation for the interest is deposited in the court. The declaration may be filed with the complaint in the action or at any time before judgment. The declaration must contain or be accompanied by—

(A) a statement of the public use for which the interest is taken;

(B) a description of the property sufficient to identify it;

(C) a statement of the interest in the property taken;

(D) a plan showing the interest taken; and

(E) a statement of the amount of money Amtrak estimates is just compensation for the interest.

(2) When the declaration is filed and the deposit is made under paragraph (1) of this subsection, title to the property vests in Amtrak in fee simple absolute or in the lesser interest shown in the declaration, and the right to the money vests in the person entitled to the money. When the declaration is filed, the court may decide—

(A) the time by which, and the terms under which, possession of the property is given to Amtrak; and

(B) the disposition of outstanding charges related to the property.

(3) After a hearing, the court shall make a finding on the amount that is just compensation for the interest in the property and enter judgment awarding that amount and interest on it. The rate of interest is 6 percent a year and is computed on the amount of the award less the amount deposited in the court from the date of taking to the date of payment.

(4) On application of a party, the court may order immediate payment of any part of the amount deposited in the court for the compensation to be awarded. If the award is more than the amount received, the court shall enter judgment against Amtrak for the deficiency.

(c) AUTHORITY TO CONDEMN RAIL CARRIER PROPERTY INTERESTS.—(1) If Amtrak and a rail carrier cannot agree on a sale to Amtrak of an interest in property of a rail carrier necessary for intercity rail passenger transportation, Amtrak may apply to the Surface Transportation Board for an order establishing the need of Amtrak for the interest and requiring the carrier to convey the interest on reasonable terms, including just compensation. The need of Amtrak is deemed to be established, and the Board, after holding an expedited proceeding and not later than 120 days after receiving the application, shall order the interest conveyed unless the Board decides that—

(A) conveyance would impair significantly the ability of the carrier to carry out its obligations as a common carrier; and

(B) the obligations of Amtrak to provide modern, efficient, and economical rail passenger transportation can be met adequately by acquiring an interest in other property, either by sale or by exercising its right of eminent domain under subsection (a) of this section.

(2) If the amount of compensation is not determined by the date of the Board's order, the order shall require, as part of the compensation, interest at 6 percent a year from the date

prescribed for the conveyance until the compensation is paid.

(3) Amtrak subsequently may reconvey to a third party an interest conveyed to Amtrak under this subsection or prior comparable provision of law if the Board decides that the reconveyance will carry out the purposes of this part, regardless of when the proceeding was brought (including a proceeding pending before a United States court on November 28, 1990).

(Pub. L. 103–272, §1(e), July 5, 1994, 108 Stat. 915; Pub. L. 112–141, div. C, title II, §32932(c)(2), July 6, 2012, 126 Stat. 829.)

§24312. LABOR STANDARDS

(a) PREVAILING WAGES AND HEALTH AND SAFETY STANDARDS.—Amtrak shall ensure that laborers and mechanics employed by contractors and subcontractors in construction work financed under an agreement made under section 24308(a) of this title will be paid wages not less than those prevailing on similar construction in the locality, as determined by the Secretary of Labor under sections 3141–3144, 3146, and 3147 of title 40. Amtrak may make such an agreement only after being assured that required labor standards will be maintained on the construction work. Health and safety standards prescribed by the Secretary under section 3704 of title 40 apply to all construction work performed under such an agreement, except for construction work performed by a rail carrier.

(b) WAGE RATES.—Wage rates in a collective bargaining agreement negotiated under the Railway Labor Act (45 U.S.C. 151 et seq.) are deemed to comply with sections 3141–3144, 3146, and 3147 of title 40.

(c) AVAILABILITY OF STATION AGENTS.—

(1) IN GENERAL.—Except as provided in paragraph (2), beginning on the date that is 1 year after the date of enactment of the Passenger Rail Expansion and Rail Safety Act of 2021, Amtrak shall ensure that at least 1 Amtrak ticket agent is employed at each station building—

(A) that Amtrak owns, or operates service through, as part of a long-distance or Northeast Corridor passenger service route;

(B) where at least 1 Amtrak ticket agent was employed on or after October 1, 2017; and

(C) for which an average of 40 passengers boarded or deboarded an Amtrak train per day during all of the days in fiscal year 2017 when the station was serviced by Amtrak, regardless of the number of Amtrak trains servicing the station per day.

(2) EXCEPTION.—Paragraph (1) shall not apply to any station building in which a commuter rail ticket agent has the authority to sell Amtrak tickets.

(Pub. L. 103–272, §1(e), July 5, 1994, 108 Stat. 916; Pub. L. 105–134, title I, §§101(f), 105(c), 121(a), Dec. 2, 1997, 111 Stat. 2572–2574; Pub. L. 107–217, §3(n)(4), Aug. 21, 2002, 116 Stat. 1302; Pub. L. 117–58, div. B, title II, §22203, Nov. 15, 2021, 135 Stat. 698.)

§24313. RAIL SAFETY SYSTEM PROGRAM

In consultation with rail labor organizations, Amtrak shall maintain a rail safety system program for employees working on property owned by Amtrak. The program shall be a model for other rail carriers to use in developing safety programs. The program shall

[§24314. Repealed. Pub. L. 105–134, title IV,
§404, Dec. 2, 1997, 111 Stat. 2586]

CHAPTER 243—AMTRAK

include—

(1) periodic analyses of accident information, including primary and secondary causes;

(2) periodic evaluations of the activities of the program, particularly specific steps taken in response to an accident;

(3) periodic reports on amounts spent for occupational health and safety activities of the program;

(4) periodic reports on reduced costs and personal injuries because of accident prevention activities of the program;

(5) periodic reports on direct accident costs, including claims related to accidents; and

(6) reports and evaluations of other information Amtrak considers appropriate.

(Pub. L. 103–272, §1(e), July 5, 1994, 108 Stat. 917.)

[§24314. Repealed. Pub. L. 105–134, title IV, §404, Dec. 2, 1997, 111 Stat. 2586]

Section, Pub. L. 103–272, §1(e), July 5, 1994, 108 Stat. 917; Pub. L. 104–287, §5(48), Oct. 11, 1996, 110 Stat. 3393, related to Amtrak developing plan for demonstrating new technology that may increase train speed in intercity rail passenger system.

§24315. Reports and audits

(a) Amtrak Annual Operations Report.—Not later than February 15 of each year, Amtrak shall submit to Congress a report that—

(1) for each route on which Amtrak provided intercity rail passenger transportation during the prior fiscal year, includes information on—

(A) ridership;

(B) passenger-miles;

(C) the short-term avoidable profit or loss for each passenger-mile;

(D) the revenue-to-cost ratio;

(E) revenues;

(F) the United States Government subsidy;

(G) the subsidy not provided by the United States Government;

(H) on-time performance; and

(I) any change made to a route's or service's frequency or station stops;

(2) provides relevant information about a decision to pay an officer of Amtrak more than the rate for level I of the Executive Schedule under section 5312 of title 5; and

(3) specifies—

(A) significant operational problems Amtrak identifies; and

(B) proposals by Amtrak to solve those problems.

(b) Amtrak General and Legislative Annual Report.—(1) Not later than February 15 of each year, Amtrak shall submit to the President and Congress a complete report of its operations, activities, and accomplishments, including a statement of revenues and expenditures for the prior fiscal year. The report—

(A) shall include a discussion and accounting of Amtrak's success in meeting the goal described in section 24902(a);

(B) may include recommendations for legislation, including the amount of financial assistance needed for operations and capital improvements, the method of computing the assistance, and the sources of the assistance;

(C) shall incorporate the category described in section 24319(c)(2)(C);

(D) shall include an action plan for bringing Amtrak-served stations that are not in compliance with the Americans with Disabilities Act of 1990 (42 U.S.C. 12101 et seq.) into compliance with such Act, as required by the settlement agreement entered into in 2020 between Amtrak and the Department of Justice;

(E) shall include a status report on—

(i) Amtrak-served stations for which Amtrak is solely responsible for compliance with such Act based on a station assessment carried out by Amtrak, including a timeline for any required compliance with such Act, as required by the settlement agreement;

(ii) Amtrak-served stations for which Amtrak has a shared responsibility for compliance with such Act based on a station assessment carried out by Amtrak or by the party responsible for such compliance, including a timeline for any required compliance with such Act for the portions of the station for which Amtrak is the responsible party consistent with the terms of the settlement agreement, identifying who is responsible for compliance (and the status of the compliance of each responsible party with such Act) for such portions and the timeline for compliance in cases in which Amtrak is not the responsible party; and

(iii) the status of compliance with such Act for all Amtrak-served stations for which Amtrak is not the responsible party, nor is responsible for a portion of the station, and identify the entity or entities that have responsibility for compliance with such Act, based on a station assessment carried out by Amtrak or the party responsible under such Act.

(2) Amtrak may submit reports to the President and Congress at other times Amtrak considers desirable.

(3) Amtrak may meet the requirements described in clauses (ii) and (iii) of paragraph (1)(E) by demonstrating that Amtrak took reasonable measures to obtain cooperation from responsible entities.

(4) Amtrak shall submit the action plan and status report required under subparagraphs (D) and (E) of paragraph (1)—

(A) annually while the settlement agreement referred to in paragraph (1)(D) is in effect; and

(B) every 5 years beginning on the first day the settlement is no longer in effect.

(c) SECRETARY'S REPORT ON EFFECTIVENESS OF THIS PART.—The Secretary of Transportation shall prepare a report on the effectiveness of this part in meeting the requirements for a balanced transportation system in the United States. The report may include recommendations for legislation. The Secretary shall include this report as part of the annual report the Secretary submits under section 308(a) of this title.

(d) INDEPENDENT AUDITS.—An independent certified public accountant shall audit the financial statements of Amtrak each year. The audit shall be carried out at the place at which the financial statements normally are kept and under generally accepted auditing standards. A report of the audit shall be included in the report required by subsection (a) of this section.

(e) COMPTROLLER GENERAL AUDITS.—The Comptroller General may conduct performance audits of the activities and transactions of Amtrak. Each audit shall be conducted at the place at which the Comptroller General decides and under generally accepted management principles. The Comptroller General may prescribe regulations governing the audit.

(f) AVAILABILITY OF RECORDS AND PROPERTY OF AMTRAK AND RAIL CARRIERS.—Amtrak and, if required by the Comptroller General, a rail carrier with which Amtrak has made a contract for intercity rail passenger transportation shall make available for an audit under subsection (d) or (e) of this section all records and property of, or used by, Amtrak or the carrier that are necessary for the audit. Amtrak and the carrier shall provide facilities for verifying transactions with the balances or securities held by depositories, fiscal agents, and custodians. Amtrak and the carrier may keep all reports and property.

(g) COMPTROLLER GENERAL'S REPORT TO CONGRESS.—The Comptroller General shall submit to Congress a report on each audit, giving comments and information necessary to inform Congress on the financial operations and condition of Amtrak and recommendations related to those operations and conditions. The report also shall specify any financial transaction or undertaking the Comptroller General considers is carried out without authority of law. When the Comptroller General submits a report to Congress, the Comptroller General shall submit a copy of it to the President, the Secretary, and Amtrak at the same time.

(h) ACCESS TO RECORDS AND ACCOUNTS.—A State shall have access to Amtrak's records, accounts, and other necessary documents used to determine the amount of any payment to Amtrak required of the State.

(Pub. L. 103–272, §1(e), July 5, 1994, 108 Stat. 918; Pub. L. 105–134, title II, §206, Dec. 2, 1997, 111 Stat. 2584; Pub. L. 117–58, div. B, title II, §§22204(a), 22206(c)(1), Nov. 15, 2021, 135 Stat. 699, 702; Pub. L. 118–205, §2, Dec. 23, 2024, 138 Stat. 2697.)

§24316. PLANS TO ADDRESS NEEDS OF FAMILIES OF PASSENGERS INVOLVED IN RAIL PASSENGER ACCIDENTS

(a) SUBMISSION OF PLAN.—Not later than 6 months after the date of the enactment of the Rail Safety Improvement Act of 2008, a rail passenger carrier shall submit to the Chairman of the National Transportation Safety Board, the Secretary of Transportation, and the Secretary of Homeland Security a plan for addressing the needs of the families of passengers involved in any rail passenger accident involving a rail passenger carrier intercity train and resulting in any loss of life.

(b) CONTENTS OF PLANS.—A plan to be submitted by a rail passenger carrier under subsection (a) shall include, at a minimum, the following:

(1) A process by which a rail passenger carrier will maintain and provide to the National Transportation Safety Board, the Secretary of Transportation, and the Secretary of Homeland Security immediately upon request, a list (which is based on the best

available information at the time of the request) of the names of the passengers aboard the train (whether or not such names have been verified), and will periodically update the list. The plan shall include a procedure, with respect to unreserved trains and passengers not holding reservations on other trains, for the rail passenger carrier to use reasonable efforts to ascertain the names of passengers aboard a train involved in an accident.

(2) A process for notifying the families of the passengers, before providing any public notice of the names of the passengers, either by utilizing the services of the organization designated for the accident under section 1139(a)(2) of this title or the services of other suitably trained individuals.

(3) A plan for creating and publicizing a reliable, toll-free telephone number within 4 hours after such an accident occurs, and for providing staff, to handle calls from the families of the passengers.

(4) A process for providing the notice described in paragraph (2) to the family of a passenger as soon as the rail passenger carrier has verified that the passenger was aboard the train (whether or not the names of all of the passengers have been verified).

(5) An assurance that, upon request of the family of a passenger, the rail passenger carrier will inform the family of whether the passenger's name appeared on any preliminary passenger manifest for the train involved in the accident.

(6) A process by which the family of each passenger will be consulted about the disposition of all remains and personal effects of the passenger within the control of the rail passenger carrier and by which any possession of the passenger within the control of the rail passenger carrier (regardless of its condition)—

(A) will be retained by the rail passenger carrier for at least 18 months; and

(B) will be returned to the family unless the possession is needed for the accident investigation or any criminal investigation.

(7) A process by which the treatment of the families of nonrevenue passengers will be the same as the treatment of the families of revenue passengers.

(8) An assurance that the rail passenger carrier will provide adequate training to the employees and agents of the carrier to meet the needs of survivors and family members following an accident.

(9) An assurance that the family of each passenger or other person killed in the accident will be consulted about construction by the rail passenger carrier of any monument to the passengers, including any inscription on the monument.

(10) An assurance that the rail passenger carrier will work with any organization designated under section 1139(a)(2) of this title on an ongoing basis to ensure that families of passengers receive an appropriate level of services and assistance following each accident.

(11) An assurance that the rail passenger carrier will provide reasonable compensation to any organization designated under section 1139(a)(2) of this title for services provided by the organization.

(c) Use of Information.—Neither the National Transportation Safety Board, the Secretary of Transportation, the Secretary of Homeland Security, nor a rail passenger carrier may release to the public any personal information on a list obtained under subsection (b)(1), but may provide information on the list about a passenger to the passenger's family members to the extent that the Board or a rail passenger carrier considers appropriate.

(d) LIMITATION ON STATUTORY CONSTRUCTION.—

(1) RAIL PASSENGER CARRIERS.—Nothing in this section may be construed as limiting the actions that a rail passenger carrier may take, or the obligations that a rail passenger carrier may have, in providing assistance to the families of passengers involved in a rail passenger accident.

(2) INVESTIGATIONAL AUTHORITY OF BOARD AND SECRETARY.—Nothing in this section shall be construed to abridge the authority of the Board or the Secretary of Transportation to investigate the causes or circumstances of any rail accident, including the development of information regarding the nature of injuries sustained and the manner in which they were sustained, for the purpose of determining compliance with existing laws and regulations or identifying means of preventing similar injuries in the future.

(e) LIMITATION ON LIABILITY.—A rail passenger carrier shall not be liable for damages in any action brought in a Federal or State court arising out of the performance of the rail passenger carrier in preparing or providing a passenger list, or in providing information concerning a train reservation, pursuant to a plan submitted by the rail passenger carrier under subsection (b), unless such liability was caused by conduct of the rail passenger carrier which was grossly negligent or which constituted intentional misconduct.

(f) DEFINITIONS.—In this section, the terms "passenger" and "rail passenger accident" have the meaning given those terms by section 1139 of this title.

(g) FUNDING.—Out of funds appropriated pursuant to section 20117(a)(1)(A), there shall be made available to the Secretary of Transportation $500,000 for fiscal year 2010 to carry out this section. Amounts made available pursuant to this subsection shall remain available until expended.

(Added Pub. L. 110–432, div. A, title V, §502(a), Oct. 16, 2008, 122 Stat. 4897; amended Pub. L. 118–63, title XII, §1215(d), May 16, 2024, 138 Stat. 1430.)

§24317. ACCOUNTS

(a) PURPOSE.—The purpose of this section is to—

(1) promote the effective use and stewardship by Amtrak of Amtrak revenues, Federal, State, and third party investments, appropriations, grants and other forms of financial assistance, and other sources of funds; and

(2) enhance the transparency of the assignment of revenues, including Federal grant funds, and costs among Amtrak service lines while ensuring the health of the Northeast Corridor and National Network.

(b) ACCOUNT STRUCTURE.—

(1) IN GENERAL.—The Secretary of Transportation, in consultation with Amtrak, shall define, maintain, and periodically update an account structure and improvements to accounting methodologies, as necessary, to support the Northeast Corridor and the National Network.

(2) NOTIFICATION OF SUBSTANTIVE CHANGES.—The Secretary shall notify the Committee on Commerce, Science, and Transportation of the Senate, the Committee on Appropriations of the Senate, the Committee on Transportation and Infrastructure of the House of Representatives, and the Committee on Appropriations of the House of Representatives regarding any substantive changes made to the account structure, including changes to—

(A) the service lines described in section 24320(b)(1); and

(B) the asset lines described in section 24320(c)(1).

(c) FINANCIAL SOURCES.—In defining, maintaining, and updating the account structure and improvements to accounting methodologies required under subsection (b), the Secretary shall ensure, to the greatest extent practicable, that Amtrak assigns the following:

(1) For the Northeast Corridor account, all revenues, appropriations, grants and other forms of financial assistance, compensation, and other sources of funds associated with the Northeast Corridor, including—

(A) grant funds appropriated for the Northeast Corridor pursuant to section 11101(a) of the Passenger Rail Reform and Investment Act of 2015 or any subsequent Act;

(B) compensation received from commuter rail passenger transportation providers for such providers' share of capital and operating costs on the Northeast Corridor provided to Amtrak pursuant to section 24905(c); and

(C) any operating surplus of the Northeast Corridor, as allocated pursuant to section 24318.

(2) For the National Network account, all revenues, appropriations, grants and other forms of financial assistance, compensation, and other sources of funds associated with the National Network, including—

(A) grant funds appropriated for the National Network pursuant to section 11101(b) of the Passenger Rail Reform and Investment Act of 2015 or any subsequent Act;

(B) compensation received from States provided to Amtrak pursuant to section 209 of the Passenger Rail Investment and Improvement Act of 2008 (42 U.S.C. 24101 note); [1] and

(C) any operating surplus of the National Network, as allocated pursuant to section 24318.

(d) FINANCIAL USES.—In defining, maintaining, and updating the account structure and improvements to accounting methodologies required under subsection (b), the Secretary shall ensure, to the greatest extent practicable, that amounts assigned to the Northeast Corridor and National Network accounts shall be used by Amtrak for the following:

(1) For the Northeast Corridor, all associated costs, including—

(A) operating activities;

(B) capital activities as described in section 24904(a)(2)(E);

(C) acquiring, rehabilitating, manufacturing, remanufacturing, overhauling, or improving equipment and associated facilities used for intercity rail passenger transportation by Northeast Corridor train services;

(D) payment of principal and interest on loans for capital projects described in this paragraph or for capital leases attributable to the Northeast Corridor;

(E) other capital projects on the Northeast Corridor, determined appropriate by the Secretary, and consistent with section 24905(c)(1)(A)(i); and

(F) if applicable, capital projects described in section 24904(b).

(2) For the National Network, all associated costs, including—

(A) operating activities;

(B) capital activities; and

(C) the payment of principal and interest on loans or capital leases attributable to the National Network.

(e) IMPLEMENTATION AND REPORTING.—

(1) IN GENERAL.—Amtrak, in consultation with the Secretary of Transportation, shall maintain and implement any account structures and improvements defined under subsection (b) to enable Amtrak to produce sources and uses statements for each of the service lines described in section 24320(b)(1) and, as appropriate, each of the asset lines described in section 24320(c)(1), that identify sources and uses of revenues, appropriations, and transfers between accounts.

(2) UPDATED SOURCES AND USES STATEMENTS.—Not later than 30 days after the implementation of subsection (b), and monthly thereafter, Amtrak shall submit to the Secretary of Transportation updated sources and uses statements for each of the service lines and asset lines referred to in paragraph (1). The Secretary and Amtrak may agree to a different frequency of reporting.

(f) ACCOUNT MANAGEMENT.—For the purposes of account management, Amtrak may transfer funds between the Northeast Corridor account and National Network account without prior notification and approval under subsection (g) if such transfers—

(1) do not materially impact Amtrak's ability to achieve its anticipated financial, capital, and operating performance goals for the fiscal year; and

(2) would not materially change any grant agreement entered into pursuant to section 24319(d), or other agreements made pursuant to applicable Federal law.

(g) TRANSFER AUTHORITY.—

(1) IN GENERAL.—If Amtrak determines that a transfer between the accounts defined under subsection (b) does not meet the account management standards established under subsection (f), Amtrak may transfer funds between the Northeast Corridor and National Network accounts if—

(A) Amtrak notifies the Amtrak Board of Directors, including the Secretary, at least 10 days prior to the expected date of transfer; and

(B) solely for a transfer that will materially change a grant agreement, the Secretary approves.

(2) REPORT.—Not later than 5 days after the Amtrak Board of Directors receives notification from Amtrak under paragraph (1)(A), the Board shall transmit to the Secretary, the Committee on Transportation and Infrastructure and the Committee on

Appropriations of the House of Representatives, and the Committee on Commerce, Science, and Transportation and the Committee on Appropriations of the Senate, a report that includes—

(A) the amount of the transfer; and

(B) a detailed explanation of the reason for the transfer, including—

(i) the effects on Amtrak services funded by the account from which the transfer is drawn, in comparison to a scenario in which no transfer was made; and

(ii) the effects on Amtrak services funded by the account receiving the transfer, in comparison to a scenario in which no transfer was made.

(3) NOTIFICATIONS.—Not later than 5 days after the date that Amtrak notifies the Amtrak Board of Directors of a transfer under paragraph (1) to or from an account, Amtrak shall transmit to the State-Supported Route Committee and Northeast Corridor Commission a letter that includes the information described under subparagraphs (A) and (B) of paragraph (2).

(h) DEFINITION OF NORTHEAST CORRIDOR.—Notwithstanding section 24102, for purposes of this section, the term "Northeast Corridor" means the Northeast Corridor main line between Boston, Massachusetts, and the District of Columbia, and facilities and services used to operate and maintain that line.

(Added Pub. L. 114–94, div. A, title XI, §11201(a), Dec. 4, 2015, 129 Stat. 1625; amended Pub. L. 117–58, div. B, title II, §22205, Nov. 15, 2021, 135 Stat. 699.)

[1] *See References in Text note below.*

§24318. COSTS AND REVENUES

(a) ALLOCATION.—Amtrak shall establish and maintain internal controls to ensure Amtrak's costs, revenues, and other compensation are appropriately allocated to the Northeast Corridor, including train services or infrastructure, or the National Network, including proportional shares of common and fixed costs.

(b) RULE OF CONSTRUCTION.—Nothing in this section shall be construed to limit the ability of Amtrak to enter into an agreement with 1 or more States to allocate operating and capital costs under section 209 of the Passenger Rail Investment and Improvement Act of 2008 (49 U.S.C. 24101 note).

(c) DEFINITION OF NORTHEAST CORRIDOR.—Notwithstanding section 24102, for purposes of this section, the term "Northeast Corridor" means the Northeast Corridor main line between Boston, Massachusetts, and the District of Columbia, and facilities and services used to operate and maintain that line.

(Added Pub. L. 114–94, div. A, title XI, §11202(a), Dec. 4, 2015, 129 Stat. 1628; amended Pub. L. 117–58, div. B, title II, §22206(a), Nov. 15, 2021, 135 Stat. 700.)

§24319. GRANT PROCESS AND REPORTING

(a) PROCEDURES FOR GRANT REQUESTS.—The Secretary of Transportation shall—

(1) establish and maintain substantive and procedural requirements, including schedules, for grant requests under this section; and

(2) report any changes to such procedures to—

(A) the Committee on Commerce, Science, and Transportation of the Senate;

(B) the Committee on Appropriations of the Senate;

(C) the Committee on Transportation and Infrastructure of the House of Representatives; and

(D) the Committee on Appropriations of the House of Representatives.

(b) GRANT REQUESTS.—Amtrak shall transmit to the Secretary a grant request annually, or as additionally required, for Federal funds appropriated to the Secretary of Transportation for the use of Amtrak.

(c) CONTENTS.—

(1) IN GENERAL.—Each grant request under subsection (b) shall, as applicable—

(A) categorize and identify, by source, the Federal funds and program income that will be used for the upcoming fiscal year for each of the Northeast Corridor and National Network in 1 of the categories or subcategories set forth in paragraph (2);

(B) describe the operations, services, programs, projects, and other activities to be funded within each of the categories set forth in paragraph (2), including—

(i) the estimated scope, schedule, and budget necessary to complete each project and program; and

(ii) the performance measures used to quantify expected and actual project outcomes and benefits, aggregated by fiscal year, project milestone, and any other appropriate grouping; and

(C) describe the status of efforts to improve Amtrak's safety culture.

(2) GRANT CATEGORIES.—

(A) OPERATING EXPENSES.—Each grant request to use Federal funds for operating expenses shall—

(i) include estimated net operating costs not covered by other Amtrak revenue sources;

(ii) specify Federal funding requested for each service line described in section 24320(b)(1); and

(iii) be itemized by route.

(B) DEBT SERVICE.—A grant request to use Federal funds for expenses related to debt, including payment of principle and interest, as allowed under section 205 of the Passenger Rail Investment and Improvement Act of 2008 (Public Law 110–432; 49 U.S.C. 24101 note).

(C) CAPITAL.—A grant request to use Federal funds and program income for capital expenses shall include capital projects and programs primarily associated with—

(i) normalized capital replacement programs, including regularly recurring work programs implemented on a systematic basis on classes of physical railroad assets, such as track, structures, electric traction and power systems, rolling stock, and communications and signal systems, to maintain and sustain the condition and performance of such assets to support continued railroad operations;

(ii) improvement projects to support service and safety enhancements, including discrete projects implemented in accordance with a fixed scope, schedule, and budget that result in enhanced or new infrastructure, equipment, or facilities;

(iii) backlog capital replacement projects, including discrete projects implemented in accordance with a fixed scope, schedule, and budget that primarily replace or rehabilitate major infrastructure assets, including tunnels, bridges, stations, and similar assets, to reduce the state of good repair backlog on the Amtrak network;

(iv) strategic initiative projects, including discrete projects implemented in accordance with a fixed scope, schedule, and budget that primarily improve overall operational performance, lower costs, or otherwise improve Amtrak's corporate efficiency; and

(v) statutory, regulatory, or other legally mandated projects, including discrete projects implemented in accordance with a fixed scope, schedule, and budget that enable Amtrak to fulfill specific legal or regulatory mandates.

(D) CONTINGENCY.—A grant request to use Federal funds for operating and capital expense contingency shall include—

(i) contingency levels for specified activities and operations; and

(ii) a process for the utilization of such contingency.

(3) MODIFICATION OF CATEGORIES.—The Secretary of Transportation and Amtrak may jointly agree to modify the categories set forth in paragraph (2) if such modifications are necessary to improve the transparency, oversight, or delivery of projects funded through grant requests under this section.

(d) REVIEW AND APPROVAL.—

(1) THIRTY-DAY APPROVAL PROCESS.—

(A) IN GENERAL.—Not later than 30 days after the date that Amtrak submits a complete grant request under this section, the Secretary of Transportation shall finish a review of the request and provide notice to Amtrak that—

(i) the request is approved; or

(ii) the request is disapproved, including the reason for the disapproval and an explanation of any deficient items.

(B) GRANT AGREEMENT.—If a grant request is approved, the Secretary shall enter into a grant agreement with Amtrak.

(2) FIFTEEN-DAY MODIFICATION PERIOD.—Not later than 15 days after the date of a notice under paragraph (1)(A)(ii), Amtrak shall submit a modified request for the Secretary's review.

(3) MODIFIED REQUESTS.—Not later than 15 days after the date that Amtrak submits a modified request under paragraph (2), the Secretary shall either approve the modified

request, or, if the Secretary finds that the request is still incomplete or deficient, the Secretary shall identify in writing to the Committee on Commerce, Science, and Transportation and the Committee on Appropriations of the Senate and the Committee on Transportation and Infrastructure and the Committee on Appropriations of the House of Representatives the remaining deficiencies and recommend a process for resolving the outstanding portions of the request.

(e) PAYMENTS TO AMTRAK.—

(1) IN GENERAL.—A grant agreement entered into under subsection (d) shall specify the operations, services, programs, projects, and other activities to be funded by the grant, consistent with the categories required for Amtrak in a grant request under subsection (c)(1)(A). The grant agreement shall include provisions, consistent with the requirements of this chapter, to measure Amtrak's performance and ensure accountability in delivering the operations, services, programs, projects, and other activities to be funded by the grant.

(2) SCHEDULE.—Except as provided in paragraph (3), in each fiscal year for which amounts are appropriated to the Secretary for the use of Amtrak, and for which the Secretary and Amtrak have entered into a grant agreement under subsection (d), the Secretary shall disburse grant funds to Amtrak on the following schedule:

(A) 50 percent on October 1.

(B) 25 percent on January 1.

(C) 25 percent on April 1.

(3) EXCEPTIONS.—The Secretary may make a payment to Amtrak of appropriated funds—

(A) using an otherwise allowable approach to the method prescribed for a specific project or category of projects under paragraph (2) if the Secretary and Amtrak agree that a different payment method is necessary to more successfully implement and report on an operation, service, program, project, or other activity;

(B) more frequently than the schedule under paragraph (2) if Amtrak, for good cause, requests more frequent payment before the end of a payment period; or

(C) with a different frequency or in different percentage allocations in the event of a continuing resolution or in the absence of an appropriations Act for the duration of a fiscal year.

(f) AVAILABILITY OF AMOUNTS AND EARLY APPROPRIATIONS.—Amounts appropriated to the Secretary for the use of Amtrak shall remain available until expended. Amounts for capital acquisitions and improvements may be appropriated for a fiscal year before the fiscal year in which the amounts will be obligated.

(g) LIMITATIONS ON USE.—Amounts appropriated to the Secretary for the use of Amtrak may not be used to cross-subsidize operating losses or capital costs of commuter rail passenger or freight rail transportation.

(h) APPLICABLE LAWS AND REGULATIONS.—

(1) SINGLE AUDIT ACT OF 1984.—Notwithstanding section 24301(a)(3) of this title and section 7501(a)(13) of title 31, Amtrak shall be deemed a "non-Federal entity" for

purposes of chapter 75 of title 31.

(2) REGULATIONS AND GUIDANCE.—The Secretary of Transportation may apply some or all of the requirements set forth in the regulations and guidance promulgated by the Secretary relating to the management, administration, cost principles, and audit requirements for Federal awards.

(i) AMTRAK GRANT REPORTING.—The Secretary of Transportation shall determine the varying levels of detail and information that will be included in reports for operations, services, program, projects, program income, cash on hand, and other activities within each of the grant categories described in subsection (c)(2).

(j) DEFINITION OF NORTHEAST CORRIDOR.—Notwithstanding section 24102, for purposes of this section, the term "Northeast Corridor" means the Northeast Corridor main line between Boston, Massachusetts, and the District of Columbia, and facilities and services used to operate and maintain that line.

(Added Pub. L. 114–94, div. A, title XI, §11202(a), Dec. 4, 2015, 129 Stat. 1628; amended Pub. L. 115–420, §4(b)(1), Jan. 3, 2019, 132 Stat. 5444; Pub. L. 117–58, div. B, title II, §22206(b), Nov. 15, 2021, 135 Stat. 700.)

§24320. AMTRAK 5-YEAR SERVICE LINE AND ASSET LINE PLANS

(a) IN GENERAL.—

(1) FINAL PLANS.—Not later than February 15, 2020, and biennially thereafter, Amtrak shall submit to Congress and the Secretary of Transportation final 5-year service line plans and 5-year asset line plans prepared in accordance with this section. These final plans shall form the basis for Amtrak's general and legislative annual report to the President and Congress required by section 24315(b). Each plan shall cover a period of 5 fiscal years, beginning with the first fiscal year after the date on which the plan is completed. During each year in which Amtrak is not required to submit a plan under this paragraph, Amtrak shall submit to Congress updated financial sources and uses statements and forecasts with the annual report required under section 24315(b).

(2) FISCAL CONSTRAINT.—Each plan prepared under this section shall be based on funding levels authorized or otherwise available to Amtrak in a fiscal year. In the absence of an authorization or appropriation of funds for a fiscal year, the plans shall be based on the amount of funding available in the previous fiscal year, plus inflation. Amtrak may include an appendix to the asset line plan required under subsection (c) that describes any funding needs in excess of amounts authorized or otherwise available to Amtrak in a fiscal year.

(b) AMTRAK 5-YEAR SERVICE LINE PLANS.—

(1) AMTRAK SERVICE LINES.—Amtrak shall prepare a 5-year service line plan for each of the following service lines and services:

(A) Northeast Corridor train services.

(B) Amtrak State-supported train services.

(C) Long-distance train services operated by Amtrak.

(D) Ancillary services operated by Amtrak, including commuter operations and other revenue generating activities as determined by the Secretary in coordination with Amtrak.

(E) Infrastructure access services for use of Amtrak-owned or Amtrak-controlled infrastructure and facilities.

(2) CONTENTS OF 5-YEAR SERVICE LINE PLANS.—The 5-year service line plan for each service line shall include, at a minimum—

(A) a statement of Amtrak's objectives, goals, and service plan for the service line, in consultation with any entities that are contributing capital or operating funding to support passenger rail services within those service lines, and aligned with Amtrak's 5-year asset line plans under subsection (c);

(B) a detailed description of any plans to permanently change a route's or service's frequency or station stops for the service line;

(C) all projected revenues and expenditures for the service line, including identification of revenues and expenditures incurred by—

(i) passenger operations;

(ii) non-passenger operations that are directly related to the service line; and

(iii) governmental funding sources, including revenues and other funding received from States;

(D) projected ridership levels for all passenger operations;

(E) estimates of long-term and short-term debt and associated principal and interest payments (both current and forecasts);

(F) annual sources and uses statements and forecasts and balance sheets;

(G) a statement describing the methodologies and significant assumptions underlying estimates and forecasts;

(H) specific performance measures that demonstrate year over year changes in the results of Amtrak's operations;

(I) financial performance for each route, if deemed applicable by the Secretary, within each service line, including descriptions of the cash operating loss or contribution;

(J) specific costs and savings estimates resulting from reform initiatives;

(K) prior fiscal year and projected equipment reliability statistics; and

(L) an identification and explanation of any major adjustments made from previously-approved plans.

(3) 5-YEAR SERVICE LINE PLANS PROCESS.—In meeting the requirements of this section, Amtrak shall—

(A) not later than 180 days after the date of enactment of the Passenger Rail Expansion and Rail Safety Act of 2021, submit to the Secretary, for approval, a consultation process for the development of each service line plan that requires Amtrak to—

(i) consult with the Secretary in the development of the service line plans;

(ii) for the Northeast Corridor service line plan, consult with the Northeast Corridor Commission and transmit to the Commission the final plan under subsection (a)(1), and consult with other entities, as appropriate;

(iii) for the State-supported route service line plan, consult with the State-Supported Route Committee established under section 24712 and submit the final service line plan required under subsection (a)(1) to the State-Supported Route Committee;

(iv) for the long-distance route service line plan, consult with any States or Interstate Compacts that provide funding for such routes, as appropriate; and

(v) for the infrastructure access service line plan, consult with the Northeast Corridor Commission and other entities, as appropriate, and submit the final asset line plan under subsection (a)(1) to the Northeast Corridor Commission;

(B) ensure that Amtrak's general and legislative annual report, required under section 24315(b), to the President and Congress is consistent with the information in the 5-year service line plans; and

(C) identify the appropriate Amtrak officials that are responsible for each service line.

(4) 5-YEAR SERVICE LINE PLANS UPDATES.—Amtrak may modify the content to be included in the service line plans described in paragraph (1), upon the approval of the Secretary, if the Secretary determines that such modifications are necessary to improve the transparency, oversight, and delivery of Amtrak services and the use of Federal funds by Amtrak.

(5) DEFINITION OF NORTHEAST CORRIDOR.—Notwithstanding section 24102, for purposes of this section, the term "Northeast Corridor" means the Northeast Corridor main line between Boston, Massachusetts, and the District of Columbia, and facilities and services used to operate and maintain that line.

(c) AMTRAK 5-YEAR ASSET LINE PLANS.—

(1) ASSET LINES.—Amtrak shall prepare a 5-year asset line plan for each of the following asset lines:

(A) Transportation, including activities and resources associated with the operation and movement of Amtrak trains, onboard services, and amenities.

(B) Infrastructure, including all Amtrak-controlled Northeast Corridor assets and other Amtrak-owned infrastructure, and the associated facilities and maintenance-of-way equipment that support the operation, maintenance, and improvement of those assets.

(C) Equipment, including all Amtrak-controlled rolling stock, locomotives, and mechanical shop facilities that are used to overhaul equipment.

(D) Stations, including all Amtrak-controlled passenger rail stations and elements of other stations for which Amtrak has legal responsibility or intends to make capital investments.

(E) National assets, including national reservations, security, training and training centers, and other assets associated with Amtrak's national rail passenger transportation system.

(2) Contents of 5-year asset line plans.—Each asset line plan shall include, at a minimum—

(A) a summary of Amtrak's 5-year strategic plan for each asset line, including goals, objectives, any relevant performance metrics, and statutory or regulatory actions affecting the assets;

(B) an inventory of existing Amtrak capital assets, to the extent practicable, including information regarding shared use or ownership, if applicable;

(C) a prioritized list of proposed capital investments that—

(i) categorizes each capital project as being primarily associated with—

(I) normalized capital replacement;

(II) backlog capital replacement;

(III) improvements to support service enhancements or growth;

(IV) strategic initiatives that will improve overall operational performance, lower costs, or otherwise improve Amtrak's corporate efficiency; or

(V) statutory, regulatory, or other legal mandates;

(ii) identifies each project or program that is associated with more than 1 category described in clause (i); and

(iii) describes the anticipated business outcome of each project or program identified under this subparagraph, including an assessment of—

(I) the potential effect on passenger operations, safety, reliability, and resilience;

(II) the potential effect on Amtrak's ability to meet regulatory requirements if the project or program is not funded; and

(III) the benefits and costs;

(D) annual sources and uses statements and forecasts for each asset line; and

(E) other elements that Amtrak elects to include.

(3) 5-year asset line plan process.—In meeting the requirements of this subsection, Amtrak shall—

(A) not later than 180 days after the date of enactment of the Passenger Rail Expansion and Rail Safety Act of 2021, submit to the Secretary, for approval, a consultation process for the development of each asset line plan that requires Amtrak to—

(i) consult with each service line described in subsection (b)(1) in the preparation of each 5-year asset line plan and ensure integration of each 5-year asset line plan with the 5-year service line plans; and

(ii) consult with the Secretary of Transportation in the development of asset line plans and, as applicable, consult with the Northeast Corridor Commission, the State-Supported Route Committee, and owners of assets affected by 5-year asset line plans; and

(B) identify the appropriate Amtrak officials that are responsible for each asset line.

(4) 5-YEAR ASSET LINE PLAN UPDATES.—Amtrak may modify the content to be included in the asset line plans described in paragraph (1), on approval of the Secretary, if the Secretary determines that such modifications are necessary to improve the transparency, oversight, and delivery of Amtrak services and the use of Federal funds by Amtrak.

(5) EVALUATION OF NATIONAL ASSETS COSTS.—The Secretary shall—

(A) evaluate the costs and scope of all national assets, but shall not include corporate services (as defined pursuant to section 24317(b)); and

(B) determine the activities and costs that are—

(i) required in order to ensure the efficient operations of a national rail passenger system;

(ii) appropriate for allocation to 1 of the other Amtrak business lines; and

(iii) extraneous to providing an efficient national rail passenger system or are too costly relative to the benefits or performance outcomes they provide.

(6) DEFINITION OF NATIONAL ASSETS.—In this section, the term "national assets" means the Nation's core rail assets shared among Amtrak services, including national reservations, security, training and training centers, and other assets associated with Amtrak's national rail passenger transportation system.

(7) RESTRUCTURING OF NATIONAL ASSETS.—Not later than 1 year after the date of completion of the evaluation under paragraph (5), the Administrator of the Federal Railroad Administration, in consultation with the Amtrak Board of Directors, the governors of each relevant State, and the Mayor of the District of Columbia, or their designees, shall restructure or reallocate, or both, the national assets costs in accordance with the determination under that section, including making appropriate updates to Amtrak's cost accounting methodology and system.

(8) EXEMPTION.—

(A) IN GENERAL.—Upon written request from the Amtrak Board of Directors, the Secretary may exempt Amtrak from including in a plan required under this subsection any information described in paragraphs (1) and (2).

(B) PUBLIC AVAILABILITY.—The Secretary shall make available to the public on the Department's Internet Web site any exemption granted under subparagraph (A) and a detailed justification for granting such exemption.

(C) INCLUSION IN PLAN.—Amtrak shall include in the plan required under this subsection any request granted under subparagraph (A) and justification under subparagraph (B).

(d) STANDARDS TO PROMOTE FINANCIAL STABILITY.—In preparing plans under this section, Amtrak shall—

(1) apply sound budgetary practices, including reducing costs and other expenditures, improving productivity, increasing revenues, or combinations of such practices; and

(2) use the categories specified in the financial accounting and reporting system developed under section 203 of the Passenger Rail Investment and Improvement Act of 2008 (49 U.S.C. 24101 note).

(Added Pub. L. 114–94, div. A, title XI, §11203(a), Dec. 4, 2015, 129 Stat. 1630; amended Pub. L. 117–58, div. B, title II, §§22204(b), 22207(a), Nov. 15, 2021, 135 Stat. 699, 703.)

§24321. FOOD AND BEVERAGE SERVICE

(a) WORKING GROUP.—

(1) ESTABLISHMENT.—Not later than 180 days after enactment of the Passenger Rail Expansion and Rail Safety Act of 2021, Amtrak shall establish a working group to provide recommendations to improve Amtrak's onboard food and beverage service.

(2) MEMBERSHIP.—The working group shall consist of individuals representing—

(A) Amtrak;

(B) the labor organizations representing Amtrak employees who prepare or provide on-board food and beverage service;

(C) nonprofit organizations representing Amtrak passengers; and

(D) States that are providing funding for State-supported routes.

(b) REPORT.—Not later than 1 year after the establishment of the working group pursuant to subsection (a), the working group shall submit a report to the Committee on Commerce, Science, and Transportation of the Senate and the Committee on Transportation and Infrastructure of the House of Representatives containing recommendations for improving Amtrak's food and beverage service, including—

(1) ways to improve the financial performance of Amtrak;

(2) ways to increase and retain ridership;

(3) the differing needs of passengers traveling on long-distance routes, State supported routes, and the Northeast Corridor;

(4) Amtrak passenger survey data about the food and beverages offered on Amtrak trains;

(5) ways to incorporate local food and beverage items on State-supported routes; and

(6) any other issue that the working group determines to be appropriate.

(c) IMPLEMENTATION.—Not later than 180 days after the submission of the report pursuant to subsection (b), Amtrak shall submit a plan for implementing the recommendations of the working group, and an explanation for any of the working group's recommendations it does not agree with and does not plan on implementing to the Committee on Commerce, Science, and Transportation of the Senate and the Committee on Transportation and Infrastructure of the House of Representatives.

(d) SAVINGS CLAUSE.—Amtrak shall ensure that no Amtrak employee who held a position on a long-distance or Northeast Corridor route as of the date of enactment of the Passenger Rail Expansion and Rail Safety Act of 2021, is involuntarily separated because of the development and implementation of the plan required under this section.

(Added Pub. L. 114–94, div. A, title XI, §11207(a), Dec. 4, 2015, 129 Stat. 1638; amended Pub. L. 116–159, div. B, title I, §1104(a), Oct. 1, 2020, 134 Stat. 727; Pub. L. 117–58, div. B, title II, §22208(b)(1), Nov. 15, 2021, 135 Stat. 706.)

§24322. ROLLING STOCK PURCHASES

(a) IN GENERAL.—Prior to entering into any contract in excess of $100,000,000 for rolling stock and locomotive procurements Amtrak shall submit a business case analysis to the Secretary of Transportation, the Committee on Commerce, Science, and Transportation and the Committee on Appropriations of the Senate and the Committee on Transportation and Infrastructure and the Committee on Appropriations of the House of Representatives, on the utility of such procurements.

(b) CONTENTS.—The business case analysis shall—

(1) include a cost and benefit comparison that describes the total lifecycle costs and the anticipated benefits related to revenue, operational efficiency, reliability, and other factors;

(2) set forth the total payments by fiscal year;

(3) identify the specific source and amounts of funding for each payment, including Federal funds, State funds, Amtrak profits, Federal, State, or private loans or loan guarantees, and other funding;

(4) include an explanation of whether any payment under the contract will increase Amtrak's funding request in its general and legislative annual report required under section 24315(b) in a particular fiscal year; and

(5) describe how Amtrak will adjust the procurement if future funding is not available.

(c) RULE OF CONSTRUCTION.—Nothing in this section shall be construed as requiring Amtrak to disclose confidential information regarding a potential vendor's proposed pricing or other sensitive business information prior to contract execution or prohibiting Amtrak from entering into a contract after submission of a business case analysis under subsection (a).

(Added Pub. L. 114–94, div. A, title XI, §11208(a), Dec. 4, 2015, 129 Stat. 1639.)

§24323. PROHIBITION ON SMOKING ON AMTRAK TRAINS

(a) PROHIBITION.—Beginning on the date of enactment of this section, Amtrak shall prohibit smoking, including the use of electronic cigarettes, onboard all Amtrak trains.

(b) ELECTRONIC CIGARETTE DEFINED.—In this section, the term "electronic cigarette" means a device that delivers nicotine or other substances to a user of the device in the form of a vapor that is inhaled to simulate the experience of smoking.

(Added Pub. L. 117–58, div. B, title II, §22209(a), Nov. 15, 2021, 135 Stat. 707.)

[CHAPTER 244—TRANSFERRED]

[§§24401 TO 24408. RENUMBERED §§22901 TO 22908]

[§§24501 to 24506. Repealed. Pub. L. 105–134, title I, §106(a), Dec. 2, 1997, 111 Stat. 2573]

[CHAPTER 245—REPEALED]

[CHAPTER 245—REPEALED]

[§§24501 TO 24506. REPEALED. PUB. L. 105–134, TITLE I, §106(A), DEC. 2, 1997, 111 STAT. 2573]

Section 24501, Pub. L. 103–272, §1(e), July 5, 1994, 108 Stat. 919; Pub. L. 103–429, §6(21), Oct. 31, 1994, 108 Stat. 4379; Pub. L. 104–88, title III, §308(h), Dec. 29, 1995, 109 Stat. 947, related to status of Amtrak Commuter and applicable laws.

Section 24502, Pub. L. 103–272, §1(e), July 5, 1994, 108 Stat. 920, related to board of directors of Amtrak Commuter.

Section 24503, Pub. L. 103–272, §1(e), July 5, 1994, 108 Stat. 921, related to appointment and service of officers of Amtrak Commuter.

Section 24504, Pub. L. 103–272, §1(e), July 5, 1994, 108 Stat. 921, related to general authority of Amtrak Commuter.

Section 24505, Pub. L. 103–272, §1(e), July 5, 1994, 108 Stat. 921, related to Amtrak's rights and responsibilities as relating to commuter rail passenger transportation.

Section 24506, Pub. L. 103–272, §1(e), July 5, 1994, 108 Stat. 922, provided that certain powers and duties of Consolidated Rail Corporation were not affected by this chapter.

CHAPTER 247—AMTRAK ROUTE SYSTEM

---

[1] *So in original. Probably should be followed by a period.*

[2] *So in original. Does not conform to section catchline.*

§24701. NATIONAL RAIL PASSENGER TRANSPORTATION SYSTEM

Amtrak shall operate a national rail passenger transportation system which ties together existing and emergent regional rail passenger service and other intermodal passenger service.

(Pub. L. 103–272, §1(e), July 5, 1994, 108 Stat. 923; Pub. L. 105–134, title I, §101(a)(1), Dec. 2, 1997, 111 Stat. 2572.)

§24702. TRANSPORTATION REQUESTED BY STATES, AUTHORITIES, AND OTHER PERSONS

(a) CONTRACTS FOR TRANSPORTATION.—Amtrak may enter into a contract with a State, a regional or local authority, or another person for Amtrak to operate an intercity rail service or route not included in the national rail passenger transportation system upon such terms as the parties thereto may agree.

(b) DISCONTINUANCE.—Upon termination of a contract entered into under this section, or the cessation of financial support under such a contract by either party, Amtrak may discontinue such service or route, notwithstanding any other provision of law.

(Added Pub. L. 110–432, div. B, title II, §201(b)(1), Oct. 16, 2008, 122 Stat. 4910.)

[§§24703 TO 24705. REPEALED. PUB. L. 105–134, TITLE I, §§103–105(A), DEC. 2, 1997, 111 STAT. 2572, 2573]

Section 24703, Pub. L. 103–272, §1(e), July 5, 1994, 108 Stat. 924, provided route and service criteria for modifying or discontinuing routes.

Section 24704, Pub. L. 103–272, §1(e), July 5, 1994, 108 Stat. 925, related to application by States, regional or local authorities, or other persons requesting Amtrak to provide passenger rail service and criteria for decision.

Section 24705, Pub. L. 103–272, §1(e), July 5, 1994, 108 Stat. 926; Pub. L. 104–88, title III, §308(i), Dec. 29, 1995, 109 Stat. 947, related to providing service on routes recommended to be discontinued, criteria for deferring Secretary's recommendation, and providing short haul demonstration routes.

§24706. DISCONTINUANCE

(a) NOTICE OF DISCONTINUANCE.—(1) Except as provided in subsection (c), not later than 180 days before discontinuing service over a route, Amtrak shall give notice of the discontinuance in the way Amtrak decides will give a State, a regional or local authority, or another person the opportunity to agree to share or assume the cost of any part of the train, route, or service to be discontinued.

(2) Notice of the discontinuance under paragraph (1) shall be posted in all stations served by the train to be discontinued at least 14 days before the discontinuance.

(b) DISCONTINUANCE OR SUBSTANTIAL ALTERATION OF LONG-DISTANCE ROUTES.—Except as provided in subsection (c), in an emergency, or during maintenance or construction outages impacting Amtrak routes, Amtrak may not discontinue, reduce the frequency of, suspend, or substantially alter the route of rail service on any segment of any long-distance route in any fiscal year in which Amtrak receives adequate Federal funding for such route on the National Network.

(c) DISCONTINUANCE FOR LACK OF APPROPRIATIONS.—(1) Amtrak may discontinue service under subsection (a)(1) during—

(A) the first month of a fiscal year if the authorization of appropriations and the appropriations for Amtrak are not enacted at least 90 days before the beginning of the fiscal year; and

(B) the 30 days following enactment of an appropriation for Amtrak or a rescission of an appropriation.

(2) Amtrak shall notify each affected State or regional or local transportation authority of a discontinuance under this subsection as soon as possible after Amtrak decides to discontinue the service.

(d) CONGRESSIONAL NOTIFICATION OF DISCONTINUANCE.—Except as provided in subsection (c), not later than 210 days before discontinuing service over a route, Amtrak shall give written notice of such discontinuance to all of the members of Congress representing any State or district in which the discontinuance would occur.

(e) APPLICABILITY.—This section applies to all service over routes provided by Amtrak, notwithstanding any provision of section 24701 of this title or any other provision of this title except section 24702(b).

(Pub. L. 103–272, §1(e), July 5, 1994, 108 Stat. 927; Pub. L. 105–134, title I, §§101(c), 142(a), Dec. 2, 1997, 111 Stat. 2572, 2576; Pub. L. 110–432, div. B, title II, §201(d), Oct. 16, 2008, 122 Stat. 4910; Pub. L. 114–94, div. A, title XI, §11316(n)(1), Dec. 4, 2015, 129 Stat. 1678; Pub. L. 117–58, div. B, title II, §22210, Nov. 15, 2021, 135 Stat. 708.)

[§§24707, 24708. Repealed. Pub. L. 105–134, title I, §101(d), (e), Dec. 2, 1997, 111 Stat. 2572]

Section 24707, Pub. L. 103–272, §1(e), July 5, 1994, 108 Stat. 928, required annual route, financial, and performance reviews.

Section 24708, Pub. L. 103–272, §1(e), July 5, 1994, 108 Stat. 929, related to continuing, modifying, or discontinuing passenger transportation routes.

§24709. International transportation

Amtrak may develop and operate international intercity rail passenger transportation between the United States and Canada and between the United States and Mexico. The Secretary of Homeland Security, in cooperation with Amtrak, shall maintain, consistent with the effective enforcement of the immigration and customs laws, en route customs inspection and immigration procedures for international intercity rail passenger transportation that will—

(1) be convenient for passengers; and

(2) result in the quickest possible international intercity rail passenger transportation.

(Pub. L. 103–272, §1(e), July 5, 1994, 108 Stat. 929; Pub. L. 114–94, div. A, title XI, §11316(n)(2), Dec. 4, 2015, 129 Stat. 1679.)

§24710. Long-distance routes

(a) Annual Evaluation.—Using the financial and performance metrics developed under section 207 of the Passenger Rail Investment and Improvement Act of 2008, Amtrak shall—

(1) evaluate annually the financial and operating performance of each long-distance passenger rail route operated by Amtrak; and

(2) rank the overall performance of such routes for 2008 and identify each long-distance passenger rail route operated by Amtrak in 2008 according to its overall performance as belonging to the best performing third of such routes, the second best performing third of such routes, or the worst performing third of such routes.

(b) Performance Improvement Plan.—Amtrak shall develop and post on its website a performance improvement plan for its long-distance passenger rail routes to achieve financial and operating improvements based on the data collected through the application of the financial and performance metrics developed under section 207 of that Act. The plan shall address—

(1) on-time performance;

(2) scheduling, frequency, routes, and stops;

(3) the feasibility of restructuring service into connected corridor service;

(4) performance-related equipment changes and capital improvements;

(5) on-board amenities and service, including food, first class, and sleeping car service;

(6) State or other non-Federal financial contributions;

(7) improving financial performance;

(8) anticipated Federal funding of operating and capital costs; and

(9) other aspects of Amtrak's long-distance passenger rail routes that affect the financial, competitive, and functional performance of service on Amtrak's long-distance passenger rail routes.

(c) IMPLEMENTATION.—Amtrak shall implement the performance improvement plan developed under subsection (b)—

(1) beginning in fiscal year 2010 for those routes identified as being in the worst performing third under subsection (a)(2);

(2) beginning in fiscal year 2011 for those routes identified as being in the second best performing third under subsection (a)(2); and

(3) beginning in fiscal year 2012 for those routes identified as being in the best performing third under subsection (a)(2).

(d) ENFORCEMENT.—The Federal Railroad Administration shall monitor the development, implementation, and outcome of improvement plans under this section. If the Federal Railroad Administration determines that Amtrak is not making reasonable progress in implementing its performance improvement plan or, after the performance improvement plan is implemented under subsection (c)(1) in accordance with the terms of that plan, Amtrak has not achieved the outcomes it has established for such routes, under the plan for any calendar year, the Federal Railroad Administration—

(1) shall notify Amtrak, the Inspector General of the Department of Transportation, the Committee on Transportation and Infrastructure of the House of Representatives, and the Committee on Commerce, Science, and Transportation of the Senate of its determination under this subsection;

(2) shall provide Amtrak with an opportunity for a hearing with respect to that determination; and

(3) may withhold appropriated funds otherwise available to Amtrak for the operation of a route or routes from among the worst performing third of routes currently served by Amtrak on which Amtrak is not making reasonable progress, other than funds made available for passenger safety or security measures.

(Added Pub. L. 110–432, div. B, title II, §210(a), Oct. 16, 2008, 122 Stat. 4918.)

§24711. COMPETITIVE PASSENGER RAIL SERVICE PILOT PROGRAM

(a) IN GENERAL.—Not later than 18 months after the date of enactment of the Passenger Rail Reform and Investment Act of 2015, the Secretary of Transportation shall promulgate a rule to implement a pilot program for competitive selection of eligible petitioners described in subsection (b)(3) in lieu of Amtrak to operate not more than 3 long-distance routes (as defined in section 24102) operated by Amtrak on the date of enactment of such Act.

(b) PILOT PROGRAM REQUIREMENTS.—

(1) IN GENERAL.—The pilot program shall—

(A) allow a petitioner described in paragraph (3) to petition the Secretary to provide intercity rail passenger transportation over a long-distance route described in subsection (a) for an operation period of 4 years from the date of commencement of service by the winning bidder and, at the option of the Secretary, consistent with the rule promulgated under subsection (a), allow the contract to be renewed for 1 additional operation period of 4 years;

(B) require the Secretary to—

(i) notify the petitioner and Amtrak of receipt of the petition under subparagraph (A) and to publish in the Federal Register a notice of receipt not later than 30 days after the date of receipt;

(ii) establish a deadline, of not more than 120 days after the notice of receipt is published in the Federal Register under clause (i), by which both the petitioner and Amtrak, if Amtrak chooses to do so, would be required to submit a complete bid to provide intercity rail passenger transportation over the applicable route; and

(iii) upon selecting a winning bid, publish in the Federal Register the identity of the winning bidder, the long distance route that the bidder will operate, a detailed justification of the reasons why the Secretary selected the bid, and any other information the Secretary determines appropriate for public comment for a reasonable period of time not to exceed 30 days after the date on which the Secretary selects the bid;

(C) require that each bid—

(i) describe the capital needs, financial projections, and operational plans, including staffing plans, for the service, and such other factors as the Secretary considers appropriate; and

(ii) be made available by the winning bidder to the public after the bid award with any appropriate redactions for confidential or proprietary information;

(D) for a route that receives funding from a State or States, require that for each bid received from a petitioner described in paragraph (3), other than such State or States, the Secretary have the concurrence of the State or States that provide funding for that route; and

(E) for a winning bidder that is not or does not include Amtrak, require the Secretary to execute a contract not later than 270 days after the deadline established under subparagraph (B)(ii) and award to the winning bidder—

(i) subject to paragraphs (4) and (5), the right and obligation to provide intercity rail passenger transportation over that route subject to such performance standards as the Secretary may require; and

(ii) an operating subsidy, as determined by the Secretary, for—

(I) the first year at a level that does not exceed 90 percent of the level in effect for that specific route during the fiscal year preceding the fiscal year in which the petition was received, adjusted for inflation; and

(II) any subsequent years at the level calculated under subclause (I), adjusted for inflation.

(2) LIMITATION.—The requirements under paragraph (1)(E), including the amounts of operating subsidies in the first and any subsequent years under paragraph (1)(E)(ii), shall not apply to a winning bidder that is or includes Amtrak.

(3) ELIGIBLE PETITIONERS.—The following parties are eligible to submit petitions under paragraph (1):

(A) A rail carrier or rail carriers that own the infrastructure over which Amtrak operates a long-distance route, or another rail carrier that has a written agreement with a rail carrier or rail carriers that own such infrastructure.

(B) A State, group of States, or State-supported joint powers authority or other sub-State governance entity responsible for provision of intercity rail passenger transportation with a written agreement with the rail carrier or rail carriers that own the infrastructure over which Amtrak operates a long-distance route and that host or would host the intercity rail passenger transportation.

(C) A State, group of States, or State-supported joint powers authority or other sub-State governance entity responsible for provision of intercity rail passenger transportation and a rail carrier with a written agreement with another rail carrier or rail carriers that own the infrastructure over which Amtrak operates a long-distance route and that host or would host the intercity rail passenger transportation.

(4) PERFORMANCE STANDARDS.—The performance standards required under paragraph (1)(E)(i) shall meet or exceed the performance required of or achieved by Amtrak on the applicable route during the last fiscal year.

(5) AGREEMENT GOVERNING ACCESS ISSUES.—Unless the winning bidder already has applicable access rights or agreements in place or includes a rail carrier that owns the infrastructure used in the operation of the route, a winning bidder that is not or does not include Amtrak shall enter into a written agreement governing access issues between the winning bidder and the rail carrier or rail carriers that own the infrastructure over which the winning bidder would operate and that host or would host the intercity rail passenger transportation.

(c) ACCESS TO FACILITIES; EMPLOYEES.—If the Secretary awards the right and obligation to provide intercity rail passenger transportation over a route described in this section to an eligible petitioner—

(1) the Secretary shall, if necessary to carry out the purposes of this section, require Amtrak to provide access to the Amtrak-owned reservation system, stations, and facilities directly related to operations of the awarded routes to the eligible petitioner awarded a contract under this section, in accordance with subsection (g);

(2) an employee of any person, except as provided in a collective bargaining agreement, used by such eligible petitioner in the operation of a route under this section shall be considered an employee of that eligible petitioner and subject to the applicable Federal laws and regulations governing similar crafts or classes of employees of Amtrak; and

(3) the winning bidder shall provide hiring preference to qualified Amtrak employees displaced by the award of the bid, consistent with the staffing plan submitted by the bidder, and shall be subject to the grant conditions under section 22905.

(d) CESSATION OF SERVICE.—If an eligible petitioner awarded a route under this section ceases to operate the service or fails to fulfill an obligation under a contract required under subsection (b)(1)(E), the Secretary, in collaboration with the Surface Transportation Board, shall take any necessary action consistent with this title to enforce the contract and ensure the continued provision of service, including—

(1) the installment of an interim rail carrier;

(2) providing to the interim rail carrier under paragraph (1) an operating subsidy necessary to provide service; and

(3) rebidding the contract to operate the intercity rail passenger transportation.

(e) BUDGET AUTHORITY.—

(1) IN GENERAL.—The Secretary shall provide to a winning bidder that is not or does not include Amtrak and that is selected under this section any appropriations withheld under section 11101(e) of the Passenger Rail Reform and Investment Act of 2015, or any subsequent appropriation for the same purpose, necessary to cover the operating subsidy described in subsection (b)(1)(E)(ii).

(2) ATTRIBUTABLE COSTS.—If the Secretary selects a winning bidder that is not or does not include Amtrak, the Secretary shall provide to Amtrak an appropriate portion of the appropriations under section 11101(b) of the Passenger Rail Reform and Investment Act of 2015, or any subsequent appropriation for the same purpose, to cover any cost directly attributable to the termination of Amtrak service on the route and any indirect costs to Amtrak imposed on other Amtrak routes as a result of losing service on the route operated by the winning bidder. Any amount provided by the Secretary to Amtrak under this paragraph shall not be deducted from or have any effect on the operating subsidy described in subsection (b)(1)(E)(ii).

(f) REPORTING.—If the Secretary does not promulgate the final rule before the deadline under subsection (a), the Secretary shall, not later than 19 months after the date of enactment of the Passenger Rail Reform and Investment Act of 2015 and every 90 days thereafter until the rule is complete, notify the Committee on Commerce, Science, and Transportation of the Senate and the Committee on Transportation and Infrastructure of the House of Representatives in writing—

(1) the reasons why the rule has not been issued;

(2) a plan for completing the rule as soon as reasonably practicable; and

(3) the estimated date of completion of the rule.

(g) DISPUTES.—

(1) PETITIONING SURFACE TRANSPORTATION BOARD.—If Amtrak and the eligible petitioner awarded a route under this section cannot agree upon terms to carry out subsection (c)(1), either party may petition the Surface Transportation Board for a determination as to—

(A) whether access to Amtrak's facility or equipment, or the provisions of services by Amtrak, is necessary under subsection (c)(1); and

(B) whether the operation of Amtrak's other services will not be unreasonably impaired by such access.

(2) SURFACE TRANSPORTATION BOARD DETERMINATION.—If the Surface Transportation

Board determines access to Amtrak's facilities or equipment, or the provision of services by Amtrak, is necessary under paragraph (1)(A) and the operation of Amtrak's other services will not be unreasonably impaired under paragraph (1)(B), the Board shall issue an order that—

(A) requires Amtrak to provide the applicable facilities, equipment, and services; and

(B) determines reasonable compensation, liability, and other terms for the use of the facilities and equipment and the provision of the services.

(h) LIMITATION.—Not more than 3 long-distance routes may be selected under this section for operation by a winning bidder that is not or does not include Amtrak.

(i) PRESERVATION OF RIGHT TO COMPETITION ON STATE-SUPPORTED ROUTES.—Nothing in this section shall be construed as prohibiting a State from introducing competition for intercity rail passenger transportation or services on its State-supported route or routes.

(j) SAVINGS CLAUSE.—Nothing in this section shall affect Amtrak's access rights to railroad rights-of-way and facilities.

(Added Pub. L. 110–432, div. B, title II, §214(a), Oct. 16, 2008, 122 Stat. 4927; amended Pub. L. 114–94, div. A, title XI, §11307(a), Dec. 4, 2015, 129 Stat. 1660; Pub. L. 115–420, §7(b)(3)(A)(i)(III), Jan. 3, 2019, 132 Stat. 5447.)

§24712. STATE-SUPPORTED ROUTES OPERATED BY AMTRAK

(a) STATE-SUPPORTED ROUTE COMMITTEE.—

(1) ESTABLISHMENT.—There is established the State-Supported Route Committee (referred to in this section as the "Committee") to promote mutual cooperation and planning pertaining to the current and future rail operations of Amtrak and related activities of trains operated by Amtrak on State-supported routes and to further implement section 209 of the Passenger Rail Investment and Improvement Act of 2008 (49 U.S.C. 24101 note).

(2) MEMBERSHIP.—

(A) IN GENERAL.—The Committee shall consist of—

(i) members representing Amtrak;

(ii) members representing the Department of Transportation, including the Federal Railroad Administration; and

(iii) members representing States.

(B) NON-VOTING MEMBERS.—The Committee may invite and accept other non-voting members to participate in Committee activities, as appropriate.

(3) DECISIONMAKING.—The Committee shall establish a bloc voting system under which, at a minimum—

(A) there are 3 separate voting blocs to represent the Committee's voting members, including—

(i) 1 voting bloc to represent the members described in paragraph (2)(A)(i);

(ii) 1 voting bloc to represent the members described in paragraph (2)(A)(ii); and

(iii) 1 voting bloc to represent the members described in paragraph (2)(A)(iii);

(B) each voting bloc has 1 vote;

(C) the vote of the voting bloc representing the members described in paragraph (2)(A)(iii) requires the support of at least two-thirds of that voting bloc's members; and

(D) the Committee makes decisions by unanimous consent of the 3 voting blocs.

(4) ABILITY TO CONDUCT CERTAIN BUSINESS.—If all of the members of 1 voting bloc described in paragraph (3) abstain from a Committee decision, agreement between the other 2 voting blocs consistent with the procedures set forth in such paragraph shall be deemed sufficient for purpose of achieving unanimous consent.

(5) MEETINGS; RULES AND PROCEDURES.—The Committee shall define and periodically update the rules and procedures governing the Committee's proceedings. The rules and procedures shall—

(A) incorporate and further describe the decisionmaking procedures to be used in accordance with paragraph (3); and

(B) be adopted in accordance with such decisionmaking procedures.

(6) COMMITTEE DECISIONS.—Decisions made by the Committee in accordance with the Committee's rules and procedures, once established, are binding on all Committee members.

(7) COST METHODOLOGY POLICY.—

(A) IN GENERAL.—Subject to subparagraph (B), the Committee may amend the cost methodology policy required and previously approved under section 209 of the Passenger Rail Investment and Improvement Act of 2008 (49 U.S.C. 24101 note).

(B) REVISIONS TO COST METHODOLOGY POLICY.—

(i) REQUIREMENT TO REVISE AND UPDATE.—Subject to rules and procedures established pursuant to clause (iii), not later than March 31, 2022, the Committee shall revise and update the cost methodology policy required and previously approved under section 209 of the Passenger Rail Investment and Improvement Act of 2008 (49 U.S.C. 20901 [1] note). The Committee shall implement a revised cost methodology policy during fiscal year 2023. Not later than 30 days after the adoption of the revised cost methodology policy, the Committee shall submit a report documenting and explaining any changes to the cost methodology policy and plans for implementation of such policy, including a description of the improvements to the accounting information provided by Amtrak to the States, to the Committee on Commerce, Science, and Transportation of the Senate and the Committee on Transportation and Infrastructure of the House of Representatives. The revised cost methodology policy shall ensure that States will be responsible for costs attributable to the provision of service for their routes.

(ii) IMPLEMENTATION IMPACTS ON FEDERAL FUNDING.—To the extent that a revision developed pursuant to clause (i) assigns to Amtrak costs that were previously allocated to States, Amtrak shall request with specificity such additional funding in the general and legislative annual report required under section 24315 or in any appropriate subsequent Federal funding request for the fiscal year in which the revised cost methodology policy will be implemented.

(iii) PROCEDURES FOR CHANGING METHODOLOGY.—Notwithstanding section 209(b) of the Passenger Rail Investment and Improvement Act of 2008 (49 U.S.C. 20901 [1] note), the rules and procedures implemented pursuant to paragraph (5) shall include—

(I) procedures for changing the cost methodology policy in accordance with clause (i); and

(II) procedures or broad guidelines for conducting financial planning, including operating and capital forecasting, reporting, data sharing, and governance.

(C) REQUIREMENTS.—The cost methodology policy shall—

(i) ensure equal treatment in the provision of like services of all States and groups of States;

(ii) assign to each route the costs incurred only for the benefit of that route and a proportionate share, based upon factors that reasonably reflect relative use, of costs incurred for the common benefit of more than 1 route; and

(iii) promote increased efficiency in Amtrak's operating and capital activities.

(D) INDEPENDENT EVALUATION.—Not later than March 31 of each year, the Committee shall ensure that an independent entity selected by the Committee has completed an evaluation to determine whether State payments for the most recently concluded fiscal year are accurate and comply with the applicable cost allocation methodology.

(8) STAFFING.—The Committee may—

(A) appoint, terminate, and fix the compensation of an executive director and other Committee employees necessary for the Committee to carry out its duties; and

(B) enter into contracts necessary to carry out its duties, including providing Committee employees with retirement and other employee benefits under the condition that Non-Federal members or officers, the executive director, and employees of the Committee are not Federal employees for any purpose.

(9) AUTHORIZATION OF APPROPRIATIONS.—Amounts made available by the Secretary of Transportation for the Committee may be used to carry out this section.

(b) INVOICES AND REPORTS.—

(1) INVOICES.—Amtrak shall provide monthly invoices to the Committee and to each State that sponsors a State-supported route that identify the operating costs for such route, including fixed costs and third-party costs.

(2) REPORTS.—

(A) IN GENERAL.—The Committee shall determine the frequency and contents of—

(i) the financial and performance reports that Amtrak is required to provide to the Committee and the States; and

(ii) the planning and demand reports that the States are required to provide to the Committee and Amtrak.

(B) MONTHLY STATISTICAL REPORT.—

(i) DEVELOPMENT.—Consistent with the revisions to the policy required under subsection (a)(7)(B), the Committee shall develop a report that contains the general ledger data and operating statistics from Amtrak's accounting systems used to calculate payments to States.

(ii) PROVISION OF NECESSARY DATA.—Not later than 30 days after the last day of each month, Amtrak shall provide to the States and to the Committee the necessary data to complete the report developed pursuant to clause (i) for such month.

(c) DISPUTE RESOLUTION.—

(1) REQUEST FOR DISPUTE RESOLUTION.—If a dispute arises with respect to the rules and procedures implemented under subsection (a)(5), an invoice or a report provided under subsection (b), implementation or compliance with the cost allocation methodology developed under section 209 of the Passenger Rail Investment and Improvement Act of 2008 (49 U.S.C. 24101 note) or amended under subsection (a)(7) of this section, either Amtrak or the State may request that the Surface Transportation Board conduct dispute resolution under this subsection.

(2) PROCEDURES.—The Surface Transportation Board shall establish procedures for resolution of disputes brought before it under this subsection, which may include provision of professional mediation services.

(3) BINDING EFFECT.—A decision of the Surface Transportation Board under this subsection shall be binding on the parties to the dispute.

(4) OBLIGATION.—Nothing in this subsection shall affect the obligation of a State to pay an amount related to a State-supported route that a State sponsors that is not in dispute.

(d) ASSISTANCE.—

(1) IN GENERAL.—The Secretary may provide assistance to the parties in the course of negotiations for a contract for operation of a State-supported route.

(2) FINANCIAL ASSISTANCE.—From among available funds, the Secretary shall provide—

(A) financial assistance to Amtrak or 1 or more States to perform requested independent technical analysis of issues before the Committee; and

(B) administrative expenses that the Secretary determines necessary.

(e) PERFORMANCE METRICS.—In negotiating a contract for operation of a State-supported route, Amtrak and the State or States that sponsor the route shall consider including provisions that provide penalties and incentives for performance, including incentives to increase revenue, reduce costs, finalize contracts by the beginning of the fiscal year, and require States to promptly make payments for services delivered.

(f) STATEMENT OF GOALS AND OBJECTIVES.—

(1) IN GENERAL.—The Committee shall develop, and review and update, as necessary,

a statement of goals, objectives, and associated recommendations concerning the future of State-supported routes operated by Amtrak. The statement shall identify the roles and responsibilities of Committee members and any other relevant entities, such as host railroads, in meeting the identified goals and objectives, or carrying out the recommendations. The Committee may consult with such relevant entities, as the Committee considers appropriate, when developing the statement.

(2) TRANSMISSION OF STATEMENT OF GOALS AND OBJECTIVES.—As applicable, based on updates, the Committee shall submit an updated statement developed under paragraph (1) to the Committee on Commerce, Science, and Transportation of the Senate and the Committee on Transportation and Infrastructure of the House of Representatives.

(3) SENSE OF CONGRESS.—It is the sense of Congress that—

(A) the Committee shall be the forum where Amtrak and the States collaborate on the planning, improvement, and development of corridor routes across the National Network; and

(B) such collaboration should include regular consultation with interstate rail compact parties and other regional planning organizations that address passenger rail.

(g) NEW STATE-SUPPORTED ROUTES.—

(1) CONSULTATION.—In developing a new State-supported route, Amtrak shall consult with—

(A) the State or States and local municipalities through which such new service would operate;

(B) commuter authorities and regional transportation authorities in the areas that would be served by the planned route;

(C) host railroads;

(D) the Administrator of the Federal Railroad Administration; and

(E) other stakeholders, as appropriate.

(2) STATE COMMITMENTS.—Notwithstanding any other provision of law, before beginning construction necessary for, or beginning operation of, a State-supported route that is initiated on or after the date of enactment of the Passenger Rail Expansion and Rail Safety Act of 2021, Amtrak shall enter into a memorandum of understanding, or otherwise secure an agreement, with each State that would be providing funding for such route for sharing—

(A) ongoing operating costs and capital costs in accordance with the cost methodology policy referred to in subsection (a)(7) then in effect; or

(B) ongoing operating costs and capital costs in accordance with the maximum funding limitations described in section 22908(e).

(3) APPLICATION OF TERMS.—In this subsection, the terms "capital costs" and "operating costs" shall apply in the same manner as such terms apply under the cost methodology policy developed pursuant to subsection (a)(7).

(h) COST METHODOLOGY POLICY UPDATE IMPLEMENTATION REPORT.—Not later than 18 months after the updated cost methodology policy required under subsection (a)(7)(B) is implemented, the Committee shall submit a report to the Committee on Commerce, Science, and Transportation of the Senate and the Committee on Transportation and Infrastructure of the House of Representatives that assesses the implementation of the updated policy.

(i) IDENTIFICATION OF STATE-SUPPORTED ROUTE CHANGES.—Amtrak shall—

(1) not later than 120 days before the submission of the general and legislative annual report required under section 24315(b), consult with the Committee and any additional States through which a State-supported route may operate regarding any proposed changes to such route; and

(2) include in such report an update of any planned or proposed changes to State-supported routes, including the introduction of new State-supported routes, including—

(A) the timeframe in which such changes would take effect; and

(B) whether Amtrak has entered into commitments with the affected States pursuant subsection (g)(2).

(j) ECONOMIC ANALYSIS.—Not later than 3 years after the date of enactment of the Passenger Rail Expansion and Rail Safety Act of 2021, the Committee shall submit a report to the Committee on Commerce, Science, and Transportation of the Senate and the Committee on Transportation and Infrastructure of the House of Representatives that—

(1) describes the role of the State-supported routes in economic development; and

(2) examines the impacts of the State-supported routes on local station areas, job creation, transportation efficiency, State economies, and the national economy.

(k) RULE OF CONSTRUCTION.—The decisions of the Committee—

(1) shall pertain to the rail operations of Amtrak and related activities of trains operated by Amtrak on State-sponsored routes; and

(2) shall not pertain to the rail operations or related activities of services operated by other rail carriers on State-supported routes.

(l) DEFINITION OF STATE.—In this section, the term "State" means any of the 50 States, including the District of Columbia, that sponsor the operation of trains by Amtrak on a State-supported route, or a public entity that sponsors such operation on such a route.

(Added Pub. L. 114–94, div. A, title XI, §11204(a), Dec. 4, 2015, 129 Stat. 1634; amended Pub. L. 117–58, div. B, title II, §22211, Nov. 15, 2021, 135 Stat. 708; Pub. L. 117–328, div. L, title I, §158, Dec. 29, 2022, 136 Stat. 5125.)

---

[1] *So in original. Probably should be "24101".*

CHAPTER 249—NORTHEAST CORRIDOR IMPROVEMENT PROGRAM

[1] *So in original. Does not conform to section catchline.*

§24901. DEFINITIONS

In this chapter—

(1) "final system plan" means the final system plan (including additions) adopted by the United States Railway Association under the Regional Rail Reorganization Act of 1973 (45 U.S.C. 701 et seq.).

(2) "rail carrier" means an express carrier and a rail carrier as defined in section 10102 of this title, including Amtrak.

(Pub. L. 103–272, §1(e), July 5, 1994, 108 Stat. 930.)

§24902. GOALS AND REQUIREMENTS

(a) MANAGING COSTS AND REVENUES.—Amtrak shall manage its operating costs, pricing policies, and other factors with the goal of having revenues derived each fiscal year from providing intercity rail passenger transportation over the Northeast Corridor route between the District of Columbia and Boston, Massachusetts, equal at least the operating costs of providing that transportation in that fiscal year.

(b) PRIORITIES IN SELECTING AND SCHEDULING PROJECTS.—When selecting and scheduling specific projects, Amtrak shall apply the following considerations, in the following order of priority:

(1) Safety-related items should be completed before other items because the safety of the passengers and users of the Northeast Corridor is paramount.

(2) Activities that benefit the greatest number of passengers should be completed before activities involving fewer passengers.

(3) Reliability of intercity rail passenger transportation must be emphasized.

(4) Trip-time requirements of this section must be achieved to the extent compatible with the priorities referred to in paragraphs (1)–(3) of this subsection.

(5) Improvements that will pay for the investment by achieving lower operating or maintenance costs should be carried out before other improvements.

(6) Construction operations should be scheduled so that the fewest possible passengers are inconvenienced, transportation is maintained, and the on-time performance of Northeast Corridor commuter rail passenger and rail freight transportation is optimized.

(7) Planning should focus on completing activities that will provide immediate benefits to users of the Northeast Corridor.

(c) COMPATIBILITY WITH FUTURE IMPROVEMENTS AND PRODUCTION OF MAXIMUM LABOR BENEFITS.—Improvements under this section shall be compatible with future improvements in transportation and shall produce the maximum labor benefit from hiring individuals presently unemployed.

(d) AUTOMATIC TRAIN CONTROL SYSTEMS.—A train operating on the Northeast Corridor main line or between the main line and Atlantic City shall be equipped with an automatic train control system designed to slow or stop the train in response to an external signal.

(e) HIGH-SPEED TRANSPORTATION.—If practicable, Amtrak shall establish intercity rail passenger transportation in the Northeast Corridor that carries out section 703(1)(E) of the Railroad Revitalization and Regulatory Reform Act of 1976 (Public Law 94–210, 90 Stat. 121).

(f) EQUIPMENT DEVELOPMENT.—Amtrak shall develop economical and reliable equipment compatible with track, operating, and marketing characteristics of the Northeast Corridor, including the capability to meet reliable trip times under section 703(1)(E) of the Railroad Revitalization and Regulatory Reform Act of 1976 (Public Law 94–210, 90 Stat. 121) in regularly scheduled revenue transportation in the Corridor, when the Northeast Corridor improvement program is completed. Amtrak must decide that equipment complies with this subsection before buying equipment with financial assistance of the Government. Amtrak shall submit a request for an authorization of appropriations for production of the equipment.

(g) AGREEMENTS FOR OFF-CORRIDOR ROUTING OF RAIL FREIGHT TRANSPORTATION.—(1) Amtrak may make an agreement with a rail freight carrier or a regional transportation authority under which the carrier will carry out an alternate off-corridor routing of rail freight transportation over rail lines in the Northeast Corridor between the District of Columbia and New York metropolitan areas, including intermediate points. The agreement shall be for at least 5 years.

(2) Amtrak shall apply to the Surface Transportation Board for approval of the agreement and all related agreements accompanying the application as soon as the agreement is made. If the Board finds that approval is necessary to carry out this chapter, the Board shall approve the application and related agreements not later than 90 days after receiving the application.

(3) If an agreement is not made under paragraph (1) of this subsection, Amtrak, with the consent of the other parties, may apply to the Surface Transportation Board. Not later than 90 days after the application, the Board shall decide on the terms of an agreement if it decides that doing so is necessary to carry out this chapter. The decision of the Board is binding on the other parties.

(h) COORDINATION.—(1) The Secretary of Transportation shall coordinate—

(A) transportation programs related to the Northeast Corridor to ensure that the programs are integrated and consistent with the Northeast Corridor improvement program; and

(B) amounts from departments, agencies, and instrumentalities of the Government to achieve urban redevelopment and revitalization in the vicinity of urban rail stations in the Northeast Corridor served by intercity and commuter rail passenger transportation.

(2) If the Secretary finds significant noncompliance with this section, the Secretary may deny financing to a noncomplying program until the noncompliance is corrected.

(i) COMPLETION.—Amtrak shall give the highest priority to completing the program.

(j) APPLICABLE PROCEDURES.—No State or local building, zoning, subdivision, or similar or related law, nor any other State or local law from which a project would be exempt if undertaken by the Federal Government or an agency thereof within a Federal enclave wherein Federal jurisdiction is exclusive, including without limitation with respect to all such laws referenced herein above requirements for permits, actions, approvals or filings, shall apply in connection with the construction, ownership, use, operation, financing, leasing, conveying, mortgaging or enforcing a mortgage of (i) any improvement undertaken by or for the benefit of Amtrak as part of, or in furtherance of, the Northeast Corridor Improvement Project (including without limitation maintenance, service, inspection or similar facilities acquired, constructed or used for high speed trainsets) or chapter 241, 243, or 247 of this title or (ii) any land (and right, title or interest created with respect thereto) on which such improvement is located and adjoining, surrounding or any related land. These exemptions shall remain in effect and be applicable with respect to such land and improvements for the benefit of any mortgagee before, upon and after coming into possession of such improvements or land, any third party purchasers thereof in foreclosure (or through a deed in lieu of foreclosure), and their respective successors and assigns, in each case to the extent the land or improvements are used, or held for use, for railroad purposes or purposes accessory thereto. This subsection shall not apply to any improvement or related land unless Amtrak receives a Federal operating subsidy in the fiscal year in which Amtrak commits to or initiates such improvement.

(Pub. L. 103–272, §1(e), July 5, 1994, 108 Stat. 930; Pub. L. 104–205, title III, §334, Sept. 30, 1996, 110 Stat. 2974; Pub. L. 105–134, title IV, §405(b)(1), Dec. 2, 1997, 111 Stat. 2586; Pub. L. 112–141, div. C, title II, §32932(c)(3), July 6, 2012, 126 Stat. 829.)

§24903. GENERAL AUTHORITY

(a) GENERAL.—To carry out this chapter and the Regional Rail Reorganization Act of 1973 (45 U.S.C. 701 et seq.), Amtrak may—

(1) acquire, maintain, and dispose of any interest in property used to provide improved high-speed rail transportation under section 24902 of this title;

(2) acquire, by condemnation or otherwise, any interest in real property that Amtrak considers necessary to carry out the goals of section 24902;

(3) provide for rail freight, intercity rail passenger, and commuter rail passenger transportation over property acquired under this section;

(4) improve rail rights of way between Boston, Massachusetts, and the District of Columbia (including the route through Springfield, Massachusetts, and routes to

Harrisburg, Pennsylvania, and Albany, New York, from the Northeast Corridor main line) to achieve the goals of section 24902 of providing improved high-speed rail passenger transportation between Boston, Massachusetts, and the District of Columbia, and intermediate intercity markets;

(5) acquire, build, improve, and install passenger stations, communications and electric power facilities and equipment, public and private highway and pedestrian crossings, and other facilities and equipment necessary to provide improved high-speed rail passenger transportation over rights of way improved under clause (4) of this subsection;

(6) make agreements with other carriers and commuter authorities to grant, acquire, or make arrangements for rail freight or commuter rail passenger transportation over, rights of way and facilities acquired under the Regional Rail Reorganization Act of 1973 (45 U.S.C. 701 et seq.), the Railroad Revitalization and Regulatory Reform Act of 1976 (45 U.S.C. 801 et seq.), and chapter 224 of this title; and

(7) appoint a general manager of the Northeast Corridor improvement program.

(b) COMPENSATORY AGREEMENTS.—Rail freight and commuter rail passenger transportation provided under subsection (a)(3) of this section shall be provided under compensatory agreements with the responsible carriers.

(c) COMPENSATION FOR TRANSPORTATION OVER CERTAIN RIGHTS OF WAY AND FACILITIES.—(1) An agreement under subsection (a)(6) of this section shall provide for reasonable reimbursement of costs but may not cross-subsidize intercity rail passenger, commuter rail passenger, and rail freight transportation.

(2) If the parties do not agree, the Surface Transportation Board shall order that the transportation continue over facilities acquired under the Regional Rail Reorganization Act of 1973 (45 U.S.C. 701 et seq.), the Railroad Revitalization and Regulatory Reform Act of 1976 (45 U.S.C. 801 et seq.), and chapter 224 of this title and shall determine compensation (without allowing cross-subsidization between commuter rail passenger and intercity rail passenger and rail freight transportation) for the transportation not later than 120 days after the dispute is submitted. The Board shall assign to a rail carrier obtaining transportation under this subsection the costs Amtrak incurs only for the benefit of the carrier, plus a proportionate share of all other costs of providing transportation under this paragraph incurred for the common benefit of Amtrak and the carrier. The proportionate share shall be based on relative measures of volume of car operations, tonnage, or other factors that reasonably reflect the relative use of rail property covered by this subsection.

(3) This subsection does not prevent the parties from making an agreement under subsection (a)(6) of this section after the Board makes a decision under this subsection.

(Pub. L. 103–272, §1(e), July 5, 1994, 108 Stat. 934, §24904; Pub. L. 103–429, §6(22), Oct. 31, 1994, 108 Stat. 4380; Pub. L. 105–134, title IV, §405(b)(2), Dec. 2, 1997, 111 Stat. 2586; Pub. L. 110–432, div. B, title II, §212(b)(2), Oct. 16, 2008, 122 Stat. 4924; Pub. L. 112–141, div. C, title II, §32932(c)(4), July 6, 2012, 126 Stat. 829; renumbered §24903, Pub. L. 114–94, div. A, title XI, §11306(a)(1), Dec. 4, 2015, 129 Stat. 1658; Pub. L. 117–58, div. B, title I, §21301(j)(4)(F), Nov. 15, 2021, 135 Stat. 693.)

§24904. NORTHEAST CORRIDOR PLANNING

(a) NORTHEAST CORRIDOR SERVICE DEVELOPMENT PLAN.—

(1) IN GENERAL.—Not later than March 31, 2022, the Northeast Corridor Commission established under section 24905 (referred to in this section as the "Commission") shall submit a service development plan to Congress.

(2) CONTENTS.—The plan required under paragraph (1) shall—

(A) identify key state-of-good-repair, capacity expansion, and capital improvement projects planned for the Northeast Corridor;

(B) provide a coordinated and consensus-based plan covering a 15-year period;

(C) identify service objectives and the capital investments required to meet such objectives;

(D) provide a delivery-constrained strategy that identifies—

(i) capital investment phasing;

(ii) an evaluation of workforce needs; and

(iii) strategies for managing resources and mitigating construction impacts on operations; and

(E) include a financial strategy that identifies funding needs and potential funding sources.

(3) UPDATES.—The Commission shall update the service development plan not less frequently than once every 5 years.

(b) NORTHEAST CORRIDOR CAPITAL INVESTMENT PLAN.—

(1) IN GENERAL.—Not later than November 1 of each year, the Commission shall—

(A) develop an annual capital investment plan for the Northeast Corridor; and

(B) submit the capital investment plan to—

(i) the Secretary of Transportation;

(ii) the Committee on Commerce, Science, and Transportation of the Senate; and

(iii) the Committee on Transportation and Infrastructure of the House of Representatives.

(2) CONTENTS.—The plan required under paragraph (1) shall—

(A) reflect coordination across the entire Northeast Corridor;

(B) integrate the individual capital plans developed by Amtrak, States, and commuter authorities in accordance with the cost allocation policy developed and approved under section 24905(c);

(C) cover a period of 5 fiscal years, beginning with the fiscal year during which the plan is submitted;

(D) notwithstanding section 24902(b), document the projects and programs being undertaken to advance the service objectives and capital investments identified in the Northeast Corridor service development plan developed under subsection (a), and the asset condition needs identified in the Northeast Corridor asset management plans, after considering—

(i) the benefits and costs of capital investments in the plan;

(ii) project and program readiness;

(iii) the operational impacts; and

(iv) Federal and non-Federal funding availability;

(E) categorize capital projects and programs as primarily associated with 1 of the categories listed under section 24319(c)(2)(C);

(F) identify capital projects and programs that are associated with more than 1 category described in subparagraph (E); and

(G) include a financial plan that identifies—

(i) funding sources and financing methods;

(ii) the status of cost sharing agreements pursuant to the cost allocation policy developed under section 24905(c);

(iii) the projects and programs that the Commission expects will receive Federal financial assistance; and

(iv) the eligible entity or entities that the Commission expects—

(I) to receive the Federal financial assistance referred to in clause (iii); and

(II) to implement each capital project.

(3) REVIEW AND COORDINATION.—The Commission shall require that the information described in paragraph (2) be submitted in a timely manner to allow for a reasonable period of review by, and coordination with, affected agencies before the Commission submits the capital investment plan pursuant to paragraph (1).

(c) FAILURE TO DEVELOP A CAPITAL INVESTMENT PLAN.—If a capital investment plan has not been developed by the Commission for a given fiscal year, then the funds assigned to the Northeast Corridor account established under section 24317(b) for that fiscal year may be spent only on capital projects and programs contained in the Commission's capital investment plan for the prior fiscal year.

(d) NORTHEAST CORRIDOR CAPITAL ASSET MANAGEMENT SYSTEM.—

(1) IN GENERAL.—Amtrak and other infrastructure owners that provide or support intercity rail passenger transportation along the Northeast Corridor shall develop an asset management system and use and update such system, as necessary, to develop submissions to the Northeast Corridor capital investment plan described in subsection (b).

(2) FEATURES.—The system required under paragraph (1) shall develop submissions that—

(A) are consistent with the transit asset management system (as defined in section 5326(a)(3)); and

(B) include—

(i) an inventory of all capital assets owned by the developer of the plan;

(ii) an assessment of condition of such capital assets;

(iii) a description of the resources and processes that will be necessary to bring or to maintain such capital assets in a state of good repair; and

(iv) a description of changes in the condition of such capital assets since the submission of the prior version of the plan.

(e) DEFINITION OF NORTHEAST CORRIDOR.—In this section, the term "Northeast

Corridor" means the main line between Boston, Massachusetts, and the District of Columbia, and the Northeast Corridor branch lines connecting to Harrisburg, Pennsylvania, Springfield, Massachusetts, and Spuyten Duyvil, New York, including the facilities and services used to operate and maintain those lines.

(Added Pub. L. 114–94, div. A, title XI, §11306(a)(2), Dec. 4, 2015, 129 Stat. 1658; amended Pub. L. 117–58, div. B, title II, §22301, Nov. 15, 2021, 135 Stat. 714.)

§24905. Northeast Corridor Commission; Safety Committee

(a) NORTHEAST CORRIDOR COMMISSION.—

(1) Within 180 days after the date of enactment of the Passenger Rail Investment and Improvement Act of 2008, the Secretary of Transportation shall establish a Northeast Corridor Commission (referred to in this section as the "Commission") to promote mutual cooperation and planning pertaining to the rail operations, infrastructure investments, and related activities of the Northeast Corridor. The Commission shall be made up of—

(A) members representing Amtrak;

(B) members representing the Department of Transportation, including the Office of the Secretary, the Federal Railroad Administration, and the Federal Transit Administration;

(C) 1 member from each of the States (including the District of Columbia) that constitute the Northeast Corridor as defined in section 24102, designated by, and serving at the pleasure of, the chief executive officer thereof; and

(D) non-voting representatives of freight and commuter railroad carriers authorities using the Northeast Corridor selected by the Secretary.

(2) The Secretary shall ensure that the membership belonging to any of the groups enumerated under paragraph (1) shall not constitute a majority of the Commission's memberships.

(3) The Commission shall establish a schedule and location for convening meetings, but shall meet no less than four times per fiscal year, and the Commission shall develop rules and procedures to govern the Commission's proceedings.

(4) A vacancy in the Commission shall be filled in the manner in which the original appointment was made.

(5) Members shall serve without pay but shall receive travel expenses, including per diem in lieu of subsistence, in accordance with sections 5702 and 5703 of title 5.

(6) The members of the Commission shall elect co-chairs consisting of 1 member described in paragraph (1)(B) and 1 member described in paragraph (1)(C).

(7) The Commission may appoint and fix the pay of such personnel as it considers appropriate.

(8) Upon request of the Commission, the head of any department or agency of the United States may detail, on a reimbursable basis, any of the personnel of that department or agency to the Commission to assist it in carrying out its duties under this section.

(9) Upon the request of the Commission, the Administrator of General Services shall

provide to the Commission, on a reimbursable basis, the administrative support services necessary for the Commission to carry out its responsibilities under this section.

(10) The Commission shall consult with other entities as appropriate.

(b) STATEMENT OF GOALS AND RECOMMENDATIONS.—

(1) STATEMENT OF GOALS.—The Commission shall develop and periodically update a statement of goals concerning the future of Northeast Corridor rail infrastructure and operations based on achieving expanded and improved intercity, commuter, and freight rail services operating with greater safety and reliability, reduced travel times, increased frequencies and enhanced intermodal connections designed to address airport and highway congestion, reduce transportation energy consumption, improve air quality, and increase economic development of the Northeast Corridor region.

(2) RECOMMENDATIONS.—The Commission shall develop recommendations based on the statement developed under this section addressing, as appropriate—

(A) short-term and long-term capital investment needs;

(B) future funding requirements for capital improvements and maintenance;

(C) operational improvements of intercity passenger rail, commuter rail, and freight rail services;

(D) opportunities for additional non-rail uses of the Northeast Corridor;

(E) scheduling and dispatching;

(F) safety and security enhancements;

(G) equipment design;

(H) marketing of rail services;

(I) future capacity requirements; and

(J) potential funding and financing mechanisms for projects of corridor-wide significance.

(3) SUBMISSION OF STATEMENT OF GOALS, RECOMMENDATIONS, AND PERFORMANCE REPORTS.—The Commission shall submit to the Committee on Commerce, Science, and Transportation of the Senate and the Committee on Transportation and Infrastructure of the House of Representatives—

(A) any updates made to the statement of goals developed under paragraph (1) not later than 60 days after such updates are made; and

(B) annual performance reports and recommendations for improvements, as appropriate, issued not later than March 31 of each year, for the prior fiscal year, which summarize—

(i) the operations and performance of commuter, intercity, and freight rail transportation, including ridership trends, along the Northeast Corridor;

(ii) the delivery of the first year of the capital investment plan described in section 24904; and

(iii) progress in assessing and eliminating the state-of-good-repair backlog.

(c) ALLOCATION OF COSTS.—

(1) POLICY.—The Commission shall—

(A) develop and maintain the standardized policy first approved on September

17, 2015, and update, as appropriate, for determining and allocating costs, revenues, and compensation for Northeast Corridor commuter rail passenger transportation, as defined in section 24102 of this title, on the Northeast Corridor main line between Boston, Massachusetts, and Washington, District of Columbia, and the Northeast Corridor branch lines connecting to Harrisburg, Pennsylvania, Springfield, Massachusetts, and Spuyten Duyvil, New York, that use Amtrak facilities or services or that provide such facilities or services to Amtrak that ensures that—

(i) there is no cross-subsidization of commuter rail passenger, intercity rail passenger, or freight rail transportation;

(ii) each service is assigned the costs incurred only for the benefit of that service, and a proportionate share, based upon factors that reasonably reflect relative use, of costs incurred for the common benefit of more than 1 service; and

(iii) all financial contributions made by an operator of a service that benefit an infrastructure owner other than the operator are considered, including but not limited to, any capital infrastructure investments and in-kind services;

(B) develop timetables for implementing and maintaining the policy;

(C) submit updates to the policy and timetables developed under subparagraph (B) to the Surface Transportation Board, the Committee on Commerce, Science, and Transportation of the Senate, and the Committee on Transportation and Infrastructure of the House of Representatives;

(D) support the efforts of the members of the Commission to implement the policy in accordance with the timetables developed pursuant to subparagraph (B); [1]

(E) with the consent of a majority of its members, petition the Surface Transportation Board to appoint a mediator to assist the Commission members through nonbinding mediation to reach an agreement under this section.

(2) IMPLEMENTATION.—

(A) IN GENERAL.—In accordance with the timetables developed pursuant to paragraph (1)(B), Amtrak and commuter authorities on the Northeast Corridor shall implement the policy developed under paragraph (1) in their agreements for usage of facilities or services.

(B) EFFECT OF FAILURE TO IMPLEMENT OR COMPLY WITH POLICY.—If the entities referred to in subparagraph (A) fail to implement the policy in accordance with paragraph (1)(D) or fail to comply with the policy thereafter, the Surface Transportation Board shall—

(i) determine the appropriate compensation in accordance with the procedures and procedural schedule applicable to a proceeding under section 24903(c), after taking into consideration the policy developed under paragraph (1); and

(ii) enforce its determination on the party or parties involved.

(3) REVISIONS.—The Commission may make necessary revisions to the policy developed under paragraph (1), including revisions based on Amtrak's financial accounting system developed pursuant to section 203 of the Passenger Rail Investment and Improvement Act of 2008.

(4) REQUEST FOR DISPUTE RESOLUTION.—If a dispute arises with the implementation of, or compliance with, the policy developed under paragraph (1), the Commission, Amtrak, or commuter authorities on the Northeast Corridor may request that the Surface Transportation Board conduct dispute resolution. The Surface Transportation Board shall establish procedures for resolution of disputes brought before it under this paragraph, which may include the provision of professional mediation services.

(d) AUTHORIZATION OF APPROPRIATIONS.—There are authorized to be appropriated to the Secretary for the use of the Commission and the Northeast Corridor Safety Committee such sums as may be necessary to carry out this section during fiscal years 2022 through 2026, in addition to any amounts withheld under section 22101(e) of the Passenger Rail Expansion and Rail Safety Act of 2021.

(e) NORTHEAST CORRIDOR SAFETY COMMITTEE.—

(1) IN GENERAL.—The Secretary shall establish a Northeast Corridor Safety Committee composed of members appointed by the Secretary. The members shall be representatives of—

(A) the Department of Transportation, including the Federal Railroad Administration;

(B) Amtrak;

(C) freight carriers operating more than 150,000 train miles a year on the main line of the Northeast Corridor;

(D) commuter rail agencies;

(E) rail passengers;

(F) rail labor; and

(G) other individuals and organizations the Secretary decides have a significant interest in rail safety or security.

(2) SUNSET.—The Committee established under this subsection ceases to exist on the date that the Secretary determines positive train control, as required by section 20157, is fully implemented along the Northeast Corridor.

(Pub. L. 103–272, §1(e), July 5, 1994, 108 Stat. 935; Pub. L. 110–432, div. B, title II, §212(a), Oct. 16, 2008, 122 Stat. 4921; Pub. L. 114–94, div. A, title XI, §11305(a)–(d)(1), Dec. 4, 2015, 129 Stat. 1656, 1657; Pub. L. 115–420, §§4(a), 6(a), Jan. 3, 2019, 132 Stat. 5444, 5445; Pub. L. 117–58, div. B, title II, §22302, Nov. 15, 2021, 135 Stat. 716.)

[1] So in original. Probably should be followed by "and".

§24906. ELIMINATING HIGHWAY AT-GRADE CROSSINGS

(a) PLAN.—In consultation with the States on the main line of the Northeast Corridor, the Secretary of Transportation shall develop a plan not later than September 30, 1993, to eliminate all highway at-grade crossings of the main line by not later than December 31, 1997. The plan may provide that eliminating a crossing is not required if—

(1) impracticable or unnecessary; and

(2) using the crossing is consistent with conditions the Secretary considers appropriate to ensure safety.

(b) AMTRAK'S SHARE OF COSTS.—Amtrak shall pay 20 percent of the cost of eliminating each highway at-grade crossing under the plan.

(Pub. L. 103–272, §1(e), July 5, 1994, 108 Stat. 936.)

§24907. NOTE AND MORTGAGE

(a) GENERAL AUTHORITY.—To secure amounts expended by the United States Government to acquire and improve rail property designated under section 206(c)(1)(C) and (D) of the Regional Rail Reorganization Act of 1973 (45 U.S.C. 716(c)(1)(C) and (D)), the Secretary of Transportation may obtain a note of indebtedness from, and make a mortgage agreement with, Amtrak to establish a mortgage lien on the property for the Government. The note and mortgage may not supersede section 24903.

(b) EXEMPTIONS FROM LAWS AND REGULATIONS.—The note and agreement under subsection (a) of this section, and a transaction related to the note or agreement, are exempt from any United States, State, or local law or regulation that regulates securities or the issuance of securities. The note, agreement, or transaction under this section has the same immunities from other laws that section 601 of the Act (45 U.S.C. 791) gives to transactions that comply with or carry out the final system plan. The transfer of rail property because of the note, agreement, or transaction has the same exemptions, privileges, and immunities that the Act (45 U.S.C. 701 et seq.) gives to a transfer ordered or approved by the special court under section 303(b) of the Act (45 U.S.C. 743(b)).

(c) IMMUNITY FROM LIABILITY AND INDEMNIFICATION.—Amtrak, its board of directors, and its individual directors are not liable because Amtrak has given or issued the note or agreement to the Government under subsection (a) of this section. Immunity granted under this subsection also applies to a transaction related to the note or agreement. The Government shall indemnify Amtrak, its board, and individual directors against costs and expenses actually and reasonably incurred in defending a civil action testing the validity of the note, agreement, or transaction.

(Pub. L. 103–272, §1(e), July 5, 1994, 108 Stat. 936; Pub. L. 114–94, div. A, title XI, §11306(b)(1), Dec. 4, 2015, 129 Stat. 1660.)

§24908. TRANSFER TAXES AND LEVIES AND RECORDING CHARGES

A transfer of an interest in rail property under this chapter is exempt from a tax or levy related to the transfer that is imposed by the United States Government, a State, or a political subdivision of a State. On payment of the appropriate and generally applicable charge for the service performed, a transferee or transferor may record an instrument and, consistent with the final system plan, the release or removal of a pre-existing lien or encumbrance of record related to the interest transferred.

(Pub. L. 103–272, §1(e), July 5, 1994, 108 Stat. 937.)

§24909. AUTHORIZATION OF APPROPRIATIONS

(a) GENERAL.—(1) Not more than $2,313,000,000 may be appropriated to the Secretary of Transportation to achieve the goals of section 24902(a)(1) [1] of this title. From this amount, the following amounts shall be expended by Amtrak:

(A) at least $27,000,000 for equipment modification and replacement that a State or a local or regional transportation authority must bear because of the electrification conversion system of the Northeast Corridor under this chapter.

(B) $30,000,000—

(i) to improve the main line track between the Northeast Corridor main line and Atlantic City, New Jersey, to ensure that the track, consistent with a plan New Jersey developed in consultation with Amtrak to provide rail passenger transportation between the Northeast Corridor main line and Atlantic City, New Jersey, would be of sufficient quality to allow safe rail passenger transportation at a minimum of 79 miles an hour not later than September 30, 1985; and

(ii) to promote rail passenger use of the track.

(C) necessary amounts to—

(i) develop Union Station in the District of Columbia;

(ii) install 189 track-miles, and renew 133 track-miles, of concrete ties with continuously welded rail between the District of Columbia and New York, New York;

(iii) install reverse signaling between Philadelphia, Pennsylvania, and Morrisville, Pennsylvania, on numbers 2 and 3 track;

(iv) restore ditch drainage in concrete tie locations between the District of Columbia and New York, New York;

(v) undercut 83 track-miles between the District of Columbia and New York, New York;

(vi) rehabilitate bridges between the District of Columbia and New York, New York (including Hi line);

(vii) develop a maintenance of way equipment repair facility between the District of Columbia and New York, New York, and build maintenance of way bases at Philadelphia, Pennsylvania, Sunnyside, New York, and Cedar Hill, Connecticut;

(viii) stabilize the roadbed between the District of Columbia and New York, New York;

(ix) automate the Bush River Drawbridge at milepost 72.14;

(x) improve the New York Service Facility to develop rolling stock repair capability;

(xi) install a rail car washer facility at Philadelphia, Pennsylvania;

(xii) restore storage tracks and buildings at the Washington Service Facility;

(xiii) install centralized traffic control from Landlith, Delaware, to Philadelphia, Pennsylvania;

(xiv) improve track, including high speed surfacing, ballast cleaning, and associated equipment repair and material distribution;

(xv) rehabilitate interlockings between the District of Columbia and New York, New York;

(xvi) paint the Connecticut River, Groton, and Pelham Bay bridges;

(xvii) provide additional catenary renewal and power supply upgrading between the District of Columbia and New York, New York;

(xviii) rehabilitate structural, electrical, and mechanical systems at the William H. Gray III 30th Street Station in Philadelphia, Pennsylvania;

(xix) install evacuation and fire protection facilities in tunnels in New York, New

York;

(xx) improve the communication and signal systems between Wilmington, Delaware, and Boston, Massachusetts, on the Northeast Corridor main line, and between Philadelphia, Pennsylvania, and Harrisburg, Pennsylvania, on the Harrisburg Line;

(xxi) improve the electric traction systems between Wilmington, Delaware, and Newark, New Jersey;

(xxii) install baggage rack restraints, seat back guards, and seat lock devices on 348 passenger cars operating in the Northeast Corridor;

(xxiii) install 44 event recorders and 10 electronic warning devices on locomotives operating within the Northeast Corridor; and

(xxiv) acquire cab signal test boxes and install 9 wayside loop code transmitters for use within the Northeast Corridor.

(2) The following additional amounts may be appropriated to the Secretary for expenditure by Amtrak:

(A) not more than $150,000,000 to achieve the goal of section 24902(a)(3) [1] of this title.

(B) not more than $120,000,000 to acquire interests in property in the Northeast Corridor.

(C) not more than $650,000 to develop and use mobile radio frequencies for passenger radio mobile telephone service on high-speed rail passenger transportation.

(D) not more than $20,000,000 to acquire and improve interests in rail property designated under section 206(c)(1)(D) of the Regional Rail Reorganization Act of 1973 (45 U.S.C. 716(c)(1)(D)).

(E) not more than $37,000,000 to carry out section 24902(a)(7) and (j) [1] of this title.

(b) EMERGENCY MAINTENANCE.—Not more than $25,000,000 of the amount appropriated under the Act of February 28, 1975 (Public Law 94–6, 89 Stat. 11), may be used by Amtrak for emergency maintenance on rail property designated under section 206(c)(1)(C) of the Regional Rail Reorganization Act of 1973 (45 U.S.C. 716(c)(1)(C)).

(c) PRIORITY IN USING CERTAIN AMOUNTS.—Amounts appropriated under subsection (a)(2)(B) and (D) of this section shall be used first to repay, with interest, obligations guaranteed under section 602 of the Rail Passenger Service Act, if the proceeds of those obligations were used to pay the expenses of acquiring interests in property referred to in subsection (a)(2)(B) and (D).

(d) PROHIBITION ON SUBSIDIZING COMMUTER AND FREIGHT OPERATING LOSSES.—Amounts appropriated under this section may not be used to subsidize operating losses of commuter rail or rail freight transportation.

(e) SUBSTITUTING AND DEFERRING CERTAIN IMPROVEMENTS.—(1) A project for which amounts are authorized under subsection (a)(1)(C) of this section is a part of the Northeast Corridor improvement program and is not a substitute for improvements specified in the document "Corridor Master Plan II, NECIP Restructured Program" of January, 1982. However, Amtrak may defer the project to carry out the improvement and rehabilitation for which amounts are authorized under subsection (a)(1)(B) of this section. The total cost of the project that Amtrak defers may not be substantially more than the amount Amtrak is required to expend or reserve under subsection (a)(1)(B).

(2) Section 24902 of this title is deemed not to be fulfilled until the projects under subsection (a)(1)(C) of this section are completed.

(f) AVAILABILITY OF AMOUNTS.—Amounts appropriated under subsection (a)(1) and (2)(A) and (C)–(E) of this section remain available until expended.

(g) AUTHORIZATIONS INCREASED BY PRIOR YEAR DEFICIENCIES.—An amount greater than that authorized for a fiscal year may be appropriated to the extent that the amount appropriated for any prior fiscal year is less than the amount authorized for that year.

(Pub. L. 103–272, §1(e), July 5, 1994, 108 Stat. 937; Pub. L. 113–158, §2, Aug. 8, 2014, 128 Stat. 1838.)

[1] *See References in Text note below.*

§24910. RAIL COOPERATIVE RESEARCH PROGRAM

(a) IN GENERAL.—The Secretary shall establish and carry out a rail cooperative research program. The program shall—

(1) address, among other matters, intercity rail passenger and freight rail services, including existing rail passenger and freight technologies and speeds, incrementally enhanced rail systems and infrastructure, and new high-speed wheel-on-rail systems;

(2) address ways to expand the transportation of international trade traffic by rail, enhance the efficiency of intermodal interchange at ports and other intermodal terminals, and increase capacity and availability of rail service for seasonal freight needs;

(3) consider research on the interconnectedness of commuter rail, passenger rail, freight rail, and other rail networks; and

(4) give consideration to regional concerns regarding rail passenger and freight transportation, including meeting research needs common to designated high-speed corridors, long-distance rail services, and regional intercity rail corridors, projects, and entities.

(b) CONTENT.—The program to be carried out under this section shall include research designed—

(1) to identify the unique aspects and attributes of rail passenger and freight service;

(2) to develop more accurate models for evaluating the impact of rail passenger and freight service, including the effects on highway and airport and airway congestion, environmental quality, and energy consumption;

(3) to develop a better understanding of modal choice as it affects rail passenger and freight transportation, including development of better models to predict utilization;

(4) to recommend priorities for technology demonstration and development;

(5) to meet additional priorities as determined by the advisory board established under subsection (c), including any recommendations made by the National Research Council;

(6) to explore improvements in management, financing, and institutional structures;

(7) to address rail capacity constraints that affect passenger and freight rail service through a wide variety of options, ranging from operating improvements to dedicated new infrastructure, taking into account the impact of such options on operations;

(8) to improve maintenance, operations, customer service, or other aspects of intercity

rail passenger and freight service;

(9) to recommend objective methodologies for determining intercity passenger rail routes and services, including the establishment of new routes, the elimination of existing routes, and the contraction or expansion of services or frequencies over such routes;

(10) to review the impact of equipment and operational safety standards on the further development of high-speed passenger rail operations connected to or integrated with non-high-speed freight or passenger rail operations;

(11) to recommend any legislative or regulatory changes necessary to foster further development and implementation of high-speed passenger rail operations while ensuring the safety of such operations that are connected to or integrated with non-high-speed freight or passenger rail operations;

(12) to review rail crossing safety improvements, including improvements using new safety technology;

(13) to review and develop technology designed to reduce train horn noise and its effect on communities, including broadband horn technology; and

(14) to improve overall safety of intercity passenger and freight rail operations.

(c) ADVISORY BOARD.—

(1) ESTABLISHMENT.—In consultation with the heads of appropriate Federal departments and agencies, the Secretary shall establish an advisory board to recommend research, technology, and technology transfer activities related to rail passenger and freight transportation.

(2) MEMBERSHIP.—The advisory board shall include—

(A) representatives of State transportation agencies;

(B) transportation and environmental economists, scientists, and engineers; and

(C) representatives of Amtrak, the Alaska Railroad, freight railroads, transit operating agencies, intercity rail passenger agencies, railway labor organizations, and environmental organizations.

(3) SUNSET.—The advisory board established under this subsection ceases to exist effective January 1, 2019.

(d) NATIONAL ACADEMY OF SCIENCES.—The Secretary may make grants to, and enter into cooperative agreements with, the National Academy of Sciences to carry out such activities relating to the research, technology, and technology transfer activities described in subsection (b) as the Secretary deems appropriate.

(e) AUTHORIZATION OF APPROPRIATIONS.—There are authorized to be appropriated to the Secretary of Transportation $5,000,000 for each of fiscal years 2010 through 2013 for carrying out this section.

(Added Pub. L. 110–432, div. B, title III, §306(a), Oct. 16, 2008, 122 Stat. 4952; amended Pub. L. 114–94, div. A, title XI, §11316(o), Dec. 4, 2015, 129 Stat. 1679; Pub. L. 115–420, §6(b), Jan. 3, 2019, 132 Stat. 5445.)

§24911. FEDERAL-STATE PARTNERSHIP FOR INTERCITY PASSENGER RAIL

(a) DEFINITIONS.—In this section:

(1) APPLICANT.—The term "applicant" means—

(A) a State (including the District of Columbia);

(B) a group of States;

(C) an Interstate Compact;

(D) a public agency or publicly chartered authority established by 1 or more States;

(E) a political subdivision of a State;

(F) Amtrak, acting on its own behalf or under a cooperative agreement with 1 or more States;

(G) a federally recognized Indian Tribe; or

(H) any combination of the entities described in subparagraphs (A) through (G).

(2) INTERCITY RAIL PASSENGER TRANSPORTATION.—The term "intercity rail passenger transportation" has the meaning given the term in section 24102.

(3) NORTHEAST CORRIDOR.—The term "Northeast Corridor" means—

(A) the main rail line between Boston, Massachusetts and the District of Columbia;

(B) the branch rail lines connecting to Harrisburg, Pennsylvania, Springfield, Massachusetts, and Spuyten Duyvil, New York; and

(C) facilities and services used to operate and maintain lines described in subparagraphs (A) and (B).

(b) GRANT PROGRAM AUTHORIZED.—The Secretary of Transportation shall develop and implement a program for issuing grants to applicants, on a competitive basis, to fund capital projects that reduce the state of good repair backlog, improve performance, or expand or establish new intercity passenger rail service, including privately operated intercity passenger rail service if an eligible applicant is involved;.[1]

(c) ELIGIBLE PROJECTS.—The following capital projects, including acquisition of real property interests, are eligible to receive grants under this section:

(1) A project to replace, rehabilitate, or repair infrastructure, equipment, or a facility used for providing intercity passenger rail service to bring such assets into a state of good repair.

(2) A project to improve intercity passenger rail service performance, including reduced trip times, increased train frequencies, higher operating speeds, improved reliability, expanded capacity, reduced congestion, electrification, and other improvements, as determined by the Secretary.

(3) A project to expand or establish new intercity passenger rail service.

(4) A group of related projects described in paragraphs (1) through (3).

(5) The planning, environmental studies, and final design for a project or group of projects described in paragraphs (1) through (4).

(d) PROJECT SELECTION CRITERIA.—In selecting a project for funding under this section—

(1) for projects located on the Northeast Corridor, the Secretary shall—

(A) make selections consistent with the Northeast Corridor Project Inventory published pursuant to subsection (e)(1), unless when necessary to address materially changed infrastructure or service conditions, changes in project sponsor capabilities or commitments, or other significant changes since the completion of the most recently issued Northeast Corridor Project Inventory; and

(B) for projects that benefit intercity and commuter rail services, only make such selections when Amtrak and the public authorities providing commuter rail passenger transportation at the eligible project location—

(i) are in compliance with section 24905(c)(2); and

(ii) identify funding for the intercity passenger rail share, the commuter rail share, and the local share of the eligible project before the commencement of the project;

(2) for projects not located on the Northeast Corridor, the Secretary shall—

(A) give preference to eligible projects—

(i) for which Amtrak is not the sole applicant;

(ii) that improve the financial performance, reliability, service frequency, or address the state of good repair of an Amtrak route; and

(iii) that are identified in, and consistent with, a corridor inventory prepared under the Corridor Identification and Development Program pursuant to section 25101; and

(B) take into account—

(i) the cost-benefit analysis of the proposed project, including anticipated private and public benefits relative to the costs of the proposed project, including—

(I) effects on system and service performance, including as measured by applicable metrics set forth in part 273 of title 49, Code of Federal Regulations (or successor regulations);

(II) effects on safety, competitiveness, reliability, trip or transit time, greenhouse gas emissions, and resilience;

(III) anticipated positive economic and employment impacts, including development in areas near passenger stations, historic districts, or other opportunity zones;

(IV) efficiencies from improved connections with other modes; and

(V) ability to meet existing or anticipated demand;

(ii) the degree to which the proposed project's business plan considers potential private sector participation in the financing, construction, or operation of the proposed project;

(iii) the applicant's past performance in developing and delivering similar projects, and previous financial contributions;

(iv) whether the applicant has, or will have—

(I) the legal, financial, and technical capacity to carry out the project;

(II) satisfactory continuing access to the equipment or facilities; and

(III) the capability and willingness to maintain the equipment or facilities;

(v) if applicable, the consistency of the project with planning guidance and documents set forth by the Secretary or otherwise required by law;

(vi) whether the proposed project serves historically unconnected or underconnected communities; and

(vii) any other relevant factors, as determined by the Secretary; and

(3) the Secretary shall reserve—

(A) not less than 45 percent of the amounts appropriated for grants under this section for projects not located along the Northeast Corridor, of which not less than 20 percent shall be for projects that benefit (in whole or in part) a long-distance route; and

(B) not less than 45 percent of the amounts appropriated for grants under this section for projects listed on the Northeast Corridor project inventory published pursuant to subsection (e)(1).

(e) LONG-TERM PLANNING.—Not later than 1 year after the date of enactment of the Passenger Rail Expansion and Rail Safety Act of 2021, and every 2 years thereafter, the Secretary shall create a predictable project pipeline that will assist Amtrak, States, and the public with long-term capital planning by publishing a Northeast Corridor project inventory that—

(1) identifies capital projects for Federal investment, project applicants, and proposed Federal funding levels under this section;

(2) specifies the order in which the Secretary will provide grant funding to projects that have identified sponsors and are located along the Northeast Corridor, including a method and plan for apportioning funds to project sponsors for the 2-year period, which may be altered by the Secretary, as necessary, if recipients are not carrying out projects in accordance with the anticipated schedule;

(3) takes into consideration the appropriate sequence and phasing of projects described in the Northeast Corridor capital investment plan developed pursuant to section 24904(a); [2]

(4) is consistent with the most recent Northeast Corridor service development plan update described in section 24904(d);[3]

(5) takes into consideration the existing commitments and anticipated Federal, project applicant, sponsor, and other relevant funding levels for the next 5 fiscal years based on information currently available to the Secretary; and

(6) is developed in consultation with the Northeast Corridor Commission and the owners of Northeast Corridor infrastructure and facilities.

(f) FEDERAL SHARE OF TOTAL PROJECT COSTS.—

(1) TOTAL PROJECT COST.—The Secretary shall estimate the total cost of a project under this section based on the best available information, including engineering studies, studies of economic feasibility, environmental analyses, and information on the expected use of equipment or facilities.

(2) FEDERAL SHARE.—The Federal share of total costs for a project under this section shall not exceed 80 percent, except as specified under paragraph (4).

(3) TREATMENT OF AMTRAK REVENUE.—If Amtrak is an applicant under this section,

Amtrak may use ticket and other revenues generated from its operations and other sources to satisfy the non-Federal share requirements.

(g) LETTERS OF INTENT; PHASED FUNDING AGREEMENTS.—

(1) LETTERS OF INTENT.—The Secretary may issue a letter of intent to a grantee under this section that—

(A) announces an intention to obligate, for a major capital project under this section, an amount from future available budget authority specified in law that is not more than the amount stipulated as the financial participation of the Secretary in the project; and

(B) states that the contingent commitment—

(i) is not an obligation of the Federal Government; and

(ii) is subject to the availability of appropriations for grants under this section and subject to Federal laws in force or enacted after the date of the contingent commitment.

(2) PHASED FUNDING AGREEMENTS.—

(A) IN GENERAL.—The Secretary may enter into a phased funding agreement with an applicant if—

(i) the project is highly rated, based on the evaluations and ratings conducted pursuant to this section and the applicable notice of funding opportunity; and

(ii) the Federal assistance to be provided for the project under this section is more than $80,000,000.

(B) TERMS.—A phased funding agreement shall—

(i) establish the terms of participation by the Federal Government in the project;

(ii) establish the maximum amount of Federal financial assistance for the project;

(iii) include the period of time for completing the project, even if such period extends beyond the period for which Federal financial assistance is authorized;

(iv) make timely and efficient management of the project easier in accordance with Federal law; and

(v) if applicable, specify when the process for complying with the National Environmental Policy Act of 1969 (42 U.S.C. 4321 et seq.) and related environmental laws will be completed for the project.

(C) SPECIAL FINANCIAL RULES.—

(i) IN GENERAL.—A phased funding agreement under this paragraph obligates an amount of available budget authority specified in law and may include a commitment, contingent on amounts to be specified in law in advance for commitments under this paragraph, to obligate an additional amount from future available budget authority specified in law.

(ii) STATEMENT OF CONTINGENT COMMITMENT.—The agreement shall state that the contingent commitment is not an obligation of the Government.

(iii) INTEREST AND OTHER FINANCING COSTS.—Interest and other financing costs of efficiently carrying out a part of the project within a reasonable time are a cost of carrying out the project under a phased funding agreement, except that eligible costs may not be more than the cost of the most favorable financing terms reasonably available for the project at the time of borrowing. The applicant shall certify, to the satisfaction of the Secretary, that the applicant has shown reasonable diligence in seeking the most favorable financing terms.

(iv) FAILURE TO CARRY OUT PROJECT.—If an applicant does not carry out the project for reasons within the control of the applicant, the applicant shall repay all Federal grant funds awarded for the project from all Federal funding sources, for all project activities, facilities, and equipment, plus reasonable interest and penalty charges allowable by law or established by the Secretary in the phased funding agreement. For purposes of this clause, a process for complying with the National Environmental Policy Act of 1969 (42 U.S.C. 4321 et seq.) that results in the selection of the no build alternative is not within the applicant's control.

(v) CREDITING OF FUNDS RECEIVED.—Any funds received by the Government under this paragraph, except for interest and penalty charges, shall be credited to the appropriation account from which the funds were originally derived.

(3) CONGRESSIONAL NOTIFICATION.—

(A) IN GENERAL.—Not later than 30 days before issuing a phased funding agreement under paragraph (2) or a letter under paragraph (1), the Secretary shall submit written notification to—

(i) the Committee on Commerce, Science, and Transportation of the Senate;

(ii) the Committee on Appropriations of the Senate;

(iii) the Committee on Transportation and Infrastructure of the House of Representatives; and

(iv) the Committee on Appropriations of the House of Representatives.

(B) CONTENTS.—The notification submitted pursuant to subparagraph (A) shall include—

(i) a copy of the phased funding agreement or the proposed letter;

(ii) the criteria used under subsection (d) for selecting the project for a grant award; and

(iii) a description of how the project meets such criteria.

(4) APPROPRIATIONS REQUIRED.—

(A) IN GENERAL.—The Secretary may enter into phased funding agreements under this subsection that contain contingent commitments to incur obligations in such amounts as the Secretary determines are appropriate.

(B) APPROPRIATIONS REQUIRED.—An obligation or administrative commitment may be made under this section only when amounts are appropriated for such purpose.

(h) AVAILABILITY.—Amounts appropriated for carrying out this section shall remain available until expended.

(i) GRANT CONDITIONS.—Except as specifically provided in this section, the use of any amounts appropriated for grants under this section shall be subject to the grant conditions under sections 22903 and 22905.

(j) ANNUAL REPORT ON PHASED FUNDING AGREEMENTS AND LETTERS OF INTENT.—Not later than the first Monday in February of each year, the Secretary shall submit a report to the Committee on Commerce, Science, and Transportation of the Senate, the Committee on Appropriations of the Senate, the Committee on Transportation and Infrastructure of the House of Representatives, and the Committee on Appropriations of the House of Representatives that includes—

(1) a proposal for the allocation of amounts to be available to finance grants for projects under this section among applicants for such amounts;

(2) evaluations and ratings, as applicable, for each project that has received a phased funding agreement or a letter of intent; and

(3) recommendations for each project that has received a phased funding agreement or a letter of intent for funding based on the evaluations and ratings, as applicable, and on existing commitments and anticipated funding levels for the next 3 fiscal years based on information currently available to the Secretary.

(k) REGIONAL PLANNING GUIDANCE CORRIDOR PLANNING.—The Secretary may withhold up to 5 percent of the total amount made available for this section to carry out planning and development activities related to section 25101, including—

(1) providing funding to public entities for the development of service development plans selected under the Corridor Identification and Development Program;

(2) facilitating and providing guidance for intercity passenger rail systems planning; and

(3) providing funding for the development and refinement of intercity passenger rail systems planning analytical tools and models.

(Added Pub. L. 114–94, div. A, title XI, §11302(a), Dec. 4, 2015, 129 Stat. 1648; amended Pub. L. 115–141, div. L, title I, Mar. 23, 2018, 132 Stat. 994; Pub. L. 115–420, §7(b)(3)(A)(i)(IV), Jan. 3, 2019, 132 Stat. 5447; Pub. L. 117–58, div. B, title II, §22307(a), Nov. 15, 2021, 135 Stat. 725.)

[1] So in original. The semicolon preceding the period probably should not appear.

[2] So in original. Probably should be "section 24904(b);".

[3] So in original. Probably should be "section 24904(a)(3);".

416

CHAPTER 251—PASSENGER RAIL PLANNING

Sec.

25101.   Corridor Identification and Development Program.

§25101. CORRIDOR IDENTIFICATION AND DEVELOPMENT PROGRAM

(a) IN GENERAL.—Not later than 180 days after the date of enactment of the Passenger Rail Expansion and Rail Safety Act of 2021, the Secretary of Transportation shall establish a program to facilitate the development of intercity passenger rail corridors. The program shall include—

(1) a process for eligible entities described in subsection (b) to submit proposals for the development of intercity passenger rail corridors;

(2) a process for the Secretary to review and select proposals in accordance with subsection (c);

(3) criteria for determining the level of readiness for Federal financial assistance of an intercity passenger rail corridor, which shall include—

(A) identification of a service operator which may include Amtrak or private rail carriers;

(B) identification of a service sponsor or sponsors;

(C) identification capital project sponsors;

(D) engagement with the host railroads; and

(E) other criteria as determined appropriate by the Secretary;

(4) a process for preparing service development plans in accordance with subsection (d), including the identification of planning funds, such as funds made available under section 24911(k) and interstate rail compact grants established under section 22210; [1]

(5) the creation of a pipeline of intercity passenger rail corridor projects under subsection (g);

(6) planning guidance to achieve the purposes of this section, including guidance for intercity passenger rail corridors not selected under this section; and

(7) such other features as the Secretary considers relevant to the successful development of intercity passenger rail corridors.

(b) ELIGIBLE ENTITIES.—The Secretary may receive proposals under this section from Amtrak, States, groups of States, entities implementing interstate compacts, regional passenger rail authorities, regional planning organizations, political subdivisions of a State, federally recognized Indian Tribes, and other public entities, as determined by the Secretary.

(c) CORRIDOR SELECTION.—In selecting intercity passenger rail corridors pursuant to subsection (a), the Secretary shall consider—

(1) whether the route was identified as part of a regional or interregional intercity passenger rail systems planning study;

(2) projected ridership, revenues, capital investment, and operating funding requirements;

(3) anticipated environmental, congestion mitigation, and other public benefits;

(4) projected trip times and their competitiveness with other transportation modes;

(5) anticipated positive economic and employment impacts, including development in the areas near passenger stations, historic districts, or other opportunity zones;

(6) committed or anticipated State, regional transportation authority, or other non-Federal funding for operating and capital costs;

(7) benefits to rural communities;

(8) whether the corridor is included in a State's approved State rail plan developed pursuant to chapter 227;

(9) whether the corridor serves historically unserved or underserved and low-income communities or areas of persistent poverty;

(10) whether the corridor would benefit or improve connectivity with existing or planned transportation services of other modes;

(11) whether the corridor connects at least 2 of the 100 most populated metropolitan areas;

(12) whether the corridor would enhance the regional equity and geographic diversity of intercity passenger rail service;

(13) whether the corridor is or would be integrated into the national rail passenger transportation system and whether the corridor would create benefits for other passenger rail routes and services; and

(14) whether a passenger rail operator, including a private rail carrier, has expressed support for the corridor.

(d) SERVICE DEVELOPMENT PLANS.—For each corridor proposal selected for development under this section, the Secretary shall partner with the entity that submitted the proposal, relevant States, and Amtrak, as appropriate, to prepare a service development plan (or to update an existing service development plan), which shall include—

(1) a detailed description of the proposed intercity passenger rail service, including train frequencies, peak and average operating speeds, and trip times;

(2) a corridor project inventory that—

(A) identifies the capital projects necessary to achieve the proposed intercity passenger rail service, including—

(i) the capital projects for which Federal investment will be sought;

(ii) the likely project applicants; and

(iii) the proposed Federal funding levels;

(B) specifies the order in which Federal funding will be sought for the capital projects identified under subparagraph (A), after considering the appropriate sequence and phasing of projects based on the anticipated availability of funds; and

(C) is developed in consultation with the entities listed in subsection (e);

(3) a schedule and any associated phasing of projects and related service initiation or changes;

(4) project sponsors and other entities expected to participate in carrying out the plan;

(5) a description of how the corridor would comply with Federal rail safety and

security laws, orders, and regulations;

(6) the locations of existing and proposed stations;

(7) the needs for rolling stock and other equipment;

(8) a financial plan identifying projected—

(A) annual revenues;

(B) annual ridership;

(C) capital investments before service could be initiated;

(D) capital investments required to maintain service;

(E) annual operating and costs; and

(F) sources of capital investment and operating financial support;

(9) a description of how the corridor would contribute to the development of a multi-State regional network of intercity passenger rail;

(10) an intermodal plan describing how the new or improved corridor facilitates travel connections with other passenger transportation services;

(11) a description of the anticipated environmental benefits of the corridor; and

(12) a description of the corridor's impacts on highway and aviation congestion, energy consumption, land use, and economic development in the service area.

(e) CONSULTATION.—In partnering on the preparation of a service development plan under subsection (d), the Secretary shall consult with—

(1) Amtrak;

(2) appropriate State and regional transportation authorities and local officials;

(3) representatives of employee labor organizations representing railroad and other appropriate employees;

(4) host railroads for the proposed corridor; and

(5) other stakeholders, as determined by the Secretary.

(f) UPDATES.—Every 5 years, after the initial development of the service development plan under subsection (d), if at least 40 percent of the work to implement a service development plan prepared under subsection (d) has not yet been completed, the plan's sponsor, in consultation with the Secretary, shall determine whether such plan should be updated.

(g) PROJECT PIPELINE.—Not later than 1 year after the establishment of the program under this section, and by February 1st of each year thereafter, the Secretary shall submit to the Committee on Commerce, Science, and Transportation of the Senate, the Committee on Appropriations of the Senate, and the Committee on Transportation and Infrastructure of the House of Representatives, and the Committee on Appropriations of the House of Representatives a project pipeline, in accordance with this section, that—

(1) identifies intercity passenger rail corridors selected for development under this section;

(2) identifies capital projects for Federal investment, project applicants, and proposed Federal funding levels, as applicable, consistent with the corridor project inventory;

(3) specifies the order in which the Secretary would provide Federal financial assistance, subject to the availability of funds, to projects that have identified sponsors,

including a method and plan for apportioning funds to project sponsors for a 5-year period, which may be altered by the Secretary, as necessary, if recipients are not carrying out projects on the anticipated schedule;

(4) takes into consideration the appropriate sequence and phasing of projects described in the corridor project inventory;

(5) takes into consideration the existing commitments and anticipated Federal, project applicant, sponsor, and other relevant funding levels for the next 5 fiscal years based on information currently available to the Secretary;

(6) is prioritized based on the level of readiness of the corridor; and

(7) reflects consultation with Amtrak.

(h) DEFINITION.—In this section, the term "intercity passenger rail corridor" means—

(1) a new intercity passenger rail route of less than 750 miles;

(2) the enhancement of an existing intercity passenger rail route of less than 750 miles;

(3) the restoration of service over all or portions of an intercity passenger rail route formerly operated by Amtrak; or

(4) the increase of service frequency of a long-distance intercity passenger rail route.

(Added Pub. L. 117–58, div. B, title II, §22308(a), Nov. 15, 2021, 135 Stat. 730.)

---

[1] So in original. Probably should be "section 22910;".

PART D—HIGH-SPEED RAIL

CHAPTER 261—HIGH-SPEED RAIL ASSISTANCE

§26101. HIGH-SPEED RAIL CORRIDOR PLANNING

(a) CORRIDOR PLANNING ASSISTANCE.—(1) The Secretary may provide under this section financial assistance to a public agency or group of public agencies for corridor planning for up to 50 percent of the publicly financed costs associated with eligible activities.

(2) No less than 20 percent of the publicly financed costs associated with eligible activities shall come from State and local sources, which State and local sources may not include funds from any Federal program.

(b) ELIGIBLE ACTIVITIES.—(1) A corridor planning activity is eligible for financial assistance under subsection (a) if the Secretary determines that it is necessary to establish appropriate engineering, operational, financial, environmental, or socioeconomic projections for the establishment of high-speed rail service in the corridor and that it leads toward development of a prudent financial and institutional plan for implementation of specific high-speed rail improvements, or if it is an activity described in subparagraph (M). Eligible corridor planning activities include—

(A) environmental assessments;

(B) feasibility studies emphasizing commercial technology improvements or applications;

(C) economic analyses, including ridership, revenue, and operating expense forecasting;

(D) assessing the impact on rail employment of developing high-speed rail corridors;

(E) assessing community economic impacts;

(F) coordination with State and metropolitan area transportation planning and corridor planning with other States;

(G) operational planning;

(H) route selection analyses and purchase of rights-of-way for proposed high-speed rail service;

(I) preliminary engineering and design;

(J) identification of specific improvements to a corridor, including electrification, line straightening and other right-of-way improvements, bridge rehabilitation and replacement, use of advanced locomotives and rolling stock, ticketing, coordination with other modes of transportation, parking and other means of passenger access, track, signal, station, and other capital work, and use of intermodal terminals;

(K) preparation of financing plans and prospectuses;

(L) creation of public/private partnerships; and

(M) the acquisition of locomotives, rolling stock, track, and signal equipment.

(2) No financial assistance shall be provided under this section for corridor planning with respect to the main line of the Northeast Corridor, between Washington, District of Columbia, and Boston, Massachusetts.

(c) CRITERIA FOR DETERMINING FINANCIAL ASSISTANCE.—Selection by the Secretary of recipients of financial assistance under this section shall be based on such criteria as the Secretary considers appropriate, including—

(1) the relationship of the corridor to the Secretary's national high-speed ground transportation policy;

(2) the extent to which the proposed planning focuses on systems which will achieve sustained speeds of 125 mph or greater;

(3) the integration of the corridor into metropolitan area and statewide transportation planning;

(4) the potential interconnection of the corridor with other parts of the Nation's transportation system, including the interconnection with other countries;

(5) the anticipated effect of the corridor on the congestion of other modes of transportation;

(6) whether the work to be funded will aid the efforts of State and local governments to comply with the Clean Air Act (42 U.S.C. 7401 et seq.);

(7) the past and proposed financial commitments and other support of State and local governments and the private sector to the proposed high-speed rail program, including the acquisition of rolling stock;

(8) the estimated level of ridership;

(9) the estimated capital cost of corridor improvements, including the cost of closing, improving, or separating highway-rail grade crossings;

(10) rail transportation employment impacts;

(11) community economic impacts;

(12) the extent to which the projected revenues of the proposed high-speed rail service, along with any financial commitments of State or local governments and the private sector, are expected to cover capital costs and operating and maintenance expenses;

(13) whether a specific route has been selected, specific improvements identified, and capacity studies completed; and

(14) whether the corridor has been designated as a high-speed rail corridor by the Secretary.

(Added Pub. L. 103–440, title I, §103(a)(2), Nov. 2, 1994, 108 Stat. 4616; amended Pub. L. 109–59, title IX, §9001(a)(1), Aug. 10, 2005, 119 Stat. 1918; Pub. L. 110–432, div. B, title V, §501(a), Oct. 16, 2008, 122 Stat. 4959.)

§26102. High-speed rail technology improvements

(a) Authority.—The Secretary may undertake activities for the improvement, adaptation, and integration of proven technologies for commercial application in high-speed rail service in the United States.

(b) Eligible Recipients.—In carrying out activities authorized by subsection (a), the Secretary may provide financial assistance to any United States private business, educational institution located in the United States, State or local government or public authority, or agency of the Federal Government.

(c) Consultation With Other Agencies.—In carrying out activities authorized by subsection (a), the Secretary shall consult with such other governmental agencies as may be necessary concerning the availability of appropriate technologies for commercial application in high-speed rail service in the United States.

(Added Pub. L. 103–440, title I, §103(a)(2), Nov. 2, 1994, 108 Stat. 4617.)

§26103. Safety regulations and evaluation

The Secretary—

(1) shall promulgate such safety regulations as may be necessary for high-speed rail services;

(2) shall, before promulgating such regulations, consult with developers of new high-speed rail technologies to develop a method for evaluating safety performance; and

(3) may solicit feedback from relevant safety experts or representatives of rail employees who perform work on similar technology or who may be expected to perform work on new technology, as appropriate.

(Added Pub. L. 103–440, title I, §103(a)(2), Nov. 2, 1994, 108 Stat. 4618; amended Pub. L. 117–58, div. B, title II, §22419(a), Nov. 15, 2021, 135 Stat. 749.)

§26104. Authorization of appropriations

(a) Fiscal Years 2006 Through 2013.—There are authorized to be appropriated to the Secretary—

(1) $30,000,000 for carrying out section 26101; and

(2) $30,000,000 for carrying out section 26102,

for each of the fiscal years 2006 through 2013.

(b) Funds To Remain Available.—Funds made available under this section shall remain available until expended.

(Added Pub. L. 103–440, title I, §103(a)(2), Nov. 2, 1994, 108 Stat. 4618; amended Pub. L. 105–178, title VII, §7201(a), June 9, 1998, 112 Stat. 469; Pub. L. 109–59, title IX, §9001(b), Aug. 10, 2005, 119 Stat. 1919; Pub. L. 110–432, div. B, title V, §501(b), Oct. 16, 2008, 122 Stat. 4960.)

§26105. Definitions

For purposes of this chapter—

(1) the term "financial assistance" includes grants, contracts,,[1] cooperative agreements, and other transactions;

(2) the term "high-speed rail" means all forms of nonhighway ground transportation that run on rails or electromagnetic guideways providing transportation service which is—

(A) reasonably expected to reach sustained speeds of more than 125 miles per hour; and

(B) made available to members of the general public as passengers,

but does not include rapid transit operations within an urban area that are not connected to the general rail system of transportation;

(3) the term "publicly financed costs" means the costs funded after April 29, 1993, by Federal, State, and local governments;

(4) the term "Secretary" means the Secretary of Transportation;

(5) the term "State" means any of the several States, the District of Columbia, Puerto Rico, the Northern Mariana Islands, the Virgin Islands, Guam, American Samoa, and any other territory or possession of the United States; and

(6) the term "United States private business" means a business entity organized under the laws of the United States, or of a State, and conducting substantial business operations in the United States.

(Added Pub. L. 103–440, title I, §103(a)(2), Nov. 2, 1994, 108 Stat. 4618; amended Pub. L. 105–178, title VII, §7201(b), June 9, 1998, 112 Stat. 470; Pub. L. 109–59, title IX, §9001(c), Aug. 10, 2005, 119 Stat. 1919.)

---

[1] *So in original.*

§26106. HIGH-SPEED RAIL CORRIDOR DEVELOPMENT

(a) IN GENERAL.—The Secretary of Transportation shall establish and implement a high-speed rail corridor development program.

(b) DEFINITIONS.—In this section, the following definitions apply:

(1) APPLICANT.—The term "applicant" means a State, a group of States, an Interstate Compact, a public agency established by one or more States and having responsibility for providing high-speed rail service, or Amtrak.

(2) CORRIDOR.—The term "corridor" means a corridor designated by the Secretary pursuant to section 104(d)(2)[1] of title 23.

(3) CAPITAL PROJECT.—The term "capital project" means a project or program in a State rail plan developed under chapter 227 of this title for acquiring, constructing, improving, or inspecting equipment, track, and track structures, or a facility of use in or for the primary benefit of high-speed rail service, expenses incidental to the acquisition or construction (including designing, engineering, location surveying, mapping, environmental studies, and acquiring rights-of-way), payments for the capital portions of rail trackage rights agreements, highway-rail grade crossing improvements related to high-speed rail service, mitigating environmental impacts, communication and signalization improvements, relocation assistance, acquiring replacement housing sites,

and acquiring, constructing, relocating, and rehabilitating replacement housing.

(4) HIGH-SPEED RAIL.—The term "high-speed rail" means intercity passenger rail service that is reasonably expected to reach speeds of at least 110 miles per hour.

(5) INTERCITY PASSENGER RAIL SERVICE.—The term "intercity passenger rail service" has the meaning given the term "intercity rail passenger transportation" in section 24102 of this title.

(6) STATE.—The term "State" means any of the 50 States or the District of Columbia.

(c) GENERAL AUTHORITY.—The Secretary may make grants under this section to an applicant to finance capital projects in high-speed rail corridors.

(d) APPLICATIONS.—Each applicant seeking to receive a grant under this section to develop a high-speed rail corridor shall submit to the Secretary an application in such form and in accordance with such requirements as the Secretary shall establish.

(e) COMPETITIVE GRANT SELECTION AND CRITERIA FOR GRANTS.—

(1) IN GENERAL.—The Secretary shall—

(A) establish criteria for selecting among projects that meet the criteria specified in paragraph (2);

(B) conduct a national solicitation for applications; and

(C) award grants on a competitive basis.

(2) GRANT CRITERIA.—The Secretary, in selecting the recipients of high-speed rail development grants to be provided under subsection (c), shall—

(A) require—

(i) that the project be part of a State rail plan developed under chapter 227 of this title, or under the plan required by section 211 of the Passenger Rail Investment and Improvement Act of 2008;

(ii) that the applicant or recipient has or will have the legal, financial, and technical capacity to carry out the project, satisfactory continuing control over the use of the equipment or facilities, and the capability and willingness to maintain the equipment or facilities;

(iii) that the project be based on the results of preliminary engineering studies or other planning, including corridor planning activities funded under section 26101 of this title;

(iv) that the applicant provides sufficient information upon which the Secretary can make the findings required by this subsection;

(v) that if an applicant has selected the proposed operator of its service, that the applicant provide written justification to the Secretary showing why the proposed operator is the best, taking into account costs and other factors;

(vi) that each proposed project meet all safety and security requirements that are applicable to the project under law; and

(vii) that each project be compatible with, and operated in conformance with—

(I) plans developed pursuant to the requirements of section 135 of title 23; and

(II) the national rail plan (if it is available);

(B) select high-speed rail projects—

(i) that are anticipated to result in significant improvements to intercity rail passenger service, including, but not limited to, consideration of the project's—

(I) levels of estimated ridership, increased on-time performance, reduced trip time, additional service frequency to meet anticipated or existing demand, or other significant service enhancements as measured against minimum standards developed under section 207 of the Passenger Rail Investment and Improvement Act of 2008;

(II) anticipated favorable impact on air or highway traffic congestion, capacity, or safety; and

(ii) for which there is a high degree of confidence that the proposed project is feasible and will result in the anticipated benefits, as indicated by—

(I) the project's precommencement compliance with environmental protection requirements;

(II) the readiness of the project to be commenced;

(III) the commitment of any affected host rail carrier to ensure the realization of the anticipated benefits; and

(IV) other relevant factors as determined by the Secretary;

(iii) for which the level of the anticipated benefits compares favorably to the amount of Federal funding requested under this section; and

(C) give greater consideration to projects—

(i) that are anticipated to result in benefits to other modes of transportation and to the public at large, including, but not limited to, consideration of the project's—

(I) encouragement of intermodal connectivity through provision of direct connections between train stations, airports, bus terminals, subway stations, ferry ports, and other modes of transportation;

(II) anticipated improvement of conventional intercity passenger, freight, or commuter rail operations;

(III) use of positive train control technologies;

(IV) environmental benefits, including projects that involve the purchase of environmentally sensitive, fuel-efficient, and cost-effective passenger rail equipment;

(V) anticipated positive economic and employment impacts;

(VI) encouragement of State and private contributions toward station development, energy and environmental efficiency, and economic benefits; and

(VII) falling under the description in section 5302(a)(1)(G) [1] of this title as defined to support intercity passenger rail service; and

(ii) that incorporate equitable financial participation in the project's financing, including, but not limited to, consideration of—

(I) donated property interests or services;

(II) financial contributions by intercity passenger, freight, and commuter rail carriers commensurate with the benefit expected to their operations; and

(III) financial commitments from host railroads, non-Federal governmental entities, non-governmental entities, and others.

(3) GRANT CONDITIONS.—The Secretary shall require each recipient of a grant under this chapter to comply with the grant requirements of section 22905.

(4) STATE RAIL PLANS.—State rail plans completed before the date of enactment of the Passenger Rail Investment and Improvement Act of 2008 that substantially meet the requirements of chapter 227 of this title, as determined by the Secretary pursuant to section 22506 [1] of this title, shall be deemed by the Secretary to have met the requirements of paragraph (2)(A)(i) of this subsection.

(f) FEDERAL SHARE.—The Federal share of the cost of a project financed under this section shall not exceed 80 percent of the project net capital cost.

(g) ISSUANCE OF REGULATIONS.—Within 1 year after the date of enactment of this section, the Secretary shall issue regulations to carry out this section.

(h) AUTHORIZATION OF APPROPRIATIONS.—There are authorized to be appropriated to the Secretary to carry out this section—

(1) $150,000,000 for fiscal year 2009;

(2) $300,000,000 for fiscal year 2010;

(3) $350,000,000 for fiscal year 2011;

(4) $350,000,000 for fiscal year 2012; and

(5) $350,000,000 for fiscal year 2013.

(Added Pub. L. 110–432, div. B, title V, §501(d), Oct. 16, 2008, 122 Stat. 4960; amended Pub. L. 115–420, §7(b)(3)(A)(ii), Jan. 3, 2019, 132 Stat. 5447.)

[1] See References in Text note below.

PART E—MISCELLANEOUS

CHAPTER 281—LAW ENFORCEMENT

§28101. RAIL POLICE OFFICERS

(a) IN GENERAL.—Under regulations prescribed by the Secretary of Transportation, a rail police officer who is directly employed by or contracted by a rail carrier and certified or commissioned as a police officer under the laws of a State may enforce the laws of any jurisdiction in which the rail carrier owns property, to the extent of the authority of a police officer certified or commissioned under the laws of that jurisdiction, to protect—

(1) employees, passengers, or patrons of the rail carrier;

(2) property, equipment, and facilities owned, leased, operated, or maintained by the rail carrier;

(3) property moving in interstate or foreign commerce in the possession of the rail carrier; and

(4) personnel, equipment, and material moving by rail that are vital to the national defense.

(b) ASSIGNMENT.—A railroad police officer directly employed by or contracted by a railroad carrier and certified or commissioned as a police officer under the laws of a State may be temporarily assigned to assist a second railroad carrier in carrying out law enforcement duties upon the request of the second railroad carrier, at which time the police officer shall be considered to be an employee or agent, as applicable, of the second railroad carrier and shall have authority to enforce the laws of any jurisdiction in which the second railroad carrier owns property to the same extent as provided in subsection (a).

(c) TRANSFERS.—

(1) IN GENERAL.—If a railroad police officer directly employed by or contracted by a rail carrier and certified or commissioned as a police officer under the laws of a State transfers primary employment or residence from the certifying or commissioning State to another State or jurisdiction, the railroad police officer, not later than 1 year after the date of transfer, shall apply to be certified or commissioned as a police office [1] under the laws of the State of new primary employment or residence.

(2) INTERIM PERIOD.—During the period beginning on the date of transfer and ending 1 year after the date of transfer, a railroad police officer directly employed by or contracted by a rail carrier and certified or commissioned as a police officer under the laws of a State may enforce the laws of the new jurisdiction in which the railroad police officer resides, to the same extent as provided in subsection (a).

(d) TRAINING.—

(1) IN GENERAL.—A State may recognize as meeting that State's basic police officer certification or commissioning requirements for qualification as a rail police officer under this section any individual who successfully completes a program at a State-recognized police training academy in another State or at a Federal law enforcement training center and who is certified or commissioned as a police officer by that other State.

(2) RULE OF CONSTRUCTION.—Nothing in this subsection shall be construed as superseding or affecting any State training requirements related to criminal law, criminal procedure, motor vehicle code, any other State law, or State-mandated comparative or annual in-service training academy or Federal law enforcement training center.

(Pub. L. 103–272, §1(e), July 5, 1994, 108 Stat. 939, §26101; renumbered §28101, Pub. L. 103–440, title I, §103(a)(1), Nov. 2, 1994, 108 Stat. 4616; amended Pub. L. 110–53, title XV, §1526(a), Aug. 3, 2007, 121 Stat. 452; Pub. L. 114–94, div. A, title XI, §11412(a), Dec. 4, 2015, 129 Stat. 1687.)

[1] *So in original. Probably should be "officer".*

§28102. LIMIT ON CERTAIN ACCIDENT OR INCIDENT LIABILITY

(a) GENERAL.—When a publicly financed commuter transportation authority established under Virginia law makes a contract to indemnify Amtrak for liability for operations conducted by or for the authority or to indemnify a rail carrier over whose tracks those operations are conducted, liability against Amtrak, the authority, or the carrier for all claims (including punitive damages) arising from an accident or incident in the District of Columbia related to those operations may not be more than the limits of the liability coverage the authority maintains to indemnify Amtrak or the carrier.

(b) MINIMUM REQUIRED LIABILITY COVERAGE.—A publicly financed commuter transportation authority referred to in subsection (a) of this section must maintain a total minimum liability coverage of at least $200,000,000.

(c) EFFECTIVENESS.—This section is effective only after Amtrak or a rail carrier seeking an indemnification contract under this section makes an operating agreement with a publicly financed commuter transportation authority established under Virginia law to provide access to its property for revenue transportation related to the operations of the authority.

(Pub. L. 103–272, §1(e), July 5, 1994, 108 Stat. 940, §26102; renumbered §28102, Pub. L. 103–440, title I, §103(a)(1), Nov. 2, 1994, 108 Stat. 4616.)

§28103. LIMITATIONS ON RAIL PASSENGER TRANSPORTATION LIABILITY

(a) LIMITATIONS.—(1) Notwithstanding any other statutory or common law or public policy, or the nature of the conduct giving rise to damages or liability, in a claim for personal injury to a passenger, death of a passenger, or damage to property of a passenger arising from or in connection with the provision of rail passenger transportation, or from or in connection with any rail passenger transportation operations over or rail passenger transportation use of right-of-way or facilities owned, leased, or maintained by any high-speed railroad authority or operator, any commuter authority or operator, any rail carrier, or any State, punitive damages, to the extent permitted by applicable State law, may be awarded in connection with any such claim only if the plaintiff establishes by clear and convincing evidence that the harm that is the subject of the action was the result of conduct carried out by the defendant with a conscious, flagrant indifference to the rights or safety of others. If, in any case wherein death was caused, the law of the place where the act or omission complained of occurred provides, or has been construed to provide, for damages only punitive in nature, this paragraph shall not apply.

(2) The aggregate allowable awards to all rail passengers, against all defendants, for all claims, including claims for punitive damages, arising from a single accident or incident, shall not exceed $200,000,000.

(b) CONTRACTUAL OBLIGATIONS.—A provider of rail passenger transportation may enter into contracts that allocate financial responsibility for claims.

(c) MANDATORY COVERAGE.—Amtrak shall maintain a total minimum liability coverage for claims through insurance and self-insurance of at least $200,000,000 per accident or incident.

(d) EFFECT ON OTHER LAWS.—This section shall not affect the damages that may be recovered under the Act of April 27, 1908 (45 U.S.C. 51 et seq.; popularly known as the "Federal Employers' Liability Act") or under any workers compensation Act.

(e) DEFINITION.—For purposes of this section—

(1) the term "claim" means a claim made—

(A) against Amtrak, any high-speed railroad authority or operator, any commuter authority or operator, any rail carrier, or any State; or

(B) against an officer, employee, affiliate engaged in railroad operations, or agent, of Amtrak, any high-speed railroad authority or operator, any commuter authority or operator, any rail carrier, or any State;

(2) the term "punitive damages" means damages awarded against any person or entity to punish or deter such person or entity, or others, from engaging in similar behavior in the future; and

(3) the term "rail carrier" includes a person providing excursion, scenic, or museum train service, and an owner or operator of a privately owned rail passenger car.

(Added Pub. L. 105–134, title I, §161(a), Dec. 2, 1997, 111 Stat. 2577.)

CHAPTER 283—STANDARD WORK DAY

§28301. GENERAL

(a) EIGHT HOUR DAY.—In contracts for labor and service, 8 hours shall be a day's work and the standard day's work for determining the compensation for services of an employee employed by a common carrier by railroad subject to subtitle IV of this title and actually engaged in any capacity in operating trains used for transporting passengers or property on railroads from—

(1) a State of the United States or the District of Columbia to any other State or the District of Columbia;

(2) one place in a territory or possession of the United States to another place in the same territory or possession;

(3) a place in the United States to an adjacent foreign country; or

(4) a place in the United States through a foreign country to any other place in the United States.

(b) APPLICATION.—Subsection (a) of this section—

(1) does not apply to—

(A) an independently owned and operated railroad not exceeding one hundred miles in length;

(B) an electric street railroad; and

(C) an electric interurban railroad; but

(2) does apply to an independently owned and operated railroad less than one hundred miles in length—

(A) whose principal business is leasing or providing terminal or transfer facilities to other railroads; or

(B) engaged in transfers of freight between railroads or between railroads and industrial plants.

(Added Pub. L. 104–287, §5(56)(A), Oct. 11, 1996, 110 Stat. 3394.)

§28302. PENALTIES

A person violating section 28301 of this title shall be fined under title 18, imprisoned not more than one year, or both.

(Added Pub. L. 104–287, §5(56)(A), Oct. 11, 1996, 110 Stat. 3394.)

CHAPTER 285—COMMUTER RAIL MEDIATION

[1] *So in original. Probably should be followed by a period.*

§28501. Definitions

In this chapter—

(1) the term "Board" means the Surface Transportation Board;

(2) the term "capital work" means maintenance, restoration, reconstruction, capacity enhancement, or rehabilitation work on trackage that would be treated, in accordance with generally accepted accounting principles, as a capital item rather than an expense;

(3) the term "commuter rail passenger transportation" has the meaning given that term in section 24102;

(4) the term "public transportation authority" means a local governmental authority (as defined in section 5302) established to provide, or make a contract providing for, commuter rail passenger transportation;

(5) the term "rail carrier" means a person, other than a governmental authority, providing common carrier railroad transportation for compensation subject to the jurisdiction of the Board under chapter 105;

(6) the term "segregated fixed guideway facility" means a fixed guideway facility constructed within the railroad right-of-way of a rail carrier but physically separate from trackage, including relocated trackage, within the right-of-way used by a rail carrier for freight transportation purposes; and

(7) the term "trackage" means a railroad line of a rail carrier, including a spur, industrial, team, switching, side, yard, or station track, and a facility of a rail carrier.

(Added Pub. L. 110–432, div. B, title IV, §401(a), Oct. 16, 2008, 122 Stat. 4955; amended Pub. L. 117–58, div. C, §30001(b)(4), Nov. 15, 2021, 135 Stat. 890.)

§28502. Surface Transportation Board mediation of trackage use requests

If, after a reasonable period of negotiation, a public transportation authority cannot reach agreement with a rail carrier to use trackage of, and have related services provided by, the rail carrier for purposes of commuter rail passenger transportation, the public transportation authority or the rail carrier may apply to the Board for nonbinding mediation. The Board shall conduct the nonbinding mediation in accordance with the mediation process of section 1109.4 of title 49, Code of Federal Regulations, as in effect on the date of enactment of this section.

(Added Pub. L. 110–432, div. B, title IV, §401(a), Oct. 16, 2008, 122 Stat. 4955.)

§28503. SURFACE TRANSPORTATION BOARD MEDIATION OF RIGHTS-OF-WAY USE REQUESTS

If, after a reasonable period of negotiation, a public transportation authority cannot reach agreement with a rail carrier to acquire an interest in a railroad right-of-way for the construction and operation of a segregated fixed guideway facility to provide commuter rail passenger transportation, the public transportation authority or the rail carrier may apply to the Board for nonbinding mediation. The Board shall conduct the nonbinding mediation in accordance with the mediation process of section 1109.4 of title 49, Code of Federal Regulations, as in effect on the date of enactment of this section.

(Added Pub. L. 110–432, div. B, title IV, §401(a), Oct. 16, 2008, 122 Stat. 4956.)

§28504. APPLICABILITY OF OTHER LAWS

Nothing in this chapter shall be construed to limit a rail transportation provider's right under section 28103(b) to enter into contracts that allocate financial responsibility for claims.

(Added Pub. L. 110–432, div. B, title IV, §401(a), Oct. 16, 2008, 122 Stat. 4956.)

§28505. RULES AND REGULATIONS

Within 1 year after the date of enactment of this section, the Board shall issue such rules and regulations as may be necessary to carry out this chapter.

(Added Pub. L. 110–432, div. B, title IV, §401(a), Oct. 16, 2008, 122 Stat. 4956.)

REGIONAL RAIL REORGANIZATION ACT OF 1973

PUBLIC LAW 93-236
AS AMENDED THROUGH P.L. 105178

REGIONAL RAIL REORGANIZATION ACT OF 1973

[Public Law 93-236]

[As Amended Through P.L. 105–178, Enacted June 9, 1998]

AN ACT To authorize and direct the maintenance of adequate and efficient rail services in the Midwest and Northeast region of the United States, and for other purposes.

Be it enacted by the Senate and House of Representatives of the United States of America in Congress assembled,

That this Act, divided into titles and sections according to the following table of contents, may be cited as the "Regional Rail Reorganization Act of 1973".

TITLE I—GENERAL PROVISIONS

DECLARATION OF POLICY

SEC. 101. (a) FINDINGS.—The Congress finds and declares that—

(1) Essential rail service in the midwest and northeast region of the United States is provided by railroads which are today insolvent and attempting to undergo reorganization under the Bankruptcy Act.

(2) This essential rail service is threatened with cessation or significant curtailment because of the inability of the trustees of such railroads to formulate acceptable plans of reorganization. This rail service is operated over rail properties which were acquired for a public use, but which have been permitted to deteriorate and now require extensive rehabilitation and modernization.

(3) The public convenience and necessity require adequate and efficient rail service in this region and throughout the Nation to meet the needs of commerce, the national defense, the environment, and the service requirements of passengers, United States mail, shippers, States and their political subdivisions, and consumers.

(4) Continuation and improvement of essential rail service in this region is also necessary to preserve and maintain adequate national rail services and an efficient national rail transportation system.

(5) Rail service and rail transportation offer economic and environmental advantages with respect to land use, air pollution, noise levels, energy efficiency and conservation, resource allocation, safety, and cost per ton-mile of movement to such extent that the preservation and maintenance of adequate and efficient rail service is in the national interest.

(6) These needs cannot be met without substantial action

441

by the Federal Government.

(b) PURPOSES.—It is therefore declared to be the purpose of Congress in this Act to provide for—

(1) the identification of a rail service system in the midwest and northeast region which is adequate to meet the needs and service requirements of this region and of the national rail transportation system;

(2) the reorganization of railroads in this region into an economically viable system capable of providing adequate and efficient rail service to the region;

(3) the establishment of the United States Railway Association, with enumerated powers and responsibilities;

(4) the establishment of the Consolidated Rail Corporation, with enumerated powers and responsibilities;

(5) assistance to States and local and regional transportation authorities for continuation of local rail services threatened with cessation; and

(6) necessary Federal financial assistance at the lowest possible cost to the general taxpayer.

[45 U.S.C. 701]

DEFINITIONS

SEC. 102. As used in this Act, unless the context otherwise requires—

(1) "Association" means the United States Railway Association, established under section 201 of this Act;

(2) "Commission" means the Interstate Commerce Commission;

(3) "Commuter authority" means any State, local, or regional authority, corporation, or other entity established for purposes of providing commuter service, and includes the Metropolitan Transportation Authority, the Connecticut Department of Transportation, the Maryland Department of Transportation, the Southeastern Pennsylvania Transportation Authority, the New Jersey Transit Corporation, the Massachusetts Bay Transportation Authority, the Port Authority Trans-Hudson Corporation, any successor agencies, and any entity created by one or more such agencies for the

purpose of operating, or contracting for the operation of, commuter service;

(4) "Commuter service" means short-haul rail passenger service operated in metropolitan and suburban areas, whether within or across the geographical boundaries of a State, usually characterized by reduced fare, multiple-ride, and commutation tickets, and by morning and evening peak period operations;

(5) "Corporation" means the Consolidated Rail Corporation required to be established under section 301 of this Act or its successor by merger, consolidation or other form of succession carried out under applicable law for the purpose of changing the State of its incorporation;

(6) "effective date of the final system plan" means the date on which the final system plan or any revised final system plan is deemed approved by Congress, in accordance with section 208 of this Act;

(7) "employees stock ownership plan" means a technique of corporate finance that uses a stock bonus trust or a company stock money purchase pension trust which qualifies under section 401(a) of the Internal Revenue Code of 1954 (26 U.S.C. 401(a)) in connection with the financing of corporate improvements, transfers in the ownership of corporate assets, and other capital requirements of a corporation and which is designed to build beneficial equity ownership of shares in the employer corporation into its employees substantially in proportion to their relative incomes, without requiring any cash outlay, any reduction in pay or other employee benefits, or the surrender of any other rights on the part of such employees;

(8) "final system plan" means the plan of reorganization for the restructure, rehabilitation, and modernization of railroads in reorganization prepared pursuant to section 206 and approved pursuant to section 208 of this Act;

(9) "Finance Committee" means the Finance Committee of the Board of Directors of the Association established under section 201(i) of this Act;

(10) "includes" and variants thereof should be read as if the phrase "but is not limited to" were also set forth;

(11) "local or regional transportation authority" includes a political subdivision of a State.[1]

(12) "Office" means the Rail Services Planning Office established under section 205 of this Act;

(13) "profitable railroad" means a railroad which is not a railroad in reorganization. The term does not include the Corporation, the National Railroad Passenger Corporation, or a railroad leased, operated, or controlled by a railroad in reorganization in the region;

(14) "rail properties" means assets or rights owned, leased, or otherwise controlled by a railroad (or a person owned, leased, or otherwise controlled by a railroad) which are used or useful in rail transportation service; except that the term, when used in conjunction with the phrase "railroads leased, operated, or controlled by a railroad in reorganization", shall not include assets or rights owned, leased, or otherwise controlled by a Class I railroad which is not wholly owned, operated, or leased by a railroad in reorganization but is controlled by a railroad in reorganization;

(15) "railroad" means a rail carrier subject to part A of subtitle IV of title 49, United States Code. The term includes the Corporation and the National Railroad Passenger Corporation;

(16) "railroad in reorganization" means a railroad which is subject to a bankruptcy proceeding and which has not been determined by a court to be reorganizable or not subject to reorganization pursuant to this Act as prescribed in section 207(b) of this Act. A "bankruptcy proceeding" includes a proceeding pursuant to section 77 of the Bankruptcy Act (11 U.S.C. 205) and an equity receivership or equivalent proceeding;

(17) "Region" means the States of Maine, New Hampshire, Vermont, Massachusetts, Connecticut, Rhode Island, New York, New Jersey, Pennsylvania, Delaware, Maryland, Virginia, West Virginia, Ohio, Indiana, Michigan, and Illinois; the District of Columbia; and those portions of contiguous States in which are located rail properties owned or operated by railroads doing business primarily in the aforementioned jurisdictions (as determined by the Commission by order);

(17A) "sale date" means the date on which the initial public offering of the securities of the Corporation is closed under the Conrail Privatization Act;

(18) "Secretary" means the Secretary of Transportation or the designated representative of the Secretary;

(19) "State" means any State or the District of Columbia;

(20) "subsidiary" means any corporation 100 percent of whose total combined voting shares are, directly or indirectly, owned or controlled by the Corporation; and

(21) "supplemental transaction" means any transaction set forth in a proposal under section 305 of this Act under section 303(b) of this Act, under which the Corporation or a subsidiary thereof would (A) acquire rail properties not designated for transfer or conveyance to it under the final system plan, (B) convey rail properties to a profitable railroad, a subsidiary of the Corporation or, other than as designated in the final system plan, to the National Railroad Passenger Corporation or to a State or a local or regional transportation authority, or to any other responsible person for use in providing rail service, or (C) enter into contractual or other arrangements with any person for the joint use of rail properties or the coordination or separation of rail operations or services.

[45 U.S.C. 702]

TITLE II—UNITED STATES RAILWAY ASSOCIATION

FORMATION AND STRUCTURE

SEC. 201. (a) ESTABLISHMENT.—There is established in accordance with the provisions of this section, an incorporated nonprofit association to be known as the United States Railway Association.

(b) ADMINISTRATION.—The Association shall be directed by a Board of Directors. The individuals designated, pursuant to subsection (d)(2) of this section, as the Government members of such Board shall be deemed the incorporators of the Association and shall take whatever steps are necessary to establish the Association, including filing of articles of incorporation, and serving as an acting Board of Directors for a period of not more than 45 days after the date of incorporation of the Association.

(c) STATUS.—The Association shall be a government corporation of the District of Columbia subject, to the extent not inconsistent with this title, to the District of Columbia Nonprofit Corporation

Act (D.C. Code, sec. 29–1001 et seq.). Except as otherwise provided, employees of the Association shall not be deemed employees of the Federal Government. The Association shall have succession until dissolved by Act of Congress, shall maintain its principal office in the District of Columbia, and shall be deemed to be a resident of the District of Columbia with respect to venue in any legal proceeding.

(d) BOARD OF DIRECTORS.—(1) The Board of Directors of the Association shall consist of five individuals, as follows:

(A) The Chairman, who shall be the individual serving as Chairman on the effective date of this subsection, until the expiration of his term of office or his resignation, or his replacement, who shall be selected by the outgoing Chairman and the other members of the Board.

(B) The Secretary of Transportation.

(C) The Comptroller General of the United States.

(D) The Chairman of the Commission.

(E) The Chairman of the Board of Directors of the Corporation.

(2) The Chairman may not have any employment or other direct financial relationship with any freight railroad. The Chairman shall receive $300 per diem when engaged in the actual performance of his duties plus reimbursement for travel, subsistence, and other necessary expenses incurred in the performance of such duties.

(e) TERM OF OFFICE.—The term of office of the Chairman of the Board of Directors of the Association shall expire on December 31, 1987. The Chairman may be reappointed and the term of the Chairman shall be 3 years.

(f) QUORUM.—Three members of the Board of Directors, or their representatives, shall constitute a quorum for the transaction of any function of the Association.

(g) The Board of Directors shall, on the effective date of this subsection, assume the functions previously performed by the Finance Committee.

(h) The members of the Board of Directors may send representatives to meetings of such Board, and such representatives may exercise full powers of the members.

(g)[1] MISCELLANEOUS.—(1) The Association shall have a seal

which shall be judicially recognized.

---

[1]   As designated by section 1147 of P.L. 97–35; probably should have been designated as subsection (i).

---

(2) The Administrator of General Services shall furnish the Association with such offices, equipment, supplies, and services as he is authorized to furnish to any other agency or instrumentality of the United States.

(3) The Secretary is authorized to transfer to the Association or the Corporation rights in intellectual property which are directly related to the conduct of the functions of the Association or the Corporation, to the extent that the Federal Government has such rights and to the extent that transfer is necessary to carry out the purposes of this Act.

(4) Any reference in this Act to the Chairman of the Commission is to the Chairman of the Commission or the person who is at the time performing the duties of the Chairman of the Commission in accordance with law.

(h)[1] USE OF NAMES.—No person, except the Association, shall hereafter use the words "United States Railway Association" as a name for any business purpose. Violations of this provision may be enjoined by any court of general jurisdiction in an action commenced by the Association. In any such action, the Association may recover any actual damages flowing from such violation, and, in addition, shall be entitled to punitive damages (regardless of the existence or nonexistence of actual damage) in an amount not to exceed $100 for each day during which such violation was committed. The district courts of the United States shall have jurisdiction over actions brought under this subsection, without regard to the amount in controversy or the citizenship of the parties.

---

[1]   As designated by section 1147 of P.L. 97–35; probably should have been designated as subsection (j).

[45 U.S.C. 711]

FUNCTIONS OF THE ASSOCIATION

SEC. 202. (a) GENERAL.—The Association is authorized to—

(1) monitor the financial performance of the Corporation;

(2) review whether the goals and requirements of this Act

are met;

(3) purchase or otherwise acquire or receive, and hold and dispose of securities (whether debt or equity) of the Corporation under sections 216 and 217 of this Act and exercise all of the rights, privileges, and powers of a holder of any such securities;

(4) purchase accounts receivable of the Corporation in accordance with section 217 of this Act; and

(5) appoint and fix the compensation of such personnel as the Association considers necessary and appropriate.

(11)[2] determine the value of the Alaska Railroad, as required by section 605 of the Alaska Railroad Transfer Act of 1982.

---

[2]   As added by section 605(e) of the Rail Safety and Service Improvement Act of 1982: probably should have been designated paragraph (6).

(b) INVESTMENT OF FUNDS.—Uncommitted funds of the Association shall be kept in cash on hand or on deposit, or invested in obligations of the United States or guaranteed thereby, or in obligations, participations, or other investments which are lawful investments for fiduciary, trust, or public funds.

(c) EXEMPTION FROM TAXATION.—The Association, including its franchise, capital reserves, surplus, security holdings, and income shall be exempt from all taxation now or hereafter imposed by the United States, any commonwealth, territory, dependency, or possession thereof, or by any State or political subdivision thereof, except that any real property of the Association shall be subject to taxation to the same extent according to its value as other real property is taxed.

(d) REPORTS.—(1)[1] The Association shall transmit to the Congress and the President, not later than 90 days after the end of each fiscal year, a comprehensive and detailed report on all activities of the Association during the preceding fiscal year. Each such report shall include (A) the Association's statement of specific and detailed objectives for the activities and programs conducted and assisted under this Act; (B) statements of the Association's conclusions as to the effectiveness of such activities and programs in meeting the stated objectives and the purposes of this Act, measured through the end of the preceding fiscal year; (C) recommendations with respect to any legislation or administrative action which the Association deems necessary or desirable; (D) a statistical compilation of the obligations issued, certificates of value issued, securities purchased, and loans made under this Act; (E) a summary of outstanding problems confronting the Association, in order of priority; (F) all other information required to be submitted to the Congress pursuant to any other provision of this Act; and (G) the Association's projections and plans for its activities and programs during the next fiscal year.

---

[1] The paragraph (1) designation was supplied editorially.

---

(2) For the fiscal year beginning October 1, 1977, and ending September 30, 1978, the Association shall transmit to the Congress and the President, not later than 30 days after the end of each quarter of such fiscal year, a comprehensive and detailed report on all expenditures and use of funds during the preceding fiscal quarter, including an assessment of the status of projects for such preceding fiscal quarter and a projection of activities proposed for the next fiscal quarter.

(3) The Association shall transmit to the Congress, no later than 30 days after the end of each fiscal quarter, a report with respect to the proceedings before the special court to determine the valuation of rail properties conveyed to the Corporation under section 303 of this Act. Each such report shall include—

(A) a detailed accounting of the Federal funds expended during such quarter in connection with such proceedings, and the purposes for which such funds were expended;

(B) an explanation of the status of such proceedings, including the prospects for settlement or conclusion; and

(C) an identification of which responsibilities in connection with such proceedings are being carried out directly by the Association, and which are being carried out by contract with private organizations.

(e) BUDGET.—The receipts and disbursements of the Association (other than administrative expenses referred to in subsection (g)[1] of this section and receipts and disbursements under section 216 of this title and section 306 of this Act) in the discharge of its functions shall not be included in the totals of the budget of the United States Government, and shall be exempt from any annual expenditure and net lending (budget outlays) limitations imposed on a budget of the United States Government. The Chairman of the Association shall transmit annually to the Congress a budget for program activities and for administrative expenses of the Association. The Chairman shall report annually to the Congress the amount of net lending of the Association, which would be included in the totals of the budgets of the United States Government, if the Association's activities were not excluded from those totals as a result of this section.

---

[1] Probably should read "subsection (f)".

(f) ACCOUNTABILITY.—(1) Section 201 of the Government Corporation Control Act (31 U.S.C. 856) is amended by striking out "and" at the end of clause (6) and by inserting immediately before the period at the end thereof the following: ", (8) the United States Railway Association".

(2) The Chairman of the Association shall transmit annually to the Office of Management and Budget a budget for administrative expenses of the Association. Whenever the Association submits any budget estimate or request to the Office of Management and Budget, it shall concurrently transmit a copy of the estimate or request to the Congress. Within budgetary constraints of the Congress, the maximum feasible and prudent budgetary flexibility shall be provided to the Association to permit effective operations.

(g) TRANSFER OF LITIGATION.—No later than March 1, 1980, the Association and the Attorney General of the United States shall develop and submit to the Congress a feasibility study for the transfer, to the appropriate department or agency of the Federal Government, of all responsibility for representing the United States in the proceedings before the special court to determine the valuation of rail properties conveyed to the Corporation under section 303 of this Act.

(h) TRANSFER OF OTHER FUNCTIONS.—No later than March 1, 1980, the Association and the Secretary of Transportation shall develop and submit to the Congress a feasibility study for the transfer of all functions of the Association, other than those referred to in subsection (h)[1] of this section, to the appropriate department or agency of the Federal Government, including the abolition of those functions which will no longer be necessary.

---

[1] Probably should read "subsection (g)".

(i) MONITORING OF CONTRACTORS.—The Board of Directors of the Association shall adopt procedures to insure (1) that contractors, including law firms, provide reports containing written verification of tasks assigned, work performed, time worked, and costs incurred, including periodic status reports on work performed, (2) that such reports are audited by the Association, (3) that no funds are paid to contractors without written reports complying with the requirements of this subsection, and (4) that the Association applies such procedures uniformly to all contractors.

[45 U.S.C. 712]

ACCESS TO INFORMATION

SEC. 203. The Corporation shall make available to the Association such information as the Association determines necessary for the Association to carry out its functions under this Act. The Association shall request from other parties which are affected by this Act information which will enable the Association to fulfill its functions under this Act.

[45 U.S.C. 713]

REPORT

SEC. 204. (a) PREPARATION.—Within 30 days after the date of enactment of this Act, the Secretary shall prepare a comprehensive report containing his conclusions and recommendations with respect to the geographic zones within the region in and between which rail service should be provided and the criteria upon which such conclusions and recommendations are based. The Secretary may use as a basis for the identification of such geographic zones the standard metropolitan statistical areas, groups of such areas, counties, or groups of counties having similar economic characteristics such as mining, manufacturing, or farming.

(b) SUBMISSION.—The Secretary shall submit the report required by subsection (a) of this section to the Office, the Association, the Governor and public utilities commission of each State studied in the report, local governments, consumer organizations, environmental groups, the public, and the Congress. The Secretary shall further cause a copy of the report to be published in the Federal Register.

[45 U.S.C. 714]

[Section 205 repealed by section 4(b) of Public Law 95–473 (92 Stat. 1466).]

FINAL SYSTEM PLAN

SEC. 206. (a) GOALS.—The final system plan shall be formulated in such a way as to effectuate the following goals:

(1) the creation, through a process of reorganization, of a financially self-sustaining rail and express service system in the region;

(2) the establishment and maintenance of a rail service system adequate to meet the rail transportation needs and service requirements of the region;

(3) the establishment of improved high-speed rail passenger service, consonant with the recommendations of the Secretary in his report of September 1971, entitled "Recommendations for Northeast Corridor Transportation";

(4) the preservation, to the extent consistent with other goals, of existing patterns of service by railroads (including short-line and terminal railroads), and of existing railroad trackage in areas in which fossil fuel natural resources are located, and the utilization of those modes of transportation in the region which require the smallest amount of scarce energy resources and which can most efficiently transport energy resources;

(5) the retention and promotion of competition in the provision of rail and other transportation services in the region;

(6) the attainment and maintenance of any environmental standards, particularly the applicable national ambient air quality standards and plans established under the Clean Air Act Amendments of 1970, taking into consideration the environmental impact of alternative choices of action;

(7) the movement of passengers and freight in rail transportation in the region in the most efficient manner consistent with safe operation, including the requirements of commuter and intercity rail passenger service; the extent to which there should be coordination with the National Railroad Passenger Corporation and similar entities; and the identification of all short-to-medium distance corridors in

densely populated areas in which the major upgrading of rail lines for high-speed passenger operation would return substantial public benefits; and

(8) the minimization of job losses and associated increases in unemployment and community benefit costs in areas in the region presently served by rail service.

(b) FACTORS.—The final system plan shall be based upon due consideration of all factors relevant to the realization of the goals set forth in subsection (a) of this section. Such factors include the need for and the cost of rehabilitation and modernization of track, equipment, and other facilities; methods of achieving economies in the cost of rail operations in the region; means of achieving rationalization of rail services and the rail service system in the region; marketing studies; the impact on railroad employees; consumer needs; traffic analyses; financial studies; and any other factors identified by the Association under section 202(b) of this title or in the report of the Secretary required under section 204(a) of this title.

(c) DESIGNATIONS.—The final system plan shall designate—

(1) which rail properties of railroads in reorganization in the region or of railroads leased, operated, or controlled by any railroad in reorganization in the region—

(A) shall be transferred to the Corporation: *Provided,* That the Corporation shall, within 95 days after the effective date of the final system plan, give notice to the Association of which such rail properties, if any, are to be transferred to a subsidiary of the Corporation in the event that the Board of Directors of the Association finds that such transfer would be consistent with the final system plan;

(B) shall be offered for sale to a profitable railroad operating in the region and, if such offer is accepted, operated by such railroad; the plan shall designate what additions shall be made to the designation under subparagraph (A) of this paragraph and what alternative designations shall be made under this paragraph in the event such profitable railroad fails to accept such offer;

(C) shall be purchased, leased, or otherwise acquired from the Corporation by the National Railroad Passenger

Corporation in accordance with the exercise of its option under section 601(d) of this Act for improvement to achieve the goal set forth in subsection (a)(3) of this section;

(D) may be purchased or leased from the Corporation by (i) a State or a local or regional transportation authority to meet the needs of commuter and intercity rail passenger service, or (ii) the National Railroad Passenger Corporation to meet the needs of improved rail passenger service over intercity routes, other than properties designated pursuant to subparagraph (C) of this paragraph; and

(E) if not otherwise required to be operated by the Corporation, a government entity, or a responsible person, are suitable for use for other public purposes, including highways, other forms of transportation, conservation, energy transmission, education or health care facilities, or recreation. In carrying out this subparagraph, the Association shall solicit the views and recommendations of the Secretary, the Secretary of the Interior, the Administrator of the Environmental Protection Agency, and other agencies of the Federal Government and of the States and political subdivisions thereof within the region, and the general public; and

(2) which rail properties of profitable railroads operating in the region may be offered for sale to the Corporation or to other profitable railroads operating in the region subject to paragraphs (3) and (4) of subsection (d) of this section. Any rail properties designated to be offered for sale to the Corporation may be sold instead to a subsidiary of the Corporation.

(d) TRANSFERS.—All transfers or conveyances pursuant to the final system plan shall be made in accordance with, and subject to, the following principles:

(1) All rail properties to be transferred to the Corporation or any subsidiary thereof by a profitable railroad, by trustees of a railroad in reorganization, or by any railroad leased, operated, or controlled by a railroad in reorganization in the region, shall be transferred in exchange for stock and other securities of the Corporation or any subsidiary thereof (including obligations of the Association) and the other benefits accruing to such railroad by reason of such transfer.

(2) All rail properties to be conveyed to a profitable railroad

operating in the region by trustees of a railroad in reorganization, or by any railroad leased, operated, or controlled by a railroad in reorganization in the region, shall be conveyed in exchange for compensation from the profitable railroad.

(3) Notwithstanding any other provision of this Act, no acquisition under this Act shall be made by any profitable railroad operating in the region without a determination with respect to each such transaction and all such transactions cumulatively (A) by the Association, upon adoption and release of the preliminary system plan, that such acquisition or acquisitions will not materially impair the profitability of any other profitable railroad operating in the region or of the Corporation, and (B) by the Commission, which shall be made within 90 days after adoption and release by the Association of the preliminary system plan, that such acquisition or acquisitions will be in full accord and comply with the provisions and standards of section 5 of part I of the Interstate Commerce Act (49 U.S.C. 5). All determinations made by the Association in the correction to the preliminary system plan published on April 11, 1975 (40 Fed. Reg. 16377), shall be treated for all purposes as if they had been made upon adoption and release by the Association of the preliminary system plan. All determinations made by the Commission with respect to such correction shall be treated for all purposes as if they had been made within 90 days after adoption and release by the Association of the preliminary system plan. All determinations made by the Commission with respect to acquisitions by profitable railroads referred to in any supplement to the preliminary system plan published under section 207(b)(2) of this title shall be deemed to be timely if made prior to the adoption of the final system plan under section 207(c) of this title. The determination by the Association shall not be reviewable in any court. The determination by the Commission shall not be reviewable in any court.

(4) Where the final system plan designates specified rail properties of a railroad in reorganization in the region, or of a railroad leased, operated, or controlled by a railroad in reorganization in the region, to be offered for sale to and operated by a profitable railroad operating in the region, such designation shall terminate 7 days after the date of the

enactment of the Railroad Revitalization and Regulatory Reform Act of 1976 unless, prior to such date, such profitable railroad has notified the Association in writing of its acceptance of such offer. Any such offer may be modified until the date of acceptance thereof, unless such modification results in an offer for the sale of rail properties at less than the net liquidation value thereof. Where the final system plan designates specified rail properties of a profitable railroad operating in the region as authorized to be offered for sale or lease to the Corporation or to other profitable railroads operating in the region, such designation and authorization shall terminate 95 days after the effective date of the final system plan unless, prior to such date, a binding agreement with respect to such properties has been entered into and concluded.

(5) All properties—

(A) transferred by the Corporation pursuant to sections 206(c)(1)(C) and 601(d) of this Act;

(B) transferred by the Corporation to any State (or local or regional transportation authority), pursuant to subsection (c)(1)(D) of this section, or

(C) transferred by the Corporation to any State, local or regional transportation authority, or the National Railroad Passenger Corporation, within 3 years after the date of conveyance, pursuant to section 303(b)(1) of this Act, to meet the needs of commuter or intercity rail passenger service, shall be transferred at a value related to the value received from the Corporation pursuant to the final system plan for the transfer to such Corporation of such properties. The value of any such properties, which are transferred pursuant to subparagraph (B) or (C) of this paragraph, shall be adjusted to reflect the value attributable to any applicable maintenance and improvement provided by the Corporation (to the extent the Corporation has not been released from the obligation to pay for such improvements) and the cost to the Corporation of transferring such properties. The Corporation, its Board of Directors, and its individual directors shall not be liable to any party, for money damages or in any other manner, solely by reason of the fact that the Corporation transferred property pursuant to section 303 of this Act to meet the needs of commuter or intercity rail passenger service or for purposes of providing rail marine freight floating service, except as otherwise provided with respect to the Corporation pursuant to section 303(c)(2) of this Act.

(6) Notwithstanding any statement to the contrary in the final system plan, a State (or a local or regional transportation authority) shall not be required to deliver to the Corporation a firm commitment to acquire rail properties designated to such State or authority prior to 7 days after the date of enactment of this paragraph.

(7) Notwithstanding any contrary provision in the options conveyed to the Corporation by railroads in reorganization, or railroads leased, operated, or controlled by a railroad in reorganization, with respect to the acquisition by the Corporation pursuant to the final system plan, on behalf of a State (or a local or regional transportation authority) of rail properties designated under section 206(c)(1)(D) of this title, such options shall not be deemed to have expired prior to 7 days after the date of enactment of this paragraph. The exercise by the Corporation of any such option shall be effective if it is made, prior to the expiration of such 7-day period, in the manner prescribed in such options.

(e) CORPORATION FEATURES.—The final system plan shall set forth—

(1) pro forma earnings for the Corporation, as reasonably projected and considering the additions or changes in the designation of rail properties to be operated by the Corporation which may be made under subsection (d)(4) of this section;

(2) the capital structure of the Corporation, based on the pro forma earnings of the Corporation as set forth, including such debt capitalization as shall be reasonably deemed to conform to the requirements of the public interest with respect to railroad debt securities, including the adequacy of coverage of fixed charges; and

(3) the manner in which employee stock ownership plans may, to the extent practicable, be utilized for meeting the capitalization requirements of the Corporation, taking into account (A) the relative cost savings compared to conventional methods of corporate finance; (B) the labor cost savings; (C)

the potential for minimizing strikes and producing more harmonious relations between labor organizations and railway management; (D) the projected employee dividend incomes; (E) the impact on quality of service and prices to railway users; and (F) the promotion of the objectives of this Act of creating a financially self-sustaining railway system in the region which also meets the service needs of the region and the Nation.

(f) VALUE.—The final system plan shall designate the value of all rail properties to be transferred under the final system plan and the value of the securities and other benefits to be received for transferring those rail properties to the Corporation in accordance with the final system plan.

(g) OTHER PROVISIONS.—The final system plan may recommend arrangements among various railroads for joint use or operation of rail properties on a shared ownership, cooperative, pooled, or condominium-type basis, subject to such terms and conditions as may be specified in the final system plan. The final system plan shall also make such designations as are determined to be necessary in accordance with the provisions of section 402 or 403 of this Act.

(h) OBLIGATIONAL AUTHORITY.—The final system plan shall recommend the amount of obligations of the Association which are necessary to enable it to implement the final system plan.

(i) TERMS AND CONDITIONS FOR SECURITIES.—The final system plan may include terms and conditions for any securities to be issued by the Corporation in exchange for the conveyance of rail properties under the final system plan which in the judgment of the Association will minimize any actual or potential debt burden on the Corporation. Any such terms and conditions for securities of the Corporation which purport to directly obligate the Association shall not become effective without affirmative approval, with or without modification by a joint resolution of the Congress.

(j) Any rail properties over which rail service was being provided as of the date of enactment of this Act, and which were recommended in the preliminary system plan for transfer to the Corporation, shall be deemed to be designated in the final system plan for transfer to the Corporation under subsection (c)(1)(A) of this section. Any designation in the final system plan, pursuant to subsection (c)(1)(B) of this section, of overhead trackage rights to be acquired by a profitable railroad operating in the region over specified rail properties to be acquired by the Corporation, where such designation does not (1) authorize such profitable railroad to interchange traffic with at least one railroad, or (2) provide for the connection of portions of such profitable railroad's rail properties, and where the transfer of ownership of such rail properties (including trackage rights) to such profitable railroad was recommended in the preliminary system plan, and the Commission has made a determination with respect thereto, in accordance with subsection (d)(3) of this section, shall be deemed to authorize such profitable railroad to interchange traffic with the Corporation and any other profitable railroad connecting with such specified rail properties.

[45 U.S.C. 716]

ADOPTION OF FINAL SYSTEM PLAN

SEC. 207. (a) PRELIMINARY SYSTEM PLAN.—(1) Within 420 days after the date of enactment of this Act, the Association shall adopt and release a preliminary system plan prepared by it on the basis of reports and other information submitted to it by the Secretary, the Office, and interested persons in accordance with this Act and on the basis of its own investigations, consultations, research, evaluation, and analysis pursuant to this Act. Copies of the preliminary system plan shall be transmitted by the Association to the Secretary, the Office, the Governor and public utility commission of each State in the region, the Congress, each court having jurisdiction over a railroad in reorganization in the region, the special court, and interested persons, and a copy shall be published in the Federal Register. The Association shall invite and afford interested persons an opportunity to submit comments on the preliminary system plan to the Association within 60 days after the date of its release.

(2) The Office is authorized and directed to hold public hearings on the preliminary system plan and to make available to the association a summary and analysis of the evidence received in the course of such proceedings, together with its critique and evaluation of the preliminary system plan, not later than 60 days after the date of release of such plan. The Office is authorized to hold public hearings on any supplement to the preliminary system plan and to make available to the Association a summary and analysis of the evidence received in the course of such proceedings, together with its critique and

evaluation of such supplement, not later than 30 days after the release of such supplement.

(b) APPROVAL.—(1) Within 120 days after the date of enactment of this Act each United States district court or other court having jurisdiction over a railroad in reorganization shall decide whether the railroad is reorganizable on an income basis within a reasonable time under section 77 of the Bankruptcy Act (11 U.S.C. 205) and that the public interest would be better served by continuing the present reorganization proceedings than by a reorganization under this Act. Within 60 days after the submission of the report by the Office, under section 205(d)(1) of this title, on the Secretary's report on rail services in the region, each United States disctrict court or other court having jurisdiction over a railroad in reorganization shall decide whether or not such railroad shall be reorganized by means of transferring some of its rail properties to the Corporation pursuant to the provisions of this Act. Because of the strong public interest in the continuance of rail transportation in the region pursuant to a system plan devised under the provisions of this Act, each such court shall order that the reorganization be proceeded with pursuant to this Act unless it (1) has found that the railroad is reorganizable on an income basis within a reasonable time under section 77 of the Bankruptcy Act (11 U.S.C. 205) and that the public interest would be better served by such a reorganization than by a reorganization under this Act, or (2) finds that this Act does not provide a process which would be fair and equitable to the estate of the railroad in reorganization in which case it shall dismiss the reorganization proceeding. If a court does not enter an order or make a finding as required by this subsection, the reorganization shall be proceeded with pursuant to this Act. An appeal from an order made under this section may be made only to the special court. Appeal to the special court shall be taken within 10 days following entry of an order pursuant to this subsection, and the special court shall complete its review and render its decision within 80 days after such appeal is taken. There shall be no review of the decision of the special court.

(2) Whenever it has been finally determined pursuant to the procedures of paragraph (1) of this subsection, that the reorganization of a railroad subject to reorganization under section 77 of the Bankruptcy Act (11 U.S.C. 205) shall not be proceeded with pursuant to this Act, the court having jurisdiction over such railroad may, upon a petition which is

filed within 10 days after the date of enactment of this subsection by the trustees of such railroad, reconsider such order. Such reorganization court shall (i) affirm its previous order or (ii) issue an order that the reorganization of such railroad be proceeded with pursuant to this Act unless it finds that this Act does not provide a process which would be fair and equitable. The provisions of paragraph (1) of this subsection are applicable in such reconsideration, except that (A) such reorganization court shall make its decision within 30 days after such petition is filed, and (B) any decision by the special court on appeal from such a decision shall be rendered within 30 days after such reorganization court decision is made. There shall be no review of the decision of the special court. The Association shall take any steps it finds necessary, consistent with time limitations and other provisions of this Act, to effectuate the consequences of such a revised order, including the preparation and submission of any necessary or appropriate supplements to the preliminary system plan.

(c) ADOPTION.—Within 540 days after the date of enactment of this Act, the executive committee of the Association shall prepare and submit a final system plan for the approval of the Board of Directors of the Association. A copy of such submission shall be simultaneously presented to the Commission. The submission shall reflect evaluation of all responses and summaries of responses received, testimony at any public hearings, and the results of additional study and review. Within 30 days thereafter, the Board of Directors of the Association shall by a majority vote of all its members approve a final system plan which meets all of the requirements of section 206 of this title.

(d) REVIEW OF COMMISSION.—Within 30 days following the adoption of the final system plan by the Association under subsection (c) of this section and the submission of such plan to Congress under section 208(a) of this title, the Commission shall submit to the Congress an evaluation of the final system plan delivered to both Houses of Congress.

[45 U.S.C. 717]

REVIEW BY CONGRESS

SEC. 208. (a) GENERAL.—The Board of Directors of the Association shall deliver the final system plan adopted by the Association to both Houses of Congress and to the Committee on Interstate and Foreign Commerce of the House of Representatives and the Committee on Commerce of the Senate. The final system plan shall be deemed approved at the end of the first period of 60 calendar days of continuous session of Congress after such date of transmittal unless either the House of Representatives or the Senate passes a resolution during such period stating that it does not favor the final system plan.

(b) REVISED PLAN.—If either the House or the Senate passes a resolution of disapproval under subsection (a) of this section, the Association, with the cooperation and assistance of the Secretary and the Office, shall prepare, determine, and adopt a revised final system plan. Each such revised plan shall be submitted to Congress for review pursuant to subsection (a) of this section.

(c) COMPUTATION.—For purposes of this section—

(1) continuity of session of Congress is broken only by an adjournment sine die; and

(2) the days on which either House is not in session because of an adjournment of more than 3 days to a day certain are excluded in the computation of the 60-day period.

(d) ADDITIONS.—(1) The supplemental report, dated September 18, 1975, to the final system plan, and the provisions of the Association's official errata supplement to the final system plan, dated December 1, 1975, including all designations made therein, shall be treated for all purposes as if they had been part of and included in the final system plan adopted by the Association and reviewed by the Congress. The final system plan shall, for all purposes, be deemed to be approved as modified and amended by such supplemental report and such supplement.

(2) The Association may, upon petition of any State, modify the final system plan to make further designations with respect to rail properties of railroads in reorganization in the region designated for transfer to the Corporation under such plan, if such designations (A) are likely to result in improved rail service on such rail properties and connecting rail properties, and (B) would not materially impair the profitability of the Corporation. Such designations, including designations of such rail properties to a State, a profitable railroad, or a responsible person, may be made at any time prior to delivery of the final system plan to the special court under section 209(c) of this

title. Such further designations shall be treated for all purposes as if they had been included in the final system plan adopted by the Association and reviewed by the Congress, and the final system plan shall for all purposes be deemed to be approved as modified by such designations. Any action of the Association with respect to any such petition shall not be subject to review by any court.

(3)(A) Within 20 days after the date of enactment of the Railroad Revitalization and Regulatory Reform Act of 1976, the Association may, by notice to the Congress and by publication in the Federal Register, modify, supplement, or add to the designations of rail properties in the final system plan if the Association finds such actions are necessary to—

(i) achieve the efficient implementation of the final system plan, or

(ii) provide for the offer to profitable railroads of rail properties designated in the final system plan to the Corporation, if such properties are not essential in the operation of other rail properties of the Corporation but are or would be integrally related to the operation of rail properties of (or which are offered pursuant to the final system plan to) such profitable railroad, or

(iii) provide for the designation of additional rail properties to the Corporation or to a subsidiary thereof to enable the Corporation to serve efficiently a line of railroad designated to the Corporation in the final system plan if such line does not connect with any other line of railroad so designated to the Corporation or if such line would be served more efficiently as a consequence of such designation.

Any designation to a profitable railroad pursuant to this paragraph shall comply with the second sentence of section 206(d)(4) of this title, and shall only be made upon a finding by the Association that such designation is integrally related to an offer of rail properties to a profitable railroad in the final system plan, that the goals of the final system plan require that the rail properties be operated as a part of the rail properties included in such offer, and that the implementation of such designation will not materially and adversely affect the impact of such offer on the profitability of the Corporation or any profitable railroad operating in the region. Any designation to a profitable railroad pursuant to this subsection, which amends any prior offer, shall terminate 30 days after the date of enactment of this paragraph unless, prior to such date, such profitable railroad has notified the Association in writing of its acceptance of such amendment to the prior offer.

(B) If a line of railroad or any segment thereof is designated for rail service in the final system plan, no designation may be made by the Association pursuant to this paragraph which would result in such line or segment not being so designated. Any designations made pursuant to this paragraph shall be treated for all purposes as if they had been included in the final system plan adopted by the Association and reviewed by the Congress. The final system plan shall for all purposes be deemed to be approved as amended by such designations.

(C) Any designations made pursuant to this paragraph shall not be subject to review by any court.

(D) Any labor agreements entered into under section 508 of this Act shall be subject to further negotiations for any modifications which may be necessary to implement designations made pursuant to this paragraph.

[45 U.S.C. 718]

JUDICIAL REVIEW

SEC. 209. (a) GENERAL.—Notwithstanding any other provision of law, the final system plan which is adopted by the Association and which becomes effective after review by the Congress is not subject to review by any court except in accordance with this section. After the final system plan becomes effective under section 208 of this title, it may be reviewed with respect to matters concerning the value of the rail properties to be conveyed under the plan and the value of the consideration to be received for such properties.

(b) SPECIAL COURT.—(1) Within 30 days after the date of enactment of this Act, the Association shall make application to the judicial panel on multi-district litigation authorized by section 1407 of title 28, United States Code, for the consolidation in a single, three-judge district court of the United States of all judicial proceedings with respect to the final system plan. Within 30 days after such application is received, the panel shall make the consolidation in a district court (cited herein as the "special court") which the panel determines to be convenient to the parties and the one most likely to be able to conduct any proceedings under this section with the least delay and the greatest possible fairness and ability. Such proceedings shall be conducted by the special court which shall be composed of three Federal judges who shall be selected by the panel, except that none of the judges selected may be a judge assigned to a proceeding involving any railroad in reorganization in the region under section 77 of the Bankruptcy Act (11 U.S.C. 205). The special court is authorized to exercise the powers of a district judge in any judicial district with respect to such proceedings and such powers shall include those of a reorganization court. The special court shall have the power to order the conveyance of rail properties of railroads leased, operated, or controlled by a railroad in reorganization in the region. The special court may issue rules for the conduct of any proceedings under this section and under section 305 of this Act, including rules with respect to the time within which motions may be filed, and with respect to appropriate representation of interests not otherwise represented (including the Secretary with respect to a petition by the Association in the case of a proposal developed by the Secretary, under such section 305). No determination by the panel under this subsection may be reviewed in any court.

(2) The special court referred to in paragraph (1) of this subsection is abolished effective 90 days after the date of enactment of the Federal Courts Improvement Act of 1996. On such effective date, all jurisdiction and other functions of the special court shall be assumed by the United States District Court for the District of Columbia. With respect to any proceedings that arise or continue after the date on which the special court is abolished, the references in the following provisions to the special court established under this subsection shall be deemed to refer to the United States District Court for the District of Columbia:

(A) Subsections (c), (e)(1), (e)(2), (f) and (g) of this section.

(B) Sections 202 (d)(3), (g), 207 (a)(1), (b)(1), (b)(2), 208(d)(2), 301 (e)(2), (g), (k)(3), (k)(15), 303 (a)(1), (a)(2), (b)(1), (b)(6)(A), (c)(1), (c)(2), (c)(3), (c)(4), (c)(5), 304 (a)(1)(B), (i)(3), 305 (c), (d)(1), (d)(2), (d)(3), (d)(4), (d)(5), (d)(8), (e), (f)(1), (f)(2)(B), (f)(2)(D), (f)(2)(E), (f)(3), 306 (a), (b), (c)(4), and 601 (b)(3), (c) of this Act (45 U.S.C. 712 (d)(3), (g), 717 (a)(1), (b)(1), (b)(2), 718(d)(2), 741 (e)(2), (g), (k)(3), (k)(15), 743 (a)(1), (a)(2), (b)(1), (b)(6)(A), (c)(1), (c)(2), (c)(3), (c)(4), (c)(5), 744 (a)(1)(B), (i)(3), 745 (c), (d)(1), (d)(2), (d)(3), (d)(4), (d)(5), (d)(8), (e), (f)(1), (f)(2)(B), (f)(2)(D), (f)(2)(E), (f)(3), 746 (a), (b), (c)(4), 791 (b)(3), (c)).

(C) Sections 1152(a) and 1167(b) of the Northeast Rail Service Act of 1981 (45 U.S.C. 1105(a), 1115(a)).

(D) Sections 4023 (2)(A)(iii), (2)(B), (2)(C), (3)(C), (3)(E), (4)(A) and 4025(b) of the Conrail Privatization Act (45 U.S.C. 1323 (2)(A)(iii), (2)(B), (2)(C), (3)(C), (3)(E), (4)(A), 1324(b)).

(E) Section 24907(b) of title 49, United States Code.

(F) Any other Federal law (other than this subsection and section 605 of the Federal Courts Improvement Act of 1996), Executive order, rule, regulation, delegation of authority, or document of or relating to the special court as previously established under paragraph (1) of this subsection.

(c) DELIVERY OF PLAN TO SPECIAL COURT.—Within 90 days after its effective date, the Association shall deliver a certified copy of the final system plan to the special court and shall certify to the special court—

(1) which rail properties of the respective railroads in reorganization in the region and of any person leased, operated, or controlled by such railroads in reorganization are to be transferred to the Corporation, or any subsidiary thereof, in accordance with the final system plan;

(2) which rail properties of the respective railroads in reorganization in the region or person leased, operated, or controlled by such railroads in reorganization are to be conveyed to profitable railroads, in accordance with the final system plan;

(3) the amount, terms, and value of the securities of the Corporation or any subsidiary thereof (including any certificates of value of the Association) to be exchanged for those rail properties to be transferred to the Corporation or any subsidiary thereof pursuant to the final system plan, and as

indicated in paragraph (1) of this subsection; and

(4) that the transfer of rail properties in exchange for securities of the Corporation or any subsidiary thereof (including any certificates of value of the Association) and other benefits is fair and equitable and in the public interest.

Notwithstanding any other provisions of this subsection and subsection (d) of this section, the time for the delivery of a certified copy of the final system plan shall be March 12, 1976, and may be extended to a date not more than 30 days thereafter, prescribed in a notice filed by the Association not later than February 17, 1976, with the special court, the Congress, and each court referred to in such subsection (d). Such notice shall contain the certification of the Association that an orderly conveyance of rail properties cannot reasonably be effected before the date for conveyance determined with respect to such notice. The time prescribed in section 303(a) of this Act shall be determined with respect to the date prescribed in such notice.

(d) BANKRUPTCY COURTS.—Within 90 days after its effective date, the Association shall deliver a certified copy of the final system plan to each district court of the United States or any other court having jurisdiction over a railroad in reorganization in the region and shall certify to each such court—

(1) which rail properties of that railroad in reorganization are to be transferred to the Corporation or any subsidiary thereof under the final system plan; and

(2) which rail properties of that railroad in reorganization, if any, are to be conveyed to profitable railroads operating in the region, under the final system plan.

(e) ORIGINAL AND EXCLUSIVE JURISDICTION.—(1) Notwithstanding any other provision of law, any civil action—

(A) for injunctive or other relief against the Association from the enforcement, operation, or execution of this Act or any provision thereof, or from any action taken by the Association pursuant to authority conferred or purportedly conferred under this Act;

(B) challenging the constitutionality of this Act or any provision thereof;

(C) challenging the legality of any action of the Association, or any failure of the Association to take any action, pursuant to authority conferred or purportedly conferred under this Act;

(D) to obtain, inspect, copy, or review any document in the possession or control of the Association that would be discoverable in litigation pursuant to section 303(c) of this Act;

(E) brought after a conveyance, pursuant to section 303(b) of this Act, to set aside or annul such conveyance or to secure in any way the reconveyance of any rail properties so conveyed; or

(F) with respect to continuing reorganization and supplemental transactions, in accordance with section 305 of this Act;

shall be within the original and exclusive jurisdiction of the special court. The special court shall not hear or determine any such action prior to the date of conveyance, pursuant to section 303(b)(1) of this Act, except as the Constitution may require. Relief shall not be granted in any action referred to in subparagraph (A), (C), or (E) unless the person seeking such relief establishes that the Association acted in reckless or deliberate disregard of applicable law.

(2) The original and exclusive jurisdiction of the special court shall include any action, whether filed by any interested person or initiated by the special court itself, to interpret, alter, amend, modify or implement any of the orders entered by such court pursuant to section 303(b) of this Act in order to effect the purposes of this Act or the goals of the final system plan. During the pendency of any proceeding described in this paragraph, the special court may enter such orders as it determines to be appropriate, including orders enjoining, restraining, conditioning, or limiting any conveyance, transfer, or use of any asset or right which is subject to such an order or which is at issue in such a proceeding, or which involves the enforcement of any liens or encumbrances upon such assets or rights. Any orders pursuant to this paragraph which interpret, alter, amend, modify, or implement orders entered by the special court shall be final and shall not be restrained or enjoined by any court.

(3)[1] An order or judgment of the United States District Court for the District of Columbia in any action referred to in this section shall be reviewable in accordance with sections 1291, 1292, and 1294 of title 28, United States Code.

---

¹ Section 605(d) of the Federal Courts Improvement Act of 1996 provided that this paragraph shall not apply to any final order or judgement entered into by the special court established under section 209(b) of the Regional Rail Reorganization Act of 1973 for which—

(1) a petition for writ of certiorari has been filed before the date on which the special court is abolished [February 16, 1997]; or

(2) the time for filing a petition for writ of certiorari has not expired before that date.

(f) DISPOSITION OF CASH DEPOSITS.—Whenever the compensation which is deposited with the special court under section 303(a) of this Act is in the form of cash, such cash shall be invested and reinvested upon such terms and conditions as the special court shall determine, pending the making of the findings referred to paragraphs (1), (2), and (3) of section 303(c) of this Act. Notwithstanding section 303(c)(4) of this Act, the special court may order (1) the income from such investments, (2) the dividends or interest, if any, received on any securities or obligations deposited with the special court under such section 303(a), and (3) the income, if any, received with respect to any other form of compensation so deposited, to be distributed to the trustee of each railroad in reorganization and to any person leased, operated or controlled by such a railroad which conveyed the right, title, and interest in the rail properties with respect to which such cash, securities, obligations, or other compensation have been so deposited with the special court. Notwithstanding 303(c)(4) of this Act, the special court may, within 90 days after the date of conveyance of rail properties pursuant to section 303(b) of this Act, order up to 25 percent of any cash (including investments made with cash) and other compensation deposited with the special court to be distributed to such trustee or person. On petition of the applicable trustee or person, the special court may order such additional distributions as it finds reasonable and appropriate, prior to the making of the findings referred to in paragraphs (1), (2), and (3) of such section 303(c).

(g) STAY OF COURT PROCEEDINGS.—The special court may stay or enjoin any action or proceeding in any State court or in any court of the United States other than the Supreme Court or Court of Appeals for the District of Columbia Circuit if such action or proceeding is contrary to any provision of this Act, impairs the effective implementation of this Act, or interferes with the execution of any order of the special court pursuant to this Act.

[45 U.S.C. 719]

OBLIGATIONS OF THE ASSOCIATION

SEC. 210. (a) GENERAL.—To carry out the purposes of this Act, the Association is authorized to issue bonds, debentures, trust certificates, securities, or other obligations (herein cited as "obligations") in accordance with this section. Such obligations shall have such maturities and bear such rate or rates of interest as are determined by the Association with the approval of the Secretary of the Treasury. Such obligations shall be redeemable at the option of the Association prior to maturity in the manner stipulated in each such obligation, and may be purchased by the Association in the open market at a price which is reasonable.

(b) MAXIMUM OBLIGATIONAL AUTHORITY.—The aggregate principal amount (exclusive of interest or additions to principal on account of accrual of interest) of obligations issued by the Association under this section which may be outstanding at any one time shall not exceed $395,000,000. No obligations or proceeds thereof shall be issued or made available after the date of enactment of the Railroad Revitalization and Regulatory Reform Act of 1976 except—

(1) to meet existing or potential commitments for loans under section 211 of this title made or applied for prior to January 1, 1976; and

(2) for the purpose of providing loans pursuant to subsections (g) and (h) of section 211 of this title.

(c) GUARANTEES.—The Secretary shall guarantee the payment of principal and interest on all obligations issued by the Association in accordance with this Act and which the Association requests be guaranteed. All guarantees entered into by the Secretary under this section shall constitute general obligations of the United States for the payment of which its full faith and credit are pledged.

(d) VALIDITY.—No obligation issued by the Association under this section shall be terminated, canceled, or otherwise revoked, except in accordance with lawful terms and conditions prescribed by the Association. Such an obligation shall be conclusive evidence that it is in compliance with this section, has been approved, and is legal as to principal, interest, and other terms. An obligation of the Association shall be valid and incontestable in the hands of a holder, except as to fraud, duress, mutual mistake of fact, or material misrepresentation by or involving such holder.

(e) THE SECRETARY OF THE TREASURY.—If at any time the moneys available to the Secretary are insufficient to enable him to discharge his responsibilities under subsection (c) of this section or under subsection (a) of section 306 of this Act, he shall issue notes or other obligations to the Secretary of the Treasury in such forms and denominations, bearing such maturities, and subject to such terms and conditions as may be prescribed by the Secretary of the Treasury. Such obligations shall bear interest at a rate to be determined by the Secretary of the Treasury taking into consideration the current average market yield on outstanding marketable obligations of the United States of comparable maturities during the month preceding the issuance of such obligations. The Secretary of the Treasury is authorized and directed to purchase any such obligations and for such purpose is authorized to use as a public debt transaction the proceeds from the sale of any securities issued under the Second Liberty Bond Act, as amended. The purposes for which securities may be issued under such Act are extended to include any purchase of notes or other obligations issued under this subsection. At any time, the Secretary of the Treasury may sell any such obligations, and all sales, purchases, and redemptions of such obligations by the Secretary of the Treasury shall be treated as public debt transactions of the United States.

(f) AUTHORIZATION FOR APPROPRIATIONS.—There are hereby authorized to be appropriated to the Secretary such amounts as are necessary to discharge the obligations of the United States arising under this section.

(g) LAWFUL INVESTMENTS.—All obligations issued by the Association shall be lawful investments and may be accepted as security for all fiduciary, trust, and public funds, the investment or deposit of which shall be under the authority and control of the United States or any officer or officers thereof. All such obligations issued pursuant to this section shall be exempt securities within the meaning of laws administered by the Securities and Exchange Commission.

[45 U.S.C. 720]

LOANS

SEC. 211. (a) GENERAL.—The Association is authorized, in

accordance with the provisions of this section and such rules and regulations as it shall prescribe, to make loans to the Corporation, the National Railroad Passenger Corporation, and other railroads (including a railroad in reorganization which has been found to be reorganizable under section 77 of the Bankruptcy Act pursuant to section 207(b) of this title) in the region, for purposes of achieving the goals of this Act; to a State or local or regional transportation authority pursuant to section 403 of this Act; and to provide assistance in the form of loans to any railroad which (A) connects with a railroad in reorganization, and (B) is in need of financial assistance to avoid reorganization proceedings under section 77 of the Bankruptcy Act (11 U.S.C. 205). No such loan shall be made by the Association to a railroad unless such loans shall, where applicable, be treated as an expense of administration. The rights referred to in the last sentence of section 77(j) of the Bankruptcy Act (11 U.S.C. 205(j)) shall in no way be affected by this Act.

(b) APPLICATIONS.—Each application for such a loan shall be made in writing to the Association in such form and with such content and other submissions as the Association shall prescribe to protect reasonably the interests of the United States. The Association shall publish a notice of the receipt of each such application in the Federal Register and shall afford interested persons an opportunity to comment thereon.

(c) TERMS AND CONDITIONS.—Each loan shall be extended in such form, under such terms and conditions, and pursuant to such regulations as the Association deems appropriate. Such loan shall bear interest at a rate not less than the greater of a rate determined by the Secretary of the Treasury taking into consideration (1) the rate prevailing in the private market for similar loans as determined by the Secretary of the Treasury, or (2) the current average yield on outstanding marketable obligations of the Association with remaining periods of maturity comparable to the average maturities of such loans, plus such additional charge, if any, toward covering costs of the Association as the Association may determine to be consistent with the purposes of this Act.

(d) MODIFICATIONS.—The Association is authorized to approve any modification of any provision of a loan under this section, including the rate of interest, time of payment of interest or principal, security, or any other term or condition, upon agreement of the recipient of the loan and upon a finding by the Association that such modification is equitable and necessary or appropriate to achieve the policy declared in subsection (f) of this section. Notwithstanding any other provision of this section, in the case of a loan made under subsection (a) of this section to a railroad in the region, the Association is not required to make the findings with respect to subsections (e)(3) and (f) and may, upon the request of such railroad—

(1) continue to make advances to such railroad pursuant to such loan, up to the total principal provided, as of the date of enactment of this sentence, under the agreement between such railroad and the Association under this section, upon finding only that (A) a good faith effort has been commenced by such railroad toward the establishment of an employee stock ownership plan, and (B) such continued advances will permit the continuation of rail service determined by the Association, in the Final System Plan or under the goals of this Act, to be desirable; and

(2) increase the principle amount of such loan to such railroad, in an amount not to exceed $7,500,000, only if the Association makes the finding referred to in paragraph (1)(B) of this subsection and determines that such railroad is making a good faith effort to establish an employee stock ownership plan for review and approval by the Association. Any such approval shall be conditioned upon a written commitment that by December 31, 1980, the railroad will adopt an employee stock ownership plan which will acquire qualifying employer securities with a fair market value of $250,000.

The Association may not take any action pursuant to the preceding sentence of this subsection after December 31, 1981.

(e) PREREQUISITES.—The Association shall make a finding in writing, before making a loan to any applicant under this section, that—

(1) the loan is necessary to achieve the goals of this Act or to prevent insolvency;

(2) it is satisfied that the business affairs of the applicant will be conducted in a reasonable and prudent manner; and

(3) the applicant has offered such security as the Association deems necessary to protect reasonably the interests of the United States.

(f) POLICY.—It is the intent of Congress that loans made under this section shall be made on terms and conditions which furnish reasonable assurance that the Corporation or the railroads to which such loans are granted will be able to repay them within the time fixed and that the goals of this Act are reasonably likely to be achieved.

(g) PRE-CONVEYANCE LOANS TO THE CORPORATION.—During the period between the effective date of the final system plan and the date of the conveyance of rail properties pursuant to section 303(b) of this Act, the Association may make such loans in such amounts to the Corporation as the Association deems essential to provide for the purchase by the Corporation of material, supplies, equipment, and services necessary to permit the orderly and efficient implementation of the final system plan. Notwithstanding any inability of the Association during such period to make the finding required by subsection (e)(3) of this section because of any existing contingencies, the Association may make any such loans to the Corporation, subject to—

(1) the most favorable terms and conditions for assuring timely repayment and security as may then be reasonably available, and

(2) the requirement that any loan to the Corporation under this subsection be refinanced immediately out of the proceeds of the first sale by the issuance of debentures under section 216 of this title.

In order to assure that necessary funds are available to the Corporation for implementation of the final system plan, the Corporation is authorized to accept such loans as may be approved by the Association under this subsection, and any such acceptance shall be deemed for all purposes to constitute a reasonable and prudent business judgment in compliance with any fiduciary obligations imposed on the Corporation or its directors. For purposes of this subsection, the term "Corporation" includes a subsidiary of the Corporation.

(h) LOANS FOR PAYMENT OF OBLIGATIONS.—(1)(A) The Association is authorized, subject to the limitations set forth in section 210(b) of this title, to enter into loan agreements, in amounts not to exceed, at any given time, $350,000,000 in the aggregate principal amount, with the Corporation, the National Railroad Passenger Corporation, and any profitable railroad to which rail properties are transferred or conveyed pursuant to section 303(b)(1) of this Act, under which the Corporation, the National Railroad Passenger Corporation, and any profitable railroad entering into such agreement will agree to meet existing or prospective obligations of the railroads in reorganization in the region which the Association, in accordance with procedures established by the Association, determines should be paid by the Corporation, the National Railroad Passenger Corporation, or a profitable railroad, on behalf of such railroads in reorganization, in order to avoid disruptions in ordinary business relationships. Such obligations shall be limited to—

(i) amounts claimed by suppliers (including private car lines) of materials or services utilized or purchased in current rail operations;

(ii) claims by shippers arising from current rail services;

(iii) payments to railroads for settlement of current interline accounts and all other current accounts and obligations;

(iv) claims of employees arising under the collective-bargaining agreements of the railroads in reorganization in the region and subject to section 3 of the Railway Labor Act (including claims for accrued vacation and wages and similar claims arising in connection with labor and services performed);

(v) claims of all employees or their personal representatives for personal injuries or death and subject to the provisions of Employers' Liability Act (45 U.S.C. 51–60);

(vi) amounts required for adequate funding of accrued pension benefits existing at the time of a conveyance or discontinuance of service under employee pension benefit plans described in section 505(a) of this Act;

(vii) amounts required to provide adequate funding for payment, when due, of claims deriving from membership in any employee voluntary relief plan which provides benefits to its members and their beneficiaries in the event of sickness, accident, disability, or death, and to which both a railroad in reorganization and employee members have made contributions;

(viii) amounts required to provide adequate funding for continuation, by the Corporation, of medical and life insurance coverage and benefits for retired employees of railroads in reorganization as required and limited by section 303(b)(6)(B) of this Act.[1]

---

[1] So in law. The period probably should be a semicolon.

(ix) amounts required to discharge the obligations of each such railroad in reorganization to nonemployee claimants for personal injuries suffered during the period such railroad has been in reorganization; and

(x) amounts required to discharge any obligation of a railroad in reorganization in the region to the National Railroad Passenger Corporation, arising out of a contract between such railroad in reorganization and such Corporation under which such railroad in reorganization is required to provide a suitable rail passenger station, in any case in which such railroad in reorganization sold a rail passenger station pursuant to a judicial order of condemnation prior to April 1, 1976.

(B) The Association shall make a loan pursuant to subparagraph (A) of this paragraph if, notwithstanding any other requirement of this subsection, it finds that the Corpration,[1] the National Railroad Passenger Corporation, or a profitable railroad is entitled to a loan pursuant to section 303(b)(6), 504(e), or 504(g) of this Act, or if, with respect to an obligation referred to in subparagraph (A) of this paragraph, it finds that—

---

[1] So in law. Probably should be "Corporation".

(i) provision for the payment of such obligation was not included in the financial projections of the final system plan;

(ii) such obligations arose from rail operations prior to the date of conveyance of rail properties pursuant to section 303 (b)(1) of this Act and is, under other applicable law, the responsibility of a railroad in reorganization in the region, and a claim is presented to a railroad in reorganization in the region, or the Corporation within 2 years after the date of enactment of the Rail Amendments of 1976;

(iii) the Corporation, the National Railroad Passenger

Corporation, or a profitable railroad has advised the Association that the direct payment of such obligation by the Corporation, the National Railroad Passenger Corporation, or a profitable railroad is for services or materials, the furnishing of which served to avoid disruptions in ordinary business relationships prior to the date of conveyance of rail properties pursuant to section 303 (b)(1) of this Act, or is necessary to avoid postconveyance disruptions in ordinary business relationships;

(iv) the transferor is unable to pay such obligation within a reasonable period of time; and

(v) with respect to loans made to the Corporation, the procedures to be followed by the Corporation, in seeking reimbursement from a railroad in reorganization in the region for an obligation paid on its behalf under this subsection, have been jointly agreed to by the Finance Committee and the Corporation, and the joint agreement—

(I) provides for the Corporation to receive reimbursement from the Association for any expenses incurred in seeking reimbursement from any railroad in reorganization in the region for an obligation paid on its behalf under this subsection; and

(II) includes a stipulation of the exact procedures the Corporation shall undertake to avoid the finding, referred to in paragraph (6)(A)(i) of this subsection, that it has not exercised due diligence.

(2) The trustees of each railroad in reorganization in the region shall attempt to negotiate agency agreements with the Corporation, the National Railroad Passenger Corporation, or a profitable railroad for the processing of all accounts receivable and accounts payable attributable to operations prior to the conveyance of property pursuant to section 303(b)(1) of this Act and for the payment of only those accounts payable which relate to obligations of the estates identified in paragraph (1) of this subsection. If any railroad in reorganization in the region fails to conclude such an agreement within a reasonable time prior to such conveyance, the applicable reorganization courts, after giving all parties an opportunity to be heard, shall prescribe the terms of such an agency arrangement by order, giving due

consideration to the need, wherever possible, to make such agreements uniform among the various estates. Nothing in this subsection shall be construed as permitting any district court of the United States having jurisdiction over the reorganization of a railroad in reorganization in the region to enjoin, restrain, or limit the Corporation, the National Railroad Passenger Corporation, or a profitable railroad from applying, to payment of the obligations of the estates identified in paragraph (1) of this subsection, amounts collected as (A) accounts receivable pursuant to this paragraph, (B) cash or other current assets identified pursuant to paragraph (3) of this subsection, or (C) proceeds of loans pursuant to paragraph (1) of this subsection. Any agency agreement executed prior to the date of the enactment of the Rail Transportation Improvement Act shall be deemed amended to the extent necessary to conform such agreement or order to the provisions of this paragraph. Nothing in this paragraph shall be construed to affect any payment made prior to such date of enactment with respect to obligations other than those identified in paragraph (1) of this subsection.

(3) The Association may, not less than 30 days prior to the date of conveyance pursuant to section 303(b)(1) of this Act, petition each district court of the United States having jurisdiction over the reorganization of a railroad in reorganization in the region for an order, which shall be entered prior to such conveyance, and which—

(A) identifies that cash and other current assets of the estate of such railroad which shall be utilized to satisfy obligations of the estates identified in paragraph (1) of this subsection; and

(B) provides for the application by the trustees of such railroads and their agents, consistent with the principles of reorganization under section 77 of the Bankruptcy Act (11 U.S.C. 205) and with the agency agreement specified in paragraph (2) of this subsection, of all such current assets, including cash available as of or subsequent to such date of conveyance, to the payment in the postconveyance period of the obligations of the estates identified in paragraph (1) of this subsection.

(4)(A) Each obligation of a railroad in reorganization in the region which is paid with financial assistance under paragraph

(1) of this subsection shall be processed, on behalf of such railroad, by the Corporation, the National Railroad Passenger Corporation, or a profitable railroad, whichever is appropriate. An obligation of a railroad in reorganization in the region shall be paid, on behalf of such railroad, by the Corporation, the National Railroad Passenger Corporation, or a profitable railroad, whichever is appropriate, if—

(i) such obligation is deemed by the Corporation, the National Railroad Passenger Corporation, or a profitable railroad, whichever is appropriate, to have been, on the date of conveyance of rail properties pursuant to section 303(b)(1) of this Act, the obligation of a railroad in reorganization in the region;

(ii) such obligation accrues after such date of conveyance but as a result of rail operations conducted prior to such date, and the trustees of such railroad in reorganization acknowledge that it is an obligation of such railroad; or

(iii) the district court of the United States having jurisdiction over such railroad in reorganization in the region approves such obligation as a valid administrative claim against such railroads;

to the extent that payment is required under a loan agreement with the Association under such paragraph (1).

(B) The Association shall resolve any disputes among the Corporation, the National Railroad Passenger Corporation, and a profitable railroad concerning which of them shall process and pay any particular obligation on behalf of a particular railroad in reorganization.

(C) The Corporation, the National Railroad Passenger Corporation, or a profitable railroad shall have a direct claim, as a current expense of administration, for reimbursement from the estate of a railroad in reorganization in the region for all obligations of such estate (plus interest thereon) which are paid by the Corporation, the National Railroad Passenger Corporation, or a profitable railroad, as the case may be. The right of the Corporation or the National Railroad Passenger Corporation to receive reimbursement under this subparagraph from the estate of a railroad in reorganization in the region shall be reduced by the amount, if any, of loans, plus interest forgiven under paragraph (5) of this subsection.

(D)(i) Except as provided in clause (ii) of this subparagraph, any funds held in an escrow account by a railroad in reorganization on the date of enactment of the Rail Transportation Improvement Act which are thereafter determined to be cash and other current assets of the estate of such railroad in reorganization, for purposes of paragraph (3) of this subsection, shall be applied as follows—

(I) first, to the reduction of any outstanding loans to the Corporation by the Association, pursuant to paragraph (1) of this subsection, the proceeds of which were used to discharge obligations of such railroad in reorganization;

(II) second, to the Association to the extent of any such loans which have been forgiven pursuant to paragraph (5) of this subsection; and

(III) third, to the payment of any remaining obligations of such railroad in reorganization, in accordance with the provision of the agency agreement entered into pursuant to paragraph (2) of this subsection.

(ii) The manner of disposition set forth in clause (i) of this subparagraph shall not apply with respect to a railroad in reorganization if the Secretary (I) determines that a different disposition of assets is necessary to carry out a reorganization plan of such railroad in reorganization, and that such different disposition adequately protects the interests of the United States, and (II) transmits his determination to the court having jurisdiction over the reorganization of such railroad.

(5)(A) If, at any time, the Finance Committee of the Association determines that the failure of the Corporation to receive full reimbursement with interest from the estate of a railroad in reorganization in the region for any obligation of such estate paid pursuant to this subsection could adversely affect the fairness and equity of the transfers and conveyances pursuant to section 303(b)(1) of this Act, or that the failure of the National Railroad Passenger Corporation to receive such full reimbursement plus interest for any such obligation would be contrary to the public interest, the Association shall forgive the indebtedness, plus accrued interest, of the Corporation or of the National Railroad Passenger Corporation incurred pursuant to paragraph (1) of this subsection in the amount recommended by the Finance Committee. The Association shall have a direct claim, as a current expense of administration of the estate of such railroad in reorganization, equal to the amount by which loans of the Corporation or of the National Railroad Passenger Corporation, plus interest, have been forgiven. Such direct claim shall not be subject to any reduction by way of setoff, cross-claim, or counter-claim which the estate of such railroad in reorganization may be entitled to assert against the Corporation, the National Railroad Passenger Corporation, the Association, or the United States.

(B) The direct claim of the association under this paragraph, and any direct claim authorized under paragraph (4) of this subsection, shall be prior to all other administrative claims of the estate of a railroad in reorganization, except claims arising under trustee's certificates or from default on the payment of such certificates. The Corporation, the National Rail Passenger Corporation, or a profitable railroad, as the case may be, shall, with respect to each direct claim for reimbursement pursuant to paragraph (4) of this subsection, file a proof of administrative expense claim with the trustees of the railroad in reorganization from whom reimbursement is sought. Each such proof of administrative expense claim shall set forth, by category and amount, the obligations of such railroad in reorganization which were paid pursuant to such paragraph (4).

(6)(A) Notwithstanding any other provision of this subsection, the Association shall forgive any loan made to the Corporation or the National Railroad Passenger Corporation pursuant to this subsection, plus accrued interest thereon, on the 3rd anniversary date of any such loan, except that the Association shall not forgive any loan or portion thereof, in accordance with this paragraph, if—

(i) the Finance Committee makes an affirmative finding, with respect to such loan or portion thereof, that—

(I) the Corporation has not exercised due diligence in executing the procedures adopted pursuant to paragraph (1)(B)(v) of this subsection, and

(II) the failure of the Association to forgive such loan or portion thereof will not adversely affect the ability of the Corporation to become financially self-sustaining;

(ii) the Finance Committee so directs the Association; and

(iii) neither House of the Congress disapproves such affirmative finding and direction, in accordance with the following provisions of this paragraph.

A copy of each such finding, the reasons therefor, and such direction made by the Finance Committee, together with the comments and recommendations thereon of the Board of Directors of the Association, shall be transmitted to the Congress by the Association within 10 days after the date on which the Finance Committee makes such finding and direction, or if not so transmitted, shall be transmitted by the Finance Committee. Each such finding and direction so transmitted shall become effective immediately, and shall remain in effect, unless, within the first period of 30 calendar days of continuous session of Congress after the date of transmittal of such finding and direction to Congress, either House of Congress disapproves such finding and direction in accordance with the procedures specified in section 1017 of the Congressional Budget and Impoundment Control Act of 1974 (31 U.S.C. 1407). For purposes of this paragraph, continuity of session of Congress is broken only in the circumstances described in section 1011(5) of that Act (31 U.S.C. 1401 (5)).

(B) The Association shall have a direct claim, as a current expense of administration of the estate of the railroad in reorganization whose obligations were paid with the proceeds of loans forgiven under this paragraph, equal to the amount by which the loans, plus interest, have been forgiven. Such direct claim shall not be subject to any reduction by way of setoff, cross-claim, or counterclaim which the estate of such railroad in reorganization may be entitled to assert against the Corporation, the National Railroad Passenger Corporation, the Association, or the United States. The direct claim of the Association under this paragraph shall be prior to all other administrative claims of the estate of the railroad in reorganization, except claims arising under trustee's certificates or from default on the payment of such certificates.

(7) For purposes of this subsection, the term "Corporation" includes a subsidiary of the Corporation.

[45 U.S.C. 721]

RECORDS, AUDIT, AND EXAMINATION

SEC. 212. (a) RECORDS.—Each recipient of financial assistance under this title, whether in the form of loans, obligations, or other arrangements, shall keep such records as the Association or the Secretary shall prescribe, including records which fully disclose the amount and disposition by such recipient of the proceeds of such assistance and such other records as will facilitate an effective audit.

(b) AUDIT AND EXAMINATION.—The Association, the Secretary, and the Comptroller General of the United States, or any of their duly authorized representatives shall, until the expiration of 3 years after the implementation of the final system plan, have access for the purpose of audit and examination to any books, documents, papers, and records of such recipients which in the opinion of the Association, the Secretary, or the Comptroller General may be related or pertinent to the loans, obligations or other arrangements referred to in subsection (a) of this section. The Association or any of its duly authorized representatives shall, until any financial assistance received under this title has been repaid to the Association, have access to any such materials which concern any matter that may bear upon—

(1) the ability of the recipient of such financial assistance to make repayment within the time fixed therefor;

(2) the effectiveness with which the proceeds of such assistance is used; and

(3) the implementation of the final system plan and the realization of the declaration of policy of this Act.

[45 U.S.C. 722]

EMERGENCY ASSISTANCE PENDING IMPLEMENTATION

SEC. 213. (a) EMERGENCY ASSISTANCE.—The Secretary is authorized, pending the implementation of the final system plan, to pay to the trustees of railroads in reorganization such sums as are necessary for the continued provision of essential transportation services by such railroads. Such payments shall be made by the Secretary upon such reasonable terms and conditions as the Secretary establishes, except that recipients must agree to maintain and provide service at a level no less than that in effect on the date of enactment of this Act. Where the Secretary and the trustees agree that funds provided pursuant to this section are to be used (together with funds provided pursuant to section 215 of this Act, if any) to perform program maintenance on designated rail properties until the date rail properties are conveyed under this Act or to improve such designated properties, such agreement shall contain the conditions set forth in section 215(b) of this Act.

(b) AUTHORIZATION FOR APPROPRIATIONS.—There are authorized to be appropriated to the Secretary for carrying out this section such sums as are necessary, not exceed $282,000,000, to remain available until expended. Of amounts authorized to be appropriated under this subsection, $50,000,000 shall be available solely to pay to the trustees of railroads in reorganization such sums as may be necessary to provide such railroads with amounts equal to revenues attributable to tariff increases proposed by such railroads and suspended by the Interstate Commerce Commission during the calendar year 1975, if the Secretary determines that such payments are necessary to carry out this section.

[45 U.S.C. 723]

AUTHORIZATION FOR APPROPRIATIONS

SEC. 214. (a) SECRETARY.—There are authorized to be appropriated to the Secretary for purposes of preparing the reports and exercising other functions to be performed by him under this Act such sums as are necessary, not to exceed $12,500,000, to remain available until expended. There are authorized to be appropriated to the Secretary such sums as may be necessary to discharge the obligations of the United States arising under section 303(c)(5) of this Act.

(b) OFFICE.—There are authorized to be appropriated to the Commission for the use of the Office in carrying out its functions under this Act such sums as are necessary, not to exceed $7,000,000, to remain available until expended. The budget for the Office shall be submitted by the Commission directly to the Congress and shall not be subject to review of any kind by any other agency or official of the United States. Moneys appropriated for the Office shall not be withheld by any agency or official of the United States or used by the Commission for any purpose other than the use of the Office. No part of any other moneys appropriated to the Commission shall be withheld by any other agency or official of the United States to offset any moneys appropriated pursuant to this subsection.

(c) ASSOCIATION.—There are authorized to be appropriated to the Association for purposes of carrying out its administrative expenses under this Act not to exceed $13,000,000 for the fiscal year ending September 30, 1982, and not to exceed $4,000,000 for the fiscal year ending September 30, 1983. Sums appropriated under this subsection are authorized to remain available until expended.

[45 U.S.C. 724]

INTERIM AGREEMENTS

SEC. 215. (a) PURPOSES.—Prior to the date upon which rail properties are conveyed to the Corporation under this Act, the Secretary, with the approval of the Association, is authorized to enter into agreements with the trustees of the railroads in reorganization in the region (or railroads leased, operated, or controlled by railroads in reorganization)—

(1) to perform the program maintenance on designated rail properties of such railroads until the date rail properties are conveyed under this Act;

(2) to improve rail properties of such railroads; and

(3) to acquire rail properties for lease or loan to any such railroads until the date such rail properties are conveyed under this Act, and subsequently for conveyance pursuant to the final system plan, or to acquire interests in such rail properties owned by or leased to any such railroads or in purchase money obligations therefor.

(b) CONDITIONS.—Agreements pursuant to subsection (a) of this section shall contain such reasonable terms and conditions as the Secretary may prescribe. In addition, agreements under paragraphs (1) and (2) of subsection (a) of this section shall provide that—

(1) to the extent that physical condition is used as a basis

for determining, under section 206(f) or 303(c) of this Act, the value of properties subject to such an agreement and designated for transfer to the Corporation under the final system plan, the physical condition of the properties on the effective date of the agreement shall be used; and

(2) in the event that property subject to the agreement is sold, leased, or transferred to an entity other than the Corporation, the trustees or railroad shall pay or assign to the Secretary that portion of the proceeds of such sale, lease, or transfer which reflects value attributable to the maintenance and improvement provided pursuant to the agreement.

(c) OBLIGATIONS.—Notwithstanding section 210(b) of this title, the Association shall issue obligations under section 210(a) of this title in an amount sufficient to finance such agreements and shall require the Corporation to assume any such obligations. The aggregate amount of obligations issued under this section and outstanding at any one time shall not exceed $300,000,000. The Association, with the approval of the Secretary, shall designate in the final system plan that portion of such obligations issued or to be issued which shall be refinanced and the terms thereof, and that portion from which the Corporation shall be released of its obligations.

(d) CONVEYANCE.—The Secretary may convey to the Corporation or any subsidiary thereof with or without receipt of consideration, any property or interests acquired by, transferred to, or otherwise held by the Secretary pursuant to this section or section 213 of this Act.

[45 U.S.C. 725]

DEBENTURES AND SERIES A PREFERRED STOCK

SEC. 216. (a) GENERAL.—The Association is authorized, in accordance with the provisions of this section, and such rules and regulations as it may prescribe, to invest from time to time in the securities of the Corporation by purchasing (1) up to $1,000,000,000 of debentures issued by the Corporation, and (2) after the acquisition of such debentures, up to $2,629,000,000 of the Series A preferred stock of the Corporation.

(b) PURPOSES AND PROCEDURE FOR INVESTMENT.—(1) The Association is authorized to purchase debentures and, thereafter, series A preferred stock of the Corporation at such times and in such amounts as may be required and requested by the Corporation in accordance with the terms and conditions governing such purchases (which shall be prescribed by the Association), to provide—

(A) for the modernization, rehabilitation and maintenance of rail properties of the Corporation;

(B) for the acquisition of equipment and other capital needs;

(C) for the refinancing of indebtedness which was incurred by the Corporation under section 211 of this title or which was incurred under section 215 of this title and assumed by the Corporation; or

(D) working capital as contemplated by the final system plan.

(2) Purchases of up to $1,000,000,000 of debentures and, thereafter, of up to $2,300,000,000 of series A preferred stock shall be made by the Association as required and requested by the Corporation, unless the Finance Committee makes an affirmative finding that—

(A) the Corporation has failed in any material respect to comply with any covenants or undertakings made to the Association and such failure remains uncorrected;

(B) the Corporation has failed substantially (as determined by performance within the margins prescribed by the Board of Directors) to attain the overall operating (including rehabilitation) and financial results projected for the Corporation in the final system plan (including any modifications of such projected results and of the performance margins applicable to such projected results which are jointly approved by the Finance Committee and the Board of Directors and which would improve the possibility that the Corporation will attain such projected results and perform within such margins, as modified); or

(C) it is not reasonably likely, taking into consideration all relevant factors including the overall operating (including rehabilitation) and financial results achieved by the Corporation, that the Corporation will be able to become financially self-sustaining without requiring Federal financial assistance substantially in excess of the amounts authorized in this section.

(3)(A) Amounts transferred to the Association pursuant to section 509(b)(1) of the Railroad Revitalization and Regulatory Reform Act of 1976 may be used to purchase series A preferred stock of the Corporation to provide for the implementation by the Corporation of a program to reduce the Corporation's work force, if the Finance Committee finds that the implementation of such program will result in substantial savings to the United States.

(B) An employee who ceases to be an employee as a result of the reduction of work force under a program implemented pursuant to this paragraph shall not, by reason of so ceasing to be an employee, or by reason of any work or employment entered into after so ceasing to be an employee, lose such employee's current connection with the railroad industry for the purposes of the Railroad Retirement Act of 1974.

(4) Purchases of up to $329,000,000 of a series A preferred stock shall be made by the Association, subject to the availability of appropriations, as required and requested by the Corporation, if the Finance Committee makes an affirmative finding that the Corporation has taken appropriate action to eliminate losses on light density lines and other lines which are unprofitable. Such action shall include the imposition of surcharges on such lines, the abandonment of such lines, and the transfer of such lines.

(5) The authority of the Association to purchase debentures or series A preferred stock of the Corporation shall terminate upon the date of the enactment of the Conrail Privatization Act.

(c) FINDING, DIRECTION, AND REVIEW BY CONGRESS.—(1) If the Finance Committee makes an affirmative finding pursuant to subsection (b)(2) of this section, it may direct the Association—

(A) not to purchase any debentures or series A preferred stock of the Corporation after the date of such affirmative finding; or

(B) to purchase debentures or series A preferred stock of the Corporation, after the date of such affirmative finding, only in such amounts, at such times, and on such terms and conditions (notwithstanding subsection (e)(1) of this section) as the Finance Committee determines to be appropriate to the role of the Association as an investor in such debentures and series

A preferred stock.

(2) A copy of each affirmative finding, the reasons thereof, and each direction made by the Finance Committee under paragraph (1) of this subsection, together with the comments and recommendations thereon of the Board of Directors of the Association, shall be transmitted to the Congress by the Association within 10 days after the date on which the Finance Committee makes such finding and direction, or if not so transmitted, shall be transmitted by the Finance Committee. Each such direction so transmitted shall become finally effective and is required to be implemented by the Association, unless within the first period of 30 calendar days of continuous session of Congress after the date of its transmittal to Congress either House of Congress disapproves such direction (except that such direction shall become finally effective immediately upon approval of such direction by both Houses of Congress) in accordance with the procedures specified in section 1017 of the Congressional Budget and Impoundment Control Act of 1974 (31 U.S.C. 1407). For purposes of this paragraph, continuity of session of Congress is broken only in the circumstances described in section 1011(5) of that Act (31 U.S.C. 1401(5)). During review by the Association and Congress, the Association shall take no action inconsistent with the direction of the Finance Committee pursuant to paragraph (c)(1) of this section, except to the extent the Association finds necessary, in its discretion, to assure continuous orderly operation of the Corporation.

(3) If the Congress, pursuant to paragraph (2) of this subsection, disapproves a direction submitted to the Association pursuant to paragraph (1) of this subsection, the Association shall continue to purchase the debentures or series A preferred stock of the Corporation as otherwise provided in this title until such time as a direction is submitted under this section which is not so disapproved (or affirmatively approved). The powers of the Association and of the Board of Directors of the Association shall remain in effect except to the extent modified by any such direction. If any such direction is disapproved by either House of Congress, the Finance Committee may, not earlier than 30 days after the date of such disapproval, make (and the Board of Directors of the Association shall transmit) any additional affirmative finding

and direction with respect to the same matter, which direction shall become effective in accordance with paragraph (2) of this subsection. An affirmative finding and direction under this subsection, or action by the Association during a review thereof by the Congress, may not be held unlawful or set aside by any reviewing court on the ground that such finding and direction or action were not adequate to meet the requirements of subparagraph (A), (E), or (F) of section 706(2) of title 5, United States Code.

(4) Notwithstanding any other provision of this section, or any terms and conditions governing its purchase of securities of the Corporation, the Association shall, upon written application by the Corporation at least 30 days prior to such investment, make an initial investment in debentures of the Corporation within 60 days after the date of conveyance of rail properties pursuant to section 303(b)(1) of this Act. Such initial investment shall be limited to such amounts as the Association and Finance Committee, acting jointly, determine are necessary for the continued and orderly operations of the Corporation prior to any additional investment.

(5) Not later than 60 days after the date of conveyance pursuant to section 303(b)(1) of this Act, the Association shall select 6 individuals to serve as members of the Board of Directors of the Corporation, subject to the provisions of section 301(d) of this Act.

(d) TERMS AND CONDITIONS.—Notwithstanding any other provision of State law, the debentures and the series A preferred stock of the Corporation shall have such terms and conditions, not inconsistent with the final system plan or this title, as may be prescribed by the Association, except as follows:

(1) The Corporation shall not be required to issue to the Association additional shares of series A preferred stock of the Corporation as a dividend on any such stock.

(2) The dividends payable on series A preferred stock of the Corporation shall not be cumulative and shall be paid in cash when and to the extent that there is "cash available for restricted cash payments", as that term is defined in the final system plan.

(3) After the Association calls for redemption of the certificates of value, no shares of series A preferred stock of the

Corporation shall be issued in lieu of interest on the debentures of the Corporation and, to the extent such interest is not payable in cash by reason of the absence of sufficient "cash available for restricted cash payment", the Corporation shall deliver to the holders of the debentures contingent interest notes in a face amount equal to such unpaid interest.

(4) If the Board of Directors of the Association and the Finance Committee, acting jointly, modify the terms or conditions governing the purchase of debentures or series A preferred stock of the Corporation pursuant to subsection (e)(1) of this section, or if the Finance Committee waives compliance with any term, condition, provision, or covenant of such securities pursuant to subsection (e)(2) of this section, the Finance Committee may require the Corporation to issue contingent interest notes in such amount as, in the determination of the Finance Committee, will provide protection for the United States, in the event of bankruptcy, reorganization, or receivership of the Corporation, equal to the protection of the United States would have had in the absence of such modification or waiver.

(5) The contingent interest notes issued pursuant to this section shall bear interest compounded annually at the rate of 8 percent per annum and such notes and the accumulated interest thereon shall be payable only in the event of bankruptcy, reorganization, or receivership of the Corporation occurring prior to the repayment and redemption of all outstanding debentures and accumulated series A preferred stock of the Corporation. The contingent interest notes and the accumulated interest thereon shall have the same priority in bankruptcy, reorganization, or receivership as the debentures of the Corporation. The other terms and conditions of the contingent interest notes shall be as set forth in an agreement to be entered into between the Association and the Corporation prior to issuance of any debentures.

(e) MODIFICATIONS, WAIVERS, AND CONVERSIONS.—(1) The Board of Directors of the Association and the Finance Committee, acting jointly, may agree with the Corporation to modify any of the terms and conditions governing the purchase by the Association of securities of the Corporation, upon a finding that such action is necessary or appropriate to achieve the purposes of this Act or the goals of the final system plan.

(2) The Finance Committee may, in its discretion and upon a finding that such action is necessary or appropriate to achieve the purposes of this Act or the goals of the final system plan, waive compliance with any term, condition, provision, or covenant of the securities of the Corporation held by the Association, including any provision of such securities with respect to redemption of principal or issuance price, payment of interest or dividends, or any term or condition governing the purchase of such securities.

(3) Notwithstanding any provision of State law, there shall be no conversion of the debentures of the Corporation into series A preferred stock of the Corporation, as provided in the terms and conditions of the debentures and pursuant to the final system plan, unless the Board of Directors of the Association and the Finance Committee jointly determine to effect such conversion.

(f)(1) The Association shall not invest the final $345,000,000 of the additional investment in the Corporation authorized by the Regional Rail Reorganization Act Amendments of 1978 unless and until (A) the Corporation has in effect an employee stock ownership plan which satisfies the requirements of paragraphs (2) and (3), and (B) the requirements of the other paragraphs of this subsection have been satisfied.

(2) The employee stock ownership plan shall:

(A) provide:

(i) for a transfer to the plan and allocation to the accounts of plan participants in periodic installments of Series A preferred stock of the Corporation with a stated redemption value of at least $345,000,000 or any other securities in an amount determined by the Association, with the concurrence of the Finance Committee, as constituting a meaningful interest in the Corporation, or any combination thereof so determined by the Association, with the concurrence of the Finance Committee. The use of Series A preferred stock to fund the Employee Stock Ownership Plan shall not be interpreted to relieve ConRail of the responsibility for repaying in full to the United States Railway Association its indebtedness as represented by all shares originally issued under Public Law 94–210 and this Act;

(ii) for immediate vesting of the rights of participants to such securities upon allocation, subject to defeasance as a result of the plan's termination which termination shall occur in the event that, by the end of the 120th month beginning after the month in which securities or interests therein are first allocated to participants' accounts, the Corporation has not attained for two consecutive quarters positive net income and a freight labor cost to freight revenue ratio equal to the average such ratio for all Class I railroads in 1977, as determined pursuant to procedures adopted by the Corporation pursuant to regulations promulgated by the Association with the concurrence of the Finance Committee;

(B) be an employee benefit plan which is designed to invest primarily in employer securities;

(C) meets such other requirements (similar to requirements applicable to employee stock ownership plans as defined in section 4975(e)(7) of the Internal Revenue Code of 1954) as the Secretary of the Treasury or his delegate may describe;

(D) have been approved by the Board of Directors of the Corporation to the extent and in the manner which may be required by the Corporation's articles of incorporation and bylaws then in effect; and

(E) have been prepared in consultation with, and been approved by, the Association and the Finance Committee.

(3) Notwithstanding any other provision of law, if a plan does not meet the requirements of section 401 of the Internal Revenue Code of 1954—

(A) stock transferred under paragraph (2) and allocated to the account of any participant under paragraph (2) shall not be considered income of the participant or his beneficiary under the Internal Revenue Code of 1954 until such stock or dividends are actually distributed or made available to the participant or his beneficiary and, at such time, shall be taxable under section 72 of the Internal Revenue Code of 1954 (treating the participant or his beneficiary as having a basis of 0 in the stock);

(B) no amount shall be allocated to any participant under the plan in excess of the amount which might be allocated if the plan met the requirements of section 401 of the Internal Revenue Code of 1954; and

(C) the plan must meet the requirements of sections 410 and 415 of the Internal Revenue Code of 1954.

(4) The Corporation shall adopt such terms and conditions governing the securities or interests therein to be transferred to the plan (including limitations on voting rights) as the Association, with the concurrence of the Finance Committee, determines are necessary to protect reasonably the interests of the United States in the litigation pursuant to section 303(c) of this Act and in the event of any action to further reorganize or restructure the Corporation's assets or capital structure.

(5) The Corporation, the Association, and a representative appointed by the Chairman of the Railway Labor Executives' Association as representative of all the classes or crafts of employees of the Corporation shall engage in negotiations to agree upon a plan in accordance with the provisions of this subsection. For purposes of this subsection, the Railway Labor Executives' Association shall be deemed to represent all of the representatives of crafts or classes of employees of the Corporation and its subsidiaries as though that organization held powers of attorney from each representative of a craft or class for the limited purposes of negotiating and agreeing upon an employee stock ownership plan. The parties shall incorporate their agreement into a written plan instrument specifying the terms and conditions set forth in this subsection and such other terms and conditions as they may decide upon, with the concurrence of the Finance Committee, unless the parties are unable to reach on an[1] agreement on the plan following the exertion of every reasonable effort to do so, in accordance with the Railway Labor Act, in which event, the Corporation and the Association, with the concurrence of the Finance Committee, shall establish a written plan with such terms and conditions as they may agree upon in accordance with this subsection. The plan shall not be subject to change

under the provisions of section 6 of the Railway Labor Act until after such time as securities have been distributed from the plan to the participants in the plan or their beneficiaries pursuant to the terms of the plan. Within one year after the effective date of this subsection, the Corporation shall transmit a draft of such plan to the Congress and shall report on its progress in establishing and administering the plan. The report shall include recommendations of contractual and statutory provisions necessary to reasonably (A) exempt any Trustee of the plan, the Corporation, the Association, any member of the Finance Committee, and any other person from any fiduciary duty, responsibility or liability for the acquisition of, investment in, or retention of any security or interest therein of the Corporation or for any other transaction contemplated by this subsection and (B) provide for the United States to indemnify, defend, and hold harmless such persons against any and all liabilities, claims, actions, judgments, amounts paid in settlement, and costs and expenses actually incurred in connection with any matter so exempted in which it is determined that such persons were acting in good faith and in a manner they believed to not be opposed to the best interests of the plan.

---

[1] So in law. The phrase "reach on an" probably should read "reach an".

(6) Within fourteen months of the effective date of this subsection, the Association shall report to the Congress on the draft plan and on any legal obstacle to the ability of the Corporation to effectuate and implement an employee stock ownership plan of the nature contemplated by this subsection, including specific recommendations on amendments to this subsection and other relevant laws which would harmonize the requirements of this subsection with those other laws. The Department of Transportation and the Department of the Treasury, as each finds appropriate, shall provide separate comments to the Association for inclusion with such report.

(7) For the purposes of this subsection, the officers of each duly authorized representative of the crafts or classes of the employees of the Corporation who have been given leaves of absence by the Corporation to serve as such officers, are to be eligible to participate in such plan on the same basis as

are employees whose employment is governed by a collective bargaining agreement with the Corporation.

(8)(A) Except as provided in subparagraph (B) of this paragraph, no person described in subparagraph (C) of this paragraph shall have or be subject to any fiduciary responsibility, obligation, or duty, nor shall any such person be subject to civil liability, under any Federal or State law, as a fiduciary or otherwise—

(i) in connection with the employee stock ownership plan and related trust established by the Corporation pursuant to the requirements of this subsection or with ConRail Equity Corporation (I) on account of any reorganization or restructuring of the Corporation, its successors or assigns, or their assets or capital structure, or (II) on account of any action taken or not taken by the Corporation which may affect its ability to attain the performance levels established in connection with the plan pursuant to paragraph (2)(A)(ii) of this subsection;

(ii) for or in connection with the establishment, continuation or implementation of the plan and related trust or of ConRail Equity Corporation or the acquisition of, investment in or retention of any security of the Corporation or ConRail Equity Corporation, or of any of their successors and assigns, by the plan or ConRail Equity Corporation, or the disposition of any such security to the extent that such disposition is made in connection with a reorganization or restructuring of the Corporation, its successors and assigns, or their assets or capital structure, as directed or approved by or on behalf of the Association or the United States, or the acquisition or retention of any cash, security or other property received in connection with any such reorganization or restructuring; or

(iii) for or in connection with any other action taken or not taken pursuant to any term or condition of the plan or related trust agreement or of the articles of incorporation or bylaws of ConRail Equity Corporation.

Any directions described in clauses (i)(I), (ii), or (iii) shall be taken at the direction, or with the consent, of the Association or of the Secretary or his designate.

(B) Subparagraph (A) of this paragraph shall not be

interpreted to relieve any person from any fiduciary or other responsibility, obligation or duty under any Federal or State law to take or not to take actions with respect to the plan in connection with (i) receiving contributions, (ii) exercising custodial responsibilities, (iii) determining eligibility to participate in the plan, (iv) calculating, determining and paying benefits, (v) processing and deciding claims, (vi) preparing and distributing plan information, benefit statements, returns and reports, (vii) maintaining plan records, (viii) appointing plan fiduciaries and other persons to advise or assist in plan administration and (ix) other than as provided in subparagraph (A), acquiring, holding or disposing of plan assets.

(C) For purposes of subparagraph (A) of this paragraph, the term "person" includes each of the following:

(i) the trustee or trustees of the plan, the Corporation and its subsidiaries, ConRail Equity Corporation, the Association, and any of their successors and assigns;

(ii) each director, officer, employee and agent of the Corporation of[1] any of its subsidiaries, of ConRail Equity Corporation, of the plan, of the Association or of any of their successors and assigns; and

---

[1]   So in law. The word "of" probably should read "or".

(iii) each member of the Finance Committee and any of their employees and agents.

(D) Neither this paragraph nor paragraph (9) of this subsection shall be construed to grant immunity from any criminal law of the United States or of any State or the District of Columbia.

(9) The United States shall indemnify, defend, and hold harmless the persons described in paragraph (8)(C) of this subsection from and against any and all liabilities, claims, actions, judgments, amounts paid in settlement, and costs and expenses (including reasonable fees of accountants, experts, and attorneys) actually incurred in connection with the establishment, implementation, or operation of the plan or

ConRail Equity Corporation or with any transaction which is required by or is appropriate to effectuate fully the provisions of this subsection, except as may arise in connection with the execution of a responsibility, obligation, or duty excluded from paragraph (8)(A) by paragraph (8)(B), if it is determined that such persons were acting in good faith. The indemnity provided in this paragraph shall be a full faith and credit obligation of the United States.

(10) All securities of the Corporation, all securities of any subsidiary of the Corporation and of ConRail Equity Corporation, and all interests in the employee stock ownership plan which are issued or transferred in connection with the employee stock ownership plan established by the Corporation pursuant to the requirements of this subsection shall be deemed for all purposes to have been issued subject to and authorized and approved pursuant to section 11301(b) of title 49 of the United States Code and any corresponding provision of any successor statute.

(g) APPROPRIATION.—(1) There is authorized to be appropriated to the Association $3,629,000,000 to be used for the purchase of securities of the Corporation in accordance with this section. All sums received by the Association on account of the holding or disposition of any such securities shall be deposited in the general fund of the Treasury.

(2) To the extent provided in appropriation Acts, any funds appropriated under the authority of paragraph (1) of this subsection prior to the date of enactment of the Rail Safety and Service Improvement Act of 1982 may be reappropriated to the Secretary, to facilitate the transfer of rail commuter services from the Corporation to other operators, for distribution under the statutory provisions of section 1139(b) of the Northeast Rail Service Act of 1981.

[45 U.S.C. 726]

ADDITIONAL PURCHASES OF SERIES A PREFERRED STOCK

SEC. 217. (a) FEDERAL INVESTMENT.—In addition to the authority provided under section 216 of this Act, the Association shall purchase shares of Series A preferred stock and accounts receivable of the Corporation after the effective date of the Northeast Rail Service Act of 1981, in amounts not to exceed a total of

$137,000,000.

(b) ACCOUNTS RECEIVABLE.—(1) In any further purchase under this section or section 216 of this title the Association shall purchase accounts receivable of the Corporation attributable to the dispute over the right-of-way related costs described in section 1163 of the Northeast Rail Service Act of 1981 until the Commission resolves such dispute under such section, and accounts receivable of the Corporation attributable to delays in reimbursement from commuter authorities.

(2) From funds provided under this section or section 216 of this Act, the Association shall purchase Series A preferred stock of the Corporation, to the extent of losses on commuter service, in an amount not to exceed $15,000,000.

(c) STATES AND LOCALITIES.—The Corporation shall be exempt from liability for any State tax, except for any tax imposed by any political subdivision of a State, applicable to any taxable period commencing before January 1, 1987.

(d) Debentures.—The Association shall return debentures to the Corporation in an amount equal to the value of the properties conveyed by the Corporation to Amtrak Commuter and any commuter authority.

(e) RIGHTS RETAINED.—The Corporation shall retain the right to collect any accounts receivable attributable to delays in reimbursement from commuter authorities that are purchased by the Association under this section. No agency or instrumentality of the United States shall be required to collect such accounts.

(f) AUTHORIZATION OF APPROPRIATIONS.—(1) There is authorized to be appropriated not to exceed $262,000,000—

(A) of which not to exceed $137,000,000 shall be appropriated to the Association for purposes of purchasing securities and accounts receivable of the Corporation under this section, such sums to remain available until the Secretary transfers the Corporation under title IV of this Act;

(B) of which not to exceed $75,000,000 shall be appropriated to the Secretary, to facilitate the transfer of rail commuter services from the Corporation to other operators, for distribution under the statutory provisions of section 1139(b) of the Northeast Rail Service Act of 1981;

(C) of which not to exceed $35,000,000 shall be

appropriated to the Secretary to be allocated for employee protection under section 106 of the Rock Island Railroad Transition and Employee Assistance Act (45 U.S.C. 1005); and

(D) of which not to exceed $15,000,000 shall be appropriated to the Secretary to facilitate the transfer of rail commuter services from railroads that entered reorganization after calendar year 1974 to any commuter authority that was providing commuter service, operated by a railroad that entered reorganization after calendar year 1974, as of January 1, 1979.

(2) All sums received on account of the holding or disposition of any securities or accounts receivable referred to in paragraph (1)(A) of this subsection shall be deposited in the general fund of the Treasury.

(3) The amount authorized to be appropriated under paragraph (1)(B) of this subsection shall be reduced, in an amount equal to any amounts reappropriated under the authority of section 216(g)(2) of this Act, upon the date of enactment of any Act which reappropriates such amounts.

[45 U.S.C. 727]

UNITED STATES RAILWAY ASSOCIATION REPORTS

SEC. 218. (a) PROGRESS AND EVALUATION.—(1) The Association shall prepare and submit to Congress periodic reports on the progress of the Secretary in carrying out the provisions of titles II, III, and IV of this Act.

(2) Reports submitted under paragraph (1) of this subsection shall also include an evaluation of the performance of the Corporation in order to keep the Congress informed as to matters which may affect the quality of rail service in the Northeast and which may affect the security of Federal funds invested in the Corporation.

(b) TRANSFER AGREEMENTS.—(1) The Association shall prepare and submit to Congress a final report on the transfer agreements which the Secretary is required to transmit to Congress under section 407 of the Regional Rail Reorganization Act of 1973. Such report shall be submitted on the same date as the Secretary's transmittal of such agreements to Congress.

(2) The report submitted under paragraph (1) of this

subsection shall include an evaluation of the effect of the transfer agreements on rail service in the Northeast, railroad employees, the economy of the Region, other railroads in the Northeast and elsewhere, and any other matter which the Association considers appropriate. Such report shall also include recommendations with respect to approval, disapproval, or modification of the transfer agreements.

[45 U.S.C. 728]

ADVISORY BOARD

SEC. 219. Members of the Board of Directors of the Association serving on the day before the effective date of the Northeast Rail Service Act of 1981, shall serve as an Advisory Board to the Association. A member of the Advisory Board who is not otherwise an employee of the Federal Government shall receive reimbursement for travel, subsistence, and other necessary expenses incurred in the performance of such duties. The Chairman of the Association shall serve as Chairman of the Advisory Board. Any vacancy on the Advisory Board shall be filled by the Association with a representative from the group which had a representative in the vacant position.

[45 U.S.C. 729]

TITLE III—CONSOLIDATED RAIL CORPORATION

FORMATION AND STRUCTURE

SEC. 301. (a) ESTABLISHMENT.—There shall be established within 300 days after the date of enactment of this Act, in accordance with the provisions of this section, a corporation to be known as the Consolidated Rail Corporation or such other corporate name as may be duly adopted by the Corporation.

(b) STATUS.—The Corporation shall be a for-profit corporation establishment under the laws of a State and shall not be an agency or instrumentality of the Federal Government. The Corporation shall be deemed a rail carrier subject to part A of subtitle IV of title 49, United States Code, shall be subject to the provisions of this Act and, to the extent not inconsistent with such Acts, shall be subject to applicable State law. The principal office of the Corporation or of its principal railroad operating subsidiary shall be located in

Philadelphia in the Commonwealth of Pennsylvania.

(c) INCORPORATORS.—(1) The members of the executive committee of the Association shall be the incorporators of the Corporation and shall take whatever steps are necessary to establish the Corporation, including the filing of articles of incorporation.

(2) Notwithstanding any provision of State law, after the date of enactment of this paragraph, the members of the executive committee of the Association (including duly authorized representatives of members who are authorized by this Act to be represented) and the chief executive officer and chief operating officer of the Corporation shall adopt the bylaws of the Corporation and serve as the Board of Directors of the Corporation until all members of the Board of Directors of the Corporation have been selected in accordance with subsection (d) of this section. The chief executive officer shall serve as chairman of such Board until a chairman thereof is selected pursuant to subsection (d) of this section, after which time such chairman shall serve at the pleasure of such Board.

(d) BOARD OF DIRECTORS.—(1) Notwithstanding any provision of State law, the articles of incorporation and bylaws of the Corporation shall provide that the Board of Directors of the Corporation shall consist of 13 members selected in accordance with the articles and bylaws of the Corporation, as follows:

(A) six individuals selected by the holders of the Corporation's debentures and series A preferred stock voting as one class, with every $100 principal amount of debentures, and every $100 liquidation amount of series A preferred stock each receiving one vote for directors;

(B) three individuals selected by the holders of the Corporation's series B preferred stock; and

(C) two individuals selected by the holders of the Corporation's common stock.

(2) The chief executive officer and the chief operating officer of the Corporation shall also serve on the Board, but the chief executive officer and chief operating officer of the Corporation shall not be entitled to vote on the election or removal of either. In the event a vacancy occurs on the Board of Directors due to death, disability, or resignation of a director, such vacancy shall

be filled only by a vote of the holders of the class of securities that initially elected such director.

(e) INITIAL CAPITALIZATION.—(1) The Corporation is authorized to issue debentures series A preferred stock, series B preferred stock, common stock, contingent interest notes, and other securities.

(2) Debentures and series A preferred stock shall be issued initially to the Association. Series B preferred stock and common stock shall be issued initially to the estates of railroads in reorganization in the region, to railroads leased, operated, and controlled by railroads in reorganization in the region, and to other persons leased, operated or controlled by a railroad in reorganization who are transferors of rail properties in exchange for rail properties transferred to the Corporation pursuant to the final system plan. Notwithstanding any other provisions of State or Federal law, the series B preferred stock and common stock shall have terms and conditions not inconsistent with the final system plan. As a condition of its investment in the Corporation, the Association may require that the Corporation adopt limitations consistent with the final system plan on the circumstances under which dividends on the series B preferred stock and common stock are payable so long as any of the debentures or series A preferred stock are outstanding. Notwithstanding anything to the contrary in the final system plan, the initial authorized number of shares of series B preferred stock may be 35,000,000, and the Corporation may issue initially for the purpose of the deposit required under section 303(a)(1) of this Act such numbers of shares of series B preferred and common stock as the Association shall certify to the Special Court pursuant to section 209(c)(1)(3)[1] of this Act, including any modifications in such numbers of shares as may be ordered by the Special Court for the purpose of, and in connection with, such deposit and certification.

---

[1] So in law. The reference to "209(c)(1)(3)" probably should be to "209(c)(3)".

(f) OFFICERS.—The officers of the Corporation shall include a chief executive officer and a chief operating officer, who shall be appointed by the Board of Directors and who shall serve at the pleasure of the Board; and such other officers as shall be provided for in the bylaws of the Corporation.

(g) VOTING TRUSTEES.—For and during the period between the deposit of securities of the Corporation with the special court, in accordance with section 303(a) of this title, and the distribution of such securities, in accordance with section 303(c) of this title, the special court shall, within 30 days after the date of conveyance pursuant to section 303(b)(1) of this Act, appoint one or more voting trustees for each class of securities which is so deposited. Such voting trustees shall, on behalf of the distributees, exercise the rights of the holders of such securities as their interests may appear. Within 30 days after such appointment, such voting trustees shall select members of the Board of Directors of the Corporation on behalf of the holders of the class of securities whose rights they exercise pursuant to this subsection.

(h) ANNUAL REPORT.—The Corporation shall transmit to the Congress and the President, not later than 90 days after the end of each fiscal year, a comprehensive and detailed report on all activities and accomplishments of the Corporation during the preceding fiscal year.

(i) LIABILITY OF DIRECTORS.—No director of the Corporation shall be liable, for money damages or otherwise, to any party by reason of the fact that such person is or was a director, if, with respect to the subject matter of the action, suit, or proceeding, such person was fulfilling a duty which he in good faith reasonably believed to be required by law or vested in him in his capacity as a director of the Association or as an officer of the United States. The United States shall indemnify such person against all judgments, amounts paid in settlement, and costs and expenses (including fees of accountants, experts, and attorneys), actually and reasonably incurred in connection with any such action, suit, or proceeding in which such person is determined to have met such standard of conduct. This subsection shall not be construed to grant any immunity from any criminal law of the United States.

(j) SIGNAL SYSTEMS.—If, within two years after the effective date of this subsection, the Corporation applies for the permission of the Secretary to substitute manual block signal systems for automatic block signal systems on lines on which less than 20,000,000 gross tons of freight are carried annually, the Secretary shall approve or disapprove such application within 90 days of its submission.

(k) GOVERNING PROVISIONS AFTER SALE.—The provisions of this Act shall not apply to the Corporation and to activities and other actions and responsibilities of the Corporation and its directors and employees after the sale date, other than with regard to—

(1) section 102;

(2) section 201(d);

(3) section 203, but only with respect to information relating to proceedings before the special court established under section 209(b);

(4) section 209, other than subsection (f) thereof;

(5) section 216(f)(8), but only as such authority applies to activities related to the ESOP and related trust before the sale date;

(6) section 216(f)(9), but only as such indemnification applies to activities relating to the ESOP and related trust before the sale date;

(7) section 216(f)(10) with respect to all securities of the Corporation issued or transferred in connection with the public offering under the Conrail Privatization Act and all securities of ConRail Equity Corporation and all interests in the ESOP;

(8) section 217 (c) and (e);

(9) subsection (b) of this section, but only with respect to matters covered by the last sentence of such subsection;

(10) subsection (i) of this section, but only as such authority applies to service as a director of the Corporation before the sale of the interest of the United States in the common stock of the Corporation;

(11) section 302, but only to the extent of (A) the creation and maintenance of the power and authority of the Corporation to operate rail service and to rehabilitate, improve, and modernize rail properties, and (B) the creation and maintenance of the powers of the Corporation as a railroad in any State in which it operates as of the sale date;

(12) section 303(b) (1) and (2), but only to the extent of establishing the legal effect of the conveyance of property ordered and of the deeds and other instruments executed, acknowledged, delivered, or recorded in connection therewith

and the quality of title acquired in such property;

(13) section 303(b)(3)(B) with respect to the effect of an assignment, conveyance, or assumption as set forth in the last sentence of such subparagraph (B);

(14) section 303(b)(5);

(15) section 303(b)(6), but only with respect to establishing and maintaining the rights of the Corporation with respect to, limiting its obligations with respect to, and establishing the status of, the employee pension and welfare benefit plans transferred to the Corporation thereunder and with respect to the exclusivity of the jurisdiction of the special court and the limitation of jurisdiction of other courts;

(16) Section 303(e);

(17) section 304, but only with respect to the finality of abandonments completed before the sale date pursuant to the authority thereof;

(18) section 305, but only as to the effect, and continuing administration, of supplemental transactions consummated before the sale date;

(19) section 308, but only (A) as to the finality of abandonments completed before the sale date and (B) as to abandonments of lines where a notice or notices of insufficient revenues with respect to such lines have been filed before November 1, 1985;

(20) section 601(a)(2), but only with respect to activities before the sale date;

(21) section 601 (b)(2) and (b)(3), but only with respect to issuance of and transactions in any security of the Corporation before the sale date;

(22) section 702(e);

(23) section 703;

(24) section 704;

(25) sections 706(a), 707, and 708(a), but only insofar as they establish part of the prevailing status quo for the Corporation's employees' rates of pay, rules, and working conditions, such provisions to continue to apply unless changed pursuant to section 6 of Railway Labor Act (45 U.S.C. 156);

(26) section 709;

(27) section 710(b)(1);

(28) section 711; and

(29) section 714, but only with regard to disputes or controversies specified in such section that arose before the sale date.

[45 U.S.C. 741]

POWERS AND DUTIES OF THE CORPORATION

SEC. 302. The Corporation shall have all of the powers and is subject to all of the duties vested in it under this Act, in addition to the powers conferred upon it under the laws of the State or States in which it is incorporated and the powers of a railroad in any State in which it operates. The Corporation is authorized and directed to—

(a) acquire rail properties designated in the final system plan to be transferred or conveyed to it;

(b) operate rail service over such rail properties except as provided under sections 304(e) and 601(d)(3) of this Act;

(c) rehabilitate, improve, and modernize such rail properties; and

(d) maintain adequate and efficient rail services.

So long as 50 per centum or more, as determined by the Secretary of the Treasury, of the outstanding indebtedness of the Corporation consists of obligations of the Association or other debts owing to or guaranteed by the United States, the Corporation shall not engage in activities which are not related to transportation.

[45 U.S.C. 742]

VALUATION AND CONVEYANCE OF RAIL PROPERTIES

SEC. 303. (a) DEPOSIT WITH COURT.—Within 10 days after delivery of a certified copy of a final system plan pursuant to section 209(c) of this Act—

(1) the Corporation, in exchange for the rail properties of the railroads in reorganization in the region and of railroads leased, operated, or controlled by railroads in reorganization in the region to be transferred to the Corporation or any subsidiary thereof, shall deposit with the special court all of the stock and other securities of the Corporation and certificates of value issued by the Association designated in the final system plan to be exchanged for such rail properties;

(2) each profitable railroad operating in the region and each State or responsible person (including a government entity) purchasing rail properties from a railroad in reorganization in the region, or from a railroad leased, operated, or controlled by a railroad in reorganization in the region, as provided in the final system plan shall deposit with the special court the compensation to be paid for such rail properties.

(b) CONVEYANCE OF RAIL PROPERTIES.—(1) The special court shall, within 10 days after deposit under subsection (a) of this section of the securities of the Corporation, certificates of value issued by the Association, and compensation from the profitable railroads operating in the region, States, and responsible persons, order the trustee or trustees of each railroad in reorganization in the region to convey forthwith to the Corporation or any subsidiary thereof, the respective profitable railroads operating in the region, States, and responsible persons, all right, title, and interest in the rail properties of such railroad in reorganization and shall itself order the conveyance of all right, title, and interest in the rail properties of any person leased, operated, or controlled by such railroad in reorganization that are to be conveyed to them under the final system plan as certified to such court under section 209(d) of this Act. In any case where the special court orders the trustee or trustees of a railroad in reorganization in the region to execute and deliver deeds or other instruments conveying rail properties to the Corporation or a subsidiary thereof or to a profitable railroad operating in the region or a State or responsible person, those deeds or other instruments may be executed, acknowledged, and delivered on behalf of the trustee or trustees by any person or persons who have been duly authorized to perform such acts on behalf of the trustee or trustees by the district court of the United States or any other court having jurisdiction over the respective railroad in reorganization in the region. Notwithstanding any provision of State or local law, in any case where deeds or other instruments have been executed, acknowledged, or delivered by a representative of the trustee or trustees of a railroad in reorganization in the region in accordance with the previous sentence, such execution, acknowledgment, and delivery, and the deeds or other instruments to which they pertain, shall have the same legal effect as they would have had if the trustee or trustees had themselves executed, acknowledged and delivered such deeds or other instruments.

(2) All rail properties conveyed to the Corporation or any

subsidiary thereof, the respective profitable railroads operating in the region, States, and responsible persons under this section shall be conveyed free and clear of any liens or encumbrances, but subject to such leases and agreements as shall have previously burdened such properties or bound the owner or operator thereof in pursuance of an arrangement with any State, or local or regional transportation authority under which financial support from such State, or local or regional transportation authority was being provided at the time of enactment of this Act for the continuance of rail passenger service or any lien or encumbrance of no greater than 5 years' duration which is necessary for the contractual performance by any person of duties related to public health or sanitation. Such conveyances shall not be restrained or enjoined by any court.

(3)(A)(i) Notwithstanding any other provision of this Act, if an interest in railroad rolling stock is included in the rail properties conveyed pursuant to subsection (b)(1) of this section, and if such conveyance is in accordance with the requirements of clause (ii) of this subparagraph, the conveyance of such properties shall be deemed an assignment. Any such assignment shall relieve the assignor of liability for any breach which occurs after the date of such conveyance, except that such assignor shall remain liable for any breach, event of default, or violation of covenant which occurred (and any charges or obligations which accrued) prior to the date of such conveyance, regardless of whether the assignee thereof assumes such liabilities, charges or obligations. If any such liabilities, charges, or obligations (accrued prior to the date of such conveyance) are paid by or on behalf of any person or entity other than such assignor, such person or entity shall have a claim to direct reimbursement, as a current expense of administration, from such assignor, together with interest on the amount so paid.

(ii) A conveyance referred to in clause (i) of this subparagraph may be effected only if—

(I) the Corporation or a subsidiary thereof, the profitable railroad operating in the region, or the State or responsible person to whom such conveyance is made assumes all of the obligations under any applicable conditional sale agreement, equipment trust agreement, or lease with respect to such rolling stock (including any obligations which accrued prior to the date on which such properties are conveyed), and

(II) such conveyance is made subject to such obligations.

As used in this subparagraph, the term "railroad rolling stock" means assets which could be carried in Interstate Commerce Commission account numbers 52, 53, 54, and 57.

(B) Subject to the provisions of this paragraph, the provisions of this Act shall not affect the title and interests of any lessor, equipment trust trustee, or conditional sale vendor under any conditional sale agreement, equipment trust agreement, or lease under section 77(j) of the Bankruptcy Act (11 U.S.C. 205(j)). A profitable railroad operating in the region, the Corporation or a subsidiary thereof, or a State or responsible person, to whom such a conveyance is made as assignee or as lessee, shall assume all liability under such conditional sale agreement, equipment trust agreement, or lease. Such an assignment or conveyance to, and such an assumption of liability by, such a profitable railroad, Corporation, subsidiary, State, or responsible person shall not be deemed a breach, an event of default, or a violation of any covenant of any such conditional sale agreement, equipment trust agreement, or lease so assigned or conveyed, notwithstanding any provisions of any such agreement or lease.

(4) Notwithstanding anything to the contrary contained in this Act, if a railroad in reorganization has leased rail properties from a lessor that is neither a railroad nor controlled by or affiliated with a railroad, and such lease has been approved by the lessee railroad's reorganization court prior to the date of enactment of this Act, conveyance of such lease may only be effected if the Corporation, profitable railroad, State, or responsible person to whom the conveyance is made assumes all future liability under such lease and all of the terms and conditions specified in the lease, including the obligation to pay the specified rent to the non-railroad lessor.

(5) Notwithstanding any covenant, undertaking, condition, or provision of any sort in any lease, agreement, or contract, the

conveyance, transfer, assignment, or other disposition of such lease, agreement, or contract or of any interest therein to, or the assumption by, the Corporation or any subsidiary thereof, or a profitable railroad of obligations thereunder, shall not be deemed a breach, an event of default, or a violation of any covenant of such lease, agreement, or contract.

(6)(A) Notwithstanding anything to the contrary contained in this Act or any other other[1] provision of law, the special court shall include in its order such further directions as may be necessary to assure (i) that the operation and administration of the employee pension benefit plans described in section 505(a) of this Act shall be continued, without termination or interruption, by the Corporation until such time as the Corporation elects to amend or terminate any such plan, in whole or in part; and (ii) that appropriate transfers and assignments with respect to all rights and obligations relating to such plans shall be made to the Corporation for such purposes, without prejudice to payment of consideration for whatever rights any railroad in reorganization may have in any residual assets under any such employee pension benefit plan. No court shall enter any judgment against the Corporation with respect to any such rights, except that the special court may enter such a judgment in an order issued by it pursuant to subsection (c) of this section, after taking into consideration the rights and obligations transferred pursuant to this paragraph. All liabilities as an employer shall be imposed solely upon the railroad in reorganization in the event such plan is terminated, in whole or in part, by the Corporation within 1 year after the date of such transfer or assignment (except liabilities as an employer under the Employee Retirement Income Security Act of 1974 for benefits accruing during such period), except that in any case in which the Corporation, on or after the date of transfer or assignment as provided by this paragraph, terminates in whole or in part any such plan, the benefits under which are not guaranteed under title IV of the Employee Retirement Income Security Act of 1974, the Corporation shall guarantee the payment when due of the accrued pension benefits provided for thereunder at the time of termination. The Corporation shall be entitled to a loan pursuant to section 211(h) of this Act in an amount required for the adequate funding of accrued pension benefits under all plans transferred or assigned to the Corporation in accordance with this paragraph (whether or not terminated by the Corporation). For purposes of such section 211(h) and notwithstanding any other provision of Federal or State law, amounts required for such adequate funding shall be deemed to be expenses of administration of the respective estates of the railroads in reorganization, due and payable as of the date of transfer or assignment of the plans to the Corporation.

---

[1] So in law.

(B) The Corporation shall, through the purchase of insurance or otherwise, maintain in effect any medical insurance coverage or so much of any life insurance coverage that does not exceed in death benefits an amount equal to twice the employee's annual salary at the time of retirement or $60,000, whichever is lower, which coverage was maintained by a railroad in reorganization in the region immediately prior to April 1, 1976, and which provides insurance benefits to employees who retired, prior to April 1, 1976, from service with such a railroad. With respect to any such employee whose medical or life insurance coverage lapsed after April 1, 1976, due to nonpayment of premiums, the Corporation shall—

(i) through the purchase of insurance or otherwise, provide medical insurance benefits or life insurance benefits at the same level as were provided by the employer railroad in reorganization and in effect with respect to such employees immediately prior to April 1, 1976, except that the life insurance benefits so provided shall not exceed in death benefits an amount equal to twice the employee's annual salary at the time of retirement or $60,000, whichever is lower; and

(ii) assume and pay any claim for such employee (or his personal representative) for any such insurance benefits, if—

(I) such claim arose during the period beginning April 1, 1976, and ending on the date insurance coverage is provided pursuant to clause (i) of this subparagraph;

(II) such benefits were not paid by an insurer solely because of the lapse of the insurance coverage during such period,

except that such death benefits shall not be paid for any such employee in excess of an amount equal to twice the employee's annual salary at the time of retirement or $60,000, whichever is lower.

The Corporation shall be entitled to a loan pursuant to section 211(h) of this Act in an amount required for the payment of insurance premiums and benefits described in this subparagraph. For purposes of section 211(h)(4)(A)(iii), amounts required for the payment of such premiums and benefits shall be deemed to be valid administrative claims against the respective estates of the railroads in reorganization, due and payable as of April 1, 1976, or, in the case of a railroad in reorganization which is not subject to a bankruptcy proceeding, such amounts shall be deemed to be obligations of such railroad, due and payable as of such date, and shall be reimbursable in accordance with the procedures set forth in paragraphs (4) and (5) of such section 211(h). As used in this subparagraph, the term "railroad in reorganization" includes any railroad which is controlled by a railroad in reorganization but is not itself subject to a bankruptcy proceeding, if such railroad conveyed substantially all of its rail properties to the Corporation pursuant to paragraph (1) of this subsection and conducted operations over such rail properties prior to the date of such conveyance.

(c) FINDINGS AND DISTRIBUTION.—(1) After the rail properties have been conveyed to the Corporation or any subsidiary thereof, profitable railroads operating in the region, States, and responsible persons under subsection (b) of this section, the special court, giving due consideration to the findings contained in the final system plan, shall decide—

(A) whether the transfers or conveyances—

(i) of rail properties of each railroad in reorganization, or of each railroad leased, operated, or controlled by a railroad in reorganization, to the Corporation or any subsidiary thereof in exchange for the certificates of value and the other benefits accruing to such railroad as a result of such exchange (taking into consideration compensable unconstitutional erosion, if any, which the special court finds to have occurred in the estate of each such railroad, during the bankruptcy proceeding with respect to such railroad), as provided in the final system plan and this Act, and

(ii) of rail properties of each railroad in reorganization, or of each railroad leased, operated, or controlled by a railroad in reorganization, to a profitable railroad operating in the region, State, or responsible person in exchange for compensation and other benefits accruing to such transferor as a result of such exchange (taking into consideration compensable unconstitutional erosion, if any, which the special court finds to have occurred in the estate of each such railroad, during the bankruptcy proceeding with respect to such railroad) in accordance with the final system plan,

are in the public interest and are fair and equitable to the estate of each railroad in reorganization in accordance with the standard of fairness and equity applicable to the approval of a plan of reorganization or a step in such a plan under section 77 of the Bankruptcy Act (11 U.S.C. 205), or fair and equitable to a railroad that is not itself in reorganization but which is leased, operated or controlled by a railroad in reorganziation;

(B) whether the transfers or conveyances are more fair and equitable than is required as a constitutional minimum; and

(C) what portion of the proceeds received by a railroad in reorganization from an entity other than the Corporation or any subsidiary thereof for the sale, lease, or transfer of property subject to an agreement under section 213 or section 215(a) (1) or (2) of this Act reflects value attributable to the maintenance or improvement provided pursuant to the agreement.

(2) If the special court finds that the terms of one or more exchanges for certificates of value and other benefits are not fair and equitable to an estate of a railroad in reorganization, or to a railroad leased, operated, or controlled by a railroad in reorganization (taking into consideration compensable unconstitutional erosion, if any, which the special court finds to have occurred in the estate of each such railroad, during the bankruptcy proceeding with respect to such railroad), which

has transferred rail properties pursuant to the final system plan, it may—

(A) enter a judgment reallocating the certificates of value in a fair and equitable manner if they have not been fairly allocated among the railroads transferring rail properties to the Corporation or any subsidiary thereof, except that one certificate of value shall be allocated to each such railroad; and

(B) if the lack of fairness and equity cannot be completely cured by a reallocation of the certificates of value, order the Corporation to provide for the transfer to the railroad of certificates of value issued by the Association as designated in the final system plan in such nature and amounts as would make the exchange or exchanges fair and equitable; and

(C) enter a judgment against the Corporation if the judgment would not endanger the viability or solvency of the Corporation.

(3) If the special court finds that the terms of one or more conveyances of rail properties to a profitable railroad operating in the region, State, or responsible person in accordance with the final system plan are not fair and equitable, it shall enter a judgment against such profitable railroad, State, or responsible person. If the special court finds that the terms of one or more conveyances or exchanges for certificates of value or other benefits are fairer and more equitable than is required as a constitutional minimum, then it shall order the return of any excess certificates of value, or compensation to the Corporation or a profitable railroad, State, or responsible person so as not to exceed the constitutional minimum standard of fairness and equity. The special court shall also find the amount of the payments, if any, which each profitable railroad has made on behalf of a transferor railroad in reorganization in accordance with section 211(h) of this Act, for which payment the profitable railroad has not been reimbursed, as provided in section 211(h). Notwithstanding any other provision of this paragraph or of paragraph (4), the special court shall order the return to any such profitable railroad from compensation deposited by such profitable railroad pursuant to subsection (a)(2) of this section, of any such amount so found together with interest at the

rate provided in section 211(h). In making any finding under this paragraph, the special court shall take into consideration compensable unconstitutional erosion, if any, which it finds to have occurred in the estate of a railroad in reorganization in the region, or of a railroad leased, operated, or controlled by such a railroad, during the bankruptcy proceeding with respect to such railroad.

(4) Upon making the findings referred to in this subsection, the special court shall order distribution of the certificates of value, and compensation deposited with it under subsection (a) of this section to the trustee or trustees of each railroad in reorganization in the region and to persons leased, operated, or controlled by such railroads who so transferred or conveyed rail properties who conveyed right, title, and interest in rail properties to the Corporation and the respective profitable railroads, States, and responsible persons under such subsection.

(5) Whenever the special court, pursuant to section 303(b)(1) of this title, orders the transfer or conveyance of rail properties—

(A) designated under section 206(c)(1) (C) or (D) of this Act, to the Corporation or any subsidiary thereof, the United States shall indemnify the Corporation against any costs or liabilities imposed on the Corporation as the result of any judgment entered against the Corporation, with respect to such properties, under paragraph (2) of this subsection; and

(B) to the National Railroad Passenger Corporation, a profitable railroad operating in the region, a State, or any other responsible person (including a governmental entity), the United States shall indemnify such Corporation, railroad, State, or person against any costs or liabilities imposed thereon as the result of any judgment entered against such Corporation, railroad, State, or person under paragraph (3) of this subsection;

plus interest on the amount of such judgment at such rate as is constitutionally required. The United States may, in its discretion, represent the Corporation or the National Railroad Passenger Corporation, such profitable railroad, State or responsible person, in any proceedings before the special court that could result in such a judgment against the Corporation under paragraph (2) of this subsection or against the National Railroad Passenger Corporation, such profitable railroad, State or responsible person, under paragraph (3) of this subsection. The Corporation, the National Railroad Passenger Corporation, any profitable railroad, State, or responsible person, which is represented by the United States of America shall cooperate diligently in whatever manner the United States shall reasonably request of it in connection with such proceedings. Neither the Corporation or its subsidiaries, nor the National Railroad Passenger Corporation, any profitable railroad, State or responsible person, shall be obligated to reimburse the United States for any moneys paid by the United States pursuant to this section.

(6) Whenever the Corporation exercises an option to acquire, or acquires, interests in rail marine freight floating equipment pursuant to the recommendations of the final system plan, and the Corporation thereafter makes such floating equipment available to a profitable railroad operating in the region, a State, or a responsible person including a government entity)[1], the United States shall indemnify—

---

[1] So in law. An opening parenthesis probably should appear before the phrase "including a government entity".

(A) the Corporation against any costs or liabilities imposed on the Corporation as the result of any judgment entered against it, with respect to such equipment, under paragraph (2) of this subsection; and

(B) such profitable railroad, State, or responsible person against any costs or liabilities imposed thereon as the result of any judgment entered against such profitable railroads, State, or responsible person under paragraph (3) of this subsection,

plus interest on the amount of such judgment at such rate as is constitutionally required.

(d)[1] APPEAL.—An order or judgment entered by the United States District Court for the District of Columbia pursuant to subsection (c) of this section or section 306 shall be reviewable in accordance with sections 1291, 1292, and 1294 of title 28, United States Code.

[1] Section 605(d) of the Federal Courts Improvement Act of 1996 provided that this subsection shall not apply to any final order or judgement entered into by the special court established under section 209(b) of the Regional Rail Reorganization Act of 1973 for which—
    (1) a petition for writ of certiorari has been filed before the date on which the special court is abolished [February 16, 1997]; or
    (2) the time for filing a petition for writ of certiorari has not expired before that date.

(e) TRANSFER AND OTHER TAXES AND RECORDING FEES.—All transfers or conveyances of rail properties (whether real, personal, or mixed) which are made under this Act (including transfers and conveyances which are made in accordance with a supplemental transaction pursuant to the section 305 of this title or which are made at any time to carry out the purposes of section 601(d) of this Act) shall be exempt from any taxes, imposts, or levies now or hereafter imposed, by the United States or by any State or any political subdivision of a State, on or in connection with such transfers or conveyances or on the recording of deeds, bills of sale, liens, encumbrances, or other instruments evidencing, effectuating, or incident to any such transfers or conveyances, whether imposed on the transferor or on the transferee. Such transferors and transferees shall be entitled to record any such deeds, bills of sale, liens, encumbrances, or other instruments and, consistent with the designations and applicable principles in the final system plan, to record the release or removal of any pre-existing liens or encumbrances of record with respect to properties so transferred or conveyed, upon payment of any appropriate and generally applicable charges to compensate for the cost of service performed.

[45 U.S.C. 743]

TERMINATION AND CONTINUATION OF RAIL SERVICES

SEC. 304. (a) DISCONTINUANCE.—(1) Except as provided in subsections (c) and (f) of this section, rail service on rail properties of a railroad in reorganization in the region, or of a person leased, operated, or controlled by such a railroad, which transfers to the Corporation or to profitable railroads operating in the region all or substantially all of its rail properties designated for such conveyance in the final system plan, and rail service on rail properties of a profitable railroad operating in the region which transfers substantially all of its rail properties to the Corporation or to other railroads pursuant to the final system plan, may be discontinued, to the extent such discontinuance is not precluded by the terms of the leases and agreements referred to in section 303(b)(2) of this title, if—

(A) the final system plan does not designate rail service to be operated over such rail properties;

(B) not sooner than 30 days following the effective date of the final system plan, the trustee or trustees of the applicable railroad in reorganization or a profitable railroad give notice in writing of intent to discontinue such service on a date certain which is not less than 60 days after the date of such notice or on the date of any conveyance ordered by the special court pursuant to section 303(b)(1) of this title, whichever is later; and

(C) the notice required by subparagraph (B) of this paragraph is sent by certified mail to the Commission; to the chief executive officer, the transportation agencies, and the government of each political subdivision of each State in which such rail properties are located; and to each shipper who has used such rail service during the previous 12 months.

(2)(A) If rail properties are not, in accordance with the designations in the final system plan, required to be operated, as a consequence of a recommended arrangement for joint use or operation of rail properties (under section 206(g) of this Act) or as part of a coordination project (under sections 206 (c) and (g) of this Act), rail service on such properties may be discontinued, subsequent to the date of conveyance of rail properties pursuant to such section 303(b)(1), if the Commission determines that such rail service on such rail properties is not compensatory and if—

(i) the petitioner and any other railroad involved in such arrangement or coordination project have, prior to filing an application for such discontinuance, entered into a binding agreement (effective on or before the effective date of such discontinuance) to carry out such arrangement or project;

(ii) such application is filed with the Commission not later than 1 year after the effective date of the final system plan; and

(iii) such discontinuance is not precluded by the terms

of the leases and agreements referred to in such section 303(b)(2).

(B) For purposes of this paragraph, rail service on rail properties is compensatory if the revenue attributable to such properties from such service equals or exceeds the sum of the avoidable costs of providing such service on such properties plus a reasonable return on the value of such rail properties, as determined in accordance with the standards developed pursuant to section 10362(b)(6) of title 49, United States Code.

(C) The Commission shall make its final determination, with respect to any discontinuance requested under this paragraph, not later than 120 days after the date of filing of an application therefor. The applicant shall have the burden of proving that the service involved is not compensatory. If the Commission fails to make a final determination within such time, the application shall be deemed to be granted.

(D) The Commission may issue such rules, regulations, and procedures as it deems necessary for the conduct of its functions under this paragraph.

(b) ABANDONMENT.—(1) Except as provided in subsections (c) and (f) of this section, rail properties over which rail service has been discontinued under subsection (a) of this section may not be abandoned sooner than 120 days after the effective date of the discontinuance. Thereafter, except as provided in subsection (c) of this section, such rail properties may be abandoned upon 30 days' notice in writing to any person (including a government entity) required to receive notice under subsection (a)(1)(C) of this section.

(2) In any case in which rail properties proposed to be abandoned under this section are designated by the final system plan as rail properties which are suitable for use for other public purposes (including roads or highways, other forms of mass transportation, conservation, and recreation), such rail properties shall not be sold, leased, exchanged, or otherwise disposed of during the 240-day period beginning on the date of notice of proposed abandonment under this section unless such rail properties have first been offered, upon reasonable terms, for acquisition for public purposes.

(3) Rail service may be discontinued, under subsection (a)

of this section, and rail properties may be abandoned, under this section, notwithstanding any provision of part A of subtitle IV of title 49, United States Code, the constitution or law of any State, or the decision of any court of administrative agency of the United States or of any State.

(c) CONTINUATION OF RAIL SERVICES.—No rail service may be discontinued and no rail properties may be abandoned, pursuant to this section—

(1) in the case of service and properties referred to in subsections (a)(1) and (b)(1) of this section, after 2 years from the effective date of the final system plan or more than 2 years after the date on which the final rail service continuation payment is received, whichever is later; or

(2) if a financially responsible person (including a government entity) offers—

(A) to provide a rail service continuation payment which is designed to cover the difference between the revenue attributable to such rail properties and the avoidable costs of providing rail service on such properties, together with a reasonable return on the value of such properties;

(B) to provide a rail service continuation payment which is payable pursuant to a lease or agreement with a State or with a local or regional transportation authority under which financial support was being provided on January 2, 1974 for the continuation of rail passenger service; or

(C) to purchase, pursuant to subsection (f) of this section, such rail properties in order to operate rail services thereon.

If a rail service continuation payment is offered, pursuant to paragraph (2)(A) of this subsection, for both freight and passenger service on the same rail properties, the owner of such properties may not be entitled to more than one payment of a reasonable return on the value of such properties.

(d) RAIL FREIGHT SERVICE.—(1) If a rail service continuation payment is offered, pursuant to subsection (c)(2)(A) of this section, for rail freight service, the person offering such payment shall designate the operator of such service and enter into an operating agreement with such operator. The person offering such payment shall designate as the operator of such service—

(A) the Corporation, if rail properties of the Corporation connect with the line of railroad involved, unless the Commission determines that such rail service continuation could be performed more efficiently and economically by another railroad;

(B) any other railroad whose rail properties connect with such line, if the Corporation's rail properties do not so connect or if the Commission makes a determination in accordance with subparagraph (A) of this paragraph; or

(C) any responsible person (including a government entity) which is willing to operate rail service over such rail properties.

A designated railroad may refuse to enter into such an operating agreement only if the Commission determines, on petition by any affected party, that the agreement would substantially impair such railroad's ability to serve adequately its own patrons or to meet its outstanding common carrier obligations. The designated operator shall, pursuant to each such operating agreement (i) be obligated to operate rail freight service on such rail properties, and (ii) be entitled to receive, from the person offering such payment, the difference between the revenue attributable to such properties and the avoidable costs of providing service on such rail properties, together with a reasonable management fee, as determined by the Office.

(2) The trustees of a railroad in reorganization shall permit rail service to be continued on any rail properties with respect to which a rail service continuation payment operating agreement has been entered into under this subsection. Such trustees shall receive a reasonable return on the values of such properties, as determined in accordance with the standards developed pursuant to section 205(d)(6) of this Act.

(3) If necessary to prevent any disruption or loss of rail service, at any time after the date of conveyance, pursuant to section 303(b)(1) of this title, the Commission shall take such action as may be appropriate under its existing authority (including the enforcement of common carrier requirements applicable to railroads in reorganization in the region) to ensure compliance with obligations imposed under this subsection. The district courts of the United States shall have jurisdiction, upon

petition by the Commission or any interested person (including a government entity), to enforce any order of the Commission issued pursuant to the exercise of its authority under this subsection, or to enjoin any designated entity or the trustees of a railroad in reorganization in the region from refusing to comply with the provisions of this subsection.

(4) No determination of reasonable payment for the use of rail properties of a railroad in reorganization in the region, and no determination of value of rail properties of such a railroad (including supporting or related documents or reports of any kind) which is made in connection with any lease agreement, contract of sale, or other agreement or understanding which is entered into after the date of enactment of the Rail Transportation Improvement Act—

(A) pursuant to this section; or

(B) pursuant to section 402 of this Act or section 17 of the Urban Mass Transportation Act of 1964 (49 U.S.C. 1613),

shall be admitted as evidence, or used for any other purpose, in any civil action, or any other proceeding for damages or compensation, arising under this Act.

(e) RAIL PASSENGER SERVICE.—(1) The Corporation (or a profitable railroad) shall provide rail passenger service for a period of 180 days immediately following the date of conveyance (pursuant to section 303(b)(1) of this title), with respect to any rail properties over which a railroad in reorganization in the region, or a person leased, operated, or controlled by such a railroad, was providing rail passenger service immediately prior to such date of conveyance. Such service shall be provided on such properties regardless of whether or not such properties are designated in the final system plan as rail properties over which rail service is required to be operated, except with respect to properties over which such service is provided by the National Railroad Passenger Corporation.

(2) If a State (or a local or regional transportation authority) was providing financial assistance to support the operation of rail passenger service, pursuant to a lease or agreement which was in effect immediately prior to the date of conveyance (pursuant to such section 303(b)(1)), the Corporation (or a profitable railroad) shall be bound by the service provisions of such lease or agreement for the duration of

the 180-day mandatory operation period specified in paragraph (1) of this subsection. If a State or such an authority was providing financial assistance for the continuation of rail passenger service on rail properties immediately prior to such date of conveyance, it shall provide the same level of financial assistance during such 180-day mandatory operation period. If no such financial assistance was being provided or if no such lease or agreement was in effect immediately prior to such date of conveyance, with respect to any such rail properties, the Corporation (or a profitable railroad) shall provide the same level of rail passenger service, for the duration of such 180-day mandatory operation period, that was provided prior to such date by the applicable railroad. If—

(A) such financial assistance is not provided;

(B) a State (or a local or regional transportation authority) has not, by the end of such 180-day mandatory operation period, offered a rail service continuation payment pursuant to subsection (c)(2)(A) of this section;

(C) an applicable rail service continuation payment pursuant to such subsection (c)(2)(A) is not paid when it is due; or

(D) a payment required under a lease or agreement, pursuant to section 303(b)(2) of this title or subsection (c)(2)(B) of this section, is not paid when it is due,

the Corporation (or, where applicable, the National Railroad Passenger Corporation, a profitable railroad, or the trustee or trustees of a railroad in reorganization in the region) may (i) discontinue such rail passenger service, and (ii) with respect to rail properties not designated for inclusion in the final system plan, abandon such properties pursuant to subsections (a) and (b) of this section.

(3) Nothing in this subsection shall be construed to affect the obligation of the Corporation (or a profitable railroad), or of the trustees of the railroads in reorganization in the region, to provide rail passenger service pursuant to section 303(b)(2) of this title or subsection (c)(2)(B) of this section.

(4) If a State (or a local or regional transportation authority)—

(A) offers a rail service continuation payment,

pursuant to subsection (c)(2)(A) of the section[1], for the operation of rail passenger service after the 180-day mandatory operation period, and

(B) provides compensation, pursuant to paragraph (2) of this subsection, for operations conducted during the 180-day mandatory operation period; or

---

[1]   So in law. The phrase "of the section" probably should read "of this section".

(C) offers a rail service continuation payment, pursuant to subsection (c)(2)(A) of this section, for the operation of rail passenger service provided under an agreement or lease pursuant to section 303(b)(2) of this title or subsection (c)(2)(B) of this section where such offer is made for the continuation of the service beyond the period required by such agreement or lease, except that such services shall not be eligible for assistance under section 17(a)(2) of the Urban Mass Transportation Act of 1964 (49 U.S.C. 1613(a)(2)),

the Corporation (or a profitable railroad) shall continue to provide such service after the end of such period, except as otherwise provided in this subsection.

(5)(A) The Secretary shall reimburse the Corporation (or a profitable railroad) for any loss which is incurred by it during the 180-day mandatory operation period specified in paragraph (1) of this subsection which is not compensated for by a State (or a local or regional transportation authority). The amount of such reimbursement shall be determined pursuant to section 17(a)(1) of the Urban Mass Transportation Act of 1964.

(B) The Secretary shall reimburse States, local public bodies, and agencies thereof for additional costs incurred by such States, bodies, and agencies for rail service continuation payments for rail passenger service pursuant to section 17(a)(2) of the Urban Mass Transportation Act of 1964.

(C) For purposes of the obligation of the Secretary to reimburse the Corporation (or a profitable railroad) or States, local public bodies, and agencies thereof under subparagraphs (A) and (B) of this paragraph, the level of rail passenger service shall be determined on the basis of train miles, car miles, or some other appropriate indicia of scheduled train movements. Programs to correct deferred maintenance on rolling stock, right-of-way, and other facilities which are designed to maintain service, meet on-time performance, and maintain a reasonable degree of passenger comfort (and costs incurred incident thereto) shall be included within the meaning of the term "loss" as used in subparagraph (A) of this paragraph and within the meaning of the term "additional costs" as used in subparagraph (B) of this paragraph and section 17(A)(2) of the Urban Mass Transportation Act of 1964 (49 U.S.C. 1613(a)(2)).

(D) If a dispute arises with respect to the application of any such regulations, the parties to such dispute may submit such dispute to arbitration by a third party. If the parties are unable to agree upon the selection of an arbitrator, the Chairman of the Commission shall serve in that capacity (except as to matters required to be decided by the Commission, pursuant to section 402(a) of the Rail Passenger Service Act (45 U.S.C. 562(a))).

(6) Notwithstanding any other provision of this subsection, the Corporation is not obligated to provide rail passenger service on rail properties if a State (or a local or regional transportation authority) contracts for such service to be provided on such properties by an operator other than the Corporation, except that the Corporation shall, where appropriate, provide such operator with access to such properties for such purpose.

(7)(A) If a State (or a local or regional transportation authority) in the region offers to provide payment for the provision of additional rail passenger service, the Corporation shall undertake to provide such service pursuant to this subsection (including the discontinuance provisions of paragraph (2) of this subsection). An offer to provide payment for the provision of additional rail passenger service shall be made in accordance with subsection (c)(2)(A) of this section, and shall be designed to avoid any additional costs to the Corporation arising from the construction or modification of capital facilities or from any additional operating delays or costs arising from the absence of such construction or modification. The State (or local or regional transportation authority) shall demonstrate that it has acquired, leased, or otherwise obtained access to all rail properties, other than those designated for conveyance to the National Railroad Passenger Corporation pursuant to sections 206(c)(1)(C) and 206(c)(1)(D) of this Act and to the Corporation pursuant to section 303(b)(1) of this title, necessary to provide the additional rail passenger service and that it has completed, or will complete prior to the inception of the additional rail service, all capital improvements necessary to avoid significant costs which cannot be avoided by improved scheduling or other means on other existing rail services (including rail freight service) and to assure that the additional service will not detract from the level and quality of existing rail passenger and freight service.

(B) As used in this paragraph, the term "additional rail passenger service" means rail passenger service (other than rail passenger service provided pursuant to the provisions of paragraphs (2) and (4) of this subsection), including extended or expanded service and modified routings, which is to be provided over rail properties conveyed to the Corporation pursuant to section 303(b)(1) of this title, or over (i) rail properties contiguous thereto conveyed to the National Railroad Passenger Corporation pursuant to this Act, or (ii) any other rail properties contiguous thereto to which a State (or local or regional transportation authority) has obtained access.

(C) Notwithstanding any other provision of this paragraph, the Corporation shall not be required to operate additional rail passenger service over rail properties leased or acquired from or owned or leased by a profitable railroad in the region.

(8) The Secretary shall, in consultation with the Association, conduct a study to determine the best means of compensating the Corporation for liabilities which it may incur for damages to persons or property, resulting from the operation of rail passenger service required to be operated pursuant to this subsection or section 303(b)(2) of this title, which are not underwritten by private insurance carriers or are not indemnified by a State (or local or regional transportation

authority). Such study shall identify the nature of the risks to the Corporation, the probable degree of uninsurability of such risks, and the desirability and feasibility of various indemnification programs, including subsidy offers made pursuant to this section, self-insurance through a passenger tax or other mechanism, or government indemnification for such liabilities. Within one year after the date of enactment of this paragraph, the Secretary shall prepare a report with appropriate recommendations and shall submit such report to the Congress. Such report shall specify the most appropriate means of indemnifying the Corporation for such liabilities in a manner which shall prevent the cross-subsidization of passenger services with revenues from freight services operated by the Corporation.

(f) PURCHASE.—If an offer to purchase is made under subsection (c)(2)(C) of this section, such offer shall be accompanied by an offer of a rail service continuation payment. Such payment shall continue until the purchase transaction is completed, unless a railroad assumes operations over such rail properties of its own account pursuant to an order or authorization of the Commission. Whenever a railroad in reorganization in the region or a profitable railroad gives notice of intent to discontinue service pursuant to subsection (a) of this section, such railroad shall, upon the request of anyone apparently qualified to make an offer to purchase or to provide a rail service continuation payment, promptly make available its most recent reports on the physical condition of such property, together with such traffic and revenue data as would be required under subpart B of part 1121 of chapter X of title 49 of the Code of Federal Regulations and such other data as are necessary to ascertain the avoidable costs of providing service over such rail properties.

(g) ABANDONMENT BY CORPORATION.—After the rail system to be operated by the Corporation or a subsidiary thereof under the final system plan has been in operation for 2 years, the Commission may authorize the Corporation or a subsidiary thereof to abandon any rail properties as to which it determines that rail service over such properties is not required by the public convenience and necessity, if the Corporation or a subsidiary thereof can demonstrate that no State (or local or regional transportation authority), is willing to offer a rail service continuation payment pursuant to subsection (c) of this section. The Commission may, at any time after the effective date of the final system plan, authorize additional rail service in the region or authorize the abandonment of rail properties which are not being operated by the Corporation or any subsidiary or affiliate thereof or by any other person. Determinations by the Commission under this subsection shall be made pursuant to applicable provisions of part A of subtitle IV of title 49, United States Code.

(h) INTERIM ABANDONMENT.—After the date of enactment of this section and prior to the date of conveyance (pursuant to section 303(b)(1) of this title), no railroad in reorganization in the region may discontinue service or abandon any line of railroad other than in accordance with the provisions of this Act, unless (1) it is authorized to do so by the Association, and (2) no affected State (or local or regional transportation authority) reasonably opposes such action, notwithstanding any provision of any other Federal law, the constitution or law of any State, or the decision or order of, or the pendency of any proceeding before any Federal or State court, agency, or authority.

(i) DISPOSITION OF DESIGNATED RAIL PROPERTIES.—No railroad in reorganization in the region and no person leased, operated or controlled by such a railroad shall sell, transfer, encumber, or otherwise dispose of rail property, or any right or interest therein, designated for transfer to the Corporation or conveyance to a profitable railroad in the final system plan, except pursuant to section 303(b) of this title. The provisions of this subsection shall not apply to any such sale, transfer, encumbrance, or other disposition—

(1) as to which the Association generally or specifically consents in writing;

(2) which, prior to enactment of the Railroad Revitalization and Regulatory Reform Act of 1976, had been specifically approved by a United States district court having jurisdiction over the reorganization of a railroad in reorganization under section 77 of the Bankruptcy Act (11 U.S.C. 205); or

(3) following certification to the special court, pursuant to section 209(c) of the Regional Rail Reorganization Act of 1973, of any such rail properties not previously so certified.

[45 U.S.C. 744]

CONTINUING REORGANIZATION; SUPPLEMENTAL TRANSACTIONS

SEC. 305. (a) PROPOSALS.—If the Secretary or the Association determines that, as part of continuing reorganization, further restructuring of rail properties in the region through transactions supplemental to the final system plan would promote the establishment and retention of a financially self-sustaining rail system in the region adequate to meet the needs of the region, the Secretary or the Association, as the case may be, may develop proposals for such supplemental transactions as are necessary or appropriate to implement the needed restructuring. Transfers of rail properties included in proposals developed by the Association shall be limited to (1) rail properties which would have qualified for designation under section 206(c)(1)(A) of this Act but which were not transferred or conveyed under the final system plan, and which the Association finds to be essential to the efficient operations of the Corporation, and (2) transfers, consistent with the final system plan, of rail properties from the Corporation to a subsidiary thereof. Each proposal (other than a proposal developed by the Association) shall be submitted in writing to the Association and shall state and describe any transactions proposed, the rail properties involved, the parties to such transactions, the financial and other terms of such transactions, the purposes of the Act or the goals of the final system plan intended to be effectuated by such transactions, and such other information incidental thereto as the Association may prescribe. Within 10 days after receipt of a proposal developed by the Secretary, and upon the development of a proposal developed by the Association, the Association shall publish a summary of such proposal in the Federal Register, and shall afford interested persons (including the Corporation when property is to be transferred to or from the Corporation) an opportunity to comment thereon.

(b) EVALUATION BY ASSOCIATION.—The Association shall analyze each proposal containing one or more supplemental transactions, taking into account the comments of interested persons and statements and exhibits submitted at any public hearings which may have been held. The Association shall, within 120 days after the publication of a summary thereof under subsection (a) of this section, publish in the Federal Register a report evaluating such proposal. Such evaluation shall state whether the supplemental transactions contained in such proposal, considered in their entirety, are (1) in the public interest and consistent with the purpose[1] of this Act and the goals of the final system plan, and (2) fair and equitable. If the Corporation opposes, or seeks modification of, any such proposed transfer, its written comments shall be given due consideration by the Association and shall be published as part of the evaluation. Within 30 days after the Association publishes its report, each proposed transferor or transferee shall notify the Association in writing as to whether any proposed supplemental transaction requiring the transfer of any property from or to such transferor or transferee is acceptable to such proposed transferor or transferee. If any such proposed transferor (other than the Corporation) or transferee fails to notify the Association that any proposed supplement[2] transaction requiring the transfer of any property from such transferor or to such transferee is acceptable to it, no further administrative or judicial proceedings shall be conducted with respect to such proposed supplemental transaction.

---

[1] So in law. Probably should read "purposes".

---

[2] So in law. Probably should read "supplemental".

(c) REVIEW BY THE COMMISSION.—Within 90 days after the publication in the Federal Register of each report referred to in subsection (b) of this section, the Commission shall determine whether the supplemental transactions referred to in the report, considered in their entirety, would be in the public interest and consistent with the purposes of this Act and the goals of the final system plan. In making such determination, the Commission shall give due consideration to the views received by it, within 30 days after the publication of the applicable report, from the Corporation and the Secretary. The Commission may condition its approval of such supplemental transactions on such reasonable terms and conditions as it may deem necessary in the public interest. The approval by the Commission of such supplemental transactions shall not be a prerequisite to the consummation of such transactions, but any determination of the Commission modifying, approving, or disapproving any proposed supplemental transactions shall be given due weight and consideration by the special court in the proceedings prescribed in subsection (d) of this section. If the Commission fails to act within the time period provided in this subsection, the supplemental transactions involved shall be deemed to have been approved by the Commission. The Commission may prescribe such regulations as may be necessary for the administration of this section.

(d) SPECIAL COURT PROCEEDINGS.—(1) If the Association has made the determination pursuant to subsection (b) of this section that a proposal for supplemental transactions is in the public interest and consistent with the purposes of this Act and the goals of the final system plan, and is fair and equitable, the Association shall, within 40 days after the date of the Commission's determination under subsection (c) of this section, or after the expiration of the 90-day period referred to in such subsection (c), whichever is applicable, petition the special court for an order of such court finding that such proposal for supplemental transactions is in the public interest and consistent with the purposes of this Act and the goals of the final system plan, and is fair and equitable, and directing the Corporation to carry out the supplemental transactions specified in such proposal. If the Association has determined, pursuant to subsection (b) of this section that a proposal made by the Secretary is not in the public interest or is not consistent with the purposes of this Act and the goals of the final system plan or is not fair and equitable, the Secretary may, if he determines that such proposal is in the public interest and consistent with the purposes of this Act and the goals of the final system plan and is fair and equitable, petition the special court for an order of such court finding that such proposal for supplemental transactions is in the public interest and consistent with the purposes of this Act and the goals of the final system plan and is fair and equitable, and directing the Corporation to carry out any supplemental transactions specified in such proposal. Such a petition shall be submitted to the special court within 90 days after the date of the Commission's determination under such subsection (c), or after the expiration of the 90-day period referred to in such section (c)[1], whichever is applicable.

---

[1]   So in law. Probably should read "subsection (c)".

---

(2) After the filing of a petition under paragraph (1) of this subsection, the special court shall decide, after a hearing, whether the proposed supplemental transactions contained in such petition, considered in their entirety, are in the public interest and consistent with the purposes of this Act and the goals of the final system plan and are fair and equitable. If the special court determines that such proposed supplemental

transactions, considered in their entirety, are in the public interest and consistent with the purposes of this Act and the goals of the final system plan and are fair and equitable, it shall, upon making such determination, issue such orders as may be necessary to direct the Corporation to consummate the transactions. If the special court determines that such proposed supplemental transactions, considered in their entirety, are not in the public interest or not consistent with the purposes of this Act and the goals of the final system plan, or are not fair and equitable, it shall file an opinion stating its conclusion and the reasons therefor. In such event the Association (in the case of a proposal developed by the Association) or the Secretary (in the case of a proposal developed by the Secretary) may, within 120 days after the filing of such opinion, certify to the special court that the terms and conditions of the proposal have been modified consistent with the opinion of the court and are acceptable to each proposed transferor (other than the Corporation) or transferee, and may petition the special court for reconsideration of the proposal as so modified. After the filing of such petition, the special court shall decide, after a hearing, whether the proposal as modified by the certification is in the public interest and consistent with the purposes of this Act and the goals of the final system plan and is fair and equitable, and shall enter such further orders as are consistent with its determination.

(3) The Corporation is authorized to petition the special court and to be represented regarding any proposed supplemental transaction, contained in a proposal developed by either the Association or the Secretary, which involves the properties of the Corporation.

(4) In proceedings under this subsection, the special court is authorized to exercise the powers of a reorganization court[1].

---

[1]   Section 605(c)(2) of the Federal Courts Improvement Act of 1996 (P.L. 104–317; 110 Stat. 3859) amended this paragraph by striking "a judge of the United States district court with respect to such proceedings and such powers shall include those of". The word "the" probably should have been "a". The amendment was executed to reflect the probable intent of Congress.

---

(5) Any evaluation by the Association, the Secretary, or the Commission shall not be reviewable in any court except the

special court in accordance with the provisions of this section. The supplemental transactions shall not be restrained or enjoined by any court nor shall they be otherwise reviewable by any court other than by the special court to the extent provided in this section.

(6) Notwithstanding any other provision of this Act, no findings, determinations, or proceedings shall be required with respect to any proposal for supplemental transactions other than as expressly set forth in this section.

(7) A final order or judgment of the special court entering or denying an order pursuant to this subsection shall be reviewable in the same manner as provided in section 209(e)(3) of this Act.

(e) DEFINITION.—As used in this section, the term "fair and equitable" means fair and equitable, in accordance with the standards applicable to the approval of a plan of reorganization (or a step in such plan) under section 77 of the Bankruptcy Act (11 U.S.C. 205) to—

(1) the estates of railroads in reorganization in the region and persons leased, operated, or controlled by such railroads who have conveyed rail properties, under section 303(b)(1) of this title, in exchange for securities of the Corporation, the Association, or profitable railroads and other benefits provided as a consequence of this Act and to any subsequent holders of such securities at the time of the supplemental transaction involved; and

(2) the holders of other securities of the Corporation.

Whenever any property or securities of the Corporation are required to be valued in order to determine whether the terms of a supplemental transaction are fair and equitable, the special court shall give proper recognition to the contributions to the Corporation by all classes of security holders, except that such court shall not assign to the series B preferred stock or the common stock of the Corporation any values added to those securities, by reason of investment by the Association in debentures and series A preferred stock of the Corporation, in excess of any value required by constitutional principles applicable to a reorganization process.

(f) EXPEDITED PROPOSALS.—(1) Within 240 days after the effective date of the Staggers Rail Act of 1980, the Secretary, after providing an opportunity for comments from interested parties, shall determine whether to initiate a proposal for a supplemental transaction under this section for the transfer of all rail properties of the Corporation in the States of Connecticut and Rhode Island to another railroad in the region. If the Secretary determines that—

(A) the proposed transferee railroad is financially and operationally capable of assuming the freight operations and freight service obligations of the Corporation on a financially self-sustaining basis;

(B) the proposed transfer would promote the establishment and retention of a financially self-sustaining rail system in the States of Connecticut and Rhode Island adequate to meet the needs of such States; and

(C) the proposed transfer is consistent with the goals set forth in section 206(a)(8) of this Act,

the Secretary shall develop such a proposal and may, after providing the Association, the Commission, and the States of Connecticut and Rhode Island an opportunity to review and comment on such proposal, petition the special court for an order to carry out such proposal.

(2)(A) Within 10 days after the effective date of the Northeast Rail Service Act of 1981, the Secretary shall initiate discussions and negotiations for the transfer of some or all of the Corporation's rail properties and freight service obligations in the States of Connecticut and Rhode Island to one or more parties under a plan which provides for continued rail freight service on all lines operated by the Corporation on the effective date of the Northeast Rail Service Act of 1981 for at least four years.

(B) Within 120 days after the effective date of the Northeast Rail Service Act of 1981, the Secretary shall petition the special court for an order to transfer all of the Corporation's rail properties and freight service obligations in the States of Connecticut and Rhode Island to one or more railroads in the Region—

(i) which have under subparagraph (A) of this paragraph completed negotiations and submitted to the Secretary a proposal to assume all of the freight operations and freight service obligations of the

Corporation in such States on a financially self-sustaining basis for a period of at least four years; or

(ii) which have developed a proposal to assume all of the freight operations and freight service obligations of the Corporation in such States under an agreement by and between the Corporation and such railroad or railroads; or

(iii) which have, prior to May 1, 1981, submitted a proposal to the Secretary for such a transfer.

For the purpose of this section, an order to transfer may include the Corporation if the Corporation agrees to maintain service over lines retained by the Corporation for four years.

(C) To permit efficient and effective rail operations consistent with the public interest, as a part of any transfer under paragraph (2)(B) of this subsection, the Secretary shall promote the transfer of additional non-mainline Corporation properties in adjoining States that connect with properties that are the subject of such transfer.

(D) The special court shall determine a fair and equitable price for the rail properties to be transferred under this subsection, and shall, unless the parties otherwise agree, establish divisions of joint rates for through routes over such properties which are fair and equitable to the parties. The special court shall establish a method to ensure that such divisions are promptly paid.

(E) Notwithstanding any other provision of law or agreement in effect on May 1, 1981, the special court shall require that the railroad or railroads to which properties are to be transferred under this subsection assume all charges payable to the Corporation by Amtrak for the carriage of property by rail over those portions of the Northeast Corridor in Connecticut and Rhode Island. If the Corporation operates any rail freight service over those portions of the Northeast Corridor in Connecticut and Rhode Island after the date of such transfer, the Corporation shall pay Amtrak any compensation that may be separately agreed upon by the Corporation and Amtrak, and the railroad or railroads to which properties are transferred under this subsection shall not be obligated to pay any compensation owed by the Corporation to Amtrak for such post-transfer operations by the Corporation.

(3) If the special court determines that a proposal developed under this subsection is fair and equitable, meets the requirements of this subsection, and is in the public interest, it shall issue such orders as may be necessary to carry out such proposal. The provisions of paragraphs (2)–(6) of subsection (d) of this section shall apply to the determination of the special court under this subsection, except that the standards for such determination shall be those set forth in this paragraph.

(4)(A) Any employee who was protected by the compensatory provisions of title V of this Act immediately prior to the effective date of the Northeast Rail Service Act of 1981, and who is deprived of employment as a result of the transfer of rail properties under this subsection shall be eligible for benefits under section 701 of this Act.

(B) As used in this paragraph, "employee deprived of employment" means any employee who is unable to secure employment through the normal exercise of seniority rights, but does not include any employee who refuses an offer of employment with a railroad acquiring properties under this subsection.

(g)(1) Within 20 days after the effective date of the Northeast Rail Service Act of 1981, the Secretary shall initiate discussions and negotiations for the expedited transfer of all properties and freight service obligations of the Corporation with respect to the following lines: Canaan, Connecticut, to Pittsfield, Massachusetts; North Adams Junction, Massachusetts, to North Adams, Massachusetts; Hazardville, Connecticut, to Springfield, Massachusetts; Westfield, Massachusetts, to Easthampton, Massachusetts; Westfield, Massachusetts, to Holyoke, Massachusetts.

(2) Within 120 days after the effective date of the Northeast Rail Service Act of 1981, the Secretary shall transfer, provided a qualified purchaser offers to purchase, the Corporation's properties and freight service obligations described in paragraph (1) of this subsection to another railroad or railroads in the Region which are determined by the Secretary to be qualified. A qualified purchaser is defined as a railroad financially self-sustaining which guarantees continuous service

for at least four years.

(3) The Secretary shall determine a fair and equitable price for the rail properties to be transferred under this subsection, and shall, unless the parties otherwise agree, establish divisions of joint rates for through routes over such properties which are fair and equitable to the parties.

(4) The Secretary shall determine fair and equitable terms for the provision of such trackage rights, on segments of the Corporation's lines not to exceed 5 miles per line transferred, to acquiring carriers as may be necessary to operate such transferred lines in an efficient manner.

[45 U.S.C. 745]

CERTIFICATES OF VALUE

SEC. 306. (a) GENERAL.—On the date when the Corporation is required to deposit securities with the special court pursuant to section 303(a)(1) of this title, the Association shall deposit with the special court the certificates of value of the Association required by this section. The Secretary shall guarantee the payment of all certificates of value delivered in accordance with this title. All guarantees entered by the Secretary under this section shall constitute general obligations of the United States of America for the payment or redemption of which its full faith and credit are pledged. Such guarantees shall be valid and incontestable except as to mutual mistake of fact or as to fraud or material misrepresentation by the holder of such certificates or the transferor of rail properties to which certificates of value of any series so guaranteed are issued.

(b) NUMBER AND DISTRIBUTION.—A separate series of certificates of value shall be issued to each railroad in reorganization in the region and each person leased, operated, or controlled by such a railroad that transfers rail properties to the Corporation or a subsidiary thereof. The number of certificates of value of each series to be deposited pursuant to subsection (a) shall be equal to the number of shares of series B preferred stock of the Corporation which are required to be deposited by the Corporation with the special court, pursuant to section 303(a)(1) of this title in exchange for the rail properties transferred to the Corporation or a subsidiary thereof by such transferor. Certificates of value of the appropriate series shall be distributed by the special court, pursuant to section 303(c)(4) of this title, at the same time to the same transferors, and in the same numbers of units as shares of such series B preferred stock are distributed to such transferor.

(c) REDEMPTION.—(1) Certificates of value, of any series, shall be redeemed by the Association on December 31, 1987, or on such earlier date as the Board of Directors of the Association and the Finance Committee jointly may determine and specify.

(2) Each certificate of value of each series shall be redeemable for an amount, payable in cash, equal to its base value on the redemption date, minus—

(A) the sum of the fair market value of the series B preferred stock applicable to such certificate, the fair market value of the common stock applicable to such certificate, and all cash dividends theretofore paid on any such series B preferred stock and on any such common stock; and

(B) any sums paid to a transferor of rail properties to whom such series of certificates of value was issued resulting from sales or leases by the Corporation of properties transferred to it by such transferor divided by the number of certificates of value distributed to such transferor.

(3) The number of shares of series B preferred stock and common stock applicable to each certificate of value of any series, pursuant to paragraph (2) of this subsection, shall be—

(A) one share of series B preferred stock (adjusted to reflect any stock splits, stock combinations, reclassifications or similar transactions affecting the number of shares of outstanding series B preferred stock following the date of distribution pursuant to section 303(c)(4) of this title); and

(B) the number of shares of common stock determined by dividing the total number of shares of common stock distributed pursuant to section 303(c)(4) of this Act to the transferor receiving such series of certificates of value (adjusted to reflect any stock splits, stock combinations, reclassifications, or similar transactions affecting the number of shares of outstanding common stock following the date of distribution pursuant to section 303(c)(4) of this title) by the total number of certificates of value in the series so distributed to such transferor.

(4) The base value of each certificate of value of any series shall be the value obtained by (A) taking the net liquidation value, as determined by the special court, to which the transferor to whom such series of certificates of value is issued is entitled by virtue of transfers of rail properties, under section 303(b)(1) of this title to the Corporation or a subsidiary thereof; (B) subtracting the value of other benefits provided under this Act, as determined by the special court; (C) adding such amount, if any, as the special court may determine shall be required after taking into consideration compensable unconstitutional erosion, if any, in the estate of a railroad in reorganization, of a railroad leased, operated, or controlled by such a railroad, which the special court finds to have occurred during any bankruptcy proceeding with respect to such railroad; (D) adding interest from the transfer date to the redemption date to be compounded annually at a rate of 8 percent per annum; and (E) dividing the resulting value by the number of certificates of value of such series distributed to such transferor. In determining such base value, the special court shall give due weight and consideration to the finding of the Association as to the net liquidation value to which each transferor is entitled by virtue of conveyances of rail properties under sectio 303(b)(1) of this title. For purposes of this paragraph, the term "rail properties" includes all rights with respect to employee benefit plans transferred and assigned to the Corporation pursuant to section 303(b)(6) of this title. Net liquidation value with respect to such rights shall be determined after taking into account all obligations finally transferred or assigned to the Corporation pursuant to such section.

(5) The fair market value of series B preferred stock and of common stock of the Corporation shall be determined in accordance with regulations prescribed by the Association, on the basis of the average price of each such security in the primary established market in which such securities are traded over a period of 120 consecutive trading days ending not less than 20 nor more than 40 trading days preceding the redemption date, or, in the case of a security for which there is not an established trading market, on the basis of the fair

market value thereof as determined by the majority vote of three experts in the valuation of securities, one to be selected by the Association, one to be selected by the directors of the Corporation elected by the holders of the security to be valued, and one to be selected by the two first selected.

(d) AUTHORIZATION FOR APPROPRIATIONS.—There are authorized to be appropriated to the Secretary such sums as are necessary to discharge the obligations of the United States arising under this section.

[45 U.S.C. 746]

PROTECTION OF FEDERAL FUNDS

SEC. 307. (a) AUDIT.—(1) The Comptroller General of the United States is authorized to audit the programs, activities, and financial operations of the Corporation for any period during which (A) Federal funds provided pursuant to this Act are being used to finance any portion of its operations, or (B) Federal funds have been invested therein pursuant to this Act. Any such audit may be conducted under such rules and regulations as the Comptroller General may prescribe. The Comptroller General shall report to the Congress at such times and to such extent as he considers necessary to keep the Congress informed on the security of such Federal funds and guarantees and, to the extent appropriate, make recommendations for achieving greater economy, efficiency, and effectiveness in such programs, activities, and operations.

(2) For the purpose of any audit conducted pursuant to subsection (a) of this section, the Comptroller General, or a designated representative of the Comptroller General, shall have access to and the right to examine all books, accounts, records, reports, files, and other papers, items, or property belonging to or in use by the Corporation.

(b) REPORT.—The Association shall prepare and submit an annual report to Congress on the performance of the Corporation in order to keep the Congress informed as to matters which may affect the quality of rail services in the region and which may affect the security of Federal funds referred to in subsection (a) of this section. Each such report shall be submitted within 150 days after the end of the fiscal year of the Corporation. Each such report shall include an evolution of—

(1) the degree to which the goals of section 206(a) of this

Act are being met;

(2) the amounts and causes of deviations, if any, from the financial projections of the final system plan;

(3) the amount of Federal funds made available to the Corporation and a clear description of the uses of such funds;

(4) the projected financial needs of the Corporation;

(5) the projected sources from which such financial needs are likely to be met; and

(6) the ability of the Corporation to become financially self-sustaining without requiring Federal funds in excess of those authorized by section 216(f) of this Act.

(c) MONITORING OF THE CORPORATION.—(1) The Association shall also report to the Congress, in accordance with this subsection, on the policies of the Corporation and the results of such policies with respect to operations, cost containment, and marketing.

(2) Within 90 days after the date of enactment of this subsection, the Association shall (A) subdivide each such policy area into constituent parts or groups of parts which are specific and significant, (B) identify the most appropriate indicia to reflect accurately such parts or groups of parts, and (C)(i) determine any and all deficiencies in data used to compute the values of such indicia including consistency and clarity of definitions, timeliness of data entry, editing and validation of input data, and processing, and (ii) outline the efforts of the Association and Corporation to correct the deficiencies and the results of such efforts. On or before the end of such 90-day period, the Association shall submit to the Congress such methodological information and additional information which the Association deems necessary or appropriate to further the purpose of this title.

(3) Using such indicia, the Association shall report on (A) the relationship of each constituent part or groups of parts to the Corporation's revenue and capital and operating expenses, (B) the extent to which such parts or group of parts contributes to profits or losses, (C) the efforts of management to contain or reduce the contribution of such part or group of parts to losses, (D) the results of such efforts, and (E) such other information as the Association deems necessary or appropriate.

(4) The Association shall (A) transmit to the Congress the

first such monitoring report pursuant to paragraph (3) at the end of the first calendar quarter which begins after the end of the 90-day period for preparation and submission of the methodological information pursuant to paragraph (2), (B) report such monitoring information to the Congress at the end of the first quarter of each calendar year thereafter, (C) update methodological and monitoring information periodically as the Association deems necessary or appropriate, but in no case less frequently than once a year, and (D) where the results of such updating are statistically significant or relevant to Congressional policymaking, report them and the reasons for their significance at the end of the calendar quarter in which the updating occurred.

[45 U.S.C. 747]

ABANDONMENTS

SEC. 308. (a) GENERAL.—The Corporation may, in accordance with this section, file with the Commission an application for a certificate of abandonment for any line which is part of the system of the Corporation. Any such application shall be governed by this section and shall not, except as specifically provided in this section, be subject to the provisions of chapter 109 of title 49, United States Code.

(b) APPLICATIONS FOR ABANDONMENT.—Any application for abandonment that is filed by the Corporation under this section before December 1, 1981, shall be granted by the Commission within 90 days after the date such application is filed unless, within such 90-day period, an offer of financial assistance is made in accordance with subsection (d) of this section with respect to the line to be abandoned.

(c) NOTICE OF INSUFFICIENT REVENUES.—(1) The Corporation may, prior to November 1, 1985, file with the Commission a notice of insufficient revenues for any line which is part of the system of the Corporation.

(2) At any time after the 90-day period beginning with the filing of a notice of insufficient revenues for a line, the Corporation may file an application for abandonment for such line. An application for abandonment that is filed by the Corporation under this subsection for a line for which a notice of insufficient revenues was filed under paragraph (1) shall be

granted by the Commission within 90 days after the date such application is filed unless, within such 90-day period, an offer of financial assistance is made in accordance with subsection (d) of this section with respect to such line.

(d) OFFERS OF FINANCIAL ASSISTANCE.—(1) The provisions of section 10904 of title 49, United States Code (including the timing requirements of subsection (d) thereof), shall apply to any offer of financial assistance under subsection (b) or (c) of this section.

(2) The Corporation shall provide any person that intends to make an offer of financial assistance under subsection (b) or (c) of this section with such information as the Commission may require.

(e) LIQUIDATION.—(1) If any application for abandonment is granted under subsection (b) of this section, the Commission shall, as soon as practicable, appraise the net liquidation value of the line to be abandoned, and shall publish notice of such appraisal in the Federal Register.

(2) Appraisals made under paragraph (1) shall not be appealable.

(3)(A) If, within 120 days after the date on which an appraisal is published in the Federal Register under paragraph (1) , the Corporation receives a bona fide offer for the sale, for 75 percent of the amount at which the liquidation value of such line was appraised by the Commission, of the line to be abandoned, the Corporation shall sell such line and the Commission shall, unless the parties otherwise agree, establish an equitable division of joint rates for through routes over such lines.

(B) If the Corporation receives no bona fide offer under subparagraph (A), within such 120-day period, the Corporation may abandon or dispose of the line as it chooses, except that the Corporation may not dismantle bridges, or other structures (not including rail, signals, and other rail facilities) for 120 days thereafter. The Secretary may require that bridges or other structures (not including rail, signals, and other rail facilities), not be dismantled for an additional 8 months if he assumes all liability of any sort related to such property.

(4) If the purchaser under paragraph (3)(A) of this

subsection of any line of the Corporation abandons such line within five years after such purchase, the proceeds of any track liquidations shall be paid into the general fund of the Treasury of the United States.

(f) EMPLOYEE PROTECTION.—The provisions of section 10903(b)(3)[1] of title 49, United States Code, shall not apply to any abandonment granted under this section. Any employee who was protected by the compensatory provisions of title V of this Act immediately prior to the effective date of the Northeast Rail Service Act of 1981, who is deprived of employment by such an abandonment shall be eligible for employee protection under section 701 of this Act.

---

[1]   Section 10903(b) of title 49, United States Code, does not have a paragraph (3). Probably should refer to section 10903(b)(2).

[45 U.S.C. 748]

TITLE IV—TRANSFER OF FREIGHT SERVICE [Repealed by P.L. 99–509, section 4033(a)(1)]

TITLE V—EMPLOYEE PROTECTION
[Repealed by P.L. 97–1981, P.L. 97–35, Section 1144(a)(1), 95 Stat. 669]

TITLE VI—MISCELLANEOUS PROVISIONS

RELATIONSHIP TO OTHER LAWS

SEC. 601. (a) ANTITRUST.—(1) Except as specifically provided in paragraph (2) of this subsection, no provision of this Act shall be deemed to convey to any railroad or employee or director thereof any immunity from civil or criminal liability, or to create defenses to actions, under the antitrust laws.

(2) The antitrust laws are inapplicable with respect to any action taken to formulate or implement the final system plan where such action was in compliance with the requirements of such plan and with respect to any action taken to formulate or implement any supplemental transaction.

(3) As used in this subsection, "antitrust laws" includes the Act of July 2, 1890 (ch. 647, 26 Stat. 209), as amended; the Act of October 15, 1914 (ch. 323, 38 Stat. 730), as amended; the Federal Trade Commission Act (38 Stat. 717), as amended; sections 73 and 74 of the Act of August 27, 1894 (28 Stat. 570), as amended; the Act of June 19, 1936 (ch. 592, 49 Stat. 1526), as amended; and the antitrust laws of any State or subdivision thereof.

(b) COMMERCE, SECURITIES, AND BANKRUPTCY.—(1) The provisions of the Interstate Commerce Act (49 U.S.C. 1 et seq.) and the Bankruptcy Act (11 U.S.C. 205 et seq.) are inapplicable (A) to actions taken under this Act to formulate and implement the final system plan which such action was in compliance with the requirements of such plan, and (B) to actions taken under this Act to formulate or implement any supplemental transaction.

(2) All securities of the Corporation which are issued to the Association as the initial holder, or which are issued in connection with the transfer to the Corporation or a subsidiary thereof of rail properties under this Act, shall be deemed for all purposes to have been issued subject to and authorized pursuant to section 20a of the Interstate Commerce Act (49 U.S.C. 20a).

(3) The provisions of section 5 of the Securities Act of 1933 (15 U.S.C. 77e), shall not apply to transactions involving the issuance of any security of the Corporation to the Association, transactions involving the issuance of any security of the Corporation that is deposited with the special court pursuant to section 303(a) of this Act, or transactions involving the issuance or distribution of any security of the Corporation, where the terms and conditions of such issuance or distribution are approved by the special court pursuant to section 303(c) of this Act.

(4) The powers and duties of the Commission under section 77 of the Bankruptcy Act (11 U.S.C. 205), with respect to a railroad in reorganization in the region which conveys all or substantially all of its designated rail properties to the Corporation or a subsidiary thereof, or to profitable railroads in the region, pursuant to the final system plan, and the requirement that plans of reorganization be filed with the Commission, shall cease upon the date of such conveyance.

The powers and duties of the Commission under section 77 of the Bankruptcy Act shall also so terminate, as of the date of enactment of this paragraph, with respect to any railroad reorganization under such section 77 but not subject to this Act which (1) does not operate any line of railroad, and (2) has transferred all or substantially all of its rail properties to a railroad in reorganization in the region which was subject to this Act prior to the date of enactment of this paragraph. Thereafter, such powers and duties of the Commission shall be vested in the district court of the United States which has jurisdiction of the estate of any such railroad in reorganization at the time of such conveyance. Such court shall proceed to reorganize or liquidate such railroad in reorganization pursuant to such section 77 on such terms as the court deems just and reasonable, or pursuant to any other provisions of the Bankruptcy Act, if the court finds that such action would be in the best interests of such estate. This paragraph does not affect any obligation of any carrier by railroad subject to regulation under the Interstate Commerce Act. The powers and duties of the Commission under section 77 of the Bankruptcy Act shall continue in effect only to the extent that the railroad in reorganization continues to operate any line of railroad.

(c) ENVIRONMENT.—The provisions of section 102(2)(C) of the National Environmental Policy Act of 1969 (42 U.S.C. 4332(2)(C)) shall not apply with respect to any action taken under authority of this Act before, and including, the conveyance of rail properties ordered by the special court under section 303(b)(1) of this Act, and shall not apply thereafter to any action taken in compliance with the requirements of the final system plan.

(d) NORTHEAST CORRIDOR.—(1) Rail properties designated in accordance with section 206(c)(1)(C) of this Act shall be purchased or leased by the National Railroad Passenger Corporation. The Corporation shall negotiate an appropriate sale or lease agreement with the National Railroad Passenger Corporation for the properties designated for transfer pursuant to section 206(c)(1)(C) of this Act (45 U.S.C. 716(c)(1)(C)), which shall take effect on the date of conveyance of such properties to the Corporation.

(2) Properties acquired by purchase, lease, or otherwise pursuant to this subsection shall be improved in order to meet the goal set forth in section 206(a)(3) of this Act, relating to

improved high-speed passenger service, by the earliest practicable date after the date of enactment of this Act.

(3) The Secretary shall begin the necessary engineering studies and improvements upon enactment.

(4) The final system plan shall provide for any necessary coordination with freight or commuter services of uses of the facilities designated in section 206(c)(1)(C) of this Act. Such coordination may be effectuated through a single operating entity, designated in the final system plan, or as mutually agreed upon by the interested parties.

(5) Construction or improvements made pursuant to this subsection may be made in consultation with the Corps of Engineers.

(e) EMERGENCY SERVICE.—[Subsection (e) amended section 1(16) of the Interstate Commerce Act, relating to directed service, now repealed.]

[45 U.S.C. 791]

SEPARABILITY

SEC. 604. If any provision of this Act or the application thereof to any person or circumstances is held invalid, the remainder of this Act and the application of such provision to other persons or circumstances shall not be affected thereby.

[45 U.S.C. 701 note]

TAX PAYMENTS TO STATES

SEC. 605. (a) Notwithstanding any other provision of law, no railroad in reorganization shall withhold from any State, or any political subdivision thereof, the payment of the portion of any tax owned by such railroad to such State or subdivision, which portion has been collected by such railroad from any tenant thereof.

(b) Any railroad which violates the provisions of subsection (a) of this section by withholding any portion of a tax referred to in such subsection shall be fined not more than $10,000 for each such violation.

[45 U.S.C. 794]

TITLE VII—PROTECTION OF EMPLOYEES [P.L. 99–509, §4024(c) provided that section

701 of the Regional Rail Reorganization Act of 1973 is repealed effective on the sale date (April 2, 1987).]

TERMINATION ALLOWANCE

SEC. 702. (a) GENERAL.—The Corporation may terminate the employment of certain employees, in accordance with this section, upon the payment of an allowance of $350 for each month of active service with the Corporation or with a railroad in reorganization, but in no event may any such termination allowance exceed $25,000.

(b) EMPLOYMENT NEEDS.—Within 90 days after the effective date of this title, the Corporation shall determine, for each location, the number of employees that the Corporation intends to separate under subsection (a) of this section.

(c) NOTIFICATION AND SEPARATION PROCEDURE.—(1) Within 90 days after the effective date of this title, the Corporation shall notify its employees of their rights and responsibilities under this section.

(2) Within 90 days after the effective date of this title, the Corporation shall notify each train and engine service employee eligible to be separated under paragraph (3) that such employee may be entitled to receive a separation payment under this section if such employee files a written request to be separated. Such notice may be revised from time to time.

(3) If the number of employees who request to be separated pursuant to paragraph (2) of this subsection is greater, in engine service at any location, than the number of excess firemen at the location, and in train service at the location than the number of excess second and third brakemen, as determined by the Corporation, the Corporation shall separate the employees described in paragraph (2) of this subsection in order of seniority beginning with the most senior employee, until the excess firemen and second and third brakemen positions at that location, as determined by the Corporation, have been eliminated.

(d) DESIGNATED SEPARATIONS.—If the number of employees who are separated pursuant to subsection (c)(3) is less at any location than the number of excess firemen in freight and commuter service and second and third brakemen in freight service at such location, as determined by the Corporation, the Corporation may, after 210 days after the effective date of this title, designate for separation employees in engine service or train service respectively in inverse order of seniority, beginning with the most junior employee in active service at such location until the excess firemen in freight and commuter service and second and third brakemen in freight service, at that location have been eliminated. An employee designated under this subsection may choose (1) to furlough himself voluntarily, in which case the next most junior employee protected under the fireman manning or crew consist agreements or any other agreement or law, in the same craft or class at such location may be separated instead and receive the separation allowance, or (2) to exercise his seniority to another location, in which case the Corporation may separate, under the provisions of this subsection, the next most junior protected employee in active service at the location to which seniority ultimately is exercised.

(e) EFFECT ON POSITIONS.—(1) The Corporation shall refrain from filling one fireman position in freight service, or in commuter service where applicable, for each employee in engine service separated in accordance with this section.

(2) The Corporation may refrain from filling one brakeman position in excess of one conductor and one brakeman on one crew in freight service for each employee in train service who is separated in accordance with this section.

(3) Positions permitted to be not filled under this subsection shall be not filled in different types of freight service actually operated at or from the location in a sequence to be agreed upon between the Corporation and the general chairman representative of classes or crafts of employees having jurisdiction over the position to be not filled. If no such agreement is reached, the Corporation may designate the position to be not filled.

(4) Notwithstanding paragraphs (1) and (2) of this subsection, the Corporation shall retain all rights it has under any provision of law or agreement to refrain from filling any position of employment.

(f) PROCEDURES.—The Corporation and representatives of the various classes and crafts of employees to be separated may agree on procedures to implement this section, but the absence of such agreement shall not interfere with implementation of the separations authorized by this section.

(g) COMMUTER EMPLOYEES.—The provisions of this section

shall apply to the separation of firemen in commuter service, except that with respect to such employees the Corporation is required to make the separations authorized by this section.

[45 U.S.C. 797a]

PREFERENTIAL HIRING[1]

SEC. 703. (a) GENERAL.—Any employee who is deprived of employment shall have the first right of hire by any other railroad for a vacancy for which he is qualified in a class or craft (or in the case of a non-agreement employee, for a non-agreement vacancy) in which such employee was employed by the Corporation or a predecessor carrier for not less than one year, except where such a vacancy is covered by (1) an affirmative action plan, or a hiring plan designed to eliminate discrimination, that is required by Federal or State statute, regulation, or Executive order, or by the order of a Federal court or agency, or (2) a permissible voluntary affirmative action plan. For purposes of this section, a railroad shall not be considered to be hiring new employees when it recalls any of its own furloughed employees.

---

[1] Section 4011(c) of the Consolidated Omnibus Budget Reconciliation Act of 1985 (P.L. 99–272; 100 Stat. 109; April 7, 1986) provided as follows:

"(c) Exemption.—The provisions of section 703 of the Regional Rail Reorganization Act of 1973 (45 U.S.C. 797b), section 8 of the Milwaukee Railroad Restructuring Act (45 U.S.C. 907), and section 105 of the Rock Island Railroad Transition and Employee Assistance Act (45 U.S.C. 1004) shall not apply to the National Railroad Passenger Corporation in the hiring of qualified train and engine employees who hold seniority rights to work in intercity rail passenger service in connection with the assumption by such Corporation of functions previously performed under contract by other carriers.".

(b) STATUS.—The first right of hire afforded to employees under this section shall be coequal to the first right of hire afforded under section 8 of the Milwaukee Railroad Restructuring Act (45 U.S.C. 907) and section 105 of the Rock Island Transition and Employee Assistance Act (45 U.S.C. 1004).

CENTRAL REGISTER OF RAILROAD EMPLOYMENT

SEC. 704. (a) REGISTER.—(1) The Railroad Retirement Board (hereafter in this section referred to as the "Board") shall prepare and maintain a register of persons separated from railroad employment after at least one year of completed service with a railroad who have declared their current availability for employment in the railroad industry. The register shall be subdivided by class and craft of prior employment and shall be updated periodically to reflect current availability.

(2) Each entry in the register shall include, or provide access to, basic information concerning the individual's experience and qualifications.

(3) The Board shall place at the top of the register those former railroad employees entitled to priority under applicable provisions of law, including this Act.

(b) CORPORATION EMPLOYEES.—As soon as is practicable after the effective date of this title, the Corporation shall provide to the Board the names of its former employees who elect to appear on the register and who have not been offered employment with acquiring railroads.

(c) VACANCY NOTICES.—(1) Each railroad shall timely file with the Board a notice of vacancy with respect to any position for which the railroad intends to accept applications from persons other than current employees of that carrier.

(2)(A) As soon as the Board becomes aware of any failure on the part of a railroad to comply with paragraph (1), the Board shall issue a warning to such railroad of its potential liability under subparagraph (B).

(B) Any railroad failing to comply with paragraph (1) of this subsection after being warned by the Board under subparagraph (A) shall be liable for a civil penalty in the amount of $500 for each subsequent vacancy with respect to which such railroad has so failed to comply.

(d) PLACEMENT.—The Board shall, through distribution of copies of the central register (or portions thereof) to railroads and representatives of classes or crafts of employees and through publication of employment information derived from vacancy notices filed with the Board, promote the placement of former railroad employees possessing requisite skills and experience in appropriate positions with other railroads.

(e) EMPLOYMENT APPLICATIONS.—In addition to its responsibilities under subsections (a) through (d) of this section, the Board shall facilitate the filing of employment applications with respect to current vacancies in the industry by former railroad employees entitled to priority under applicable provisions of law, including this Act.

(f) EXPIRATION.—The provisions of this section shall cease to be effective on the expiration of the 6-year period beginning on the effective date of this title.

(g) RESOLUTION OF DISPUTES.—Any dispute, grievance, or claim arising under this section, section 703 of this Act, section 8 of the Milwaukee Railroad Restructuring Act (45 U.S.C. 907), or section 105 of the Rock Island Railroad Transition and Employee Assistance Act (45 U.S.C. 1004) shall be subject to resolution in accordance with the following procedures:

(1) Any employee with such a dispute, grievance, or claim may petition the Board to review and investigate the dispute, grievance, or claim.

(2) The Board shall investigate the dispute, grievance, or claim, and if it concludes that the employee's rights under this section, section 703 of this Act, section 8 of the Milwaukee Railroad Restructuring Act (45 U.S.C. 907), or section 105 of the Rock Island Railroad Transition and Employee Assistance Act (45 U.S.C. 1004) may have been violated, the dispute, grievance, or claim shall be subject to resolution in accordance with the procedures set forth in section 3 of the Railway Labor Act (45 U.S.C. 153).

(3) In the case of any violation of this section, section 703 of this Act, section 8 of the Milwaukee Railroad Restructuring Act (45 U.S.C. 907), or section 105 of the Rock Island Railroad Transition and Employee Assistance Act (45 U.S.C. 1004), the Adjustment Board (or any division or delegate thereof) or any other board of adjustment created under section 3 of the Railway Labor Act shall, where appropriate, award such relief, including back pay, as may be necessary to enforce the employee's rights.

[45 U.S.C. 797c]

ELECTION AND TREATMENT OF BENEFITS

SEC. 705. (a) ELECTION.—(1) Any employee who accepts any benefits under an agreement entered into under section 701 of this Act or a termination allowance under section 702 of this Act, shall, except as provided in paragraph (2) of this subsection, be deemed to waive any employee protection benefits otherwise available under any other provision of law or any contract or agreement in effect on the effective date of this title, except benefits under sections 703 and 704 of this Act, and shall be deemed to waive any cause of action for any alleged loss of benefits resulting from the provisions of or the amendments made by the Northeast Rail Service Act of 1981.

(2) Nothing in paragraph (1) of this subsection shall affect the right of any employee described in such paragraph to benefits under the Railroad Retirement Act of 1974 or the Railroad Unemployment Insurance Act.

(b) TREATMENT OF BENEFITS.—Any benefits received by an employee under an agreement entered into pursuant to section 701 of this Act and any termination allowance received under section 702 of this Act shall be considered compensation solely for purposes of—

(1) the Railroad Retirement Act of 1974 (45 U.S.C. 231 et seq.); and

(2) determining the compensation received by such employee in any base year under the Railroad Unemployment Insurance Act (45 U.S.C. 351 et seq.).

[45 U.S.C. 797d]

ASSIGNMENT OF WORK

SEC. 706. (a) GENERAL.—With respect to any craft or class of employees not covered by a collective bargaining agreement that provides for a process substantially equivalent to that provided for in this section, the Corporation shall have the right to assign, allocate, reassign, reallocate, and consolidate work formerly performed on the rail properties acquired pursuant to the provisions of this Act from a railroad in reorganization to any location, facility, or position on its system if it does not remove such work from coverage of a collective bargaining agreement and does not infringe upon the existing classification of work rights of any craft or class of employees at the location or facility to which such work is assigned, allocated, reassigned, reallocated, or consolidated. Prior to the exercise of authority under this subsection, the Corporation shall negotiate an agreement with the representatives of the employees involved permitting such employees the right to follow their work.

(b) EXPIRATION.—The authority granted by this section shall apply only for as long as benefits are provided under this title with funds made available under section 713 of this Act.

[45 U.S.C. 797e]

CONTRACTING OUT

SEC. 707. All work in connection with the operation or services provided by the Corporation on the rail lines, properties, equipment, or facilities acquired pursuant to the provisions of this Act and the maintenance, repair, rehabilitation, or modernization of such lines, properties, equipment, or facilities which has been performed by practice or agreement in accordance with provisions of the existing contracts in effect with the representatives of the employees of the classes or crafts involved shall continue to be performed by the Corporation's employees, including employees on furlough. Should the Corporation lack a sufficient number of employees, including employees on furlough, and be unable to hire additional employees, to perform the work required, it shall be permitted to subcontract that part of such work which cannot be performed by its employees, including those on furlough, except where agreement by the representatives of the employees of the classes or crafts involved is required by applicable collective-bargaining agreements. The term "unable to hire additional employees" as used in this section contemplates establishment and maintenance by the Corporation of an apprenticeship, training, or recruitment program to provide an adequate number of skilled employees to perform the work.

[45 U.S.C. 797f]

NEW COLLECTIVE-BARGAINING AGREEMENTS

SEC. 708. (a) AGREEMENT.—Not later than 60 days after the effective date of any conveyance pursuant to the provisions of this Act, the representatives of the various classes or crafts of employees of a railroad in reorganization involved in a conveyance and representatives of the Corporation shall commence negotiation of a new single collective bargaining agreement for each class and craft of employees covering the rate of pay, rules, and working conditions of employees who are the employees of the Corporation. Such collective bargaining agreement shall include appropriate provisions concerning rates of pay, rules, and working conditions, but shall not, before April 1, 1984, include any provisions for job stabilization which may exceed or conflict with those established herein. Negotiations with respect to such single collective bargaining agreement, and any successor thereto, shall be conducted systemwide.

(b) PROCEDURE.—(1) Any procedure for finally determining the components of the first single collective bargaining agreement for any class or craft, agreed upon before the effective date of this title, shall be completed no later than 45 days after such effective date. Such agreed upon procedure shall be deemed to satisfy the requirements of sections 7 and 8 of the Railway Labor Act. The National Mediation Board shall appoint any person as provided for by such agreements.

(2) Nothing in this section shall be construed to require the parties to enter into a new single collective bargaining agreement if the agreement between the parties in effect immediately prior to the effective date of this title complied with section 504(d) of this Act as in effect immediately prior to such date.

(c) RAILWAY LABOR ACT NOTICES.—Employees of the Corporation may not serve notices under section 6 of the Railway Labor Act for the purpose of negotiating job stabilization or other protective agreements with the Corporation until after April 1, 1984.

[45 U.S.C. 797g]

EMPLOYEE AND PERSONAL INJURY CLAIMS

SEC. 709. (a) LIABILITY FOR EMPLOYEE CLAIMS.—In all cases of claims, prior to April 1, 1976, by employees, arising under the collective bargaining agreements of the railroads in reorganization in the Region, and subject to section 3 of the Railway Labor Act (45 U.S.C. 153), the Corporation, the National Railroad Passenger Corporation, or an acquiring carrier, as the case may be, shall assume responsibility for the processing of any such claims, and payment of those which are sustained or settled on or subsequent to the date of conveyance, under section 303(b)(1) of this Act, and shall be entitled to direct reimbursement from the Association pursuant to section 211(h) of this Act, to the extent that such claims are determined by the Association to be the obligation of a railroad in reorganization in the Region. Any liability of an estate of a railroad in reorganization to its employees which is assumed, processed, and paid pursuant to this subsection by the Corporation, the National Railroad Passenger Corporation, or an acquiring carrier shall remain the preconveyance obligation of the estate of such railroad for purposes of section 211(h)(1) of this Act. The Corporation, the National Railroad Passenger Corporation, an acquiring carrier, or the Association, as the case may be, shall be entitled to a direct claim as a current expense of administration, in accordance with the provisions of section 211(h) of this Act (other than paragraph (4)(A) thereof), for reimbursement (including costs and expenses of processing such claims) from the estate of the railroad in reorganization on whose behalf such obligations are discharged or paid. In those cases in which claims for employees were sustained or settled prior to such date of conveyance, it shall be the obligation of the employees to seek satisfaction against the estate of the railroads in reorganization which were their former employers.

(b) ASSUMPTION OF PERSONAL INJURY CLAIMS.—All cases or claims by employees or their personal representatives for personal injuries or death against a railroad in reorganization in the Region arising prior to the date of conveyance of rail properties, pursuant to section 303 of this Act, shall be assumed by the Corporation or an acquiring railroad, as the case may be. The Corporation or the acquiring railroad shall process and pay any such claims that are sustained or settled, and shall be entitled to direct reimbursement from the Association pursuant to section 211(h) of this Act, to the extent that such claims are determined by the Association or its successor authority to be the obligation of such railroad. Any liability of an estate of a railroad in reorganization which is assumed, processed, and paid, pursuant to this subsection, by the Corporation or an acquiring railroad shall remain the preconveyance obligation of the estate of such railroad for purposes of section 211(h)(1) of this Act. The Corporation, an acquiring railroad, or the Association, as the case may be, shall be entitled to a direct claim as a current expense of administration, in accordance with the provisions of section 211(h) of this Act (other than paragraph (4)(A) thereof), for reimbursement (including costs and expenses of processing such claims) from the estate of the railroad in reorganization on whose behalf such obligations were discharged or paid.

[45 U.S.C. 797h]

LIMITATIONS ON LIABILITY

SEC. 710. (a) FEDERAL GOVERNMENT.—The liability of the United States under an agreement entered into or benefit schedule prescribed under section 701 of this Act or for payment of a termination allowance under section 702 of this Act shall be limited to amounts appropriated under section 713 of this Act.

(b) THE CORPORATION.—(1) The Corporation, Amtrak Commuter, and commuter authorities shall incur no liability under an agreement entered into or benefit schedule prescribed under section 701 of this Act or for the payment of a termination allowance under section 702 of this Act.

(2) Notwithstanding any other provision of law, until April 1, 1984, the Corporation shall have no liability for employee protection in the event of a sale of any asset to a purchaser, and such purchaser shall assume the liability for the application of employee protection conditions imposed by the Commission for all employees adversely affected by such sale.

[45 U.S.C. 797i]

PREEMPTION

SEC. 711. No State may adopt or continue in force any law, rule, regulation, order, or standard requiring the Corporation to employ any specified number of persons to perform any particular task, function, or operation, or requiring the Corporation to pay protective benefits to employees, and no State in the Region may adopt or continue in force any such law, rule, regulation, order, or standard with respect to any railroad in the Region.

[45 U.S.C. 797j]

FACTFINDING PANEL

SEC. 712. (a) PURPOSE.—The Corporation shall enter into collective bargaining agreements with it employees which provide for the establishment of one or more advisory factfinding panels, chaired by a neutral expert in industrial relations, for purposes of recommending changes in operating practices and procedures which result in greater productivity to the maximum extent practicable.

(b) NATIONAL MEDIATION BOARD.—The National Mediation Board shall appoint public members to any panel established by an agreement entered into under this subparagraph, and shall perform such functions contained in the agreement as are consistent with the duties of such Board under the Railway Labor Act.

(c) OTHER FUNCTIONS.—The factfinding panel may, before making its report to the parties, provide mediation, conciliation, and other assistance to the parties.

[45 U.S.C. 797k]

CLASS II RAILROADS RECEIVING FEDERAL ASSISTANCE

SEC. 713. The Surface Transportation Board shall impose no labor protection conditions in approving an application under section 10902 of title 49, United States Code, when the application involves a Class II rail carrier which—

(1) is headquartered in a State, and operates in at least one State, with a population of less than 1,000,000 persons, as determined by the 1990 census; and

(2) has, as of January 1, 1996, been a recipient of repayable Federal Railroad Administration assistance in excess of $5,000,000.

[45 U.S.C. 797l]

ARBITRATION

SEC. 714. Any dispute or controversy with respect to the interpretation, application, or enforcement of the provisions of this title, except sections 703, 704, 708 and 713, or section 1144 of the Northeast Rail Service Act of 1981, and except those matters subject to judicial review under section 1152 of the Northeast Rail Service Act of 1981, which have not been resolved within 90 days, may be submitted by either party to an Adjustment Board for a final and binding decision thereon as provided in section 3 of the Railway Labor Act, in which event the burden of proof on all issues so presented shall be on the Corporation, or the Association, where appropriate.

[45 U.S.C. 797m]

Title 49 U.S.C. — Transportation

www.ingramcontent.com/pod-product-compliance
Lightning Source LLC
Chambersburg PA
CBHW070047030426
42335CB00016B/1822